Lecture Notes in Computer Science 14663

Founding Editors

Gerhard Goos
Juris Hartmanis

Editorial Board Members

The series Lecture Notes in Computer Science (LNCS), including its subseries Lecture Notes in Artificial Intelligence (LNAI) and Lecture Notes in Bioinformatics (LNBI), has established itself as a medium for the publication of new developments in computer science and information technology research, teaching, and education.

LNCS enjoys close cooperation with the computer science R & D community, the series counts many renowned academics among its volume editors and paper authors, and collaborates with prestigious societies. Its mission is to serve this international community by providing an invaluable service, mainly focused on the publication of conference and workshop proceedings and postproceedings. LNCS commenced publication in 1973.

Giancarlo Guizzardi · Flavia Santoro ·
Haralambos Mouratidis · Pnina Soffer
Editors

Advanced Information Systems Engineering

36th International Conference, CAiSE 2024
Limassol, Cyprus, June 3–7, 2024
Proceedings

 Springer

Editors
Giancarlo Guizzardi [ID]
University of Twente
Enschede, The Netherlands

Flavia Santoro [ID]
State University of Rio de Janeiro
Rio de Janeiro, Rio de Janeiro, Brazil

Haralambos Mouratidis [ID]
University of Essex
Colchester, UK

Pnina Soffer [ID]
University of Haifa
Haifa, Israel

ISSN 0302-9743 ISSN 1611-3349 (electronic)
Lecture Notes in Computer Science
ISBN 978-3-031-61056-1 ISBN 978-3-031-61057-8 (eBook)
https://doi.org/10.1007/978-3-031-61057-8

Discovery; Session Trust, Security and Risk; Social Aspects and LLMs; Model-Driven Engineering and Quantum Workflows.

The two invited keynote presentations were "The colour of cognition: from abstract computation to the lived mind" by J. Mark Bishop, Professor Emeritus at Goldsmiths, University of London, UK, and "Two Projects on Human Interaction with AI" by David Harel, The William Sussman Professorial Chair at the Department of Computer Science and Applied Mathematics at the Weizmann Institute of Science, Israel. On behalf of the information systems engineering community, we would like to thank our keynote speakers for their time dedicated to preparing profound, timely, and insightful talks.

After an open call for tutorials, we accepted the following five proposals: "Data-driven Business Process Simulation: From Event Logs to Tools and Techniques", "Designing Virtual Knowledge Graphs", "How to Conduct Valid Information Systems Engineering Research?", "FAIR Data Train: A FAIR-compliant distributed data and services platform", and "Engineering Information Systems with LLMs and AI-based techniques". Together these tutorials make for an interesting coverage of the core interests of the CAiSE community, combining a selection of disjoint and extremely relevant topics.

As the editors of this volume, we would like to express our immense gratitude to: all authors who chose CAiSE as a forum for submitting their research contributions; the members of the Program Committee for their professional and timely work; the members of the Program Board for their dedication and expertise in helping to shape an essential part of the final program of the conference; all the chairs of the conference for selecting an interesting program that complements the contributions collected here; the Organization Committee for professionally taking care of all the multiple details of running an international and sufficiently large conference like CAiSE, but also for bringing the conference to fantastic Limassol, in Cyprus.

April 2024

Giancarlo Guizzardi
Flavia Santoro
Haralambos Mouratidis
Pnina Soffer

Organization

General Chairs

Haralambos Mouratidis   University of Essex, UK
Pnina Soffer   University of Haifa, Israel

Local Organizing and Finance Chair

George A. Papadopoulos   University of Cyprus, Cyprus

Program Chairs

Giancarlo Guizzardi   University of Twente, the Netherlands
Flavia Maria Santoro   University of the State of Rio de Janeiro, Brazil

Workshop Chairs

João Paulo A. Almeida   Federal University of Espírito Santo, Brazil
Claudio di Ciccio   Utrecht University, the Netherlands
Christos Kalloniatis   University of the Aegean, Greece

Forum Chairs

Shareeful Islam   Anglia Ruskin University, UK
Arnon Sturm   Ben-Gurion University of the Negev, Israel

Journal First Chairs

Paolo Giorgini   University of Trento, Italy
Jeffrey Parsons   Memorial University of Newfoundland, Canada

Tutorial and Panel Chairs

Adela de Rio Ortega	University of Seville, Spain
Tiago Sales	University of Twente, the Netherlands

Doctoral Consortium Chairs

Iris Reinhartz-Berger	University of Haifa, Israel
Chiara Di Francescomarino	University of Trento, Italy
Aggeliki Tsohou	Ionian University, Greece

Publicity Chairs

Achilleas Achilleos	Frederick University, Cyprus
Palash Bera	Saint Louis University, USA
Dominik Bork	TU Wien, Austria
Georg Grossmann	University of South Australia, Australia
Lucineia Heloisa Thom	Federal University of Rio Grande do Sul, Brazil

Sponsor Chairs

Andreas Andreou	Cyprus University of Technology, Cyprus
Massimo Mecella	Sapienza Università di Roma, Italy

Proceedings Chair

Sander J. J. Leemans	RWTH Aachen University, Germany

PhD Award Chair

Andreas Opdahl	University of Bergen, Norway

Industry and Projects@CAiSE Chairs

Raimundas Matulevičius	University of Tartu, Estonia
Henderik A. Proper	TU Wien, Austria

Web and Social Media Chair

Christos Therapontos	EasyConferences Ltd, Cyprus

Program Board

João Paulo Almeida	Universidade Federal do Espírito Santo, Brazil
Xavier Franch	Universitat Politècnica de Catalunya, Spain
Renata Guizzardi	University of Twente, the Netherlands
Marta Indulska	University of Queensland, Australia
John Krogstie	Norwegian University of Science and Technology, Norway
Wolfgang Maass	Deutsches Forschungszentrum für Künstliche Intelligenz, Germany
Marco Montali	Free University of Bozen-Bolzano, Italy
Oscar Pastor	Universidad Politécnica de Valencia, Spain
Barbara Pernici	Politecnico di Milano, Italy
Geert Poels	Ghent University, Belgium
Henderik Proper	TU Wien, Austria
Jolita Ralyté	University of Geneva, Switzerland
Hajo Reijers	Utrecht University, the Netherlands
Iris Reinhartz-Berger	University of Haifa, Israel
Stefanie Rinderle-Ma	Technische Universitat München, Germany
Shazia Sadiq	University of Queensland, Australia
Maribel Santos	University of Minho, Portugal
Monique Snoeck	KU Leuven, Belgium
Barbara Weber	University of St. Gallen, Switzerland
Mathias Weske	HPI, University of Potsdam, Germany
Jelena Zdravkovic	Stockholm University, Sweden

Program Committee

Raian Ali	Hamad Bin Khalifa University, Qatar
João Araújo	Universidade NOVA de Lisboa, Portugal

Fernanda Baião — PUC-Rio, Brazil
Marko Bajec — University of Ljubljana, Slovenia
Monalessa Barcellos — UFES, Brazil
Pedro Paulo F. Barcelos — University of Twente, the Netherlands & Ghent University, Belgium
Boualem Benatallah — UNSW, Australia
Palash Bera — Saint Louis University, USA
Anna Bernasconi — Politecnico di Milano, Italy
Devis Bianchini — University of Brescia, Italy
Luiz Olavo Bonino Da Silva Santos — University of Twente, the Netherlands
Dominik Bork — TU Wien, Austria
Andrea Burattin — Technical University of Denmark, Denmark
Corentin Burnay — University of Namur, Belgium
Istvan David — McMaster University, Canada
Johannes De Smedt — KU Leuven, Belgium
Adela Del Río Ortega — University of Seville, Spain
Claudio Di Ciccio — Utrecht University, the Netherlands
Chiara Di Francescomarino — University of Trento, Italy
Oscar Diaz — University of the Basque Country, Spain
Schahram Dustdar — Vienna University of Technology, Austria
Johann Eder — Alpen-Adria-Universität Klagenfurt, Austria
Sergio España — Universitat Politècnica de València, Spain & Utrecht University, The Netherlands
Marcelo Fantinato — University of São Paulo, Brazil
Luís Ferreira Pires — University of Twente, the Netherlands
Claudenir Fonseca — University of Twente, the Netherlands
Ulrich Frank — Universität Duisburg-Essen, Germany
Mattia Fumagalli — Free University of Bozen-Bolzano, Italy
Chiara Ghidini — Fondazione Bruno Kessler, Italy
Asif Qumer Gill — University of Technology Sydney, Australia
Paolo Giorgini — University of Trento, Italy
Maria Teresa Gómez López — University of Seville, Spain
Jaap Gordijn — Vrije Universiteit Amsterdam, the Netherlands
Georg Grossmann — University of South Australia, Australia
Simon Hacks — Stockholm University, Sweden
Jennifer Horkoff — Chalmers University of Technology, Sweden
Mirjana Ivanovic — University of Novi Sad, Serbia
Matthias Jarke — RWTH Aachen University, Germany
Paul Johannesson — Royal Institute of Technology, Sweden
Ashwin Viswanathan Kannan — Oklahoma State University, USA
Marite Kirikova — Riga Technical University, Latvia

Julio Cesar Leite — UFBA, Brazil

Massimiliano Leoni — University of Padua, Italy

Henrik Leopold — Kühne Logistics University, Germany

Sebastian Link — University of Auckland, New Zealand

Fabrizio Maria Maggi — Free University of Bozen-Bolzano, Italy

Felix Mannhardt — Eindhoven University of Technology, the Netherlands

Andrea Marrella — Sapienza University of Rome, Italy

Raimundas Matulevičius — University of Tartu, Estonia

Massimo Mecella — Sapienza University of Rome, Italy

Jan Mendling — Humboldt-Universität zu Berlin, Germany

Selmin Nurcan — Université Paris 1 Panthéon – Sorbonne, France

Jeffrey Parsons — Memorial University of Newfoundland, Canada

Pierluigi Plebani — Politecnico di Milano, Italy

Artem Polyvyanyy — University of Melbourne, Australia

Tiago Prince Sales — University of Twente, the Netherlands

Luise Pufahl — TU Munich, Germany

Manfred Reichert — University of Ulm, Germany

Kate Revoredo — Humboldt-Universität zu Berlin, Germany

Marcela Ruiz — Zurich University of Applied Sciences, Switzerland

Antonio Ruiz-Cortés — University of Seville, Spain

Sareh Sadeghianasl — Queensland University of Technology, Australia

Camile Salinesi — Université Paris 1 Panthéon-Sorbonne, France

Michael Sheng — Macquarie University, Australia

Janis Stirna — Stockholm University, Sweden

Veda Storey — GSU, USA

Arnon Sturm — Ben-Gurion University, Israel

Sagar Sunkle — Tata Consultancy Services, USA

Yutian Tang — University of Glasgow, UK

Ernest Teniente — UPC, Spain

Han van der Aa — University of Mannheim, Spain

Seppe Vanden Broucke — Katholieke Universiteit Leuven, Belgium

Tony Wasserman — Carnegie Mellon Silicon Valley, USA

Matthias Weidlich — Humboldt-Universität zu Berlin, Germany

Hans Weigand — Tilburg University, the Netherlands

Manuel Wimmer — Johannes Kepler University Linz, Austria

Veruska Zamborlini — Universidade Federal do Espírito Santo, Brazil

Additional Reviewers

Abasi-Amefon Obot Affia
Abhimanyu Gupta
Adam Banham
Adam Burke
Adnan Mahmood
Aleksandar Gavric
Alfonso Marquez Chamorro
Anandi Sethunga Mudiyanselage
Andrei Buliga
Daniel Ayala
Felix Schumann
Finn Klessascheck
Francesca Meneghello
Hanan Alkhammash
Inma Hernandez
Jelena Zdravkovic
José María García
Kerstin Andree
Leon Bein
Marco Roveri

Mari Seeba
Mariia Bakhtina
Matthias Ehrendorfer
Michel Kunkler
Mubashar Iqbal
Nedo Bartels
Patrizio Bellan
Qian Chen
Rebecca Morgan
Robert Andrews
Rodrigo Calhau
Simone Agostinelli
Subhash Sagar
Syed Juned Ali
Vjatšeslav Antipenko
Wenjun Zhou
Xavier Oriol
Yang Zhang
Zihang Su

Abstracts of the Invited Talks

The Colour of Cognition: From Abstract Computation to the Lived Mind

J. Mark Bishop[1,2,3]

[1]Cognitive Computing at Goldsmiths, University of London, UK
ProfJMarkBishop@outlook.com
[2]Karel Čapek Center, Praha, Czech Republic
[3]FACT360, London, Guildford, UK

Abstract. Ever since CPP Snow's Rede Lecture of 1959, there has been a general perception amongst educated people of life lived in two cultures: "On the one hand the departments of the arts and humanities dealing with 'the living and experiential' in a world of meaningful cognition; information as semantics; communication through language; signs and interpretations and on the other hand the sciences and mathematics dealing with the non-living and mechanical in a world of artificial cognition; information as statistics; communication through signals; energy, forces and matter all governed by strict laws. In this light these two cultures live in enforced ontological separation; they do not share the same reality". Conversely, modern approaches to cognitive science, emphasising the body and its interactions with environment and society, offer new tools with which to bridge this ontological gap and in so doing open up a new, shared reality: a reality of neurons living in the brain; the brain living in the body; the body living in the world & society. This radical, holistic approach to cognition focuses on the development of four research themes in cognitive science – the so-called '4E's; the 'embodied, embedded, enactive and ecological' – each of which has its own vibrant research programme; but which also come together to form a larger, coherent, trans-disciplinary whole. In this talk I will present my evidence concerning Artificial Intelligence and [Turing Machine] Functionalism, which fatally undermines the idea of mind as mere computational mathesis, and contrast with modern cognitive science, wherein mind is coextensive with life.

Two Projects on Human Interaction with AI

David Harel

Department of Computer Science and Applied Mathematics, The Weizmann Institute
of Science, Israel
david.harel@weizmann.ac.il

Abstract. I will present two projects that attempt to shed new light on
the role computers will be playing in the future. The first we term "The
Human-or-Machine Issue". Turing's imitation game addresses the question of whether a machine can be labeled intelligent. We explore a related,
yet quite different, challenge: in everyday interactions with an agent, how
will knowing whether the agent is human or machine affect that interaction? In contrast to Turing's test, this is not a thought experiment, but
is directly relevant to human behavior, human-machine interaction and
also system development. I will argue that exploring the issue now is useful even if machines will end up not attempting to disguise themselves
as humans. In the second project, we propose a systematic programming methodology that consists of three main components: (1) a modular incremental specification approach (specifically, scenario-based programming); (2) a powerful, albeit error-prone, AI-based software development assistant; and (3) systematic iterative articulation of requirements
and system properties, amid testing and verification. The preliminary
results we have obtained show that one can indeed use an AI chatbot
as an integral part of an interactive development method, during which
one constantly verifies each new artifact contributed by the chatbot in the
context of the evolving system (This represents joint work with Assaf
Marron, Guy Katz and Smadar Szekely.).

Contents

Process Alignment, Comparison and Discovery

Object-Centric Conformance Alignments with Synchronization 3
    Alessandro Gianola, Marco Montali, and Sarah Winkler

Process Comparison Based on Selection-Projection Structures 20
    Tobias Brockhoff, Merih Seran Uysal, and Wil M. P. van der Aalst

Stochastic Process Discovery: Can It Be Done Optimally? 36
    Sander J. J. Leemans, Tian Li, Marco Montali, and Artem Polyvyanyy

Process Discovery, Monitoring and Correction

Reinforcement Learning-Based Streaming Process Discovery Under
Concept Drift 55
    Rujian Cai, Chao Zheng, Jian Wang, Duantengchuan Li, Chong Wang,
    and Bing Li

Enhancing Predictive Process Monitoring with Time-Related Feature
Engineering 71
    Rafael Seidi Oyamada, Gabriel Marques Tavares,
    Sylvio Barbon Junior, and Paolo Ceravolo

Stochastic Directly-Follows Process Discovery Using Grammatical
Inference 87
    Hanan Alkhammash, Artem Polyvyanyy, and Alistair Moffat

Graphs and Graph Networks

A Graph Language Modeling Framework for the Ontological Enrichment
of Conceptual Models 107
    Syed Juned Ali and Dominik Bork

PGTNet: A Process Graph Transformer Network for Remaining Time
Prediction of Business Process Instances 124
    Keyvan Amiri Elyasi, Han van der Aa, and Heiner Stuckenschmidt

Multi-perspective Concept Drift Detection: Including the Actor Perspective 141
    Eva L. Klijn, Felix Mannhardt, and Dirk Fahland

Process Modelling and Management

On the Flexibility of Declarative Process Specifications 161
Carl Corea, Paolo Felli, Marco Montali, and Fabio Patrizi

Towards a Multi-model Paradigm for Business Process Management 178
Anti Alman, Fabrizio Maria Maggi, Stefanie Rinderle-Ma,
Andrey Rivkin, and Karolin Winter

Model-Based Recommendations for Next-Best Actions
in Knowledge-Intensive Processes 195
Anjo Seidel, Stephan Haarmann, and Mathias Weske

Prediction, Monitoring and Planning

Towards Learning the Optimal Sampling Strategy for Suffix Prediction
in Predictive Monitoring 215
Efrén Rama-Maneiro, Fabio Patrizi, Juan Vidal, and Manuel Lama

HOEG: A New Approach for Object-Centric Predictive Process Monitoring ... 231
Tim K. Smit, Hajo A. Reijers, and Xixi Lu

A Context-Aware Framework to Support Decision-Making in Production
Planning 248
Simone Agostinelli, Dario Benvenuti, Angelo Casciani,
Francesca De Luzi, Matteo Marinacci, Andrea Marrella,
and Jacopo Rossi

Data Preparation, Sharing, and Architecture

Implementation Patterns for Zone Architectures in Enterprise-Grade Data
Lakes 267
Corinna Giebler, Christoph Gröger, Eva Hoos, Holger Schwarz,
and Bernhard Mitschang

Improving Understandability and Control in Data Preparation:
A Human-Centered Approach 284
Emanuele Pucci, Camilla Sancricca, Salvatore Andolina,
Cinzia Cappiello, Maristella Matera, and Anna Barberio

Data Friction: Physics-Inspired Metaphor to Evaluate the Technical
Difficulties in Trustworthy Data Sharing 300
Matteo Falconi, Giacomo Lombardo, Pierluigi Plebani,
and Sebastian Werner

Requirements

Assuring Runtime Quality Requirements for AI-Based Components 319
Dan Chen, Jingwei Yang, Shuwei Huang, and Lin Liu

Designing Military Command and Control Systems as System
of Systems – An Analysis of Stakeholder Needs and Challenges 336
Jan Lundberg, Janis Stirna, and Kent Andersson

Improving Requirement Traceability by Leveraging Video Game
Simulations in Search-Based Software Engineering 352
Javier Verón, Raúl Lapeña, Carlos Cetina, Óscar Pastor,
and Francisca Pérez

Process and Decision Mining

From Loss of Interest to Denial: A Study on the Terminators of Process
Mining Initiatives 371
Vinicius Stein Dani, Henrik Leopold, Jan Martijn E. M. van der Werf,
Iris Beerepoot, and Hajo A. Reijers

Variants of Variants: Context-Based Variant Analysis for Process Mining 387
Christoffer Rubensson, Jan Mendling, and Matthias Weidlich

Towards a Comprehensive Evaluation of Decision Rules and Decision
Mining Algorithms Beyond Accuracy 403
Beate Wais and Stefanie Rinderle-Ma

Event and Process Discovery

Making Sense of Temporal Event Data:A Framework for Comparing
Techniques for the Discovery of Discriminative Temporal Patterns 423
Chiara Di Francescomarino, Ivan Donadello, Chiara Ghidini,
Fabrizio Maria Maggi, Williams Rizzi, and Sergio Tessaris

Improving Simplicity by Discovering Nested Groups in Declarative Models ... 440
Vlad Paul Cosma, Axel Kjeld Fjelrad Christfort,
Thomas T. Hildebrandt, Xixi Lu, Hajo A. Reijers, and Tijs Slaats

Discovering Two-Level Business Process Models from User Interface
Event Logs 456
Irene Barba, Carmelo Del Valle, Andrés Jiménez-Ramírez,
Barbara Weber, and Manfred Reichert

Session Trust, Security and Risk

The Power of Many: Securing Organisational Identity Through Distributed
Key Management 475
    Mariia Bakhtina, Jan Kvapil, Petr Švenda, and Raimundas Matulevičius

Configuring and Validating Multi-aspect Risk Knowledge for Industry 4.0
Information Systems 492
    *Stefan Biffl, Sebastian Kropatschek, Kristof Meixner, David Hoffmann,
    and Arndt Lüder*

Trusted Execution Environment for Decentralized Process Mining 509
    Valerio Goretti, Davide Basile, Luca Barbaro, and Claudio Di Ciccio

Social Aspects and LLMs

Identifying Citizen-Related Issues from Social Media Using LLM-Based
Data Augmentation 531
    *Vitor Gaboardi dos Santos, Guto Leoni Santos, Theo Lynn,
    and Boualem Benatallah*

Kicking Prejudice: Large Language Models for Racism Classification
in Soccer Discourse on Social Media 547
    *Guto Leoni Santos, Vitor Gaboardi dos Santos, Colm Kearns,
    Gary Sinclair, Jack Black, Mark Doidge, Thomas Fletcher,
    Dan Kilvington, Patricia Takako Endo, Katie Liston, and Theo Lynn*

Infonomics of Autonomous Digital Twins 563
    Istvan David and Dominik Bork

Model-Driven Engineering and Quantum Workflows

Comparing MDD and CcD in the Bug Localization Context: An Empirical
Evaluation in Video Games 581
    *Isis Roca, África Domingo, Óscar Pastor, Carlos Cetina,
    and Lorena Arcega*

A Model-Driven Framework to Support Portfolio Management Under
Uncertainties 596
    *Clara Le Duff, Yohann Chasseray, Audrey Fertier, Raphaël Falco,
    Anouck Adrot, Benoit Montreuil, and Frederick Benaben*

Observability for Quantum Workflows in Heterogeneous Multi-cloud
Environments 612
  *Martin Beisel, Johanna Barzen, Frank Leymann, Lavinia Stiliadou,
  and Benjamin Weder*

Tutorials

Data-Driven Business Process Simulation: From Event Logs to Tools
and Techniques 631
  Orlenys López-Pintado and David Chapela-Campa

Designing Virtual Knowledge Graphs 633
  Diego Calvanese and Davide Lanti

How to Conduct Valid Information Systems Engineering Research? 635
  Jan Mendling, Henrik Leopold, Henning Meyerhenke, and Benoit Depaire

FAIR Data Train: A FAIR-Compliant Distributed Data and Services
Platform 637
  Luiz Olavo Bonino da Silva Santos

Engineering Information Systems with LLMs and AI-Based Techniques 639
  Massimo Mecella

Author Index 641

Process Alignment, Comparison
and Discovery

Object-Centric Conformance Alignments
with Synchronization

Alessandro Gianola[1], Marco Montali[2(✉)], and Sarah Winkler[2]

[1] INESC-ID/Instituto Superior Técnico, Universidade de Lisboa, Lisbon, Portugal
alessandro.gianola@tecnico.ulisboa.pt
[2] Free University of Bozen-Bolzano, Bolzano, Italy
{montali,winkler}@inf.unibz.it

Abstract. Real-world processes operate on objects that are inter-dependent. To accurately reflect the nature of such processes, object-centric process mining techniques are needed, notably conformance checking. However, while the object-centric perspective has recently gained traction, few concrete process mining techniques have been presented so far. Moreover, existing approaches are severely limited in their abilities to keep track of object identity and object dependencies. Consequently, serious problems in event logs with object information remain undetected. This paper, presents a new formalism that combines the key modelling features of two existing approaches, notably the ability of object-centric Petri nets to capture one-to-many relations and the ability of Petri nets with identifiers to compare and synchronize objects based on their identity. We call the resulting formalism *object-centric Petri nets with identifiers*, and define alignments and the conformance checking task for this setting. We propose a conformance checking approach for such nets based on an encoding in satisfiability modulo theories (SMT), and illustrate how it serves to effectively overcome shortcomings of earlier work. To assess its practicality, we evaluate it on data from the literature.

Keywords: BPM · conformance checking · object-centric processes · object-centric process mining · SMT

1 Introduction

In information systems engineering, business/work processes are classically captured with a case-centric approach: every process instance focuses on the evolution of a main case object (such as an order, a claim, a patient), in isolation to other case objects. This approach falls short in a variety of real-life, so-called *object-centric processes*, where multiple objects are co-evolved depending on their

Gianola was partially supported by national funds through FCT, Fundação para a Ciência e a Tecnologia, under projects UIDB/50021/2020 (DOI:10.54499/UIDB/50021/2020). Montali and Winkler acknowledge the UNIBZ project ADAPTERS and the PRIN MIUR project PINPOINT Prot. 2020FNEB27.

G. Guizzardi et al. (Eds.): CAiSE 2024, LNCS 14663, pp. 3–19, 2024.
https://doi.org/10.1007/978-3-031-61057-8_1

mutual, many-to-many and one-to-many relations. A prime scenario witnessing this intricacy, which we use as main motivation throughout the paper, is the one of order-to-delivery processes, where an order consists of multiple items.

The need of capturing this class of processes has emerged in modelling, verification and enactment [4,11,13,16,18]. In particular, a number of different Petri net-based formalisms have been developed to deal with object-centricity, where one can distinguish: *(i)* implicit object manipulation as in synchronous proclets [11] and object-centric Petri nets [3]; and *(ii)* explicit object manipulation as in [13,16,21], which extend Petri nets with names [17] with the ability of manipulating tuples of identifiers, to handle object relations.

Even more vehemently, the same call for object-centricity has been recently advocated in process mining [2,5]. Many information systems (e.g., ERP systems [6,8]) store event data related to several objects without any explicit reference to a single case object. Artificially introducing or selecting one such object as the case during the extraction phase leads to misleading process mining outputs, in particular when dealing with convergence (events that simultaneously operate over multiple objects) and divergence (concurrent flows of related objects) [1].

This paradigm shift calls for novel, object-centric process mining techniques, able to cope with process models that fully support the following features:

1. activities creating and manipulating objects, as well as one-to-one and one-to-many relations among them—for example, the insertion of multiple items in an order, or the split of an order into multiple packages;[1]
2. concurrent flows evolving related objects separately—for example, the concurrent evolution of package shipments and order notifications;
3. object-aware synchronization points dictating that an object o can flow through an activity only if some (*subset synchronization*) or all (*exact synchronization*) objects related to o simultaneously flow as well—e.g., enabling order billing only when some/all its packages have been delivered.

Interestingly, while all aforementioned formalisms cope with the first two aspects, object-aware synchronization is completely missing in object-centric Petri nets [3], subset synchronization is tackled by Petri nets with identifiers [21], while synchronous proclets [11] handle both subset and exact synchronization.

Unfortunately, the existing, few techniques for object-centric process discovery [3] and conformance checking [15] (two cornerstone problems in process mining) are unable to track the identity of objects and their relations, and in turn to deal with synchronization. In conformance checking, which is the focus of this paper, this means that serious deviations between the recorded and the expected behaviour remain undetected, as shown in the following example:

Example 1. Consider the order process specified as an *object centric Petri net* [3] in Fig. 1(a), with sorts *order* (blue) and *product* (yellow). The following (partial) log uses two orders o_1, o_2 and two product items p_1, p_2. Intuitively, it should not conform to the process, since the items are shipped with the wrong order:

---

[1] Many-to-many relations are typically reified into corresponding one-to-many relations, which is essential to properly handle synchronization constraints [4,11,13].

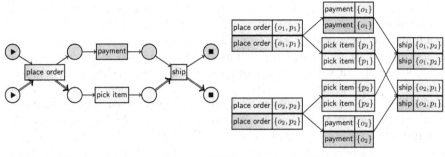

(a) Object-centric Petri net in the formalism of [15].   (b) Optimal alignment.

Fig. 1. Order process and alignment.

(place order, $\{o_1, p_1\}$), (payment, $\{o_1\}$), (pick item, $\{p_1\}$), (place order, $\{o_2, p_2\}$), (payment, $\{o_2\}$), (pick item, $\{p_2\}$), (ship, $\{o_1, p_2\}$), (ship, $\{o_2, p_1\}$)

However, according to the approach of [15], this log has an alignment with cost 0 (cf. Fig. 1(b)), i.e., the mismatch is not detected. Essentially, the problem is that their formalism does not keep track of object identity for synchronization.

Our goal is to remedy problems like the one just presented, introducing a comprehensive framework for alignment-based conformance checking of Petri net-based object-centric processes, where object identity and synchronization are fully accommodated. Precisely, we tackle the following research questions:

(1) How to obtain a lightweight formalism for Petri net-based object-centric processes, capable to track object identity and express synchronization?
(2) How to formalise conformance checking for such a model?
(3) Is it possible to obtain a feasible, algorithmic technique tackling this form of conformance checking?

We answer all these questions affirmatively. Pragmatically, we start from the approach in [15], notably from the object-centric Petri nets used therein, which provide two essential features: the presence of multiple object types, and a special type of arc expressing that *many* tokens flow at once through it (how many is decided at binding time). We infuse these nets with explicit object manipulation as originally introduced in *Petri nets with identifiers* [21]. The resulting, novel model of *object-centric Petri nets with identifiers* (OPIDs) combines simultaneous operations over multiple objects with one-to-many relations, and subset synchronisation based on the identity of objects and their mutual relations.

We then show how the notion of alignment originally introduced in [15] can be suitably lifted to the much richer formalism of OPIDs. We discuss relevant examples showing how non-conformance like the case of Example 1 can be detected. A side-result of independent interest arises as a result of this discussion: even though, from the modelling point of view, OPIDs are only capable of expressing subset synchronisation, if the model does not provide a way to progress objects that missed the synchronization point, then alignments enforce the exact synchronization semantics.

Finally, we show how the problem of computing optimal object-centric alignments can be cast as a Satisfiability/Optimization Modulo Theory problem, in the style of [12], but with a much more complex logical encoding, due to object-centricity. We prove correctness of our encoding, implement it in a new tool oCoCoMoT, and experimentally validate the feasibility of our implementation.

The remainder of this paper is structured as follows: We first recall relevant background about object-centric event logs (Sect. 2), before we compare object-centric process models from the literature (Sect. 3). We then introduce our notion of object-centric Petri nets with identifiers, and its conformance checking task (Sect. 4). Next, we present our encoding of this task as an SMT problem (Sect. 5). We then sketch the implementation of our approach in the tool oCoCoMoT and present experiments (Sect. 6), before we conclude (Sect. 7).

2   Object-Centric Event Logs

We recall basic notions on object-centric event logs [3]. Let Σ be a set of object types, $\mathcal{A}$ a set of activities, and $\mathbb{T}$ a set of timestamps with a total order $<$.

Definition 1. *An* event log *is a tuple* $L = \langle E, \mathcal{O}, \pi_{act}, \pi_{obj}, \pi_{time} \rangle$ *where*

- *E is a set of event identifiers,*
- *$\mathcal{O}$ is a set of object identifiers that are typed by a function* type$: \mathcal{O} \to \Sigma$,
- *the functions $\pi_{act}\colon E \to \mathcal{A}$, $\pi_{obj}\colon E \to \mathcal{P}(\mathcal{O})$, and $\pi_{time}\colon E \to \mathbb{T}$ associate each event $e \in E$ with an activity, a set of affected objects, and a timestamp, respectively, such that for every $o \in \mathcal{O}$ the timestamps $\pi_{time}(e)$ of all events e such that $o \in \pi_{obj}(e)$ are all different.*

Given an event log and an object $o \in \mathcal{O}$, we write $\pi_{trace}(o)$ for the tuple of events involving o, ordered by timestamps. Formally, $\pi_{trace}(o) = \langle e_1, \ldots, e_n \rangle$ such that $\{e_1, \ldots, e_n\}$ is the set of events in E with $o \in \pi_{obj}(e)$, and $\pi_{time}(e_1) < \cdots < \pi_{time}(e_n)$ (by assumption these timestamps can be totally ordered).

In examples, we often leave $\mathcal{O}$ and $\mathcal{A}$ implicit and present an event log L as a set of tuples $\langle e, \pi_{act}(e), \pi_{obj}(e), \pi_{time}(e) \rangle$ representing events. Timestamps are shown as natural numbers, and concrete event ids as $\#_0, \#_1, \ldots$.

Example 2. Let $\mathcal{O} = \{o_1, o_2, o_3, p_1, \ldots, p_4\}$ with type$(o_i) = order$ and type$(p_j) = product$ for all i, j. The following is an event log with $E = \{\#_0, \#_1, \ldots, \#_9\}$:

$\langle \#_0, \mathsf{place\ order}, \{o_1, p_1\}, 1 \rangle, \langle \#_1, \mathsf{payment}, \{o_1\}, 3 \rangle, \langle \#_2, \mathsf{pick\ item}, \{o_1, p_1\}, 2 \rangle,$

$\langle \#_3, \mathsf{place\ order}, \{o_2, p_2\}, 3 \rangle, \langle \#_4, \mathsf{payment}, \{o_2\}, 4 \rangle, \langle \#_5, \mathsf{pick\ item}, \{o_2, p_2\}, 5 \rangle,$

$\langle \#_6, \mathsf{ship}, \{o_1, p_2\}, 6 \rangle, \langle \#_7, \mathsf{ship}, \{o_2, p_1\}, 9 \rangle, \langle \#_8, \mathsf{payment}, \{o_3\}, 2 \rangle, \langle \#_9, \mathsf{ship}, \{o_3, p_3, p_4\}, 5 \rangle$

For instance, we have $\pi_{trace}(o_1) = \langle \#_0, \#_1, \#_2, \#_6 \rangle$.

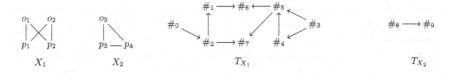

Fig. 2. Object graph for Example 2 and the respective trace graphs.

Given an event log $L = \langle E, \mathcal{O}, \pi_{act}, \pi_{obj}, \pi_{time} \rangle$, the *object graph* $\mathcal{G}_L$ of L is the undirected graph with node set $\mathcal{O}$, and an edge from o to o' if there is some event $e \in E$ such that $o \in \pi_{obj}(e)$ and $o' \in \pi_{obj}(e)$. Thus, the object graph indicates which objects share events. We next define a *trace graph* as the equivalent of a linear trace in our setting.

Definition 2. *Let* $L = \langle E, \mathcal{O}, \pi_{act}, \pi_{obj}, \pi_{time} \rangle$ *be an event log, and* X *a connected component in* $\mathcal{G}_L$. *The* trace graph *induced by* X *is the directed graph* $T_X = \langle E_X, D_X \rangle$ *where*

- *the set of nodes* E_X *is the set of all events* $e \in E$ *that involve objects in* X, *i.e., such that* $X \cap \pi_{obj}(e) \neq \emptyset$, *and*
- *the set of edges* D_X *consists of all* $\langle e, e' \rangle$ *such that for some* $o \in \pi_{obj}(e) \cap \pi_{obj}(e')$, *it is* $\pi_{trace}(o) = \langle e_1, \ldots, e_n \rangle$ *and* $e = e_i$, $e' = e_{i+1}$ *for some* $0 \leq i < n$.

Example 3. The object graph for the log in Example 2 is shown in Fig. 2 on the left. It has two connected components X_1 and X_2, whose trace graphs T_{X_1} and T_{X_2} are shown on the right. Note that T_{X_1} corresponds to the trace in Example 1, just that pick item now mentions also the order it is associated with.

3   Related Work and Modelling Features

To single out essential modelling features in the object-centric space, we reviewed the literature, considering seminal/survey papers [1,2,5] and papers proposing object-centric process models. For the latter, we restrict to those that rely on a Petri net-based specification [3,11,13,16,19,21]. A summary of the modelling features described next and their support in these approaches is given in Table 1.

A first essential feature is, as expected, the presence of constructs for *creating and deleting objects*. Approaches distinguish each other depending on whether objects are *explicitly referenced* in the model, or only *implicitly manipulated*. Another essential feature is to allow objects to *flow concurrently* and independently from each other—e.g., items that are picked while their order is paid (cf. *divergence* in [1]). Possibly, *multiple objects* of the same type can be *transferred* at once—e.g., a single check over multiple items. At the same time, it is also crucial to capture single transitions that manipulate multiple objects of the same or different type at once (cf. *convergence* in [1]). A first form of convergence is when a single transition takes a single, (parent) object and *spawns unboundedly many (child) objects* of a different type, all related to that parent—e.g., placing an order attaches unboundedly many items to it. If such a parent-children, *one-to-many relation* is tracked, also convergence in the form of synchronizing transitions can be supported. Such transitions allow a parent object to evolve only if some or all its child objects are in a certain state; these two forms are resp. called *subset* or *exact synchronization*. Finally, advanced forms of *coreference* can be used to inspect and evolve multiple related objects at once.

Resource-constraint ν-Petri nets [19] provide the first formalism dealing with a primitive form of object-centricity, where objects can be created and removed through the typical, explicit object-reference constructs of ν-Petri nets [17]. Objects can be related to resources (which are defined in the initial marking, and cannot be generated anew), but not to other objects. Alignment-based conformance checking is defined taking into account object identifiers and the resources they are related to, in an exact [19] and approximate [20] way.

Object-centric nets [3] provide an implicit approach to object-centric processes. Places and transitions are assigned to different object types. Simple arcs match with a single object at once, while double arcs process arbitrarily many objects of a given type. However, as already indicated, object relations are not tracked, which prohibits to capture object synchronization and coreference. Alignment-based conformance checking for this class of nets is studied in [15].

Synchronous proclets [11] provide a formalism where objects and their mutual relations are tracked implicitly. Dedicated constructs are provided to deal with the different types of convergence described above, including subset and exact synchronization (but not supporting other forms of coreference). Multi-object transfer is only approximately captured via iteration (picking objects one by one). Conformance checking has not yet been studied for proclets.

Variants of Petri nets with identifiers (PNIDs) are studied in [13,16,21], without dealing with conformance. PNIDs extend ν-Petri nets and the model in [19] by explicitly tracking objects and their relations, using tuples of identifiers. Differently from object-centric nets and proclets, no constructs are given to operate over unboundedly many objects with a single transition. As shown in [13], multi-object transfer and spawning, as well as subset synchronization, can be simulated using object coreference and iteration, while exact synchronization would require data-aware wholeplace operations, which are not supported.

4 Object-Centric Petri Nets with Identifiers

Using the literature analysis in Sect. 3, we define *object-centric Petri nets with identifiers* (OPIDs), combining the features of PNIDs with those of object-centric nets. As in PNIDs, objects can be created in OPIDs using ν variables, and tokens can carry objects or tuples of objects (accounting for object relations). In this way, objects can be associated with other objects, e.g., in situations as in Example 4, a product can "remember" the order it belongs to. Arcs are labeled with (tuples of) variables to match with objects and relations. Differently from PNIDs, OPIDs also support multi-object spawning and transfer typical of object-centric nets, by

Table 1. Comparison of Petri net-based object-centric process modelling languages along main modelling features, tracking which approaches support conformance. ✓ indicates full, direct support, ✗ no support, and ~ indirect support.

	object creation	object removal	concurrent object flows	multi-object transfer	multi-object spawning	object relations	subset sync	exact sync	coreference	object reference	conformance
resource-const. ν-PNS [19]	✓	✓	✓	✗	✗	✗	✗	✗	✗	exp.	[19,20]
object-centric nets [3]	✓	✓	✓	✓	✓	✗	✗	✗	✗	imp.	[15]
synchronous proclets [11]	✓	✓	✓	~	✓	✓	✓	✓	✗	imp.	✗
PNID variants [13,16,21]	✓	✓	✓	~	~	✓	~	✗	✓	exp.	✗
OPIDs	✓	✓	✓	✓	✓	✓	✓	~	✓	exp.	*here*

including special variables that match with *sets of objects*. All in all, as shown in the last row of Table 1, our new formalism supports all features discussed in Sect. 3, with the exception of exact synchronization, for the same reason for which this is not supported in PNIDs. However, we put ~ there, since as we will see below, this feature is implicitly supported when computing alignments.

Formal Definition. First, we assume that every object type $\sigma \in \Sigma$ has a domain $dom(\sigma) \subseteq \mathcal{O}$, given by all objects in $\mathcal{O}$ of type σ. In addition to the types in Σ, we also consider list types with a base type in σ, denoted as $[\sigma]$. As in colored Petri nets, each place has a *color*: a cartesian product of data types from Σ. More precisely, the set of colors $\mathcal{C}$ is the set of all $\sigma_1 \times \cdots \times \sigma_m$ such that $m \geq 1$ and $\sigma_i \in \Sigma$ for all $1 \leq i \leq m$. We fix a set of Σ-typed variables $\mathcal{X} = \mathcal{V} \uplus \mathcal{V}_{list} \uplus \Upsilon$ as the disjoint union of a set $\mathcal{V}$ of "normal" variables that refer to single objects, denoted by lower-case letters like v, with a type $\texttt{type}(v) \in \Sigma$, a set $\mathcal{V}_{list}$ of list variables that refer to a list of objects of the same type, denoted by upper case letters like U, with a type $\texttt{type}(U) = [\sigma]$ for some $\sigma \in \Sigma$, and a set Υ of variables referring to fresh objects, denoted as ν, with $\texttt{type}(\nu) \in \Sigma$. We assume that infinitely many variables of each kind exist, and for every $\nu \in \Upsilon$, that $dom(\texttt{type}(\nu))$ is infinite, to ensure an unbounded supply of fresh objects [17].

In OPIDs, tokens are tuples of objects, each associated with a color. E.g., for the objects in Example 2, we want to use $\langle o_1, p_1 \rangle$, $\langle o_2, p_2 \rangle$, or also just $\langle o_1 \rangle$ as tokens. To define relationships between objects in consumed and produced tokens when firing a transition, we next define *inscriptions* of arcs.

Definition 3. *An* inscription *is a tuple* $\boldsymbol{v} = \langle v_1, \ldots, v_m \rangle$ *such that* $m \geq 1$ *and* $v_i \in \mathcal{X}$ *for all* i, *but at most one* $v_i \in \mathcal{V}_{list}$, *for* $1 \leq i \leq m$. *We call* $\boldsymbol{v}$ *a* template inscription *if* $v_i \in \mathcal{V}_{list}$ *for some* i, *and a* simple inscription *otherwise.*

For instance, for $o, p \in \mathcal{V}$ and $P \in \mathcal{V}_{list}$, there are inscriptions $\langle o, P \rangle$ or $\langle p \rangle$, the former being a template inscription and the latter a simple one. However, $\langle P, P \rangle$ is not a valid inscription as it has two list variables. By allowing at most one list variable in inscriptions, we restrict to many-to-one relationships between objects, but it is known that many-to-many relationships can be modeled by many-to-one

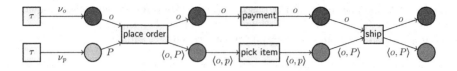

Fig. 3. OPID for a package handling process.

with auxiliary objects, through reification. Template inscriptions will be used to capture an arbitrary number of tokens of the same color: intuitively, if o is of type *order* and P of type $[product]$, then $\langle o, P \rangle$ refers to a single order with an arbitrary number of products.

We define the color of an inscription $\iota = \langle v_1, \ldots, v_m \rangle$ as the tuple of the types of the involved variables, i.e., $\texttt{color}(\iota) = \langle \sigma_1, \ldots, \sigma_m \rangle$ where $\sigma_i = \texttt{type}(v_i)$ if $v_i \in \mathcal{V} \cup \Upsilon$, and $\sigma_i = \sigma'$ if v_i is a list variable of type $[\sigma']$. Moreover, we set $vars(\iota) = \{v_1, \ldots, v_m\}$. E.g. for $\iota = \langle o, P \rangle$ with o, P as above, we have $\texttt{color}(\iota) = \langle order, product \rangle$ and $vars(\iota) = \{o, P\}$. The set of all inscriptions is denoted Ω.

Definition 4. *An* object-centric Petri net with identifiers *(OPID) is defined as a tuple $N = (\Sigma, P, T, F_{in}, F_{out}, \texttt{color}, \ell)$, where:*

1. *P and T are finite sets of places and transitions such that $P \cap T = \emptyset$;*
2. $\texttt{color} \colon P \to \mathcal{C}$ *maps every place to a color;*
3. $\ell \colon T \to \mathcal{A} \cup \{\tau\}$ *is the transition labelling where τ marks an invisible activity,*
4. $F_{in} \colon P \times T \to \Omega$ *is a partial function called* input flow, *such that $\texttt{color}(F_{in}(p, t)) = \texttt{color}(p)$ for every $(p, t) \in dom(F_{in})$;*
5. $F_{out} \colon T \times P \to \Omega$ *is a partial function called* output flow, *such that $\texttt{color}(F_{out}(t, p)) = \texttt{color}(p)$ for every $(t, p) \in dom(F_{out})$;*

We set $vars_{in}(t) = \bigcup_{p \in P} vars(F_{in}(p, t))$, and $vars_{out}(t) = \bigcup_{p \in P} vars(F_{out}(t, p))$, and require that $vars_{in}(t) \cap \Upsilon = \emptyset$ and $vars_{out}(t) \subseteq vars_{in}(t) \cup \Upsilon$, for all $t \in T$.

If $F_{in}(p, t)$ is defined, it is called a *variable* flow if $F_{in}(p, t)$ is a template inscription, and *non-variable* flow otherwise; and similar for output flows. Variable flows play the role of variable arcs in [15], they can carry multiple tokens at once. For an OPID $\mathcal{N}$ as in Definition 4, we also use the common notations $\bullet t = \{p \mid (p, t) \in dom(F_{in})\}$ and $t \bullet = \{p \mid (t, p) \in dom(F_{out})\}$.

Example 4. Figure 3 expresses the model of Example 1 as an OPID. We use variables ν_o or type *order* and ν_p of type *product*, both in Υ, to refer to new objects and products; as well as normal variables $o, p \in \mathcal{V}$ of type *order* and *product*, respectively, and a variable P of type $[product]$. For readability, we write e.g. o instead of $\langle o \rangle$. Note that in contrast to the model in Fig. 1, after place order, products now remember the order they belong to. As in Example 1, the transitions place order and ship have variable arcs, to process multiple products at once. However, we can now use tokens that combine a product p with its order o in a tuple $\langle o, p \rangle$. In Example 5 below we will see that the semantics of OPIDs ensure that in the ship transition, all consumed tokens must refer to *the same* order.

Semantics. Given the set of objects $\mathcal{O}$, the set of *tokens* $\mathcal{O}$ is the set of object tuples $\mathcal{O} = \{\mathcal{O}^m \mid m \geq 1\}$. The *color* of a token $\omega \in \mathcal{O}$ of the form $\omega = \langle o_1, \dots, o_m \rangle$ is denoted $\text{color}(\omega) = \langle \text{type}(o_1), \dots, \text{type}(o_m) \rangle$. To define the execution semantics, we first introduce a notion of a *marking* of an OPID $\mathcal{N} = \langle \Sigma, P, T, F_{in}, F_{out}, \text{color}, \ell \rangle$, namely as a function $M \colon P \to 2^{\mathcal{O}}$, such that for all $p \in P$ and $\langle o_1, \dots o_m \rangle \in M(p)$, it holds that $\text{color}(\langle o_1, \dots o_m \rangle) = \text{color}(p)$. Let $Lists(\mathcal{O})$ denote the set of objects lists of the form $[o_1, \dots, o_k]$ with $o_1, \dots, o_k \in \mathcal{O}$ such that all o_i have the same type; the type of such a list is then $[\text{type}(o_1)]$. Next, we define *bindings* to fix which objects are involved in a transition firing.

Definition 5. *A* binding *for a transition t and a marking M is a type-preserving function $b \colon vars_{in}(t) \cup vars_{out}(t) \to \mathcal{O} \cup Lists(\mathcal{O})$. To ensure freshness of created values, we demand that b is injective on $\Upsilon \cap vars_{out}(t)$, and that $b(\nu)$ does not occur in M for all $\nu \in \Upsilon \cap vars_{out}(t)$.*

For transition ship in Example 4 the mapping b that sets $b(o) = o_1$ and $b(P) = [p_1, p_2, p_3]$ is a binding (for any marking). Next, we extend bindings to inscriptions to fix which tokens (not just single objects) participate in a transition firing. The extension of a binding b to inscriptions, i.e., variable tuples, is denoted $\boldsymbol{b}$. For an inscription $\iota = \langle v_1, \dots, v_m \rangle$, let $o_i = b(v_i)$ for all $1 \leq i \leq m$. Then $\boldsymbol{b}(\iota)$ is the set of object tuples defined as follows: if ι is a simple inscription then $\boldsymbol{b}(\iota) = \{\langle o_1, \dots, o_m \rangle\}$. Otherwise, there must be one v_i, $1 \leq i \leq n$, such that $v_i \in \mathcal{V}_{list}$, and consequently o_i must be a list, say $o_i = [u_1, \dots, u_k]$ for some $u_1, \dots, u_k$. Then $\boldsymbol{b}(\iota) = \{\langle o_1, \dots, o_{i-1}, u_1, o_{i+1}, \dots, o_m \rangle, \dots, \langle o_1, \dots, o_{i-1}, u_k, o_{i+1}, \dots, o_m \rangle\}$. The set of all bindings is denoted by $\mathcal{B}$. Next, we define that a transition with a binding b is enabled if all object tuples pointed by $\boldsymbol{b}$ occur in the current marking.

Definition 6. *A transition $t \in T$ and a binding b for marking M are* enabled *in M if $\boldsymbol{b}(F_{in}(p, t)) \subseteq M(p)$ for all $p \in \bullet t$.*

E.g., the binding b with $b(o) = o_1$ and $b(P) = [p_1, p_2, p_3]$ is enabled in a marking M of the OPID in Example 4 with $\langle o_1 \rangle \in M(q_{blue})$ and $\langle o_1, p_1 \rangle, \langle o_1, p_2 \rangle, \langle o_1, p_3 \rangle \in M(q_{green})$, for q_{blue} and q_{green} the input places of ship with respective color.

Definition 7. *Let transition t be enabled in marking M with binding b. The* firing *of t yields the new marking M' given by $M'(p) = M(p) \setminus \boldsymbol{b}(F_{in}(p, t))$ for all $p \in \bullet t$, and $M'(p) = M(p) \cup \boldsymbol{b}(F_{out}(p, t))$ for all $p \in t\bullet$.*

We write $M \xrightarrow{t,b} M'$ to denote that t is enabled with binding b in M, and its firing yields M'. A sequence of transitions with bindings $\rho = \langle (t_1, b_1), \dots, (t_n, b_n) \rangle$ is called a *run* if $M_{i-1} \xrightarrow{t_i, b_i} M_i$ for all $1 \leq i \leq n$, in which case we write $M_0 \xrightarrow{\rho} M_n$. For such a binding sequence ρ, the *visible subsequence* ρ_v is the subsequence of ρ consisting of all (t_i, b_i) such that $\ell(t_i) \neq \tau$.

An *accepting* object-centric Petri net with identifiers is an object-centric Petri net $\mathcal{N}$ together with a set of initial markings M_{init} and a set of final markings M_{final}. For instance, for Example 4, M_{init} consists only of the empty marking, whereas M_{final} consists of all (infinitely many) markings in which each of the two right-most places has at least one token, and all other places have no token. The *language* of the net is given by $\mathcal{L}(\mathcal{N}) = \{\rho_v \mid m \xrightarrow{\rho} m', m \in M_{init}, \text{ and } m' \in M_{final}\}$, i.e., the set of visible subsequences of accepted sequences.

Alignments. In our approach, alignments show how a trace graph relates to a run of the model. In the remainder of this section, we consider a trace graph $T_X = \langle E_X, D_X \rangle$ and an accepting OPID with identifiers $\mathcal{N} = \langle \Sigma, P, T, F_{in}, F_{out}, \texttt{color}, \ell \rangle$, and we assume that the language of $\mathcal{N}$ is not empty.

Definition 8. *A move is a tuple that is a* model *move if it is in the set* $\{\gg\} \times ((\mathcal{A} \cup \{\tau\}) \times \mathcal{P}(\mathcal{O}))$, *and a* log *move if it is in the set* $(\mathcal{A} \times \mathcal{P}(\mathcal{O})) \times \{\gg\}$, *and a* synchronous *move if it is of the form* $\langle\langle a, O\rangle, \langle a', O'\rangle\rangle \in (\mathcal{A} \times \mathcal{P}(\mathcal{O})) \times (\mathcal{A} \times \mathcal{P}(\mathcal{O}))$ *such that* $a = a'$ *and* $O = O'$. *The set of all synchronous, model, and log moves over* X *and* $\mathcal{N}$ *is denoted* $moves(T_X, \mathcal{N})$.

In the object-centric setting, an alignment is a *graph* of moves. To define them formally, we first define log and model projections, similarly to [15]. In a graph of moves we write $\langle q_0, r_0 \rangle \xrightarrow{\gg}_{log} \langle q_k, r_k \rangle$ if there is a path $\langle q_0, r_0 \rangle \to \langle \gg, r_1 \rangle \to \dots \langle \gg, r_{k-1} \rangle \to \langle q_k, r_k \rangle$, for $q_0, q_k \neq \gg$ and $k > 0$, i.e., a path where all intermediate log components are $\gg$. Similarly, $\langle q_0, r_0 \rangle \xrightarrow{\gg}_{mod} \langle q_k, r_k \rangle$ abbreviates a path $\langle q_0, r_0 \rangle \to \langle q_1, \gg \rangle \to \dots \langle q_{k-1}, \gg \rangle \to \langle q_k, r_k \rangle$, for $r_0, r_k \neq \gg$ and $k > 0$.

Definition 9 (Projections). *Let* $G = \langle C, B \rangle$ *be a graph with* $C \subseteq moves(T_X, \mathcal{N})$.
The log *projection* $G|_{log} = \langle C_l, B_l \rangle$ *is the graph with node set* $C_l = \{q \mid \langle q, r \rangle \in C \text{ and } q \neq \gg\}$, *and an edge* $\langle q, q' \rangle$ *iff* $\langle q, r \rangle \xrightarrow{\gg}_{log} \langle q', r' \rangle$ *for some* r, r'.
The model *projection* $G|_{mod} = \langle C_m, B_m \rangle$ *is the graph with node set* $C_m = \{r \mid \langle q, r \rangle \in C, r \neq \gg\}$, *and an edge* $\langle r, r' \rangle$ *iff* $\langle q, r \rangle \xrightarrow{\gg}_{mod} \langle q', r' \rangle$ *for some* q, q'.

Basically, for a graph G over moves, the log projection is a graph that restricts to the log component of moves, omitting skip symbols. The edges are as in G, except that one also adds edges that "shortcut" over model moves, i.e. where the log component is $\gg$; the model projection is analogous for the other component. Next we define an alignment as a graph over moves where the log and model projections are a trace graph and a run, respectively.

Definition 10 (Alignment). *An* alignment *of a trace graph* T_X *and an accepting OPID* $\mathcal{N}$ *is an acyclic directed graph* $\Gamma = \langle C, B \rangle$ *with* $C \subseteq moves(T_X, \mathcal{N})$ *such that* $\Gamma|_{log} = T_X$, *there is a run* $\rho = \langle\langle t_1, b_1 \rangle, \dots, \langle t_n, b_n \rangle\rangle$ *with* $\rho_v \in \mathcal{L}(\mathcal{N})$, *and the model projection* $\Gamma|_{mod} = \langle C_m, B_m \rangle$ *admits a bijection* $f : \{\langle t_1, b_1 \rangle, \dots, \langle t_n, b_n \rangle\} \to C_m$ *such that*

- *if* $f(t_i, b_i) = \langle a, O_m \rangle$ *then* $\ell(t_i) = a$, *and* $O_m = range(b_i)$, *for all* $1 \leq i \leq n$
- *for all* $\langle r, r' \rangle \in B_m$ *there are* $1 \leq i < j \leq n$ *such that* $f(t_i, b_i) = r$ *and* $f(t_j, b_j) = r'$, *and if* $r = f(t_i, b_i)$, $r' = f(t_{i+1}, b_{i+1})$ *are in* C_m *for* $1 \leq i < n$ *then* $\langle r, r' \rangle \in B_m$.

Example 5. Figure 4 shows an alignment Γ for T_{X_1} from Example 3 w.r.t. the model in Example 4, where the log (resp. model) component is shown on top

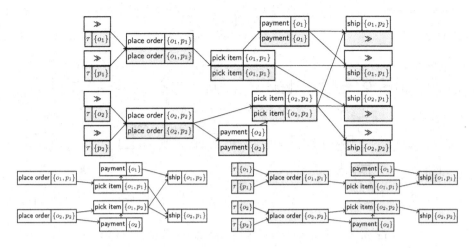

Fig. 4. Alignment with projections.

(resp. bottom) of moves. Below, the log (left) and model projections (right) of Γ are shown. One can check that the former is isomorphic to T_{X_1} in Example 3. The alignment in Example 1 is not valid in our setting: its model projection is not in the language of the net.

In the remainder of the paper, we use the following cost function based on [15]. However, the approach developed below can also be adapted to other definitions.

Definition 11. *The cost of a move M is defined as follows:*

- *if M is a log move $\langle\langle a_{log}, O_{log}\rangle, \gg\rangle$ then $cost(M) = |O_{log}|$,*
- *if M is a model move $\langle\gg, \langle a_{mod}, O_{mod}\rangle\rangle$ then $cost(M) = 0$ if $a_{mod} = \tau$, and $cost(M) = |O_{mod}|$ otherwise,*
- *if M is a synchronous move $\langle\langle a_{log}, O_{log}\rangle, \langle a_{mod}, O_{mod}\rangle\rangle$ then $cost(M) = 0$.*

For an alignment $\Gamma = \langle C, B\rangle$, we set $cost(\Gamma) = \sum_{M \in C} cost(M)$, i.e., the cost of an alignment Γ is the sum of the cost of its moves.

E.g., Γ in Fig. 4 has cost 8, as it involves two log moves and two non-silent model moves with two objects each. In fact, it is optimal in the following sense:

Definition 12. *An alignment Γ of a trace graph T_X and an accepting OPID $\mathcal{N}$ is optimal if $cost(\Gamma) \leq cost(\Gamma')$ for all alignments Γ' of T_X and $\mathcal{N}$.*

The *conformance checking task* for an accepting OPID $\mathcal{N}$ and a log L is to find optimal alignments with respect to $\mathcal{N}$ for all trace graphs in L.
Finally, OPIDs generalize the object-centric nets in [3,15]:

Remark 1. Every object-centric net *ON* in the formalism of [3,15] can be encoded into an equivalent OPID $\mathcal{N}$ by adding suitable arc inscriptions, as follows. Let $v_\sigma \in \mathcal{V}$ be a normal variable, and $V_\sigma \in \mathcal{V}_{list}$ a list variable, for each

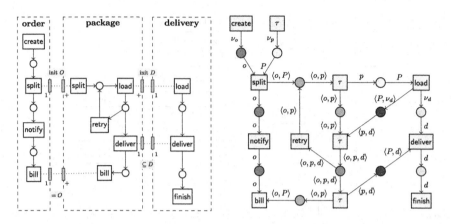

Fig. 5. A synchronous proclet and a corresponding OPID.

object type σ in ON. For every arc a that has as source or target a place p taking objects of type σ, we associate color $\langle\sigma\rangle$ with p, and add the arc inscription $\langle V_\sigma\rangle$ to a if a is a variable arc, and $\langle v_\sigma\rangle$ otherwise. This is possible as in the object-centric Petri nets of [3,15], transitions do not distinguish between objects of the same type. Initial and final markings M_{init} and M_{final} for ON can be used as such.

In [15], alignments are computed assuming that they involve exactly the set of objects mentioned in the log. The next example shows that this assumption can compromise the existence of alignments, even irrespective of optimality.

Example 6. Consider the OPID $\mathcal{N}$ from Example 4, and let M_{final} consist of all markings where the right-most two places contain at least one token, and all other places contain no token. The empty run is thus not in the language of $\mathcal{N}$. Now consider the log $L = \{\langle\#_0, \text{place order}, \{p\}, 1\rangle, \langle\#_1.\text{pick item}, \{p\}, 2\rangle, \langle\#_2, \text{ship}, \{p\}, 3\rangle\}$ where (say, due to an error in the logging system), the order was not recorded, but only an item p of type *product*. There exists no alignment involving only object p, as every run of $\mathcal{N}$ must involve an object of type *order*.

In contrast, an OPID with silent transitions and ν-inscriptions as in Example 4 to create objects, admits an optimal alignment also in this case. We next observe that synchronization in OPIDs is quite expressive when tackling conformance.

Example 7. To show the expressiveness of OPIDs, we model a proclet inspired from the running example in [11]—keeping all essential proclet features. The proclet N is shown in Fig. 5 on the left, while the OPID on the right emulates the behaviour of N with few differences: Packages are created by a silent transition instead within split, and the exact synchronization $=O$ in the bill transition of N cannot be expressed in OPIDs. Instead, all synchronizations are implicitly of subset type. Let a trace graph T consist of the events $\langle\text{create}, \{o\}, 1\rangle, \langle\text{split}, \{o, p\}, 2\rangle,$

$\langle$notify, $\{o\}, 3\rangle$, $\langle$load, $\{d, p\}, 4\rangle$, $\langle$bill, $\{o\}, 5\rangle$, $\langle$deliver, $\{o, p\}, 5\rangle$ and $\langle$finish, $\{d\}, 6\rangle$. Product p was ignored in the bill event, so the exact synchronization demanded by the proclet is violated. In our OPID, due to the implicit subset semantics, T could be matched against a valid transition sequence, but no final marking would be reached: token $\langle o, p\rangle$ is left behind in the bottom green place. Thus no alignment with a synchronous bill move exists, hence no cost 0 alignment, and the lack of synchronization is in fact detected in the alignment task.

5   Encoding

In encoding-based conformance checking, it is essential to fix upfront an upper bound on the size of an optimal alignment [12]. For OPIDs, the next lemma establishes such a bound. We assume that in runs of $\mathcal{N}$ every object used in a silent transition occurs also in a non-silent one. The precise statement with a formal proof can be found in [14, Lem. 2].

Lemma 1. *Let m be the number of object occurrences in T_X, c the number of objects in some run of $\mathcal{N}$, and k the maximal number of subsequent silent transitions without ν in $\mathcal{N}$. The number of moves in $\Gamma|_{mod}$ is linear in $|E_X|$, c, m and k, and $\Gamma|_{mod}$ has at most $2c+m$ object occurrences in non-silent transitions.*

For our encoding we also need to determine a priori a set of objects O that is a superset of the objects used in the model projection of the optimal alignment. However, we can nevertheless solve problems as in Example 6 using the bound on the number of objects in Lemma 1: e.g. in Example 6, we have $c = 3$ and $m = 6$, so the bound on object occurrences is 12, while the bound on moves is 25.

Encoding the Run. Let $\mathcal{N} = \langle \Sigma, P, T, F_{in}, F_{out}, \mathtt{color}, \ell \rangle$ an OPID and $T_X = \langle E_X, D_X \rangle$ a trace graph. In the encoding, we assume the following, using Lemma 1: *(i)* The number of nodes in the model projection of an optimal alignment is upper-bounded by a number $n \in \mathbb{N}$. *(ii)* The set $O \subseteq \mathcal{O}$ is a finite set of objects that might occur in the alignment, it must contain all objects in T_X, optionally it can contain more objects. We assume that every $o \in O$ is assigned a unique id $id(o) \in \{1, \ldots, |O|\}$ *(iii)* K is the maximum number of objects involved in any transition firing, it can be computed from O and $\mathcal{N}$.

To encode a run ρ of length at most n, we use the following SMT variables:

(a) Transition variables $\mathtt{T}_j$ of type integer for all $1 \leq j \leq n$ to identify the j-th transition in the run. To this end, we enumerate the transitions as $T = \{t_1, \ldots, t_L\}$, and add the constraint $\bigwedge_{j=1}^{n} 1 \leq \mathtt{T}_j \leq L$, with the semantics that $\mathtt{T}_j$ is assigned value l iff the j-th transition in ρ is t_l.

(b) To identify the markings in the run, we use marking variables $\mathtt{M}_{j,p,o}$ of type boolean for every time point $0 \leq j \leq n$, every place $p \in P$, and every vector o of objects with elements in O such that $\mathtt{color}(o) = \mathtt{color}(p)$. The semantics is that $\mathtt{M}_{j,p,o}$ is assigned true iff o occurs in p at time j.

(c) To keep track of which objects are used by transitions of the run, we use object variables $\mathsf{o}_{j,k}$ of type integer for all $1 \leq j \leq n$ and $0 \leq k \leq K$ with the constraint $\bigwedge_{j=1}^{n} 1 \leq \mathsf{o}_{j,k} \leq |O|$. The semantics is that if $\mathsf{o}_{j,k}$ is assigned value i then, if $i > 0$ the k-th object involved in the j-th transition is o_i, and if $i = 0$ then the j-th transition uses less than k objects.

(d) To encode the actual length of the run, we use an integer variable $\mathtt{len}$.

In addition, we use the following variables to represent alignment cost:

(e) Distance variables $\mathsf{d}_{i,j}$ of type integer for every $0 \leq i \leq m$ and $0 \leq j \leq n$, their use will be explained later.

Next we intuitively explain the used constraints: the formal description with all technical formulae of the encoding, as well as the decoding, can be found in [14].

(1) *Initial markings.* We ensure that the first marking in the run ρ is initial.

(2) *Final markings.* Next, we state that after at most n steps, but possibly earlier, a final marking is reached.

(3) *Moving tokens.* Transitions must be enabled; tokens are moved by transitions.

(4) *Tokens not moved by transitions stay in their place.* Similarly to the previous item, we capture that for every time point, place p, and token o, the marking does not change for p and o unless it is produced or consumed by some transition.

(5) *Transitions use objects of suitable type.* To this end, recall that every transition can use at most K objects, which limits instantiations of template inscriptions. For every transition $t \in T$, we can thus enumerate the objects used by it from 1 to K. Depending on the transition t_l performed in the j-th step, we thus demand that the object variables $\mathsf{o}_{j,k}$ are instantiated by an object of suitable type, using a disjunction over all possible objects.

(6) *Objects that instantiate ν-variables are fresh.* Finally, we need to require that if an object is instantiated for a ν-inscription in a transition firing, then this object does not occur in the current marking.

We denote by φ_{run} the conjunction of the constraints in (a)–(c) and (1)–(6), as they encode a valid run of $\mathcal{N}$.

Encoding Alignment Cost. Similar as in [7,12], we encode the cost of an alignment as the edit distance with respect to suitable penalty functions. Given a trace graph $T_X = (E_X, D_X)$, let $e_1, \ldots, e_m$ be an enumeration of all events in E_X such that $\pi_{time}(e_1) \leq \cdots \leq \pi_{time}(e_m)$. Let $[P_L]_i$, $[P_M]_j$, and $[P_=]_{i,j}$ be the penalty expressions, for a log move, a model move and a synchronous move, resp.

$$\mathsf{d}_{0,0} = 0 \qquad \mathsf{d}_{i+1,0} = [P_L] + \mathsf{d}_{i,0} \qquad \mathsf{d}_{0,j+1} = [P_M]_{j+1} + \mathsf{d}_{0,j} \qquad (\varphi_\delta)$$
$$\mathsf{d}_{i+1,j+1} = \min([P_=]_{i+1,j+1} + \mathsf{d}_{i,j},\ [P_L] + \mathsf{d}_{i,j+1},\ [P_M]_{j+1} + \mathsf{d}_{i+1,j})$$

Solving. We use an SMT solver to obtain a satisfying assignment α for the following constrained optimization problem (Φ): $\varphi_{run} \wedge \varphi_\delta$ *minimizing* $\mathsf{d}_{m,n}$.

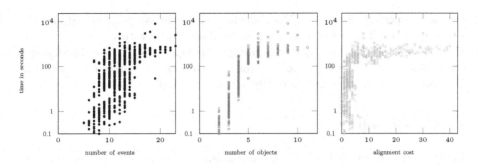

Fig. 6. Run time related to the number of events, objects, and alignment cost.

From α one can then decode the run $\rho(\alpha)$ and the optimal alignment $\Gamma(\alpha)$, similar as in [12]. In particular, $\alpha(\mathsf{d}_{m,n})$ is the cost of the optimal alignment.

Theorem 1. *Given an OPID $\mathcal{N}$, trace graph T_X, and satisfying assignment α to (Φ), $\Gamma(\alpha)$ is an optimal alignment of T_X with respect to $\mathcal{N}$ with cost $\alpha(\mathsf{d}_{m,n})$.*

6   Evaluation

Implementation. Our tool oCoCoMoT is implemented in Python as a branch of CoCoMoT.[2] oCoCoMoT uses the SMT solver Yices 2 [10] as backend. As inputs, the tool takes an OPID and an object-centric event log. The former we represent as a pnml file with minimal adaptations, namely every place has an attribute *color*, which is a tuple of types in Σ; and every arc has an *inscription* attribute that is a list of typed variables as in Definition 3. The event log is represented as a jsonocel file, in the format used in [3,15]. The tool provides a simple command-line interface, and it outputs a textual representation of the decoded run of the OPID, as well as the alignment and its cost. The encoding in our implementation is as described in Sect. 5, apart from some simple optimizations that introduce additional SMT variables for subexpressions that occur multiple times.

Experiments. We followed [15] and used the BPI 2017 event data [9] restricted to the most frequent 50% of activities. This resulted in 715 variants after applying pm4py's variant filtering as in [15]. The resulting traces have 3 to 23 events (12 on average), and 2 to 11 objects (5 on average). The OPID for the experiments was obtained by augmenting their object-centric Petri net with arc inscriptions as remarked in Remark 1. The evaluation was performed single-threaded but distributed on a 12-core Intel i7-5930K 3.50 GHz machine with 32 GB of main memory.

Figure 6 summarizes the results of the experiments, showing the runtime in seconds in relationship to the number of events, the number of objects, and the

---

[2] See https://github.com/bytekid/cocomot/tree/object-centric.

cost of the optimal alignment. Note that the scale on the y-axis is logarithmic, the x-axis is linear. The runtime is on average about 200 s, with maximal runtime of 7900 s. While the tool of [15] is faster in comparison, the overhead seems acceptable given that oCoCoMoT performs a considerably more complex task. Experiment data and examples can be found on github.

7   Conclusion

In this work we have defined the new formalism of OPIDs for object-centric processes, supporting the essential modelling features in this space, as described in Sect. 3. We have then defined alignment-based conformance for this model. We can thus answer the research questions posed in the introduction affirmatively: (1) OPIDs constitute a succinct, Petri net-based formalism for object-centric processes that supports object identity, arcs with multiplicity, and synchronization, (2) we formally defined the conformance checking problem for OPIDs, and (3) SMT encodings are a feasible, operational technique to implement this notion of conformance checking, as witnessed by our experiments.

In future work, we want to extend OPIDs along two directions. First, we aim at supporting data and data-aware conditions, exploiting the fact that our approach seamlessly integrates with CoCoMoT. Second, while exact synchronization is so far tackled only when computing alignment, we want to make it part of the model. This is non trivial: OPIDs need to be equipped with a form of wholeplace operation, which requires universal quantification in the SMT encoding.

References

1. van der Aalst, W.M.P.: Object-centric process mining: dealing with divergence and convergence in event data. In: Ölveczky, P., Salaün, G. (eds.) SEFM 2019. LNCS, vol. 11724, pp. 3–25. Springer, Cham (2019). https://doi.org/10.1007/978-3-030-30446-1_1
2. van der Aalst, W.M.P.: Twin transitions powered by event data - using object-centric process mining to make processes digital and sustainable. In: Joint Proceedings of the ATAED/PN4TT (2023)
3. van der Aalst, W.M.P., Berti, A.: Discovering object-centric Petri nets. Fundam. Informaticae **175**(1–4), 1–40 (2020)
4. Artale, A., Kovtunova, A., Montali, M., van der Aalst, W.M.P.: Modeling and reasoning over declarative data-aware processes with object-centric behavioral constraints. In: Hildebrandt, T., van Dongen, B., Röglinger, M., Mendling, J. (eds.) BPM 2019. LNCS, vol. 11675, pp. 139–156. Springer, Cham (2019). https://doi.org/10.1007/978-3-030-26619-6_11
5. Berti, A., Montali, M., van der Aalst, W.M.P.: Advancements and challenges in object-centric process mining: a systematic literature review. CoRR abs/2311.08795 (2023)
6. Berti, A., Park, G., Rafiei, M., van der Aalst, W.M.P.: An event data extraction approach from SAP ERP for process mining. In: Proceedings of the ICPM Workshops (2021)

7. Boltenhagen, M., Chatain, T., Carmona, J.: Optimized SAT encoding of conformance checking artefacts. Computing **103**(1), 29–50 (2021)
8. Calvanese, D., Jans, M., Kalayci, T.E., Montali, M.: Extracting event data from document-driven enterprise systems. In: Indulska, M., Reinhartz-Berger, I., Cetina, C., Pastor, O. (eds.) CAiSE 2023. LNCS, vol. 13901, pp. 193–209. Springer, Cham (2023). https://doi.org/10.1007/978-3-031-34560-9_12
9. van Dongen, B.: BPI challenge 2017 data set (2017)
10. Dutertre, B.: Yices 2.2. In: Biere, A., Bloem, R. (eds.) CAV 2014. LNCS, vol. 8559, pp. 737–744. Springer, Cham (2014). https://doi.org/10.1007/978-3-319-08867-9_49
11. Fahland, D.: Describing behavior of processes with many-to-many interactions. In: Donatelli, S., Haar, S. (eds.) PETRI NETS 2019. LNCS, vol. 11522, pp. 3–24. Springer, Cham (2019). https://doi.org/10.1007/978-3-030-21571-2_1
12. Felli, P., Gianola, A., Montali, M., Rivkin, A., Winkler, S.: Data-aware conformance checking with SMT. Inf. Syst. **117**, 102230 (2023)
13. Ghilardi, S., Gianola, A., Montali, M., Rivkin, A.: Petri net-based object-centric processes with read-only data. Inf. Syst. **107**, 102011 (2022)
14. Gianola, A., Montali, M., Winkler, S.: Object-centric conformance alignments with synchronization (extended version). CoRR abs/2312.08537 (2023)
15. Liss, L., Adams, J.N., van der Aalst, W.M.P.: Object-centric alignments. In: Almeida, J.P.A., Borbinha, J., Guizzardi, G., Link, S., Zdravkovic, J. (eds.) ER 2023. LNCS, vol. 14320, pp. 201–219. Springer, Cham (2023). https://doi.org/10.1007/978-3-031-47262-6_11
16. Polyvyanyy, A., van der Werf, J.M.E.M., Overbeek, S., Brouwers, R.: Information systems modeling: language, verification, and tool support. In: Giorgini, P., Weber, B. (eds.) CAiSE 2019. LNCS, vol. 11483, pp. 194–212. Springer, Cham (2019). https://doi.org/10.1007/978-3-030-21290-2_13
17. Rosa-Velardo, F., de Frutos-Escrig, D.: Decidability problems in Petri nets with names and replication. Fundam. Informaticae **105**(3), 291–317 (2010)
18. Snoeck, M., De Smedt, J., De Weerdt, J.: Supporting data-aware processes with MERODE. In: Augusto, A., Gill, A., Nurcan, S., Reinhartz-Berger, I., Schmidt, R., Zdravkovic, J. (eds.) BPMDS/EMMSAD -2021. LNBIP, vol. 421, pp. 131–146. Springer, Cham (2021). https://doi.org/10.1007/978-3-030-79186-5_9
19. Sommers, D., Sidorova, N., van Dongen, B.: Aligning event logs to resource-constrained ν-Petri nets. In: Bernardinello, L., Petrucci, L. (eds.) PETRI NETS 2022. LNCS, vol. 13288, pp. 325–345. Springer, Cham (2022). https://doi.org/10.1007/978-3-031-06653-5_17
20. Sommers, D., Sidorova, N., van Dongen, B.: Exact and approximated log alignments for processes with inter-case dependencies. In: Gomes, L., Lorenz, R. (eds.) PETRI NETS 2023. LNCS, vol. 13929, pp. 99–119. Springer, Cham (2023). https://doi.org/10.1007/978-3-031-33620-1_6
21. van der Werf, J.M.E.M., Rivkin, A., Polyvyanyy, A., Montali, M.: Data and process resonance. In: Bernardinello, L., Petrucci, L. (eds.) PETRI NETS 2022. LNCS, vol. 13288, pp. 369–392. Springer, Cham (2022). https://doi.org/10.1007/978-3-031-06653-5_19

Process Comparison Based on Selection-Projection Structures

Tobias Brockhoff[(✉)] , Merih Seran Uysal , and Wil M.P. van der Aalst

Chair of Process and Data Science, RWTH Aachen University, Aachen, Germany
{brockhoff,uysal,wvdaalst}@pads.rwth-aachen.de

Abstract. Insight into differences between different implementations of a process provides valuable information for improvement. Process comparison approaches leverage event data on process executions to provide such insight. However, state-of-the-art procedural methods are often limited to *local* differences considering activities executed within a limited number of steps (e.g., directly following activities). Thereby, detecting differences which, for instance, relate early steps of a process execution to its outcome remains challenging. In contrast, rule-based declarative approaches can detect *global* differences with respect to distant activities; yet they are limited by the *complexity of the rule templates employed*. Moreover, they are prone to yield *fragmented* diagnostics. If a subprocess occurs more frequently in one process variant, these approaches typically report each activity contained. In this work, we therefore propose a process comparison approach that detects *aggregated* likelihood differences for *global* control-flow patterns. To this end, we decompose the difference detection task into subprocesses induced by co-occurring activities. Using Earth Mover's Distance, we identify differences within individual subprocesses independent of predefined rule templates. We then aggregate and combine subprocesses which distinguish the process variants. By exploiting relations among subprocesses, we retrieve *maximal* differences affecting many activities. Reducing fragmentation caused by choice-induced frequency differences, we additionally *complement* these *maximal* differences. To compare the sensitivity of our difference detection method to existing approaches, we devise a quantitative evaluation framework. Moreover, we demonstrate the effectiveness of our method on a public, real-life event log. Ultimately, the evaluation shows that our method is accurate and capable of providing coherent, global diagnostics.

Keywords: Process Mining · Process Comparison · Process Variant Analysis · Business Process Intelligence

1 Introduction

Operational processes are at the core of companies' value chains making active process management crucial for a company's success. Often, multiple variants of the same process exist (e.g., implementations at different facilities). Process

G. Guizzardi et al. (Eds.): CAiSE 2024, LNCS 14663, pp. 20–35, 2024.
https://doi.org/10.1007/978-3-031-61057-8_2

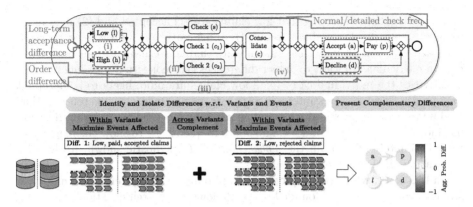

Fig. 1. Control-flow differences between process instances can be strongly entangled and concern distant parts of the process. In our approach, we decompose the difference detection in order to isolate activities and execution variants related to a difference. We then combine sets of complementary differences.

comparison methods aim to provide insight into differences between variants of a process denoting valuable information for process improvement. A common challenge is that there only exist event data of process executions where each event corresponds to a business transaction and is associated with a case (i.e., process instance), an activity, and a timestamp. Therefore, recent data-driven process comparison approaches take two event logs as input and return the (statistically significant) differences [4,7,14,19]. Yet, this can be challenging.

Consider the BPMN model of a claim management process shown in Fig. 1. Despite its simplicity, two instances of this process can differ in several ways. For example, they can differ with respect to (i) the frequency of low or high claims or (ii) in the probability of the detailed checks c_1 and c_2 being executed in a particular order. Moreover, these low-level differences might be further entangled. There can be additional dependencies between (iii) a claim's type and whether it is accepted, or (iv) the order differences of the checks is embedded in a frequency difference between normal and detailed checks. Besides, processes may differ in dimensions other than the (e.g., time). However, control flow has been the major concern of most existing works (see [20] for an overview), and we will focus on the former leaving extensions as future work.

State-of-the-art procedural approaches [4,14] are strong at identifying *local* differences—that is, differences concerning activities executed within a limited number of steps in the processes (e.g., directly following activities). However, detecting long-term differences such as the third differences illustrated in Fig. 1 is challenging. In contrast, the declarative approach proposed in [7] can detect differences for activities irrespective of their position in a case. However, it is limited to a fixed set of rule templates, and the implementation currently only supports activity pairs. Besides, reporting differences found for individual rules from a large corpus of rules is prone to yield fragmented diagnostics. For our example, considering the third—outcome-related—difference in Fig. 1, we obtain separate diagnostics showing that low claims are (1) accepted and (2) paid more frequently, but (3) declined less frequently. This motivates a process comparison approach that can provide *global* diagnostics that concern more than two activities. In particular, we want to detect differences that concern a *maximal* number of activities the individual cases (e.g., low claims are more likely to be accepted *and* paid). Besides, we want to incorporate *complementary* differences—that is, differences found for a distinct set of cases and caused by differing decision likelihoods (e.g., declining high claims more frequently)—to show the bigger picture. Ultimately, we obtain the *global, high-level* diagnostic shown in Fig. 1 by integrating all three diagnostics above.

In this work, we therefore propose an approach, which attempts to unify the strengths of both worlds, founded on the following research questions:

RQ(I)   How can we reliably detect *global* control-flow differences?
RQ(II)   How can we discover *maximal differences* that concern many activities?
RQ(III) How can we find differences across cases that complement each other?

To this end, we propose to analyze different sets of (possibly distant) activities. Thereby, we aim to isolate differences in terms of the cases and activities they concern improving the sensitivity of our approach to detect differences. Exploiting relations between the sets of activities, we aggregate sets of activities maximizing the number of activities concerned. Ultimately, we visualize differences in the process induced by each maximal set of activities. In doing so, we consider a context of complementary differences to show the bigger picture. The concept is shown on the bottom of Fig. 1 where we eventually identify a difference regarding the type and outcome of a claim. Conceptually, the approach is inspired by the variant and activity sliders implemented by most process mining tools. For process discovery, reducing the number of variants and activities reveals frequent control-flow patterns. In contrast, we consider not one but two process instances and attempt to find a configuration that shows a strong, coherent difference between the two instances.

Our contributions are as follows: we propose a method to detect *global* control flow differences based on the analysis of different sets of activities. It does not rely on predefined rule templates and proves to be highly sensitive. Moreover, we propose a two-step method *maximizing* and *combining* distinctive activity sets to reduce fragmentation of diagnostics. Compared to recent procedural approaches, latter combination step allows visualizing a particular difference in the context of other differences which can foster new interpretations.

We discuss related work and introduce preliminary concepts in Sects. 2 and 3. Next, we propose our method in Sect. 4, which we quantitatively and qualitatively evaluate in Sect. 5. Finally, we give our conclusion in Sect. 6.

2   Related Work

On a high level, one can distinguish process comparison approaches that devise differences from a process model or directly from data. Former approaches either require models as input [2,10], first discover a model [6,18], or enhance models [9]. For an in-depth discussion, we refer to the survey in [20].

An early application of graph comparison to process models proposes to visually compare them with respect to a merged, specially layouted graph [2]. In [10], Küster et al. consider change operations in the SESE-decompositions of UML activity diagrams. Yet, the authors in [1] argue that one must consider event data instead of models to make process comparison actionable.

Kriglstein et al. [9] complement structural diagnostics on model elements by differences in their use. Suriadi et al. discover process models and compare them with respect to how well they fit the other variants [18]. A similar approach, focussing on the mutual replay results, is proposed in [6]. An overview of different model-based visualizations is given in [16].

Log-based methods devise differences directly from event logs. An approach using sequential pattern mining is proposed in [11]. Van Beest et al. represent the process variants with prime event structures [3], align them, and verbalize differences. However, the approach requires a concurrency oracle. In [4], statistically significant differences are considered. The authors create a shared Transition System (TS) and apply hypothesis tests to detect performance and frequency differences. Yet, there is a trade-off between the expressiveness of the TS and its size. Taymouri et al. [19] create directly-follows graphs (DFGs), so-called Mutual Finger Prints (MFPs), from cases which they consider distinctive for each variant. To this end, they extract location- and frequency-aware features from a discrete wavelet transformation and discover the most distinctive subset of features by training and evaluating classifiers. Finally, they select the cases containing these features. However, the computational complexity of the method is high. A declarative approach is proposed in [7]. The authors instantiate a set of rule templates and test for differences. A log-based approach that allows to consider perspectives beyond control flow and performance is proposed in [14]. Finally, an interactive process comparison framework, applying filters upfront, was proposed in [21] . In contrast, we consider filtering an essential part of process comparison itself.

Our decomposition is related to concept lattices in Formal Concept Analysis (FCA) [17,22]; yet, we explicitly consider activity order.

3   Preliminaries

We denote the powerset of a set X by $\mathcal{P}(X)$ and the bags over X by $\mathcal{B}(X)$. For example, $M = [a^5, b]$ is a bag of size $|M| = 6$ containing a five times. In an abuse of notation, we overload set operators for bags (e.g., $a \in M$ and $[a^3] \subset M$). A directed graph is a tuple $G = (V, E)$ of a set of vertices and a directed edge relation $E \subseteq V \times V$. For brevity, we use an infix notation to denote edges—for example, for $v_1, v_2 \in V$, the vertex v_1 is a predecessor of v_2 if $v_1 \, E \, v_2$ holds. The transitive reduction of G is the graph $G' = (V, E')$ with the fewest edges and the same pairwise reachability of vertices as G.

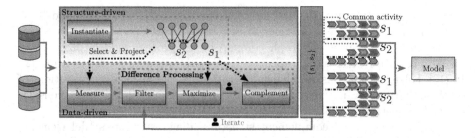

Fig. 2. Overview of the approach. We instantiate a measurement structure where vertices correspond to a subaspects of the process and edges relate the former. Using this structure, we measure differences and filter the initial results. Afterward, we maximize differences making them as specific as possible. Finally, we complement user-selected differences by related differences and use the associated variants and activities to visualize the result.

Event Data. Let $\mathcal{A}$ denote the universe of activity labels, and let $\Sigma \subseteq \mathcal{A}$ be a finite set of activities. A *trace* $\sigma = \langle \sigma_1, \ldots, \sigma_n \rangle \in \Sigma^*$ is a finite sequence of activities. The length of σ is $|\sigma| = n$. A trace $\sigma', |\sigma'| = m$ is a *subtrace* of σ, denoted by $\sigma' \sqsubseteq \sigma$, if there exist indices $1 \leq i_1 < \cdots < i_m \leq n$ such that $\sigma' = \langle \sigma_{i_1}, \ldots, \sigma_{i_m} \rangle$. Finally, we write $\{\sigma\} = \{\sigma_i \mid 1 \leq i \leq |\sigma|\}$ to denote the set of distinct activities in σ. An *event log* collects multiple executions of a process.

Definition 1 (Event Log). *Given a finite alphabet $\Sigma \subseteq \mathcal{A}$, an event log $E \in \mathcal{B}(\Sigma^*)$ is a finite bag of traces over Σ.*

For an event log $L \in \mathcal{B}(\Sigma^*)$, its empirical trace distribution is defined by the probability mass function $p_E \colon \Sigma^* \to [0,1], \sigma \mapsto \frac{E(\sigma)}{|E|}$. This is also called the *stochastic language* of E [12]. Let $\delta \colon \Sigma^* \times \Sigma^* \to [0,1]$ be a so-called *trace distance*—that is, a function that quantifies the dissimilarity between pairs of traces. Given event logs $L_1, L_2 \in \mathcal{B}(\Sigma^*)$, the Earth Mover's Distance (EMD) quantifies the dissimilarity of the associated stochastic languages [12]—that is, $\text{emd}_\delta(p_{L_1}, p_{L_2}) \in [0,1]$. In the following, we assume that normalized edit distance (edt) is used as trace distance.

4 Selection-Projection-Based Difference Discovery

We propose a two-stage process comparison approach that separates the detection and aggregation of differences. Figure 2 provides an overview and demonstrates how we distinguish between a structure-driven and data-driven aspect of our method. On the structural side, we create a lattice of commonly co-occurring sets of activities and use them to select and project control-flow variants of the process. This results in pairs of filtered sub-event logs extracted from the original event logs, representing data on subprocess executions. For example, in Fig. 2, the subprocess s_1 is associated with three activities, highlighted red, from two variants in each event log. By *measuring* the differences between each pair of sub-event logs using EMD, we then identify sets of activities for which the two process variants significantly differ in frequency or activity execution order. To consolidate differences related to the same variants, we *aggregate* them based on structural relations between subprocesses. This reduces fragmentation of frequency differences with respect to entire subprocesses such as the frequency difference regarding low and accepted as well as low and paid claims in Fig. 1. Additionally, we propose integrating complementary differences that are closely related but involve a different set of control-flow variants. For instance, in Fig. 2, we complement s_1 by s_2 since latter subprocess focuses on a distinct set of variants while sharing one activity. Ultimately, we create a model for the differential analysis of the retrieved *complementary* and *maximal* subprocesses. In the following, we illustrate our approach on the following two—left and right $(l|r)$—event logs generated from the process shown in Fig. 1:

$$L^{l|r,\text{ex}} = [\langle l, c_1, c_2, c, \text{a}, \text{p}\rangle^{42|50}, \langle l, c_1, c_2, c, \text{d}\rangle^{9|3}, \langle l, c_2, c_1, c, \text{d}\rangle^{9|7},$$
$$\langle h, c_1, c_2, c, \text{a}, \text{p}\rangle^{28|20}, \langle h, c_1, c_2, c, \text{d}\rangle^{6|7}, \langle h, c_2, c_1, c, \text{d}\rangle^{6|13}] \tag{1}$$

Selection-Projection Structure As depicted on the left of Fig. 2, one can think of an event log as a list of cases or, focusing on the control flow, variants. To isolate control-flow differences, we can "horizontally" select entries (i.e., variants) and "vertically" remove activities (i.e., activity projection). While for process discovery one typically focuses on frequent variants and activities, we suggest choosing and projecting traces based on frequently co-occurring activities for process comparison. To this end, let $L \in \mathcal{B}(\Sigma^*)$ denote an event log over an alphabet $\Sigma \subseteq \mathcal{A}$ and $\Sigma' \subseteq \Sigma$ be set of activities. *Activity projection* $\pi^{\text{act}}_{\Sigma'} \colon \Sigma^* \to \Sigma^*$ projects traces on Σ'. For a trace $\sigma \in \Sigma^*$, $\pi^{\text{act}}_{\Sigma'}(\sigma)$ is the longest subsequence of σ over Σ'—that is, $\pi^{\text{act}}_{\Sigma'}(\sigma) = \arg\max_{\tau \in (\Sigma')^*, \tau \sqsubseteq \sigma} |\tau|$. Similarly, *activity-based trace selection* $\mu^{\text{act}}_{\Sigma'} \colon \Sigma^* \to \Sigma^*$ keeps a trace σ if all activities in Σ' occur—that is, $\mu^{\text{act}}_{\Sigma'}(\sigma) = \sigma$ if $\Sigma' \subseteq \{\sigma\}$; otherwise, $\mu^{\text{act}}_{\Sigma'}(\sigma) = \langle\rangle$. Assuming that event logs initially do not contain empty traces, we do not model discarded traces by a dedicated symbol to unify the notation. Using an element-wise application, we can concatenate the functions and apply them to event logs to isolate control-flow aspects of a process For example, the event log $L^{l,\text{ex}}_{\pi^{\text{act}}_{\{l,d\}} \circ \mu^{\text{act}}_{\{l,d\}}} = [\langle l, \text{d}\rangle^{18}, \langle\rangle^{82}]$ focuses on the frequency and activity order of low and declined claims.

While can we consider different sets of activities to study different control-flow aspects, we can also use them to further process the retrieved differences. In doing so, we exploit that activity sets are naturally related in terms of specialization. To this end, consider Fig. 3 that shows the effect of selecting variants (y-axis) and projecting the selected variants on potentially different sets of activities (x-axis). In particular, we consider the case where we use the same set of activities to select and project (highlighted in orange). *The behavior* based on which we select the variant is the *same* behavior that we extract from the former. Besides, this also establishes a specialization relation regarding the data extracted for activity sets $s_1, s_2 \in \mathcal{P}(\mathcal{A}), s_1 \subset s_2$. For s_2, we consider a subset

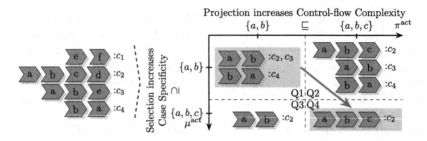

Fig. 3. By extending the activity set, we extract subtraces with increasingly complex control flow from a more specific (i.e., smaller) subset of traces. Here, we eventually isolate a single variant.

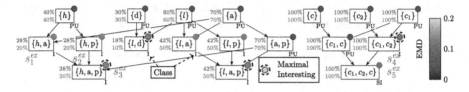

Fig. 4. SPS for our running example. Each vertex is a set of frequently co-occurring activities. It is annotated by the activity set's occurrence probability in the left and right log, its associated EMD, and class. Dashed red circle show the *maximal interesting* activity sets (comp. Definition 3). (Color figure online)

(i.e., fewer) of the variants, and the control flow becomes more complex—that is, we consider a superset of the events. In contrast, disentangling the selection and projection can blur the localization (e.g., a difference measured for Q2 might optionally involve c), or it might result in diagnostics that are less general than expected. For instance, differences found for Q3 do not necessarily concern a and b in general. Exploiting the specialization relation, we define the Selection-projection Structure (SPS)—the backbone of our approach.

Definition 2 (SPS). *Let* $L^l, L^r \in \mathcal{B}(A^*), \langle\rangle \notin L^l, \langle\rangle \notin L^r$ *denote event logs over an alphabet* $A \subseteq \mathcal{A}$. *A Selection-projection Structure (SPS)* $\mathrm{sps}_{L^l,L^r} = (S, <, m^{\mathrm{sps}}_{L^l,L^r})$ *for* L^l *and* L^r *is a triple of a set of activity sets* $S \subseteq \mathcal{P}(A)$, *an edge set* $< \subseteq S \times S$ *such that* $(S, <)$ *is the transitive reduction of the graph* $(S, \{(s_1, s_2) \in S \times S | s_1 \subset s_2\})$, *and an EMD-based vertex measurement function*

$$m^{\mathrm{sps}}_{L^l,L^r} : S \to [0,1], s \mapsto \mathrm{emd}_{\mathrm{edt}}(p_{L^l_{\pi^{\mathrm{act}}_s \circ \mu^{\mathrm{act}}_s}}, p_{L^r_{\pi^{\mathrm{act}}_s \circ \mu^{\mathrm{act}}_s}}). \tag{2}$$

Figure 4 shows an SPS for our running example comprising sets of *frequently co-occurring* activities. We measure a non-zero difference for nine vertices in total, yet multiple vertices refer to the same difference. For example, the sets $\{h, a\}$, $\{h, p\}$, and $\{h, a, p\}$ all indicate a difference regarding the acceptance (a) and payment (p) of high claims (h).

Maximization. In an SPS, many vertices may witness the same difference which can result in fragmented diagnostics. Yet, the specialization relation between vertices in the SPS gives us a means to *maximize* differences: return the more specific vertex, if it perfectly extends the differences measured for its predecessors. However, this requires an accurate characterization of the mechanisms behind the difference scores (e.g., frequency difference, order differences, or even combinations of the former). We therefore propose a relaxed difference maximization approach based on the vertices' EMD values and leave other implementation for future work. If two related activity sets have similar difference scores, they are likely to witness the same difference, and we return the more specific one (i.e., superset). However, Fig. 5 exemplifies limitations of this naive approach. To this end, consider two process instances differing in two ways: in the right process instance (1) more low claims are registered (i.e., l_1, l_2), and (2) more claims are accepted. The color of a vertex shows its frequency which is directly related to its EMD value. The activities l_1 and l_2 witness the same frequency difference and aggregating them shows a difference for a coherent branch of the process. In contrast, we argue that $\{l_1, l_2, c\}$ is not an interesting difference, despite it has the same support as $\{l_1, l_2\}$. It comprises the consolidation step c which is always executed and therefore not interesting. Moreover, we measure a strong difference for $\{l_1, l_2, a\}$. Nevertheless, the choices related to $\{l_1, l_2\}$ and $\{a\}$ might be independent making the set less interesting. Based on these considerations, we bottom-up classify the SPS vertices as *interesting* (I), *uninteresting* (U), and *sub-interesting* (SI) and retrieve the most specific, interesting differences.

Definition 3 (SPS Difference Classification). *Let $L^l, L^r \in \mathcal{B}(A^*)$, $\langle\rangle \notin L^l, \langle\rangle \notin L^r$ denote event logs over an alphabet $A \subseteq \mathcal{A}$; $\tau_m^i, \tau_i^i \in [0,1]$ be thresholds; and $\mathrm{sps}_{L^l,L^r} = (S, <, m^{\mathrm{sps}}_{L^l,L^r})$ be an SPS. The SPS difference class of a vertex is given by $\bar{\kappa} := \kappa_{\mathrm{sps}_{L^l,L^r}, \tau_m^i, \tau_i^i} \colon S \to \{U, SI, I\}$,*

$$
\bar{\kappa}(s) =
\begin{cases}
U \text{ if } \bar{m}(s) < \tau_m^i \wedge \forall s_1 \, (s_1 < s \to \bar{\kappa}(s_1) = U) & \textit{(C1 All U)} \\
I \text{ if } \bar{m}(s) \geq \tau_m^i \wedge \{[\forall s_1 \, (s_1 < s \to \bar{\kappa}(s_1) = U)] & \textit{(C2 - Pred. U)} \\
\quad \vee [\exists^{=1} s_1 \, (s_1 < s) \wedge \exists^{=1} s_1 \, (s_1 < s \wedge \bar{\kappa}(s_1) = I)] & \textit{(C3 - One Pred. I)} \\
\quad \vee [\nexists s_1 \bar{\kappa}(s_1) = SI & \textit{(C4 - No pred. SI)} \\
\quad \wedge \exists s_1, s_2 (s_1 < s \wedge s_2 < s \wedge \bar{\kappa}(s_1) = I & \textit{(C5 - Pred. I)} \\
\quad \wedge \bar{\kappa}(s_2) = I \wedge \phi_{L^l,L^r}(s_1, s_2) > \tau_i^i & \textit{(C6 - Not indep.)} \\
\quad \wedge \bigcup\limits_{s_1 < s, \bar{\kappa}(s_1) = U} s_1 \subseteq \bigcup\limits_{s_1 < s, \bar{\kappa}(s_1) = I} s_1)]\} & \textit{(C7 - Prove I)} \\
SI \text{ else}
\end{cases}
\tag{3}
$$

for $s \in S$, $\bar{m} := m^{\mathrm{sps}}_{L^l,L^r}$, and ϕ denoting the phi-coefficient of the occurrence of two given activity sets. Given a domination factor $\tau_d^i > 1$, a vertex $s \in S$ is maximal interesting if and only if

$$
\bar{\kappa}(s) = I \wedge \forall s_1 \left(s < s_1 \wedge \bar{\kappa}(s_1) = I \to m^{\mathrm{sps}}_{L^l,L^r}(s) > \tau_d^i m^{\mathrm{sps}}_{L^l,L^r}(s_1) \right). \tag{4}
$$

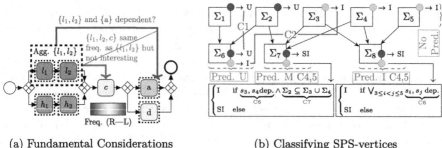

(a) Fundamental Considerations   (b) Classifying SPS-vertices

Fig. 5. Maximizing differences in the SPS graph.

Figure 5b illustrates the conditions. The EMD value determines the class of a vertex without predecessors (note that the "for all" statements in C1,2 hold). Otherwise, we consider its predecessors: if all predecessors are *uninteresting*, we again consider the EMD value (C2). For example, in Fig. 4, the vertex $\{c_1, c_2\}$ becomes interesting due to the activity order difference. If all predecessors are *interesting*, we not only consider EMD but also whether there are dependent predecessors (C 6). Similar conditions apply if the predecessors are *either interesting or uninteresting*. However, the *uninteresting* predecessors indicate that we might aggregate an uninteresting subaspect (comp. c in Fig. 5a). Therefore, we additionally require that each activity is interesting with respect to at least one subaspect (C 7). For example, we do not observe a difference regarding the acceptance subprocess $\{a, p\}$, but in the context of high claims—namely, $\{h, a\}$ and $\{h, p\}$—acceptance is more likely in the left log. A vertex with *interesting* predecessors that cannot be proved *interesting* is labeled *sub-interesting*. We found evidence that we cannot further maximize an *interesting* predecessor, and, in case of doubt, we follow Occam's razor and opt for the simpler difference.

Eventually, we report the *maximal interesting vertices*—that is, interesting vertices that do not have an interesting successor with a similar EMD value. In Fig. 4, the scores of these vertices are highlighted in red using, for example, the thresholds $\tau_m^i = 0.01, \tau_i^i = 0.2, \tau_d^i = 1.2$.

Complementary Differences. Conceptually, each *maximal interesting vertex* captures differences with respect to *observed* activities. Thinking of BPMN, this covers sequences of activities, order resolution of concurrency, and loop repetitions. However, a single set of observed activities cannot entirely explain choices. A simple difference in the likelihood of choosing between two activities a and b, results in significant EMD values for $\{a\}$ and $\{b\}$ (but not for $\{a, b\}$). Yet, showing both sets at the same time would paint a clearer picture. Note that the declarative method proposed in [7] faces a similar challenge. We therefore propose to search additional, complementary differences. Let $\mathrm{sps}_{L^l,L^r} = (S, <, m_{L^l,L^r}^{\mathrm{sps}})$ be an SPS for event logs L^l and L^r and $S_{\mathrm{sps}_{L^l,L^r}}^{\mathrm{int}}$ denote the set of maximal interesting differences. We propose a three-step filter pipeline where we assess whether two vertices $s_1, s_2 \in S^{\text{int}}_{\text{sps}_{L^l,L^r}}$ occur complementary by the Jaccard index of their co-occurrences in the event logs—namely, $J^{\text{occ}}_{L^l,L^r}(s, s_1) := \min_{x=l,r} \frac{|L^x_{\mu^{\text{act}}_{s_1 \wedge s_2}}|}{|L^x_{\mu^{\text{act}}_{s_1 \vee s_2}}|}$. A low score indicates that, in (at least) one process instances, cases that comprise one activity set do not comprise the other. Given a vertex $s \in S^{\text{int}}_{\text{sps}_{L^l,L^r}}$ and a bound on the vertices' co-occurrence $\tau^c_{jacc} \in [0,1]$, the filtering steps are:

(1) remove structurally related differences

$$S^{\text{int }1}_{\text{sps}_{L^l,L^r}} := S^{\text{int}}_{\text{sps}_{L^l,L^r}} \setminus \left\{ s_1 \in S^{\text{int}}_{\text{sps}_{L^l,L^r}} \,\middle|\, s_1 \subseteq s \vee s \subseteq s_1 \right\};$$

(2) remove co-occurring vertices

$$S^{\text{int }2}_{\text{sps}_{L^l,L^r}} := S^{\text{int }1}_{\text{sps}_{L^l,L^r}} \setminus \left\{ s_1 \in S^{\text{int }1}_{\text{sps}_{L^l,L^r}} \,\middle|\, J^{\text{occ}}_{L^l,L^r}(s, s_1) > \tau^c_{jacc} \right\};$$

(3) sort vertices $s_1 \in S^{\text{int }2}_{\text{sps}_{L^l,L^r}}$ by increasing vertex similarity $\frac{s \cap s_1}{s \cup s_1}$, decreasing co-occurrence $J^{\text{occ}}_{L^l,L^r}(s, s_1)$, and similar EMD $|m^{\text{sps}}_{L^l,L^r}(s) - m^{\text{sps}}_{L^l,L^r}(s_1)|$.

In the first step, we exploit the structural relation to discard vertices that are naturally not complementary.

Visualization. Given a set of complementary activity sets $S^{\text{co}} \subseteq S$ for an SPS $\text{sps}_{L^l,L^r} = (S, <, m^{\text{sps}}_{L^l,L^r})$, we illustrate differences using a directly follows-based visualization. Like the approach proposed in [19], we focus on the traces that constitute the difference, yet we show both logs in the same graph to facilitate the visual alignment. To create the DFG, we first generalize the trace selection to multi-activity set conditions. Given activity sets $\Sigma_i, i = 1, \ldots, n$, $\mu^{\text{act}}_{\Sigma_1 \vee \cdots \vee \Sigma_n}$ ($\mu^{\text{act}}_{\Sigma_1 \wedge \cdots \wedge \Sigma_n}$) keeps a trace if any (all) of the individual trace selections $\mu^{\text{act}}_{\Sigma_i}, i = 1, \ldots, n$ do. Selecting all relevant traces and projecting on the involved activities, we obtain two pairs of event logs:

$$L^{x,\text{co}} := L^x_{\pi^{\text{act}}_{\bigcup_{s \in S^{\text{co}}} s} \circ \mu^{\text{act}}_{\bigvee_{s \in S^{\text{co}}} s}}, L^{x,\text{co},\neq \langle\rangle} := [\sigma \in L^{x,\text{co}} \mid \sigma \neq \langle\rangle], x = l, r. \quad (5)$$

Note that the second pair of event logs only contains relevant traces. Since the initial event logs may have different sizes, we scale by the size of the logs. For $L^{x,\text{co}}$ ($L^{x,\text{co},\neq\langle\rangle}$), $x = l, r$, each DFG edge thereby shows the expected (conditional) number of occurrences in the log (given that the trace is relevant). Conditioning allows to analyze qualitative differences within the subprocess defined by the selected variants irrespective of its global frequency. We refer to these graphs as Trace-probability DFGs (TP-DFGs) as the edge values are aggregated trace likelihoods. Figure 6a shows a TP-DFG on real-life data where we added information on the considered activity sets to an artificial start vertex.

5   Evaluation

We evaluate the Java implementation of our approach (SPS)[1] with respect to the research questions, and compare it to Bolt's approach (TS-PC) [4] and Cecconi's

---

[1] https://github.com/tbr-git/procmin-apps.

method (DecPC) [7]. We quantitatively evaluate RQ(I) and assess RQ(II) and RQ(III) in a case study. In the quantitative evaluation, we also consider EMD (emd$_{edt}$) between the complete logs as we only require a score.

For SPS, we consider the 10, 000 most frequent activity sets. For TS-PC, we use the default p-value of 0.05 with the default abstraction (TS-PC-d)—i.e., 1-set history abstraction—and 2-sequence history abstraction as in [4] (TS-PC-s). For DecPC, we evaluate the default parameters (DecPC-d) and the significantly differing parameterization used for the evaluation presented in [7](DecPC-s).

5.1   Case Study

We conduct a real-life case study to compare and evaluate the considered approaches with respect to RQ(II) and RQ(III). To this end, we consider the well-known Road Traffic Fine Management log [13], split into a left and right log containing low ($< 50€$) and high fines ($\geq 50€$) [7,19], which was also investigated in [4,19]. We analyze the logs with respect to two evaluation questions:

EQ(I)   Are there execution patterns with respect to the control flow that are more likely in either variant?

EQ(II) Are there qualitative differences in the execution of certain subprocesses?

EQ(I) is related to RQ(I) and RQ(II), and RQ(III) is the foundation to assess EQ(II). We identify a subprocess by co-occurring activities where retrieving complementary difference accommodates for choices. Eventually, the conditioned TP-DFG shows qualitative differences. In contrast to DecPC, which currently only supports binary rules (e.g., if a occurs, b is more likely to occur), we implicitly condition on multiple activity sets. We run our process comparison method in an automatic mode. We consider the five strongest *maximal differences* as seeds and complement each by (at most) three additional activity sets. In doing so, we skip seeds that were already shown as complementary differences. To discover the maximal interesting SPS-vertices and complementary differences, we use the thresholds $\tau_m^i = 0.001$, $\tau_d^i = 0.9$, $\tau_s^i = 1.2$, $\tau_i^i = 0.05$, and $\tau_{jacc}^c = 0.2$. An analysis of the sensitivity of our method to these parameters as well as additional results can be found online[2].

Results. Table 1 summarizes the results obtained by our method and DecPC. Table 1a shows four sets of complementary activity sets together with each activity set's (conditional) probability. Besides, we depict the conditioned TP-DFG associated with the second set of complementary differences in Fig. 6a and the TS obtained using TS-PC in Fig. 6b.

Considering EQ(I), all approaches show that the activities SF, IFN, and AP, related to additional fining, more frequently occur for high claims (D(1)). However, DecPC splits it among multiple differences, and it remains up to the analyst to see the bigger picture. Similarly, there are more high-fine cases where an additional penalty (AP) is added *and* the fine is collected (SCC, D(2)) or

---

[2] https://doi.org/10.6084/m9.figshare.c.7167954.v1.

Table 1. Summary of results obtained for the RTFM log

(a) Discovered complementary SPS-vertex sets

No.	Activities	Prob. To./Cond.				Log
		L	R	L	R	
1	$\{SF, IFN, AP\}$ (D(1))	0.12	0.69	1	1	
	$\{P\}$ (D(4))	0.66	0.33	0.88	0.38	
3	$\{SF, IFN, AP, SCC\}$	0.09	0.51	0.12	0.58	(0.75|0.87)
	$\{SF, IFN, IDA2P, AP, SA2P\}$ (D(5))	0	0.06	0.1	0.07	
	$\{SF, AP, A2J\}$ (D(5))	0	0.01	0	0.01	
	$\{SF, P, IFN, AP, SCC\}$	0	0.02	0.41	0.21	(0.01|0.09)
4	$\{SF, IFN, IDA2P, AP, SA2P\}$ (D(5))	0	0.06	0.56	0.68	
	$\{IFN, AP, A2J\}$ (D(5))	0	0.01	0.02	0.14	
	$\{P, IDA2P\}$ (D(5))	0	0.01	0.08	0.09	

(b) Top 10 distinguishing rules [7]

No.	Rule	LLH diff.
1	P then SF (D(6))	24.8%
2	P then AP (D(6))	19.57%
3	P then IFN (D(6))	19.57%
4	AP always occurs (D(1)(2))	19.41%
5	IFN always occurs	19.41%
6	CF then AP before CF	19.41%
7	CF then IFN before CF	19.41%
8	SF always occurs (D(1)(2))	19.19%
9	CF then SF before CF (D(1)(2))	19.19%
10	SCC always occurs (D(2))	14.47%

paid (P, D(3)). In contrast, a payment is made for the majority of low-fine cases (D(4)). While our approach clearly shows this difference, it is not included in the top-ten differences obtained by DecPC. TS-PC even shows that low fines are more likely to be paid immediately after creation. Finally, SPS and TS-PC indicate that traffic offenders who receive a high fine are more likely to appeal (A2J, SA2P, IDA2P, D(5)).

Considering RQ(III), the retrieved complementary differences define coherent subaspects. While payments ($\{P\}$) might semantically complement the first difference, D(3) shows that these often occur together. The second set of differences covers the outcomes of cases with an additional penalty—namely, payment, credit collection, or appeal. Similarly, the third set gathers the general outcomes. Finally, the fourth set is again concerned with additional fining, yet, the seed are cases including credit collections despite payments were made.

Finally, we assess EQ(II) using the conditioned TP-DFG. First, DecPC finds that if payment was made, high fines are more likely to contain an additional penalty (D(6)). Note the difference to the diagnostic: even though a fine was added, payments are more likely. In fact, the order of the activities in the rule is the opposite of their intuitive order. In contrast, the conditioned TP-DFG in Fig. 6a shows only small differences considering the outcome of cases with an additional fine. While credit collection is slightly more likely for low-fine cases, high-fine cases more frequently result in a payment or in an appeal (D(7)).

5.2 Quantitative Evaluation on Scoring Concept Drift

To the best of our knowledge, there exist no frameworks that evaluate the sensitivity of process comparison approaches. Thus, we propose to quantitatively evaluate approaches based on their ability to distinguish pairs of event logs that were extracted from a stable process and those that were extracted from differing processes. To this end, we use the values returned by approaches to quantify the severity of a detected difference. For SPS, we consider the largest EMD among the maximal interesting vertices. For TS-PC, we extract the largest Cohen's d value, and DecPC returns the difference in the confidence of distinguishing rules.

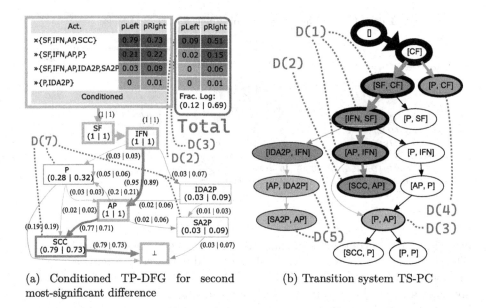

(a) Conditioned TP-DFG for second most-significant difference

(b) Transition system TS-PC

Fig. 6. Graph-based difference visualization using (a) our proposed method and (b) TS-PC. Due to the conditioning enabled by the variant selection, Subfigure (a) shows that low fines are less likely to be paid given that an additional penalty (AP) was added. In contrast, Subfigure (a) shows that additional penalties and credit collection (SCC) as well as appealing are more likely for high fines. For both graphs, additional frequency filtering has been applied.

Regarding the classification, we consider this value a "confidence" score assuming a score of zero if no difference was detected. This is also how a user might intuitively interpret the number. In particular, we create process comparison tasks from collections of artificial event logs [5,8,15] created for Process Concept Drift Detection where each event log contains sudden changes at known positions. Figure 7a shows the extraction of five process comparison tasks where each log contains 50% of the cases of a stable period, and each pair of event logs is either extracted from same period or comprises across-drift event logs.

Finally, we evaluate process comparison approaches in two ways: first, we consider the Detection Error Tradeoff (DET) graph. Thereby, we assess how reliably high scores indicate strong differences—independent of the underlying process. Second, we analyze how drifts a ranked with respect to the process before and after. In contrast to the DET graph, this only considers similar processes. We distinguish the cases: no difference was detected, a method correctly scores the across-drift task higher than the other two tasks, and a remainder class. Note that our approach and EMD always return a score, and the first case therefore never applies. The top part of Fig. 7a shows both approaches.

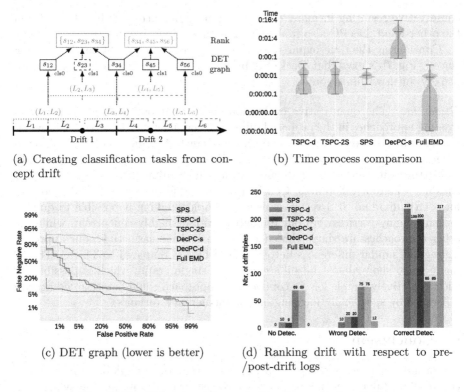

(a) Creating classification tasks from concept drift

(b) Time process comparison

(c) DET graph (lower is better)

(d) Ranking drift with respect to pre-/post-drift logs

Fig. 7. Classifying event logs whether they contain a drift.

Results. Figure 7 depicts the results for the extracted 609 classification tasks. The DET graph in Fig. 7c shows that SPS and TS-PC perform best in the global drift classification task. Compared to SPS, the false positive rate of TS-PC increases earlier meaning that TS-PC scores certain across-drift tasks lower than log pairs extracted from a stable process. EMD performs worse than the former two methods, yet it might become superior for complicated differences. For a high false positive rate, the curve falls beneath the curves for SPS and TS-PC. Finally, DecPC shows an interesting pattern. It assigns the highest scores to across-drift tasks; yet, at some point, there are many false positives. Eventually, the false negative rate drops to zero for a false positive rate larger than 20%. This can be explained by a large number of drift and non-drift process comparison tasks where no difference is detected. Such tasks receive the score zero.

The local ranking of drifts shown in Fig. 7d confirms the prior findings. SPS correctly ranks most process comparison tasks triples performing slightly better than TS-PC. Interestingly, EMD performs very well in this local context. While SPS aims to isolate differences before it scores them, EMD always considers the entire trace. Thereby, the cost contribution of a difference dependents on the trace's length. Consequently, EMD performs worse than SPS on the global drift classification task. Finally, the statistical test used by DecPC is, on the one hand, conservative resulting in many cases where no difference is detected at all. On the other hand, DecPC also ranks a couple task triples incorrectly.

Considering the time required for the comparison (i.e., excluding log loading times), Fig. 7b shows that DecPC is by far the slowest. The other approaches usually finish within seconds.

Discussion. The quantitative evaluation shows that our method outperforms existing approaches in the proposed difference classification. However, this evaluation is still based on artificial and does not assess the usefulness of the discovered differences. Besides, even though high EMD values in the SPS framework indicate strong differences, the individual value can be difficult to interpret; it may subsume different differences. Considering the performance, the EMD problem for each individual SPS vertex is usually simpler making it possible to quickly measure many vertices. Yet our implementation is highly concurrent, while the other approaches are single threaded. In the real-life case study, our approach aggregates similar differences better than DecPC. Compared to TS-PC, TS-PC manages to show almost all differences in a single graph, which is possible for such a relatively simple log. In contrast, our approach could detect an additional difference by specifically focusing on complementary variants.

6   Conclusion

We propose a process comparison approach that detects global and complex control-flow differences in event data extracted from an information system. To this end, we leverage event data projections to facilitate the comparison and to isolate differences. We then extend the isolated differences to cover larger fractions of the associated cases. Moreover, we propose an approach to complement a given difference by considering additional activities and cases. Explicitly identifying variants that induce a difference also gives a context for a refined analysis. We demonstrate the applicability of the method in a case study as well as quantitatively assess its sensitivity in a newly devised process comparison evaluation approach. For future work, we plan to improve the detection and presentation of conditional differences as well to incorporate other dimensions (e.g., time). Furthermore, we intend to explicitly test differences for statistical significance to improve the confidence in attained results.

Acknowledgments. Funded by the Deutsche Forschungsgemeinschaft (DFG, German Research Foundation) under Germany's Excellence Strategy-EXC-2023 Internet of Production-390621612. We also thank the Alexander von Humboldt (AvH) Stiftung for supporting our research.

References

1. van der Aalst, W.M.P., de Medeiros, A.K.A., Weijters, A.J.M.M.: Process equivalence: comparing two process models based on observed behavior. In: BPM, pp. 129–144 (2006)

2. Andrews, K., Wohlfahrt, M., Wurzinger, G.: Visual graph comparison. In: 13th IV, pp. 62–67 (2009)
3. van Beest, N.R.T.P., Dumas, M., García-Bañuelos, L., La Rosa, M.: Log delta analysis: interpretable differencing of business process event logs. In: BPM, pp. 386–405 (2015)
4. Bolt, A., de Leoni, M., van der Aalst, W.M.P.: A visual approach to spot statistically-significant differences in event logs based on process metrics. In: CAiSE, pp. 151–166 (2016)
5. Bose, R.P.J.C., van der Aalst, W.M.P., Žliobaitė, I., Pechenizkiy, M.: Handling concept drift in process mining. In: CAiSE, pp. 391–405 (2011)
6. Buijs, J.C.A.M., Reijers, H.A.: Comparing business process variants using models and event logs. In: BPMDS, pp. 154–168 (2014)
7. Cecconi, A., Augusto, A., Di Ciccio, C.: Detection of statistically significant differences between process variants through declarative rules. In: BPM Forum, pp. 73–91 (2021)
8. Ceravolo, P., Tavares, G.M., Junior, S.B., Damiani, E.: Evaluation goals for online process mining: a concept drift perspective. In: SERVICES, pp. 27–27 (2022)
9. Kriglstein, S., Wallner, G., Rinderle-Ma, S.: A visualization approach for difference analysis of process models and instance traffic. In: BPM, pp. 219–226 (2013)
10. Küster, J.M., Gerth, C., Förster, A., Engels, G.: Detecting and resolving process model differences in the absence of a change log. In: BPM, pp. 244–260 (2008)
11. Lakshmanan, G.T., Rozsnyai, S., Wang, F.: Investigating clinical care pathways correlated with outcomes. In: BPM, pp. 323–338 (2013)
12. Leemans, S.J.J., Syring, A.F., van der Aalst, W.M.P.: Earth movers' stochastic conformance checking. In: BPM Forum, pp. 127–143 (2019)
13. de Leoni, M., Mannhardt, F.: Road traffic fine management process (2015)
14. Nguyen, H., Dumas, M., La Rosa, M., ter Hofstede, A.H.M.: Multi-perspective comparison of business process variants based on event logs. In: Conceptual Modeling, pp. 449–459 (2018)
15. Ostovar, A., Maaradji, A., La Rosa, M., ter Hofstede, A.H.M., van Dongen, B.F.V.: Detecting drift from event streams of unpredictable business processes. In: Conceptual Modeling, pp. 330–346 (2016)
16. Pini, A., Brown, R., Wynn, M.T.: Process visualization techniques for multi-perspective process comparisons. In: AP-BPM, pp. 183–197 (2015)
17. Poelmans, J., Dedene, G., Verheyden, G., Van der Mussele, H., Viaene, S., Peters, E.: Combining business process and data discovery techniques for analyzing and improving integrated care pathways. In: ICDM, pp. 505–517 (2010)
18. Suriadi, S., Mans, R.S., Wynn, M.T., Partington, A., Karnon, J.: Measuring patient flow variations: a cross-organisational process mining approach. In: AP-BPM, pp. 43–58 (2014)
19. Taymouri, F., La Rosa, M., Carmona, J.: Business process variant analysis based on mutual fingerprints of event logs. In: CAiSE, pp. 299–318 (2020)
20. Taymouri, F., Rosa, M.L., Dumas, M., Maggi, F.M.: Business process variant analysis: survey and classification. Knowl.-Based Syst. **211**, 106557 (2021)
21. Vidgof, M., Djurica, D., Bala, S., Mendling, J.: Interactive log-delta analysis using multi-range filtering. SoSyM **21**, 847–868 (2022)
22. Wille, R.: Restructuring lattice theory: an approach based on hierarchies of concepts. In: Ordered Sets, pp. 445–470 (1982)

Stochastic Process Discovery: Can It Be Done Optimally?

Sander J. J. Leemans[1,2(✉)], Tian Li[1,4], Marco Montali[3],
and Artem Polyvyanyy[4]

[1] RWTH Aachen University, Aachen, Germany
{s.leemans,t.li}@bpm.rwth-aachen.de
[2] Fraunhofer, Frankfurt, Germany
[3] Free University of Bozen-Bolzano, Bolzano, Italy
[4] The University of Melbourne, Melbourne, Australia

Abstract. Process discovery is the problem of automatically constructing a process model from an event log of an information system that supports the execution of a business process in an organisation. In this paper, we study how to construct models that, in addition to the control flow of the process, capture the importance, in terms of probabilities, of various execution scenarios of the process. Such probabilistic aspects of the process are instrumental in understanding the process and to predict aspects of its future. We formally define the problem of stochastic process discovery, which aims to describe the processes captured in the event log. We study several implications of this definition, and introduce two discovery techniques that return optimal solutions in the presence and absence of a model of the control flow of the process. The proposed discovery techniques have been implemented and are publicly available. Finally, we evaluate the feasibility and applicability of the new techniques and show that their models outperform models constructed using existing stochastic discovery techniques.

Keywords: Stochastic process mining · stochastic process discovery

1 Introduction

The increasing complexity of modern socio-technical and cyber-physical systems is calling for a change of paradigm in their engineering, moving from pure model-driven engineering to approaches where *models and execution data are synergically connected* [16]. In enterprise information systems engineering, this practice has a long tradition when focusing on *how* organisations operate, that is, on their work processes. Specifically, process mining techniques [1] provide insights on processes by analysing the event data produced within an organisation while executing such processes. Even data yield, implicitly or explicitly,

M. Montali—This work is partially supported by the UNIBZ project ADAPTERS and the PRIN MIUR project PINPOINT Prot. 2020FNEB27.

G. Guizzardi et al. (Eds.): CAiSE 2024, LNCS 14663, pp. 36–52, 2024.
https://doi.org/10.1007/978-3-031-61057-8_3

event logs recording the historical executions of the process under scrutiny, where each execution typically corresponds, in the log, to an (execution) *trace*: a time-ordered sequence of triggered events, each referring to an activity within the process. A key process mining task is that of *process discovery*, whose goal is to learn a process model that suitably reconstructs the behaviours contained in the event log under scrutiny, and that can be used as a driver for fact-based process analysis and improvement. However, traditional process discovery techniques do not transfer into the discovered models any information regarding the relative frequency, and in turn the likelihood, of the observed traces. This hampers the possibility of using such models, as letting infrequent flows in the process influence optimisation and analysis indistinctly from frequent ones is improvident.

To tackle this limitation, *stochastic process discovery* techniques learn process models that pair traces with indications on how likely one can expect to see them in the future executions of the process. This is challenging due to a granularity mismatch in the stochastic information contained in a log or model. At the log level, the likelihood of a trace is directly obtained by dividing its frequency with the total number of log traces. At the model level, stochastic information is usually attached locally to decision points, and the likelihood of a trace is only indirectly obtained by chaining such (independent) decisions. In spite of this challenge, several stochastic process discovery techniques have been proposed [6, 7,19], empirically demonstrating their applicability and quality using real-life logs. On the downside, none of these works provides foundational insights on the problem space and on the formal properties of the proposed techniques, in terms of optimality and guarantees.

The goal of this work is to fill this gap, providing a *foundational investigation of stochastic process discovery*, in the case where the target process model is expressed using stochastic variants of Petri nets [11,15,17]. We provide a formal definition of the problem, casting it as a two-dimensional optimisation problem. The first dimension concerns the *behaviour* of the process, that is, the selection of a process model in a class of Petri nets defined based on some representational bias defining which constructs can be expressed (e.g., whether labels can be repeated). The second dimension concerns the *stochastic information* attached to the process, employing measures that define how well the distribution of traces induced by the model matches the distribution of the log. We study the implications of this definition in terms of optimality, considering two types of stochastic process discovery techniques. The techniques from the first type operate under the assumption that the control flow of the target process model is given, and the goal is to enhance it with the "best" stochastic information. The techniques of the second type relax this assumption, and entangle control-flow and stochastic information discovery in a single step. Finally, we evaluate the introduced techniques in the context of existing stochastic process discovery algorithms.

The paper is organised as follows. In Sect. 2, we discuss related work, while in Sect. 3, we introduce existing concepts. Section 4 formally introduces the problem of stochastic process discovery and discusses some inherent aspects of this definition. Sections 5 and 6 introduce two discovery techniques. Section 7 evaluates the introduced techniques before Sect. 8 concludes the paper.

2   Related Work

The representation, discovery and measurements of stochastic process models have been investigated before in several settings, leading to a variety of techniques that deal with different prerequisites, targets, advantages and limitations.

Several formalisms are used in process mining for representing stochastic process models. Generalised Stochastic Petri nets are a well-established formalism for stochastic modelling [3]. Molloy [17] introduced the first model to handle the stochastic aspect, which was extended later by Marsan et al. [15] by distinguishing timed and immediate transitions, showing how the resulting stochastic behaviour can be captured through a discrete-time Markov chain.

Several measures have been proposed to quantify the quality of a stochastic process model with respect to an event log. Entropic relevance measures the average number of bits required to compress a trace in the input event log based on the structure and information about the relative likelihoods of traces provided by the stochastic process model [18]. Consequently, a model with a lower relevance value to a given log is accepted as such that describes the traces and their likelihoods better. Earth Movers' Stochastic Conformance (EMSC) derives the stochastic languages from the input event log and model and then measures the earth movers' distance between them [14].

The ability to discover the stochastic perspective of processes has enabled new types of analyses in process mining, such as analysis tasks on the traces of labelled stochastic processes and their probabilities [11]—instrumental to provide exact methods for computing stochastic conformance measures, detection of stochastic-based changes in processes [5], and techniques for weighting alignments depending on the likelihood of model traces [4].

Existing stochastic process discovery techniques can be classified into two categories: *one-stage* techniques directly discovering a stochastic model from an event log and *two-stage* approaches that first discover a control-flow model, and then annotate it with stochastic information. To the best of our knowledge, Toothpaste Miner [7] is the only known stochastic discovery technique that automatically outputs a stochastic process model without relying on a given control flow model. However, this approach does not provide conformance-measure guarantees. Recently, several two-stage approaches have been proposed. The GDT_SPN Miner [19] is an alignment-based technique that estimates arbitrary delay distributions of stochastic Petri nets. The weight estimation framework includes deterministic and non-deterministic estimators that derive an SPN [6]. In [12], the authors proposed the discovery of stochastic dependencies, which address the likelihood of decisions influenced by earlier decisions. Two-stage discovery is reminiscent of the widely investigated problem of parameter synthesis in probabilistic models (in particular, Markov chains) [8]. The crucial difference is that in parameter synthesis there is a single probabilistic reachability/temporal property used to drive the search for parameter assignments, while in two-stage discovery this is done by considering multiple properties, expressing that the probability of each log trace according to the model should resemble the frequency with which it appears in the log. To the best of our knowledge, the limitations of stochastic process discovery have not been studied, and no stochastic process discovery technique that guarantees some kind of optimal result with respect to a conformance measure have been proposed.

3   Preliminaries

Multisets, Logs, Vectors. A multiset $X \colon S \to \mathbb{N}$ is a mapping of elements in S to the natural numbers. The multiset union is $(X_1 \uplus X_2)(a) \equiv X_1(a) + X_2(a)$, the multiset subset is $X_2 \subseteq X_1 \equiv \forall_{a \in S} X_1(a) \geq X_2(a)$, and for any multiset X over S, $X \subseteq S^\infty$. For multisets X, X', if $X \subseteq X'$ then $(X \setminus X')(a) = X(a) - X'(a)$ is the multiset difference. Thus, the multiset $X = [x^2, y^3, z^5]$ contains 10 items, and $|X| = 3$ while $||X|| = 10$. $\bar{X} = \{a \mid X(a) > 0\}$ is the corresponding set.

A *trace* is a sequence of activities that denotes the process steps executed for a particular case of a process. An *event log* is a multiset of traces. Figure 1c is an event log with 100 traces. For an (event) log L, $\tilde{L}$ denotes its prefix closure: $\tilde{L} \equiv \{\langle a_1 \dots a_m \rangle \mid \langle a_1 \dots a_m, \dots \rangle \in \bar{L}\}$. The set of all logs is $\mathcal{L}$.

Let $\vec{A} = \langle a_1, \dots, a_n \rangle$, $\vec{B} = \langle b_1, \dots, b_n \rangle$ be vectors. Then, $\vec{A} \succeq \vec{B} \equiv \forall_{1 \leq i \leq n} a_i \geq b_i$, and $\vec{A} \odot \vec{B} \equiv \langle a_1 b_1, \dots, a_n b_n \rangle$; we might omit $\odot$ if the context is clear.

Stochastic Models. A stochastic language is a weighted collection of traces, such that the sum of weights of all traces in the language is 1. A stochastic model M expresses a stochastic language. The set of all stochastic models is $\mathcal{M}$.

Definition 1 (Stochastic Petri net). *Let P be a set of places, let T be a set of transitions such that $P \cap T = \emptyset$, let $F \subseteq (P \times T \uplus T \times P)^\infty$ be a flow relation, let $w \colon T \to \mathbb{R}^+$ be a weight function and let $M_0 \subseteq P^\infty$ be an initial marking. Then, (P, T, F, w, M_0) is a stochastic Petri net (SPN).*

Definition 2 (Stochastic labelled Petri net). *Let Σ be an alphabet of activities, let (P, T, F, w, M_0) be an SPN and let $\lambda \colon T \to \Sigma \cup \tau$ be a labelling function. Then, (P, T, F, w, M_0) is a stochastic labelled Petri net (SLPN).*

An SPN or SLPN starts execution in its initial marking M_0. Let $t^\bullet = [p \mid (t, p) \in F]$ and $^\bullet t = [p \mid (p, t) \in F]$. In a marking M, the transitions $T_e = \{t \mid {}^\bullet t \subseteq M\}$ are *enabled*. An enabled transition $t \in T_e$ can *fire*, with firing probability $\mathbb{P}(t \mid M) = \frac{w(t)}{\Sigma_{t' \in T_e} w(t')}$, which results in a new marking $M' = M \uplus t^\bullet \setminus {}^\bullet t$. A *path* is a sequence of transitions $\langle t_1 \dots t_n \rangle$ such that there is a sequence of markings $\langle M_0 \dots M_n \rangle$ such that $\forall_{1 \leq i \leq n} {}^\bullet t_i \subseteq M_{i-1} \wedge M_i = M_{i-1} \uplus t_i^\bullet \setminus {}^\bullet t_i$ and M_n is a *deadlock*, that is, $\neg \exists_{t \in T} {}^\bullet t \subseteq M_n$. That is, a path brings the model from its initial marking M_0 to a deadlock marking. The probability of a path $\langle t_0 \dots t_n \rangle$ is $\prod_{1 \leq i \leq n} \mathbb{P}(t_i \mid M_i)$ where $M_i = M_{i-1} \uplus t^\bullet \setminus {}^\bullet t$.

A *trace* is a sequence of activities. For an SPN, path and trace are equivalent notions, while for an SLPN, the projection of a path by λ on the non-τ transitions is a trace. In an SLPN, there may be several (even countable-infinitely many [10]) paths that project to the same trace. For an SPN or SLPN M and a trace σ, we write $M(\sigma)$ for the probability of σ in M. For σ, we introduce an automaton that accepts σ interleaved with arbitrary silent transitions (Fig. 1d shows an example):

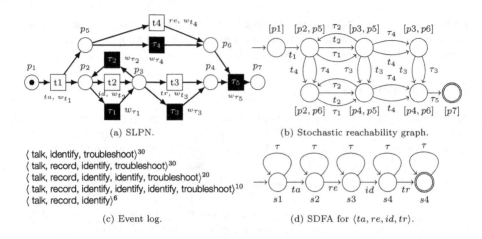

(a) SLPN.

(b) Stochastic reachability graph.

⟨ talk, identify, troubleshoot⟩[30]
⟨ talk, record, identify, troubleshoot⟩[30]
⟨ talk, record, identify, identify, troubleshoot⟩[20]
⟨ talk, record, identify, identify, identify, troubleshoot⟩[10]
⟨ talk, record, identify⟩[6]

(c) Event log.

(d) SDFA for ⟨ta, re, id, tr⟩.

Fig. 1. Example log and model.

Definition 3 (Silenced trace DFA). *Let τ be the silent label. The silenced trace deterministic finite automaton (SDFA) of trace $\sigma = \langle a_1, \ldots, a_n \rangle$ is a tuple $(\Sigma, S, s_0, S_f, \delta)$ where $\Sigma = \{a_0, \ldots, a_n\}$, $S = \{s_0, \ldots, s_{n+1}\}$, $S_f = \{s_{n+1}\}$, and $\delta = \{s_i \times a_i \to s_{i+1}$ for $1 \le i < n+1\} \cup \{s_i \times \tau \to s_i$ for $1 \le i < n+1\}$.*

Definition 4 (Stochastic Reachability Graph). *The stochastic reachability graph of an SLPN M is a labelled transition system $R = (\Sigma, S, s_0, S_f, \varrho, p)$ where Σ is a finite set of labels, S is a set of states (reachable markings in M), $s_0 \in S$ is the initial state, $S_f \subseteq S$ is the set of accepting states, $\varrho: S \times \Sigma \to S$ is a transition function, and $p: \varrho \to [0,1]$ is a probability function that maps each transition in ϱ to a probability value, such that for every transition $t = \langle s, l, s' \rangle \in \varrho$, $p(t) = \mathbb{P}(t|s)$, and for every non-deadlock marking $s \in S$, $\sum_{t=\langle s,l,s_2 \rangle \in \varrho} p(t) = 1$.*

If we disregard labels in the stochastic reachability graph and only consider firing probabilities, the graph is a discrete-time absorbing Markov chain, by mapping the final states to the absorbing states, non-final states to the transient states, and strip off transition labels, while keeping the probabilities.

Definition 5 (Absorbing Markov Chain for Stochastic Reachability Graph). *Let R be a stochastic reachability graph, its absorbing Markov chain is a tuple $C = (S, \varrho, p)$ where $S = S_t \cup S_a$, such that S_t is the set of transient states, and S_a is a set of absorbing states, $\varrho \subseteq S \times S$ is a transition relation, such that $\langle S, \varrho \rangle$ is a connected graph, and $p: S \times S \to [0,1]$ is a probability function, such that for all states $s \in S_a$: $\sum_{t=\langle s,s' \rangle} p(t) = 1$.*

Stochastic Conformance Measures. A stochastic conformance measure δ compares an event log and a stochastic model, that is, $\delta: \mathcal{L} \times \mathcal{M} \to \mathbb{R}$. In this work, we use two such measures: unit earth movers' stochastic conformance (uEMSC [14]) and inverted entropic relevance (ER^{-1} [2]).

uEMSC captures the agreement mass between the distributions of L and M.

Definition 6 (Unit Earth Movers' Stochastic Conformance [14]). *Let L be an event log and let M be an SLPN. Then, the* unit Earth Movers' Stochastic Conformance *is* $\text{uEMSC}(L, M) = 1 - \sum_{\sigma \in \bar{L}} \max(L(\sigma) - M(\sigma), 0)$.

An entropic relevance of a stochastic process model M to an event log L measures the average number of bits required to describe a trace in L given the information available in M.[1] The lower the relevance, the better the model describes the stochastic language of the log. To allow consistent discussions, in this work, we invert entropic relevance to obtain a conformance measure.

Definition 7 (Inverted Entropic Relevance [2]). *Let L be a non-empty event log and let M be an SLPN. Let Λ be the set of all activities appearing in the traces of L. Then, the* inverted entropic relevance *(ER^{-1}) of M to L is defined as follows:*

$$ER^{-1}(L, M) = \frac{1}{H_0\left(\sum_{\sigma \in \bar{L}, \, M(\sigma) > 0} L(\sigma)\right) + \sum_{\sigma \in \bar{L}} L(\sigma) J(\sigma, M)}$$

$$J(\sigma, M) = \begin{cases} -\log_2 M(\sigma) & M(\sigma) > 0 \\ (1 + |\sigma|) \log_2(1 + |\Lambda|)) & otherwise \end{cases}$$

$$H_0(x) = -x \log_2 x - (1 - x) \log_2(1 - x) \text{ with } H_0(0) = H_0(1) = 0$$

4 The Stochastic Discovery Problem

In this section, we formally define the stochastic discovery problem, show several direct implications of our definition, and prove a generic result for uEMSC.

Definition 8 (Stochastic process discovery problem). *Let L be an event log and let $\delta \colon \mathcal{L} \times \mathcal{M} \to \mathbb{R}^{\geq 0}$ be a stochastic conformance measure. Then, the stochastic discovery problem is to find a model M of a class of models $\mathcal{M}'$ such that M maximises stochastic conformance with L:*

$$\delta(L, M) = \max_{M' \in \mathcal{M}'} \delta(L, M')$$

For the representational bias $\mathcal{M}'$ of all *SLPNs*, this definition is prone to over-fitting, and trivial solutions exist. For instance, for $\delta = $ uEMSC and representational bias $\mathcal{M}'$ of all SLPNs, a technique that satisfies this definition would be to return an SLPN representing every trace of L with the likelihood of that trace (a *stochastic trace model*), which would be a useless exercise as nothing new would have been learned and the model would be too complex for

---

[1] We use entropic relevance that relies on the uniform background coding model [2].

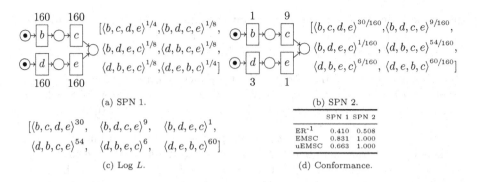

(a) SPN 1. (b) SPN 2.

$[\langle b, c, d, e\rangle^{30}, \quad \langle b, d, c, e\rangle^{9}, \quad \langle b, d, e, c\rangle^{1},$

$\langle d, b, c, e\rangle^{54}, \quad \langle d, b, e, c\rangle^{6}, \quad \langle d, e, b, c\rangle^{60}]$

(c) Log L.

	SPN 1	SPN 2
ER^{-1}	0.410	0.508
EMSC	0.831	1.000
uEMSC	0.663	1.000

(d) Conformance.

Fig. 2. Example of frequencies vs. weights.

human analysis. Furthermore, in evaluation settings, to avoid over-fitting, one should either separate evaluation and training data, or consider an appropriate representational bias, and obviously the definition given here does not guarantee optimality in such cases. As such, this definition is rather limited, but allows us to discuss stochastic process discovery in more detail, and obtain techniques that nevertheless perform competitively in evaluations, even though the optimality does not extend to these evaluation settings.

4.1   Implications

Weights vs. Frequencies. Regardless of the representational bias, how often a transition is executed (its *frequency*) is not necessarily proportional to its weight in a stochastic model.

Figure 2 shows an example of two SPNs with concurrency, only differing in their stochastic perspective. In the SPNs and the log, all activities occur exactly once per trace. Thus, an estimator technique based on frequencies, such as [6], will assign equal weights to all transitions, for instance SPN 1. However, next to *which* activities are executed, the weights in an SPN also influence the *order* of activities. As such, intuitively SPN 2 is a much more likely explanation for the log than SPN 1. This is reflected in the stochastic conformance measures, shown in Fig. 2d, all of which assign higher scores to SPN 2.

Another example is shown in Fig. 4. SPN 5 is frequency-based, while in SPN 6, b has twice the weight of a. The latter model has higher uEMSC and EMSC scores, as it prioritises the trace $\langle b, d\rangle$ at the expense of the a traces, which, in this case, proves beneficial for these measures. ER^{-1} of SPN 6 is lower than that of SPN 5, though. Despite traces $\langle a, d\rangle$ and $\langle b, d\rangle$ are modelled by SPN 6 perfectly, the probabilities of traces $\langle a, c\rangle$ and $\langle b, c\rangle$ as per SPN 6 deviate further from those in the log, as compared to their probabilities in SPN 5, causing non-linear effects on ER^{-1}. This example shows that frequency-based weight estimators are also challenged by dependent choices.

Loops. In the representational bias of SPNs, a model with loops is unlikely to be the result of stochastic process discovery according to Definition 8.

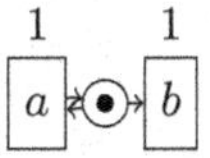

(a) SPN 3.

$[\langle b \rangle^{1/2}, \quad \langle a,b \rangle^{1/4},$
$\langle a,a,b \rangle^{1/8}, \quad \ldots]$

(b) SPN 4.

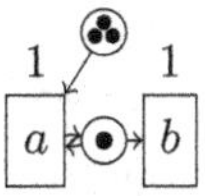

$[\langle b \rangle^{1/2}, \quad \langle a,b \rangle^{1/4},$
$\langle a,a,b \rangle^{1/8}, \quad \langle a,a,a,b \rangle^{1/8}]$

$[\langle b \rangle^{8}, \quad \langle a,b \rangle^{4},$
$\langle a,a,b \rangle^{2}, \quad \langle a,a,a,b \rangle^{1}]$

(c) Log L.

	SPN 3	SPN 4
ER^{-1}	0.577	0.600
EMSC $\approx$	0.958	0.965
uEMSC	0.938	0.942

(d) Conformance measures.

Fig. 3. Example of the influence of bounding loops.

For instance, consider Fig. 3. In SPN 3, $1/16$ probability mass is included in traces with 4 or more as, which does not appear in the event log. In SPN 4, the loop is bounded by an extra place with 3 tokens, such that this probability mass is not "lost" on traces that are not in the event log, but instead is put on the longest trace. This is reflected in the conformance measures shown in Fig. 3d.

In Lemma 1, we will prove that in general, uEMSC can only go up when adding such bounding places that do not restrict the behaviour in the log.

This example also shows the limitations of Definition 8: even though uEMSC may increase a little by adding such places, the model also gets more complex.

Two-Stage Approach. Regardless of the representational bias, existing stochastic process discovery approaches can be categorised by that the technique either (i) discovers control flow itself (one-stage, e.g. [7]) or (ii) leverages a control flow model as input (two-stage, e.g. [6]).

Figure 4 shows an example of the limitations of a two-stage approach, that is, first discovering a process model and then estimating the weights on top of it. In this example, the likelihoods of c and d depend on the choice between a and b. Comparing SPN 5 to SPN 7, we observe that SPN 5 (without its stochastic perspective) is a fully fitting model, but is less precise than SPN 7, whereas SPN 7 has a slightly lower fitness but a higher precision.

The stochastic measures, as shown in Fig. 4e, clearly prefer SPN 7. Thus, a control-flow trade-off needs to be made, with implications on the stochastic perspective. Hence, in this example, the stochastic perspective needs to be considered to decide on the control flow structure of the model.

The example shows that a lower fitness does not guarantee lower stochastic quality, and a higher fitness does not guarantee a higher stochastic quality. Therefore, it may be challenging to choose a model if stochastic quality is to be optimised. Thus, a two-stage approach may not always yield the best results.

4.2 uEMSC and Precision

Next, we establish the relation between control-flow precision and uEMSC. That is, we show that if non-log traces are removed from a model, uEMSC can only improve (which is conceptually linked to precision in [20, A2]).

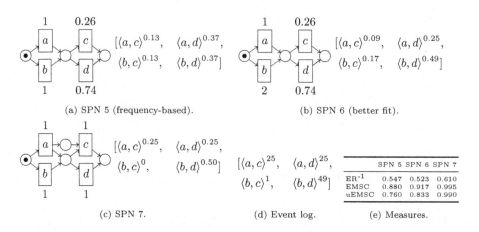

(a) SPN 5 (frequency-based).

(b) SPN 6 (better fit).

(c) SPN 7.

(d) Event log.

(e) Measures.

Fig. 4. Example of the interplay between places and weights.

Lemma 1 (Precision - uEMSC monotonicity). *Let L be an event log, and let M and M' be SPNs, such that $M = (P, T, F, w, M_0)$ and $M' = (P', T, F', w, M_0)$, such that $\tilde{L} \cap \tilde{M} = \tilde{L} \cap \tilde{M}'$, and such that $\tilde{M}' \subset \tilde{M}$. Then, $\mathrm{uEMSC}(L, M) \leq \mathrm{uEMSC}(L, M')$.*

Proof. Let $\sigma \in \tilde{M}$, $\sigma \notin \tilde{M}'$, $\sigma \notin \tilde{L}$. Let $\rho = M(\sigma)$ be the probability of σ in M. As σ does not contribute to $\mathrm{uEMSC}(L, M)$, it holds that $\mathrm{uEMSC}(L, M) \leq 1 - \rho$. As M' is a SPN, the probability mass ρ is accounted for in traces other than σ. As some of these traces may be in L, by definition of uEMSC, $\mathrm{uEMSC}(L, M) \leq \mathrm{uEMSC}(L, M')$. $\qquad\square$

Informally, ρ gets distributed from traces allowed by M that are not in the event log (that is, imprecise traces), to other traces in M'. Some traces in M' therefore get extra probability, and for some traces σ, this may increase the difference between $L(\sigma)$ and $M(\sigma)$, which leaves uEMSC unchanged as ρ already fully counted against $\mathrm{uEMSC}(L, M)$. However, for some traces σ' it may be that this difference gets smaller, thereby increasing $\mathrm{uEMSC}(L, M')$.

5   Stochastic Discovery as a Decision Problem

In this section, we translate stochastic process discovery with the representational bias of SPNs to a decision problem for uEMSC. That is, in this section, we consider the setting in which we do not have a control-flow model yet, and we aim to discover a fully stochastic model in one go, where we limit ourselves to the unlabelled transitions of SPNs. We start with the given set of transitions T. Then, we need to decide on four sets of variables: (i) the set of places P, (ii) the initial marking $M_0 \in P^\infty$, (iii) for every place $p \in P$ and transition $t \in T$, the arc multiplicities $t^\bullet_p \in \mathbb{N}$ and $^\bullet t_p \in \mathbb{N}$, and (iv) for every transition $t \in T$, a weight: $W_t \in (0, 1]$. For ease of notation, we write these variables as vectors, that is, $\vec{M}_0$, $t^{\bullet}$, ${}^{\bullet}t$ and $\vec{W}$. If $M_0(p) = t^{\bullet}{}_p = {}^{\bullet}t_p = 0$, a place p has no influence on the result, and thus the set of places P is a dependent variable and will be ignored further on.

We do not require that every trace of the log fits the model, so we need to keep track of which of the traces are supported by the model. Inspired by the ILP miner [21], if the net supports a trace σ, it should support all its prefixes, and the net should be in a deadlock after σ.

We introduce helper variables $\vec{E}$ indicating whether a pre-fix is supported by the model. As a base case, the empty pre-fix is supported by the model in any case (1), and a non-empty pre-fix $\sigma \cdot \langle t \rangle$ is supported if and only if the shorter pre-fix σ is supported and after executing all transitions in σ, t is enabled (2).

$$E_{\langle\rangle} = \text{true} \tag{1}$$

$$\forall_{\sigma \cdot \langle t \rangle \in \bar{L}} E_{\sigma \cdot \langle t \rangle} = E_\sigma \wedge \vec{M}_0 + \left(\sum_{t'' \in \sigma'} (t''^{\vec{\bullet}} - {}^{\bullet}\vec{t}'') \right) \succeq {}^{\bullet}\vec{t} \tag{2}$$

Furthermore, we introduce helper variables $\vec{D}$ indicating whether a trace is supported by the model. That is, for every trace $\sigma \in \bar{L}$ in the log, D_σ is true if and only if the net supports σ and after σ the net is in a deadlock:

$$\forall_{\sigma \in \bar{L}} D_\sigma = E_\sigma \wedge \forall_{t \in T} \left(\vec{M}_0 + \sum_{t'' \in \sigma'} t''^{\vec{\bullet}} - {}^{\bullet}\vec{t}'' \right) \not\succeq {}^{\bullet}\vec{t} \tag{3}$$

An optimal solution for Definition 8 can then be obtained by maximising uEMSC directly in the objective function. This function multiplies the probability of a trace by whether the trace is enabled (assuming false = 0 and true = 1):

$$1 - \sum_{\sigma \in \bar{L}} \max \left(L(\sigma) - D_\sigma \prod_{\sigma' \cdot \langle t \rangle \cdot \sigma'' = \sigma} \frac{W_t}{\sum_{(\vec{M}_0 + \sum_{t'' \in \sigma'} (t''^{\vec{\bullet}} - {}^{\bullet}\vec{t}'')) \succeq {}^{\bullet}\vec{t}} W_{t'}}, 0 \right) \tag{4}$$

Then, the full problem can be written as maximising (4) such that (1)$\wedge$(2)$\wedge$(3). By construction, the optimal solution to this problem corresponds to a SPN that maximises uEMSC, satisfying the problem of Definition 8.

Irrelevant Places. Next to an event log L, the optimisation problem requires a parameter of the maximum number of places the optimiser can utilise. Even if we do not consider arc multiplicities, there are $2^{2|T|}$ potential places in an SPN with transitions T. For 10 transitions, this would already yield $1\,048\,576$ candidate places. The optimisation problem uses $2|T|+1$ variables for each place, thus for practical computabilty, the number of places needs to be limited.

Observe that if an optimal SPN has $|P|$ places, then allowing for more places in will not decrease uEMSC: the optimisation problem can, for instance, simply duplicate places, which obviously does not change the behaviour of the resulting net. We refer to such places as *irrelevant* places:

Definition 9 (Irrelevant place). *Let L be a log and let M, M' be SPNs with places P and P', such that $P = P' \setminus \{p\}$ and* uEMSC(L, M) = uEMSC(L, M'). *Then, p is an* irrelevant *place.*

To check whether a place in an SPN is irrelevant, we can remove this place and compare the uEMSC of the SPN before and after the place removal. We conjecture that if the optimiser returns a net with irrelevant places, then adding more places will not improve uEMSC, and consequently Definition 8 is satisfied.

Conjecture 1. If the optimiser returns a irrelevant place, then adding even more places $|P|$ will not increase the uEMSC score.

We use these two results to guide the optimisation: we simply attempt with a number of places $|P|$ and check for irrelevant places. If no such place is found, we repeat the optimisation with a larger number of places, until an optimisation yields an irrelevant place. Then, we have a lower bound and an upper bound for the number of places $|P|$, and we can apply a binary search to find the model with the smallest number of places that satisfies Definition 8. While to the best of our knowledge this is the first stochastic discovery technique that guarantees an as-high-as-possible uEMSC score, it requires a mixed-integer non-convex solver and would probably need further consideration to be practically applicable. Therefore, we leave its implementation as future work. Instead, we proceed with a more practically applicable technique that works on the more generic representational bias of *labelled* Petri nets, and that uses a separately discovered control flow model as input.

6   Stochastic Discovery Given the Control-Flow Structure

In this section, we address a different setting: we assume that a control flow model is given, and we need to assign the stochastic perspective to it that gives us the highest uEMSC. As a trade-off for being given the control flow model, the method of this section can handle labelled transitions. Given a log and a labelled Petri net N, we discover an SLPN that best represents the stochastic information in L with the control flow of N. Our strategy is to turn the net into an SLPN M that assigns a *weight parameter* to every transition. Then, stochastic discovery is posed as an optimisation problem, where values for the weights must be found so that a stochastic conformance measure is maximised.

To set up the optimisation problem, for every trace σ in the log, we extract a symbolic formula characterising the parametric probability of σ according to M, by adapting the trace probability calculation given in [10,11]. First, σ is turned into an SDFA to account for silent transitions. Then, the cross product of the SDFA and a parametric stochastic reachability graph of M is constructed. The cross product is a parametric absorbing Markov chain, from which a system of equations accounting for step-wise probabilities can be extracted, in turn allowing to obtain the probability of σ according to M as the absorption probability of the Markov chain - which can be solved symbolically, considering the

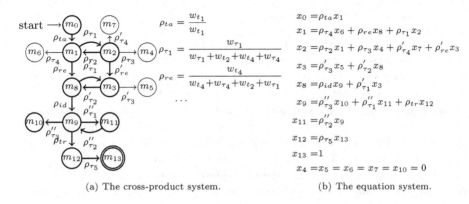

(a) The cross-product system.

(b) The equation system.

Fig. 5. Example for the trace ⟨talk, record, identify, troubleshoot⟩.

parameters. This is then repeated for every trace, combining all the so-obtained symbolic formulae together using a stochastic conformance measure. We detail these steps in the remainder of the section.

Note that we cannot equate the symbolic formulae to the observed trace probabilities in the log, as due to the representational bias of the given control flow, that solution may not exist.

Constructing the Cross-Product System. We convert the given net N into a parametric SLPN M by associating each transition in N to a weight parameter. To compare M with the input log L, we characterise the probability of each trace σ in L according to M. This cannot be done directly: if the input N contains silent transitions, the same trace might correspond to infinitely many different paths in M [10,11]. We therefore follow the steps of [10,11], with as main difference that while in [10,11] the weights of the SLPN are given, and the only unknown variable is the trace probability, here also the weights are parameters. So, instead of getting a solution for the trace probability, we will obtain a symbolic formula describing how the trace probability relates to the weight parameters of M.

The first step towards this is to turn each trace σ into an SDFA (cf. Definition 3), then computing the cross-product system of such an SDFA and the stochastic reachability graph (cf. Definition 4) of M, recalled here:

Definition 10. (Cross-Product System). *Let $R = (\Sigma^1, S^1, s_0^1, S_f^1, \varrho, p)$ be the stochastic reachability graph of an SLPN M, and $D(\sigma) = (\Sigma^2, S^2, s_0^2, S_f^2, \delta)$ be an SDFA describing all and only those runs whose corresponding trace is σ. The* cross-product system *of M and σ is an absorbing Markov chain $\mathcal{E}_M^\sigma = M \otimes \sigma = (s_0^\otimes, \varrho^\otimes, p^\otimes, S^\otimes, S_f^\otimes)$ where:*

- $s_0^\otimes = (s_0^1, s_0^2)$,
- *for every $s = (s^1, s^2) \in S^\otimes$, we have $s^1 \in S^1 \wedge s^2 \in S^2$,*
- *for every $s = (s^1, s^2)$ and $s' = (s^{1'}, s^{2'}) \in S^\otimes$ with $\exists_{l \in \Sigma^1 \cap \Sigma^2} \langle s^1, l, s^{1'} \rangle \in \varrho \wedge \delta(s^2, l) = s^{2'}$, we have $\langle s, l, s' \rangle \in \varrho^\otimes$, $p^\otimes(s, l, s') = p(s^1, l, s^{1'})$,*

– for every $(s_f^1, s_f^2) \in S_f^\otimes$, we have $s_f^1 \in S_f^1 \wedge s_f^2 \in S_f^2$,

For example, Fig. 5a shows the cross-product system of the trace $\langle talk, record, identify, troubleshoot \rangle$ and the stochastic reachability graph in Fig. 1b. It has multiple paths whose label sequence corresponds to the trace, and we omit the parts of the system that do not lead to the accepting state m_{13}.

Describing Trace Probabilities. Given the cross-product system $\mathcal{E}_M^\sigma = (s_0^\otimes, \varrho^\otimes, p^\otimes, S^\otimes, S_f^\otimes)$, we denote $S_n^\otimes$ as the set of non-target accepting states. To describe how the probability of trace σ according to M depends on the parameters of M, we recast [10,11], which uses standard techniques from literature on absorbing Markov chain to turn the cross-product into a corresponding system $\mathcal{E}_M^\sigma$ of step-wise equations, where every state $s \in S^\otimes$ corresponds to a probability variable x_s, and equations are defined based on $M \otimes \sigma$ as follows:

$$x_{s_i} = 1 \qquad \text{for each } s_i \in S_f^\otimes \setminus S_n^\otimes$$

$$x_{s_j} = 0 \qquad \text{for each } s_j \in S_n^\otimes$$

$$x_{s_k} = \sum_{(s_k, s_k') \in \varrho} p(s_k, s_k') \cdot x_{s_k'} \qquad \text{for each } s_k \in S^\otimes \setminus S_f^\otimes$$

Recall that the state probability variables and the parameters of M are unknown. In addition, in $\mathcal{E}_M^\sigma$, variable $x_{s_0^\otimes}$ denotes the probability of σ according to M. We can then solve the system symbolically, obtaining a formula that relates $x_{s_0^\otimes}$ to (only) the weight parameters from M. We denote this formula with $\widetilde{p}_M(\sigma)$.

In our running example, the system of equations for the cross-product system of Fig. 5a is given in Fig. 5b. By symbolically solving the equation system, we derive $(\rho_{re} + \rho_{\tau_1} \cdot \rho_{re}' \cdot \rho_{\tau_2}') \cdot \rho_{ta} \cdot \rho_{id} \cdot \rho_{tr} \cdot \rho_{\tau_5} / ((1 - \rho_{\tau_1} \cdot \rho_{\tau_2}) \cdot (1 - \rho_{\tau_1}' \cdot \rho_{\tau_2}') \cdot (1 - \rho_{\tau_1}'' \cdot \rho_{\tau_2}''))$, where each ρ is a division of weight parameters; e.g. $\rho_{re} = w_{t_4} / (w_{t_4} + w_{\tau_4} + w_{t_2} + w_{\tau_1})$.

Estimating Weights Through Optimisation. We now combine into a single system all the symbolic probability descriptions derived, as shown before, for every trace in the input log L. For every trace σ in L, we compute the trace probability of σ according to the relative frequency of σ in L (denoted $L(\sigma)$) and compare it with the corresponding symbolic formula $\widetilde{p}_M(\sigma)$. We do so by imposing, overall, optimisation against a stochastic conformance measure applied to M and L, such as uEMSC or ER^{-1}, which is a substitution of the trace probability of $M(\sigma)$ by our symbolic formula $\widetilde{p}_M(\sigma)$. For uEMSC, we get:

$$\text{maximise } 1 - \sum_{\sigma \in \bar{L}} \max(L(\sigma) - \widetilde{p}_M(\sigma), 0) \qquad (5)$$

This problem is non-convex due to the many divisions. However, the max can be rewritten into linear constraints, and all parameters are numeric, which makes it suitable for standard solvers. A solution to this problem satisfies Definition 8, when taking the representational bias of SLPNs and uEMSC. Another optimal solution for Definition 8 can be obtained by maximising ER^{-1} in a similar way.

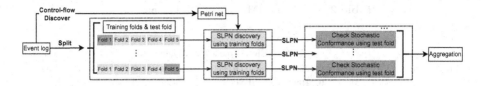

Fig. 6. Experimental setup for evaluation.

Table 1. Results for DFMM [13] control-flow models.

Log	Measure	Stochastic discovery technique						
		d-uEMSC	d-ER	Frequency	Alignment	LH	RH	Scaled
BPIC2013_close	uEMSC	**0.5745**	0.5358	0.0000	0.4273	0.0000	0.0000	0.0000
	EMSC	**0.9059**	0.8820	0.4576	0.4701	0.4600	0.4712	0.4716
	ER⁻¹	0.0881	**0.0906**	0.0397	0.0751	0.0650	0.0650	0.0650
BPIC2013_open	uEMSC	0.3659	0.3910	0.0000	**0.4164**	0.0000	0.0000	0.0000
	EMSC	**0.4897**	0.4541	0.4482	0.4207	0.4209	0.4156	0.4212
	ER⁻¹	0.1082	0.1059	0.0449	**0.1141**	0.1000	0.1000	0.1000
BPIC2017_application	uEMSC	**0.5832**	0.5072	0.2785	0.4117	0.3214	0.3214	0.3214
	EMSC	0.6804	**0.8673**	0.8605	0.8672	0.8672	0.8672	0.8672
	ER⁻¹	0.1134	0.1106	0.1110	**0.1137**	0.1110	0.1110	0.1110
BPIC2017_offer	uEMSC	**0.6563**	0.5828	0.5388	0.5811	0.5373	0.5373	0.5373
	EMSC	**0.9155**	0.9101	0.9026	0.9102	0.9010	0.9010	0.9010
	ER⁻¹	0.2312	0.2330	0.1091	**0.3115**	0.1092	0.1092	0.1092
BPIC2020_domestic	uEMSC	**0.8079**	0.8064	0.0000	0.3575	0.0000	0.0000	0.0000
	EMSC	**0.9158**	0.8596	timeout	timeout	timeout	timeout	timeout
	ER⁻¹	0.1543	**0.1569**	0.0428	0.1144	0.0384	0.0384	0.0384
BPIC2020_request	uEMSC	**0.7537**	0.7151	0.0000	0.6256	0.0000	0.0000	0.0000
	EMSC	0.2830	0.1978	**0.4116**	0.4026	0.3991	0.3990	0.4006
	ER⁻¹	**0.1610**	0.1538	0.0386	0.1220	0.0389	0.0389	0.0389
road traffic fines	uEMSC	**0.8196**	0.3048	0.0139	0.2940	0.0000	0.0000	0.0000
	EMSC	**0.9061**	0.7054	0.5159	0.5311	0.5311	0.5566	0.5403
	ER⁻¹	0.1938	**0.1955**	0.0627	0.1675	0.0590	0.0590	0.0590

7 Evaluation

The two-stage SLPN discovery approaches were implemented in the ProM framework; their source code and the experiments' scripts are publicly available[2]. A 60-second timeout is applied to each trace probability calculation. In this section, we compare the quality of models of our techniques with existing stochastic discovery techniques on 7 publicly available real-life event logs[3].

Set-Up. Figure 6 shows the experiment setup. Firstly, two control flow discovery algorithms (IMf [9] and DFMM [13]; chosen as they guarantee livelock-freedom) are applied to each full log to obtain a control-flow model. Next, each log is

---

[2] https://github.com/promworkbench/SLPNMiner.
[3] https://www.tf-pm.org/resources/logs.

Table 2. Results for IMf [9] control-flow models.

Log	Measure	Stochastic discovery technique						
		d-uEMSC	d-ER	Frequency	Alignment	LH	RH	Scaled
BPIC2013_close	uEMSC	**0.4989**	0.3860	0.0000	0.4273	0.0000	0.0000	0.0000
	EMSC	**0.7199**	0.7140	0.4568	0.6569	0.4681	0.4615	0.4609
	ER^{-1}	**0.0856**	0.0835	0.0397	0.0751	0.0650	0.0650	0.0650
BPIC2013_open	uEMSC	0.4391	**0.4518**	0.0000	0.4165	0.0000	0.0000	0.0000
	EMSC	**0.7041**	0.7005	0.4208	0.4483	0.4482	0.4465	0.4385
	ER^{-1}	0.1396	**0.1475**	0.0449	0.1141	0.0999	0.0999	0.0999
BPIC2017_application	uEMSC	0.3256	**0.3753**	0.2785	0.4117	0.3214	0.3214	0.3214
	EMSC	0.8068	**0.8917**	0.8650	0.8663	0.8649	0.8650	0.8590
	ER^{-1}	0.1431	0.1574	0.0609	**0.1686**	0.0457	0.0457	0.0457
BPIC2017_offer	uEMSC	**0.6564**	0.5829	0.5388	0.5811	0.5373	0.5373	0.5373
	EMSC	**0.9155**	0.9101	0.9026	0.9102	0.9010	0.9010	0.9010
	ER^{-1}	0.1080	0.1042	0.1091	0.1037	**0.1092**	**0.1092**	**0.1092**
BPIC2020_domestic	uEMSC	0.0231	0.0152	0.0001	**0.5799**	0.0000	0.0000	0.0000
	EMSC	0.6187	0.5940	0.4342	**0.9361**	timeout	timeout	timeout
	ER^{-1}	0.0763	0.0791	**0.1472**	0.1277	0.0384	0.0384	0.0384
BPIC2020_request	uEMSC	0.2830	0.1978	0.0000	**0.6256**	0.0000	0.0000	0.0000
	EMSC	**0.7537**	0.7151	0.4020	0.3987	0.4093	0.4092	0.3991
	ER^{-1}	0.0701	0.0637	0.0386	**0.1220**	0.0386	0.0386	0.0386
road traffic fines	uEMSC	**0.1729**	0.1407	0.0140	0.0700	0.0000	0.0000	0.0000
	EMSC	0.6148	**0.7473**	0.5567	0.5291	0.5292	0.5310	0.5389
	ER^{-1}	0.1188	0.1389	0.0627	**0.1493**	0.0590	0.0590	0.0590

randomly split using 5-fold cross-validation to measure how well the techniques can represent a non-changing process; stochastic discovery (our "d-uEMSC" and "d-ER" discovery techniques, as well as 5 estimators from [6]) are applied to 4 folds and the remaining fold is used to evaluate the SLPN using uEMSC [14], EMSC [14] and ER^{-1} [18]. A 100-second timeout was applied to each conformance measure. The evaluation was repeated 3 times to eliminate random effects: each reported number is thus the average over 15 models.

Results. The results are shown in Tables 1 and 2. We could not compute EMSC on several estimators for the BPIC2020-domestic declations log. Even though d-uEMSC and d-ER optimise for uEMSC and ER^{-1} respectively, training data was not used for measuring, thus in this experiment they are not guaranteed to yield the highest scores. Nevertheless, d-uEMSC got the highest uEMSC value in 9 cases and d-ER got the highest ER^{-1} in 4 cases. On the EMSC measure, for which the techniques did not optimise, d-uEMSC was highest in 9 cases and d-ER in 3 cases. The closest existing technique was the alignment-based estimator, which got a highest EMSC score once, which highlights the trade-offs that need to be made in stochastic discovery, even when optimising for a single measure.

When comparing the control-flow discovery techniques, DFMM combines well with our d-uEMSC and d-ER, as a highest measure (of all stochastic discovery techniques) is achieved in 16 out of 21 log-measure combinations, while for IMf this is 13. We manually inspected the results for the BPIC2020 domestic log on IMf, where the alignment-based estimator fared better than d-uEMSC and d-ER. We found that the many silent transitions in the model led to a large state space for the cross-product system, which made the derivation of a symbolic representation of trace probability time out. Consequently, these trace probabilities were not considered during optimisation. We also re-ran some instances multiple times, and found that our solver may return different values over different runs and, as expected, does not guarantee optimality on our non-convex problem.

In summary, the estimators proposed in this paper can be applied to real-life logs and discover better SLPNs, considering common stochastic conformance measures, even the ones they did not optimise for. Thus, they provide alternative estimation approaches to existing two-stage stochastic discovery techniques.

8   Conclusion

In this paper, we formally defined stochastic process discovery as finding a model with an optimal conformance checking measure over a given representation bias. We studied the implications of this definition in detail, and introduced techniques for two biases: one for SPNs (a one-stage approach), and one that takes a control-flow model for SLPNs (a two-stage approach). We implemented and evaluated the latter one for uEMSC and ER^{-1}, and found that they perform well compared to existing techniques, even evaluating stochastic measures on test logs they did not optimise for. A direction for future work is to improve the implementation of symbolic trace probabilities, and to implement the one-stage approach. Furthermore, stochastic discovery can be extended to optimisation problems over further conformance measures, and on combinations of such measures. In particular, considering simplicity measures, which must be invented first for stochastic models, may prove beneficial for stochastic process discovery.

References

1. van der Aalst, W.M.P.: Process Mining - Data Science in Action, 2nd edn. Springer, Cham (2016)
2. Alkhammash, H., Polyvyanyy, A., Moffat, A., García-Bañuelos, L.: Entropic relevance: a mechanism for measuring stochastic process models discovered from event data. Inf. Syst. **107**, 101922 (2022)
3. Bause, F., Kritzinger, P.S.: Stochastic Petri Nets - An Introduction to the Theory, 2nd edn. Vieweg, Braunschweig (2002)
4. Bergami, G., Maggi, F.M., Montali, M., Peñaloza, R.: Probabilistic trace alignment. In: ICPM. IEEE (2021)
5. Brockhoff, T., Uysal, M.S., van der Aalst, W.M.P.: Time-aware concept drift detection using the earth mover's distance. In: ICPM. IEEE (2020)
6. Burke, A., Leemans, S.J.J., Wynn, M.T.: Stochastic process discovery by weight estimation. In: Leemans, S., Leopold, H. (eds.) Process Mining Workshops. Lecture Notes in Business Information Processing, vol. 406, pp. 260–272. Springer, Cham (2020). https://doi.org/10.1007/978-3-030-72693-5_20

7. Burke, A., Leemans, S.J.J., Wynn, M.T.: Discovering stochastic process models by reduction and abstraction. In: Buchs, D., Carmona, J. (eds.) Application and Theory of Petri Nets and Concurrency. Lecture Notes in Computer Science(), vol. 12734, pp. 312–336. Springer, Cham (2021). https://doi.org/10.1007/978-3-030-76983-3_16

8. Jansen, N., Junges, S., Katoen, J.: Parameter synthesis in Markov models: a gentle survey. In: Raskin, J.F., Chatterjee, K., Doyen, L., Majumdar, R. (eds.) Principles of Systems Design. Lecture Notes in Computer Science, vol. 13660, pp. 407–437. Springer, Cham (2022). https://doi.org/10.1007/978-3-031-22337-2_20

9. Leemans, S.J.J., Fahland, D., van der Aalst, W.M.P.: Discovering block-structured process models from incomplete event logs. In: Ciardo, G., Kindler, E. (eds.) Application and Theory of Petri Nets and Concurrency. Lecture Notes in Computer Science, vol. 8489, pp. 91–110. Springer, Cham (2014). https://doi.org/10.1007/978-3-319-07734-5_6

10. Leemans, S.J.J., Maggi, F.M., Montali, M.: Reasoning on labelled Petri nets and their dynamics in a stochastic setting. In: Di Ciccio, C., Dijkman, R., del Rio Ortega, A., Rinderle-Ma, S. (eds.) Business Process Management. Lecture Notes in Computer Science, vol. 13420, pp. 324–342. Springer, Cham (2022). https://doi.org/10.1007/978-3-031-16103-2_22

11. Leemans, S.J.J., Maggi, F.M., Montali, M.: Enjoy the silence: analysis of stochastic Petri nets with silent transitions. CoRR **abs/2306.06376** (2023)

12. Leemans, S.J.J., Mannel, L.L., Sidorova, N.: Significant stochastic dependencies in process models. Inf. Syst. **118**, 102223 (2023)

13. Leemans, S.J.J., Poppe, E., Wynn, M.T.: Directly follows-based process mining: exploration & a case study. In: ICPM. IEEE (2019)

14. Leemans, S.J.J., Syring, A.F., van der Aalst, W.M.P.: Earth movers' stochastic conformance checking. In: Hildebrandt, T., van Dongen, B., Roglinger, M., Mendling, J. (eds.) Business Process Management Forum. Lecture Notes in Business Information Processing, vol. 360, pp. 127–143. Springer, Cham (2019). https://doi.org/10.1007/978-3-030-26643-1_8

15. Marsan, M.A., Conte, G., Balbo, G.: A class of generalized stochastic Petri nets for the performance evaluation of multiprocessor systems. ACM Trans. Comput. Syst. **2**(2), 93–122 (1984)

16. Mazak, A., Wolny, S., Wimmer, M.: On the need for data-based model-driven engineering. In: Biffl, S., Eckhart, M., Luder, A., Weippl, E. (eds.) Security and Quality in Cyber-Physical Systems Engineering, pp. 103–127. Springer, Cham (2019). https://doi.org/10.1007/978-3-030-25312-7_5

17. Molloy, M.K.: Performance analysis using stochastic Petri nets. IEEE Trans. Comput. **31**(9) (1982)

18. Polyvyanyy, A., Moffat, A., García-Bañuelos, L.: An entropic relevance measure for stochastic conformance checking in process mining. In: ICPM. IEEE (2020)

19. Rogge-Solti, A., van der Aalst, W.M.P., Weske, M.: Discovering stochastic Petri nets with arbitrary delay distributions from event logs. In: Lohmann, N., Song, M., Wohed, P. (eds.) Business Process Management Workshops. Lecture Notes in Business Information Processing, vol. 171, pp. 15–27. Springer, Cham (2013). https://doi.org/10.1007/978-3-319-06257-0_2

20. Tax, N., Lu, X., Sidorova, N., Fahland, D., van der Aalst, W.M.P.: The imprecisions of precision measures in process mining. Inf. Process. Lett. **135**, 1–8 (2018)

21. van der Werf, J.M.E.M., van Dongen, B.F., Hurkens, C.A.J., Serebrenik, A.: Process discovery using integer linear programming. Fundam. Inform. **94**(3-4) (2009)

Process Discovery, Monitoring
and Correction

Reinforcement Learning-Based Streaming Process Discovery Under Concept Drift

Rujian Cai, Chao Zheng, Jian Wang$^{(\boxtimes)}$, Duantengchuan Li, Chong Wang, and Bing Li$^{(\boxtimes)}$

School of Computer Science, Wuhan University, Wuhan, China
{cai-r-j,chaozheng,jianwang,dtclee1222,cwang,bingli}@whu.edu.cn

Abstract. Streaming process discovery aims to discover a process model that may change over time, coping with the challenges of concept drift in business processes. Existing studies update process models with fixed strategies, neglecting the highly dynamic nature of trace streams. Consequently, they fail to accurately reveal the process evolution caused by concept drift. This paper proposes RLSPD (**R**einforcement **L**earning-based **S**treaming **P**rocess **D**iscovery), a dynamic process discovery approach for constructing an online process model on a trace stream. RLSPD leverages conformance-checking information to characterize trace distribution and employs a reinforcement learning policy to capture fluctuations in the trace stream. Based on the dynamic parameters provided by reinforcement learning, we extract representative trace variants within a memory window using frequency-based sampling and perform concept drift detection. Upon detecting concept drift, the process model is updated by process discovery. Experimental results on real-life event logs demonstrate that our approach effectively adapts to the high dynamics of trace streams, improving the conformance of constructed process models to upcoming traces and reducing erroneous model updates. Additionally, the results highlight the significance of the pre-trained policy in dealing with unknown environments.

Keywords: Process discovery · Concept drift · Trace stream · Reinforcement learning

1 Introduction

Process mining aims to understand the business processes of organizations by analyzing event data recorded in information systems [1]. Process discovery is the primary task of process mining. It explicitly constructs a process model based on the execution records of a business process, providing insights for subsequent process monitoring and improvement. Early process discovery methods [2–4] employ the entire event log to construct a process model by analyzing the execution relationships among activities. These methods operate under the assumption that the business process is in a steady state, and the process model

G. Guizzardi et al. (Eds.): CAiSE 2024, LNCS 14663, pp. 55–70, 2024.
https://doi.org/10.1007/978-3-031-61057-8_4

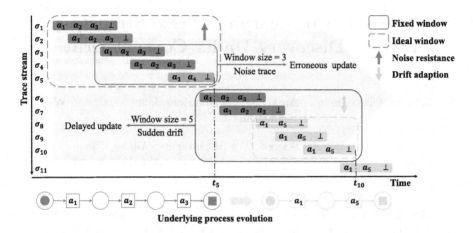

Fig. 1. Illustration of dynamic parameter adjustments in streaming process discovery

extracted from historical event logs can describe the execution of the future process. However, real-life processes may undergo changes over time due to shifts in business environments, such as evolving requirements and policies, herein called concept drift [5]. Organizations must treat the real-time event logs generated by business systems as data streams and handle concept drifts within them [6]. When the underlying business process changes, the distribution of the traces representing different process variants changes. Once a concept drift is detected, the online process model must be updated to ensure high conformance with upcoming traces.

Prior studies [7–12] primarily focus on detecting and locating concept drifts, delving into when they occur, their characteristics, and the root causes. However, the process evolution before and after concept drifts is not explicitly revealed. Several approaches have recently explored dynamic process discovery on event streams. In [13–16], process discovery is performed whenever new data arrives or at regular intervals, without considering potential changes in the process execution. Consequently, the process model is updated solely upon detecting concept drifts in [17]. Nevertheless, it uses the same fixed detection parameters for diverse trace streams or segments within the same trace stream, failing to effectively adapt to the highly dynamic nature of trace streams. This may result in erroneous or delayed updates to the process model.

Figure 1 illustrates a fluctuating trace stream that contains underlying process evolution and noise caused by misoperations. For instance, at time t_5, utilizing a fixed small window (e.g., window size = 3) may mistakenly identify the fluctuation caused by the noise trace σ_5 as a concept drift, leading to an erroneous model update. This issue can be addressed by enlarging the window to filter out noise, thereby enhancing resistance to interference. Conversely, at time t_{10}, the underlying business process has changed. If the fixed window is large (e.g., window size = 5), the discovered model is influenced by distant historical traces, resulting in a delayed detection of the sudden drift. This issue can be mitigated by reducing the window size to focus exclusively on the most recent traces, facilitating a rapid and accurate update of the process model. In summary, dynamically adjusting parameters is crucial for streaming process discovery.

This paper proposes RLSPD (Reinforcement Learning-based Streaming Process Discovery), a novel dynamic process discovery approach designed to discover an online process model over the trace stream. We utilize the conformance-checking information of the process model for the upcoming traces to characterize the trace distribution. Subsequently, we employ a reinforcement learning policy to dynamically determine the required parameters (i.e., memory window and sampling rate) for identifying the most representative trace variants through frequency-based sampling. A change in the representative variants signifies a significant shift in the trace distribution, indicating the detection of a concept drift. At this point, the process discovery is re-performed based on the new trace variants, and the online process model is promptly updated.

The main contributions of this work are summarized as follows: **1)** We propose a streaming process discovery approach that improves the conformance of the online process model to the upcoming traces under concept drifts, and reduces the number of incorrect model updates. **2)** We characterize trace distribution with conformance-checking information and employ reinforcement learning to capture the dynamic nature of trace streams. This enables the acquisition of robust online process models, even in the presence of totally new trace streams. **3)** We conduct experiments on several real-life event logs treated as trace streams, and the results show the effectiveness of RLSPD.

The rest of this paper is organized as follows. Section 2 reviews related work. Section 3 introduces preliminary concepts, while Sect. 4 describes the proposed RLSPD approach. The experimental results and discussions are reported in Sect. 5. Finally, Sect. 6 draws conclusions and sketches future work.

2   Related Work

Concept Drift in Process Mining. Traditional process mining algorithms, such as Inductive Miner [2], ILP Miner [3] and Split Miner [4], operate under the assumption that business processes always remain stable. However, real-world business processes often change over time due to factors like customer requirements and market trends.

Concept drift in process mining was initially explored in [7], where three critical issues were identified: drift detection, drift localization, and unraveling process evolution. Most research has primarily focused on the first two problems. Hypothesis testing is a prevalent method for detecting concept drift [7-9]. It involves extracting features at both the log and trace levels and conducting hypothesis tests on consecutive sub-logs to determine whether there is statistical evidence of significant differences in feature sets before and after the drift point. Another category of concept drift detection methods is trace clustering [10-12]. This technique involves mapping traces into a vector space and clustering them within fixed-size windows. Drift is detected when there are notable differences between two consecutive clusters. Drift localization approaches typically analyze variations in feature sets or trace clusters before and after concept drifts, identifying the drift type and the changed activities or transitions.

These methods focus on detecting and locating concept drifts, but do not reveal the process evolution before and after concept drifts. This necessitates a mechanism for dynamic process discovery within event streams.

Streaming Process Discovery. In recent years, researchers have been dedicated to discovering evolving process models in dynamic business scenarios. In [13–16], various static process discovery algorithms are applied to stream settings. By introducing classic data stream mining techniques like Sliding Window and Lossy Counting, the event stream is managed to continuously update the underlying data structure with the latest observations. The process model is then reconstructed based on this updated representation. Despite addressing the challenge of processing infinite event stream data with limited memory, these approaches do not explicitly detect concept drifts. This leads to restarting process discovery periodically or upon the arrival of each new event, potentially resulting in unchanged process models and unnecessary time consumption.

Combining process discovery with concept drift detection becomes crucial. By capturing the high dynamics of the log stream, it is possible to update the process model only when necessary. STARDUST [17] designs a streamlined drift detection method specifically for streaming process discovery. It monitors the trace stream and detects concept drifts when high-frequency trace variants changes, and then uses these trace variants to discover a new process model. However, its fixed window size and sampling rate cannot effectively adapt to the dynamic changes in trace distribution, potentially resulting in false detections of concept drifts and impacting model fitness and precision for upcoming traces.

Using identical and fixed parameters may result in poor performance when confronted with various trace streams or diverse segments within a single trace stream. While grid search is a prevalent approach for parameter optimization, it is inefficient in highly dynamic real-time scenarios. Hence, we introduce reinforcement learning to adapt to changes in trace streams, dynamically adjusting parameters for concept drift detection and process discovery.

3   Preliminaries

3.1   Event and Trace Stream

A process is a series of interrelated and ordered activities executed according to specific rules and conditions to achieve a particular goal. Each case represents an instance of process execution. Let $\mathcal{A}$ be the set of activities, $\mathcal{C}$ be the set of case identifiers, and $\mathcal{T}$ be the set of timestamps.

Definition 1 (Event). An event e is a triple, $e = (c, a, t) \in \mathcal{C} \times \mathcal{A} \times \mathcal{T}$ representing that in case c, activity a is executed at timestamp t.

To identify the case, activity, and timestamp of an event $e = (c, a, t)$, we introduce the functions: $I_{case}(e) = c$, $I_{activity}(e) = a$, $I_{time}(e) = t$, respectively. Let $\perp$ denote the end activity, an event e with $I_{case}(e) = c$ and $I_{activity}(e) = \perp$ represents the completion of case c.[1] Then, the complete execution trace σ_c of case c can be extracted.

Definition 2 (Trace). A trace σ_c is a sequence of all events within the same case c in time order, $\sigma_c = \langle e_1, e_2, ..., e_n \rangle$, where $I_{case}(e_i) = I_{case}(e_{i+1}) = c$, $I_{time}(e_i) < I_{time}(e_{i+1})$, $i \in \{1, 2, ..., n-1\}$, and $I_{activity}(e_n) = \perp$.

For trace $\sigma_c = \langle e_1, e_2, ..., e_n \rangle$, let $\sigma_c(i) = e_i$ be the i-th event of trace σ_c, $|\sigma_c| = n$ be the total number of events in completed case c, and the completion time of trace σ_c be $t_c = I_{time}(\sigma_c(|\sigma_c|)) = I_{time}(e_n)$. Different cases are executed as the business process system runs, generating an online stream of traces.

Definition 3 (Trace stream). A trace stream Σ is an infinite sequence of traces in order of trace completion time, i.e., $\Sigma = \sigma_1, \sigma_2, ...$, where for each $c \in \mathcal{C}$, σ_c denotes the complete execution trace of case c, and $t_c \leq t_{c+1}$.

To adapt to the dynamic nature of streaming data, it is necessary to introduce a memory window that only considers the traces from the most recent period.

Definition 4 (Memory window). Let w be the memory size. Given a trace stream Σ and the current trace σ_c, a memory window extracts a trace subset S_c^w that records the most recent w traces, $S_c^w = \{\sigma_{c-w+1}, \sigma_{c-w+2}, ..., \sigma_c\}$.

When analyzing a trace set to discover a process model, the focus is on the execution order of different activities in each trace and the frequency of distinct trace variants.

Definition 5 (Trace variant). A trace variant v is a unique activity execution sequence, $v = \langle a_1, a_2, ..., a_n \rangle$, where $a_i \in \mathcal{A}$ and $a_n = \perp$.

Let $v(i)$ be the i-th activity of trace variant v, and $|v|$ be the total number of activities in v. The trace σ_c belongs to the trace variant v only if $|\sigma_c| = |v|$ and $I_{activity}(e_i) = v(i)$ for each $i = 1, 2, ..., |\sigma_c|$.

Definition 6 (Trace variant counter). A trace variant counter V_S is a counter that records distinct trace variants and their frequency in the trace set S.

Taking the trace stream $\Sigma = \sigma_1, \sigma_2, ..., \sigma_{11}, ...$ in Fig. 1 as an example, traces $\sigma_1 - \sigma_4, \sigma_6 - \sigma_7$ belong to trace variant $\langle a_1, a_2, a_3, \perp \rangle$ and traces $\sigma_8 - \sigma_{11}$ belong to trace variant $\langle a_1, a_5, \perp \rangle$. With memory size $w = 10$ and the current trace σ_{11}, the trace set $S_{11}^{10} = \{\sigma_2, \sigma_3, ..., \sigma_{11}\}$ can be transformed into trace variant counter $V_{S_{11}^{10}} = \{\langle a_1, a_2, a_3, \perp \rangle^5, \langle a_1, a_5, \perp \rangle^4, \langle a_1, a_4, \perp \rangle^1\}$.

---

[1] Business processes usually declare the completion of a case, such as ticket resolution in help desk processes. Business processes that do not explicitly declare the completion of a case cannot be handled in this study and require further investigation in future work.

Before constructing a process model, it is a common practice to filter the input traces to extract essential information and reduce noise interference. An intuitive solution is to sample high-frequency trace variants from the trace variant counter as a preprocessing step for process discovery.

Definition 7 (Frequency-based sampling). Let ρ be the sampling rate. Given a trace variant counter V_S, the frequency-based sampling algorithm is a function $\Phi(\rho, V_S)$ that sorts the trace variants of V_S in descending order of frequency and generates V_S^ρ, which comprises the smallest counter set of the top-frequent trace variants of V_S so that $\frac{\Gamma(V_S^\rho)}{\Gamma(V_S)} \geq \rho$.

The function $\Gamma()$ counts the total occurrences of trace variants recorded in a trace variant counter. For example, given $\rho = 0.8$ and $V_S = \{\langle a_1, a_2, a_3, \perp\rangle^5, \langle a_1, a_5, \perp\rangle^4, \langle a_1, a_4, \perp\rangle^1\}$, $V_S^\rho = \Phi(\rho, V_S) = \{\langle a_1, a_2, a_3, \perp\rangle^5, \langle a_1, a_5, \perp\rangle^4\}$, sampling the top two most frequent trace variant of V_S. In this case, $\frac{\Gamma(V_S^\rho)}{\Gamma(V_S)} = \frac{9}{10} > 0.8$.

3.2 Process Discovery and Conformance Checking

Using a trace variant counter as input, process discovery algorithms abstract the order of activity execution, generating a summarized representation to construct a process model.

Definition 8 (Process model discovery). A process discovery algorithm $\Omega : V_S \mapsto M$ is a function that constructs a process model M from a trace variant counter V_S.

Process models come in various forms (e.g., Petri nets, process trees, and BPMN). Still, they exhibit similar behaviors in executing and generating a set of traces based on the represented processes. For a given process model M, its behavior B_M refers to the set of traces that can be generated through its execution.

To evaluate a model, the typical practice involves checking its conformance with a given trace variant counter, examining the model's behavior against the counter to measure its appropriateness.

Definition 9 (Conformance checking). Given a process model M and a trace variant counter V_S, a conformance-checking algorithm $\Psi(M, V_S)$ measures the appropriateness of M for V_S, denoted as $\alpha = \{\alpha^f, \alpha^p\}$. α^f represents fitness, quantifying how much of V_S can be reproduced in M, while α^p represents precision, quantifying the proportion of B_M can be observed in V_S.

Alignment [18] and Token Replay [19] are two widely used conformance-checking algorithms. The former identifies inconsistencies by comparing traces and executable paths of the model. Although intuitive and accurate, it exhibits high computational complexity for large-scale models and traces. Conversely, the latter employs tokens in a Petri net to simulate the execution of traces, identifying errors or rule violations during the replay of traces in the model. It achieves approximate alignment results with higher computational efficiency but only applies to process models that can be converted into standard Petri nets.

Table 1. Example of concept drift detected between t_{10} and t_{11} in Σ of Fig. 1

Timestamp	V_S	V_S^ρ with $\rho = 0.8$	$\Delta(V_S^\rho)$
t_9	$\{\langle a_1, a_2, a_3, \bot\rangle^2, \langle a_1, a_5, \bot\rangle^2, \langle a_1, a_4, \bot\rangle^1\}$	$\{\langle a_1, a_2, a_3, \bot\rangle^3, \langle a_1, a_5, \bot\rangle^2\}$	$\{\langle a_1, a_2, a_3, \bot\rangle, \langle a_1, a_5, \bot\rangle\}$
t_{10}	$\{\langle a_1, a_2, a_3, \bot\rangle^2, \langle a_1, a_5, \bot\rangle^3\}$	$\{\langle a_1, a_2, a_3, \bot\rangle^2, \langle a_1, a_5, \bot\rangle^3\}$	$\{\langle a_1, a_2, a_3, \bot\rangle, \langle a_1, a_5, \bot\rangle\}$
t_{11}	$\{\langle a_1, a_2, a_3, \bot\rangle^1, \langle a_1, a_5, \bot\rangle^4\}$	$\{\langle a_1, a_5, \bot\rangle^4\}$	$\{\langle a_1, a_5, \bot\rangle\}$

3.3 Streaming Process Discovery

When conducting process discovery tasks on a trace stream, the expectation is that the process model discovered based on existing historical traces exhibits high conformance with upcoming traces, thereby providing insights for downstream tasks such as process monitoring, prediction, and enhancement. However, in the presence of concept drifts, the existing model may fail to effectively depict the ongoing business process. In such cases, it becomes necessary to dynamically restart the process discovery for model updates.

We introduce function $\Delta(V_S)$ to identify distinct trace variants recorded in a trace variant counter V_S, e.g., $\Delta(\{\langle a_1, a_2, a_3, \bot\rangle^5, \langle a_1, a_5, \bot\rangle^4\}) = \{\langle a_1, a_2, a_3, \bot\rangle, \langle a_1, a_5, \bot\rangle\}$. When the high-frequency trace variants $\Delta(V_S^\rho)$ differ between two memory windows, we consider that there is a significant change in the trace distribution between these two memory windows, that is, a concept drift occurs.

Definition 10 (Concept drift). Considering two trace sets S_i^w and S_j^w recorded by a memory window in a trace stream Σ at timestamps t_i and t_j, if $\Delta(V_{S_i^w}^\rho) \neq \Delta(V_{S_j^w}^\rho)$, a concept drift is detected in Σ between t_i and t_j.

According to the definition, a concept drift is detected when a particular trace variant in the trace stream experiences a substantial increase or decrease in frequency. Table 1 illustrates a scenario of a concept drift detected between t_{10} and t_{11} in the trace stream Σ of Fig. 1, considering a memory size $w = 5$. This drift is attributed to the emergence of a newly frequent trace variant $\langle a_1, a_5, \bot\rangle$.

4 Methodology

This section introduces RLSPD, as illustrated in Fig. 2, with four modules: Process Discovery, Conformance Checking, RL-based Parameter Selector, and Concept Drift Detection. Detailed descriptions of each module are provided below.

4.1 Process Discovery

In the initialization phase, we observe the trace stream Σ to obtain the initial set $S_0 = \{\sigma_1, \sigma_2, ..., \sigma_w\}$ consisting of the first w traces. We then extract the most representative trace variants $V_{S_0}^\rho = \Phi(\rho, V_{S_0})$ by frequency-based sampling. In this way, the online process model is initialized to $M = \Omega(V_{S_0}^\rho)$.

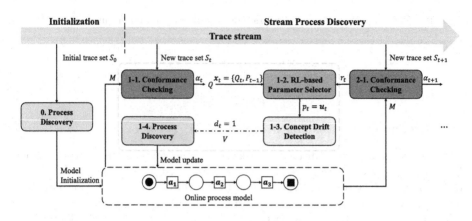

Fig. 2. The framework of RLSPD

After completing the initialization step, we continuously monitor the trace stream. Once a concept drift is detected, we re-run the process discovery algorithm and update the online process model $M = \Omega(V)$ according to the latest representative trace variants V provided by the concept drift detection module. Otherwise, the model M remains unchanged.

4.2   Conformance Checking

After initialization, we evaluate the online process model by checking its conformance with upcoming traces. Considering computational efficiency, we choose Token Replay [19] as the conformance-checking algorithm Ψ. To maintain evaluation stability, we calculate the appropriateness with the upcoming trace set rather than a single trace, avoiding drastic fluctuations cause by noise traces.

Let o be the observation window size. At each time step t, we observe the trace stream Σ and record the next o arriving traces, obtaining the set $S_t = \{\sigma_{i+1}, \sigma_{i+2}, ..., \sigma_{i+o}\}$, where i represents the count of traces already seen in the trace stream. Then, we transform S_t to a trace variant counter V_{S_t}, perform a conformance-checking algorithm $\Psi(M, V_{S_t})$ to calculate the appropriateness $\alpha_t = \{\alpha_t^f, \alpha_t^p\}$ and insert it into the historical queue Q.

4.3   RL-Based Parameter Selector

We aim to use the appropriateness queue Q as a feature to capture the fluctuations in the trace stream, dynamically providing parameters p_t to extract the currently most representative trace variants for streaming process discovery. This can be considered as an agent in reinforcement learning making real-time adaptive adjustments to the dynamic environment.

In reinforcement learning, an agent learns how to make optimal decisions in interacting with the environment. At each time step $t \in [1, T]$, the agent takes an action $\mathbf{u}_t$ according to its current policy $\pi(\mathbf{u}_t | \mathbf{x}_t)$ and state $\mathbf{x}_t$ of the environment. The environment interacts with this action, gives a feedback reward $r_t = \mathcal{R}(\mathbf{x}_t, \mathbf{u}_t)$, and proceeds to the next state. According to this new state, the agent moves into the next time step and decides a new action. The goal of reinforcement learning is to train an agent with policy π to maximize the expected sum of rewards.

For streaming process discovery, the key is to find the optimal parameters to select the most representative trace variants in the trace stream, thus properly characterizing the trace distribution and detecting concept drift. The trace stream and the online model can be viewed as the environment in reinforcement learning, and parameter adjusting can be viewed as the action. Then, parameter optimization can be considered as training an adjusting agent to learn a policy for finding the optimal action. In streaming process discovery, we evaluate the appropriateness of the online process model with the upcoming traces in the trace stream, which shows how the trace stream fluctuates and hence offers rich information for adjusting the parameters. Having observed this, we apply the appropriateness queue Q at time step t (denoted as Q_t) to construct the state $\mathbf{x}_t$, denoted as

$$\mathbf{x}_t = \{Q_t, P_{t-1}\}, \tag{1}$$

where $Q_t = \langle \alpha_{t-h+1}, \alpha_{t-h+2}, ..., \alpha_t \rangle$ and $P_{t-1} = \langle p_{t-h}, p_{t-h+1}, ..., p_{t-1} \rangle$ are queues consisting of appropriateness and parameters of the history window with length h, respectively. Note that one time step of reinforcement learning corresponds to o new arrival traces observed in trace stream Σ.

Given the state $\mathbf{x}_t$, the agent will take an action, that is, choose a parameter vector $\mathbf{u}_t \in \mathbb{R}^{N_u}$, where N_u is the number of parameters to be adjusted. This is a user-defined variable that varies with different streaming process discovery methods. We choose two key parameters, including memory size w_t and sampling rate ρ_t. Thus, the action is defined as

$$\mathbf{u}_t = \{w_t, \rho_t\}. \tag{2}$$

The memory size determines how many recent traces in the trace stream should be considered, while the sampling rate determines how frequently a trace variant should appear to be considered representative. After taking the action, the parameters are updated with $\mathbf{u}_t$, formulated as $p_t = \{w_t, \rho_t\}$.

Based on the updated parameters p_t, we detect whether a concept drift has occurred, indicated by a binary variable d_t. If $d_t = 1$, we perform process discovery and update the online process model. Then, we continue to observe the trace stream and perform conformance checking on the model and the set of traces within the next observation window, calculating the appropriateness α_{t+1}. After that, the reward function $\mathcal{R}(\mathbf{x}_t, \mathbf{u}_t)$ is defined as

$$\mathcal{R}(\mathbf{x}_t, \mathbf{u}_t) = \alpha_{t+1} - \beta \cdot d_t - \gamma \cdot w_t, \tag{3}$$

where β and γ denote penalty coefficients. The purpose of doing this is to maintain high appropriateness while reducing the occurrence of concept drift to save computational resources and decrease time consumption, and reducing the memory window size to minimize memory consumption. Finally, the environment proceeds to the next time step and updates the state to $\mathbf{x}_{t+1} = \{Q_{t+1}, P_t\}$.

We train the agent with the Twin Delayed Deep Deterministic policy gradient algorithm (TD3) [20]. Each episode corresponds to a trace stream transformed from a historical event log. Both the actor and critic networks adopt Gate Recurrent Unit (GRU) [21] to capture time-series features of the state.

During the online execution phase of streaming process discovery, the trained actor network is used for inference. At each time step t, it takes an environmental state $\mathbf{x}_t$ as input and outputs the considered optimal parameter $p_t = \mathbf{u}_t$.

4.4   Concept Drift Detection

As defined in **Definition** 10, we believe that a concept drift has occurred when the representative trace variants change in the trace stream.

At each time step t, after calculating the appropriateness α_t of the online process model with the newly arrived trace set $S = \{\sigma_{i+1}, \sigma_{i+2}, ..., \sigma_{i+o}\}$, the RL agent gives parameter $p_t = \{w_t, \rho_t\}$. Then, the trace set to be considered in the memory window w_t can be extracted as $S_{i+o}^{w_t} = \{\sigma_{i+o-w_t+1}, \sigma_{i+o-w_t+2}, ..., \sigma_{i+o}\}$, and the current representative trace variant counter is $V_{S_{i+o}^{w_t}}^{\rho_t} = \Phi(\rho_t, V_{S_{i+o}^{w_t}})$. Similarly, the trace set in the previous memory window w_{t-1} is $S_i^{w_{t-1}} = \{\sigma_{i-w_{t-1}+1}, \sigma_{i-w_{t-1}+2}, ..., \sigma_i\}$ and the previous representative trace variant counter is $V_{S_i^{w_{t-1}}}^{\rho_{t-1}} = \Phi(\rho_{t-1}, V_{S_i^{w_{t-1}}})$. If these two are not the same, we believe that the trace distribution has changed significantly, indicating a concept drift has occurred. We use a binary variable d_t to denote whether a concept drift is detected at time step t, formulated as

$$
d_t = \begin{cases} 1, \Delta\left(V_{S_i^{w_{t-1}}}^{\rho_{t-1}}\right) \neq \Delta\left(V_{S_{i+o}^{w_t}}^{\rho_t}\right) \\ 0, \Delta\left(V_{S_i^{w_{t-1}}}^{\rho_{t-1}}\right) = \Delta\left(V_{S_{i+o}^{w_t}}^{\rho_t}\right) \end{cases} \tag{4}
$$

If a concept drift occurs(i.e., $d_t = 1$), the process discovery module is triggered, updating the online process model; otherwise (i.e., $d_t = 0$), the model remains unchanged. After that, we go to the next time step $t + 1$ and continue monitoring the trace stream.

5   Experiment

The proposed RLSPD is implemented in Python, and the source code is available in the GitHub repository[2]. We evaluate the effectiveness of RLSPD on several benchmark event logs.

---

[2] https://github.com/WHU-Process-Mining/RLSPD.

Table 2. Statistics of event logs: number of activities, events, traces and trace variants

Event log	#Activities	#Events	#Traces	#Variants
BPIC2013Incidents(BPIC13I)	4	65533	7554	1511
BPIC2020DomesticDeclarations(BPIC20DD)	17	56437	10500	99
BPIC2020InternationalDeclarations(BPIC20ID)	34	72151	6449	753
BPIC2020PermitLog(BPIC20PL)	51	86581	7065	1478
BPIC2020PrepaidTravelCost(BPIC20PC)	29	18246	2099	202
BPIC2020RequestForPayment(BPIC20RP)	19	36796	6886	89

5.1 Experimental Setting

Datasets. We generate trace streams from six real-life event logs available in 4TU. ResearchData[3] for experiments. These logs record the execution of business processes related to travel reimbursement and traffic management. Table 2 provides the characteristics of these logs.

Hyperparameters. For each trace stream, an initial model is constructed using the first 200 traces (i.e., $w_0 = 200$). According to [17], the initial sampling rate ρ_0 is set to 0.8. Subsequently, continuously observing the trace stream to obtain the next trace, conformance checks are performed between the model and the next ten traces ($o = 10$). Then, parameters are given based on ten historical evaluations ($h = 10$) by the reinforcement learning agent, and the online process model is updated through process discovery if a concept drift is detected. The process discovery algorithms we employed are Inductive Miner (IND) [2] and ILP Miner (ILP) [3], both conveniently imported from PM4PY[4]. The hyperparameters w_0, o, h are chosen based on experience and preliminary experimental results as better values.

Comparison Methods. To validate the effectiveness of RLSPD, we compare it with STARDUST [17], the state-of-the-art method that employs fixed parameters for concept drift detection and process discovery. Additionally, we use the STATIC process discovery as a baseline, which keeps the process model discovered in the initialization step without updates upon detecting concept drifts.

Evaluation Metrics. To evaluate the performance of different methods, we use the average F-measure of fitness and precision, denoted as

$$F = \frac{1}{T} \sum_{t=1}^{T} F_t = \frac{1}{T} \sum_{t=1}^{T} \frac{2\alpha_t^f \alpha_t^p}{\alpha_t^f + \alpha_t^p}, \tag{5}$$

where F_t is the F1-score of α_t^f and α_t^p, and it is calculated together with appropriateness in the online process discovery phase. In addition, we record the number of model updates (i.e., detected concept drifts) and the computation time

---

[3] https://data.4tu.nl/.
[4] https://github.com/pm4py/pm4py-core.

Table 3. Overall performance

Trace stream	Method	F-measure		Update count		Time(s)	
		IND	ILP	IND	ILP	IND	ILP
BPIC13I	STATIC	0.73	0.65	0	0	**10**	9
	STARDUST	0.68	0.62	329	329	14	12
	RLSPD	**0.75**	**0.67**	67	345	**10**	11
BPIC20DD	STATIC	0.72	0.72	0	0	**2**	**2**
	STARDUST	0.93	0.89	8	8	**2**	**2**
	RLSPD	**0.95**	**0.95**	65	141	**2**	5
BPIC20ID	STATIC	0.46	0.61	0	0	10	8
	STARDUST	0.50	0.63	487	487	25	140
	RLSPD	**0.90**	**0.90**	35	45	**6**	**8**
BPIC20PL	STATIC	0.30	0.59	0	0	25	15
	STARDUST	0.16	0.32	630	630	442	1895
	RLSPD	**0.83**	**0.84**	50	55	**10**	**12**
BPIC20PC	STATIC	0.48	0.50	0	0	2	**2**
	STARDUST	0.57	0.77	134	134	3	14
	RLSPD	**0.88**	**0.88**	12	15	**1**	**2**
BPIC20RP	STATIC	0.69	0.69	0	0	**1**	**1**
	STARDUST	0.92	0.89	12	12	**1**	2
	RLSPD	**0.94**	**0.94**	6	4	**1**	2

spent in seconds when processing the entire trace stream. The computation time reflects the duration of a full episode during the testing phase of reinforcement learning. This encompasses model initialization and the online phase (including conformance checking, adaptive parameter adjustment by the trained RL agent, concept drift detection, and potential restart of process discovery). The computation time is collected through experiments conducted on a workstation with Intel(R) Core(TM) i7-12700 CPU, NVIDIA GeForce GTX 1080 Ti GPU and 125 GB RAM Memory, operating on Ubuntu 20.04.4 LTS.

5.2 Results and Discussions

Overall Performance Evaluation. To evaluate RLSPD's overall performance, we train the RL agent and conduct testing on the same dataset. We investigate the impact of updating process models when concept drifts are detected through a comparison with STATIC. Additionally, we explore the effectiveness of leveraging reinforcement learning for dynamically adjusting parameters in streaming process discovery by comparing RLSPD with STARDUST. Table 3 reports the average F-measure, as well as the update counts and computational time for the online process model handling the entire trace stream.

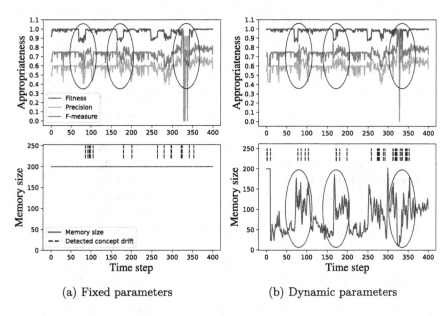

(a) Fixed parameters   (b) Dynamic parameters

Fig. 3. The model's appropriateness using fixed and dynamic parameters on BPIC13I

The results highlight a substantial performance boost of RLSPD compared to the baselines. Continuous updates to the online process model, as evidenced by the F-measure, prove to be more effective in adapting to the trace stream and aligning with upcoming traces than maintaining the initial model unchanged. Notably, on BPIC13I and BPIC20PL, STARDUST's fixed parameter strategy results in delayed or erroneous model updates due to numerous trace variants, leading to adverse effects. Regarding computation time, STATIC generally requires less time due to its non-updating nature. However, in cases involving a complex initial model followed by subsequent process simplification, STATIC consumes more time due to conformance checking. In general, RLSPD excels in capturing trace distribution fluctuations through dynamic parameter adjustments, which not only enhances conformance with upcoming traces but also reduces unnecessary model updates and time consumption.

Dynamic Parameter Analysis. To further explore the effectiveness of dynamic parameters, we analyze the adjustment of the memory window in RLSPD while processing the trace stream BPIC13I as an illustrative example. We record the appropriateness of the online model at each time step (as shown in Fig. 3(b)) and compare it with the fixed parameter strategy ($w_0 = 200$) depicted in Fig. 3(a).

The observations indicate that RLSPD tends to use smaller memory windows, enabling it to promptly adapt to the numerous trace variants and significant fluctuations in BPIC13I. Around time steps 100 and 200, a slight decline in the appropriateness is noticeable. RLSPD swiftly detects and mitigates this

Table 4. Zero-shot performance

Trace stream	Method	Memory size	Sampling rate	F-measure		Update count	
				IND	ILP	IND	ILP
BPIC13I	STARDUST	800	0.8	0.68	0.62	329	329
	Grid Search	10	0.1	**0.75**	**0.67**	341	341
	RLSPD-Z	200	0.8	**0.75**	**0.67**	107	226
BPIC20DD	STARDUST	1000	0.8	0.93	0.89	8	8
	Grid Search	200	0.2	**0.95**	**0.95**	5	5
	RLSPD-Z	200	0.8	**0.95**	**0.95**	12	15
BPIC20ID	STARDUST	600	0.8	0.50	0.63	487	487
	Grid Search	50	0.1	**0.89**	0.89	66	66
	RLSPD-Z	200	0.8	**0.89**	**0.90**	28	47
BPIC20PL	STARDUST	700	0.8	0.16	0.32	630	630
	Grid Search	50	0.1	**0.83**	**0.84**	105	105
	RLSPD-Z	200	0.8	0.82	**0.84**	79	15
BPIC20PC	STARDUST	200	0.8	0.57	0.77	134	134
	Grid Search	700	0.1	**0.89**	**0.89**	0	0
	RLSPD-Z	200	0.8	0.88	0.88	15	17
BPIC20RP	STARDUST	700	0.8	0.92	0.89	12	12
	Grid Search	200	0.2	**0.94**	**0.94**	3	3
	RLSPD-Z	200	0.8	**0.94**	**0.94**	6	4

change by increasing the memory window, thereby reducing noise interference and preventing erroneous model updates. Around time step 300, a sharp appropriateness decline prompts RLSPD to infer a sudden concept drift, reducing the memory window for rapid adaptation and timely model updates. This suggests that RLSPD adeptly captures trace stream fluctuations through evaluation metrics, effectively enhancing the model's conformance with future traces.

Zero-shot Performance Assessment. To assess RLSPD's zero-shot capability with entirely new trace streams, we conduct transfer reinforcement learning on RLSPD-Z. The RL agent is trained on five trace streams and tested on the remaining new ones. In contrast, STARDUST employs a fixed strategy when handling different trace streams, setting the memory window to 10% of the trace stream size and the sampling rate to 0.8. In addition, we perform a grid search on STARDUST's parameters, varying them in the grid $w_0 = \{10, 50, 100, 200, 300, 400, 500, 600, 700, 800, 900, 1000\}$ and $\rho_0 = \{0.1, 0.2, 0.3, 0.4, 0.5, 0.6, 0.7, 0.8, 0.9, 1.0\}$ to find the best fixed parameters (labeled as Grid Search). Table 4 presents the initial parameters for different methods, along with the process model's average F-measure and update counts.

The results indicate that RLSPD-Z achieves comparable performance to Grid Search regarding the F-measure and effectively reduces the number of model updates. The optimal parameters identified through Grid Search suggest varying memory window requirements for different trace streams, with sampling rates favoring lower values such as 0.1 or 0.2. This implies diverse fluctuation patterns among trace streams, where a small number of high-frequency trace variants can represent the overall trace distribution. In practical and various business scenarios, STARDUST exhibits poor performance with a fixed parameter strategy. Additionally, Grid Search requires partial data collection before searching and becomes time-consuming as the search space expands. In contrast, RLSPD, based on reinforcement learning with offline pre-training, demonstrates the ability to achieve satisfactory zero-shot results on entirely new trace streams.

6   Conclusion

In this paper, we propose RLSPD, a streaming process discovery approach for dynamically adapting to evolving business processes. It leverages feedback from conformance checking by reinforcement learning and updates the online process model upon detecting concept drifts. Experimental results demonstrate that RLSPD, through dynamic parameter adjustments, effectively improves model conformance with upcoming traces and reduces unnecessary model updates.

Currently, our approach relies on event stream data partitioning into complete traces, which is only suitable for business processes with declared completion activities. We plan to introduce predictive process monitoring to predict completion marks for ongoing cases. Additionally, our method only detects whether concept drifts occur, lacking an analysis of drift characteristics and root causes. Future work involves integrating relevant concept drift analysis methods. Furthermore, our future research will explore how activity sequence information in traces can be exploited in reinforcement learning, providing a more comprehensive understanding of trace stream dynamics.

Acknowledgments. This work is supported by the National Key Research and Development Program of China (No. 2022YFF0902701) and the National Natural Science Foundation of China (No. 62032016).

References

1. Van Der Aalst, W.: Process mining: overview and opportunities. ACM Trans. Manag. Inf. Syst. **3**(2), 1–17 (2012)
2. Leemans, S.J., Fahland, D., Van Der Aalst, W.M.: Discovering block-structured process models from event logs-a constructive approach. In: Colom, J.M., Desel, J. (eds.) Application and Theory of Petri Nets and Concurrency. Lecture Notes in Computer Science, vol. 7927, pp. 311–329. Springer, Berlin (2013). https://doi.org/10.1007/978-3-642-38697-8_17
3. van Zelst, S.J., van Dongen, B.F., van der Aalst, W.M., Verbeek, H.: Discovering workflow nets using integer linear programming. Computing **100**, 529–556 (2018)
4. Augusto, A., Conforti, R., Dumas, M., La Rosa, M., Polyvyanyy, A.: Split miner: automated discovery of accurate and simple business process models from event logs. Knowl. Inf. Syst. **59**, 251–284 (2019)
5. Sato, D.M.V., De Freitas, S.C., Barddal, J.P., Scalabrin, E.E.: A survey on concept drift in process mining. ACM Comput. Surv. **54**(9), 1–38 (2021)

6. Burattin, A.: Streaming process mining. In: Process Mining Handbook, vol. 349 (2022)
7. Bose, R.J.C., van der Aalst, W.M., Žliobaitė, I., Pechenizkiy, M.: Handling concept drift in process mining. In: Mouratidis, H., Rolland, C. (eds.) Advanced Information Systems Engineering. Lecture Notes in Computer Science, vol. 6741, pp. 391–405. Springer, Berlin (2011). https://doi.org/10.1007/978-3-642-21640-4_30
8. Maaradji, A., Dumas, M., La Rosa, M., Ostovar, A.: Detecting sudden and gradual drifts in business processes from execution traces. IEEE Trans. Knowl. Data Eng. **29**(10), 2140–2154 (2017)
9. Adams, J.N., van Zelst, S.J., Rose, T., van der Aalst, W.M.: Explainable concept drift in process mining. Inf. Syst. **114**, 102177 (2023)
10. Barbon Junior, S., Tavares, G.M., da Costa, V.G.T., Ceravolo, P., Damiani, E.: A framework for human-in-the-loop monitoring of concept-drift detection in event log stream. In: Companion Proceedings of the the Web Conference 2018, pp. 319–326 (2018)
11. de Sousa, R.G., Peres, S.M., Fantinato, M., Reijers, H.A.: Concept drift detection and localization in process mining: an integrated and efficient approach enabled by trace clustering. In: Proceedings of the 36th Annual ACM Symposium on Applied Computing, pp. 364–373 (2021)
12. Zellner, L., Richter, F., Sontheim, J., Maldonado, A., Seidl, T.: Concept drift detection on streaming data with dynamic outlier aggregation. In: Leemans, S., Leopold, H. (eds.) Process Mining Workshops. Lecture Notes in Business Information Processing, vol. 406, pp. 206–217. Springer, Cham (2021). https://doi.org/10.1007/978-3-030-72693-5_16
13. van Zelst, S.J., van Dongen, B.F., van der Aalst, W.M.: Event stream-based process discovery using abstract representations. Knowl. Inf. Syst. **54**, 407–435 (2018)
14. Batyuk, A., Voityshyn, V.: Streaming process discovery for lambda architecture-based process monitoring platform. In: 2018 IEEE 13th International Scientific and Technical Conference on Computer Sciences and Information Technologies, vol. 1, pp. 298–301. IEEE (2018)
15. Leno, V., Armas-Cervantes, A., Dumas, M., La Rosa, M., Maggi, F.M.: Discovering process maps from event streams. In: Proceedings of the 2018 International Conference on Software and System Process, pp. 86–95 (2018)
16. Batyuk, A., Voityshyn, V.: Streaming process discovery method for semi-structured business processes. In: 2020 IEEE Third International Conference on Data Stream Mining & Processing, pp. 444–448. IEEE (2020)
17. Pasquadibisceglie, V., Appice, A., Castellano, G., Fiorentino, N., Malerba, D.: Stardust: a novel process mining approach to discover evolving models from trace streams. IEEE Trans. Serv. Comput. **16**(4), 2970–2984 (2023)
18. Adriansyah, A., Munoz-Gama, J., Carmona, J., van Dongen, B.F., van der Aalst, W.M.: Alignment based precision checking. In: La Rosa, M., Soffer, P. (eds.) Business Process Management Workshops. Lecture Notes in Business Information Processing, vol. 132, pp. 137–149. Springer, Berlin (2013). https://doi.org/10.1007/978-3-642-36285-9_15
19. Berti, A., van der Aalst, W.M.: Reviving token-based replay: increasing speed while improving diagnostics. ATAED@ Petri Nets/ACSD **2371**, 87–103 (2019)
20. Fujimoto, S., Hoof, H., Meger, D.: Addressing function approximation error in actor-critic methods. In: International Conference on Machine Learning, pp. 1587–1596. PMLR (2018)
21. Chung, J., Gulcehre, C., Cho, K., Bengio, Y.: Empirical evaluation of gated recurrent neural networks on sequence modeling. arXiv preprint: arXiv:1412.3555 (2014)

Enhancing Predictive Process Monitoring with Time-Related Feature Engineering

Rafael Seidi Oyamada[1]([⊠]), Gabriel Marques Tavares[2,3],
Sylvio Barbon Junior[4], and Paolo Ceravolo[1]

[1] Università degli Studi di Milano, Milan, Italy
{rafael.oyamada,paolo.ceravolo}@unimi.it
[2] LMU Munich, Munich, Germany
tavares@dbs.ifi.lmu.de
[3] Munich Center for Machine Learning (MCML), Munich, Germany
[4] Università degli Studi di Trieste, Trieste, Italy
sylvio.barbonjunior@units.it

Abstract. Predictive process monitoring plays a critical role in process mining by predicting the dynamics of ongoing processes. Recent trends employ deep learning techniques that use event sequences to make highly accurate predictions. However, this focus often overshadows the significant advantages of lightweight, transparent algorithms. This study explores the potential of traditional regression algorithms, namely kNN, SVM, and RF, enhanced by event time feature engineering. We integrate existing and novel time-related features to augment these algorithms and compare their performance against the well-known LSTM network. Our results show that these enhanced lightweight models not only compete with LSTM in terms of predictive accuracy but also excel in scenarios requiring online, real-time decision-making and explanation. Furthermore, despite incorporating additional feature extraction processes, these algorithms maintain superior computational efficiency compared to their deep learning counterparts, making them more viable for time-critical and resource-constrained environments.

Keywords: Process Mining · Predictive Monitoring · Event feature engineering · Explainable artificial intelligence

1 Introduction

Predictive Process Monitoring (PPM) is a key element within Process Mining (PM), as it enables the prediction of upcoming behaviors or outcomes of ongoing process executions. Current state-of-the-art approaches mainly rely on deep learning methods to exploit the sequential knowledge encoded in event sequences [24]. However, there is a growing need to explore the potential benefits offered by traditional machine learning algorithms due to their lightweight and more transparent nature [7]. These lightweight models ensure transparency and

G. Guizzardi et al. (Eds.): CAiSE 2024, LNCS 14663, pp. 71–86, 2024.
https://doi.org/10.1007/978-3-031-61057-8_5

computational efficiency, which is particularly important in resource-constrained environments or online applications.

In this paper, we explore the potential of these algorithms combined with engineered time features to enhance PPM. The motivation for this study stems from the observation that deep learning-based approaches such as Long Short-Term Memory (LSTM), while known for their high predictive performance [4,24], often (i) operate as black boxes, (ii) are computationally expensive, and (iii) are difficult to tune. This opacity challenges stakeholders and practitioners in extracting meaningful insights or efficiently integrating results into online decision processes. For example, continuous model retraining to avoid the concept drift problem is a common practice in PM [5], which reinforces the need for efficient and lightweight algorithms. Furthermore, the Explainable Artificial Intelligence (XAI) community has recently introduced the problem that explanations provided by different tools are less reliable when the trained algorithms have a higher level of complexity [10,11], which is the case of deep neural networks. This is of concern because explaining the behavior of algorithms is crucial to understanding underlying process characteristics [13] and to improving decision-making [18].

We conduct this study by comparing the performance of traditional shallow regression algorithms from different families, including k-Nearest Neighbours (KNN), Support Vector Machines (SVM), and Random Forests (RF), with the LSTM. In addition, this research introduces novel event features, developed from well-known time-related features from the PM literature, to improve the performance of traditional algorithms in a computationally efficient manner and provide deeper insights into process behavior. By incorporating event features explicitly tailored to process data, we aim to incrementally improve the predictive capabilities of shallow learning algorithms, thereby leveraging their computational efficiency and being able to extract more reliable insights using XAI tools. Specifically, we focus our experimental setup on the task of residual time prediction [24] and demonstrate how the complete pipeline of extraction and development of time-related features improves the final predictive performance while consuming significantly less computational resources than neural networks.

Our findings provide essential insights for practitioners and researchers seeking a balance between predictive accuracy, interpretability, and computational efficiency in their modeling efforts. We present a comprehensive profile for each algorithm, providing valuable tools for the deliberate selection of the most appropriate algorithm based on specific needs. In this sense, our study contributes to the state of the art by (i) introducing innovative time-related event features designed to enhance the capabilities of predictive algorithms, and (ii) presenting a method for profiling algorithms based on their response to an enriched feature space. This method allows for a systematic evaluation of the impact of the developed features on prediction accuracy and interpretability, exploring it at both event log and case level.

The following sections outline the organization of this work. Section 2 provides the necessary background and definitions for this work. Section 3 describes the context in which this research is being developed and the problem that is being addressed. We then present our methodology in Sect. 4 and discuss our results in Sect. 5. Section 6 presents related work, and we leave the final remarks in Sect. 7.

2 Background

PM stands as a research domain focused on the analysis of process execution data [1]. PM encompasses a suite of tools designed for extracting insights from historical data originating from information systems and subsequently stored in event logs. An event log consists of a collection of cases, with each case characterized by a sequential arrangement of events, also known as a trace. This trace captures the sequential execution of system activities, defined by a specific set of features. Primarily, these features encompass the activity label and the associated execution timestamp. However, alternative features could include resource requirements for the activity or the associated execution cost. Precisely, we define an event and its features as follows.

Definition 1 (Event, Feature). *Let $\mathcal{FN}$ denote the set of feature names. For any event $e \in \Sigma$ and an attribute $f \in \mathcal{FN}$, $\#_f(e)$ represents the value of feature f for event e. The values are typically confined to a specific domain. For instance, $\#_{activity} \in A$, where A encompasses the range of legitimate activities within a business process, e.g., $\{a, b, c, d, e\}$.*

An event can also be denoted by its position in the sequence, such as e_i, with e_n signifying the final event in the sequence. A sequence of events forms a *trace* $t \in \Sigma^*$, defined as follows.

Definition 2 (Trace, Prefix). *Within a trace, each event occurs only once, and the chronological order of events is maintained. In mathematical terms, for $1 \leq i < j \leq |t| : t(i) \leq t(j)$. A trace can also be represented as a function that generates the corresponding event for each position in the sequence: $t(i \to n) \mapsto \langle e_i, ..., e_n \rangle$. As such, a prefix represents a subtrace $t(i \to j)$ where $0 < i \leq j < n$.*

A trace combined with a unique identifier forms a case, and a collection of cases constitutes an event log.

Definition 3 (Case, Event Log). *A case $c_i \in C$ is denoted as a sequence of unique events, e.g., $\langle \#_{case}(e1), \#_{case}(e2), \#_{case}(e3) \rangle$. An event log L is a set of cases $\mathbf{L} \subseteq \Sigma^*$ where each event appears only once in the log. In other words, for any two distinct cases, their event intersection is empty.*

PPM encompasses a set of tasks within process monitoring that aims to predict future behaviors. This includes tasks like next activity prediction, which involves suffix prediction or simulation of remaining traces [4,17], outcome prediction [23], and remaining time prediction [24]. In this study, we focus on the latter task to showcase our contributions. In this context, we follow the definitions presented in [23] and establish a learning pipeline composed of two stages: trace encoding and learning phases.

Definition 4 (Trace Encoder). *A trace encoder is a function that maps a (sub)sequence of events to a d-dimensional feature vector:* $f : t(i \rightarrow n) \rightarrow X^d$.

The order of events corresponds to the control-flow within an event log. However, the encoded data can be enhanced by incorporating additional event features associated with the data flow, including timestamps, resources, and cost. Each event is encoded individually first and then aggregated in the end to compose a single numerical feature vector [23]. After completing the encoding stage, a regressor can predict the remaining time for a (partial) trace.

Definition 5 (Regressor). *A regressor maps an encoded trace to its numerical target:* $reg : X_n^d \rightarrow \mathcal{Y}$.

The remaining time is defined as the time difference between the current event timestamp and the timestamp of the last event.

3   Problem Definition

In this section, we aim to highlight the need for dedicated research in enriching event logs with advanced feature engineering techniques tailored for PPM. Shallow models, known for their computational efficiency compared to deep learning models, prove indispensable in scenarios where resources are limited and rapid model training and deployment are crucial [7]. Besides, the power of PPM can be greatly enhanced by assimilating both pre-existing and newly created inter- and intra-case features from event logs [9,15,16,19].

PM is often characterized by dynamic environments where rapid data processing and model updates are critical. For instance, a commonly employed strategy to tackle concept drift involves retraining the model with the most recent data [5]. However, this approach becomes cumbersome when the learning phase is time-intensive. Despite the remarkable predictive capabilities demonstrated by deep neural networks in PPM [24], they are not suited for frequent model updates, due to their very time-consuming nature. As a result, shallow learning algorithms are preferred for their computational efficiency, offering a notable reduction in elapsed time, as exemplified in Sect. 5. Thus, the challenge before us is to explore how shallow algorithms can be effectively and efficiently enhanced to achieve superior predictive performance.

In addition, the challenges of explaining deep neural networks could create bottlenecks for business stakeholders, even with the use of model-agnostic explainability methods prevalent in the PPM community [6,18]. Liu et al. [11] have detailed how data characteristics and model hyperparameter settings affect empirical explainability metrics. The authors emphasize that changes in these aspects can lead to noticeable variations in the metrics, highlighting concern about the stability of explanations. Therefore, assuming the data characteristics are fixed for any learning algorithm given a PPM setup, this issue is particularly pertinent as deep learning models exhibit greater sensitivity to hyperparameters and require more computational resources for optimal configuration [7].

Krishna et al. [10] introduce a metric to measure the level of disagreement among different explainable methods when applied to the same trained model. Their findings indicate that as the model complexity increases, such as regarding neural networks, there is a higher level of disagreement among the explanations provided by traditional explainability tools. Moreover, despite some shallow learning models being composed of ensembles that could be perceived as black-box models, they generally offer greater transparency than deep learning models. This transparency is particularly valuable in domains where understanding the decision-making process of the model is as important as the accuracy of its predictions.

Therefore, considering the drawbacks addressed in this section regarding deep learning models, we aim to improve the predictive performances of shallow learning algorithms by **proposing new feature engineering techniques** tailored for PM. We show in the next sections that even adding more effort to the preprocessing phase, the end-to-end learning pipeline using shallow algorithms (i.e., preprocessing plus training) is still one order of magnitude faster than a pipeline using deep learning.

4   Engineering Time-Related Features

In this study, our primary objective is to evaluate the extent to which time-related features, derived from event logs, can improve the performance of the predictive task and the interpretability of the generated predictions. To accomplish this, we delve into a comprehensive examination of existing features documented in the literature, while also introducing novel features that we have developed.

First, we employ the three distinct features (always described in seconds) outlined by Tax et al. [22]: the *execution time*, which is the timestamp of the current event $\#_{time}(e_i)$ minus the previous one $\#_{time}(e_{i-1})$ (0 if $i = 0$, i.e. for initial activities, the execution time is zero); the time *within the day* with midnight as a reference, i.e. current timestamp minus midnight; and the elapsed time *within the week*, with respect to the midnight of Sunday. Furthermore, we extend the authors' approach by including the *accumulated time*, which is obtained by subtracting the current timestamp of an event from the first one $(\#_{time}(e_i) - \#_{time}(e_0))$; and the *weekday* as a categorical feature. In Sect. 5 we refer to these features as *TF*.

Second, it is well-known in the machine learning community that expanding the information provided by the raw data through statistical measures improves predictive performance [2]. In PM, a similar strategy has been introduced by Tavares et al. [21] to enhance the descriptive power to represent event log behavior. However, the authors focus only on control-flow aspects and ignore other attributes, such as timestamps, thus limiting the impact on predictive performance. Inspired by these works and the vast machine learning literature, we consider statistical-, distribution-, and dispersion-based features to capture the time dimension.

Therefore, after extracting the aforementioned temporal features at each trace position denoted as t_i, we proceed to extract statistical measures for each position. This extraction involves an interactive process, in which various measures are computed, such as the average execution time between $\#_{exec\_time}(e_0)$ and $\#_{exec\_time}(e_n)$, denoted as $avg_{exec\_time} = \frac{\sum_{i=0}^{n} \#_{exec\_time}(e_i)}{n}$. Other measures include variance, entropy, and kurtosis, which go beyond simple mean values. All the statistical measures are detailed in Table 1. Finally, we follow the aggregation approach outlined in [23] to aggregate the (sub)traces and their event attributes (including both activities and time-related features) to obtain the corresponding vector representations. In Sect. 5 we refer to TF features plus these engineered features as *ALL*.

Table 1. Acronym and a brief description of each statistical measure employed in this work.

Acronym	Description	Acronym	Description
min	Minimum value	*geometric_mean*	Geometric mean
max	Maximum value	*geometric_std*	Geometric Std
mean	Mean value	*harmonic_mean*	Harmonic mean
median	Median value	*skewness*	Skewness
mode	Mode	*kurtosis*	Kurtosis
std	Standard deviation	*coefficient_variation*	Coefficient of variation
variance	Variance	*entropy*	Entropy
q1	25th percentile	*hist*	Histogram (10 bins)
q3	75th percentile	*skewness_hist*	Skewness histogram
iqr	Interquartile range	*kurtosis_hist*	Kurtosis histogram

5   Experimental Analysis

This section presents the benefits of using time-based features for remaining time prediction using shallow methods, and how these features help us better understand underlying behaviors. We start by explaining how adding more features can make predictions more accurate. We also show that while shallow methods need a lot of data preparation, LSTMs still perform better even without the same preprocessing although they require more computational resources. However, shallow methods demonstrate errors within a narrow time unit (in days), and in a specific dataset, they even surpass LSTM performance. These features are also great for deeper analysis of behavior in the data, which helps with online decision-making.

5.1   Experimental Setup

We chose three shallow baseline algorithms from distinct families for their unique strengths: SVM for handling complex data with kernel functions, KNN for its quick inference by identifying nearest neighbors, and RF for its robust training and ability to highlight key features. We picked different baseline algorithms to test if our event feature engineering boosts their performance by seeing how they handle various feature sets. Research shows advanced simple algorithms can outperform basic ones [6, 24], with some like CatBoost benefiting from GPU multithreading for speed [8]. However, this study doesn't include these algorithms, focusing instead on how well feature engineering works in general, not on maxing out performance with advanced shallow algorithms.

For the shallow algorithms, we utilized Python's Scikit-learn library[1]. Hyperparameters were initially tuned using Grid Search. Since the tuning presented low variance across different settings, we reported results using the default hyperparameters from the library to ensure fairness. Regarding the deep learning algorithm, we adopted the LSTM architecture specified in Camargo et al. [3], modifying its output layer for remaining time prediction. Optimal hyperparameters were determined through Bayesian optimization, resulting in the following settings for all event logs: $batch\_size = 32$, $epochs = 50$, $learning\_rate = 0.0005$, $prefix\_len = 5$. For evaluation, we employ the root mean squared error (RMSE) metric (the lower the better), which is given by the formula $RMSE = \sqrt{\frac{1}{n} \sum_{i=1}^{n} (y_i - \hat{y}_i)^2}$, where y_i is the true value and $\hat{y}_i$ is the predicted value. The main reason for employing this metric is that it is measured in the same units as the original target (days), allowing a more realistic interpretation of predictions. To interpret and explain the effects of features, we used the feature importance derived from the RF, which identifies features that are influential for models' decisions; and the SHAP method [12], which explains the contribution of each feature to an individual prediction. Despite the recent explosion of new XAI tools proposals [10, 11], we use the aforementioned methods due to their popularity in PM [6, 18].

Our methodology involves the application of two coding methods (*one-hot* and *node2vec*, denoted *OH* and *n2v*, respectively) that present good results in the PM literature [20], along with a feature extraction process. We follow the aggregation strategy proposed in [23] to assemble each subtrace from each trace. Our approach involves an incremental investigation, starting by evaluating the performance of the encoding scheme (i.e., control flow data only) without additional features. Next, we augment the encoded data with time features extracted from the literature (*encoding+TF*), and finally we end up with the fusion of the encoded data with features from the literature and those proposed in this paper (*encoding+ALL*). This systematic approach results in six different pipelines.

The event logs employed in this work are the BPI12 and BPI20, described and benchmarked in [25]. The former is an event log of loan application processes[2] and the latter describes two years of expense claims from a university[3]. They are both collections of smaller event logs, which allow us to test seven different scenarios (4 BPI12 and 3 BPI20), as illustrated in Fig. 1 and Table 2. Due to the

---

[1] https://scikit-learn.org/.

[2] https://data.4tu.nl/articles/dataset/BPI_Challenge_2012/12689204.

[3] https://data.4tu.nl/collections/_/5065541/1.

lack of space, we included the full details of these event logs in our repository, along with all the code for this paper[4]. It is important to note that our study focused on timestamps and did not cover all event attributes like resources and costs, as not all event logs include these features.

5.2 The Impact of Time-Related Features

Figure 1 illustrates the significant progress made in improving predictive performance by incorporating time-related features, particularly concerning the RMSE metric. The inclusion of all features consistently yields the lowest error rates, despite the resulting increase in dimensionality. In the context of Random Forest (RF), this result aligns seamlessly with expectations given the inherent robustness of the algorithm, which prevents a decrease in predictive performance with the inclusion of additional features. Notably, the k-Nearest Neighbors (KNN) algorithm also shows improvements when using all features, despite its traditional susceptibility to the curse of dimensionality. In contrast, the Support Vector Machine (SVM), despite achieving competitive results in predictive monitoring as reported by Polato et al. [16], encounters challenges with high dimensionality and doesn't necessarily exhibit improvements through various preprocessing techniques, as evidenced by the *RequestForPayment* event log. The SVM algorithm's task of identifying a hyperplane for class separation becomes increasingly difficult as the dimensionality of the feature space increases. This analysis highlights that the robustness of machine learning predictions greatly benefits from carefully integrating comprehensive time-related features. In the next section, we introduce a discussion on computational complexity and the trade-off between complexity and predictive performance.

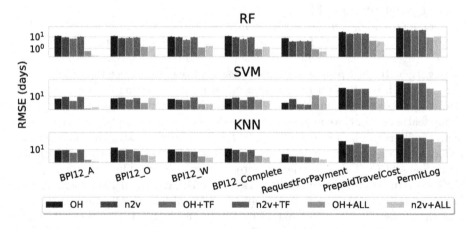

Fig. 1. Predictive performance of remaining time according to different combinations of preprocessing methods for each learning algorithm (row) and event log (column).

---

[4] https://github.com/raseidi/log-engineering.

5.3   Analysis of Elapsed Times

Putting extra effort into the preprocessing phase improves predictive performance for any algorithm. However, deep neural networks are still capable of overcoming shallow methods for remaining time prediction without any extra effort in preprocessing. The better predictive accuracy of LSTMs is depicted in Table 2. The table shows the RMSE achieved by the best pipeline of each shallow method. We can see poorer predictive performance regarding shallow methods for all cases except for the *PrepaidTravelCost* event log using RF.

Although LSTMs can achieve better performances without extra preprocessing effort, this method has a more expensive pipeline since it demands more time and computational resources for training and tuning [7]. We illustrate the elapsed time for each pipeline, including the preprocessing and training/testing phase, for all event logs in Fig. 2. It becomes evident that there exists a substantial discrepancy in the averaged elapsed times since LSTMs require approximately an order of magnitude more time compared to RF and KNN. This discrepancy highlights the inherent complexity and resource-intensive nature of neural networks. Nonetheless, the SVM takes even longer due to the fact it suffers from the high dimensionality caused by the proposed feature extraction.

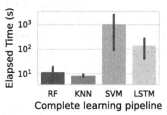

Fig. 2. Elapsed time using *n2v+ALL* pipeline against the complete LSTM pipeline.

Among the shallow algorithms, the SVM exhibits consistently poor performance across various metrics, including both elapsed time and predictive accuracy. This underscores the necessity for fine-tuning to mitigate its high RMSE, as well as additional preprocessing measures for dimensionality reduction. In this case, these steps are aimed at slightly increasing preprocessing time but significantly reducing the training duration. On the other hand, the KNN algorithm demonstrates the shortest average elapsed time and minimal variation. However, it also exhibits higher error rates in terms of RMSE (as indicated in Table 2). This behavior can be attributed to the algorithm's intrinsic susceptibility to the curse of dimensionality. While the new event features contribute to enhancing predictive performance, the KNN algorithm could benefit from a subsequent feature selection stage, particularly considering the impact of dimensionality. Lastly, the RF algorithm showcases a notably low average elapsed time despite considerable variation. Remarkably, it achieves the best predictive performance among the shallow algorithms, with errors below the single time unit (a day). Notably, it surpasses LSTM performance in a specific event log scenario and maintains competitive performance for other event logs.

Employing a statistical approach, we conduct the Nemenyi test to determine the optimal pipeline concerning the elapsed time and RMSE showcased in Fig. 3a and Fig. 3b, respectively. In terms of RMSE, the pipelines that incorporate all time-related features (*n2v+ALL* and *OH+ALL*) outperform others, regardless of the encoding method employed. A clear trade-off is observed as both pipelines are

Table 2. RMSE scores, in days, for each model and each event log.

	BPI12_A	BPI12_Complete	BPI12_O	BPI12_W	PrepaidTravelCost	RequestForPayment
KNN	2.7077	4.2951	4.85	4.1232	12.0898	3.4464
LSTM	**0.0785**	**0.4348**	**1.4561**	**1.0097**	4.7497	**0.3839**
RF	0.2817	1.5617	1.6475	1.7889	**4.4131**	0.6338
SVM	3.5933	6.6551	8.8416	4.8422	9.0235	10.3065

statistically slower, according to Fig. 3a. Therefore, improved predictive power comes at the cost of higher resource consumption but yet lower than deep neural nets. Consequently, we further consider the second statistical analysis and focus exclusively on the $n2v{+}ALL$ pipeline in the remaining paper since there is no statistical difference between $OH{+}ALL$ and $n2v{+}ALL$.

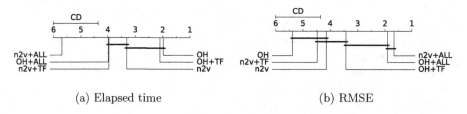

(a) Elapsed time   (b) RMSE

Fig. 3. Post-hoc Nemenyi test of both preprocessing and training model. Groups that are not significantly different (p = 0.05 and CD = 1.62) are connected.

5.4   Interpretability

In this section, we highlight an additional advantage related to transparency offered by the optimal shallow method presented in this study. The RF, in addition to low inference time and reasonable predictive performance, provides us with the ability to identify which feature has the most significant impact on the predicted value. Thus, the temporal features presented in this study not only demonstrate improvements in predictive performance but also provide transparency and interpretability through the RF. We then examine the overall impact of all the time-based features across all the event logs. We then select one specific event log to gain a deeper understanding of the scenario and conclude by reinforcing the feature explainability using the SHAP method.

In order to evaluate the impact of the presented features from a global point of view, we select the 10 features with the highest importance averages according to the RF. We show their distributions as box plots in Fig. 4. The suffix integers in the features' names represent the n-th dimension of the *node2vec* or the i-th statistical measure (see Sect. 4) extracted from the time-related feature, whereas the feature names without those suffixes refer to the time feature itself. The *n2v3* is the third feature (dimension) generated by the *node2vec* encoder and is the most important one. Although the control-flow of a (sub)trace is encoded

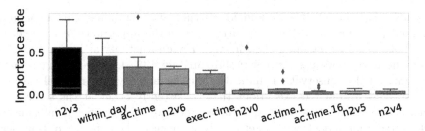

Fig. 4. Top 10 averaged feature (x-axis) importance (y-axis) for all event logs. *n2v* refers to the nth-dimension of node2vec, *ac.time* to accumulated time, and *exec.time* to execution time. The numerical suffixes for time features refer to the index of a statistical measure (described in our repository).

into a new latent space, we can implicitly save the current activity from the ongoing trace before encoding the respective data, which could further support the user in interpreting the model's decision. On the other hand, the *within_ day* is the second most impactful feature across all datasets and it regards the time within a day (in seconds as described in Sect. 4). With respect to the proposed features, we notice a lower importance rate, which leads us to conclude they have a thorough and refined participation in the final prediction since we showed in the previous section their significant improvement in predictive accuracy.

Intuitively, the *within_ day* feature is important for all datasets since it refers to commercial working time; the *BPI12* dataset describes events related to banks, and the *BPI20* describes events related to a university. We further investigate the initial intuition and assert it in Fig. 5. We select the *BPI20 Prepaid-TravelCost* to illustrate that most events are indeed executed within the time intervals 7:00 and 17:00.

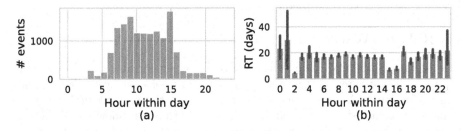

Fig. 5. Getting insights from the most important time-related feature: (a) number of events that occurred within each hour of a day; and (b) remaining time (RT) distribution for each hour of the day.

Given the importance of the *time within day* feature, we filtered out activities with noticeable error rates measured by the absolute differences between predictions and actuals by comparing average true and predicted remaining times.

Our investigation revolves around identifying, understanding, and explaining the poor performance of these activities despite the importance of the feature. Initial observations highlight the *Payment Handled* activity as having the most pronounced absolute error rates (approximately 135%) in predicting remaining time. Further observations indicate that this activity has minimal variance due to likely automated executions that consistently occur at the same daily time. Consequently, this reduced variance does not add significant information to the prediction model. Subsequent analysis suggests the influence of European summertime on event log timestamps, resulting in a temporal pattern: between October and March, timestamps are consistently recorded around 16:30, deviating from the 15:30 pattern observed in other months.

Lastly, we utilize SHAP values to quantify the impact of introduced features on individual cases. We select a trace with the lowest average prediction error and examine three distinct subtraces (prefixes) extracted from it. This chosen trace has a length of $|t| = 7$, and we denote its evaluated subtraces as $t(0 \rightarrow i)$, where $i \in 1, 4, 7$. Refer to Fig. 6a for the $i = 1$ subtrace, Fig. 6b for $i = 4$, and Fig. 6c for $i = 7$. In these figures, the base value represents the model's average predicted value across the entire event log, while $f(x)$ signifies the predicted value for the specific subtrace. A higher positive SHAP value for a particular feature indicates that this feature has a positive impact on increasing the output of the model for the given instance. In other words, it helps increase the predicted value. Conversely, a higher negative SHAP value for a feature indicates that this feature has a negative impact on the model's output for the given instance. It contributes to decreasing the predicted value. Importantly, the latent space (referred to as prefix *n2v*, encoding the control-flow), literature-based features, and newly introduced time-related features consistently contribute to predictions, regardless of the case's position (i.e., subtrace length). This detailed analysis holds critical value for decision-making. As depicted in Fig. 6, users can receive per-case insights into the features influencing predictions, facilitating informed actions based on predictions.

6 Related Works

The literature on PPM includes several research papers that examine various aspects of how different features, at event, case, or inter-case level, affect predictive performance. A recent survey [17] reveals that the best predictive performances are achieved by methods incorporating both control-flow and data-flow features. In another study, Camargo et al. [3] incorporate a resource role discovery algorithm, demonstrating its significant contribution to improving predictive performances. Senderovich et al. [19] emphasize the addition of inter-case information, leading to increased accuracy across different datasets. Furthermore, [9] proposes a novel framework that compares the performance of tree-based models trained with and without resource experience features, highlighting their value in achieving superior results. Kernel-based and time-series models have also been employed and combined [16], and these methods also improve when data-flow features are added to the training.

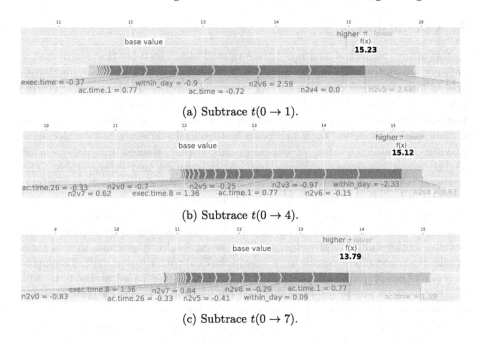

(a) Subtrace $t(0 \rightarrow 1)$.

(b) Subtrace $t(0 \rightarrow 4)$.

(c) Subtrace $t(0 \rightarrow 7)$.

Fig. 6. SHAP analysis for different subtraces.

It is also worth noting that recent advancements in the field rely on the predictive capabilities provided by deep learning methods [15, 22], which are boosted by overabundance of data and can improve their performance when data dimensionality is increased [15]. However, such models do not offer means to interpret the prediction results, which is of utmost importance in business process environments [18]. Furthermore, the combination of high computational resource consumption and the challenging fine-tuning process, which often requires expertise, is a barrier to the seamless application of these models in production environments [14]. In addition, a recent paper has highlighted scenarios where shallow algorithms can outperform or be comparable to deep algorithms [6].

While it's true that the issues addressed in our paper have been recognized in the existing literature, our work stands out by its detailed examination of the impact of temporal features on both the prediction and explanatory power of an algorithm. What truly distinguishes our research is the introduction of a novel method to expand the feature space and methodically evaluate the effects of temporal features on prediction accuracy and interpretability. Importantly, our approach operates at both the event log and case levels, allowing for the profiling of different algorithms based on these crucial aspects.

7   Conclusion

In this study, we introduced novel time-related event features that significantly enhance predictive capabilities in shallow learning algorithms. This highlights how tailored feature extraction can substantially improve accuracy and effectiveness in PPM tasks. On the one hand, deep learning methods excel at capturing intricate process dynamics and complex relationships, resulting in lower prediction errors. However, their black-box nature limits interpretability, decision-making, and understanding of behavior. In contrast, shallow methods provide slightly lower predictive accuracy but are lightweight and interpretable. The trade-off between predictive performance and interpretability must be carefully considered based on specific PM needs. Strategically investing more time in preprocessing for shallow methods proves beneficial. This additional effort, even when compared to deep learning methods, remains time-efficient and yields notable performance improvements. This is especially important in real-time applications and model retraining scenarios to deal with concept drift. The introduction of newly proposed event features alongside tree-based methods significantly improves model interpretability. This integrated approach transparently quantifies feature importance, facilitating PM decision-making.

While our findings contribute to the advancement of predictive performance and interpretability for decision support and behavioral understanding, it's important to note that our study did not explore all event attributes, such as resources and costs. Future research will thoroughly investigate PM preprocessing techniques and their implications in other emerging applications, such as process simulation.

Acknowledgements. Supported by Università degli Studi di Milano (PON DM 1061/2021, action IV.5, FSE REACT-EU CUP: G45F21002100006), LMU Munich, and the Munich Center for Machine Learning.

Disclosure of Interests. The authors have no competing interests to declare that are relevant to the content of this article.

References

1. van der Aalst, W.M.P.: Process Mining - Data Science in Action, 2nd edn. (2016)
2. Alcobaça, E., Siqueira, F., Rivolli, A., Garcia, L.P.F., Oliva, J.T., de Carvalho, A.C.P.L.F.: MFE: towards reproducible meta-feature extraction. J. Mach. Learn. Res. (2020)
3. Camargo, M., Dumas, M., González-Rojas, O.: Learning accurate LSTM models of business processes. In: Hildebrandt, T., van Dongen, B.F., Röglinger, M., Mendling, J. (eds.) BPM 2019. LNCS, vol. 11675, pp. 286–302. Springer, Cham (2019). https://doi.org/10.1007/978-3-030-26619-6_19
4. Camargo, M., Dumas, M., González-Rojas, O.: Learning accurate business process simulation models from event logs via automated process discovery and deep learning. In: Franch, X., Poels, G., Gailly, F., Snoeck, M. (eds.) CAiSE 2022. LNCS, vol. 13295, pp. 55–71. Springer, Cham (2022). https://doi.org/10.1007/978-3-031-07472-1_4

5. Ceravolo, P., Tavares, G.M., Junior, S.B., Damiani, E.: Evaluation goals for online process mining: a concept drift perspective. IEEE Trans. Serv. Comput. (2022)
6. Galanti, R., et al.: An explainable decision support system for predictive process analytics. Eng. Appl. Artif. Intell. (2023)
7. Grinsztajn, L., Oyallon, E., Varoquaux, G.: Why do tree-based models still outperform deep learning on typical tabular data? In: NIPS (2022)
8. Hancock, J.T., Khoshgoftaar, T.M.: Catboost for big data: an interdisciplinary review. J. Big Data (2020)
9. Kim, J., Comuzzi, M., Dumas, M., Maggi, F.M., Teinemaa, I.: Encoding resource experience for predictive process monitoring. Decis. Support Syst. (2022)
10. Krishna, S., et al.: The disagreement problem in explainable machine learning: a practitioner's perspective. CoRR (2022)
11. Liu, Y., Khandagale, S., White, C., Neiswanger, W.: Synthetic benchmarks for scientific research in explainable machine learning. In: Vanschoren, J., Yeung, S. (eds.) NIPS (2021)
12. Lundberg, S.M., Lee, S.: A unified approach to interpreting model predictions. In: Guyon, I., et al. (eds.) NIPS (2017)
13. Mozafari Mehr, A.S., de Carvalho, R.M., van Dongen, B.: Explainable conformance checking: understanding patterns of anomalous behavior. Eng. Appl. Artif. Intell. (2023)
14. Munappy, A., Bosch, J., Olsson, H.H., Arpteg, A., Brinne, B.: Data management challenges for deep learning. In: SEAA (2019)
15. Navarin, N., Vincenzi, B., Polato, M., Sperduti, A.: LSTM networks for data-aware remaining time prediction of business process instances. In: SSCI (2017)
16. Polato, M., Sperduti, A., Burattin, A., de Leoni, M.: Time and activity sequence prediction of business process instances. Computing (2018)
17. Rama-Maneiro, E., Vidal, J., Lama, M.: Deep learning for predictive business process monitoring: review and benchmark. IEEE TSC (2021)
18. Rizzi, W., Di Francescomarino, C., Maggi, F.M.: Explainability in predictive process monitoring: when understanding helps improving. In: Fahland, D., Ghidini, C., Becker, J., Dumas, M. (eds.) BPM 2020. LNBIP, vol. 392, pp. 141–158. Springer, Cham (2020). https://doi.org/10.1007/978-3-030-58638-6_9
19. Senderovich, A., Di Francescomarino, C., Ghidini, C., Jorbina, K., Maggi, F.M.: Intra and inter-case features in predictive process monitoring: a tale of two dimensions. In: Carmona, J., Engels, G., Kumar, A. (eds.) BPM 2017. LNCS, vol. 10445, pp. 306–323. Springer, Cham (2017). https://doi.org/10.1007/978-3-319-65000-5_18
20. Tavares, G.M., Oyamada, R.S., Barbon, S., Ceravolo, P.: Trace encoding in process mining: a survey and benchmarking. Eng. Appl. Artif. Intell. (2023)
21. Tavares, G.M., Barbon Junior, S., Damiani, E., Ceravolo, P.: Selecting optimal trace clustering pipelines with meta-learning. Intell. Syst. (2022)
22. Tax, N., Verenich, I., La Rosa, M., Dumas, M.: Predictive business process monitoring with LSTM neural networks. In: Dubois, E., Pohl, K. (eds.) CAiSE 2017. LNCS, vol. 10253, pp. 477–492. Springer, Cham (2017). https://doi.org/10.1007/978-3-319-59536-8_30
23. Teinemaa, I., Dumas, M., Rosa, M.L., Maggi, F.M.: Outcome-oriented predictive process monitoring: review and benchmark. ACM Trans. Knowl. Discov. Data (2019)

24. Verenich, I., Dumas, M., Rosa, M.L., Maggi, F.M., Teinemaa, I.: Survey and cross-benchmark comparison of remaining time prediction methods in business process monitoring. ACM Trans. Intell. Syst. Technol. (2019)
25. Weytjens, H., De Weerdt, J.: Creating unbiased public benchmark datasets with data leakage prevention for predictive process monitoring. In: Marrella, A., Weber, B. (eds.) BPM 2021. LNBIP, vol. 436, pp. 18–29. Springer, Cham (2022). https://doi.org/10.1007/978-3-030-94343-1_2

Stochastic Directly-Follows Process Discovery Using Grammatical Inference

Hanan Alkhammash[✉][iD], Artem Polyvyanyy[iD], and Alistair Moffat[iD]

The University of Melbourne, Parkville, VIC 3010, Australia
halkhammash@student.unimelb.edu.au,
{artem.polyvyanyy,ammoffat}@unimelb.edu.au

Abstract. Starting with a collection of traces generated by process executions, process discovery is the task of constructing a simple model that describes the process, where simplicity is often measured in terms of model size. The challenge of process discovery is that the process of interest is unknown, and that while the input traces constitute positive examples of process executions, no negative examples are available. Many commercial tools discover Directly-Follows Graphs, in which nodes represent the observable actions of the process, and directed arcs indicate execution order possibilities over the actions. We propose a new approach for discovering sound Directly-Follows Graphs that is grounded in grammatical inference over the input traces. To promote the discovery of small graphs that also describe the process accurately we design and evaluate a genetic algorithm that supports the convergence of the inference parameters to the areas that lead to the discovery of interesting models. Experiments over real-world datasets confirm that our new approach can construct smaller models that represent the input traces and their frequencies more accurately than the state-of-the-art technique. Reasoning over the frequencies of encoded traces also becomes possible, due to the stochastic semantics of the action graphs we propose, which, for the first time, are interpreted as models that describe the stochastic languages of action traces.

Keywords: Process mining · stochastic process discovery · directly-follows graphs

1 Introduction

Process mining is a discipline that studies data-driven methods and techniques to analyze and optimize processes by leveraging the event data extracted from information systems during process execution. Process mining approaches can uncover inefficiencies, bottlenecks, and deviations within processes, empowering analysts to make well-informed decisions and formulate hypotheses about future processes [3].

A fundamental problem studied in process mining is *process discovery*, which involves constructing process models from event data [3]. The discovered models aim to describe the process that generated the data and can vary in detail and accuracy. The event data used as input often takes the form of an *event log*, a collection of *traces*, each captured as a sequence of executed *actions* in a single instance of the process. As the same sequence of actions can be executed multiple times by the process, an event log can contain multiple instances of the same trace.

G. Guizzardi et al. (Eds.): CAiSE 2024, LNCS 14663, pp. 87–103, 2024.
https://doi.org/10.1007/978-3-031-61057-8_6

A plethora of discovery techniques have been proposed, employing a range of options to represent the constructed models. Among these languages, Directly-Follows Graphs (DFGs) stand out for their intuitiveness, and are a preferred choice for practitioners seeking insights [4,13,24]. A DFG is a directed graph in which nodes denote actions and arcs encode "can follow" relations between them. The nodes and arcs of a DFG are annotated with numbers reflecting the frequencies of the actions and "occurs next" dependencies inferred from the data.

In this paper, we present an approach grounded in stochastic grammar inference for constructing a Stochastic Directed Action Graph (SDAG), a special type of DFG defined to capture the likelihood of traces, from an event log. The problem of stochastic grammar inference from a language consists of learning a grammar representing the strings of the language and their probabilities, which indicate their importance in the language [17]. Hence, discovering a process model from an event log is akin to grammar inference, where traces of actions in the event log can be seen as words in the language strings. There are several reasons why one might choose to use stochastic inference for process discovery. First, noisy traces are, in general, infrequent and can thus be identified and suppressed during inference, noting that noise is intrinsic to event data and poses challenges to discovery [14]. Second, stochastic grammars can be used to predict the next trace or deduce the probability of the next action given an observed sequence of actions, information which can inform process simulations [26], decision-making by analysts [2], and future process design [3]. Third, grammar inference is performed based on positive example strings, aiming to: (i) learn the input examples; (ii) favor simpler explanations of the strings, known as Occam's razor or the parsimony principle; and to (iii) generalize to *all* positive examples of the target unknown language [17]. These aims naturally coincide with the goals of process discovery to construct models that: (i) are fitting and precise; (ii) simple; and that (iii) generalize to *all* of the traces the (unknown) process can support [10].

We use *ALERGIA* to perform stochastic grammar inference. *ALERGIA* identifies any stochastic regular language from positive example strings in the limit with probability one [12], with a runtime bounded by a cubic polynomial in the number of input strings. In practice the runtime grows only linearly with the size of the sample set [12,17]. When performing process discovery, to support process exploration at different abstraction levels [29], one is often interested in creating a range of models of various sizes. In general, the problem of determining whether there is a representation of a language of a given size is NP-complete [15]. To control the level of detail in the models it constructs, *ALERGIA* makes use of two parameters. A key contribution in this paper is a genetic algorithm that evolves an initial random population toward parameter pairs that result in better models. Even though SDAGs (unlike DFGs) can have multiple nodes that refer to the same action, we were able to discover SDAGs that are both smaller than the DFGs constructed by a state-of-the-art discovery algorithm and also yield more faithful encodings.

Specifically, we contribute:

1. The first formal semantics of SDAGs (and DFGs) grounded in stochastic languages;
2. A Genetic Algorithm for Stochastic Process Discovery (*GASPD*) that discovers a family of SDAGs from an input event log;

3. A heuristic for focusing genetic mutations to areas likely to accelerate convergence, resulting in SDAGs of superior quality; and
4. An evaluation of *GASPD* over real-life event logs that both demonstrates its benefits and also suggests future improvements.

The remainder of this paper is structured as follows. The next section discusses related work. Section 3 introduces basic notions required to understand the subsequent sections. Then, Sect. 4 presents SDAGs and their formal semantics. Section 5 proposes our approach for discovering SDAGs from event logs, while Sect. 6 discusses the results of an evaluation of this approach over real-world datasets using our open-source implementation. The paper concludes with final remarks and discussions in Sect. 7.

2   Related Work

ALERGIA, introduced by Carrasco and Oncina [12], and its variant, *Minimum Divergence Inference (MDI)* by Thollard et al. [32], are state-merging algorithms for learning *stochastic deterministic finite automata* (SDFA) from positive examples. *MDI* extends *ALERGIA* with different heuristics and compatibility tests during state merging. Stolcke and Omohundro [31] proposed *Bayesian Model Merging (BMM)*, which deduces a model through structure merging guided by posterior probabilities.

Work by Herbst [16], inspired by *BMM*, was the first application of grammatical inference for stochastic process discovery. The approach consists of two routines: model merging and model splitting. The former generalizes the most specific model by merging processes, using log-likelihood as a heuristic, while the latter refines a general model through iterative splits. The resulting models are then converted to ADONIS, permitting concurrent behavior.

Recent research in stochastic process mining resulted in several advancements. Rogge-Solti et al. [30] proposed a technique that lays stochastic performance data over given non-stochastic Petri nets. Improvements of the algorithm by Burke et al. [11] introduce five methods to estimate transition probabilities in Petri nets. An approach developed by Mannhardt et al. [25] discovers data dependencies between Petri net transitions, and Leemans et al. [22] extend the approach to capture stochastic long-dependencies triggered by the earlier actions in processes. To assess the quality of stochastic process models, several quantification techniques have been developed using the Earth Mover's Distance [19], entropy-based conformance checking [23], and the Minimum Description Length principle [6,28].

Directly-Follows Graphs emerged as an alternative modeling notation to deterministic automata. van der Aalst et al. [5] laid the foundation for process discovery by defining the directly-follows relation within a workflow, capturing the inherent dependencies among activities. Algorithms like α-Miner [5], *Flexible Heuristics Miner* [33], and *Fodina* [9] discover and map these relations onto Petri nets or BPMN models.

Directly-Follows visual Miner (DFvM) discovers DFGs, aiming to visually represent the direct dependencies between actions in the input log. Designed by Leemans et al. [24], *DFvM* also filters out less frequent relations, focusing on significant and regular behaviors. *DFvM* consistently constructs high-quality small-sized models comparable to models produced by top software vendors in the field [28], and is the method we use as a baseline in the experiments described in Sect. 6.

Chapela-Campa et al. [13] proposed a Directly-Follows Graphs filter technique to enhance the understandability of DFGs. The technique formulates the simplification task as an optimization problem, aiming to identify a sound spanning subgraph that minimizes the number of edges while maximizing the sum of edge frequencies.

Widely recognized algorithms like *Inductive Miner* (*IM*) by Leemans et al. [20] and *Split Miner* (*SM*) by Augusto et al. [7] discover DFGs as an intermediate step, mapping them to well-defined modeling notations. *IM* discovers block-structured workflow nets using process trees by computing log cuts based on identified dominant operators such as exclusive choice, sequence, parallel, and loop within the directly-follows graph. Building upon this approach, *Inductive Miner-directly follows* (*IMd*) [21] handles scalability by employing a single-pass directly-follows graph approach for incomplete logs, and those with infrequent behavior. *SM* transforms logs into graphical Directly-Follows Graphs. The algorithm detects concurrency, prunes the graph, and models it in BPMN, balancing precision and fitness and keeping the model complexity low.

The adaptive metaheuristic framework [8] optimizes the accuracy of DFG-based process discovery using three strategies that guide exploring the solution space of discoverable DFGs. The framework iteratively refines DFGs through metaheuristics, evaluates their performance using an objective function, and selects optimal process models.

3   Preliminaries

An SDFA is a representation of the traces of a process and their likelihoods.

Definition 3.1 (Stochastic deterministic finite automata)
A *stochastic deterministic finite automaton* (SDFA) is a tuple $(S, \Lambda, \delta, p, s_0)$, where S is a finite set of *states*, Λ is a finite set of *actions*, $\delta : S \times \Lambda \rightarrow S$ is a *transition function*, $p : S \times \Lambda \rightarrow [0, 1]$ is a *transition probability function*, and $s_0 \in S$ is the *initial state*, such that $\forall s \in S : (\sum_{\lambda \in \Lambda} p(s, \lambda) \leq 1.0)$. ⌟

A *trace* is a sequence $t \in \Lambda^*$. We use ϵ to denote the empty trace. Given two traces t_1 and t_2, their concatenation $t_1 \circ t_2$ is obtained by joining t_1 and t_2 consecutively; for example $\epsilon \circ \epsilon = \epsilon$, $\epsilon \circ \langle b,b \rangle = \langle b,b \rangle$, and $\langle b,b \rangle \circ \langle b,d \rangle = \langle b,b,b,d \rangle$.

An SDFA $A = (S, \Lambda, \delta, p, s_0)$ encodes *stochastic language* L_A defined using recursive function $\pi_A : S \times \Lambda^* \rightarrow [0, 1]$, that is, $L_A(t) = \pi_A(s_0, t)$, $t \in \Lambda^*$, where:

$$\pi_A(s, \epsilon) := 1.0 - \sum_{\lambda \in \Lambda} p(s, \lambda), \text{ and}$$

$$\pi_A(s, \lambda \circ t') := p(s, \lambda) \ \pi_A(\delta(s, \lambda), t'), \lambda \in \Lambda, t = \lambda \circ t'.$$

Note that $\pi_A(s, \epsilon)$ denotes the probability of terminating a trace in state $s \in S$. It holds that $\sum_{t \in \Lambda^*} L_A(t) = 1.0$. Figure 1 shows an example SDFA in which $L_A(\langle a,c,e,c \rangle) = 0.664$, $L_A(\langle a,b,c,e \rangle) \approx 0.028$, and $L_A(\langle b,b,b,d \rangle) = 0$. The probability associated with a trace is an indication of its importance in the language.[1]

---

[1] A common mistake is to confuse this with the probability of the trace being in the language.

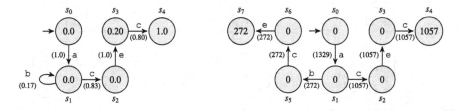

Fig. 1. An SDFA A.   **Fig. 2.** A PAT T.

An *event log* L is a finite multiset of traces, where each trace encodes a sequence of observed and recorded actions executed in the corresponding process. The multiplicity of t in L, denoted by $n(t, L)$, indicates how frequently it has been observed and recorded; we thus have $|L| = \sum_{t \in L} n(t, L)$. The empirical finite support distribution associated with L, denoted as $\mathcal{P}_L$, is given by $\mathcal{P}_L(t) = n(t, L)/|L|$. For example, suppose that $L = [\langle a, c, e, c\rangle^{1057}, \langle a, b, c, e\rangle^{272}, \langle b, b, b, d\rangle^{164}]$ is an event log. It holds that $|L| = 1493$, $\mathcal{P}_L(\langle a,c,e,c\rangle) \approx 0.708$, $\mathcal{P}_L(\langle a,b,c,e\rangle) \approx 0.182$, and $\mathcal{P}_L(\langle b,b,b,d\rangle) \approx 0.110$.

Entropic relevance relies on the minimum description length principle to measure the number of bits required to compress a trace in an event log using the structure and information about the relative likelihoods of traces described in a model, for instance, an SDFA [6]. Models with lower relevance values to a given log are preferred because they describe the traces and their likelihoods better. For example, the entropic relevance of SDFA A from Fig. 1 to event log L is 3.275 bits per trace.[2]

4 Stochastic Directed Action Graphs

We now describe SDAGs, their stochastic semantics, and their relationship to DFGs.

Definition 4.1 (Stochastic directed action graphs) A *stochastic directed action graph* (SDAG) is a tuple $(N, \Lambda, \beta, \gamma, q, i, o)$, where N is a finite set of *nodes*, Λ is a finite set of *actions*, $\beta : N \to \Lambda$ is a *labeling function*, $\gamma \subseteq (N \times N) \cup (\{i\} \times N) \cup (N \times \{o\})$ is the *flow relation*, $q : \gamma \to [0, 1]$ is a *flow probability function*, and $i \notin N$ and $o \notin N$ are the *input* node and the *output* node, such that $\forall\, n \in N \cup \{i\}$: $(\sum_{m \in \{k \in N \cup \{o\} \mid (n,k) \in \gamma\}} q(n, m) = 1)$.   ⌐

An *execution* of an SDAG is a finite sequence of its nodes beginning with i and ending with o, such that for every two consecutive nodes x and y in the sequence there is an arc $(x, y) \in \gamma$. A *trace* of an SDAG is a sequence of actions such that there is an execution that *confirms* the trace in which the nodes, excluding the input and output nodes, are the actions of the trace in the order they appear. Figure 3 shows example SDAG G. The sequence of nodes $\langle i, n_1, n_3, n_5, n_4, o\rangle$ is an execution of G that confirms trace $\langle a, c, e, c\rangle$.

An SDAG G encodes stochastic language L_G such that for a trace t of G it holds that $L_G(t)$ is equal to the sum of probabilities of all the executions of G that confirm t, where the probability of an execution is equal to the product of the probabilities, as per function q, of all the arcs, as per γ, defined by all pairs of consecutive nodes in the execution. In addition, if $t \in \Lambda^*$ is not a trace of G, it holds that $L_G(t) = 0$.

---

[2] We use the uniform background coding model throughout this work [6].

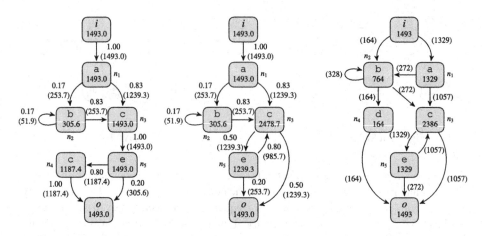

Fig. 3. SDAG G.   **Fig. 4.** SDAG G'.   **Fig. 5.** DFG.

Given an SDFA, one can obtain its corresponding SDAG.

Definition 4.2 (SDAG of SDFA)
Let A be an SDFA $(S, \Lambda, \delta, p, s_0)$. Then, $(N, \Lambda, \beta, \gamma, q, i, o)$, where it holds that:
- $N = \delta$, $i \notin N$, $o \notin N$,
- $\beta = \{((x, \lambda, y), \lambda) \mid (x, \lambda, y) \in \delta\}$,
- $q = \{((x, \lambda_1, y), (y, \lambda_2, z), p(y, \lambda_2)) \mid (x, \lambda_1, y) \in \delta \wedge (y, \lambda_2, z) \in \delta\} \cup$
  $\{(i, (s_0, \lambda, y), p(s_0, \lambda)) \mid (s_0, \lambda, y) \in \delta\} \cup$
  $\{((x, \lambda, y), o, 1.0 - \sum_{\mu \in \Lambda} p(y, \mu)) \mid (x, \lambda, y) \in \delta \wedge \sum_{\mu \in \Lambda} p(y, \mu) < 1.0\} \cup$
  $\{(i, o, 1.0 - \sum_{\mu \in \Lambda} p(s_0, \mu)) \mid \sum_{\mu \in \Lambda} p(s_0, \mu) < 1.0\}$, and
- $\gamma = \{(x, y) \mid (x, y, z) \in q \wedge z \in [0, 1]\}$,
is the *SDAG* of A, denoted by *SDAG(A)*.   ⌐

If A is an SDFA, then *SDAG(A)* is *sound* [1] by construction, as every node of *SDAG(A)* is on a directed walk from the input node to the output node while the directed walks in *SDAG(A)* define all and only its executions. Hence, one can reach the output node from every node of *SDAG(A)* (option to complete property), once a directed walk, and thus the corresponding execution, reaches the output node, it completes (proper completion), and the output node is the only deadlock in *SDAG(A)* (no dead actions).

In addition, an SDAG of an SDFA has a special structure; that is, it is deterministic.

Definition 4.3 (Deterministic SDAGs) An SDAG $(N, \Lambda, \beta, \gamma, q, i, o)$ is *deterministic* if and only if for every two arcs that start at the same node and lead to two distinct nodes it holds that the labels of the nodes are different, that is, it holds that: $\forall n \in N \cup \{i\} \; \forall n_1, n_2 \in N : (((n, n_1) \in \gamma \wedge (n, n_2) \in \gamma \wedge n_1 \neq n_2) \Rightarrow \beta(n_1) \neq \beta(n_2))$.   ⌐

In a deterministic SDAG, every distinct arc originating at a node must lead to a node with a different action. Consequently, every trace of a deterministic SDAG has only one execution that confirms it, significantly simplifying the computation of the stochastic language of the action graph. The SDAG of an SDFA is deterministic.

Lemma 4.1 (Deterministic SDAGs) *If A is a SDFA then SDAG(A) is deterministic.*   ⌐

Lemma 4.1 holds by construction of Definition 4.2. The SDAG G from Fig. 3 is an SDAG of SDFA A in Fig. 1, i.e., it holds that $G = SDAG(A)$. As G is deterministic, it holds that $L_G(\langle a,c,e,c \rangle) = 0.664$, which is equal to the product of the probabilities on all the arcs of the corresponding execution $\langle i,n_1,n_3,n_5,n_4,o \rangle$.

Definition 4.4 (SFA of SDAG) Let G be an SDAG $(N,\Lambda,\beta,\gamma,q,i,o)$. Then, (S,Λ,δ,p,s_0), where it holds that $S = N \cup \{i\}$, $\delta = \{(x,\lambda,y) \in (N \cup \{i\}) \times \Lambda \times N \mid (x,y) \in \gamma \wedge \lambda = \beta(y)\}$, $p = \{(x,\lambda,\sum_{\beta(y)=\lambda,y\in N} q(x,y)) \mid x \in N \cup \{i\} \wedge \lambda \in \Lambda \wedge \exists z \in N : (x,\lambda,z) \in \delta\}$, and $s_o = i$, is the *stochastic finite automaton* (SFA) of G, denoted by $SFA(G)$.   ⌐

Definition 4.4 generalizes Definition III.5 from [28] to account for the fact that an SDAG can have multiple nodes that refer to the same action.

Note that $SFA(G)$ is indeed an SDFA if G is deterministic.

Lemma 4.2 (Determinism) *If G is a deterministic SDAG then $SFA(G)$ is an SDFA.*   ⌐

Lemma 4.2 holds by construction of Definition 4.4. The SDAG of an SDFA and the SDFA of a deterministic SDAG have the same stochastic languages.

Lemma 4.3 (Equivalence) *Let A be an SDFA and let G be an SDAG. Then, it holds that (i) $L_A = L_{SDAG(A)}$, and (ii) $L_G = L_{SFA(G)}$.*   ⌐

The stochastic language of the SDFA of a deterministic SDAG defines the stochastic semantics of the SDAG. In turn, the stochastic semantics of the SDAG of an SDFA is specified by the stochastic language of the SDFA.

In a DFG discovered by a conventional discovery technique, every action has only a single corresponding node. Every SDAG with a pair of distinct nodes that refer to the same action λ can be transformed to an SDAG in which those two nodes are removed, a fresh node for λ is added, all the incoming (outgoing) arcs of the removed nodes get rerouted to reach (originate at) the fresh node, and the probabilities on the outgoing arcs of the fresh node are normalized. Repeated application of this transformation until no further reductions are feasible yields an SDAG that is a DFG.[3] It is straightforward to show that different maximal sequences of feasible transformations do indeed lead to the same resulting DFG. Figure 4 shows the DFG G' obtained in this way from SDAG G in Fig. 3; we denote this relationship between the graphs by $G' = DFG(G)$.

An SDAG can be annotated with frequencies of actions and flows, thereby providing information on the rate at which the corresponding concepts arise in the event log from which the SDAG was constructed. Given a number n of cases that should "flow" through the graph, frequencies can be derived from the probabilities by solving a system of equations comprising two types. Each node of the graph defines a *conservation* equation that requires that the sum of frequencies on the incoming arcs equal the sum of the frequencies on the outgoing arcs, except for the input (output) node, for which the sum of frequencies on the outgoing (incoming) arcs is equal to n. Finally, each arc emanating from a node s defines an *arc* equation that specifies that the frequency of the arc is equal to its probability times the sum of frequencies of all the incoming arcs of s. Such

---

[3] Noting that in a DFG nodes and arcs are annotated with occurrence frequencies.

Table 1. A system of equations used to obtain frequencies of nodes and arcs in Fig. 4.

Node	Equation	Arc	Equation
		$\gamma(n_1, n_2)$	$0.17 f(i, n_1) = f(n_1, n_2)$
i	$1493.0 = f(i, n_1)$	$\gamma(n_1, n_3)$	$0.83 f(i, n_1) = f(n_1, n_3)$
n_1	$f(i, n_1) = f(n_1, n_2) + f(n_1, n_3)$	$\gamma(n_2, n_2)$	$0.17 \, (f(n_1, n_2) + f(n_2, n_2)) = f(n_2, n_2)$
n_2	$f(n_1, n_2) = f(n_2, n_3)$	$\gamma(n_2, n_3)$	$0.83 \, (f(n_1, n_2) + f(n_2, n_2)) = f(n_2, n_3)$
n_3	$f(n_1, n_3) + f(n_2, n_3) + f(n_5, n_3) = f(n_3, o) + f(n_3, n_5)$	$\gamma(n_3, n_5)$	$0.50 \, (f(n_1, n_3) + f(n_2, n_3) + f(n_5, n_3)) = f(n_3, n_5)$
n_5	$f(n_3, n_5) = f(n_5, n_3) + f(n_5, o)$	$\gamma(n_3, o)$	$0.50 \, (f(n_1, n_3) + f(n_2, n_3) + f(n_5, n_3)) = f(n_3, o)$
o	$f(n_3, o) + f(n_5, o) = 1493.0$	$\gamma(n_5, n_3)$	$0.80 f(n_3, n_5) = f(n_5, n_3)$
		$\gamma(n_5, o)$	$0.20 f(n_3, n_5) = f(n_5, o)$

a system of equations always has a solution as it contains one unknown per arc and at least as many equations as arcs.

The annotations in Figs. 3 and 4 show frequencies for nodes and arcs, obtained from the probabilities by following that process. For instance, the annotations in Fig. 4 were obtained by solving the fourteen simultaneous equations in Table 1.[4] Notice that in the figures, all frequencies are rounded to one decimal place. The frequency of a node is derived as the sum of the frequencies of all its incoming (or outgoing) arcs.

The SDAG in Fig. 3 is of size 16 and has an *entropic relevance* of 3.267 bits per trace relative to the example event log L from Sect. 3, with the small difference with the relevance of the SDFA in Fig. 1 due to the integer frequencies used in the SDAG. The DFG in Fig. 5 constructed from the same log using the *DFvM* algorithm [24] has size 19 and an *entropic relevance* to L of 4.168. That is, the SDAG is smaller and also describes the event log more faithfully than the DFG. Nor does varying the *DFvM* filtering threshold in steps of 0.01 from zero to 1.0 find any outcomes that alter that relativity: 70 of those 100 generated DFGs have a size of 10 and relevance of 6.062; 19 DFGs are of size 14 and relevance of 4.804; and the remaining 11 DFGs (as in Fig. 5) have size of 19 and relevance of 4.168. Finally, the relevance of the SDAG in Fig. 4 to L is 4.865 bits per trace, illustrating the desirability of permitting duplicate action nodes in the discovered models.

5   Stochastic Process Discovery

Our approach to discovering stochastic process models consists of two fundamental components: a *grammar inference* algorithm coupled with a *genetic optimization* mechanism. We build on *ALERGIA* to construct representations of stochastic language models encoded in the given event data. Complementing that model discovery, we employ *Multi-Objective Genetic Search* to fine-tune the parameters associated with the learning process. This section explains these two fundamental components.

ALERGIA, an instantiation of the *Red-Blue* algorithm, is introduced by Carrasco and Oncina [12] for learning SDFAs from a multiset of strings. The algorithm starts by constructing a *Prefix Acceptor Tree* (PAT) from the multiset of traces, with nodes

---

[4] In which $f(x, y)$ is the frequency of arc $(x, y) \in \gamma$.

representing prefixes of traces and edges indicating transitions between the nodes. Each edge is labeled with the frequency of the corresponding trace prefix in the input log. *ALERGIA* then generalizes and compacts that PAT by merging states that exhibit similar behavior. The merging aims to identify sets of states with similar probabilistic distributions of outgoing edges, and consolidates each such set into a single state, thereby seeking to create a more concise representation of the underlying language of the model.

Two subsets of nodes are maintained while the compaction process is carried out. The *Red* set initially contains only the root of the prefix tree, while the *Blue* set contains all direct successors of the *Red* set. At each cycle of operation, *ALERGIA* iteratively selects a state from the *Blue* set, taking into account a threshold parameter t that determines the minimum number of strings necessary for a state to be considered for merging. Compatibility for merging is determined by comparing final-state frequencies and outgoing transitions of states in the *Red* and *Blue* sets.

Hoeffding's inequality [18] is a statistical test that bounds the extent to which the mean of a set of observations can deviate from its expected value. This inequality can be used to test if an observed outcome g significantly deviates from a probability value p given a confidence level α and n observations:

$$\left| p - \frac{g}{n} \right| < \sqrt{\frac{1}{2n} \log \frac{2}{\alpha}}. \tag{1}$$

ALERGIA approximates that inequality to compare the observed frequencies of pairs of states drawn from the *Red* and *Blue* sets, taking into account final-state frequencies and the frequencies of outgoing transitions:

$$\left| \frac{g_1}{n_1} - \frac{g_2}{n_2} \right| < \omega \cdot \left(\sqrt{\frac{1}{n_1}} + \sqrt{\frac{1}{n_2}} \right). \tag{2}$$

In Eq. (2), n_1 and n_2 are the frequencies of arriving sequences at the compared states, and g_1 and g_2 are the frequencies of ending sequences at those states. This Hoeffding bound assesses the significance of the difference between the two estimates. It ensures that the difference in frequencies is within a statistically acceptable range, as determined by the value of ω. If the observed frequencies fall within the permitted range, the states are deemed compatible, and *ALERGIA* merges them. Conversely, if the observed differences exceed the bounds, the states are considered incompatible, and the algorithm preserves that difference by converting the *Blue* member of the pair to *Red*. These compatibility checks are not limited to the states but also extend to their respective successors in the tree structure. To merge states, the algorithm redirects transitions and folds subtrees rooted at an identified *Blue* state onto the outgoing edges of the corresponding *Red* state. Based on the merged transitions, the automaton is then updated, with the process iterated until no more mergings can be identified.

As a pre-processing step, we employ a simple filtering technique that selectively retains a certain percentage, as a predefined threshold f, of the most frequent traces from the event log. This filtering reduces the complexity of the discovered model, particularly in scenarios where noise and infrequent traces might detract from the overall view of the process. Varying the filtering threshold f also allows altering the level of detail preserved in the log, allowing alignment with specific analytical goals.

Algorithm 1: *ALERGIA*

Data: A multiset of traces L, parameters $\omega > 0$, $t > 0$, and $f \in [0, 1]$
Result: An SDFA A

1 $L' \leftarrow FILTER(L, f)$;
2 $T \leftarrow PAT(L')$;
3 $Red \leftarrow \{q_0\}$;
4 $Blue \leftarrow \{\delta(q_0, a) : \forall a \in \Sigma\}$;
5 **while** $\exists q_b \in Blue : FREQ(q_b) \geq t$ **do**
6 $\quad$ **if** $\exists q_r \in Red : COMPATIBLE(q_r, q_b, \omega)$ **then**
7 $\quad\quad$ $A \leftarrow MERGE(q_r, q_b)$;
8 $\quad\quad$ $A \leftarrow FOLD(q_r, q_b)$;
9 $\quad$ **else**
10 $\quad\quad$ $Red \leftarrow Red \cup \{q_b\}$;
11 $\quad\quad$ $Blue \leftarrow (Blue - \{q_b\}) \cup \{\delta(q_b, a) : a \in \Sigma$ **and** $\delta(q_b, a) \notin Red\}$;
12 $A \leftarrow CONVERT(T)$;
13 **return** A;

Algorithm 2: *GASPD*

Data: Initial population size n, number of generations *GenLim*, and
$\quad\quad\quad$ number of parents k to generate offspring
Result: A Pareto frontier F, captured as a set of parameter triples

1 $g \leftarrow 0$;
2 $P \leftarrow POPULATION(n)$;
3 **while** $g < GenLim$ **do**
4 $\quad$ $F \leftarrow SELECT(P)$;
5 $\quad$ $U \leftarrow CROSSOVER\text{-}MUTATION(F, k)$;
6 $\quad$ $P \leftarrow REPLACE\text{-}ELITE(U, F)$;
7 $\quad$ $g \leftarrow g + 1$;
8 **return** F;

Algorithm 1 provides an overview of *ALERGIA*. The *FILTER* function, called at line 1, filters the input log based on the supplied threshold. The filtered log is then used to construct PAT T, refer to line 2. Figure 2 shows the prefix tree constructed from example log L from Sect. 3 after applying the filtering using the threshold of $f = 0.89$. At line 5, the *FREQ* function computes the frequency of arriving at state q_b to check if the state is reached sufficiently frequently, as per the threshold t. The compatibility test between states q_r and q_b is performed by the *COMPATIBLE* function at line 6. The *MERGE* function is then called at line 7 to merge two states and, subsequently, the *FOLD* function folds the tree. Finally, the *CONVERT* function maps T to its corresponding automaton A. For a detailed description of the algorithm, refer to [12]. The SDFA A in Fig. 1 is discovered from the example event log by *ALERGIA* using parameters $\omega = 1$, $t = 1$, and $f = 0.89$.

The initialization phase sets the foundation for the genetic algorithm. At line 2 of Algorithm 2, the *POPULATION* function creates a population of n seed solutions $P = \{p_1, p_2, \ldots, p_n\}$, where $p_i = (\omega_i, t_i, f_i)$, $i \in [1 .. n]$, is a parameter triple. The values of these parameters are independently and randomly generated within specified bounds, with each triple determining a model using Algorithm 1. A large initial population enhances exploration but increases the computational cost. Conversely, a small initial population is computationally more efficient but may compromise the ability to find good solutions.

The quality of each solution p_i is then assessed to determine how well it performs with respect to the objective functions. In Algorithm 2, this is done in function *SELECT* at line 4, which applies *ALERGIA* to obtain a process model as a function of each parameter triple in the current population P. This gives rise to a set of models, where each model has an associated size and an *entropic relevance* score computed using *Entropia* [27]. The selection of relevance as a quality metric stems from its ability to rapidly score models, a feature that harmonizes effectively with the genetic framework.

As part of each selection phase, the individuals from the current population that form the *Pareto frontier F* are identified, noting the individuals that are not dominated by other solutions in terms of the two objectives, with Pareto efficient points leading to models having small *size* and *entropic relevance*. Each such point represents a unique trade-off between the objectives, providing decision-makers with a set of alternative options. One such frontier is associated with each *generation*, with the generations counted in Algorithm 2 by the variable g. While we use *ALERGIA*, *size*, and *entropic relevance*, the *GASPD* procedure is not tied to a specific discovery algorithm or quality measure.

In function *CROSSOVER-MUTATION* at line 5 of Algorithm 2, each generation is constructed from the previous one by applying crossover and mutation operations to create a set of offspring, new individuals that (with luck) inherit beneficial traits from previous generations. The *crossover* operation mimics natural genetic recombination, combining information from selected parents, with both single- and double-point crossover techniques employed in our approach. Specifically, to produce offspring, two parents (ω_1, t_1, f_1) and (ω_2, t_2, f_2) are selected from frontier F. In the single-point crossover, one crossover position in the parent triples is selected. Then, the parameters at and to the left of the crossover point in both parents remain unchanged, while the parameters to the right of the crossover point are swapped between the parents. Hence, six offspring are produced, namely (ω_1, t_2, f_2) and (ω_2, t_1, f_1) at position one, (ω_1, t_1, f_2) and (ω_2, t_2, f_1) at position two, and (ω_1, t_1, f_1) and (ω_2, t_2, f_2) at position three. In the double-point crossover, two additional offspring (ω_1, t_2, f_1) and (ω_2, t_1, f_2) are produced by swapping parameters of the parents twice, once after the first crossover point and then after the second crossover point. *GASPD* includes all such offspring stemming from all pairs in k randomly selected parents from front F (or $|F|$ selected parents, if $|F| < k$) when generating the set of offspring U.

The *mutation* component of the *CROSSOVER-MUTATION* function then alters the "genetic makeup" of new individuals in U by randomly modifying their three defining parameters, restricted to certain predefined bounds. The random nature of these mutations ensures that the algorithm does not converge prematurely to a limited subset of solutions and allows for the exploration of a broader range of possibilities, crucial when the global optimum may not be immediately apparent. For each individual (ω, t, f) in U, its mutated twin defined as $(\omega + \Delta_\omega, t + \Delta_t, f + \Delta_f)$, where Δ_ω, Δ_t, and Δ_f

are random positive or negative mutation values within specified bounds, is created and added to U.

Our approach here (implemented in the *REPLACE-ELITE* function at line 6 of Algorithm 2) is that each generation retains the items that were on the Pareto frontier of any previous generation, and then adds any new parameter triples that establish new points on the frontier. That is, we always preserve solutions that, at some stage, have appeared promising, and seek to add any new solutions that outperform them.

The SDFAs constructed by *ALERGIA* using the parameters discovered by *GASPD* can be translated to sound SDAGs using the principles laid out in Definition 4.2.

6   Evaluation

We have implemented *GASPD*[5] and conducted experiments using twelve publicly available real-world event logs shared by the IEEE Task Force on Process Mining[6], derived from IT systems executing business processes. These experiments assess the feasibility of using *GASPD* in industrial settings, and compare the quality of its models with the ones constructed by *DFvM* [24]. A wide range of *DFvM* filtering parameters were considered, establishing a reference curve for each log showing the versatility of *DFvM* across the spectrum of possible model sizes. We also explored the effectiveness of the genetic search in guiding the selection of parameters to identify desirable solutions.

For each of the twelve event logs *GASPD* was seeded with an initial population of 50 parameter triples, each containing random values for ω (from 0 to 15); for t (from 0 to the most frequent PAT branch); and for f (from 0 to 1). The genetic search was then iterated for 50 generations, with mutation achieved by random adjustments to parameter values within the same defined ranges.

Figures 6a to 6c show model relevance scores as a function of model size, taking three snapshots during the course of *GASPD* when executed on the BPIC17 log. After one generation the models are a mixed bag, a result of the random starting point; but with broad coverage of the search space achieved, and already with individuals (yellow dots) identified that outperform the baseline set by the red *DFvM* frontier. By the tenth generation, mutation and breeding have taken the population toward improved performance, with many solutions now below the previous frontier, and convergence towards promising regions in the parameter space. Then, by generation 50, the situation has stabilized, with additional individuals identified that lead to attractive models that outperform the *DFvM* frontier used here as a reference.

Figure 7 shows *GASPD* performance at the 50 generation point for three other logs. In each case *GASPD* constructs models that outperform the *DFvM* ones over at least some fraction of the range of sizes being considered, noting that smaller and more accurate models are preferable for human analysis. Table 2 then summarizes *GASPD* when applied to all twelve event logs, further supporting our contention that *GASPD*

---

[5] https://github.com/jbpt/codebase/tree/master/jbpt-pm/gaspd.
[6] https://www.tf-pm.org/resources/logs.

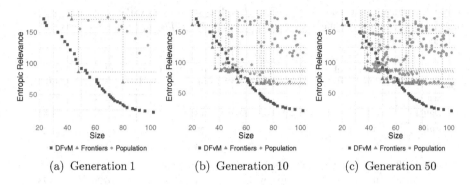

(a) Generation 1   (b) Generation 10   (c) Generation 50

Fig. 6. Size and relevance of SDAG models discovered by *GASPD* from the BPIC17 log.

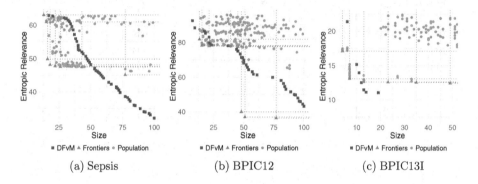

(a) Sepsis   (b) BPIC12   (c) BPIC13I

Fig. 7. Size and relevance of SDAG models discovered by *GASPD* after 50 generations.

finds useful new models. In the first seven rows we focus on human-scale models of up to 100 nodes/edges, and then relax that to a limit of size 1000 for the BPIC15 tasks, which tend to give rise to more complex models. As can be seen, in ten of the twelve cases *GASPD* generates models of better relevance for at least part of the size range, with *DFvM* tending to discover models of better relevance for large sizes. In future work, it would be interesting to study if grammar inference techniques can be useful in discovering large, accurate models.

As already described, *GASPD* employs evolutionary search as part of the discovery algorithm. To focus the search onto good candidates, the individuals in each generation P are split into two classes: "good", and "bad". An individual is "good" if it has been on the Pareto frontier in any previous generation; and it is "bad" if has never been part of any Pareto frontier. In Algorithm 2 each generation is derived solely from the "good" individuals of the previous population, with the aim of iterating towards better solutions. Only new individuals that are also "good" are then retained into the next population.

To verify the usefulness of that heuristic, we also experimented with breeding from "bad" parents, recording at each generation the fractions of "good" offspring from pairs of "bad" parents, and then likewise the fraction arising from pairs of "good" parents. Figure 8 shows the result, with the four dotted lines at the top the "good parents" success

Table 2. Relative performance of SDAG models discovered by *GASPD* after 50 generations, including the size range of interest, the size interval(s) of *GASPD* superiority, min/max size, and min/max relevance.

Event log	Size interval From	To	Size interval of superior performance	Size within interval Min	Max	Entropic relevance Min	Max
Sepsis	0	100	(0..53)	13	77	45.16	63.10
BPIC12	0	100	[13..44) ∪ [48..100]	13	77	36.39	81.84
BPIC17	0	100	(0..25) ∪ [34..62)	20	95	60.56	161.25
RTFM	0	100	[53..100]	13	69	2.71	9.07
BPIC13OP	0	100	[4..6) ∪ [8..9)	3	80	5.06	7.80
BPIC13CP	0	100	(0..9)	4	79	6.26	9.78
BPIC13I	0	100	(0..12)	4	89	12.33	17.10
BPIC15-1	0	1000	[37..44) ∪ [59..122)	37	633	380.01	384.21
BPIC15-2	0	1000	[473..641) ∪ [697..965)	149	946	428.00	469.94
BPIC15-3	0	1000	(0..27) ∪ [95..103)	11	958	298.01	370.63
BPIC15-4	0	1000	∅	475	475	386.93	386.93
BPIC15-5	0	1000	∅	695	695	445.41	445.41

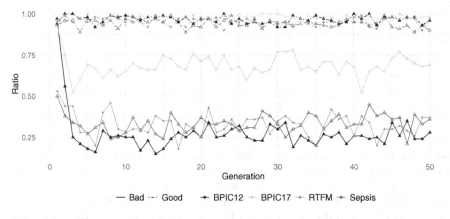

Fig. 8. The fraction of "good" individuals arising as offspring from pairs of "good" parents and pairs of "bad" parents, traced through 50 generations, for each of four logs.

rate, and the four solid lower lines the "bad parents" rate. As can be seen, the four dotted lines comprehensively outperform their solid equivalents, and good parents are much more likely to lead to interesting offspring than are bad parents. Taking a paired t-test between the 50 "dotted" points and the 50 "solid" points for the four logs gives $p < 10^{-10}$ in all four cases, confirming that filtering the population at each generation to only contain good parents is a highly beneficial strategy.

7   Discussion and Conclusion

We have presented *GASPD*, an algorithm for discovering sound Stochastic Directed Action Graphs, a variant of the DFGs often used in commercial process mining applications. The technique is grounded in grammar inference over sequences of actions, as recorded in event logs; and uses a bespoke genetic algorithm that ensures fast convergence towards models of practically interesting sizes and accuracy.

GASPD can be used to implement a user-friendly tool for exploring input logs, with interesting models often uncovered even in the first generation of random parameters, and then improved through subsequent generations. Moreover, construction of multiple such models is easily done in parallel, meaning that as the interesting models become progressively available, they can be presented to the user via a dynamic slider interface [29], ordered by size. This conjectured interface can thus present the so-far discovered Pareto-best models, while generations are extended and new models are constructed in the background, further feeding the slider. A second slider can be introduced to navigate over all the computed generations. For instance, selecting a specific generation in this slider can load all the Pareto optimal models obtained after that generation in the other slider. Such controls would support interactive exploration of the improvement in model quality observed through generations.

The exploration of alternative grammatical inference techniques stands out as a promising avenue for enhancing the quality of the discovered models. Replacing *ALERGIA* with other grammar inference methods in the genetic framework can reveal their ultimate effectiveness in generating process models from event logs. *ALERGIA* appears as a strong candidate for initiating the quest due to its acknowledged performance characteristics over a wide variety of real-world languages [17]. Additionally, there is a prospect for improvement by introducing pruning strategies over prefix acceptor trees before merging states and redesigning the merging rules. These enhancements can streamline the algorithm's convergence process, ensuring more efficient solution space exploration, resulting in more accurate and concise process models and allowing the discovery of superior models of larger sizes. Finally, new ideas to guide the genetic exploration of the parameter space of grammar inference can be explored. Some initial ideas include using simulated annealing and particle swarm optimization principles to escape parameter subspaces of local optimal models.

The evaluation in Sect. 6 made use of entropic relevance and model size to identify Pareto-optimal models. Entropic relevance ensures models that better describe the frequencies of log traces are prioritized, and strikes a balance between conventional precision and recall quality measures in process mining [6]; and model size is a standard measure of simplicity for DFGs [4]. But other measurement combinations could also be considered, and would lead to different concrete measurements and, consequently, might result in different Pareto-optimal models. Nevertheless it seems probable that measures that assess the same broad phenomena as entropic relevance and size will result in similar conclusions to those achieved here – that *GASPD* provides the ability to realize interesting and useful process models not found by other current approaches, making it an important development for process mining.

References

1. van der Aalst, W.: Verification of workflow nets. In: Azéma, P., Balbo, G. (eds.) ICATPN 1997. LNCS, vol. 1248, pp. 407–426. Springer, Heidelberg (1997). https://doi.org/10.1007/3-540-63139-9_48
2. van der Aalst, W.: Using process mining to bridge the gap between BI and BPM. Computer **44**(12) (2011)
3. van der Aalst, W.: Process Mining—Data Science in Action, 2nd edn. Springer, Cham (2016)
4. van der Aalst, W.: A practitioner's guide to process mining: Limitations of the directly-follows graph. Procedia Comput. Sci. **164** (2019)
5. van der Aalst, W., Weijters, T., Maruster, L.: Workflow mining: Discovering process models from event logs. IEEE Trans. Knowl. Data Eng. **16**(9) (2004)
6. Alkhammash, H., Polyvyanyy, A., Moffat, A., García-Bañuelos, L.: Entropic relevance: A mechanism for measuring stochastic process models discovered from event data. Inf. Syst. **107** (2022)
7. Augusto, A., Conforti, R., Dumas, M., La Rosa, M., Polyvyanyy, A.: Split miner: Automated discovery of accurate and simple business process models from event logs. Knowl. Inf. Syst. **59**(2) (2019)
8. Augusto, A., Dumas, M., La Rosa, M., Leemans, S., vanden Broucke, S.: Optimization framework for DFG-based automated process discovery approaches. Softw. Syst. Model. **20**(4) (2021)
9. vanden Broucke, S., De Weerdt, J.: Fodina: A robust and flexible heuristic process discovery technique. Decis. Support Syst. **100** (2017)
10. Buijs, J., van Dongen, B., van der Aalst, W.: Quality dimensions in process discovery: The importance of fitness, precision, generalization and simplicity. Int. J. Coop. Inf. Syst. **23**(01) (2014)
11. Burke, A., Leemans, S., Wynn, M.T.: Stochastic process discovery by weight estimation. In: Leemans, S., Leopold, H. (eds.) ICPM 2020. LNBIP, vol. 406, pp. 260–272. Springer, Cham (2021). https://doi.org/10.1007/978-3-030-72693-5_20
12. Carrasco, R.C., Oncina, J.: Learning stochastic regular grammars by means of a state merging method. In: Carrasco, R.C., Oncina, J. (eds.) ICGI 1994. LNCS, vol. 862, pp. 139–152. Springer, Heidelberg (1994). https://doi.org/10.1007/3-540-58473-0_144
13. Chapela-Campa, D., Dumas, M., Mucientes, M., Lama, M.: Efficient edge filtering of directly-follows graphs for process mining. Inf. Sci. **610** (2022)
14. Cheng, H.J., Kumar, A.: Process mining on noisy logs: Can log sanitization help to improve performance? Decis. Support Syst. **79** (2015)
15. Gold, E.M.: Complexity of automaton identification from given data. Inf. Control. **37**(3) (1978)
16. Herbst, J.: A machine learning approach to workflow management. In: López de Mántaras, R., Plaza, E. (eds.) ECML 2000. LNCS (LNAI), vol. 1810, pp. 183–194. Springer, Heidelberg (2000). https://doi.org/10.1007/3-540-45164-1_19
17. de la Higuera, C.: Grammatical Inference: Learning Automata and Grammars, 1st edn. Cambridge University Press, Cambridge (2010)
18. Hoeffding, W.: Probability inequalities for sums of bounded random variables. J. Am. Stat. Assoc. **58**(301) (1963)
19. Leemans, S., van der Aalst, W., Brockhoff, T., Polyvyanyy, A.: Stochastic process mining: earth movers' stochastic conformance. Inf. Syst. **102** (2021)
20. Leemans, S., Fahland, D., van der Aalst, W.: Discovering block-structured process models from event logs - a constructive approach. In: Colom, J.-M., Desel, J. (eds.) PETRI NETS 2013. LNCS, vol. 7927, pp. 311–329. Springer, Heidelberg (2013). https://doi.org/10.1007/978-3-642-38697-8_17

21. Leemans, S., Fahland, D., van der Aalst, W.: Scalable process discovery and conformance checking. Softw. Syst. Model. **17**(2) (2018)
22. Leemans, S., Mannel, L., Sidorova, N.: Significant stochastic dependencies in process models. Inf. Syst. **118** (2023)
23. Leemans, S., Polyvyanyy, A.: Stochastic-aware conformance checking: An entropy-based approach. In: Dustdar, S., Yu, E., Salinesi, C., Rieu, D., Pant, V. (eds.) CAiSE 2020. LNCS, vol. 12127, pp. 217–233. Springer, Cham (2020). https://doi.org/10.1007/978-3-030-49435-3_14
24. Leemans, S., Poppe, E., Wynn, M.T.: Directly follows-based process mining: exploration & a case study. In: ICPM (2019)
25. Mannhardt, F., Leemans, S., Schwanen, C., de Leoni, M.: Modelling data-aware stochastic processes - discovery and conformance checking. In: Gomes, L., Lorenz, R. (eds.) PETRI NETS 2023. LNCS, vol. 13929, pp. 77–98. Springer, Cham (2023). https://doi.org/10.1007/978-3-031-33620-1_5
26. Meneghello, F., Di Francescomarino, C., Ghidini, C.: Runtime integration of machine learning and simulation for business processes. In: ICPM (2023)
27. Polyvyanyy, A., Alkhammash, H., Di Ciccio, C., Garcáa-Bãnuelos, L., Kalenkova, A., Leemans, S., Mendling, J., Moffat, A., Weidlich, M.: Entropia: a family of entropy-based conformance checking measures for process mining. In: ICPM. CEUR-WS Proceedings, vol. 2703 (2020)
28. Polyvyanyy, A., Moffat, A., García-Bañuelos, L.: An entropic relevance measure for stochastic conformance checking in process mining. In: ICPM (2020)
29. Polyvyanyy, A., Smirnov, S., Weske, M.: Process model abstraction: A slider approach. In: ECOC (2008)
30. Rogge-Solti, A., van der Aalst, W., Weske, M.: Discovering stochastic Petri nets with arbitrary delay distributions from event logs. In: Lohmann, N., Song, M., Wohed, P. (eds.) BPM 2013. LNBIP, vol. 171, pp. 15–27. Springer, Cham (2014). https://doi.org/10.1007/978-3-319-06257-0_2
31. Stolcke, A., Omohundro, S.: Best-first model merging for hidden Markov model induction. CoRR (1994)
32. Thollard, F., Dupont, P., de la Higuera, C.: Probabilistic DFA inference using Kullback-Leibler divergence and minimality. In: ICML (2000)
33. Weijters, T., Ribeiro, J.: Flexible heuristics miner (FHM). In: CIDM (2011)

Graphs and Graph Networks

A Graph Language Modeling Framework for the Ontological Enrichment of Conceptual Models

Syed Juned Ali[✉][iD] and Dominik Bork[iD]

Business Informatics Group, TU Wien, Vienna, Austria
{syed.juned.ali,dominik.bork}@tuwien.ac.at

Abstract. Conceptual models (CMs) offer a structured way to organize and communicate information in information systems. However, current models lack adequate semantics of the terminology of the underlying domain model, leading to inconsistent interpretations and uses of information. Ontology-driven conceptual modeling languages provide primitives for articulating these domain notions based on the ontological categories, i.e., stereotypes put forth by upper-level (or foundational) ontologies. Existing CMs have been created using ontologically-neutral languages (e.g., UML, ER). Enriching these models with ontological categories can better support model evaluation, meaning negotiation, semantic interoperability, and complexity management. However, manual stereotyping is prohibitive, given the sheer size of the legacy base of ontologically-neutral models. In this paper, we present a graph language modeling framework for conceptual models that combines fine-tuning pre-trained language models to learn the vector representation of OntoUML models' data and then perform a graph neural networks-based node classification that exploits the model's graph structure to predict the stereotype of model classes and relations. We show with an extensive comparative evaluation that our approach significantly outperforms existing stereotype prediction approaches.

Keywords: Ontology-Driven Conceptual Models · Graph Neural Networks · Pre-trained Language Model · Representation Learning

1 Introduction

Conceptual models were introduced to increase understanding and communication of a system or domain among stakeholders in information systems for design, analysis, and development purposes. Ontologies proved useful in assessing whether different conceptual modeling procedures will likely lead to good representations of real-world phenomena and evaluate the ontological soundness of a conceptual modeling language and its corresponding concepts and grammar. Foundational ontologies emerged to consistently define fundamental concepts in conceptual modeling, e.g., types and taxonomic structures, roles and relational properties, part-whole relations, and multi-level structures. The Unified Foundational Ontology (UFO) was developed to provide foundations for all these major

© The Author(s), under exclusive license to Springer Nature Switzerland AG 2024
G. Guizzardi et al. (Eds.): CAiSE 2024, LNCS 14663, pp. 107–123, 2024.
https://doi.org/10.1007/978-3-031-61057-8_7

conceptual modeling constructs. UFO has been applied to design a general-purpose language OntoUML for ontology-driven conceptual modeling (ODCM) as a revised version of UML such that its modeling primitives reflect the ontological distinctions put forth by UFO, and its metamodel includes semantically-motivated syntactic constraints that reflect the axiomatization of UFO. Empirical evidence shows that OntoUML significantly contributes to improving the quality of conceptual models [11,29]. Semantically rich conceptual models created from OntoUML enable various crucial applications such as *i*) better support for semantic interoperability of the systems as shown in [13]; *ii*) for supporting ontological analysis, meaning explication and negotiation, and conceptual clarification using the fundamental ontological distinctions embodied in a foundational ontology as a conceptual toolbox; *iii*) for more sophisticated conceptual model modularization mechanism [14]; and *iv*) database design [4]. Therefore, we notice sufficient value from generating semantically rich models.

Many CMs exist, however, they are often created using ontologically-neutral languages like UML and ER. Enriching the elements of such models with ontological categories would add the aforementioned benefits. However, given the sheer size of these legacy models, manually enriching them is a prohibitive task. For this reason, in our previous work [1], we presented an automated approach using a trained Graph Neural Network (GNN) on a set of OntoUML models to predict the ontological category of classes and relations in a model. In the present work, we aim to resolve the limitations of our and other stereotype prediction approaches and significantly improve the prediction accuracy for a larger set of less frequent stereotypes. We propose a novel framework for CMs that couples the strengths of transformer-based language models [28] with GNNs [15].

We transformed the stereotype prediction of a class or a relation in an OntoUML model into a node classification task. We first transform an OntoUML model into a Knowledge Graph (KG) using a transformation mechanism described in [1]. In particular, the transformation converts an OntoUML model into a type of KG termed as Conceptual Knowledge Graph (CKG) that can comprehensively capture the CM's graph structure and the ontological stereotypes of the model. Next, the node information, which includes node label and meta properties, is encoded as vectors (i.e., node embeddings) using pre-trained language models (PLM) such as GLoVE, BERT [8,22]. The natural language semantics carry significant information about the category of a class or a relation. E.g., a class "Person" is generally of the type *kind* in OntoUML models. Therefore, the vector representation, i.e., the node embeddings of the elements in an OntoUML model that capture such linguistic semantics, can train a neural network to predict a model element's ontological stereotype.

We note three limitations in [1] that we aim to resolve in this work. Firstly, the node embeddings lack relevant contextual information, i.e., the natural language representation of the nodes' data is generated using only the individual node data. It does not use the other nodes of the model. E.g., the node embedding of the class "Person" in Fig. 1 should depend upon the neighboring nodes such as "Patient", "Adult", "Child", or "Physician", which add crucial contextual information about the *meaning* of the class "Person". We resolve this issue by extending the node data by adding contextual data from the neighboring nodes. Secondly, PLMs such as BERT or GLoVE are trained on generalized natural language text and, therefore, are not particularly aware that the node labels are specific to an OntoUML model. We resolve this limitation by finetuning the PLM for OntoUML models' data and then using the generated node embeddings to classify the stereotype of each node. Finally, [1] misses out on using the stereotype information of the nodes already labeled with a stereotype. E.g., let's consider "Person" and "Adult" as already labeled nodes and "Child" as an unlabeled node in Fig. 1. We can use the stereotype of "Person" and "Adult" to predict the stereotype "Child". In other words, the stereotype information of a node's contextual nodes can be used for the node's stereotype prediction.

In this work, we present our improved solution that tackles the above limitations of the previous work to achieve automated ontological category prediction. Consequently, we developed a **G**raph **L**anguage **M**odeling framework for Conceptual Models (**GLaM4CM**) that enables conceptual modeling applications by combining PLMs and GNNs on the KG representation of CMs, i.e., CKGs. GLaM4CM uses the CKGs as an intermediary to achieve conceptual modeling tasks such as model autocompletion, classification, and ontological enrichment using node stereotype classification, which is the task that we use to evaluate our framework in this paper. Since OntoUML and UFO are among the most used modeling languages and foundational ontologies in ODCM, our proposal makes a clear contribution to advancing the state of the art. We present an experimental evaluation to validate our approach and to provide a detailed comparative impact analysis of various design choices in our solution architecture based on the OntoUML FAIR model dataset described in [4]. We make the code available on Github[1] for (*i*) CKG creation and context generation (*ii*) finetuning PLMs and training GNN on the OntoUML CKGs and, (*iii*) reproducing the results of our work.

In the remainder of this paper, Sect. 2 introduces relevant background. Section 3 discusses the existing graph language modeling solutions and how our proposal advances the state of the art. Section 4 presents the three contributions of this paper, namely, *i*) a graph language modeling framework for an automated stereotype prediction task; *ii*) an extensive evaluation of the different parameters involved in modeling the nodes' context; and *ii*) a comparative analysis of our approach with existing approaches. Section 5 reports the results of an experimental evaluation of our approach. Section 6 discusses the obtained results, their implications, and threats to validity before we conclude this paper in Sect. 7.

2   Background

We now provide the relevant background for developing our GLaM4CM framework and its application for ontological stereotype prediction.

Conceptual Knowledge Graphs. Conceptual models facilitate detection and correction of system development errors [30]. However, error detection techniques

---

[1] https://github.com/junaidiiith/GLM-Stereotype-Prediction.

are constrained when applied to ontologically-neutral modeling languages like ER and UML as they lack an adequate semantic specification of their terminology, which leads to inconsistent interpretations and uses [12,21]. Ontologies proved useful in assessing whether different conceptual modeling procedures will likely lead to good representations of real-world phenomena and evaluate the ontological soundness of a conceptual modeling language and its corresponding concepts and grammar. ODCM extends or supports conceptual modeling techniques by ontological theories that further formalize the conceptual modeling grammars [29], thereby strengthening the ontological commitment of these languages and thus improving the semantic quality of the conceptual modeling language. Knowledge Graphs represent a collection of interlinked descriptions of entities - e.g., objects, events, and concepts. KGs provide a foundation for data integration, fusion, analytics, and sharing [24] based on linked data and semantic metadata. KGs have been recently used for the representation [25,26] of CMs. Such KG-based representations can act as the intermediary representation of CMs to enable ML-based applications on CMs. *Conceptual Knowledge Graphs* (CKG) are termed as "ontologically enriched KGs representing CMs" [1].

Transformer-Based Node Classification. Transformer architecture [28] based language models have proven to be useful in supporting natural language processing (NLP) tasks that operate by leveraging a neural network model that learns a representation of words that captures the contextual relationships between words in a text. BERT, which stands for "Bidirectional Encoder Representations from Transformers", is particularly powerful it captures how each word or token relates to the entire sentence by processing it forward and backward [8]. These transformer-based models are generally trained on a massive text corpus, called the pretraining phase to produce a PLM that provides rich contextual embeddings of text that can be used for various NLP tasks. In the finetuning phase, a PLM is further trained on a smaller dataset and adapted to specific NLP tasks by the model's parameters adjustment to make it proficient for at NLP tasks such as text classification, sentiment analysis, or question answering for a specific dataset.

In the context of graph data, a BERT model can be adapted for node label classification. By representing nodes in a graph as sequences of text or encoding their local neighborhood information into text, we can apply BERT to learn meaningful representations of graph nodes that incorporate local graph structure and semantics of the graph data. Based on the idea of transforming node labels as a sequence of texts, BERT can be finetuned on the graph data. In our work, we finetune pre-trained BERT models for two tasks, i.e., masked language modeling (MLM) and sequence classification (SC). In masked language modeling, some node labels may be masked, i.e., hidden, and the model is tasked with predicting those masked labels based on the contextual text. In sequence classification, a node label is predicted by a classification neural network layer that uses the node embedding produced by the BERT model. Note that the pre-trained embeddings from the pretraining phase are enriched with dataset (i.e., OntoUML) and task-specific (i.e., MLM and SC) embeddings during finetuning.

Graph Neural Networks are neural models that learn graph representations via *message passing* between graph nodes. A node aggregates information from its neighborhood. GNNs leverage the inherent structure and connectivity of the graph to make informed predictions about the labels or properties of individual nodes. Thereby, GNNs capture the local and global context of each node, allowing them to assign appropriate labels based on the learned representations. This approach is particularly valuable in diverse applications, such as social network analysis, recommendation systems, biology, and knowledge graphs, where nodes represent entities and relationships. Recently, variants of GNNs such as Graph Convolutional Networks (GCN), Graph Attention Networks (GAT), and Graph Recurrent Networks (GRN) have demonstrated good performance on many deep learning tasks. GraphSAGE [15] generalized the aggregation function (compared to GCN, which uses "mean" as the aggregation function) that generates node embeddings by sampling and aggregating features from a node's local neighborhood. GNNs can be combined with embeddings from pre-trained or language models-based BERT embeddings such that embeddings capture node-specific information, and the GNN can propagate the information by leveraging the graph structure.

3   Related Work

Next, we discuss existing works for ontological stereotype prediction and NLP approaches to support conceptual modeling tasks.

Ontological Category Prediction. Barcelos et al. [3] present a rule-based solution to infer the ontological stereotype of OntoUML classes. They present 37 different rules that use the UFO semantics to predict the ontological stereotype of OntoUML classes. They restrict the inference for eight categories of classes, namely, *kind, subkind, phase, role, category, mixin, roleMixin* and *phaseMixin* [3] and show, that the 37 rules can only predict the stereotype of a class accurately in 15–20% of the cases. However, the rules can predict with good confidence that the correct stereotype is within the top three predicted classes for each node.

Keet et al. [17] proposed a method leveraging a decision tree for DOLCE [5] categories to select the ontological category for their models. A survey by Trojahn et al. [27] indicates that several works enrich the domain ontologies with foundational ontology concepts. Felipe et al. [18] propose mapping rules between the noun synsets of Wordnet and the top-level constructs of UFO. RDF2Vec [23] considers entities' lexical terms for learning node embeddings; however, they treat an entity composed of multiple words as a single entity, which limits generality. OWL2Vec [6] considers word compositions and adds OWL constraints. Junior et al. [16] propose an approach that automatically classifies domain entities into top-level concepts using informal definitions and the term's word embedding.

Word Embeddings for Conceptual Modeling. A conceptual model's lexical terms contain natural language semantics. Therefore, conceptual modeling tasks can benefit from NLP techniques. Efstathiou et al. [9] released a word2vec model trained over 15GB of textual data in the software engineering context. Lopez et al. [19] present a word2vec model trained on model-driven engineering (MDE) and conceptual modeling data corpus [19].

Synopsis. Considering ontological stereotype prediction, [3] is the closest to our work. However, there are several distinctions. Their approach *i*) is based on a manually created set of non-exhaustive 37 rules compared to our data-driven approach, i.e., it uses deep learning-based patterns to infer the stereotype from the natural language semantics and graph structural information within the OntoUML model; *ii*) is restricted to predicting stereotypes only for classes whereas our approach also considers relations; and *iii*) uses only eight ontological stereotype classes, whereas our approach works for 21 classes, which includes many less frequent classes that are naturally harder to predict. Based on the related work, we present a comparative analysis of our approach with [3] and also show the comparison of using the word embeddings from [9,19] with the embeddings generated by finetuned language models from our framework.

4   The GLaM4CM Framework

We now introduce our end-to-end framework, including its architecture and the steps involved in training and finetuning language models and training GNNs.

4.1   CKG Transformation and Context Generation

First, we elaborate on transforming an OntoUML model into a CKG and generating the node data using the neighbors' node data. Figure 1 shows an example of an OntoUML model of a medical facility (left) and the transformed CKG (right). Note that only the node label and stereotype information are shown in the CKG for simplicity. Other attributes such as node type, i.e., Class or Relation, also form part of the node data (cf. the textual descriptions of the nodes "Person" and "Symptom"). Further information can be similarly added. The CKG represents classes and relations such as "reportedBy" as nodes with a stereotype label. Generalization relations, e.g., "Child" to "Person" relations, do not have a stereotype and are thus not transformed into a CKG node.

We create textual data for each node that captures its neighboring context. Given a directed graph G and a node n within G, the first step is to identify all the nearest neighbors, denoted as N_b, of node n within specified k hops. These neighbors are typically nodes within k hops or edges away from node n in the graph. Next, we create a string of shortest paths from node n to each neighbor N_b as a concatenation of the node labels of all the nodes present in the shortest path. This string effectively captures the sequence of node labels that need to be traversed to reach each neighbor within the specified k hops from node n. Figure 1 shows paths starting from node "Person" which cover nodes and edges in blue for $k = 1$ and the additional green nodes and edges for $k = 2$. The node description follows a specific format of ⟨node type⟩ ⟨node label⟩: ⟨node stereotype⟩ and the edge description is replaced by the keyword "generalizes" if the edge is between two class nodes or "relates" if the edge is between a class node

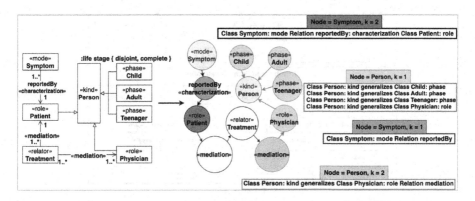

Fig. 1. An OntoUML model CKG transformation and context generation

and a relation node. Note that some relation nodes do not have a label and only stereotype information, such as the relation node with "mediation" stereotypes in Fig. 1, which makes predicting the stereotype of such a node difficult. Adding neighboring information can help in predicting the stereotype for such nodes.

4.2   Problem Description

In the following, we formally describe the node stereotype prediction problem for a set of OntoUML models. Let $\mathcal{G} = \{G_1, G_2, \ldots, G_n\}$ represent a set of CKGs that represent OntoUML models, where $G_i = (\mathcal{V}_i, \mathcal{E}_i)$ is a graph with a set of nodes $\mathcal{V}_i$ and edges $\mathcal{E}_i$. Each node in $\mathcal{V}_i$ is associated with a text content denoted as X_i. The node data vector is obtained from a language model using the node's textual content. To transform the node text labels into node embeddings, a node mapping function $\phi(\cdot)$ is employed. In this context, $\phi(\cdot)$ represents a PLM such as BERT, which generates embeddings for text sequences. A graph nodes' text labels X_i are encoded into a node embedding $\mathbf{H}_i = \{\mathbf{h}_{i1}, \mathbf{h}_{i2}, \ldots, \mathbf{h}_{i|\mathcal{V}_i|}\}$, where $\mathbf{h}_{ij} = \phi(X_{ij})$ for each node j in G_i. Subsequently, a GNN is utilized for node classification on each graph. The objective is to assign a label from a predefined set of labels $\mathcal{Y}$ to each node within a graph. This task can be formally described as finding a function $\sigma(\cdot) : \mathbb{R}^{d_h} \rightarrow \mathcal{Y}$, where k_h is the dimension of the node embeddings, and $\sigma(\mathbf{h}_{ij})$ provides the predicted label for node j in graph G_i. The objective of the problem is i) to learn a node mapping function $\phi(\cdot)$ which maps a node text to a vector by finetuning a pre-trained language model (note that node mapping function is pre-trained the language model itself if no finetuning is required), and ii) the GNN function $\sigma(\cdot)$ to optimize the accuracy of node classification across the set of graphs $\mathcal{G}$.

4.3   GLaM4CM Architecture

We start with a set of Graphs $\mathcal{G} = \{G_1, G_2, \ldots, G_n\}$ as shown in Fig. 2. Next, we extract the node data in the form of node paths and the node stereotype information as described in Sect. 4.1. Then, we prepare the training and testing

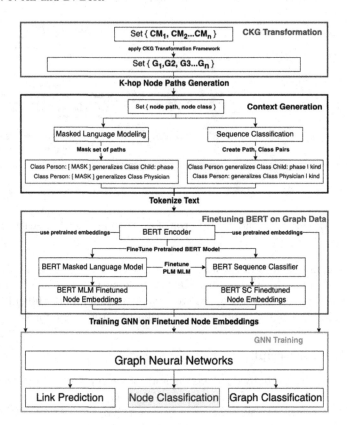

Fig. 2. Graph Language Modeling Framework for Conceptual Models

dataset from the set of node paths and labels for the MLM and SC tasks. We first divide the nodes of each graph into 80% training and 20% test nodes. Note that the path string consists of node stereotype information of the neighboring nodes. Therefore, we only keep the node stereotype information if the context node is in a training set and remove the information if the context node is in a testing set to simulate a graph where 20% of the stereotype labels of a graph are unknown. For example, if in Fig. 1 we treat the "Child" node as a training node and the "Physician" node as a test node, Fig. 1 shows that the node path string of the "Person" node contains the "phase" information for the "Child" class but does not contain the "phase" information for the "Physician" class. In case of the MLM task, we mask the stereotype label of the training node such that the node data forms the format ⟨node type⟩ ⟨node label⟩: ⟨[MASK]⟩ and in case of sequence classification task, we remove the stereotype label from the node path string such that string follows a format ⟨node type⟩ ⟨node label⟩. An example of both formats can be seen in Fig. 2 for the class node "Person".

Once we have the training and testing dataset, a pre-trained BERT model will be finetuned to the MLM and the SC tasks. After finetuning the BERT

Table 1. Stereotypes with a frequency greater than 100

Stereotype	Frequency	Stereotype	Frequency	Stereotype	Frequency
subKind	1522	category	461	derivation	195
kind	1268	event	396	participation	180
mediation	1264	characterization	357	datatype	132
role	1114	roleMixin	346	collective	129
relator	746	mode	333	type	128
material	554	phase	306	quality	128
componentOf	496	formal	272	memberOf	120

model for the MLM task, we can further finetune the BERT MLM model for the same SC task. This can be useful because the MLM task learns the contextual relationships between words in training data sequences and captures how each word relates to the entire sentence, thereby effectively modeling the nuances and subtleties of sequences in the training dataset. Afterward, another model can use this learned knowledge about contextual relationships in the OntoUML dataset to classify the text sequence. However, it is important to note that the effectiveness of using a two-step approach, i.e., first MLM finetuning and then classification, depends on the task and dataset and, therefore, does not guarantee better performance compared to directly using only a BERT for SC. After the finetuning, we can receive the node embeddings from the BERT models. Till now, BERT models were agnostic to the graph structural information of the CKG. Therefore, we now execute a GNN-based node classification using the finetuned BERT node embeddings.

5   Framework Evaluation

We now elaborate the experimental setup to evaluate the ontological stereotype prediction accuracy of GLaM4CM on a partially complete graph, i.e., when a subset of the CKG nodes do not have an OntoUML stereotype label.

5.1   Experimental Set Up

We use the OntoUML models dataset from [4] with 144 models and test our solution for three cases with respect to the number of classes. We select all the stereotypes that occur more than 1000 and 100 times across all the models, which gives us four and 21 stereotypes, respectively (cf. Table 1). We also select the eight stereotypes used by [3] to compare our approach against theirs. In this work, we show the results for 21 stereotypes classification case. Due to lack of space, we provide the complete set of results separately[2].

---

[2] https://bit.ly/onto-stp-cls.

Our framework allows the extraction of node paths from the graph based on the hyperparameter k, which is the maximum number of hops between two nodes. We test our framework with the values $k = 1, 2, 3$. Note that the case $k = 0$ does not use any contextual information. Our framework produces node embeddings from four different models, namely, 1) pre-trained BERT model; 2) finetuned MLM model; 3) finetuned SC model; and 4) finetuned for first MLM and then SC model. Furthermore, we compare the quality of the node embeddings produced by the BERT models in our approach compared to three other GLoVE language models, namely, i) the GLoVE model from [1] trained on OntoUML data; ii) GLoVE model from [19] trained on MDE and conceptual modeling research papers data; and 3) GLoVE model from [9] trained on data from the software engineering domain. We use the generated node embeddings to train a GraphSage GNN model for the node classification task. We test our framework with different hyperparameter values, such as the type of GNN model, the number of GNN layers, and the learning rate (lr). After experimentation, we eventually chose the GraphSage model from [1], two GNN layers, and a $lr = 0.01$ as the best hyperparameter values for training. We perform a five-fold cross-validation to provide robust results.

In our experiments, we test the prediction accuracy of our ML models on the nodes in the test set in each graph for a set of graphs on which ML models are trained. In this configuration, the ML model has seen the graphs during training. However, we also test how well the trained ML model transfers its learning to unseen graphs because even though different OntoUML models may differ in their graph structure and the nodes' data, they may still share some common patterns that an ML model can learn to generalize even to unseen graphs. For example, given a generalization with two specializations like "MedicalProcedure" as a generalization of "RemoteMedicalProdure" and "PresenceMedicalProduce", the generalization can be a "kind" and the specialization can be a "subkind". Therefore, we split our set of 144 graphs into 90% seen and 10% unseen graphs and then calculate the prediction accuracy of the ML model on the test nodes in both seen and unseen graphs. It is important to note that the nomenclature "seen" does not mean the ML model has seen these graphs previously before training. In our experiments, "seen" simply means the graphs used to train the ML models with 80% of nodes as training nodes and 20% nodes as testing nodes.

Lastly, we compare our approach with the most recent existing rule-based inferencing approach [3] which infers the stereotype of the classes in an OntoUML model, given a percentage of classes already labeled. We compare our approach with the same setting of 80% of the nodes already labeled. They present their results in the form of *accuracy@n* metric that evaluates the average number of times the actual class y_i is present in the top-n predicted classes out of all predicted classes $\hat{y}$ for all N nodes defined as Accuracy@n $= \frac{1}{N} \sum_{i=1}^{N} \delta(y_i, \hat{y})$ where $\delta(y_i, \hat{y}) = 1$ if $y_i \in \hat{y}$ and 0 otherwise.

We note that even though we use the same dataset, stereotypes, and percentage of already labeled nodes (80%), a direct comparison has a shortcoming. Due to the unavailability of the information to reproduce the same graphs used in [3], our results hint at the comparative performance of the two approaches. Furthermore, they divide their model files into two sets—one that follows an Open World Assumption (OWA) and the other that follows a Closed World Assumption (CWA)—and provide the accuracy scores for both these approaches. Our approach is independent of such assumptions, and we compare our results with the average score of the two scores provided for both cases in [3].

5.2   Results

Performance on Seen Graphs. For seen graphs, our approaches involving first getting embeddings from MLM and SC finetuning stages and then training a GNN model using these embeddings outperforms the other approaches that involve non-finetuned embeddings (cf. Table 2). The results clearly show the positive impact of using finetuned embeddings on the contextual information available in the node paths. We show the combined importance of contextual information and pre-trained language model finetuning. Adding contextual information in the form of node paths increases the prediction accuracy for all the approaches, including those that do not involve finetuned embeddings—i.e., GLoVE and pre-trained BERT. Moreover, the accuracy of using finetuned embeddings is significantly higher than pre-trained embeddings. Interestingly, the BERT embeddings without finetuning (BERT + GNN) perform worse than embeddings from GLoVE models (SE, Onto, MDE). This result is very much in line with the fact that the pre-trained BERT model does not have any knowledge of OntoUML models' specific knowledge as it is trained on general natural language text. However, we see that finetuning the BERT model for MLM and SC produces rich contextualized embeddings that provide significantly higher accuracy, thereby outperforming the state-of-the-art [1] by more than **25%** (from 57.4% with Onto + GNN and $k = 0$ to 83.1% with SC + GNN and $k = 2$) (Table 3).

Next, we see that using GNNs improves the classification accuracy (cf. Table 2). These results are consistent with the idea that BERT language models learn contextualized node embeddings but do not directly or only implicitly capture graph structural information. In contrast, GNNs can better capture the graph's structural information. Finally, we also note the impact of contextual information in the paths and find that using $k = 2$ provides the best results. The accuracy decreases with $k = 3$, which indicates that for larger values of k, the neighborhood of the majority of the nodes ends up having a lot of common nodes, thereby reducing the distinguishing characteristic of a neighborhood.

Performance on Unseen Graphs. We now evaluate how well the ML models transfer the learning to unseen graphs. In Table 2, the GNN models trained using node embeddings from pre-trained embeddings or GLoVE model embeddings do not generalize well with a maximum accuracy of 48.9%. However, using BERT-based finetuning models improves the prediction accuracy by more than 20%, indicating that the finetuned embeddings generalize much better and capture latent features that support the ML model in predicting the node stereotype.

Table 2. Different models accuracy comparison for top 21 stereotypes

Approach	Test Accuracy Seen				Test Accuracy Unseen			
	k = 0	k = 1	k = 2	k = 3	k = 0	k = 1	k = 2	k = 3
SE [9] + GNN	0.498	0.555	0.553	0.537	0.363	0.435	0.397	0.375
Onto [1] + GNN	0.574	0.634	0.618	0.599	0.356	0.422	0.379	0.356
MDE [19] + GNN	0.563	0.644	0.624	0.597	0.374	0.489	0.446	0.435
BERT + GNN	–	0.401	0.384	0.356	–	0.390	0.363	0.336
SC	–	0.801	0.816	0.792	–	0.646	0.625	0.609
MLM + SC	–	0.814	0.810	0.799	–	**0.656**	**0.636**	**0.634**
SC + GNN	–	**0.815**	**0.831**	**0.817**	–	0.634	0.625	0.621
MLM + SC + GNN	–	**0.827**	**0.822**	**0.813**	–	**0.661**	**0.643**	**0.627**

Table 3. Accuracy comparison with rule-based approach

Approach	accuracy@1	accuracy@2	accuracy@3
Rule-based [3]	0.181	0.303	0.917
SC + GNN	**0.820**	0.917	0.956
MLM + SC + GNN	**0.820**	**0.920**	**0.957**

We note that using GNN models improves the prediction accuracy for unseen graphs. However, the prediction accuracy does not improve as well as they did for seen graphs. Using GNNs with finetuned embeddings for seen graphs increased the prediction accuracy score by almost 2% (from 81.6% by SC and $k = 2$ to 83.1% by SC + GNN and $k = 2$). In contrast, in case of unseen graphs, the prediction accuracy increased by less than 1% in case of $k = 1, 2$ (from 65.6% by MLM + SC and $k = 1$ to 66.1% by MLM + SC + GNN and $k = 1$) and in fact decreased in case of $k = 3$. This result may be because the linguistic semantics are shared more across OntoUML graphs than the graph structural information.

Comparative Evaluation with Rule-Based Inference. Lastly, we compare our approach with the rule-based approach in [3]. We choose the top two best results from all the configurations, and use the GNN-based classification on finetuned embeddings for seen graphs. Our approach significantly outperforms the rule-based approach that predicts the exact stereotype class in 18.1% and has the correct class as one of the top two predicted classes in 30% of the cases. We see that the rule-based approach provides a quite good accuracy@3 score, i.e., the correct stereotype is amongst the top three predicted ones. Overall, we see that our approach outperforms the rule-based approach by more than **60%** in case of accuracy@1 and accuracy@2 and by around 4% in case of accuracy@3.

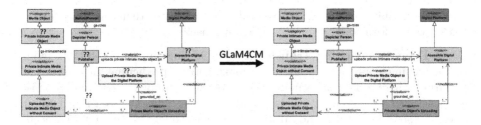

Fig. 3. GLaM4CM-based Ontological Stereotype Prediction Example

6   Discussion

In the following, we aim to discuss our results, the degree of automation provided by our work for modeling, the transferability aspects, i.e., how can a model trained for one domain transfer the learning for a different domain, and finally discuss some further applications of our framework.

Illustrative Example-Based Results Analysis. In Fig. 3, we show how GLaM4CM learned to correctly predict the stereotype from the data itself without the need for any explicit rules to infer the stereotype. The example uses the ontology from [10] that provides an ontological analysis of cyber-security cases. GLaM4CM was able to predict stereotypes accurately, notably identifying the "Upload Private Media Object to Digital Platform" as an "event" and "Accessible Digital Platform" as a "role". The correct "event" prediction could be attributed to the model's understanding of the term "Upload", highlighting the model's capability to recognize patterns beyond frequent stereotypes. Similarly, it distinguished "Accessible Digital Platform" as "role" instead of "subKind" by considering contextual clues from related classes. This indicates the model's ability to learn ontological rules, such as those from OntoUML. The shortcomings of a rule-based approach, as can be seen from our results, are that the rules are hardly exhaustive and, even if the rule-based approach does provide good top-k suggestions, such a benefit is not useful enough. Even if a rule-based approach provides the suggestion for the top 3 possible stereotypes with high confidence, if the confidence on top 1 or top 2 is poor, these suggestions are not quite useful for the domain expert because the expert can, given adequate modeling experience, narrow down on the top-3 with some effort by herself.

Degree of Automation for ODCM. The paper presents a modeling assistant, not for fully automating ODCM research, but as an ontological concept recommender aiding UML modelers in transitioning to OntoUML and assisting OntoUML modelers during model creation. Our approach does not replace the need for domain experts in UML structural class diagram modeling but supports them with recommendations based on data-driven patterns linking natural language to ontological semantics—for instance, identifying "Person" as "kind" and "Student" as "role" relative to "Person". While one could use rules to define these relationships, our comparative evaluation indicates that rule-based methods are outperformed by our data-driven approach.

Cross-Domain Learning Transfer. Despite having only 144 OntoUML models for training, our model's ability to make correct predictions in a zero-shot scenario—where it has not seen an example of the test input—is notably promising, with over 65% accuracy. This is particularly significant given that current research shows industry-standard large language models average 60–75% accuracy in zero-shot generalization across different domains [32,33]. Our approach achieving 65% accuracy aligns with these findings and signals a positive outlook on transferability rather than poor performance. The field is actively developing methods such as fine-tuning [31] and in-context learning [7] to enhance zero-shot generalization, and we plan to integrate these advancements into our approach. We are also confident that, as the adoption of OCDM increases and we get access to more ODCM models, the performance of our approach will even further improve.

Overall, we showed that our GLaM4CM framework combines pre-trained language models to learn contextually rich embeddings of OntoUML model nodes' data. It is important to note that our framework provides flexibility by being usable with *i*) different PLMs like BERT, distill-bert, LSTM, or GPT, among others, *ii*) different GNN models like GCN, GATConv, or GINConv among others, and *iii*) different modeling languages provided a CKG transformation exists as proposed in [2,25].

Further Applications. Although this paper focuses on the accuracy of predicting OntoUML stereotypes using node classification, we want to elaborate on several application areas enabled by our GLaM4CM framework.

AI-Based ODCM. GLaM4CM can be used to predict an ontologically sound metamodel element recommendations given a partially constructed metamodel.

Metamodel Domain Classification. CKG embeddings capture domain information using domain ontologies; therefore, these embeddings can be finetuned for classifying the domain of the metamodel. Metamodel domain classification can further support domain-based clustering of conceptual models.

Semantic Search. Learned representations of conceptual models can directly use the trained embeddings in semantic search for models. Semantic search can provide an efficient way of accessing and searching on and within these models, considering the ontological semantics of the queried model's semantics in search results. This would enable queries like *search all models that use UFO and that have a concept 'professor' with the stereotype 'role' assigned.*

Threats to Validity. Our research is not exempted from the following threats to validity: *Conclusion Validity: Dataset size.* The training dataset for the experiment consists only of 144 OntoUML models. Each model belongs to a specific domain, and the labels consist of domain-specific information, which makes it difficult for the model to learn generalized patterns. We mitigated this by performing a five-fold cross-validation so that the ML models learn general patterns and not domain-specific ones. *Construct Validity: Node Path String Content.* The node path string of a node n contains stereotype information of its neighboring nodes. If the neighboring node of n is a testing node, then the stereotype information of the testing node should not be present in the node path string. We mitigated this threat by adding the stereotype label only if the neighboring node is a training node. *Internal Validity.* The risk of overfitting or suboptimal configuration can impact the internal validity of the findings. Therefore, we performed an exhaustive search for different GNN models, language models, context path lengths, and hyperparameters of GNN models to mitigate these issues. *External Validity.* To enhance the generalizability of the results beyond the specific dataset we used, the approach should be tested on a more diverse set of datasets, potentially including larger graphs with varying characteristics. We aim to explore a more diverse dataset in our future work.

7   Conclusion

In this paper, we presented GLaM4CM, a Graph Language Modeling framework for Conceptual Models and showed its genericity by using different ML models, different extents of contextual information during learning, and combining fine-tuned BERT models with GNN. We used the ontological stereotype prediction task for OntoUML models to experimentally evaluate the prediction accuracy for different configurations that analyze the impact of i) adding contextual information, i.e., neighboring nodes data, ii) the quantity of contextual information, i.e., experimenting with different path lengths with k hops, iii) the language modeling architecture used to capture the natural language features, i.e., pre-trained BERT-based language models and GLoVE models, iv) using GNNs on the learned linguistic features, and, finally, v) using the learned ML models on unseen graphs to evaluate the learning transferred to new graphs. Our extensive evaluation showed that GLaM4CM significantly outperforms other GNN-based and rule-based approaches. In our future work, we aim to explore possibilities to integrate our stereotype predictor into either an existing OntoUML tool (https://ontouml.org/ or a new web-based OntoUML modeling editor by extending the currently developed GLSP-based UML editor [20]. Furthermore, concerning GLaM4CM itself, we aim to apply GLaM4CM on several applications like (meta-)model classification or model completion. We also aim to create an accessible user interface for modelers to plug and play different modeling languages, PLMs or GNN models for different conceptual modeling tasks.

References

1. Ali, S.J., Guizzardi, G., Bork, D.: Enabling representation learning in ontology-driven conceptual modeling using graph neural networks. In: Indulska, M., Reinhartz-Berger, I., Cetina, C., Pastor, O. (eds.) CAiSE 2023. LNCS, vol. 13901, pp. 278–294. Springer, Cham (2023). https://doi.org/10.1007/978-3-031-34560-9_17

2. Ali, S.J., Michael Laranjo, J., Bork, D.: A generic and customizable genetic algorithms-based conceptual model modularization framework. In: Proper, H.A., Pufahl, L., Karastoyanova, D., van Sinderen, M., Moreira, J. (eds.) EDOC 2023. LNCS, vol. 14367, pp. 39–57. Springer, Cham (2024). https://doi.org/10.1007/978-3-031-46587-1_3

3. Barcelos, P., et al.: Inferring ontological categories of owl classes using foundational rules. In: Proceedings of the 13th International Conference on Formal Ontology in Information Systems (2023)

4. Barcelos, P.P.F., et al.: A FAIR model catalog for ontology-driven conceptual modeling research. In: Ralyté, J., Chakravarthy, S., Mohania, M., Jeusfeld, M.A., Karlapalem, K. (eds.) ER 2022. LNCS, vol. 13607, pp. 3–17. Springer, Cham (2022). https://doi.org/10.1007/978-3-031-17995-2_1

5. Borgo, S., et al.: DOLCE: a descriptive ontology for linguistic and cognitive engineering. Appl. Ontol. **17**(1), 45–69 (2022)

6. Chen, J., Hu, P., Jimenez-Ruiz, E., Holter, O.M., Antonyrajah, D., Horrocks, I.: Owl2vec*: embedding of OWL ontologies. Mach. Learn. **110**, 1813–1845 (2021)

7. Coda-Forno, J., Binz, M., Akata, Z., Botvinick, M., Wang, J., Schulz, E.: Meta-in-context learning in large language models. In: Advances in Neural Information Processing Systems, vol. 36 (2024)

8. Devlin, J., Chang, M.W., Lee, K., Toutanova, K.: BERT: pre-training of deep bidirectional transformers for language understanding. arXiv preprint arXiv:1810.04805 (2018)

9. Efstathiou, V., Chatzilenas, C., Spinellis, D.: Word embeddings for the software engineering domain. In: International Conference on Mining Software Repositories, pp. 38–41 (2018)

10. Falduti, M., Griffo, C.: Modeling cybercrime with UFO: an ontological analysis of non-consensual pornography cases. In: Ralyté, J., Chakravarthy, S., Mohania, M., Jeusfeld, M.A., Karlapalem, K. (eds.) ER 2022. LNCS, vol. 13607, pp. 380–394. Springer, Cham (2022). https://doi.org/10.1007/978-3-031-17995-2_27

11. Fonseca, C.M., Porello, D., Guizzardi, G., Almeida, J.P.A., Guarino, N.: Relations in ontology-driven conceptual modeling. In: Laender, A.H.F., Pernici, B., Lim, E.-P., de Oliveira, J.P.M. (eds.) ER 2019. LNCS, vol. 11788, pp. 28–42. Springer, Cham (2019). https://doi.org/10.1007/978-3-030-33223-5_4

12. Grüninger, M., Atefi, K., Fox, M.S.: Ontologies to support process integration in enterprise engineering. Comput. Math. Organ. Theory **6**, 381–394 (2000)

13. Guizzardi, G.: The role of foundational ontologies for conceptual modeling and domain ontology representation. In: 2006 7th International Baltic Conference on Databases and Information Systems, pp. 17–25. IEEE (2006)

14. Guizzardi, G., Prince Sales, T., Almeida, J.P.A., Poels, G.: Relational contexts and conceptual model clustering. In: Grabis, J., Bork, D. (eds.) PoEM 2020. LNBIP, vol. 400, pp. 211–227. Springer, Cham (2020). https://doi.org/10.1007/978-3-030-63479-7_15

15. Hamilton, W., Ying, Z., Leskovec, J.: Inductive representation learning on large graphs. In: Advances in Neural Information Processing Systems, vol. 30 (2017)

16. Junior, A.G.L., Carbonera, J.L., Schimidt, D., Abel, M.: Predicting the top-level ontological concepts of domain entities using word embeddings, informal definitions, and deep learning. Expert Syst. Appl. **203**, 117291 (2022)

17. Keet, C.M., Khan, M.T., Ghidini, C.: Ontology authoring with FORZA. In: Proceedings of the 22nd ACM International Conference on Information & Knowledge Management, pp. 569–578 (2013)

18. Leão, F., Revoredo, K., Baião, F.: Extending wordnet with UFO foundational ontology. J. Web Semant. **57**, 100499 (2019)
19. López, J.A.H., Durá, C., Cuadrado, J.S.: Word embeddings for model-driven engineering. In: ACM/IEEE 26th International Conference on Model Driven Engineering Languages and Systems (MODELS) (2023)
20. Metin, H., Bork, D.: Introducing bigUML: a flexible open-source GLSP-based web modeling tool for UML. In: Companion Proceedings of MODELS 2023. IEEE (2023)
21. Moody, D.L.: Theoretical and practical issues in evaluating the quality of conceptual models: current state and future directions. Data Knowl. Eng. **55**(3), 243–276 (2005)
22. Pennington, J., Socher, R., Manning, C.D.: Glove: global vectors for word representation. In: Empirical Methods in NLP, pp. 1532–1543 (2014)
23. Ristoski, P., Rosati, J., Di Noia, T., De Leone, R., Paulheim, H.: RDF2Vec: RDF graph embeddings and their applications. Semant. Web **10**(4), 721–752 (2019)
24. Sequeda, J., Lassila, O.: Designing and building enterprise knowledge graphs. Synth. Lectures Data Semant. Knowl. **11**(1), 1–165 (2021)
25. Smajevic, M., Bork, D.: Towards graph-based analysis of enterprise architecture models. In: Ghose, A., Horkoff, J., Silva Souza, V.E., Parsons, J., Evermann, J. (eds.) ER 2021. LNCS, vol. 13011, pp. 199–209. Springer, Cham (2021). https://doi.org/10.1007/978-3-030-89022-3_17
26. Sun, S., Meng, F., Chu, D.: A model driven approach to constructing knowledge graph from relational database. In: Journal of Physics: Conference Series, vol. 1584, p. 012073. IOP Publishing (2020)
27. Trojahn, C., Vieira, R., Schmidt, D., Pease, A., Guizzardi, G.: Foundational ontologies meet ontology matching: a survey. Semant. Web **13**(4), 685–704 (2022)
28. Vaswani, A., et al.: Attention is all you need. In: Advances in Neural Information Processing Systems, vol. 30 (2017)
29. Verdonck, M., Gailly, F., Pergl, R., Guizzardi, G., Martins, B., Pastor, O.: Comparing traditional conceptual modeling with ontology-driven conceptual modeling: an empirical study. Inf. Syst. **81**, 92–103 (2019)
30. Wand, Y., Weber, R.: Research commentary: information systems and conceptual modeling—a research agenda. Inf. Syst. Res. **13**(4), 363–376 (2002)
31. Wei, J., et al.: Finetuned language models are zero-shot learners. arXiv preprint arXiv:2109.01652 (2021)
32. Yang, H., Zhang, Y., Xu, J., Lu, H., Heng, P.A., Lam, W.: Unveiling the generalization power of fine-tuned large language models. arXiv preprint arXiv:2403.09162 (2024)
33. Zhang, X., et al.: On the out-of-distribution generalization of multimodal large language models. arXiv preprint arXiv:2402.06599 (2024)

PGTNet: A Process Graph Transformer Network for Remaining Time Prediction of Business Process Instances

Keyvan Amiri Elyasi[1]([✉]) [iD], Han van der Aa[2] [iD], and Heiner Stuckenschmidt[1] [iD]

[1] Data and Web Science Group, University of Mannheim, Mannheim, Germany
{keyvan,heiner}@informatik.uni-mannheim.de
[2] Faculty of Computer Science, University of Vienna, Vienna, Austria
han.van.der.aa@univie.ac.at

Abstract. We present PGTNet, an approach that transforms event logs into graph datasets and leverages graph-oriented data for training Process Graph Transformer Networks to predict the remaining time of business process instances. PGTNet consistently outperforms state-of-the-art deep learning approaches across a diverse range of 20 publicly available real-world event logs. Notably, our approach is most promising for highly complex processes, where existing deep learning approaches encounter difficulties stemming from their limited ability to learn control-flow relationships among process activities and capture long-range dependencies. PGTNet addresses these challenges, while also being able to consider multiple process perspectives during the learning process.

Keywords: Predictive process monitoring · Remaining time prediction · Deep learning · Graph Transformers

1 Introduction

Predictive process monitoring (PPM) aims to forecast the future behaviour of running business process instances, thereby enabling organizations to optimize their resource allocation and planning [17], as well as take corrective actions [7]. An important task in PPM is remaining time prediction, which strives to accurately predict the time until an active process instance will be completed. Precise estimations for remaining time are crucial for avoiding deadline violations, optimizing operational efficiency, and providing estimates to customers [13,17].

A variety of approaches have been developed to tackle remaining time prediction, with recent works primarily being based on deep learning architectures. In this regard, approaches using deep neural networks are among the most prominent ones [15]. However, the predictive accuracy of these networks leaves considerable room for improvement. In particular, they face challenges when it comes to capturing long-range dependencies [2] and other control-flow relationships (such as loops and parallelism) between process activities [22], whereas they also struggle to harness information from additional process perspectives, such

G. Guizzardi et al. (Eds.): CAiSE 2024, LNCS 14663, pp. 124–140, 2024.
https://doi.org/10.1007/978-3-031-61057-8_8

as case and event attributes [13]. Other architectures can overcome some of these individual challenges. For instance, the Transformer architecture can learn long-range dependencies [2], graph neural networks (GNNs) can explicitly incorporate control-flow structures into the learning process [22], and LSTM (long short-term memory) architectures can be used to incorporate (parts of) the data perspective [13]. However, so far, no deep learning approach can effectively deal with all of these challenges simultaneously.

Therefore, this paper introduces PGTNet, a novel approach for remaining time prediction that can tackle all these challenges at once. Specifically, our approach converts event data into a graph-oriented representation, which allows us to subsequently employ a neural network based on the general, powerful, scalable (GPS) Graph Transformer architecture [16] to make predictions. Graph Transformers (GTs) have shown impressive performance in various graph regression tasks [4,10,16] and their theoretical expressive power closely aligns with our objectives: they can deal with multi-perspective data (covering various process perspectives) and can effectively capture long-range dependencies and recognize local control-flow structures. GTs achieve these latter benefits through a combination of local message-passing neural networks (MPNNs) [6] and a global attention mechanism [18]. They employ sparse message-passing within their GNN blocks to learn local control-flow relationships among process activities, while their Transformer blocks attend to all events in the running process instance to capture the global context.

We evaluated the effectiveness of PGTNet for remaining time prediction using 20 publicly available real event logs. Our experiments show that our approach outperforms current state-of-the-art deep learning approaches in terms of accuracy and earliness of predictions. We also investigated the relationship between process complexity and the performance of PGTNet, which revealed that our approach particularly achieved superior predictive performance (compared to existing approaches) for highly complex, flexible processes.

The structure of the paper is outlined as follows: Sect. 2 covers background and related work, Sect. 3 presents preliminary concepts, Sect. 4 introduces our proposed approach for remaining time prediction, Sect. 5 discusses the experimental setup and key findings, and finally, Sect. 6 summarizes our contributions and suggests future research directions.

2   Background and Related Work

This section briefly discusses related work on remaining time prediction and provides more details on Graph Transformers.

Remaining Time Prediction. Various approaches have been proposed for remaining time prediction, encompassing process-aware approaches relying on transition systems, stochastic Petri Nets, and queuing models, along with machine learning-based approaches [20]. In recent years, approaches based on deep learning have emerged as the foremost methods for predicting remaining time [15]. These approaches use different neural network architectures such as LSTMs [13,17], Transformers [2], and GNNs [3].

Vector embedding and feature vectors, constituting the data inputs for Transformers and LSTMs, face a challenge in directly integrating control-flow relationships into the learning process. To overcome this constraint, event logs can be converted into graph data, which then acts as input for training a Graph Neural Network (GNN) [22]. GNNs effectively incorporate control-flow structures by aligning the computation graph with input data. Nevertheless, they suffer from over-smoothing and over-squashing problems [10], sharing similarities with LSTMs in struggling to learn long-range dependencies [16]. Moreover, existing graph-based predictive models face limitations due to the expressive capacity of their graph-oriented data inputs. Current graph representations of business process instances, either focus solely on the control-flow perspective [7,19] or conceptualize events as nodes [3,22], leading to a linear graph structure that adversely impacts the performance of a downstream GNN.

Graph Transformers. Inspired by the successful application of self-attention mechanism in natural language processing, two distinct solutions have emerged to address the limitations of GNNs. The first approach unifies GNN and Transformer modules in a single architecture, while the second compresses the graph structure into positional (PE) and structural (SE) embeddings. These embeddings are then added to the input before feeding it into the Transformer network [16]. Collectively known as Graph Transformers (GTs), both solutions aim to overcome the limitations of GNNs, by enabling information propagation across the graph through full connectivity [10,16]. GTs also possess greater expressive power compared to conventional Transformers, as they can incorporate local context using sparse information obtained from the graph structure [4].

Building upon this theoretical foundation, we propose to convert event logs into graph datasets to enable remaining time prediction using a Process Graph Transformer Network (PGTNet), as discussed in the remainder.

3   Preliminaries

This section presents essential concepts that will be used in the remainder.

Directed and Attributed Graphs. A directed graph $G = (V, \mathcal{E})$ is defined by a set of nodes V, and a set of ordered pairs of nodes $\mathcal{E} \subseteq V \times V$ called directed edges. For an edge $\epsilon_{ij} = (v_i, v_j) \in \mathcal{E}$ pointing from v_i to v_j, nodes $v_i \in V$ and $v_j \in V$ are called source and target nodes, respectively. Setting $n = |V|$, G's adjacency matrix A is a $n \times n$ matrix with $A_{ij} = 1$ if $\epsilon_{ij} \in \mathcal{E}$ and $A_{ij} = 0$ if $\epsilon_{ij} \notin \mathcal{E}$. An attributed graph is a graph that has node attributes in the form of a node feature matrix $X \in R^{n \times d}$, with $x_v \in R^d$ representing the feature vector of node v. It may also have edge attributes in the form of $\mathcal{Z} \in R^{m \times c}$, where $m = |\mathcal{E}|$ is the number of edges, and $z_{u,v} \in R^c$ denotes the feature vector of edge (u, v).

Events. Let Γ be the event universe (i.e., set of all possible event identifiers), $\mathcal{T}$ the time domain, $\mathcal{A}$ the finite set of process activities, $\mathcal{C}$ the set of all possible case identifiers, and $V_1, V_2, ..., V_m$ sets of all possible values for data attributes

$d_1, d_2, ..., d_m$. An event e is denoted by the tuple $e = (a, c, t, D)$. We assume that every event is characterized by mandatory properties, namely an activity identifier, a case identifier (i.e., the business process instance which the event belongs to), and a timestamp. Put it differently, there are $\Pi_A : \Gamma \to \mathcal{A}$, $\Pi_C : \Gamma \to \mathcal{C}$, and $\Pi_T : \Gamma \to \mathcal{T}$ functions that map an event e to an activity, a case, and a timestamp: $\Pi_A(e) = a$, $\Pi_C(e) = c$, $\Pi_T(e) = t$. All other attribute-value pairs (e.g., transition life-cycle, organizational attributes, etc.) which may be associated to the event are denoted by $D \equiv \{(d_1, v_1), (d_2, v_2), ..., (d_m, v_m)\}$ where $\forall v_i \in V_i$. Similar projection functions can be defined to extract values of specific attributes out of an event (e.g., $\Pi_{d_i}(e) = v_i$).

Traces, Event Log, Event Prefixes. Let Γ^* be the set of all possible sequences over Γ. A finite non-empty sequence of events $\sigma = <e_1, e_2, ..., e_n> \in \Gamma^*$, of length $|\sigma| = n$, is called a trace only and only if: 1) $\forall e_i, e_j \in \sigma : \pi_C(e_i) = \pi_C(e_j)$ (i.e., all events belong to the same case), 2) $\forall 1 \leq i \leq j \leq n : \pi_T(e_i) \leq \pi_T(e_j)$ (i.e., the events are ordered by their timestamps). Each trace thus represents the execution of one business process instance. An event log refers to a collection of traces and is denoted as $L \subseteq \Gamma^*$, where every event appears only once within the entirety of the log. For the remaining time prediction problem, we also need to define partial traces, which we do through event prefixes. An event prefix of length k consists of the first k events of a trace and is denoted by $hd^k(\sigma) = <e_1, ..., e_k>$, where $k \in [1, n-1]$ is a positive integer number.

Problem Statement. Given an event log L of completed traces and an event prefix $hd^k(\sigma)$ of a trace $\sigma = <e_1, e_2, ..., e_n>$, where $\sigma \notin L$ is an unseen trace of the same process as the traces of L, then the remaining time prediction problem is defined as using the traces from L to learn a function θ_L that takes an unseen event prefix $hd^k(\sigma)$ and estimates the remaining time of the corresponding business process instance:

$$\theta_L(hd^k(\sigma)) \approx \pi_T(e_n) - \pi_T(e_k) \tag{1}$$

4   PGTNet for Remaining Time Prediction

To predict the remaining time of business process instances, we convert an event log into a graph dataset (see Sect. 4.1), and use it to train a predictive model (see Sect. 4.2). Once the model's parameters are learned, we can query the model to predict the remaining time of an active process instance based on its current partial trace.

4.1   Graph Representation of Event Prefixes

To train a predictive model, we first turn an event log L (consisting of traces of completed process instances) into a collection of event prefix-time tuples, with each tuple $(hd^k(\sigma), \pi_T(e_n) - \pi_T(e_k))$ capturing an event prefix of length k of a trace $\sigma \in L$, along with the time difference between σ's final timestamp and the last timestamp of $hd^k(\sigma)$. Then, we establish a collection of directed attributed graphs $\mathcal{G}$, where each graph $G_{hd^k(\sigma)} \in \mathcal{G}$ encodes an event prefix $hd^k(\sigma)$, with its target attribute $\pi_T(e_n) - \pi_T(e_k)$. This transformation is illustrated in Fig. 1, displaying a snapshot of an event log for case ID '27583' and the corresponding graph representation of the event prefix of a length of 6. The details of this transformation procedure are as follows:

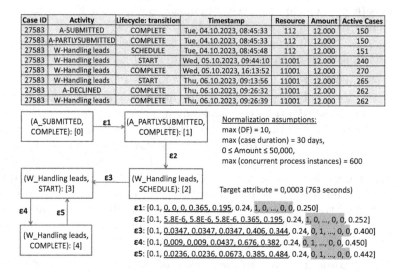

Case ID	Activity	Lifecycle: transition	Timestamp	Resource	Amount	Active Cases
27583	A-SUBMITTED	COMPLETE	Tue, 04.10.2023, 08:45:33	112	12.000	150
27583	A-PARTLYSUBMITTED	COMPLETE	Tue, 04.10.2023, 08:45:33	112	12.000	150
27583	W-Handling leads	SCHEDULE	Tue, 04.10.2023, 08:45:48	112	12.000	151
27583	W-Handling leads	START	Wed, 05.10.2023, 09:44:10	11001	12.000	240
27583	W-Handling leads	COMPLETE	Wed, 05.10.2023, 16:13:52	11001	12.000	270
27583	W-Handling leads	START	Thu, 06.10.2023, 09:13:56	11001	12.000	265
27583	A-DECLINED	COMPLETE	Thu, 06.10.2023, 09:26:32	11001	12.000	262
27583	W-Handling leads	COMPLETE	Thu, 06.10.2023, 09:26:39	11001	12.000	262

(A_SUBMITTED, COMPLETE): [0] —ε1→ (A_PARTLYSUBMITTED, COMPLETE): [1]

ε2

(W_Handling leads, START): [3] —ε3→ (W_Handling leads, SCHEDULE): [2]

ε4   ε5

(W_Handling leads, COMPLETE): [4]

Normalization assumptions:
max (DF) = 10,
max (case duration) = 30 days,
$0 \leq$ Amount $\leq 50{,}000$,
max (concurrent process instances) = 600

Target attribute = 0,0003 (763 seconds)

ε1: [0.1, 0, 0, 0, 0.365, 0.195, 0.24, 1, 0, ..., 0, 0, 0.250]
ε2: [0.1, 5.8E-6, 5.8E-6, 5.8E-6, 0.365, 0.195, 0.24, 1, 0, ..., 0, 0, 0.252]
ε3: [0.1, 0.0347, 0.0347, 0.0347, 0.406, 0.344, 0.24, 0, 1, ..., 0, 0, 0.400]
ε4: [0.1, 0.009, 0.009, 0.0437, 0.676, 0.382, 0.24, 0, 1, ..., 0, 0, 0.450]
ε5: [0.1, 0.0236, 0.0236, 0.0673, 0.385, 0.484, 0.24, 0, 1, ..., 0, 0, 0.442]

Fig. 1. Graph representation of an event prefix of length of 6, Case ID = '27583'.

Nodes. We create a node in $G_{hd^k(\sigma)}$ for each event class, i.e., each unique combination of an activity and life-cycle attribute (if any) contained in prefix $hd^k(\sigma)$. Each node has a numeric identifier, such as ('A-SUBMITTED', 'COMPLETE'): [0] in Fig. 1. Using event classes as graph nodes results in graphs with relatively few nodes, even for lengthy prefixes.

Edges and Edge Weights. We create an edge in $G_{hd^k(\sigma)}$ for each directly-follows (DF) relation in $hd^k(\sigma)$, while the edge's weight indicates the number of its occurrences within $hd^k(\sigma)$. These edge weights are normalized by the maximum number of occurrences of any directly-follows relation within the available training prefixes. In Fig. 1, this normalization coefficient (max(DF)) is equal to 10, resulting in edge weights of 0.1 (the first feature in the edge's vector).

Edge Features. To enhance the expressive capacity of the graph representation, we incorporate additional features into the edge feature vector:

- We use five different temporal features per edge. These include the total duration (t_1) and duration of the last occurrence (t_2) of the DF relation represented by the edge. Similar to other works [17], we also incorporate distances between the timestamp of the target node and the start of the case (t_3), start of the day (t_4), and start of the week (t_5) for the latest occurrence of the DF relation. While t_1, t_2, and t_3 are normalized by the largest case duration in the training data, t_4 and t_5 are normalized by the duration of days and weeks, respectively. In Fig. 1, the temporal features are underlined in the feature vectors of the edges.

- We encode case attributes and event attributes of the target node (for the last occurrence of the DF relation in $hd^k(\sigma)$). For numerical and categorical attributes, we use min-max normalization and one-hot encoding, respectively. In Fig. 1, one-hot encoding of the categorical attribute 'Resource' is highlighted with a grey shadow, while the feature before this gray part (always 0.24 in the example) captures the case attribute 'Amount'.
- To account for the overall workload of the process at a given time, we capture the number of active cases at the timestamp of the target node (for the last occurrence of the DF relation). This feature is normalized by the maximum number of concurrent process instances observed in the training data.

Note that we encode this information as edge features, rather than on the nodes, in order to preserve the simplicity of the node semantics. In this way, PGTNet can also deal with event logs with a large number of event classes, achieved by employing an embedding layer.

Target Attribute. For each graph $G_{hd^k(\sigma)} \in \mathcal{G}$, its target attribute $\pi_T(e_n) - \pi_T(e_k)$ is normalized by the longest case duration in the training data.

4.2   Training PGTNet to Predict Remaining Time

Once an event log is converted into a graph dataset, it can be used to train PGTNet to learn function θ_L in Eq. 1 in an end-to-end manner. We specifically approach the remaining time prediction problem as a graph regression task, using L1-Loss (mean absolute error between predictions and ground truth remaining times). Model training employs the backpropagation algorithm to iteratively minimize the loss function. For this, we adopt the GPS Graph Transformer recipe [16] as the underlying architecture of PGTNet.

PGTNet Architecture. PGTNet's architecture comprises embedding and processing modules, as shown in Fig. 2.

Embedding modules have two main functionalities:

- They map node and edge features into continuous spaces. To ensure that similar event classes are closer in the embedding space, an embedding layer is used to map integer node features into a continuous space. We use fully-connected layer(s) to compress edge features into the same hidden dimension and address the challenges arising from high-dimensional data attributes.
- They compress the graph structure into multiple positional and structural encodings (PE/SE), and seamlessly incorporate these PE/SEs into node and edge features [16]. This integration is achieved through diverse PE/SE initialization strategies and the utilization of several learnable modules, including MLPs (multi-layer perceptron) and batch normalization layers, as illustrated in Fig. 2.

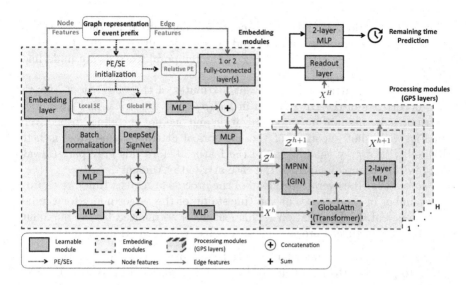

Fig. 2. PGTNet architecture: based on the GPS Graph Transformer recipe [16]. Paths to process node and edge features are specified by blue and red colors, respectively. (Color figure online)

Assuming a graph $G = (V, E)$ with adjacency matrix A, node feature matrix $\tilde{X}^0$, and edge feature matrix $\tilde{Z}^0$, embedding modules are described by Eq. 2.

$$X^0, Z^0 = \mathbf{f}_{PE/SE}(\tilde{X}^0, \tilde{Z}^0, A) \tag{2}$$

Graph Transformers vary in their choice of function $\mathbf{f}_{PE/SE}$, which is often a neural network with learnable parameters. Further insights into the PE/SEs is provided in the subsequent discussion of the design space for PGTNet.

Processing modules consist of hybrid layers combining MPNN and Transformer blocks. Each of the H layers, also referred to as GPS layers, computes a hidden representation of nodes and edges (X^{h+1}, Z^{h+1}) based on the node and edge embedding from the previous layer (X^h, Z^h), and the adjacency matrix A, as summarized in Eqs. 3a, 3b, 3c, and 3d below. Parallel computations in MPNN and Transformer blocks aim to strike a balance between local message passing and global attention mechanisms and resolve over-smoothing and over-squashing problems [16].

$$X^{h+1}, Z^{h+1} = GPS^h(X^h, Z^h, A) \quad \forall h \in \{0, 1, ..., H-1\} \tag{3a}$$

$$X_M^{h+1}, Z^{h+1} = MPNN^h(X^h, Z^h, A) \quad \forall h \in \{0, 1, ..., H-1\} \tag{3b}$$

$$X_T^{h+1} = GlobalAttn^h(X^h) \quad \forall h \in \{0, 1, ..., H-1\} \tag{3c}$$

$$X^{h+1} = MLP^h(X_M^{h+1} + X_T^{h+1}) \quad \forall h \in \{0, 1, ..., H-1\} \tag{3d}$$

After obtaining node embeddings X^H from the last GPS layer, they are aggregated in the readout layer to derive a graph-level representation that is subsequently fed into a 2-layer MLP to predict the remaining time (see Eq. 4). Since a simple permutation invariant function (e.g., mean or sum) is used for the readout function in Eq. 4, the readout layer accommodates varying node counts. Therefore, PGTNet avoids the need for zero-padding [2,13] and its computational overhead.

$$y_G = MLP(readout(X^H))$$ (4)

Note that edge features are solely processed by MPNN blocks and are not utilized by Transformer blocks or in obtaining the graph-level representation.

Design Space for PGTNet. The modular design of the GPS Graph Transformer recipe offers flexibility in choosing various types of positional/structural encodings (PE/SEs) and MPNN/Transformer blocks.

PE/SEs aim to enhance positional encoding for Transformer blocks [10], and enable GNN blocks to be more expressive [4]. The compression of graph structure into PE/SEs can be achieved through the utilization of various initialization strategies (PE/SE initialization in Fig. 2). Notably, Laplacian eigenvector encodings (LapPE) [10] furnishes node embedding with information about the overall position of the event class within the event prefix (global PE), while it enhances edge embedding with information on distance and directional relationships between nodes (relative PE). Random-walk structural encoding (RWSE) [4] incorporates local SE into node features, facilitating the recognition of cyclic control-flow patterns among event classes. Graphormer employs a combination of centrality encoding (local SE) and edge encoding (relative PE) to enhance both node and edge features [24].

Additionally, a range of learnable modules for processing PE/SEs can be integrated into PGTNet as highlighted in [16]. These design options include simple MLPs as well as more advanced networks such as DeepSet [25] and SignNet [11]. Lastly, while it is possible to use various MPNN and global attention blocks within each GPS layer [16], we exclusively used the graph isomorphism network (GIN) [9] and conventional transformer architecture [18]. Further details regarding our policy for designing PGTNet are elaborated upon in Sect. 5.1.

5   Evaluation

This section presents the experiments used to evaluate the performance of PGTNet for remaining time prediction. Table 1 summarizes the characteristics of the 20 publicly available event logs used as a basis for this. In the remainder, Sect. 5.1 describes the experimental setup, followed by the results in Sect. 5.2. Our employed implementation and additional results are available in our project's public repository.[1]

---

[1] https://github.com/keyvan-amiri/PGTNet.

Table 1. Characteristics of the employed event logs (time-related attributes in days).

Event log	Cases	Events	Event Classes	Variants	Case length		Case duration	
					Avg.	Max	Avg.	Max
Env.permit	1434	8577	27	116	5.98	25	5.4	275.8
Helpdesk	4580	21348	14	226	4.66	15	40.9	60.0
BPIC12	13087	262200	36	4366	20.04	175	8.6	137.2
BPIC12W	9658	170107	19	2643	17.61	156	11.7	137.2
BPIC12C	13087	164506	23	4336	12.57	96	8.6	91.5
BPIC12CW	9658	72413	6	2263	7.50	74	11.4	91.0
BPIC12O	5015	31244	7	168	6.23	30	17.2	89.6
BPIC12A	13087	60849	10	17	4.65	8	8.1	91.5
BPIC20I	6449	72151	34	753	11.19	27	86.5	742.0
BPIC20D	10500	56437	17	99	5.37	24	11.5	469.2
Sepsis	1050	15214	16	846	14.49	185	28.5	422.3
Hospital	100000	451359	18	1020	4.51	217	127.2	1035.4
BPIC15-1	1199	52217	398	1170	43.55	101	95.9	1486.0
BPIC15-2	832	44354	410	828	53.31	131	160.3	1326.0
BPIC15-3	1409	59681	383	1349	42.36	123	62.2	1512.0
BPIC15-4	1053	47293	356	1049	44.91	115	116.9	927.0
BPIC15-5	1156	59083	389	1153	51.11	153	98.0	1344.0
BPIC13I	7554	65533	13	2278	8.68	123	12.1	771.4
BPIC13C	1487	6660	7	327	4.48	35	178.9	2254.0
Traffic fines	150370	561470	11	231	3.73	20	341.6	4372.0

5.1 Experimental Setup

Data Preprocessing. We filter out traces with fewer than 3 events, since our approach requires an event prefix of at least length 2 to make a prediction. Aside from that, we do not apply any preprocessing to the available event logs.

Benchmark Approaches. We compare our approach against four others:

- *DUMMY*: A simple baseline that predicts the average remaining time of all training prefixes with the same length k as a given prefix.
- *DALSTM* [13]: An LSTM-based approach that was recently shown to have superior results among LSTMs used for remaining time prediction [15].
- *ProcessTransformer* [2]: A transformer-based approach designed to overcome LSTM's limitations in capturing long-range dependencies.
- *GGNN* [3]: An approach that utilizes gated graph neural networks to incorporate control-flow relationships into the learning process. It employs gated recurrent unit (GRU) within its MPNN layers, enabling the learning of the sequential nature of graph nodes.

Data Split. There is no consensus on the data split for predictive process monitoring. Some papers employed a chronological holdout split [2,17], while others opted for cross-validation [5,14,15]. The holdout split maintains chronological order but may introduce instability due to end-of-dataset bias. To avoid such instability, additional data preprocessing, as suggested by [23], is necessary.

As our benchmark approaches were not trained with such preprocessing, we avoided additional steps and chose a 5-fold cross-validation data split (CV = 5) to enhance model's robustness against the end-of-dataset bias. We randomly partition the dataset into 5 folds where each fold serves as a test set once, and the remaining four folds are used as training and validation sets. For completeness, we also report results obtained using holdout data splits in our supplementary GitHub repository.

Prefix Establishment. We turn the three sets of traces (training, validation, and test) into three sets of event prefixes by taking the event prefixes for each length $1 < k < |\sigma|$ per trace. In contrast to [2,13], we excluded event prefixes of length 1 because a minimum of two events is required to form the graph representation of an event prefix. Moreover, similar to [13], we excluded complete prefixes (i.e., $k = |\sigma|$) because predicting the remaining time for such prefixes often lacks practical value.

Training Setup and Configuration Choices. We used the AdamW optimizer [12] and cosine with warm-up learning rate scheduling [8] to train our model. Training spanned 600 epochs, including 50 warm-up epochs, with a base learning rate of 0.001 and weight decay of e^{-5}. We used a batch size of 128, with occasional adjustments for specific event logs. Similarly, the number of training epochs is adjusted to account for variations in validation loss behaviours across different event logs. The key configuration choices in our experiments include:

- *PE/SE modules:* LapPE+RWSE [4,10] serves as the default module, occasionally substituted by Graphormer [24]. By default, DeepSet [25] processes PE/SEs, with SignNet [11] replacing LapPE+RWSE and DeepSet in some experiments. PE/SEs are tested in two sizes: 8 and 16.
- *Embedding modules:* Nodes and edges use an embedding size of 64. Edge features are compressed using two fully-connected layers, though in some experiments we opt for a single layer.
- *Processing modules:* comprising 5 GPS layers (GIN + Transformer) [16] with 8 heads, utilizing a dropout of 0.0 for MPNN blocks and 0.5 for Transformer blocks. In some experiments, we used 10 GPS layers with 4 heads instead, while in others we applied a dropout of 0.2 for MPNN blocks.
- *Readout layer:* Mean pooling is the default configuration, occasionally replaced by sum pooling.

Our focus is on demonstrating PGTNet's applicability for remaining time prediction rather than an exhaustive hyperparameter search. Therefore, we evaluated a limited set of configurations per log, selecting the best based on validation loss.

Evaluation Metrics. We used Mean Absolute Error (MAE) to measure prediction accuracy. Since we are interested in models that not only have smaller

MAE but also can make accurate predictions earlier, allowing more time for corrective actions, we used the method proposed in [17], which evaluates MAE across different event prefix lengths. This approach provides insights into the predictive performance of the model as more events arrive.

5.2   Results

Overall Results. Table 2 summarizes the experimental results for the 20 event logs, providing the average and standard deviations of the MAEs obtained over experiments with three distinct, random seeds for training and evaluation. The table shows that our approach consistently outperforms the benchmark approaches across the 20 event logs, yielding an average MAE of 12.92, compared to 24.63 for the next best approach (GGNN).

Table 2. Mean Absolute Error for remaining time prediction (MAE: in days).

Event log	DUMMY	DALSTM	Process Transformer	GGNN	PGTNet
Env.permit	5.21	3.36 ± 0.04	4.26 ± 0.04	3.52 ± 0.02	$\mathbf{2.72 \pm 0.08}$
Helpdesk	9.15	8.22 ± 0.23	6.33 ± 0.01	6.21 ± 0.04	$\mathbf{4.11 \pm 0.04}$
BPIC12	9.03	9.34 ± 0.41	7.11 ± 0.02	4.78 ± 0.01	$\mathbf{2.31 \pm 0.19}$
BPIC12W	9.16	8.22 ± 0.06	7.40 ± 0.01	5.12 ± 0.02	$\mathbf{2.70 \pm 0.01}$
BPIC12C	8.92	8.21 ± 0.27	6.86 ± 0.01	5.32 ± 0.01	$\mathbf{2.77 \pm 0.02}$
BPIC12CW	9.17	8.04 ± 0.09	7.46 ± 0.01	6.99 ± 0.01	$\mathbf{5.07 \pm 0.03}$
BPIC12O	8.39	8.21 ± 0.09	7.29 ± 0.01	6.93 ± 0.04	$\mathbf{5.57 \pm 0.01}$
BPIC12A	8.17	7.62 ± 0.03	7.79 ± 0.01	7.48 ± 0.01	$\mathbf{7.38 \pm 0.01}$
BPIC20I	27.20	20.43 ± 0.39	17.06 ± 0.11	15.67 ± 0.04	$\mathbf{7.67 \pm 0.19}$
BPIC20D	4.33	4.15 ± 0.12	3.65 ± 0.01	3.25 ± 0.01	$\mathbf{3.10 \pm 0.01}$
Sepsis	41.12	25.21 ± 0.66	34.77 ± 0.18	19.44 ± 0.05	$\mathbf{16.48 \pm 0.19}$
Hospital	59.41	43.66 ± 0.10	47.00 ± 0.07	41.84 ± 0.06	$\mathbf{35.68 \pm 0.03}$
BPIC15-1	50.22	36.48 ± 2.69	31.01 ± 0.36	16.77 ± 0.01	$\mathbf{1.76 \pm 0.06}$
BPIC15-2	83.11	63.66 ± 2.36	44.04 ± 0.48	20.76 ± 0.05	$\mathbf{3.02 \pm 0.07}$
BPIC15-3	28.76	17.69 ± 1.16	15.23 ± 0.23	7.06 ± 0.03	$\mathbf{1.54 \pm 0.23}$
BPIC15-4	56.75	53.33 ± 2.63	34.40 ± 0.42	17.97 ± 0.03	$\mathbf{1.65 \pm 0.06}$
BPIC15-5	45.97	42.89 ± 3.08	27.76 ± 0.28	13.61 ± 0.08	$\mathbf{1.61 \pm 0.01}$
BPIC13I	16.18	7.60 ± 0.45	13.54 ± 0.04	11.99 ± 0.04	$\mathbf{2.23 \pm 0.05}$
BPIC13C	152.93	91.82 ± 1.48	127.01 ± 0.85	123.28 ± 0.53	$\mathbf{37.44 \pm 1.49}$
Traffic fines	196.26	187.41 ± 0.53	187.08 ± 0.11	154.56 ± 0.19	$\mathbf{113.53 \pm 0.12}$
Average	41.47	32.78 ± 0.84	31.85 ± 0.16	24.63 ± 0.06	$\mathbf{12.92 \pm 0.14}$

Next to these absolute MAE scores, we also computed the relative MAE (i.e., the MAE divided by the average case duration per log) to account for differences in the cycle times across event logs. Using these relative scores, we can visualize

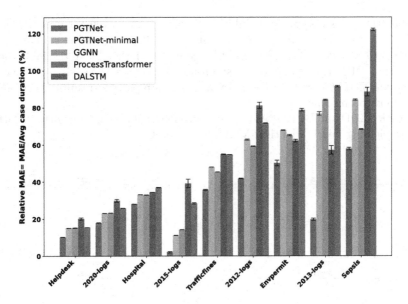

Fig. 3. Remaining time prediction accuracy in terms of relative MAE (in percentage).

the accuracy improvements across different logs, as done in Fig. 3 (for clarity, we aggregated the results of logs that stem from the same BPI collection, e.g., averaging the results of all BPIC15 logs).

PGTNet also excels in earliness of predictions, achieving lower MAE for most prefix lengths across all event logs. We illustrate some of these results in Fig. 4, which depicts MAE trends for BPIC15-1, BPIC12, BPIC13I, Sepsis, Helpdesk, and BPIC12A logs at various prefix lengths. These six logs are representative of major MAE trends that we observed across the 20 event logs (the remaining figures are available in our repository). To improve understandability, we exclude uncommonly long prefixes from the visualization, so that Fig. 4 focuses on prefixes up to a length that corresponds to 90% of all prefixes in each dataset.

Summarizing the overall results in terms of MAE, relative MAE, and prediction earliness, we obtain the following main insights:

– In 11 out of 20 logs, PGTNet achieves an MAE improvement of over 50% compared to the best baseline approach. For five BPIC15 and two BPIC13 logs, MAE trends closely mirror those of BPIC15-1 and BPIC13I as depicted in Fig. 4. In BPIC12, BPIC12W, BPIC12C, and BPIC20I, the MAE trends closely follow those observed in BPIC12. In BPIC15 and BPIC12 logs, ProcessTransformer is the best baseline approach for short prefixes, whereas GGNN exhibits competitive performance only after execution of a substantial number of events. Notably, in the BPICS13 event logs, DALSTM outperforms other baseline approaches.

- In another 7 logs, PGTNet exhibits considerable improvement in MAE (15% to 35%), with Traffic fines, Env.permit and BPIC12O showing similar MAE trends to Helpdesk log in Fig. 4. MAE trends for BPIC12CW resemble those of other BPIC12 logs in the first group. Notably, the Sepsis log shows a distinct MAE trend, where GGNN achieves comparable results to PGTNet for most prefix lengths.
- For BPIC20D and BPIC12A, the improvement is more modest, with the latter case yielding nearly identical MAEs for all prefix lengths (see Fig. 4).

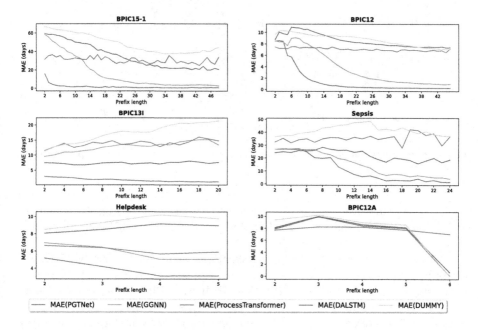

Fig. 4. MAE over different prefix lengths (selected event logs).

Ablation Study. The remarkable performance of PGTNet can be attributed to a synergy between the expressive capacity of the employed architecture and the incorporation of diverse process perspectives into the graph representation of event prefixes. To distinguish the impacts of these factors, we conducted an ablation study for which we trained a minimal PGTNet model, relying solely on edge weights (i.e., control-flow) and temporal features, thus omitting data attributes from consideration. We used identical hyperparameters and configurations as was done for the complete PGTNet model. Hence, the ablation study establishes a lower boundary for contribution of the PGTNet's architecture.

Our experiments reveal that the minimal PGTNet model consistently outperforms ProcessTransformer in terms of MAE (see Fig. 3). This underscores PGTNet's capabilities in capturing both local and global contexts, which is advantageous for predicting remaining time. However, the predictive performance of the minimal PGTNet is comparable to that of the GGNN approach, suggesting that learning from local control-flow structures in MPNN blocks (done by GGNN) holds greater significance than capturing long-range dependencies (as done by ProcessTransformer). This observation is further supported by the overall results presented in Table 2, where GGNN outperforms DALSTM and ProcessTransformer in all event logs, except for two BPIC13 logs. Additionally, the contribution of the architecture and the incorporation of extra data attributes varies across different event logs. While the PGTNet's architecture plays a decisive role for logs such as BPIC15 and BPIC20I, the improvements in MAE for logs such as BPICS12 and BPICS13 is primarily due to the incorporation of additional features. Further details regarding our ablation study can be found in our repository.

Impact of Process Complexity. The MAE improvement achieved by PGTNet varies significantly across different event logs. Investigating these variations, we correlated process complexity metrics from [1,21] with MAE improvements achieved by PGTNet. Notably, our approach outperforms alternatives when the number of process variants increases rapidly with respect to the number of cases. This trend extends to other *variation metrics*, including *'structure'* (average distinct activities per case) and *'level of detail'* (number of acyclic paths in the transition matrix) [1]. In terms of *size metrics*, PGTNet exhibits superior performance with increasing average trace length and/or number of distinct activities. The most significant positive correlation is observed for *'normalized sequence entropy'*, a graph entropy metric adept at capturing both variation and size complexity [1].

This reveals that PGTNet excels in highly flexible and complex processes, where benchmark approaches may overlook sparse but meaningful directly-follows relations among activities. The graph representation, detailed in Sect. 4.1, converts different process variants into non-isomorphic graphs with varying nodes, connectivity structures, and edge weights. Graph isomorphism network (GIN) modules, renowned for distinguishing non-isomorphic graphs [8], process this graph-oriented data. Simultaneously, Transformer blocks capture long-range dependencies. In complex processes like BPIC15, GIN blocks benefit from diverse set of non-isomorphic graphs available for learning, while Transformer blocks leverage insightful PE/SEs, thus providing a synergy that results in a remarkable reduction in MAE.

Training, and Inference Time. We conducted experiments using an Nvidia RTX A6000 GPU, with training and inference times detailed in Table 3. For training time, we computed the sum of training time for all cross-validation data splits and then averaged these times across all 20 event logs. Regarding average inference time, we compute the time to infer the remaining time per event prefix and report the average inference time across all event logs.

In terms of training time, DALSTM and ProcessTransformer, which use shallow neural networks (either with 2 LSTM layers or 1 self-attention layer), can be trained an order of magnitude faster than the graph-based approaches, though PGTNet is still trained faster than GGNN (12.93 vs. 18.56 h). We see a similar trend in terms of inference times, though essentially all approaches are reasonably fast here, with PGTNet being the slowest with an average time just below 3 ms.

Table 3. Average training and inference time for remaining time prediction.

Time	DALSTM	Process Transformer	GGNN	PGTNet
Training time (hours)	1.68	1.64	18.56	12.93
Inference time (milliseconds)	0.51	0.14	2.14	2.96

6   Conclusion and Future Work

This paper introduces a novel approach employing Process Graph Transformer Networks (PGTNet) to predict the remaining time of running business process instances. Our approach consists of a data transformation from an event log to a graph dataset, and training a neural network based on the GPS Graph Transformer recipe [16]. Our graph representation of event prefixes incorporates multiple process perspectives and also enables integration of control-flow relationships among activities into the learning process. This graph-oriented data input is subsequently processed by PGTNet, which strikes a balance between learning from local contexts and long-range dependencies.

Through experiments conducted on 20 real-world datasets, our results demonstrate the superior accuracy and earliness of predictions achieved by PGTNet compared to the existing deep learning approaches. Notably, our approach exhibits exceptional performance for highly flexible and complex processes, where the performance of LSTM, Transformer and GGNN architectures falls short.

While originally designed for predicting remaining times, our approach has the potential to learn high-level event prefix representations, rendering it applicable to other tasks, including next activity prediction and process outcome prediction. In future research, we therefore aim to apply PGTNet for these tasks, whereas we also aim to improve the predictive accuracy of our approach by investigating the potential of multi-task learning and exploring different positional and structural embeddings, as well as varying graph representations. Finally, we aim to extend our approach to also be applicable to object-centric event logs.

Reproducibility: Our source code and all evaluation results are accessible in our repository: https://github.com/keyvan-amiri/PGTNet.

References

1. Augusto, A., Mendling, J., Vidgof, M., Wurm, B.: The connection between process complexity of event sequences and models discovered by process mining. Inf. Sci. **598**, 196–215 (2022)

2. Bukhsh, Z.A., Saeed, A., Dijkman, R.M.: ProcessTransformer: predictive business process monitoring with transformer network (2021). arXiv:2104.00721
3. Duong, L.T., Travé-Massuyès, L., Subias, A., Merle, C.: Remaining cycle time prediction with Graph Neural Networks for Predictive Process Monitoring. In: International Conference on Machine Learning Technologies (ICMLT). ACM (2023)
4. Dwivedi, V.P., Luu, A.T., Laurent, T., Bengio, Y., Bresson, X.: Graph neural networks with learnable structural and positional representations (2022). arXiv:2110.07875
5. Evermann, J., Rehse, J.R., Fettke, P.: Predicting process behaviour using deep learning. Decis. Support Syst. **100**, 129–140 (2017)
6. Gilmer, J., Schoenholz, S.S., Riley, P.F., Vinyals, O., Dahl, G.E.: Neural message passing for quantum chemistry. In: Precup, D., Teh, Y.W. (eds.) Proceedings of the 34th International Conference on Machine Learning. Proceedings of Machine Learning Research, vol. 70, pp. 1263–1272. PMLR (2017)
7. Harl, M., Weinzierl, S., Stierle, M., Matzner, M.: Explainable predictive business process monitoring using gated graph neural networks. J. Decis. Syst. **29**(sup1), 312–327 (2020)
8. He, T., Zhang, Z., Zhang, H., Zhang, Z., Xie, J., Li, M.: Bag of tricks for image classification with convolutional neural networks. In: Proceedings of the IEEE/CVF Conference on Computer Vision and Pattern Recognition (CVPR) (2019)
9. Hu, W., et al.: Strategies for pre-training graph neural networks (2020). arXiv:1905.12265
10. Kreuzer, D., Beaini, D., Hamilton, W.L., Létourneau, V., Tossou, P.: Rethinking graph transformers with spectral attention (2021). arXiv:2106.03893
11. Lim, D., et al.: Sign and basis invariant networks for spectral graph representation learning (2022). arXiv:2202.13013
12. Loshchilov, I., Hutter, F.: Decoupled weight decay regularization (2019). arXiv:1711.05101
13. Navarin, N., Vincenzi, B., Polato, M., Sperduti, A.: LSTM networks for data-aware remaining time prediction of business process instances. In: 2017 IEEE Symposium series on Computational Intelligence (SSCI), pp. 1–7 (2017)
14. Polato, M., Sperduti, A., Burattin, A., de Leoni, M.: Data-aware remaining time prediction of business process instances. In: 2014 International Joint Conference on Neural Networks (IJCNN), pp. 816–823 (2014)
15. Rama-Maneiro, E., Vidal, J.C., Lama, M.: Deep learning for predictive business process monitoring: review and benchmark. IEEE Trans. Serv. Comput. **16**(1), 739–756 (2023)
16. Rampášek, L., Galkin, M., Dwivedi, V.P., Luu, A.T., Wolf, G., Beaini, D.: Recipe for a general, powerful, scalable graph transformer. In: NeurIPS, vol. 35, pp. 14501–14515 (2022)
17. Tax, N., Verenich, I., La Rosa, M., Dumas, M.: Predictive business process monitoring with LSTM neural networks. In: Dubois, E., Pohl, K. (eds.) CAiSE 2017. LNCS, vol. 10253, pp. 477–492. Springer, Cham (2017). https://doi.org/10.1007/978-3-319-59536-8_30
18. Vaswani, A., et al.: Attention is all you need. In: NeurIPS, vol. 30. Curran Associates, Inc. (2017)
19. Venugopal, I., Töllich, J., Fairbank, M., Scherp, A.: A comparison of deep-learning methods for analysing and predicting business processes. In: 2021 International Joint Conference on Neural Networks (IJCNN), pp. 1–8 (2021)

20. Verenich, I., Dumas, M., Rosa, M.L., Maggi, F.M., Teinemaa, I.: Survey and cross-benchmark comparison of remaining time prediction methods in business process monitoring. ACM Trans. Intell. Syst. Technol. **10**(4), 34:1–34:34 (2019)

21. Vidgof, M., Wurm, B., Mendling, J.: The impact of process complexity on process performance: a study using event log data (2023). arXiv:2307.06106

22. Weinzierl, S.: Exploring gated graph sequence neural networks for predicting next process activities. In: Marrella, A., Weber, B. (eds.) BPM 2021. LNBIP, vol. 436, pp. 30–42. Springer, Cham (2022). https://doi.org/10.1007/978-3-030-94343-1_3

23. Weytjens, H., De Weerdt, J.: Creating unbiased public benchmark datasets with data leakage prevention for predictive process monitoring. In: Marrella, A., Weber, B. (eds.) BPM 2021. LNBIP, vol. 436, pp. 18–29. Springer, Cham (2022). https://doi.org/10.1007/978-3-030-94343-1_2

24. Ying, C., et al.: Do transformers really perform badly for graph representation? In: NeurIPS, vol. 34, pp. 28877–28888. Curran Associates, Inc. (2021)

25. Zaheer, M., Kottur, S., Ravanbakhsh, S., Poczos, B., Salakhutdinov, R.R., Smola, A.J.: Deep sets. In: NeurIPS, vol. 30. Curran Associates, Inc. (2017)

Multi-perspective Concept Drift Detection: Including the Actor Perspective

Eva L. Klijn$^{(\boxtimes)}$ ⓘ, Felix Mannhardt ⓘ, and Dirk Fahland ⓘ

Eindhoven University of Technology, Eindhoven, The Netherlands
{e.l.klijn,f.mannhardt,d.fahland}@tue.nl

Abstract. Changes in processes manifest as *concept drift* in event logs. Drift detection aids in analyzing the nature of such change and its impact on the process. Process executions or cases are driven by actors and machines performing the actual work. Actors typically divide and structure their work into *tasks*—multiple consecutive actions performed together—before handing a case to the next actor. Process changes affect this work division and collaboration, potentially impacting performance and outcomes. However, existing research on concept drift detection from event logs has not yet focused on the behavior of actors. We generalize an existing concept drift detection technique to consider actor behavior and control-flow jointly by using a multi-layered event knowledge graph. We evaluate our proposal by comparing the theoretical properties of the newly defined actor perspective features with existing features and perform an experimental evaluation. The experiments showed actor features to be more robust with on average (up to factor 2.6) stronger signals for concept drift in two real-life datasets. Our approach led to new insights into global process changes, changes in behavior of individual actors, and change in collaborations between actors.

Keywords: concept drift · multi-perspective · knowledge graph · actors

1 Introduction

Organizations rely on insights from process analytics for the successful execution and optimization of their core processes. These processes are driven by human actors and automated resources performing work on the cases of the process. For example, multiple employees of a bank jointly check a credit application, create several loan offers, contact the client for additional information, to finally decline or prepare a contract.

Such processes are subject to change due to changes in process design (top-down) or due to actors gradually changing their way of working (bottom-up) [18]. And both kinds of changes also mutually influence each other and impact process performance and outcomes. Detecting and understanding the nature of changes in a process is therefore essential for continuous process analysis and improvement, such as envisioned in AI-augmented BPM systems [7].

Changes in processes can be detected in event data through *concept drift detection* [4,19]. Established techniques assume a traditional event log that is structured along the process' control flow and focus on detecting changes in the distribution of

G. Guizzardi et al. (Eds.): CAiSE 2024, LNCS 14663, pp. 141–157, 2024.
https://doi.org/10.1007/978-3-031-61057-8_9

some process' features within a time-window. These features describe in one way or another the control flow logic over all process executions assuming all cases and process steps are impacted equally by a change. However, this leaves bottom-up changes due to individual actors or changes only impacting individual actors undetected.

Yet, actors working on these process instances do exhibit behavior of their own leading to bottom-up changes. They jointly structure and divide work *along a case*, e.g., one actor creates and sends two loan offers to the same client, before handing it to the next actor; such a larger unit of work is called *task* [14,18] in routines research. Each actor also plans and structures their own work *across multiple cases* [15]. These bottom-up actor-based dynamics in process executions are central for realizing agent-based process management [20] and AI-augmented BPM systems [7]. However, changes in these dynamics are undetectable with drift detection on control-flow features only (detailed in Sect. 2).

In this paper, we investigate detecting changes in the perspective of the actor and control-flow together from event data and how these compare to (1) changes in the control flow only, (2) changes in individual actors and (3) changes in collaborations between actors. As actor behavior is inherently intertwined with control-flow [16], we turn to *event knowledge graphs* (EKGs) [9] as data model (recalled in Sect. 3) to translate an event log into a joint description of actor behavior, process control-flow, and their interactions.

We then address the problem of *defining features for concept drift detection over EKGs that consider the actor and the control-flow perspective jointly*. We generalize existing change point detection techniques from event logs to EKGs (Sect. 4). Such techniques detect drift by extracting multi-variate time-series of the frequency of various process features and then detect at which points the signals described by these time-series significantly change [1]. To detect changes in combined actor and control-flow behavior, we explore and compare several aggregations over EKGs [9] to construct features of multi-variate time series for change point detection. We identified task executions (subsequent actions performed by the same actor on the same case) and abstracted these to task variants (same activity sequence) or tasks (similar task variants) together with the actor and case-paths connecting them. We discuss the features' properties for drift detection in a theoretical analysis.

In our evaluation (Sect. 5), we show for two real-life event logs that including the actor perspective leads to more robust features with on average stronger signal changes, with up to a factors 2.6 stronger in BPIC'17. We also show that it revealed (1) new insights into global process changes (some performance related), (2) changes in individual actors only (some against process change) and (3) task collaborations between actors reducing in favor of actors sequencing tasks themselves. We conclude in Sect. 6.

2   Related Work

Concept drift detection and model adaptation has been extensively researched [17]. Change point detection methods [21] based on time series indicate possible drifts by finding a gradual or a sudden change in the observed distributions. We briefly review related work on concept drifts of process behavior [4] as well as the analysis of actor behavior.

A recent survey on concept drift detection in process mining [19] categorizes 45 papers based on their addressed perspectives: control-flow, data and resource. However, despite the importance of actors in organizations, who drive the process behavior, none of the papers covered the resource perspective. An earlier survey [8] also found that only a few approaches supported multiple perspectives, and those were focused on process variant comparison instead of general detection of concept drift. More recently, Adams et al. [1] proposed a detection method for concept drift that does support resources. The idea is to aggregate the information on them in the event log (e.g., workload, active resources) into a numeric feature and, then, use the PELT-algorithm [21] to detect change points. Their approach supports object-centric event logs by extracting individual process executions from an object graph; however, the actor-case interplay is not taken into account at the graph level. Additionally, their evaluation on the BPIC'17 dataset considers only the resource workload as feature. A concept drift with an increased workload for resources is found but none of the additional changes detected by our proposed approach. Thus, while we adopt PELT as change point detection from [1], their approach and proposed feature sets did not find the changes in actor-case interplay or behavior on task level.

Information on actors in processes has been previously used in process mining to analyze how resources organize their work [5,11], how they work together in collaborations [13], and to build overall organizational models [23]. Also related is a proposal on using agent mining [20] for process analysis. Agent mining puts the actor or agent driving the business process at the center of the investigation and aims to build a multi-agent system by discovering behavior of individual agents. Such agent models could show similar behavior to what we discover as tasks. None of these works investigates concept drift and the particular actor-case interplay feature on a task level that we propose to use. In previous work, we described how to detect and classify task executions by actors in processes [14] and used them to analyze the actor behavior [15]. Both [14] and [15] did not look at changes of such behavior over time in a structured manner.

3   Preliminaries

To model behavior of case and actor jointly, we make use of an event knowledge graph (EKG) data model, recalled in Sect. 3.1. Section 3.2 then recalls a way to summarize joint behavior of case and actor in a task instance layer and 3.2 recalls basic aggregation operations for EKGs; we will later use both to derive actor-control-flow features for concept drift detection in Sect. 4.

3.1   Event Knowledge Graphs

A process-aware system can record an action execution as an *event* in an event log. We require that each event records at least the *action* that occurred, the *time* of occurrence, the *case* in which the event occurred and the *resource* (or actor) executing the action.

While an event log orders events wrt. one identifier into isolated event sequences, an *event knowledge graph* (EKG) allows to model that an event is part of multiple, synchronizing paths (e.g., path of a case and path of an actor) [10]. EKGs are based on *labeled property graphs* (LPG), a graph-based data model supported by graph DB systems [3] that describes concepts as nodes and various relationships between them as edges. In an LPG $G = (X, Y, \Lambda, \#)$, each node $x \in X$ and each relationship $y \in Y$ with edge $\overrightarrow{y} = (x, x')$ from x to x' has a label $\ell \in \Lambda$, denoted $x \in \ell$ or $y \in \ell$ that describes the *concept* represented by x or y; we use $(x, x') \in \ell$ as shorthand for $y \in \ell$. $\#_{(a)}(x) = v$ and $\#_{(a)}(y) = v$ denotes that property a of x or y has value v; we use and $x.a = v$ and $y.a = v$ as short-hand.

In an EKG, each event and each entity (i.e., each case or resource) is represented by a node with label *Event* and *Entity*, respectively. Each node $e \in Event$ defines $e.action$ and $e.time$; each node $n \in Entity$ defines $n.type$ and $n.id$. While EKGs allow to model arbitrarily many entity types, we subsequently restrict ourselves to EKGs with *two* entity types: *case* (any data object or a classical case identifier) and *resource* (the actors working in the process). Figure 1 (layer 1) shows an example graph: each square node is an *Event* node; each circle is an *Entity* node of the corresponding type (blue for *case*, red for *resource*). An EKG has relationship labels:

- *corr* (correlation): $y \in corr$, $\overrightarrow{y} = (e, n)$ iff event $e \in Event$ is correlated to entity $n \in Entity$; we write $(e, n) \in corr$ as short-hand.
- *df* (directly-follows): $y \in df$, $\overrightarrow{y} = (e, e')$ iff events e, e' are correlated to the same entity n $(e, n), (e', n) \in corr$, $e.time < e'.time$ and there is no other event $(e'', n) \in corr$ with $e.time < e''.time < e'.time$; we write $(e, e')^{n.type} \in df$ as short-hand, i.e., $(e, e')^c$ for entity type case and $(e, e')^r$ for resource.

In Fig. 1 (1), *corr* relationships are shown as dashed edges, e.g., $e1, e2, e5, e6, e9$, $e11, e12$ are correlated to case $c4$ and $e5, e6, e7, e8$ are correlated to resource $r5$. *df*-relationships are shown as solid edges. The *df*-relationships between the events correlated to the same entity form a *df-path* for that entity; the graph in Fig. 1 (1) has 2 df-paths for case entities, e.g., $\sigma_{c4} = \langle (e1, e2)^c, (e2, e5)^c, (e5, e6)^c, (e6, e9)^c, (e9, e11)^c, (e11, e12)^c \rangle$ and 4 df-paths for resource entities, e.g., $\sigma_{r5} = \langle (e5, e6)^r, (e6, e7)^r, (e7, e8)^r \rangle$. See [9] for details on the creation of an EKG G from event data sources through graph DB queries.

3.2   Adding a Task Instance Layer

Events and df-edges together form an *event layer* of an EKG [10]. A maximal sub-graph of events $ti = \{e_1, ..., e_k\}$ where the df-paths of a case and of an actor synchronize is called a task instance [14] and describes the maximal sequence of activities, or unit of work, performed by the same actor in a case. In Fig. 1 (1) sub-graphs of events that meet these criteria are $\{e_1, e_2\}, \{e_3, e_4\}, \{e_5, e_6\}, \{e_7, e_8\}, \{e_9\}, \{e_{10}\}, \{e_{11}, e_{12}\}$ and $\{e_{13}, e_{14}\}$.

To aid analysis, an EKG can be extended with a *task instance layer* [10] by aggregating each task instance sub-graph $ti = \{e_1, ..., e_k\}$ into a new "high-level" event node $h_{ti} \in TaskInstance$, as shown in Fig. 1 (layer 2); h_{ti} is connected to each $e_j \in ti$ via a relationship $(h_{ti}, e_j) \in contains$. The *corr* and *df* relationships (for cases and actors) are lifted from *Event* nodes to *TaskInstance* nodes along the *contains* relationships. For example, $ti1$ over $e1, e2$ and $ti4$ over $e7, e8$ derived

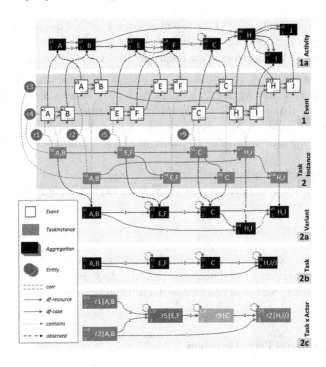

Fig. 1. Example EKG containing an event (1) and task instance (2) layer, and aggregation layers for activity (1a), variants (2a), tasks (2b) and tasks per actor (2c). (Color figure online)

from Fig. 1 (1) results in nodes $h1$ and $h4$ in Fig. 1 (2), respectively. Further, property $h_{ti}.variant = e_1.action, ..., e_k.action$ describing the sequence of actions performed in ti, and $h_{ti}.start = e_1.time$ and $h_{ti}.end = e_k.time$.

3.3 Aggregating Behavior

We recall generalized node and *df* aggregation operations on an EKG $G = (X, Y, \lambda, \#)$ (with event or task instance layers) for process analysis [15].

Node Aggregation. $Agg^N(\alpha, X', l, l')$ aggregates nodes $x \in X' \subseteq X$ with the same feature $\alpha(x)$ into concept ℓ as follows: (1) query all values $V = \{\alpha(x) \mid x \in X'\}$, (2) for each value $v \in V$ add a new node $v \in \ell$ to G with label ℓ, (3) query the nodes $X'_v = \{x \in X' \mid \alpha(x) = v\}$ and (4) add new relationship $y \in \ell', \overrightarrow{y} = (x, v)$ with label ℓ' from x to v, and (5) set $v.count = |X'_v|$. For example, applying $Agg^N(\alpha_{action}, Event, Activity, observed)$ with $\alpha_{action}(e) = e.action$ on the graph in Fig. 1 creates one new *Activity* node for each value of the *Event* nodes' *action* property, i.e., nodes $a1, \dots, a8$ shown in Fig. 1 (layer 1a), and links each event to *Activity* that was observed when the event occurred.

Directly-Follows Aggregation. $Agg^{df}(type, \ell, \ell')$ aggregates (or lifts) *df*-relationships (between *Event* or *TaskInstance* nodes) for a particular entity *type* to ℓ nodes along the ℓ' relationships as follows: (1) for any two nodes $x, x' \in \ell$ query the set $df_{x,x'}^{type} = \{(z, z')^{type} \in df \mid (z, x) \in \ell', (z', x') \in \ell'\}$ of all df-edges (z, z') for $type$ where nodes z, z' (e.g., events or task instances) are related to x, x' via ℓ', (2) if $df_{x,x'}^t \neq \emptyset$ create a new df-relationship $y^* \in df, \overrightarrow{y^*} = (x, x'), y^*.type = ttype$ and set $y^*.count = |df_{x,x'}^{type}|$. For example, first aggregating events to $Activity$ nodes via node aggregation, and then applying $Agg_{df}(type, Activity, observed)$ for $type \in \{Case, Resource\}$ on the graph in Fig. 1 yields the df-edges between $a1, \dots, a8$ in Fig. 1 (layer 1a) where, e.g., $(a4, a3)^r$ originates from $(e6, e7)^r$ while $(a3, a4)^c$ originates from $(e5, e6)^c$ and $(e7, e8)^c$.

Several aggregations using Agg^N and Agg^{df}, also limited to task instances in a specific time window, have been proposed [15] as we exploit in our method.

4   Method

We generalize an existing change point detection technique (Sect. 4.1) to EKGs (Sect. 4.2). We introduce several features for drift detection in actor behavior and control-flow together (Sect. 4.3) and analyze their theoretical properties for drift detection (Sect. 4.4).

4.1   Existing Change Point Detection

We first recall an existing technique [1] for change point detection on event logs structured along the process' control-flow and generalize it to EKGs. Afterwards, we discuss its application to actor features.

Given a log L, the technique defines a series $w_0, \dots, w_n$ of subsequent time-windows $w_i = [t_i; t_{i+1})$ of equal length, e.g., 1 day, (spanning the entire log) and a function F that extracts from L per time-window w_i a feature vector $\chi_i = F(L, w_i)$. For example, if $A = \{a_1, \dots, a_k\}$ are the actions recorded in L and $|L_{a_j}, w_i|$ denotes how many events in L in w_i refer to action a_j, then $F_A(L, w_i) = \langle |L_{a_j,w_i}| / \sum_{b \in A} |L_{b,w_i}| \rangle_{j=1}^k$ defines the feature vector of relative frequencies of activities $a_1, \dots, a_k$ in w_i. Likewise a feature vector $F_A^{df}(L, w_i)$ that defines for each pair $(a, b) \in A$ how often in a case b directly follows a in w_i can be constructed. Note that df-relations between events in different time windows are ignored.

The feature vectors $\chi = \langle \chi_1, \dots, \chi_n \rangle$ yield a multi-variate time-series. Change point detection takes χ as input and returns as output a series $0 = cp_0, cp_1, \dots, cp_{k-1}, cp_k = n - 1$ of change points where cp_i marks a change in $w_{cp_i} = [t_i; t_{i+1})$.

4.2   Generalizing Change Point Detection to EKGs

Our input for change point detection is an EKG with an event layer and a task instance layer. We generalize the above technique from event logs to EKGs by defining feature extraction functions $F(G, w_i)$ that extracts features of an EKG G in a specific time-window. For this, we first aggregate only the nodes in a specific time window $w_i = [t_i; t_{i+1})$, and the extract the $count$ properties of their aggregates as feature vectors.

Let $Event|_{w_i} = \{e \in Event \mid t_i \leq e.time < t_{i+1}\}$ be the event nodes in time window w_i. We write $Agg(\alpha, Event|_{w_i}, \mathcal{A})$ for first aggregating events in w_i by $Agg^N(\alpha, Event|_{w_i}, \mathcal{A}, observed)$ and then lifting df by $Agg^{df}(type, \mathcal{A}, observed)$ for $type \in \{case, resource\}$ as described in Sect. 3.3. For example, choosing $\alpha_{action}(e) = e.action, \mathcal{A} = Activity$ aggregates all $Event$ nodes in w_i with $e.action = a$ to $a \in Activity$ node and lifts df.

Let G_{w_i} be the result of applying $Agg(\alpha, Event|_{w_i}, \mathcal{A})$ on G. Then for each node $a \in \mathcal{A}$, $|G^N_{a,w_i}| = a.count$ defines the *frequency of a in w_i*, and for $(a,b) \in \mathcal{A} \times \mathcal{A}$ and $type$ with $y \in df$, $\vec{y} = (a,b)$, $y.type = type$, $|G^{type}_{(a,b),w_i}| = y.count$ defines the *frequency of b directly following a* for a particular entity $type$ during w_i (as the original method, we ignore df-edges that span multiple windows). The feature vector of relative frequencies of $\mathcal{A}$ and df of $type$ in w_i are $F^N_{\mathcal{A}}(G, w_i) = \langle |G^N_{a,w_i}| / \sum_{b \in \mathcal{A}} |G^N_{b,w_i}| \rangle_{a \in \mathcal{A}}$ and $F^{type}_{\mathcal{A}}(G, w_i) = \langle |G^{type}_{(a,b),w_i}| / \sum_{c,d \in \mathcal{A}} |G^{type}_{(c,d),w_i}| \rangle_{(a,b) \in \mathcal{A} \times \mathcal{A}}$ (for an arbitrary but fixed order of the $a \in \mathcal{A}$). The feature vectors $F^N_{\mathcal{A}}$ and $F^{type}_{\mathcal{A}}$ can be used in the existing change point detection technique of Sect. 4.1.

For example, if all events in Fig. 1 (layer 1) occur within one time window $w = [12; 16)$, then aggregation yields the *"activity layer"* of Fig. 1 (layer 1a) describing df-frequencies for cases and actors, e.g., $|G^c_{(E,F),w}| = 2$ and $|G^r_{(F,E),w}| = 1$. If we choose $w_1 = [12; 14)$ and $w_2 = [14; 16)$, then $|G^c_{(E,F),w_1}| = |G^c_{(E,F),w_2}| = 1$ while $|G^r_{(F,E),w_i}| = 0$ (across windows), i.e., we must choose window length with care.

4.3   Extracting Actor and Control-Flow Features

Features derived from the activity layer describe activity counts, case-df counts and even actor-df counts, but do not hold any information on the larger units of work performed, i.e., task executions in which cases and actors synchronize, nor how these are organized by the actors along the cases. To derive features that describe actor and case perspective together, we adopt functions $F_{\mathcal{A}}(G, w_i)$ to aggregate actor and case behavior in the task instance layer (Sect. 3.2).

In this layer, a task instance – formed by a path of a case and actor together – is the smallest unit describing their interaction or conjoint behavior. Consequently, df-edges describe handovers from one task to the next: a df-case edge describes the *handover of a case to another actor* while a df-resource edge describes the sequencing of tasks *across different cases for the same actor*. To detect drift in the combination of actor behavior and control-flow, we therefore study drift in the frequency of task instances and df-edges. We can lift the feature extraction on EKG G from $Event$ to $TaskInstance$ nodes: Let $TI|_{w_i} = \{h_{ti} \in TaskInstance \mid t_i \leq h_{ti}.start \leq h_{ti}.end < t_{i+1}\}$ be the task instance in time window w_i. Let G_{w_i} be the result of applying $Agg(\alpha, TI|_{w_i}, \mathcal{A})$ on G, i.e., aggregating task instances. Then $F^N_{\mathcal{A}}(G, w_i)$ and $F^{type}_{\mathcal{A}}(G, w_i)$ define the feature vectors of relative frequencies of $\mathcal{A}$ and df of $type$ in w_i.

Previous research [15] identified the following 3 aggregation-levels for *TaskInstances*, which we explore for concept drift detection.

Task Variant. Like aggregating events based on the executed action, we can aggregate task instances based on the *sequence of executed actions* (or *variant*). Using $\alpha(h_{ti}) =$

$h_{ti}.variant$ we aggregate into $\mathcal{A} = Variant$ nodes. The resulting *task variant layer* (see layer 2a in Fig. 1) distinguishes each task instance action sequence as a separate feature. Features $F^N_{Variant}$ and $F^c_{Variant}$ (short F^N_V, F^c_V) describe the relative frequency of each task variant and the handovers from one task variant to another within a case.

Task. Aggregating task instances h_{ti} of *similar variants* into one *Task* requires a "Task oracle" [15] $O(h_{ti})$ with $O(h_{ti}) = O(h'_{ti})$ whenever $h_{ti}.variant$ and $h'_{ti}.variant$ achieve the same task in similar but different ways, e.g., all variants of creating Offers. A task oracle can be any function to group task variants; this can be done using simple heuristic, e.g., all variants starting with the same activity belong to the same task, or a clustering algorithm. In any case, retrieving a meaningful grouping requires a thorough understanding of the process or domain knowledge. Using $\alpha(h_{ti}) = O(h_{ti})$ we aggregate into $\mathcal{A} = Task$ nodes. The resulting *task layer* (see layer 2b in Fig. 1) groups similar variants into tasks resulting in a more granular description of the actor and control-flow perspective. Features F^N_{Task} and F^c_{Task} (short F^N_T, F^c_T) describe the relative frequency of each task and the handovers from one task to another within a case, respectively.

Figure 2 shows how features are extracted from an example task instance layer using $F^p_T(G, w_i), i \in \{1, 2, 3\}, p \in \{N, c, r\}$ based on the task that was executed according to an oracle O where CHI and CHJ, and HI and HJ and considered the same task, respectively. For example, $F^N_T(G, w_1)$ first aggregates task instance nodes in window w_1 based on O and then extracts feature vector $\chi^N_{T,1}$ (Fig. 2 left).

Task Per Actor. We can also distinguish *Tasks* per *Actor* in the aggregation by using $\alpha(h_{ti}) = (O(h_{ti}), h_{ti}.actor)$ to aggregate into $\mathcal{A} = T \times R$ nodes; see layer 2c in Fig. 1. This *task/actor layer* distinguishes tasks for each individual actor separately.

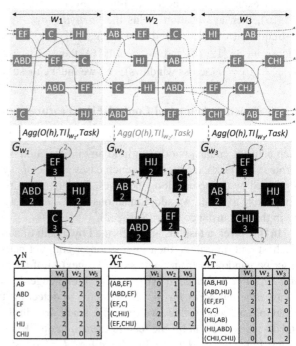

Fig. 2. Feature extraction of a task instance layer in G' for three time windows using function $F_T(G', w_i), i \in \{1, 2, 3\}$.

It therefore also distinguishes df-edges between tasks of the same actor from task handovers between a pair of actors. Hence, the aggregated feature $F^N_{T \times R}$ describes the relative frequency of each task per actor, $F^c_{T \times R}$ the handovers of cases between actors, and $F^r_{T \times R}$ the task switching per actor.

4.4 Properties of Actor and Control-Flow Features

We compare classical control-flow based features, i.e., frequency of (pairs of) activities, to features combining actor and control-flow, i.e., task (variants).

Let G_w be an EKG with event, task instance, activity, task variant, and task layers derived for window w. Intuitively, a task variant $v = \langle a_1, \ldots, a_k \rangle$ can only occur as often as the least frequent activity a_i and the least frequent df-edge (a_i, a_{i+1}) considering both df-case and df-resource edges. Formally, the frequency of task variant $v = \langle a_1, \ldots, a_k \rangle \in Variant$ in G_w is $|G_{v,w}^N| = |\{h \in TI|_w \mid (h, v) \in observed\}|$. For each such h exists a unique set $e_1, \ldots, e_k \in Event$ s.t. $(h, e_i) \in contains$ and $(e_i, e_{i+1})^c, (e_i, e_{i+1})^r \in df, i = 1, \ldots, k-1$. Moreover, $(e_i, a_i) \in observed, i = 1, \ldots, k$ and $(a_i, a_{i+1})^c, (a_i, a_{i+1})^r \in df, i = 1, \ldots, k-1$. Thus, the frequency of v is bounded by the least frequently directly following activities $(a_i, a_{i+1})^c$ or $(a_i, a_{i+1})^r$ in the case or resource perspective, i.e., $|G_{v,w}^N| \leq \min_{i=1}^{k-1}\{|G_{(a_i, a_{i+1}), w}^c|, |G_{(a_i, a_{i+1}), w}^r|\}$.

This particularly means that every single activity pair (a_i, a_{i+1}) can act as a strong "signal filter". Suppose $(a_i, a_{i+1})^c$ is frequent over all time windows but a_i and a_{i+1} were performed initially by different actors but from w on is performed by the same actor, i.e., $(a_i, a_{i+1})^r$ was initially infrequent and become frequent from w on. Then the task variant feature v changes from infrequent to frequent, i.e., is a notable change at a drift point, while the control-flow feature $(a_i, a_{i+1})^c$ shows no change.

Conversely, a task t occurs as often as all its task variants together. Formally, the frequency of $t \in Task$ in G_w is $|G_{t,w}^N| = |\{h \in TI|_w \mid O(h) = t\}|$. For each such h exists a unique variant $v, (h, v) \in observed$. Let $v_1, \ldots, v_k$ be the variants of t. Thus, $|G_{t,w}^N| = \sum_{i=1}^k |G_{v_i,w}^N|$ and $|G_{t,w}^N| \geq |G_{v_i,w}^N|, i = 1, \ldots, k$. Thus, for tasks with many variants that all change similarly in frequency, $|G_{t,w}^N|$ creates a stronger "change signal", while for tasks where some variants rise in frequency and some fall in frequency, $|G_{t,w}^N|$ creates a weaker or no "change signal" compared to $|G_{v_i,w}^N|$.

5 Experimental Results

We experimentally investigate drift detection of the actor and the control-flow perspective together compared to control-flow based drift detection on two real-life event logs. We implemented the approach of Sect. 4 in Python 3.10[1]; the script (1) generates Cypher queries from [15] for extracting features from the graph, and (2) derives multi-variate time-series and (3) detects the change points based on [1].

5.1 Experimental Setup and Procedure

Our objectives are to:

O1 Compare change points detected in the entire process using task F_T^N and task variant F_V^N features vs the activity F_A^N and activity-case-df F_A^c features that were already proposed in [1];

---

[1] https://github.com/multi-dimensional-process-mining/ekg-bpic17-concept-drift-detection-multi-perspective.

O2 Compare change points detected in individual actors using tasks $F_{T \times r}^N$ vs change points detected in the entire process using task features F_T^N;

O3 Compare change points detected in individual actors using task-actor-df features $F_{T \times r}^r$ (i.e., task switching), and between individual actors using task-case-df $F_{T \times r}^c$ (i.e., case handovers) vs change points detected in the entire process using task features F_T^N.

For (O1–O3) we compare moment of change and which feature changes in frequency (direction and magnitude). We selected the BPIC'17 data [6] and a private dataset of a small manufacturing process (MF) as these have actor information recorded on the level of detail and quantity required for our approach. For each dataset, we constructed an event knowledge graph [9] including a task instance layer [14] (see Sect. 3), which resulted in 271,815 and 20,776 task instances describing 2,023 and 549 unique variants, respectively. We removed task instances of infrequent task variants (occurring < 10 (1%) and < 25 (4%) times, resulting in 389 and 81 variants, respectively.

To derive the task and task-df features, we used agglomerative clustering of task instances into tasks [2] as task oracle (see Sect. 4): we used Euclidean distance between $h_{ti}.variant$ as distance metric and chose the number of clusters by maximizing the silhouette index [2], resulting in 21 and 17 clusters for the BPIC'17 and MF data, respectively. We subdivided clusters of leftover variants after manual inspection as follows: (1) each variant occurring at least 100 times was grouped together with all variants including the same set of activities; (2) all remaining variants were removed, resulting in 7 and 3 manually created clusters and removal of 7 and 0 variants, respectively.

We extracted multi-variate time series with window = 1 day (Sect. 4) describing (O1) tasks F_T^N, task variants F_V^N, activities F_A^N and activity-case-df F_A^c in the entire process from BPIC'17 and MF; (O2) tasks $F_{T \times r}^N$ in each individual actor r that executes at least 500 tasks in the entire process, and tasks F_T^N in the entire process from BPIC'17; (O3) task-actor-df $F_{T \times r}^r$ in each individual actor r that executes at least 500 tasks in the entire process, task-case-df $F_{T \times r}^c, r \in R$ for each pair R of individual actors that share at least 300 handovers, and tasks F_T^N in the entire process from BPIC'17.

We specifically chose a window size of 1 day for all features (O1–O3) to yield a fine-grained analysis on the level of individual actors that is comparable to the process level. While [1] argues for a window size of 7 days to overcome seasonal variability, we want to be able to detect more fine-grained dynamics and changes on an actor level. Such changes may remain undetected with a coarse granularity level of a week. By using data on actor behavior, our approach can address the issue of seasonal variability caused by weekends/holidays nonetheless by using relative counts for detecting process level drifts (O1) correcting for variable workloads, and, for detecting drift in actors and actor pairs (O2 and O3), we use absolute counts and strip the time series of the days no events were recorded for the actor (O2)/one of the actors (O3). We also tested our approach using a window size of 7 days, but found roughly the same change points.

Extracting features from the graph based on task nodes F_T^N took on average 1.63 s per time window for BPIC'17 and 0.26 per time window for MF on an Intel Xeon CPU (2x)2.4 GHz machine with 64 GB. We detected change points using the PELT-algorithm [1, 21] and varied penalty $\beta \in \{2, 3, 4\}$ to avoid overfitting.

We investigated changes at a detected change point cp_i in a feature F further[2]. We use *signal* for the value of a feature over time. We write $f \in F$ for one feature of the feature vector, e.g., frequency of activity a. We then compute $\mu_{(i,i+1),f}$ as the mean value of f in all time-windows χ_j, $cp_i \leq j < cp_{i+1}$ and $|\Delta\mu_{cp_i,f}| = |\mu_{(i,i+1),f} - \mu_{(i-1,i),f}|$ as *magnitude of the signal change* at cp_i; the signal change in a feature is *stronger* if this value is *greater*. Additionally, the signal of a feature shows a *rising trend* if $\Delta\mu_{cp_i,f} > 0$ and a *falling trend* otherwise. Measuring the magnitude and direction of each feature's signal separately allows us to qualitatively compare the changes across specific features, e.g., compare changes in tasks (actor perspective) to changes in activities contained in that task (control-flow perspective). For the average and maximum overall signal change, we write $\mu(|\Delta\mu_F|)$ and $\max(|\Delta\mu_F|)$ for the average and maximum of $|\Delta\mu_{cp_i,f}|$ for all cp_i and $f \in F$, respectively.

5.2 Results

Objective O1. Table 1 summarizes the change points detected in the entire process using feature sets $F \in \{F_T^N, F_V^N, F_A^N, F_A^c\}$ and penalty $\beta \in \{2, 3, 4\}$ for BPIC'17 and MF.

Change points. For BPIC'17 at $\beta = 3$ all detected change points (CPs) largely coincide across all feature sets (maximum time difference in CPs across features ≤ 4 days); the first and last detected change points in intervals $[9; 11]$ and $[365; 368]$ mark the start and end of the process. For $\beta = 2$, we most notably detect an additional CP in interval $[145; 146]$ in tasks F_T^N, variants F_V^N and activities F_A^N while case-df F_A^c shows no changes. In contrast, F_A^N replaces the CP at 198 by two CPs at 183 and 191 (which is not visible in the other features). From $\beta = 4$ onward, the signals in F_A^N and F_A^c are not strong enough anymore to detect changes around $[327; 330]$ and signals in F_V^N no longer detect changes at the start and end of the process. For MF, we observe in Tab. 1 that at $\beta = 4$ detected change points precisely coincide across all feature sets. At $\beta = 3$ an additional change point at 7 is detected in the task features and at $\beta = 2$ additional change points are detected at 102, 106, 137 for F_A^N and at 137 for F_A^c.

Mean Change Signal. We investigated the magnitude of the signal changes at the change points of BPIC'17 with $\beta = 3$ and of MF with $\beta = 4$ (Table 1). We chose these settings as the change points obtained largely coincide across all features, allowing for the

Table 1. Process level change points in days since the start of the log for feature sets $(F_T^N, F_V^N, F_A^N, F_A^c)$ and three penalty settings (β).

	β	F_T^N	F_V^N	F_A^N	F_A^c
BPIC17	2	11 137 145 200 328 366 386	9 146 196 330 368	11 145 183 191 327 367 385	11 198 329 366 384
	3	11 200 328 366	9 196 330 368	11 198 327 365	11 198 329 366
	4	11 200 328 366	196 330	11 198 365	11 199 366
MF	2	7 39 91	7 39 91	7 39 91 102 106 137	7 39 91 137
	3	7 39 91	39 91	39 91	39 91
	4	39 91	39 91	39 91	39 91

most fair comparison between control-flow and actor-based features. We found for BPIC'17 and MF the average signal change $\mu(|\Delta\mu_F|)$ is stronger in tasks F_T^N than in other features $F_V^N/F_A^N/F_A^c$ (1.2 vs 0.2/0.8/0.1 for BPIC'17 and 1.5 vs 0.7/0.7/0.2 for

---

[2] Full BPIC'17 results available: https://zenodo.org/doi/10.5281/zenodo.10933096.

MF). For BPIC'17 the maximum signal change $max(|\Delta\mu_F|)$ is significantly stronger in F_T^N/F_V^N vs F_A^N/F_A^c (17.4/17.3 vs 6.5/6.7), whereas for MF they were slightly stronger in F_A^N/F_A^c vs F_T^N/F_V^N (5.2/6.0 vs 4.0/4.0). Overall, using task features generally led to equal or stronger signal changes, while using activity/activity-df features in most cases led to weaker signal changes confirming the analysis in Sect. 4.4.

Comparison of Change Signals Across Features. On the four CPs ($cp_1, \ldots, cp_4$) of BPIC'17 for $\beta = 3$ shown in Table 1, we investigated how the magnitudes and directions of signal changes compare across F_T^N, F_V^N and F_A^N, F_A^c. We again use $\beta = 3$ to allow for the best comparison as for this β the obtained change points largely coincide for all feature sets. We include in Table 2 for cp_2 and cp_3 all task changes with $|\Delta\mu_{cp_i, f\in F_T^N}| = |M| > 1.0$ and limit cp_1 and cp_4 to task changes of $|M| > 10$ due to extensive drift at the process start and end. We include variants of a task if these showed opposing directions for $\Delta\mu_{cp_i, f\in F_V^N}$ (rising vs falling). For each task or variant change, we report the fraction φ of activities and of activity pairs contained in the task or variant whose signal change $\Delta\mu_{cp_i, f\in F}, F \in F_A^N, F_A^c$ has the same trend as the signal change for F_T^N/F_V^N, and the fraction that has the opposite trend (only considering signal changes > 0.1). For each, we report the strongest signal change (max).

Table 2. Comparison of change signals in F_T^N, F_V^N vs F_A^N, F_A^c at four change points (CP) detected with $\beta = 3$.

CP	F_T^N	F_V^N	M	F_A^N				F_A^c			
				Same trend φ	max	Opposite trend φ	max	Same trend φ	max	Opposite trend φ	max
cp_1	m04		**-11.19**	1.00	-2.94	0.00		0.85	-1.57	0.00	
	T03		**10.13**	0.97	4.65	0.00		0.91	2.71	0.00	
	T07		**-14.71**	0.95	-3.15	0.00		0.94	-2.32	0.00	
cp_2	m01		**3.79**	1.00	1.26	0.00		0.75	0.88	0.00	
	m03		**-5.41**	0.97	-2.34	0.03	0.33	0.40	-2.12	0.00	
	m04		**-2.06**	1.00	-0.73	0.00		0.85	-0.59	0.00	
	T01		**1.37**	0.72	0.90	0.21	-2.34	0.42	0.31	0.21	-2.12
	T02		**2.18**	0.77	1.26	0.13	-2.34	0.72	0.64	0.03	-0.49
	T03	v04	-1.13	0.17	-1.67	0.67	0.38	0.20	-0.31	0.60	0.49
		v06	1.18	0.80	0.58	0.20	-1.67	1.00	0.49	0.00	
	T10	v08	2.40	1.00	1.26	0.00		1.00	0.64	0.00	
		v13	-1.61	0.33	-2.34	0.67	1.26	0.20	-0.49	0.60	0.64
	T11		**1.28**	0.85	1.26	0.03	-2.34	0.35	0.88	0.00	
cp_3	m02		**-13.02**	1.00	-3.17	0.00		0.50	-3.60	0.00	
	m04		**1.38**	0.88	0.55	0.00		0.85	0.65	0.00	
	m05		**15.27**	1.00	3.27	0.00		1.00	4.78	0.00	
	T03	v04	-4.79	0.00		0.33	1.67	1.00	-1.57	0.00	
		v27	4.10	0.33	1.62	0.00		0.20	1.36	0.80	-0.22
	T11	v12	-2.14	0.00		0.33	1.67	0.50	-0.58	0.50	0.11
		v43	1.90	0.33	1.62	0.00		1.00	0.67	0.00	
cp_4	m05		**-11.88**	1.00	-4.23	0.00		1.00	-3.70	0.00	
	T11		**17.38**	0.86	6.50	0.11	-2.94	0.62	6.72	0.06	-0.66

In Table 2 we observe that only for few task (variants) all the contained activity and activity-df features change in the same trend ($\varphi = 1.0$), and that for 11/22 task (variants) at least some activity and activity-df features (up to 67%) show an opposite trend. In terms of magnitude, we observe that the signal changes in all tasks in F_T^N are stronger than the max signal changes measured in F_A^N, F_A^c going the same direction. We find that a few changes in tasks can to some extent be explained by changes in some F_A^N or F_A^c, e.g., the change -5.41 in m03 at cp_2 is also detected in 97% of its activities with strongest change -2.34 in "W_VA+resume". However, signals in those same activities can show conflicting changes wrt. other task changes, e.g., activity "W_VA+resume" is also contained in T01 which changes with $+1.37$ in cp_2.

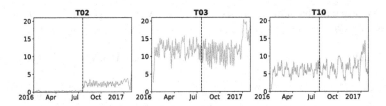

Fig. 3. Signals of T02, T03 and T10 in F_T^N.

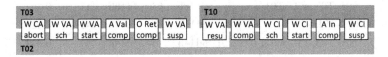

Fig. 4. Most dominant variants of T02 combining T03,T10.

Variants. Signal changes in variants in F_V^N are stronger than the max signal changes in F_A^N, F_A^c for 6/8 variants. For v04 and v12 at cp_3 no activity (F_A^N) changed in the same direction as the variants ($\varphi = 0$). Only v04 and v13 at cp_2 contained activities (F_A^N) that have a stronger max signal change, but this only holds for a minority of activities while the majority of contained activities (F_A^N) and activity-df (F_A^c) shows the opposite trend ($\varphi \geq 0.6$).

Opposing Variants. We also observe some strong (opposite) changes in variants that were not reflected in the tasks. For example, task T03 with $|M| < 1.0$ at cp_3 contains two variants v04 and v27 showing strong opposite changes, -4.79 and $+4.10$, respectively, which is also reflected in the max signal change in corresponding activity-df signals (F_A^c). Inspection of the variants showed that the activity "W_CAO+abort" as part of variant v04 was replaced by "W_CAO+withdraw".

Impact of Drift on Performance. More closely inspecting signals and contents of changing tasks in Table 2 revealed task T02 was only introduced as a regular task from cp_2, see Fig. 3. Even though T02 combines actions of existing tasks T03 and T10, illustrated by their most dominant variants in Fig. 4, the relative increase in T02 did not coincide with (significant, $|M| < 1.0$) relative decreases in T03 and T10, see Fig. 3. We investigated the effect of combining T03 and T10 into T02 after cp_2 on the processing time. Table 3 compares duration of trace suffixes $\langle X, ... \rangle$ with $X =$T03,T10 vs $X =$T02 occurring > 50 times. We observe in Table 3 that the change to T02 at cp_2 led to significantly shorter processing times in 4 out of 7 suffixes.

Objective O2. For this objective and the next (O3), we only report the changes in actors/actor pairs detected with $\beta = 4$, as these included also the more subtle changes that remained undetected with larger β.

Table 3. Average duration of trace suffixes $\langle X, ...\rangle$ with $X =$ T03, T10 vs $X =$ T02 occurring > 50 times after cp_2.

Suffix	X = T02		X = T03, T10		P-value
	μ	#	μ	#	
X, m01, T03, T01	**4d03h**	242	4d19h	526	**0.012**
X, m01, T03, T10, m01, T01	**7d20h**	134	12d04h	145	**6.950e−7**
X, m01, T03, T15	**4d07h**	155	5d16h	58	**0.001**
X, m01, T03, m03, T01	4d18h	63	**4d10h**	113	0.463
X, T03, T01	**3d11h**	33	3d17h	147	0.622
X, m01, T03, T10, m01, T03, T01	**6d14h**	74	8d14h	39	**0.049**
X, m01, m01, T03, T15	**6d22h**	58	8d19h	18	0.098

Fig. 5 summarizes the task changes detected in individual actors $F_{T\times r}^N$ with $\beta = 4$ compared to the task changes detected in the entire process; it displays 225 task changes in 65 actors. We observe a number of changes peaking around process change points; most changes follow the same trend and largely coincide with the process change, e.g. 27 task changes in actors within 5 days of cp_2 (weeks 28 and 29). We also observe 8 task changes in actors going against the trend of process changes within 25 days of the change point, one of which within 5 days (week 29). Surprisingly, we also see many task changes in individual actors only, i.e., either not happening in proximity of the process change or not reflected in process task changes.

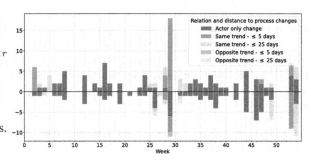

Fig. 5. Number of tasks rising (+) and falling (-) in $F_{T\times r}^N$ in individual actors with $\beta = 4$ compared to task changes in the entire process F_T^N ($\beta = 3$).

Objective O3. Table 4 summarizes the changes detected in task handovers between actors ($F_{T\times r}^c$) (left) and in task switching in individual actors ($F_{T\times r}^r$) (right) happening within 5 days of process change point cp_2 with $\beta = 4$. In Table 4 (left), we

Table 4. Number and trend of detected changes in case handovers between individual actors $F_{T\times r}^c$ (left) and in task switches in individual actors $F_{T\times r}^r$ (right) within 5 days of cp_2 with $\beta = 4$.

Case handovers $F_{T\times r}, c, c = (t_i, t_j)$

a_j	a_i m03	T01...T15
m03	-7	
T01	-5	
T02		
T03		
T10	-6	
T15	-5	

Task switches $F_{T\times r}, r, r = (t_i, t_j)$

a_j	a_i m03	T01	T02	T03	T10	T15
m03	-5	-2			-3	-3
T01	-3	+5	+2	-1	+5	+4
T02				+6	+6	
T03		+2	-1	+6	-3	
T10	-3	+5			+4	+5
T15	-1	+4			+4	+3

observe for 5–7 actors a reduction in handovers from m03 to m03, T01, T10 and T15 and observe similar reductions in task switching also between m03 and m03,...,T15; this decrease in m03 is also reflected in the process changes (see Table 2).

Conversely, we observe for 2–5 actors increases in task switching involving T01, T10 and T15, suggesting that handing over these tasks to other actors has been replaced by actors sequencing these tasks more themselves. In Fig. 4 (right), we also observe for 6 actors a uniform increase in task switches involving T02 (in line with the process change) and a non-uniform change in task-switching involving T03.

6   Conclusion

We generalized control-flow drift detection to multi-perspective drift detection by feature extraction from a multi-layered event knowledge graph (EKG). We use aggregation in an EKG with actor and case paths to extract novel features about (changes in) actor behavior along the control-flow in the form of task (variants) and handovers between actors. We rely on an existing change point detection [1] but propose an entirely new set of features that is not available in a regular event log.

The experimental evaluation showed that including features combining the actor and the control-flow perspective leads to more robust drift point detection with on average (up to 2.6×) stronger signal changes compared to an existing approach using the same detection method. The robustness of task features in drift detection arises because a task sequentially composes multiple control-flow features, thus suppressing "noisy" drift signals of individual control-flow features within the larger task, which we analyzed theoretically and confirmed experimentally. Interestingly, we observed (1) drift on the task level to be correlated with process performance, and (2) individual actors also showing drift independent of control-flow drift in various forms. This shows that actor behavior can play a significant role in real-life processes and suggests that detecting drift in the actor perspective is essential for continuous process analysis and improvement [7] and can provides new insights in the context of (changing) routines [16,18], effect of process redesign [22] or fraud detection in auditing [12]. Further research on the impact of the relationship between resource and control-flow perspective on process performance could help with the identification of root causes for performance deviations.

Our findings rely on the quality of the task clustering and to what extent clustering yields the real-life tasks in the process; doing this properly requires a detailed understanding of the process. Furthermore, the task clustering in itself still requires manual support, hindering the integration into a continuous monitoring system. A limitation shared with all other drift detection approaches is that our approach ignores edges spanning a time window, potentially leaving certain drifts undetected. An EKG based approach could consider them but this requires further research. A next step is to investigate a more systematic approach to analyze cause-effect relations in more detail, possibly including synthetic datasets and a more comprehensive parameter exploration to systematically evaluate the detection method. Moreover, our feature extraction on EKG is generic, enabling further research on drift detection in other process dimensions such as data objects, relations, or queues [10]. Finally, whereas we showed feasibility on two real-life datasets, the scalability of the approach still needs to be systematically investigated.

References

1. Adams, J.N., van Zelst, S.J., Rose, T., van der Aalst, W.M.P.: Explainable concept drift in process mining. Inf. Syst. **114**, 102177 (2023)
2. Aggarwal, C.C.: Data Mining - The Textbook. Springer, Cham (2015). https://doi.org/10.1007/978-3-319-14142-8
3. Bonifati, A., Fletcher, G.H.L., Voigt, H., Yakovets, N.: Querying Graphs. Synthesis Lectures on Data Management. Morgan & Claypool Publishers (2018)
4. Bose, R.P.J.C., van der Aalst, W.M.P., Zliobaite, I., Pechenizkiy, M.: Dealing with concept drifts in process mining. IEEE Trans. Neural Netw. Learn. Syst. **25**(1), 154–171 (2014)
5. Delcoucq, L., Lecron, F., Fortemps, P., van der Aalst, W.M.P.: Resource-centric process mining: clustering using local process models. In: SAC 2020, pp. 45–52. ACM (2020)
6. van Dongen, B.F.: BPI challenge 2017. Dataset (2017). https://doi.org/10.4121/12705737.v2
7. Dumas, M., et al.: AI-augmented business process management systems: a research manifesto. ACM Trans. Manag. Inf. Syst. **14**(1), 11:1–11:19 (2023)
8. El-Khawaga, G., Abu-Elkheir, M., Barakat, S.I., Riad, A.M., Reichert, M.: CONDA-PM - a systematic review and framework for concept drift analysis in process mining. Algorithms **13**(7), 161 (2020)
9. Esser, S., Fahland, D.: Multi-dimensional event data in graph databases. J. Data Semant. **10**, 109–141 (2021)
10. Fahland, D.: Process mining over multiple behavioral dimensions with event knowledge graphs. In: van der Aalst, W.M.P., Carmona, J. (eds.) Process Mining Handbook. LNBIP, vol. 448, pp. 274–319. Springer, Cham (2022). https://doi.org/10.1007/978-3-031-08848-3_9
11. van Hulzen, G.A.W.M., Li, C., Martin, N., van Zelst, S.J., Depaire, B.: Mining context-aware resource profiles in the presence of multitasking. Artif. Intell. Med. **134**, 102434 (2022)
12. Jans, M., Eulerich, M.: Process mining for financial auditing. In: van der Aalst, W.M.P., Carmona, J. (eds.) Process Mining Handbook. LNBIP, vol. 448, pp. 445–467. Springer, Cham (2022). https://doi.org/10.1007/978-3-031-08848-3_15
13. Jooken, L., Jans, M., Depaire, B.: Mining valuable collaborations from event data using the recency-frequency-monetary principle. In: CAiSE 2022. LNCS, vol. 13295, pp. 339–354. Springer, Cham (2022). https://doi.org/10.1007/978-3-031-07472-1_20
14. Klijn, E.L., Mannhardt, F., Fahland, D.: Classifying and detecting task executions and routines in processes using event graphs. In: BPM 2021. LNBIP, vol. 427, pp. 212–229. Springer, Cham (2021). https://doi.org/10.1007/978-3-030-85440-9_13
15. Klijn, E.L., Mannhardt, F., Fahland, D.: Aggregating event knowledge graphs for task analysis. In: Montali, M., Senderovich, A., Weidlich, M. (eds.) ICPM 2022. LNBIP, vol. 468, pp. 493–505. Springer, Cham (2022). https://doi.org/10.1007/978-3-031-27815-0_36
16. Kremser, W., Blagoev, B.: The dynamics of prioritizing: how actors temporally pattern complex role-routine ecologies. Adm. Sci. Q. **66**(2), 339–379 (2021)
17. Lu, J., Liu, A., Dong, F., Gu, F., Gama, J., Zhang, G.: Learning under concept drift: a review. IEEE Trans. Knowl. Data Eng. **31**(12), 2346–2363 (2018)
18. Pentland, B., Feldman, M., Becker, M., Liu, P.: Dynamics of organizational routines: a generative model. J. Manag. Stud. **49**, 1484–1508 (2012)
19. Sato, D.M.V., Freitas, S.C.D., Barddal, J.P., Scalabrin, E.E.: A survey on concept drift in process mining. ACM Comput. Surv. **54**(9), 189:1–189:38 (2022)

20. Tour, A., Polyvyanyy, A., Kalenkova, A.A.: Agent system mining: vision, benefits, and challenges. IEEE Access **9**, 99480–99494 (2021)
21. Wambui, G.D., Waititu, G.A., Wanjoya, A.K.: The power of the pruned exact linear time (PELT) test in multiple changepoint detection. AJTAS **4**, 581–586 (2015)
22. Wurm, B., Grisold, T., Mendling, J., vom Brocke, J.: Business process management and routine dynamics, pp. 513–524. Cambridge University Press (2021)
23. Yang, J., Ouyang, C., van der Aalst, W.M.P., ter Hofstede, A.H.M., Yu, Y.: OrdinoR: a framework for discovering, evaluating, and analyzing organizational models using event logs. Decis. Support Syst. **158**, 113771 (2022)

Process Modelling and Management

On the Flexibility of Declarative Process Specifications

Carl Corea[1(✉)], Paolo Felli[2], Marco Montali[3], and Fabio Patrizi[4]

[1] University of Koblenz, Koblenz, Germany
ccorea@uni-koblenz.de
[2] University of Bologna, Bologna, Italy
paolo.felli@unibo.it
[3] Free University of Bozen-Bolzano, Bolzano, Italy
montali@inf.unibz.it
[4] Sapienza University of Rome, Rome, Italy
patrizi@diag.uniroma1.it

Abstract. Declarative process specifications, such as Declare, provide a natural framework to capture flexible business processes. However, the specification may be more, or less flexible, depending on how much freedom it provides – for example, a specification that is so strict it allows only one exact behavior (i.e., trace) can be seen as inflexible. Surprisingly, little attention has been given to this key feature in declarative process specifications, and how to measure it. In this paper, we therefore close this gap by investigating how to measure the degree of flexibility of declarative process specifications. We show how techniques for measuring the density of infinite regular languages can be effectively employed to define a measure of flexibility for constraint-based process specifications, focusing in particular on Declare. Also, we show when our measure (which is a limit) is guaranteed to exist for Declare specifications, and present how to actually compute our measure using known techniques.

Keywords: Declarative Process Specifications · Flexibility · Language Distances

1 Introduction

Managing flexibility in business process models and their execution is a long-standing, widely studied problem [19]. In particular, *flexibility by design* aims at incorporating flexibility within process models. Since seminal works [20], one prominent line of research approached this challenge by equipping the process modelling language with (less restrictive) temporal constraints. The literature has then led to a more separate way of presenting these different modelling constructs, namely *constraint-based* approaches to process modelling, such as DCR Graphs [9] and Declare [15]. Such *declarative* approaches are usually introduced as inherently flexible, while sequence flow-based approaches, like Petri

© The Author(s), under exclusive license to Springer Nature Switzerland AG 2024
G. Guizzardi et al. (Eds.): CAiSE 2024, LNCS 14663, pp. 161–177, 2024.
https://doi.org/10.1007/978-3-031-61057-8_10

nets, are deemed as *procedural* and inherently rigid. While this is a good intuitive metaphor, it is technically misleading: whether a specification is more or less flexible does not depend on how it has been modelled, but rather on how much freedom it provides when considering the behaviours it accepts. For example, even a Declare specification can be so strict that it allows only for one trace. So, the question arises what exactly it means to be "declarative", or flexible.

Surprisingly, little attention has been given to define, characterise, and measure the *behavioural flexibility* of specifications. In this work, we aim to fill this gap, by investigating how to measure the *degree of flexibility* of a process specification, focusing in particular on infinite regular languages and using Declare. If we would be working with finite languages (i.e., finite sets of traces), flexibility would be measured quite straightforwardly by directly comparing their sizes, for example through the widely adopted Jaccard distance J, where $J(A, B) = \frac{|A \cap B|}{|A \cup B|}$. This has been already explored to compare Declare specifications on traces of a given maximum length [21]. However, our problem inherently deals with infinite regular languages: when considering specifications of processes built over a given alphabet Σ of activities, the *maximally permissive behavior* corresponds to Σ^*. Less flexible specifications of processes are typically infinite as well, as it is enough to have a loop in the process.

We hence need a meaningful way to measure flexibility of infinite regular languages, and more specifically to relate the (number of traces) accepted by a specification of interest, with those of the maximally permissive behaviour Σ^*. To our aid, mathematical techniques to compare infinite regular languages exist in the literature - but have not been applied in the context of processes. Of special interest for us is the approach developed in [13,14], which brings forward a measure that takes inspiration from the Jaccard distance, lifting it to the infinite setting by measuring the relative density of the languages to be compared. On the downside, this distance is based on a limit, which does not always exist. Based on this, we provide the following contributions:

1. We discuss desirable properties of a flexibility measure, and why notions based on the entropy of infinite languages [1,16,17] are not suitable (Sect. 2).
2. We take the distance measure for infinite regular languages introduced in [13,14], and adapt it to our setting, with the goal of measuring flexibility as a distance between the language of a given specification, and Σ^* (Sect. 4).
3. While this measure does not always exist in general (not even restricting to LTL_f) [13,14], we discuss its applicability to Declare in practice (Sect. 4).
4. We further study properties and behavior of our proposed measure (Sect. 5).
5. We show how to actually compute this measure using algorithmic techniques from the foundational literature [13,14], in particular, related to counting the number of possible walks in digraphs [22] (Sect. 6).

2   Intuitions on Flexibility

We discuss the intuition behind flexibility to introduce initial postulates for flexibility measures, discussing why existing entropy measures are not adequate.

2.1 Postulates for Flexibility

We start from the mathematical assumption that a flexibility measure is a function mapping a regular language over a given alphabet to a value in $[0, 1]$, where 0 represents *no flexibility*, while 1 represents *maximal flexibility*.

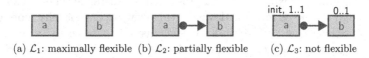

(a) $\mathcal{L}_1$: maximally flexible (b) $\mathcal{L}_2$: partially flexible   (c) $\mathcal{L}_3$: not flexible

Fig. 1. Three Declare specifications exhibiting different degrees of flexibility.

Consider the Declare specifications in Fig. 1 (we will recall syntax and semantics later). All three specifications are defined over the alphabet $\Sigma = \{a, b\}$, consisting of two activities. The one in Fig. 1(a) is maximally permissive: it does not contain any constraint, and so implicitly it allows one to execute both activities an arbitrary amount of times, and in whatever order. This specification corresponds to the regular language $\mathcal{L}_1 = \Sigma^*$, in turn yielding the maximum degree of flexibility one can hope for. This leads to a first postulate.

Postulate 1 (Maximally permissive specifications). For the language $\mathcal{L} = \Sigma^*$ over Σ, a flexibility measure should return 1.   ◁

Figure 1(c) shows a specification that is at the opposite extreme of the flexibility spectrum. $\mathcal{L}_3$ results form a Declare specification dictating that every trace must start with a (due to **init** on a), every a must be eventually followed by b (due to the **response** constraint from a to b), but a and b can occur at most once (due to ..1). Hence $\mathcal{L}_3$ only contains the single trace ab. To think about what a flexibility value should be in this case, it is important to recall that in this work we are only dealing with infinite languages. If one would deal with finite languages, it would be fair to assume that a flexibility value should be 0 iff a language accepts no traces. However, in our setting of *infinite* languages, the flexibility can only be assessed on the level of a mathematical limit (as otherwise, it would never be possible to compare two infinite languages). As a result, the language shown in Fig. 1(c) must be judged as having no flexibility, and the same must hold for *any finite* language, which in a sense only provides the (very limited) option of choosing one among their finitely many traces.

Postulate 2 (Non-infinite specifications). A flexibility measure should return 0 for every finite language $\mathcal{L}$ over Σ.   ◁

Clearly, these two initial postulates, although important, are not sufficient to fully characterize a desirable notion of flexibility, as these only address the two the extreme situations. Somewhere in-between, we have $\mathcal{L}_2$. Intuitively, $\mathcal{L}_2$ should be viewed as "half" as flexible as $\mathcal{L}_1$, as for any word of length n only those that end with one of the two possible symbols is accepted. Instead of making a case here for further postulates, we postpone to Sect. 5 the discussion of how our measure behaves when a specification enjoys *some* degree of flexibility.

2.2 Related Work on Flexibility

In the seminal work by [20], those authors define flexibility as the *"ability of the [...] process to execute on the basis of a loosely, or partially specified model, where the full specification of the model is made at runtime"*. In this sense, a model is considered as more "flexible" if it can produce more instance types (i.e., distinct paths through a process model). However, this view is conceptually more geared towards finite languages, where the set of such instance types is finite and the sets of instance types can be compared directly with standard Jaccard-like distance measures to determine which is "more flexible" (cf. [21]). The smallest amount of flexibility possible would be that no trace (or 1 trace) is accepted, and the largest degree of flexibility possible would be any infinite language. This, however, leaves out the case in which two infinite languages need to be compared, which we are dealing with in this work.

Before continuing, we discuss why a prominent approach from process mining, namely that of *language entropy* [16,17], is not applicable for our purpose. As argued already, the notion of flexibility is related to the *size* of the language accepted, compared with that of the maximally permissive specification. As we are dealing with infinite languages, this has to be interpreted in terms of *relative* density w.r.t. Σ^*. This is why related measures based on language entropy cannot be used for our purpose: while entropy measures the *growth rate* of a language, we are instead interested in measuring its *(relative) size/density*.

To substantiate this observation, consider again the specifications and languages from Fig. 1. The entropy of a language is a limit which is defined as the logarithm of the number of words with length $\leq n$ (divided by n), as n grows to infinity [1,14]. Applying this to our example, $\mathcal{L}_1$ has 2^n words of length n, and $\mathcal{L}_2$ has 2^{n-1} words of length n. For $\mathcal{L}_3$, it is immediate to see that this has an entropy of 0. So $\mathcal{L}_1$ has $1+2+\ldots+2^{n-1} = 2^n - 1$ words of length at most n and $\mathcal{L}_2$ has $1+2+\ldots+2^n = 2^{n+1} - 1$ words of length at most n. The entropy for $\mathcal{L}_1$ and $\mathcal{L}_2$ are computed as follows, showing how this notion does not capture the intuition that $\mathcal{L}_2$ is "half" as flexible as $\mathcal{L}_1$:[1]

$$\lim_{n\to\infty} \log(2^n-1)/n = \lim_{n\to\infty} \log(2^n)/n = \lim_{n\to\infty} n\log(2)/n = \log(2)$$

$$\lim_{n\to\infty} \log(2^{n+1}-1)/n = \lim_{n\to\infty} \log(2^{n+1})/n = \lim_{n\to\infty} (n+1)\log(2)/n = \log(2)$$

3 Preliminaries

Declarative process specifications define properties of process traces, i.e., sequences over an alphabet of activity labels. In this paper, we focus in particular on Declare process specifications, in which Linear Temporal Logic on finite strings (LTL_f) is used to provide semantics to Declare templates.

---

[1] This also holds for some variants of entropy as in [17] (i.e., short-circuit entropy): if we short-circuit the languages from Fig. 1, we obtain a short-circuit entropy of 1.585 for $\mathcal{L}_1$ and 1.2715 for $\mathcal{L}_2$, which again does not capture the desired behavior.

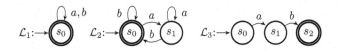

Fig. 2. DFAs for languages $\mathcal{L}_1$–$\mathcal{L}_3$, corresponding to the specifications in Fig. 1.

3.1 Deterministic Finite-State Automata

Let Σ be a finite alphabet. A trace over Σ is a finite, possibly empty sequence $\sigma_0 \ldots \sigma_n$, with $\sigma_i \in \Sigma$ for each $0 \leq i \leq n$. For $n \geq 0$, Σ^n denotes the set of all sequences over Σ of length n, while Σ^* denotes the set of all possible trace over Σ, including the empty trace ϵ. A *regular* language is a set $\mathcal{L} \subseteq \Sigma^*$ and it can be represented as a DFA [18] over Σ, as formalized next.

Definition 1 (DFA). A DFA is a tuple $A = (\Sigma, S, \delta, s_0, S_F)$, where: *(i)* Σ is the alphabet of labels; *(ii)* S is a non-empty set of states and $s_0 \in S$ the initial state; *(iii)* $\delta : S \times \Sigma \to S$ is a state-transition function which, given a state s and a label σ, specifies the next state $s' = \delta(s, \sigma)$; *(iv)* $S_F \subseteq S$ are final states.◁

A run of a DFA A is a finite sequence $\rho = s_0 \sigma_0 s_1 \sigma_1 \ldots \sigma_{n-1} s_n$, alternating states and labels, s.t. $s_{i+1} = \delta(s_i, \sigma_i)$ for all $0 \leq i < n$ and $s_n \in S_F$. Given ρ as above, its corresponding trace is $\sigma_0 \ldots \sigma_n$. We thus define the language of a DFA A as the set of traces corresponding to all its runs. A DFA is said to be *trimmed* iff its final states are reachable from each state in S.

The DFA representations of the specifications in Fig. 1 (languages $\mathcal{L}_1$–$\mathcal{L}_3$) are shown in Fig. 2. We will use these as running examples.

3.2 LTL$_f$

Linear Temporal Logic (LTL) over infinite traces is a well known specification language for declarative process specifications. As an infinite regular language is interpreted as an infinite set of finite words, it is necessary to consider LTL$_f$, i.e., a variant of LTL interpreted over finite traces [5].

Considering again a fixed alphabet Σ, LTL$_f$ formulas are built from propositions in Σ and boolean connectives, the unary operator **X** (*next*) and the binary operator **U** (*until*). The resulting grammar is as follows, where $\sigma \in \Sigma$:

$$\varphi ::= \sigma \mid \neg\varphi \mid \varphi_1 \wedge \varphi_2 \mid \mathbf{X}\,\varphi \mid \varphi_1 \,\mathbf{U}\, \varphi_2.$$

The usual propositional abbreviations for disjunction $\vee$, implication $\to$, *true*, *false* apply. We also write abbreviations $\mathbf{F}\,\varphi \equiv true\,\mathbf{U}\,\varphi$ (*eventually*) and $\mathbf{G}\,\varphi \equiv \neg\,\mathbf{F}\,\neg\varphi$ (*always*). LTL$_f$ formulae are interpreted over finite traces as follows.

Definition 2. We inductively define when a trace satisfies a formula ϕ at instant $0 \leq i \leq last(t)$, written $t, i \models \phi$. Then t satisfies ϕ, written $t \models \phi$, iff $t, 0 \models \phi$.

$t, i \models true$

$t, i \models a$ iff $t(i) = a$

$t, i \models \neg\varphi$ iff $t, i \not\models \varphi$

$t, i \models \varphi_1 \wedge \varphi_2$ iff $t, i \models \varphi_1$ and $t, i \models \varphi_2$

$t, i \models \mathbf{X}\varphi$ iff $i < n$ and $t, i + 1 \models \varphi$

$t, i \models \varphi_1 \mathbf{U} \varphi_2$ iff $t, j \models \varphi_2$ with $i \leq j \leq n$, and $t, k \models \varphi_1$ for all $k, i \leq k < j$.

◁

The set of traces satisfying a LTL$_f$ formula φ is called the language of φ, and a corresponding DFA, denoted $\mathcal{A}(\varphi)$, can be computed, s.t. given a trace t we have that $t \models \varphi$ iff $t \in \mathcal{A}(\varphi)$ [5]. Indeed, for any LTL$_f$ formula φ there exists an NFA whose language consists of all traces t so that $t \models \varphi$, and this NFA can be then determinized to a DFA (cf. Sect. 3.1).

3.3 Declarative Process Specifications

Declare is a language and graphical notation that allows one to specify constraints by using of a catalogue common templates [7]. Intuitively, a Declare template is a predicate $\kappa(x_1, \ldots, x_m)$, with variables $x_1, \ldots, x_m$, whose semantics is specified (usually) by an LTL$_f$ formula φ_κ with alphabet Σ. Through a mapping that binds each variable x_i to an element of Σ, a constraint is interpreted as imposing a restriction over the possible activity sequences, according to the semantics of φ_κ. A selection of Declare constraint templates is found in [4], together with the associated graphical notation, LTL$_f$ formula and DFA.

Definition 3. A (Declare) specification is a tuple DS $= (\mathrm{T}, X, \Sigma, K)$:

- T is a finite set of templates, i.e. predicates $\kappa(x_1, \ldots, x_m)$ with variables $x_1, \ldots, x_m \in X$, whose semantics is given as a LTL$_f$ formula φ_κ over X;
- Σ is a finite, non-empty set of labels as before;
- K is a finite set of *constraints*, namely pairs of the form $(\kappa(x_1, \ldots, x_m), \gamma)$ so that $\kappa(x_1, \ldots, x_m) \in \mathrm{T}$ and $\gamma : X \mapsto \Sigma$ is a partial function mapping each x_i, with $i \in [1, m]$, to an activity label.

◁

Given a constraint $c = (\kappa(x_1, \ldots, x_m), \gamma)$ as above, the LTL$_f$ formula obtained from φ_κ by replacing each variable occurrence $x \in X$ by $\gamma(x) \in \Sigma$, denoted φ_c, can therefore be evaluated over traces $t \in \Sigma^*$. We say that t satisfies the constraint c as above iff $t \models \varphi_c$. Similarly, by conjoining all formulas φ_c for each $c \in K$ in a specification DS, hence obtaining the formula $\varphi_{\mathrm{DS}} = \wedge_{c \in K} \varphi_c$, we say that a trace t is a *model trace* of DS iff $t \models \varphi_{\mathrm{DS}}$.

4 Flexibility of Declarative Process Specifications

We now illustrate the proposed definition of flexibility. Since it is based on the computation of a limit, in Sect. 4.2 we discuss its applicability to declarative process specifications by showing when said limit exists. We discuss and analyze further the properties and behavior of this measure in Sect. 5, and provide details on how one can compute its actual value in Sect. 6.

4.1   A Language-Theoretic Measure of Flexibility

Taking as maximally permissive the language Σ^*, we define a baseline flexibility measure as the fraction of words of length n which are supported by a regular language divided by the number of words of length n in Σ^* as n approaches infinity. We fix two important notations: (1) $W_n(\mathcal{L}) = \{w \in \mathcal{L} \mid length(w) = n\}$. (2) $W_{\leq n}(\mathcal{L}) = \bigcup_{i=0}^{n} W_i(\mathcal{L})$. Based on these, we define the baseline flexibility.

Definition 4. The *flexibility* of a regular language $\mathcal{L}$ over alphabet Σ is:

$$flex_\Sigma(\mathcal{L}) = \lim_{n \to \infty} \frac{|W_{\leq n}(\mathcal{L})|}{|W_{\leq n}(\Sigma^*)|}$$

When apparent from the context, we omit the subscript and write $flex(\mathcal{L})$.   ◁

As we view flexibility of a language $\mathcal{L}$ as the fraction of words of length n in Σ^* which are also in $\mathcal{L}$, there exists a fraction d of words of length n which are not in $\mathcal{L}$, representing the *distance* between $\mathcal{L}$ and Σ^*. As proposed in [14], a natural definition of distance between two languages can be obtained from an extension of the Jaccard distance for finite languages. This is defined as $\frac{\mathcal{L}\Delta\mathcal{L}'}{\mathcal{L}\cup\mathcal{L}'}$, where $\mathcal{L}\Delta\mathcal{L}'$ is the symmetric difference, i.e., $\mathcal{L}\Delta\mathcal{L}' = (\mathcal{L}\backslash\mathcal{L}') \cup (\mathcal{L}'\backslash\mathcal{L})$. Accordingly, as in [14], one can define a variant of the Jaccard distance that considers the words of length up to n, denoted $J_{\leq n}(\mathcal{L}, \mathcal{L}')$, so that its natural extension to infinite languages employs the limit of n to infinity:[2]

$$\lim_{n \to \infty} J_{\leq n}(\mathcal{L}, \mathcal{L}') = \lim_{n \to \infty} \frac{|W_{\leq n}(\mathcal{L}\Delta\mathcal{L}')|}{|W_{\leq n}(\mathcal{L} \cup \mathcal{L}')|}$$

As in our approach we take $\mathcal{L}' = \Sigma^*$, and $\mathcal{L}\backslash\Sigma^* = \emptyset$, we can simplify the numerator as $\Sigma^*\backslash\mathcal{L}$, i.e., the complement of $\mathcal{L}$, denoted $\mathcal{L}^C$. Likewise, the denominator is equal to Σ^*. So for the distance to Σ^*, we have the following:

$$\lim_{n \to \infty} J_{\leq n}(\mathcal{L}, \Sigma^*) = \lim_{n \to \infty} \frac{|W_{\leq n}(\mathcal{L}\Delta\Sigma^*)|}{|W_{\leq n}(\mathcal{L} \cup \Sigma^*)|} = \lim_{n \to \infty} \frac{|W_{\leq n}(\mathcal{L}^C)|}{|W_{\leq n}(\Sigma^*)|}$$

Finally, as this distance is naturally the complement to flexibility, we can define the following flexibility measure F_{J_n} based on the Jaccard distance.

Definition 5. For a regular language $\mathcal{L}$, the flexibility measure $\mathsf{F}_{J_n}(\mathcal{L})$ is:

$$\mathsf{F}_{J_n}(\mathcal{L}) = 1 - \lim_{n \to \infty} J_{\leq n}(\mathcal{L}, \Sigma^*) = 1 - \lim_{n \to \infty} \frac{|W_{\leq n}(\mathcal{L}^C)|}{|W_{\leq n}(\Sigma^*)|}$$

◁

Before showing that this in fact corresponds to our definition of $flex(\mathcal{L})$, we first apply it to our running examples (cf. Sect. 5 for further discussions).

---

[2] In this section, we assume that the limit exists. We defer the problem of establishing whether this is the case for our application domain to Sect. 4.2.

Example 1. Consider again the languages $\mathcal{L}_1$–$\mathcal{L}_3$ in Fig. 2. We start with the simple case of $\mathcal{L}_3$, which is finite. The flexibility of $\mathcal{L}_3$ is 0 as $\mathcal{L}_3$ has exactly 1 accepted word of length $\leq n$, for any $n > 2$. In the following, we will therefore focus on the more interesting cases of $\mathcal{L}_1$ and $\mathcal{L}_2$. $\mathcal{L}_1$ is the language $(a|b)^*$ (also including the empty trace ε), and $\mathcal{L}_2$ is the language $\varepsilon|(a|b)^*b$ (which only accepts words that end with b, or simply ε). The complement for $\mathcal{L}_1$ is the empty language, and the complement for $\mathcal{L}_2$ is the language accepting only words that end on a, i.e., $(a|b)^*a$. Note that the complement of a language can be obtained by simply swapping the accepting and non-accepting states of the (complete, not trimmed) DFA. For $\mathcal{L}_1^C$, there are 0 words of length n; for $\mathcal{L}_2^C$, there are 2^{n-1} words of length n; and for Σ^*, there are 2^n words of length n (We will show how to compute this for arbitrary languages in Sect. 6). So $\mathcal{L}_1^C$ has 0 words of length at most n, $\mathcal{L}_2^C$ has $1+2+4+...+2^{n-1} = 2^n - 1$ words of length at most n, and Σ^* has $1+2+4+...+2^n = 2^{n+1} - 1$ words of length at most n. Then we have:

$$\mathsf{F}_{J_n}(\mathcal{L}_1) = 1 - \lim_{n\to\infty} \frac{0}{2^{n+1}-1} = 1, \quad \mathsf{F}_{J_n}(\mathcal{L}_2) = 1 - \lim_{n\to\infty} \frac{2^n - 1}{2^{n+1}-1} = 1 - \frac{1}{2} = 0.5$$

So $\mathcal{L}_1$ has a flexibility value of 1 (as it accepts all words), and $\mathcal{L}_2$ has a flexibility value of 0.5 (as it does not accept "half" of all words from Σ^*).   ◁

Theorem 1. $flex_\Sigma(\mathcal{L}) = F_{J_n}(\mathcal{L})$ for any regular language $\mathcal{L}$ over alphabet Σ. ◁

Proof. Observe that $\mathcal{L} \subseteq \Sigma^*$. Thus, by $\mathcal{L}^C = \mathcal{L}\Delta\Sigma^*$ and $\mathcal{L} = \Sigma^*\backslash\mathcal{L}^C$ it follows that $W_{\leq n}(\mathcal{L}) = W_{\leq n}(\Sigma^*\backslash\mathcal{L}^C)$. Moreover, since $\mathcal{L} \subseteq \Sigma^*$, it follows that $|W_{\leq n}(\Sigma^*\backslash\mathcal{L}^C)| = |W_{\leq n}(\Sigma^*)| - |W_{\leq n}(\mathcal{L}^C)|$. Then $|W_{\leq n}(\mathcal{L})| = |W_{\leq n}(\Sigma^*)| - |W_{\leq n}(\mathcal{L}^C)|$, and the thesis then follows by limit linearity.   ⊣

This result shows how the needed notion of flexibility as a measure of language sizes (rather than growth) can be obtained by building on the notion of language distances. This sets the framework needed for flexibility analysis.

However, the existence of the limit in the definition of flexibility poses a major obstacle, as it is not guaranteed to exist for arbitrary regular languages. Consider for instance $(aa)^*$. When n is even, the fraction in the flexibility measure is 1, while when n is odd the fraction is 0, so the limit is not defined. Therefore, before analyzing how to actually compute the distance values (see Sect. 6), we first show that the limit indeed exists for relevant fragments of Declare specifications.

4.2   Applicability of the Flexibility Measure to Declare

As discussed in Sect. 3.3, every Declare constraint can be represented as a DFA with alphabet Σ and therefore a regular language. In this section, we discuss sufficient conditions on these "constraint" DFAs to guarantee that the limit in Definition 5 exists and is finite, and thus the flexibility measure can be computed.

Crucially, the same guarantee must hold when one takes into account at once the entire set of constraints in a Declare specification, i.e., it must hold for the cross-product of the DFAs of individual constraints.

We rely on the following fundamental result in the literature [14], reported later in this section, which states that the limit used in our definition of flexibility measure exists and is finite when the DFA is *aperiodic*. Intuitively, aperiodicity requires that there is no constant $p > 1$ so that all paths between every couple of states has length multiple of p. We proceed as follows:

1. We observe that, with the exception of CHAINRESPONSE, CHAINSUCCES-SION, the DFAs of standard Declare templates are aperiodic [4,6]. In this particular case, aperiodicity is trivially witnessed by the presence of self-loops in each strongly-connected component of the DFA, which implies aperiodicity;
2. Then we turn to the case of a DFA obtained as cross-product of DFAs for Declare templates. If the product is aperiodic, then the limit exists and is finite. This already gives us a sufficient, formal condition for being able to compute the flexibility measure of a Declare specification DS. However, since it is not possible beforehand to determine this, we comment on a rather simple, sufficient condition which can be checked directly on DS.

Aperiodicity. First, we recall the required preliminaries on aperiodic graphs [14]. The *period* of a strongly-connected graph (V, E) where V the set of vertexes and E the set of directed edges, is the largest integer p s.t. the vertices can be grouped into classes $Q_0, Q_1, \ldots, Q_{p-1}$ such that if $v \in Q_i$ then all of the out neighbors of v, namely all vertexes u such that $(v, u) \in E$, are in Q_j with $j = i + 1 \pmod{p}$. A graph as above is aperiodic iff it has period $p = 1$, and the period of a graph with multiple (strongly-connected) components is simply the least common multiple of their periods. If $|\Sigma| = 1$, results on the limit $\lim_{n \to \infty} J_{\leq n}(\mathcal{L}, \mathcal{L}')$ for cyclic languages are available in the literature [3]. However, as this case is of no particular interest here, from now we restrict to $|\Sigma| > 1$.

It is known [14, Thm. 5.7] that, given two regular languages $\mathcal{L}$ and $\mathcal{L}'$ with DFAs $\mathcal{A}$ and $\mathcal{A}'$, if all of the components of $\mathcal{A}$ and $\mathcal{A}'$ are aperiodic, then $\lim_{n \to \infty} J_{=n}(\mathcal{L}, \mathcal{L}')$ exists and is finite. Here, $J_{=n}(\mathcal{L}, \mathcal{L}')$ is the Jaccard distance that considers all the words of length n rather than up to n (as $J_{\leq n}(\mathcal{L}, \mathcal{L}')$ in Sect. 4.1). As shown in Sect. 6, from this we can compute $J_{\leq n}(\mathcal{L}, \mathcal{L}')$.

Aperiodicity and Flexibility. We now apply these notions to the DFAs for Declare constraints, noting (cf. their catalogue [4,6]) that the underlying topology of their templates (their graph structure) is aperiodic, with the exception of *chain* templates such as CHAINRESPONSE, CHAINSUCCESSION. This is immediate to prove: as we assumed $|\Sigma| > 1$, all these DFAs have a self-loop on at least one state in each of their strongly connected components, which directly implies aperiodicity, as one cannot partition their set of states as in the definition of periodicity. We call these Declare templates aperiodic templates.

Theorem 2. *Given a Declare constraint $k = (\text{K}(\cdots), \gamma)$ and its language $\mathcal{L}_k$, formula ϕ_k and DFA $\mathcal{A}(\phi_k)$, then $\lim_{n \to \infty} J_{\leq n}(\mathcal{L}_k, \Sigma^*)$ as in Definition 5 converges if $\mathcal{A}(\phi_k)$ is aperiodic or, equivalently, $\text{K}(\cdots)$ is one of the aperiodic templates.* ◁

It remains to address the case of DFAs obtained as cross-products of the set of DFAs corresponding to templates in the Declare specification, hence representing the conjunction of the constraints. By directly extending the previous result:

Theorem 3. *Given a Declare specification* DS *with corresponding language* $\mathcal{L}_{\mathrm{DS}}$, *then* $\lim_{n \to \infty} J_{\leq n}(\mathcal{L}_{\mathrm{DS}}, \Sigma^*)$ *as in Definition 5 converges if* $\mathcal{A}_{\mathrm{DS}}$ *is aperiodic.* ◁

A Simple Condition for Aperiodic Specifications. Note that even restricting to aperiodic templates does not determine an aperiodic product DFA $\mathcal{A}_{\mathrm{DS}}$ in general. Although one could simply check aperiodicity of $\mathcal{A}_{\mathrm{DS}}$ (even when the specification includes non-aperiodic templates such as CHAINRESPONSE) and, if it holds, compute its flexibility value, we identify one sufficient condition to guarantee this when only aperiodic templates are used. Since all the DFAs corresponding to Declare aperiodic templates not only have a self-loop on at least a state in each strongly-connected component, *but in fact on every state* (a self loop labelled by either Σ or a special symbol denoting "all other" unconstrained symbols – see [4]), if $\sigma \in \Sigma$ exists which is not mentioned in any constraint, then the cross-product of these DFAs is guaranteed to be aperiodic. The proof is again immediate: given DFAs $\mathcal{A}_a$ and $\mathcal{A}_b$, all self-loops in both of them are labelled by σ. For every two transitions $a = \delta_a(a, \sigma)$ in $\mathcal{A}_a$ and $b = \delta_b(b, \sigma)$ in $\mathcal{A}_b$, if (a, b) is in the product, then $(a, b) = \delta_p((a, b), \sigma)$ is included as well.

Therefore, given DS $= (\mathrm{T}, X, \Sigma, K)$, the conditions of Theorem 3 hold when T only comprises aperiodic templates and σ as above is in Σ.

5   Discussion on the Proposed Measure

In this section, we discuss and analyse further the proposed measure $\mathit{flex}_\Sigma(\mathcal{L})$, focusing on *regular languages for which the limit of Definition 4 is defined* (which, as we have seen, is true for Declare under the conditions of Theorem 3). First, we note that the two elementary postulates presented in Sect. 2 are satisfied.

Lemma 1. *Given a regular language* $\mathcal{L}$ *over* Σ, $\mathit{flex}_\Sigma(\mathcal{L}) = 1$ *if* $\mathcal{L} = \Sigma^*$, *and* $\mathit{flex}_\Sigma(\mathcal{L}) = 0$ *if* $\mathcal{L}$ *is finite.* ◁

Proof. Directly follows from Definition 4, noticing that in the case of $\mathcal{L} = \Sigma^*$, the fraction is 1 and so is the limit, while in the case of finite $\mathcal{L}$, the numerator is a fixed number, while the denominator grows exponentially, yielding a limit of 0. ⊣

Then, we discuss when our measure $\mathit{flex}_\Sigma(\mathcal{L})$ assigns positive flexibility.

5.1   Languages with Positive Flexibility Values

Consider again language $\mathcal{L}_2$ from Fig. 1(b). As commented already in Example 1, the **response** constraint from a to b, in a setting where these are the only two available activities, constrains every trace to finish with b, i.e. $\mathcal{L}_2 = \varepsilon | (a|b)^* b$. Nonetheless, $\mathcal{L}_2$ allows to select any activity in Σ unboundedly many times (although not at each step). We call Σ-*repeating* any language having this property.

Definition 6. *Given* $\Sigma' \subseteq \Sigma$, *a regular language* $\mathcal{L}$ *is* Σ'-*repeating if* $\mathcal{L}$ *is of the form* $\mathcal{L}_a; (\mathcal{L}_b; \Sigma'^*; \mathcal{L}_c)^*; \mathcal{L}_d$, *where* $\mathcal{L}_a, \mathcal{L}_b, \mathcal{L}_c, \mathcal{L}_d$ *are regular languages over* Σ. ◁

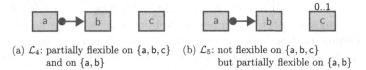

(a) $\mathcal{L}_4$: partially flexible on $\{a, b, c\}$ (b) $\mathcal{L}_5$: not flexible on $\{a, b, c\}$
and on $\{a, b\}$ but partially flexible on $\{a, b\}$

Fig. 3. Two Declare specifications that exhibit different flexibility when judged over the whole set of activities, but identical when only focusing on a and b.

We argue that allowing a free choice (1) over *the whole* Σ and (2) *unboundedly* many times, i.e. a Σ-repeating language, is the requirement for assigning flexibility greater than 0, and this is indeed the case for our measure $flex_\Sigma(\mathcal{L})$. For example, if a language $\mathcal{L}$ allows one to freely choose the activity at the beginning of the execution, but once this is done, then the execution itself is completely determined, this would be inflexible (cf. Postulate 2).

Similarly, allowing unboundedly many times a choice over $\Sigma' \subset \Sigma$ is also inflexible. Consider the examples in Fig. 3, which includes two variants of $\mathcal{L}_2$ from Fig. 1, both considering a larger alphabet including also activity c. Here, $\mathcal{L}_4$ is Σ-repeating and still retains a positive degree of flexibility ($flex_\Sigma(\mathcal{L}_4) > 0$), as it always allows one to choose between all activities a, b and c, with the only proviso that a should not be executed as last activity of the trace. Instead, $\mathcal{L}_5$ from Fig. 3(b) should have flexibility 0 (and indeed $flex_\Sigma(\mathcal{L}_5) = 0$), as it only allows for executing c once, thus restricting consequent choices to only pick between a and b. Indeed, as opposed to the unbounded opportunity of maximal freedom offered by language such as Σ^* or $\mathcal{L}_2$, at some point $\mathcal{L}_5$ *permanently* restricts the possible activities, at each step, to a subset of Σ.

Lemma 2. *Given a regular language $\mathcal{L}$ over Σ: $flex_\Sigma(\mathcal{L}) > 0$ if $\mathcal{L}$ is Σ-repeating, and $flex_\Sigma(\mathcal{L}) = 0$ if $\mathcal{L}$ is not Σ-repeating.*   ◁

Proof. Being Σ-repeating implies that, if the limit exists then the numerator of Definition 4 grows with the same exponential rate of Σ^*, thus yielding a positive fraction for $flex_\Sigma(\mathcal{L})$. Likewise, if $\mathcal{L}$ is not Σ-repeating, the exponential growth of the numerator is strictly lower than that of the denominator, yielding 0.   ⊣

5.2   A Finer-Grained Analysis

Deeming a language flexible only if it supports free decisions on the *whole* Σ unboundedly often (i.e., if Σ-repeating – see Lemma 2) may be too coarse-grained and uninformative. We discuss here how our measure can be used for more fine-grained analysis, although not *as is*. For example, we may want to grant $\mathcal{L}_4$ in Fig. 3 positive flexibility if we only focus on two activities, say, a and b. Similarly, by focussing only on a, we may even consider language a* to be in fact flexible, as it allows the process executors to decide when to end the trace.

More systematically, we can proceed by selecting one maximal set $\Sigma' \subset \Sigma$ for which $\mathcal{L}$ is Σ'-repeating. This can be done by looking into the trimmed DFA of

$\mathcal{L}$, looking for a maximal set of activities that is labeling the outgoing edges of a state in a strongly-connected component. Note that only the cardinality of such a set is relevant (not the actual activities selected therein). Then, a flexibility measure can be obtained by computing $flex_{\Sigma'}(\mathcal{L})$. Consider, e.g., $\mathcal{L}_5$ from Fig. 3, where $flex_{\Sigma}(\mathcal{L}_4) = 0$, as c can only appear at most once. However, if we restrict to two activities (i.e., $|\Sigma'| = 2$), we get $flex_{\Sigma'}(\mathcal{L}_5) = 0.5$. In fact, $\mathcal{L}_5$ can repeat two activities (in particular, a and b) unboundedly many times.

Intuitively, considering a subset Σ' when computing the limit can be understood as follows. At the numerator, the number of words in $\mathcal{L}$ of length up to n are unaffected, hence the *exact* behavior of $\mathcal{L}$ is preserved. At the denominator, the effect is instead that of simply considering as maximally flexible the possibility of choosing among $|\Sigma'|$ activities (recalling that $|\Sigma'| < |\Sigma|$). In fact, the distinction between two or more alphabet symbols is there blurred, effectively reducing the number of words of length up to n against which $W_{\leq n}(\mathcal{L})$ is compared. Indeed, note that it is not the actual identity of alphabet symbols to determine flexibility, but only the density, i.e., the *number* of words in the language. The justification for this has primarily to do with the computation of the limit, although it can also be understood within the application domain.

Assume there are in the process two or more activities that are performed by distinct agents at different times, and/or that have a natural precedence ordering in the process (for example, users log in into a web store at the beginning of the process, while delivery by the shipping department typically concludes the process). If then we accept to lose "resolution" and thus be able to distinguish between them when analyzing $\mathcal{L}$, then we can measure the flexibility of the process under this blurred lenses. Indeed, only the number of choices at each step is relevant, and one may consider the fact that some activities are not available at the same not as an indication of a too constrained, inflexible process, but simply as a natural characteristic of the domain. This may allow us to determine that the process has positive flexibility, under the assumption that we do not care to distinguish between some of the activities of customers or of the shipping department, or even more between two activities each belonging to one of these sets (as we acknowledge that these cannot possibly be executable at the same time). Hence, we reduce the total number of activities used to fix what it means to be maximally flexible, i.e., the cardinality of the alphabet in the denominator.

Operationally, when a Σ'-repeating process is found to be minimally flexible (and there is no larger subset for which it is repeating), we can remove $|\Sigma|-|\Sigma'|$ elements from Σ and check whether a positive value is obtained. Clearly, if we aim to compare the flexibility values of two or more languages, all these should be compared against a Σ' with the same cardinality. We stress that this limitation of the measure is not a consequence of an arbitrary design choice in our definitions, but rather the direct consequence of the infinite nature of these languages, in particular the fact that traces have an unbounded horizon, pushed to the limit of ∞ when measuring flexibility.

6 Computing the Flexibility Measure

In this Section, we show how to calculate the cardinality of $W_{\leq n}(\mathcal{L})$ for a regular language $\mathcal{L}$, given n, as needed to compute the flexibility values via Definition 5. We will assume that the DFAs representing languages are trimmed.

For computing $|W_{\leq n}(\mathcal{L})|$, we resort to approaches in the relevant literature. In [2,22], it is shown that the number of words of certain lengths in a language can be computed via so-called *structure functions* of digraphs, recalled next.

A digraph is a just directed graph $D = (V, E)$ where V are the vertexes and E is a multi-set of vertex pairs. Unlike a DFA, a digraph has no labelling, nor initial/final states, although the underlying topology of a DFA is in fact a digraph, so that we can directly associate to any regular language a digraph D together with initial and final state sets $I, F \subseteq V$. The words of length n in $\mathcal{L}$ are in bijection with the set of paths of length n from I to F [2].

Definition 7 (Structure function). Let $D = (V, E)$ be a digraph as above, then, the structure function for n w.r.t. D is defined via $f_{\mathcal{L}}(n) = v_I^T A^n v_F$, where: (1) A is the $|V| \times |V|$ adjacency matrix of D s.t. the entry in row i and column j is the multiplicity of $(i, j) \in E$; (2) v_I is the column vector of size $|V|$ where row i is 1 if $i \in I$ (also called characteristic vector of I), hence encoding the initial states; (3) v_F is the characteristic vector of F.   ◁

The structure function can be used to compute the number of paths of length n in a digraph. Although one could in principle directly use such enumerative computation, we need an equation in n to compute the limit. In [22], the authors show that $f_{\mathcal{L}}(n)$ can be expressed as $f_{\mathcal{L}}(n) = \sum_i \lambda_i^n p_i(n)$ where $p_i(n)$ is a polynomial with bounded degree (at most one less than the index of the eigenvalue λ_i), and how to obtain this from the characteristic equation of A.

We will exemplify this on the running examples from Fig. 2, i.e., $\mathcal{L}_1 = (a|b)^*$ and $\mathcal{L}_2 = \epsilon|(a|b)^*b$, for which we have $\mathcal{L}_1^C = \{\}$ and $\mathcal{L}_2^C = (a|b)^*a$. Then, the adjacency matrices of the digraphs associated with these languages are: $A_{\mathcal{L}_1} = [2]$, $A_{\mathcal{L}_1^C} = [0]$ and $A_{\mathcal{L}_2} = A_{\mathcal{L}_2^C} = [[1\ 1], [1\ 1]]$.

We recall that we can find the eigenvalues of a matrix A via the characteristic polynomial of its adjacency matrix. The characteristic equation of a square matrix is $det(\lambda I - A) = 0$, where I is the identity matrix, and the eigenvalues are the roots of the polynomial $det(\lambda I - A)$. We then obtain the structure function by (i) determining the linear homogeneous recurrence relation for A from its characteristic polynomial and (ii) computing its *particular* solution, using the initial conditions given by the initial and final states of the DFA.

Example 2. Consider $\mathcal{L}_1$. The characteristic equation for A is $det(A - \lambda I) = 0$, namely $-\lambda + 2 = 0$. The polynomial has root 2. From this we obtain [22] the general recurrence relation as $f(n) = 2f(n - 1)$. Its general solution can be written [22] in the form $\sum_i \lambda_i^n p_i(n)$ as $f(n) = 2^n \cdot c/2$, with polynomial $c/2$ for some constant c, for $n \geq 2$. Considering now the initial and final vectors $v_I^T = [1]$ and $v_F^T = [1]$, the initial conditions are $f(0) = v_I^T v_F = 1$ and $f(1) = v_I^T A v_F = 2$, giving $c = 2$. So the particular solution is $f(n) = 2^n$, $n \geq 0$.

We apply the same computation to $\mathcal{L}_2$. The characteristic equation for A is $\lambda^2 - 2\lambda$ with eigenvalues $\lambda_1 = 0$ and $\lambda_2 = 2$. Again the recurrence equation is $f(n) = 2f(n-1)$ and the solution as above. Considering now the initial and final vectors $v_I^T = [1\ 0]$ and $v_F^T = [1\ 0]$, the initial conditions are $f(0) = v_I^T v_F = 1$ and $f(1) = v_I^T A v_F = 1$, which give $c_1 = 1$. So $f(n) = 2^n/2 = 2^{n-1}$ for $n \geq 1$.

For $\mathcal{L}_1^C$, the structure function is $f(n) = 0$, as A is a zero matrix, so any power of A will be so. For $\mathcal{L}_2^C$, the computation is as for $\mathcal{L}_2$. Although $f(0) = 0$, we have $f(1) = 1$ and thus $c_1 = 1$, so again we obtain $f(n) = 2^{n-1}$ for $n \geq 1$. ◁

These examples show how to compute the number of words of length *exactly* n for the languages via the structure functions. We now need to compute the number of words of length *at most* n. To find the number of words of length up to n, we need to sum over all values from 0 to n, i.e., $f(0) + \ldots + f(n)$. For the structure function of $\mathcal{L}_1$ ($f(n) = 2^n$, $n \geq 0$), we can substitute this to get the geometric series $2^0 + \ldots + 2^n = 2^{n+1} - 1$. So for $\mathcal{L}_1$ with $f(n) = 2^n$, the number of words *up to* n is $|W_{\leq n}(\mathcal{L}_1)| = 2^{n+1} - 1$, which is the same as for Σ^*. For $\mathcal{L}_2$, with $f(0) = 1$ and $f(n) = 2^{n-1}$ for $n \geq 1$, we get that the number of words up to n is $|W_{\leq n}(\mathcal{L}_2)| = 1 + 2^n - 1 = 2^n$. For $\mathcal{L}_2^C$, as $f(0) = 0$ and $f(n) = 2^{n-1}$ for $n \geq 1$, we obtain $|W_{\leq n}(\mathcal{L}_2^C)| = 2^n - 1$. Finally, $|W_{\leq n}(\mathcal{L}_1^C)| = 0$.

From the above, we can compute the following flexibility values for $\mathcal{L}_1$ and $\mathcal{L}_2$, namely $flex(\mathcal{L}_1) = 1, flex(\mathcal{L}_2) = 0.5$, while trivially $flex(\mathcal{L}_3) = 0$. For instance, $\lim_{n \to \infty} |W_{\leq n}(\mathcal{L}_2)|/|W_{\leq n}(\Sigma^*)| = \lim_{n \to \infty} 2^n/(2^{n+1} - 1) = 0.5$.

We conclude by giving two additional examples.

Example 3. Consider two Declare constraints `response(a,b)`, `response(c,b)` (i.e., only accepting words ending with b), with alphabet $\Sigma = \{a, b, c\}$. For brevity we consider the minimized DFA, with adjacency matrix $A = [[1, 2], [1, 2]]$, and $v_I^T = [1, 0]$, $v_F^T = [1, 0]$. Let $\mathcal{L}$ be the corresponding language. The characteristic equation of A is $\lambda^2 - 3\lambda = 0$ hence the general structure function is $f(n) = c_1 3^n$. So, from $f(1) = v_I^T A v_F = 1$ we obtain $c_1 = 1/3$ and $f(n) = 3^{n-1}$ for $n \geq 2$. From this, $|W_{\leq n}(\mathcal{L})| = (3^n + 1)/2$. As $|\Sigma| = 3$, we have $|W_{\leq n}(\Sigma^*)| = (3^{n+1} - 1)/2$. As a result, $flex(\mathcal{L}) = \lim_{n \to \infty} \frac{(3^n + 1)}{(3^{n+1} - 1)} = 1/3$, as expected (a third of Σ^* is accepted). The non-minimized DFA gives the same structure function and result, although from polynomial $\lambda^4 - 5\lambda^3 + 7\lambda^2 - 3\lambda$. ◁

Example 4. Consider a declarative specification for a simple order-to-cash process. The customer needs to pick at least one item (`at-least-one(pick)`), which calls for a consequent reply from the seller who may refuse or accept the order (`response(pick,accept OR refuse)`). After this, no further items can be picked (`neg-succession(accept,pick)` and `neg-succession(refuse,pick)`). Also, the seller may decide to turn a refusal into acceptance, but not vice-versa (`neg-succession(accept,refuse)`). Finally, upon acceptance, a consequent payment is expected, and the customer can pay only after a prior acceptance (`succession(accept,pay)`). The specification is shown in Fig. 4 together with the corresponding (minimized, trimmed) DFA. Let $\mathcal{L}$ be the resulting language. The characteristic polynomial of the adjacency matrix is

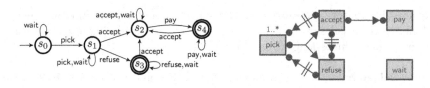

Fig. 4. Declare specification (right) and corresponding DFA (left).

$\lambda^5 - 9\lambda^4 + 31\lambda^3 - 51\lambda^2 + 40\lambda - 12$, so the recurrence relation is $f(n) = 9f(n-1) + 31f(n-2) - 51f(n-3) + 40f(n-4) - 12f(n-5)$, with initial conditions $[0, 0, 1, 6, 25]$. The characteristic equation is $f(n) = (-2^{n+1} + 3^n + 1)/2$, $n \geq 0$. Hence $|W_{\leq n}(\mathcal{L})| = (2n + 3^{n+1} - 2^{n+3} + 5)/4$.

Since $|\Sigma| = 5$ and $|W_{\leq n}(\Sigma^*)| = (5^{n+1} - 1)/4$, the limit is 0, i.e. $\mathit{flex}(\mathcal{L}) = 0$. This result was evident (see Lemma 2) by inspecting the DFA in Fig. 4: at most three distinct activities are available at the same time (and in a strongly connected component: at state s_2 in component $\{s_2, s_4\}$). Indeed, if we take Σ' so that $|\Sigma'| = 3$ (see Sect. 5.2 for a discussion), then since $|W_{\leq n}(\Sigma'^*)| = (3^{n+1} - 1)/2$ the flexibility of $\mathcal{L}$ becomes 0.5.   ◁

Regarding complexity, assume a set $\{A_1, ..., A_k\}$ of k DFA over Σ, one for each individual constraint, and each with at most q states. The (trim) product automaton is of size q^k, hence exponential in the number of constraints. The adjacency matrix can be obtained by checking at most $q^k|\Sigma|$ edges, and the same holds for complementation, if required (when a DFA is trimmed, it is not enough to swap accepting and non-accepting states). The characteristic polynomial can be computed with existing polynomial algorithms [10].

7   Conclusion

We have introduced and studied a notion of flexibility for infinite regular languages w.r.t. the maximally permissive language. Furthermore, we have given a practical way of computing flexibility of Declare specifications, showing that the limits needed for computing the measure exist in certain Declare settings.

We foresee three lines of future work. First, we intend to set up an empirical investigation, assessing to what extent the formal measure introduced here corresponds to the intuition of human experts. This is intriguing as users have troubles in understanding which traces are accepted by a declarative specification [8]. Second, we plan to build on the flexibility analysis provided in this work to single out more refined flexibility measures, which would yield fine-grained, comparative assessments. Third, we intend to investigate how measuring flexibility may be used to provide different forms of support through the business process lifecycle. For instance, when modelling declarative specifications, computing flexibility every time a constraint is added/removed may be useful to understand the impact on the whole specification due to hidden dependencies among constraints [8,12]. Also, declarative constraints can be used during enactment for run-time anticipatory monitoring [4,11], which amounts to checking whether an evolving trace satisfies an LTL_f formula of interest, considering also its possible (infinitely many, finite-length) continuations.

Acknowledgements. Work partially funded by MUR under the PNRR MUR project PE0000013-FAIR and the PRIN MUR project PINPOINT (Prot. 2020FNEB27), as well as by the Sapienza Project MARLeN, and the UNIBZ Project ADAPTERS.

References

1. Ceccherini-Silberstein, T., Machì, A., Scarabotti, F.: On the entropy of regular languages. Theor. Comput. Sci. **307**(1), 93–102 (2003)
2. Chomsky, N., Miller, G.A.: Finite state languages. Inf. Control **1**(2), 91–112 (1958)
3. Dassow, J., Martín, G.M., Vico, F.J.: A similarity measure for cyclic unary regular languages. Fundam. Informaticae **96**(1–2), 71–88 (2009)
4. De Giacomo, G., De Masellis, R., Maggi, F.M., Montali, M.: Monitoring constraints and metaconstraints with temporal logics on finite traces. ACM Trans. Softw. Eng. Methodol. **31**(4), 1–44 (2022)
5. De Giacomo, G., Vardi, M.Y.: Linear temporal logic and linear dynamic logic on finite traces. In: Proceedings of the IJCAI 2013, pp. 854–860 (2013)
6. De Smedt, J., Vanden Broucke, S., De Weerdt, J., Vanthienen, J.: A full R/I-net construct lexicon for declare constraints. Available at SSRN 2572869 (2015)
7. Di Ciccio, C., Montali, M.: Declarative process specifications: reasoning, discovery, monitoring. In: van der Aalst, W.M.P., Carmona, J. (eds.) Process Mining Handbook. LNBIP, vol. 448, pp. 108–152. Springer, Cham (2022). https://doi.org/10.1007/978-3-031-08848-3_4
8. Haisjackl, C., et al.: Understanding declare models: strategies, pitfalls, empirical results. Softw. Syst. Model. **15**(2), 325–352 (2016)
9. Hildebrandt, T.T., Mukkamala, R.R.: Declarative event-based workflow as distributed dynamic condition response graphs. In: PLACES, vol. 69, pp. 59–73 (2010)
10. Keller-Gehrig, W.: Fast algorithms for the characteristics polynomial. Theor. Comput. Sci. **36**, 309–317 (1985)
11. Maggi, F.M., Montali, M., Westergaard, M., van der Aalst, W.M.P.: Monitoring business constraints with linear temporal logic: an approach based on colored automata. In: Rinderle-Ma, S., Toumani, F., Wolf, K. (eds.) BPM 2011. LNCS, vol. 6896, pp. 132–147. Springer, Heidelberg (2011). https://doi.org/10.1007/978-3-642-23059-2_13
12. Montali, M., Pesic, M., van der Aals, W.M.P., et al.: Declarative specification and verification of service choreographies. ACM Trans. Web **4**(1), 1–62 (2010)
13. Parker, A.J., Yancey, K.B., Yancey, M.P.: Regular language distance and entropy. In: Proceedings of the MFCS 2017 (2017)
14. Parker, A.J., Yancey, K.B., Yancey, M.P.: Definitions and properties of entropy and distance for regular languages. In: Dynamical Systems and Random Processes, pp. 139–170. American Mathematical Society (2019)
15. Pesic, M., Schonenberg, H., van der Aalst, W.M.P.: Declare: full support for loosely-structured processes. In: Proceedings of the 11th IEEE International Enterprise Distributed Object Computing Conference, pp. 287–300. IEEE (2007)
16. Polyvyanyy, A., Kalenkova, A.: Conformance checking of partially matching processes: an entropy-based approach. Inf. Syst. **106**, 101720 (2022)

17. Polyvyanyy, A., Solti, A., Weidlich, M., Ciccio, C.D., Mendling, J.: Monotone precision and recall measures for comparing executions and specifications of dynamic systems. ACM Trans. Softw. Eng. Methodol. **29**(3), 1–41 (2020)
18. Rabin, M.O., Scott, D.: Finite automata and their decision problems. IBM J. Res. Dev. **3**(2), 114–125 (1959)
19. Reichert, M., Weber, B.: Enabling Flexibility in Process-Aware Information Systems - Challenges, Methods, Technologies. Springer, Heidelberg (2012). https://doi.org/10.1007/978-3-642-30409-5
20. Sadiq, S.W., Sadiq, W., Orlowska, M.E.: Pockets of flexibility in workflow specification. In: Kunii, H.S., Jajodia, S., Sølvberg, A. (eds.) ER 2001. LNCS, vol. 2224, pp. 513–526. Springer, Heidelberg (2001). https://doi.org/10.1007/3-540-45581-7_38
21. Schützenmeier, N., Corea, C., Delfmann, P., Jablonski, S.: Efficient computation of behavioral changes in declarative process models. In: van der Aa, H., Bork, D., Proper, H.A., Schmidt, R. (eds.) BPMDS EMMSAD 2023 2023. LNBIP, vol. 479, pp. 136–151. Springer, Cham (2023). https://doi.org/10.1007/978-3-031-34241-7_10
22. Yancey, M.: Three ways to count walks in a digraph (2016). arXiv:1610.01200

Towards a Multi-model Paradigm for Business Process Management

Anti Alman[1]([⊠]) [ID], Fabrizio Maria Maggi[2] [ID], Stefanie Rinderle-Ma[3] [ID],
Andrey Rivkin[4] [ID], and Karolin Winter[5] [ID]

[1] University of Tartu, Tartu, Estonia
anti.alman@ut.ee
[2] Free University of Bozen-Bolzano, Bolzano, Italy
maggi@inf.unibz.it
[3] Technical University of Munich, Munich, Germany
stefanie.rinderle-ma@tum.de
[4] Technical University of Denmark, Lyngby, Denmark
ariv@dtu.dk
[5] Eindhoven University of Technology, Eindhoven, The Netherlands
k.m.winter@tue.nl

Abstract. The design and development of information systems (IS) often requires not only software development expertise, but also a deep understanding of the multitude of business processes supported by the given IS. Such understanding is usually elicited via business process modeling and numerous, often interrelated, process models can be created even for a single IS. However, commonly used process modeling languages focus on single processes in isolation, while providing, at best, only limited support for modeling process interactions. This does enforce a clear scope on each process model, but also leads to a non-holistic view of the IS behavior. In this exploratory paper, we take the position that, instead of forcing existing "single-process-focused" models to be changed, approaches should be provided for modeling their interactions in a fine-grained and unambiguous manner. To meet this goal, we propose developing a *Multi-Model paradigm* for Business Process Management, where the same, already existing, declarative and procedural modeling languages would be used to represent both the individual processes as well as their interactions.

Keywords: Multi-Model Paradigm · Business Process Management · Business Process Modeling · Hybrid Process Model · Model Interplay

1 Introduction

The connection between information systems (IS) and business process management (BPM) can range from IS providing simple data storage to fully-fledged Process-Aware Information Systems (PAIS) [1] often directly managing multiple interconnected business processes. From the IS design and development perspective, this necessitates a deep understanding of such processes, which is commonly achieved by creating multiple, also often interrelated, process models [17].

A wide variety of languages can be used for that purpose, ranging from procedural (e.g., Petri nets [38]) to declarative (e.g., DECLARE [31]), and various combinations in between (cf. [7]). Furthermore, an object-centric view for representing processes has recently emerged in the field of process mining [2]. But despite that variety, existing languages tend to provide significantly more expressive power for modeling single processes, than for modeling their interactions.

This "single-process-focus" helps to considerably simplify modeling by giving a clear scope to each process model. However, it also contributes to the emergence of "process silos", a phenomenon recently recognized as one of the most important BPM problems yet to be solved [10]. In a nutshell, process silos often lead to multiple, potentially heterogeneous and certainly misaligned processes, that nevertheless need to be executed in combination.

In fact, interactions between business processes (and by extension, between the corresponding models) are highly relevant, as demonstrated by ongoing research in areas such as holistic BPM [9], collaborative processes [19], and process-spanning constraints [41]. Similar interactions can also be observed in hierarchical process models where some activities may refer to other process models (sub-processes) [37], customizable processes where a base model is combined with models capturing its variations [26], and even guided process discovery where (possibly interconnected) model fragments are used as an additional input [29]. While very different, all the above examples can be seen as manifestations of a single underlying research question (**RQ**): *"How to represent and handle the interactions of multiple (separately defined) business process models?"*.

Our earlier work [3,5] also began by tackling that same RQ in a narrow context (i.e., online process monitoring), but was later extended into a data-aware modeling language/approach [4], where individual processes (procedural or declarative) can still be first modeled in isolation, and then simply combined through the use of exactly the same modeling constructs.

Given the above examples, we propose that scenarios, where one or more processes are best represented as sets of smaller interconnected models, are sufficiently prevalent to warrant a dedicated line of research, which we refer to as a *Multi-Model paradigm* for BPM. Furthermore, given our experience with [3–5], we propose that already existing languages can be extended to meet modeling requirements of these scenarios in a formally well-defined manner. In this paper, we explore these ideas further by a language-agnostic analysis of four example scenarios, based on which we outline corresponding language extensions for [4].

More specifically, Sect. 2 analyzes a representative example of each scenario, leading to a set of modeling requirements presented in Sect. 3. Then, Sect. 4 discusses the requirements (not) met by [4] and the corresponding future extensions. This is followed by a discussion on the limitations of this paper in Sect. 5, and an overview of related approaches in Sect. 6. Finally, Sect. 7 concludes the paper by outlining directions for future works.

2   Multi-model Scenarios

Based on numerous discussions among the authors of this paper, we identified four types of business processes in which multi-model scenarios are, in our
opinion, likely to emerge. These types were validated by searching for concrete
examples from the literature. However, as discussed in Sect. 5, we did not aim
for completeness, instead focusing on broadness and variety. We begin with a
relatively simple hybrid model, followed by progressively more complex examples
involving multiple interconnected process models.

2.1   Hybrid Processes: Management of Funding Applications

By hybrid processes, we refer to business processes which contain both structured
and unstructured parts, and therefore, require both the strictness of procedural,
as well as, the flexibility of declarative process modeling languages. One of the
most common approaches to hybrid processes is using a hierarchical structure
of sub-processes, with each being either declarative or procedural (e.g., [37]).

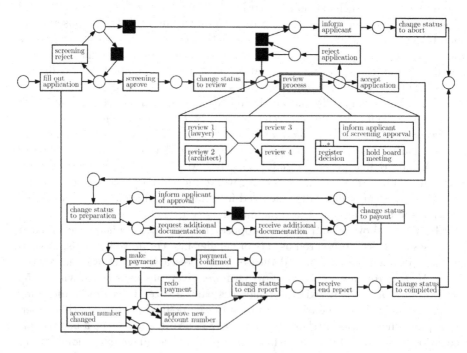

Fig. 1. Hybrid application model for the Dreyers foundation (taken from [37]).

As a concrete example, we use the application process of the Dreyer Foundation from [37]. The same source provides two process models: a fully declarative model using nested DCR Graphs [13]; and a hybrid model using a target-
branched DECLARE [14] sub-process within a Petri net. The fully declarative

model is used in practice to drive the electronic case management system of the Dreyer Foundation. However, given the complexity of that model, a hybrid solution was investigated, resulting in the model shown in Fig. 1.

Without describing the full process here (cf. [37]), we highlight the following:

- **Strict control flow** – Based on Fig. 1 it is clear that most of the application process is procedural, which is also the main reason why [37] started exploring alternatives to using a fully declarative model.
- **Flexible control flow** – In contrast, application reviews are highly flexible and therefore modeled declaratively. The corresponding model (`review process`) does not define concrete start and end activities, but does require at least one execution of `register decision`. Authors of [37] also note the flexibility related to account numbers and payments, but state that this part is modeled procedurally due to it having two entry points.
- **Sub-processes** – The declarative model is integrated into the procedural one as a sub-process. More specifically, firing the Petri net transition `review process` means executing the corresponding declarative model. The process itself does not contain a concrete activity `review process`, meaning that `review process` in the hybrid model is effectively a model reference.
- **Data conditions** – While not present in the hybrid model, the fully declarative model contains data conditions defining which reviewer should review which type of application. These conditions are in the form of variable-to-constant comparisons, e.g., $UddelingPulje = 2$.
- **Time perspective** – While not present in the hybrid model, the fully declarative model also specifies a time interval of three days between two reviews.

2.2   Orchestration Processes: Assessment of Loan Applications

By orchestration processes, we refer to scenarios where different roles, systems, artifacts, etc., have their own models to be executed in parallel with others, while following some cross-model dependencies. The most common of these dependencies stem from a shared subject (e.g., a patient) between the models, which may, for example, lead to shared data values (e.g., blood pressure of the patient) and synchronization points (e.g., admission of the patient). This is analogous to orchestration processes in BPMN [30], but with a distinct model for each lane.

As a concrete example, we rely on the loan application event log [16] of BPIC 2017 and our corresponding analysis in [4]. This event log explicitly distinguishes application state changes, offer state changes and workflow events, thus providing a natural basis for three interconnected process models as shown in Fig. 2. Each model is represented procedurally using Data Petri nets [12,20,28], while the interactions of models are defined by milestones, shared variables, and declarative constraints.

Without describing the full process here (cf. [4]), we highlight the following:

- **Strict control flow** – Based on Fig. 2, it is clear that the overall process is largely procedural. However, there is some flexibility in how the activities of the models can interleave, especially after the activity `A_Complete`.

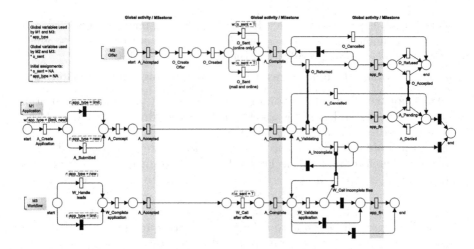

Fig. 2. Orchestration processes for loan application assessment (taken from [4]).

- **Cross-model variables** – Activity A_Create Application in M1 stores the loan application type (variable *app_type*). This stored value is then used in M1 to decide if A_Submitted will be executed. Furthermore, the same value is also used in M2 to decide if W_Handle leads will be executed.
- **System variables** – Model M2 stores a value for the variable (*o_sent*) which is required to execute W_Call after offers in M3. However, based on [4], this variable is not part of the original process, but, instead, used specifically to enforce an additional synchronization between M2 and M3.
- **Data conditions** – All three models contain variable-to-constant comparisons, with r: and w: denoting read and write operations respectively, and {...} used as a shorthand for possible matching constants.
- **Cross-model activities** – Activities A_Accepted, A_Complete, and app_fin constitute milestones of this process. These activities can only be executed when they are allowed by all models, and a single execution progresses all models concurrently, making them cross-model activities (milestones).
- **Declarative interleavings** – Interleavings of these models are further constrained by three pairs of activities (e.g., O_Accepted and A_Pending), where executing one requires executing the other at some point in the same trace.
- **Execution cardinalities** – As highlighted in [4], Fig. 2 falls short if multiple loan offers (executions of M2) are made for a single loan application (execution of M1). For example, it would fail to capture that at most one offer can be accepted (O_Accepted) per successful application (A_Pending).

2.3   Collaborative Processes: Manufacturing of Car Parts

By collaborative processes, we refer to scenarios in which multiple organizations, each having their own business processes, collaborate in a way that creates some dependencies between their processes. Such scenarios are usually tackled by modeling a message flow between process activities, such that each activity having incoming messages can only be executed after receiving all of them, thus providing a mechanism for modeling synchronizations. A prime example of this approach is the use of pools and message flows in BPMN, along with the related collaboration and choreography diagrams [30].

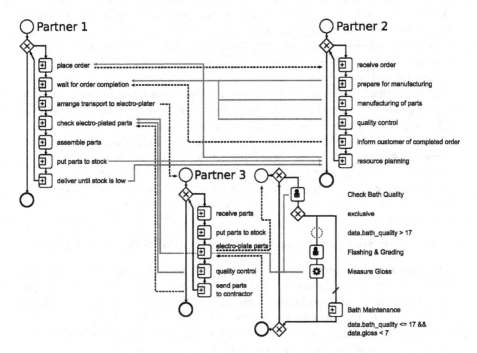

Fig. 3. Collaborative model of processes for manufacturing car parts (taken from [19]).

As a concrete example, we rely on [19], which presents the real-life collaboration of three partners involved in manufacturing of car parts, i.e., a car manufacturer, and partners responsible for injection molding and electro plating. As shown in Fig. 3 the process of each partner is modeled using BPMN, while additional black and green lines are used between the models to represent message exchanges and data dependencies respectively.

Without describing the full process here (cf. [19]), we highlight the following:

- **Strict control flow** – The overall process, as shown in Fig. 3, is largely procedural. However, some flexibility in process interleavings is possible.
- **Public representation of private tasks** – Almost all activities in Fig. 3 are modeled as complex tasks to hide internal processes from other partners.
- **Sub-processes** – While all other activities could be treated as atomic, `electro-plate parts` (Partner 3) is explicitly connected to both the start and the end event of the same concrete process model, effectively turning `electro-plate parts` into a sub-process reference.

- **Execution triggers** – The process of Partner 3 is triggered by the execution of `arrange transport to electro-plater` (Partner 1) and needs to be completed for executing the next activity of Partner 1. A sub-process is not suitable here due to the partners being different and also because the process of Partner 3 does not refer back to the same activity that triggered it.
- **Activity types** – The model for `electro-plate parts` differentiates between user and service activities.
- **Data conditions** – The model for `electro-plate parts` contains variable-to-constant conditions on variables *data.bath_quality* and *data.gloss*.
- **Cross-model variables** – As stated before, each green line represents a data dependency between the processes, i.e., data generated by one process is available for the execution of another process (possibly as shared variables).
- **Message exchange** – The data dependencies represented by the green lines can also be seen as a message exchange mechanism between the processes.
- **Cross-instance messages** – Each execution of this collaboration produces information for the next execution, as represented by the data dependency from `resource planning` (Partner 2) to `place order` (Partner 1). Here, we consider each iteration of the outer-loops as one execution.

2.4   Instance-Spanning Processes: Operation of a Printing Agency

In addition to model interactions, the examples in Sects. 2.2 and 2.3 also contain some instance-spanning behavior, and one can easily argue that the example in Sect. 2.1 is likely to contain such behavior as well (e.g., the overall funding budget is likely to be limited). In the literature, these types of behaviors/rules are referred to as *instance-spanning constraints* [18], and, in essence, they relate multiple instances of the same process to each other in some way.

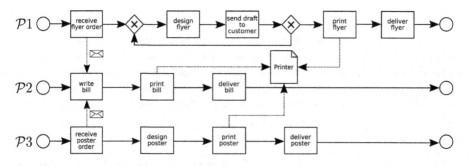

Fig. 4. Instance-spanning processes of a printing agency (taken from [41]).

As a concrete example, we rely on [41], which presents a scenario inspired by an extensive collection of real-life examples of instance-spanning constraints [34]. It consists of three interconnected processes (P1, P2, P3 in Fig. 4), where P1 and P3 describe the design, printing and delivery of fliers and posters respectively, and P2 manages the corresponding bills for both. While not explicitly modeled, [41] also describes six instance- and process-spanning constraints for this scenario, ranging from batching behavior to concurrency constraints.

Without describing the full process here (cf. [41]), we highlight the following:

- **Strict control flow** – Based on Fig. 4 all three processes are modeled procedurally and have largely linear control flows.
- **Execution triggers** – One of the constraints in [41] states that "if a flyer or poster order is received then P2 (billing process) is started", which effectively means that the first activity of either P1 or P3 triggers the execution of P2.
- **Message exchange** – Related to the above constraint, P2 receives some billing information from either P1 or P3, which is modeled as an envelope in Fig. 4.
- **Time perspective** – Two constraints in [41] relate to the time perspective. First, finished orders are delivered in the evening. Second, at least 95% printing activities must take 10 min or less. The former relates to the time of day, while the latter is basically a key performance indicator (KPI).
- **Batch activities** – Concerning deliveries, [41] also states that all completed deliveries are made simultaneously, which effectively means a single batch activity progressing multiple instances concurrently.
- **Batch conditions** – Printing is also a batch activity in [41], but with an added condition that fliers and posters must be printed separately from bills.
- **Cross-instance cardinalities** – Concerning printing, [41] also states that "printer 1 may only print 10 times per day", which means that a cross-instance cardinality constraint on an activity should hold, with added conditions on data and time.

3 Modeling Requirements

The highlights of the example scenarios in Sect. 2 directly lead to the modeling requirements for developing a Multi-Model paradigm for BPM. A corresponding overview is provided in Table 1.

Overall, we identified 16 requirements on modeling expressiveness, which we further categorize as requirements on i) individual models, ii) model interactions, and iii) instance interactions. For the individual models, the requirements cover control flow, data flow, and time perspectives. Across the use cases, a mix of strict and flexible control flow as well as support for at least constant-to-variable data conditions is needed. Support of time and system variables is also important, but depends on the use case.

Developing a multi-model paradigm demands for interaction of models. The corresponding requirements (Table 1) cover a range of interactions from nesting of models via sub-processes to interactions based on message exchanges, cross-model variables, and cross model activities. Furthermore, execution of models or activities across models can be further refined through declarative rules for interleavings, execution cardinalities, and execution triggers.

Table 1. Categorized requirements on expressiveness and their applicability to example scenarios. Highlights from Sect. 2 are marked with "+", while "+/-" marks likely applicability. The last column is used to provide an overview of Sect. 4.1.

Requirements		Hybrid Funding	Orchest. Loan	Collab. Car	Inst-Span. Printing	Supported by [4]
Individual models	Req1: Strict control flow	+	+	+	+	+
	Req2: Flexible control flow	+	+/-		+/-	+
	Req3: Data conditions	+	+	+	+/-	+
	Req4: Time perspective	+			+	
	Req5: System variables		+			+
Model interactions	Req6: Sub-processes	+		+		
	Req7: Message exchange	+/-		+	+	
	Req8: Cross-model variables		+	+/-		+
	Req9: Cross-model activities		+			+
	Req10: Execution cardinalities		+			
	Req11: Execution triggers		+/-	+	+	
	Req12: Declarative interleavings		+	+/-	+/-	+
Instance interactions	Req13: Batch activities		+/-		+	
	Req14: Batch conditions				+	
	Req15: Cross-instance messages			+		
	Req16: Cross-instance cardinalities		+/-		+	

As seen in Table 1, the particular model interactions differ between scenarios. In the hybrid example, the interaction between declarative and procedural models is based on their nesting as sub-processes. In the loan example, models are orchestrated based on shared activities and variables, together with declarative definitions of additional interleaving rules. For the collaboration, a choreography interaction style (based on message exchanges) is used, where the receiving of a message can be also seen as an (activity) execution trigger. Meanwhile, the printing example is structured similarly to an orchestration, but the models interact through message exchanges and additional rules across process instances.

Instance level interactions require at least the ability to model batch activities, which progress multiple instances concurrently, along with conditions on which instances belong to the same batch. Furthermore, messages (and possibly data values in general) may cross the instance boundary and the number of activity (and possibly process) executions may be limited across instances.

Finally, we note that two of the highlights from Sect. 2 are not present in Table 1. First, public representation of private tasks was not added since it can be solved through traditional usage of sub-processes, which is already covered by the requirements. Second, activity types are not added as they are purely informative in the corresponding example. Additionally, KPIs and resource perspective are left out of the scope of this paper (cf. Section 5).

4   Exploring a Potential Baseline Language

Given that, to the best of our knowledge, no existing modeling languages nor frameworks meet all the requirements outlined in Sect. 3, we could either design a completely new language from ground up or build on already existing works. In this paper, we opt for the latter, which, regardless of the specific works chosen, necessitates an analysis of these works w.r.t. the modeling requirements, and laying out a plan for addressing any potential shortcomings identified during that analysis. In the following, we go through these steps (Sect. 4.1 and Sect. 4.2 respectively) on the basis of [4], while noting that a similar exploration could also be undertaken on the basis of other existing works (cf. Section 5).

4.1   Current Capabilities

As stated in Sect. 1, we choose the formal modeling language of [4] as our baseline. The main reason is that it already provides means to represent multi-model scenarios by using Data Petri nets (DPNs) [12, 20, 28], accounting for procedural components, and DECLARE with "local filters" (LF-DECLARE) [4], accounting for declarative components. The latter is also used in [4] to model complex interactions between DPN components and to further refine their behavior. This fully meets **Req1**, **Req2** and **Req12**.

Activities in [4] are instantaneous and come with attributes in the form of attribute-value pairs (similarly to MP-DECLARE [11]). Both LF-DECLARE constraints and DPNs may contain conditions (in the case of DPNs, such conditions are attached to transitions) over these attributes in the form of variable-to-constant comparisons, using the comparison operators $=, <, >$ and boolean connectives $\neg, \wedge, \vee$. This meets **Req3** and **Req5**, but with some caveats (cf. Section 4.2). Meanwhile, **Req4** is not met, as [4] lacks a notion of time.

Each activity in [4] is enriched with a special provenance identifier referring to a concrete model to which the activity belongs. This allows LF-DECLARE constraints to refer to activities of specific models, even if other models have same-labeled activities, thus further reinforcing **Req12**. However, activity provenance is not required, and in such cases an activity is considered global across all models, which meets **Req9**. Furthermore, variables in [4] can similarly be either local or global, with the latter meeting **Req8**. A combination of global/local variables can also be used to mimic message-passing protocols (**Req7**), but this requires significant modeling effort (cf. Sect. 4.2).

Finally, the LF-DECLARE constraints in [4] capture complex DPN interleavings, but yet fall short of meeting **Req6**, **Req10** and **Req11** as only concrete activities (and not entire models) can be constrained. For example, **Req6** would require defining constraints on each potential start and end activity of a sub-process, and even then, the corresponding "high level" activity would effectively remain instantaneous (i.e., it is executed and the sub-process starts afterwards). Furthermore, LF-DECLARE constraints also hinder from meeting **Req13-16** as instance-spanning behavior was not originally considered in [4].

4.2   Language Extensions

While [4] meets the most crucial modeling requirements (e.g., declarative and procedural control flow, interleavings, etc.) out of the box, we also discovered that it is not sufficiently expressive to fully deal with the scenarios discussed in this paper. We have analyzed these results and identified a set of extensions which would transform the modeling language of [4] into one suitable for a Multi-Model paradigm for BPM. In the following, we discuss each of these extensions, highlighting the requirements it either solves directly or contributes to solving.

Declarative Process Models. Although LF-DECLARE constraints in [4] already meet **Req2**, there is one caveat that should be addressed. LF-DECLARE constraints use simple filters (i.e., activities are matched based on data payload values in addition to activity labels), while DPNs use more sophisticated read and write conditions that allow to store and manipulate data within DPN local or global variables. DPN conditions can precisely replicate the behavior of LF-DECLARE filters, but not the other way around, since LF-DECLARE lacks a distinction between read and write conditions and the corresponding storage capabilities. Therefore, LF-DECLARE should be enhanced with precisely the same guard language as used in DPNs, thus enabling **Req5** within declarative models.

Model References. Both DPN transitions and LF-DECLARE constraints can only refer to concrete activities in [4], which is not sufficient for meeting **Req6** and **Req11**. However, this can be overcome by allowing both LF-DECLARE constraints and DPNs to refer to entire process specifications, which would meet **Req6**, while **Req11** may also require references specifically to the beginning and end of models. Furthermore, this extension can be designed in such a way that it also addresses **Req10** through declarative cardinality constraints referencing entire models, and contributes to covering **Req7**, as message exchanges can, in some cases, also serve as execution triggers (cf. Section 2.3).

Execution Goals. In our previous works [3–5], one of the points of contention was a decision on what should drive the process execution in a multi-model setting, while having a strong requirement that all process components must successfully complete their executions. To accommodate the latter, two options have been explored: one may consider the DPN final markings and/or the satisfaction of LF-DECLARE constraints as execution goals. However, both options fall short (in the context of [4]) when the execution of a model is required only under specific conditions or constraints (e.g., a model is the sub-process of an optional higher level activity or a model may not be executed more than a certain number of times). To address such issue one may introduce process-spanning constraints, allowing for fine-grained specification of component behaviors, and complement such constraints by requiring each model to be configured as either "mandatory" or "optional". Like that, potentially multiple mandatory models can drive the execution (using the goal conditions from above), leaving the execution of other models optional according to specific execution constraints set among them. This would cover **Req10** and **Req11**, while also reinforcing **Req12**.

Richer Comparison Operations. The first two requirements on instance interactions (**Req13** and **Req14**) can possibly be solved with LF-DECLARE constraints by introducing correlation conditions. This would allow each constraint to distinguish and reliably handle activities of different executions through the implicit data condition *same case_id*, while omitting that condition would effectively result in a cross-instance constraint, thus allowing also to meet **Req16**. The solution for DPNs likely involves extending their expressive power towards formalisms like the one of colored Petri nets [23].

Arithmetic Operations. An alternative (and possibly complementary) approach to meet **Req16** is adding support for arithmetic operations (e.g., addition, multiplication) and functions (e.g., average, sum), which would also reinforce **Req3** and **Req5**. A way of achieving this is to extend the language of conditions currently used in DPNs (similarly to [20]) allowing for such expressions as $i' = i+1$, which increments a (possibly global) variable i whenever a corresponding transition is fired. By requiring this increment to happen across multiple instances (thus requiring i to be global), one also contributes to **Req15**.

Time Perspective. The most natural way of working towards **Req4** in declarative process models is extending LF-DECLARE with the already existing Timed DECLARE language [39]. However, activities in Timed DECLARE are still instantaneous and modeling truly durative activities (over, e.g., dense time intervals) is out of reach of the language and requires further investigation. As for procedural components, one may think on extending DPNs from [4] towards the support of time, similarly to Timed Petri nets [32]. This extension would also contribute to **Req3** and would be relevant for **Req13** in some cases (cf. Section 2.4).

Message Exchanges. Technically, message exchanges (**Req7**) can already be represented using the modeling language from [4]. Specifically, sending messages can be mimicked by updating values of corresponding global variables to the content of the message, while receiving and reading messages can be modeled by copying the values of the same global variables into local variables of a process. Furthermore, the same approach would likely apply to **Req15** after the addition of cross-instance variables (cf. Arithmetic operations). However, modeling these exchanges explicitly would be a significant burden for a type of interaction that is very common in many types of processes (cf. Section 2.3). Instead, a simpler modeling construct should be added, which can then be seamlessly translated into the corresponding interactions through global and local variables.

5   Limitations

In the following, we discuss the main limitations of this paper in more detail.

Selection of Multi-model Scenarios. We cannot claim any notion of completeness in our selection of example scenarios (Sect. 2) as it is primarily based on discussions between the authors of this paper. A more systematic review (e.g., based on [25]) was considered, however, we opted against it due to terminological issues. In general, interactions of process models are studied within the context of specific research areas, each using their own terminology. For example, [41] uses the term "process-spanning constraints", while [37] uses terms "hierarchical" and "sub-processes". Meanwhile, more general terms such as "model interaction" or "model interplay" are used in neither. This means that, on the one hand, any systematic review must rely on the specific terminology of the relevant research areas, but, on the other hand, these areas are difficult to systematically identify due to the lack of a common terminology. Given these reasons, we believe that the approach taken in this paper is the most feasible, and also meets the main goal of identifying a broad set of diverse multi-model scenarios.

Completeness of Modeling Requirements. The modeling requirements presented in Sect. 3 are likely to be non-exhaustive as we may have missed some research areas and other examples of the areas that we included may lead to additional requirements. Furthermore, there are two broader categories of requirements, which we decided to be out of the scope of this paper. First, the requirements on resources, partly because it was not discussed in any of the selected examples, but also because resources can be addressed, at least to some extent, through data conditions. However, we acknowledge that a more explicit representation of resources and/or roles (akin to BPMN lane constructs) can be beneficial in process models. Second, incorporating existing probabilistic languages, such as [6], could also be considered. This would allow further refinement of instance-spanning behavior within and between the individual models, and could additionally be used to represent the underlying business rules of KPIs (cf. the scenario in Sect. 2.4). However, incorporating a probabilistic dimension would increase the scope of this paper considerably and, for this reason, should be tackled separately.

Reliance on a Specific Baseline Language. Sect. 4 is focused on the analysis and extension of one specific language, namely [4], which is also developed by the authors of this paper. This choice is mainly motivated by our in-depth expertise on [4], based on which we believe it is a natural starting point for developing a multi-model paradigm for BPM. However, we acknowledge that this opinion may be biased by our involvement in [4]. For alternatives, one could consider more well-known formalisms, such as Colored Petri nets [24] and Open Petri Nets [8], or some of the approaches mentioned in Sect. 6. To accommodate that, we have structured this paper in a way that would allow reusing Sects. 2 and 3 as-is for any potential baseline language, while, Sect. 4 can be leveraged as an example of analyzing a specific language in the context of the given requirements.

6   Related Work

In this section, we highlight a variety of related works ranging from high-level modeling approaches to more detailed approaches specific to Sect. 3.

Business Process Architectures. While usually not resulting in multi-model representations akin to the ones analyzed in Sect. 2, larger collections of processes are commonly managed using business process architecture models (also referred to as enterprise maps, process ecosystems, process landscapes, process maps, etc.) [21]. In these approaches, the focus is on representing the overall structure of business processes and their relationships at a high level of abstraction, while details of the processes (e.g., control flow) are usually omitted. A notable exception, bordering between organizational and process modeling, is the DEMO methodology [15], which incorporates multiple types of models, such as interstriction model, action model, process model, etc., that collectively constitute the essential model of an organization. However, as demonstrated by the Ford case in [15], that essential model may remain exactly the same even in the case of radical reengineering of the underlying business processes.

Process Choreographies and Compositions. Authors in [22] identify problems in the synchronization of independently defined but concurrently executed workflow models. [38] discusses how to compose business processes modeled using Petri nets. In particular, the Petri nets are connected using shared places, thus enabling synchronization. The above approaches do not consider data nor declarative components. Other formally well-defined alternatives could be Colored Petri nets [24] and Open Petri Nets [8], while a less formal approach could be achieved with collaboration and choreography diagrams of BPMN [30].

Hybrid and Hierarchical Modeling. Authors in [33] highlight the need for hybrid process modeling approaches and propose a research agenda for their development. Later on, other works have defined formal semantics for hybrid processes. For example, [37] presents a formal semantics that uses a hierarchy of models, where each of model may be specified in either an imperative or declarative fashion. A conceptual framework and a common terminology for hybrid models has been proposed in [7] and a number of open research challenges related to hybrid processes have been identified in [36].

Process-Spanning and Instance-Spanning Constraints. Instance and process spanning constraints have been addressed from several perspectives like modeling and enactment [27], supporting runtime and design time verification through formalization with Event Calculus [18] and elicitation of patterns relying on Proclets and timed colored workflow nets [40]. Though these approaches provide means for handling interactions between multiple instances, they mainly require specific formalizations hampering the seamless integration of models expressed in different modeling languages. Therefore, those approaches are only contingently suitable for a multi-model paradigm as envisioned in this paper.

7   Conclusion

As highlighted in the introduction, this paper proposes that scenarios, where one or more processes are best represented as sets of smaller interconnected models, are sufficiently prevalent to warrant a dedicated line of research, which we call a *Multi-Model paradigm* for BPM. In support of this, we derived corresponding modeling requirements from four fundamentally different scenarios and, furthermore, explored a potential baseline language for meeting these requirements. In doing so, we have taken a crucial step in our overarching efforts to provide a fully-fledged framework for addressing a plethora of research areas from hybrid processes to the broader issues related to "process silos".

While the focus of this paper is on the language presented in [4], we described the characteristics of the paradigm in a language-agnostic manner. As a result, both the analysis of the modeling scenarios and also the corresponding requirements can be used as input for developing a similar multi-model solution from scratch or on the basis of any other existing approaches.

For future work, we plan to further investigate the extensions of [4] proposed in this paper with the goal of developing a corresponding complete formalization. This will, in turn, enable us to tackle concrete problems, related to IS development, such as automatic validation and execution support for multi-model scenarios. We also believe that modeling patterns in the style of [35] would need to be developed further down the line. Finally, we reiterate that the resource perspective and potential inclusion of KPIs warrants further investigation.

Acknowledgements. The work of A. Alman was supported by the Estonian Research Council grant PRG1226. F.M. Maggi was supported by the UNIBZ project PRISMA.

References

1. van der Aalst, W.M.P.: Process-aware information systems: Lessons to be learned from process mining. Trans. Petri Nets Other Model. Concurr. **2**, 1–26 (2009)
2. van der Aalst, W.M.P.: Object-centric process mining: unraveling the fabric of real processes. Mathematics **11**(12), 2691 (2023)
3. Alman, A., Maggi, F.M., Montali, M., Patrizi, F., Rivkin, A.: Multi-model monitoring framework for hybrid process specifications. In: Franch, X., Poels, G., Gailly, F., Snoeck, M. (eds.) Advanced Information Systems Engineering. CAiSE 2022. LNCS, vol. 13295, pp. 319–335. Springer, Cham (2022). https://doi.org/10.1007/978-3-031-07472-1_19
4. Alman, A., Maggi, F.M., Montali, M., Patrizi, F., Rivkin, A.: A framework for modeling, executing, and monitoring hybrid multi-process specifications with bounded global-local memory. Inf. Syst. **119**, 102271 (2023)
5. Alman, A., Maggi, F.M., Montali, M., Patrizi, F., Rivkin, A.: Monitoring hybrid process specifications with conflict management: an automata-theoretic approach. Artif. Intell. Med. **139**, 102512 (2023)
6. Alman, A., Maggi, F.M., Montali, M., Peñaloza, R.: Probabilistic declarative process mining. Inf. Syst. **109**, 102033 (2022)
7. Andaloussi, A.A., Burattin, A., Slaats, T., Kindler, E., Weber, B.: On the declarative paradigm in hybrid business process representations: a conceptual framework and a systematic literature study. Inf. Syst. **91**, 101505 (2020)
8. Baldan, P., Corradini, A., Ehrig, H., König, B.: Open petri nets: non-deterministic processes and compositionality. In: Ehrig, H., Heckel, R., Rozenberg, G., Taentzer, G. (eds.) Graph Transformations. ICGT 2008. LNCS, vol. 5214, pp. 257–273. Springer, Berlin (2008). https://doi.org/10.1007/978-3-540-87405-8_18
9. Bandara, W., Van Looy, A., Rosemann, M., Meyers, L.: A call for 'holistic' business process management. In: Problems@BPM. CEUR Workshop Proceedings, vol. 2938, pp. 6–10. CEUR-WS.org (2021)
10. Beerepoot, I., et al.: The biggest business process management problems to solve before we die. Comput. Ind. **146**, 103837 (2023)

11. Burattin, A., Maggi, F.M., Sperduti, A.: Conformance checking based on multi-perspective declarative process models. Expert Syst. Appl. **65**, 194–211 (2016)
12. de Leoni, M., Felli, P., Montali, M.: A holistic approach for soundness verification of decision-aware process models. In: Trujillo, J., et al. Conceptual Modeling. ER 2018. LNCS, vol. 11157, pp. 219–235. Springer, Cham (2018). https://doi.org/10.1007/978-3-030-00847-5_17
13. Debois, S., Hildebrandt, T., Slaats, T.: Hierarchical declarative modelling with refinement and sub-processes. In: Sadiq, S., Soffer, P., Völzer, H. (eds.) Business Process Management. BPM 2014. LNCS, vol. 8659, pp. 18–33. Springer, Cham (2014). https://doi.org/10.1007/978-3-319-10172-9_2
14. Di Ciccio, C., Maggi, F.M., Mendling, J.: Discovering target-branched declare constraints. In: Sadiq, S., Soffer, P., Völzer, H. (eds.) Business Process Management. BPM 2014. LNCS, vol. 8659. Springer, Cham (2014). https://doi.org/10.1007/978-3-319-10172-9_3
15. Dietz, J.L.G.: Understanding and modelling business processes with DEMO. In: Akoka, J., Bouzeghoub, M., Comyn-Wattiau, I., Métais, E. (eds.) Conceptual Modeling - ER 1099. ER 1999. LNCS, vol. 1728, pp. 188–202. Springer, Berlin (1999). https://doi.org/10.1007/3-540-47866-3_13
16. van Dongen, B.: Bpi challenge 2017 (2017). https://doi.org/10.4121/uuid:5f3067df-f10b-45da-b98b-86ae4c7a310b
17. Dumas, M., van der Aalst, W.M.P., ter Hofstede, A.H.M. (eds.): Process-Aware Information Systems: Bridging People and Software Through Process Technology. Wiley (2005)
18. Fdhila, W., Gall, M., Rinderle-Ma, S., Mangler, J., Indiono, C.: Classification and formalization of instance-spanning constraints in process-driven applications. In: La Rosa, M., Loos, P., Pastor, O. (eds.) Business Process Management. BPM 2016. LNCS, vol. 9850, pp. 348–364. Springer, Cham (2016). https://doi.org/10.1007/978-3-319-45348-4_20
19. Fdhila, W., Knuplesch, D., Rinderle-Ma, S., Reichert, M.: Verifying compliance in process choreographies: foundations, algorithms, and implementation. Inf. Syst. **108**, 101983 (2022)
20. Felli, P., Montali, M., Winkler, S.: Linear-time verification of data-aware dynamic systems with arithmetic. In: Proceedings of AAAI, pp. 5642–5650. AAAI Press (2022)
21. Gonzalez-Lopez, F., Bustos, G.: Business process architecture design methodologies - a literature review. Bus. Process. Manag. J. **25**(6), 1317–1334 (2019)
22. Heinlein, C.: Workflow and process synchronization with interaction expressions and graphs. In: Georgakopoulos, D., Buchmann, A. (eds.) International Conference on Data Engineering, pp. 243–252 (2001)
23. Jensen, K., Kristensen, L.M.: Coloured petri nets. In: Modelling and Validation of Concurrent Systems. Springer, Berlin (2009). https://doi.org/10.1007/B95112
24. Jensen, K., Kristensen, L.M.: Coloured Petri Nets - Modelling and Validation of Concurrent Systems. Springer (2009)
25. Kitchenham, B., Charters, S.: Guidelines for performing systematic literature reviews in software engineering (2007)
26. La Rosa, M., van der Aalst, W.M.P., Dumas, M., Milani, F.: Business process variability modeling: a survey. ACM Comput. Surv. **50**(1), 2:1–2:45 (2017)
27. Leitner, M., Mangler, J., Rinderle-Ma, S.: Definition and enactment of instance-spanning process constraints. In: Wang, X.S., Cruz, I., Delis, A., Huang, G. (eds.) Web Information Systems Engineering - WISE 2012. WISE 2012. LNCS, vol. 7651,

pp. 652–658. Springer, Berlin (2012). https://doi.org/10.1007/978-3-642-35063-4_49

28. Mannhardt, F., de Leoni, M., Reijers, H.A., van der Aalst, W.M.P.: Balanced multi-perspective checking of process conformance. Computing **98**(4), 407–437 (2016)

29. Mannhardt, F., de Leoni, M., Reijers, H.A., van der Aalst, W.M.P., Toussaint, P.J.: Guided process discovery - A pattern-based approach. Inf. Syst. **76**, 1–18 (2018)

30. OMG: Business process model and notation (BPMN). Technical report, Object Management Group (2014). https://www.omg.org/spec/BPMN/2.0.2/PDF

31. Pesic, M., Schonenberg, H., van der Aalst, W.M.P.: DECLARE: full support for loosely-structured processes. In: EDOC, pp. 287–300. IEEE Computer Society (2007)

32. Popova-Zeugmann, L.: On time petri nets. J. Inf. Process. Cybern. **27**(4), 227–244 (1991)

33. Reijers, H.A., Slaats, T., Stahl, C.: Declarative modeling-an academic dream or the future for BPM?. In: Daniel, F., Wang, J., Weber, B. (eds.) Business Process Management. LNCS, vol. 8094, pp. 307–322. Springer, Berlin (2013). https://doi.org/10.1007/978-3-642-40176-3_26

34. Rinderle-Ma, S., Gall, M., Fdhila, W., Mangler, J., Indiono, C.: Collecting examples for instance-spanning constraints. CoRR **abs/1603.01523** (2016)

35. Russell, N., van der Aalst, W.M.P., ter Hofstede, A.H.M.: Workflow Patterns: The Definitive Guide. MIT Press, Cambridge (2016)

36. Slaats, T.: Declarative and hybrid process discovery: recent advances and open challenges. J. Data Semant. **9**(1), 3–20 (2020)

37. Slaats, T., Schunselaar, D.M.M., Maggi, F.M., Reijers, H.A.: The semantics of hybrid process models. In: OTM Conferences, vol. 10033, pp. 531–551 (2016)

38. van Hee, K.M., Sidorova, N., van der Werf, J.M.E.M.: Business process modeling using petri nets. Trans. Petri Nets Other Model. Concurr. **7**, 116–161 (2013)

39. Westergaard, M., Maggi, F.M.: Looking into the future. Using timed automata to provide a priori advice about timed declarative process models. In: OTM Conferences (1). vol. 7565, pp. 250–267. Springer (2012)

40. Winter, K., Rinderle-Ma, S.: Defining instance spanning constraint patterns for business processes based on proclets. In: ER. vol. 12400, pp. 149–163. Springer (2020)

41. Winter, K., Stertz, F., Rinderle-Ma, S.: Discovering instance and process spanning constraints from process execution logs. Inf. Syst. **89**, 101484 (2020)

Model-Based Recommendations
for Next-Best Actions
in Knowledge-Intensive Processes

Anjo Seidel[1]([✉]), Stephan Haarmann[2], and Mathias Weske[1]

[1] Hasso Plattner Institute, University of Potsdam, Prof.-Dr.-Helmert-Str. 2-3,
14482 Potsdam, Germany
{anjo.seidel,mathias.weske}@hpi.de
[2] Camunda Services GmbH, Berlin, Germany
stephan.haarmann@camunda.com

Abstract. Knowledge-intensive processes are highly flexible and volatile and therefore hard to predict. During the execution of a case, knowledge workers plan their actions to reach their goals based on their expertise and traditionally without system support. This paper proposes a model-driven framework that allows combining process model analysis with existing predictive process monitoring approaches to automatically recommend the next best action to perform. The approach is based on case-specific and data-centric goals that the knowledge workers may specify during run-time. A prototypical implementation uses state space analysis based on colored Petri nets to compute recommendations, while user experiments show their value to knowledge workers.

Keywords: Knowledge-intensive Processes · Process Modeling · Predictive Process Monitoring · Fragment-based Case Management

1 Introduction

Knowledge workers are domain experts, who identify and solve problems in complex changing contexts [10]. They drive the underlying knowledge-intensive processes (KiPs) towards their goals [4]: Therefore, knowledge workers decide in any situation which action aligns best with their goals and, hence, should be executed next. These choices are rarely trivial as multiple actions may be possible, and each action can change process data and, therefore, influence the process's possible future execution. In addition, the cost of actions and temporal constraints between different actions need to be considered.

However, approaches that support knowledge workers with these decisions are missing. The research area of predictive process monitoring aims at predicting the future of a running process instance [5]. Building on top, prescriptive process monitoring recommends next-best actions or detects situations that require intervention [9]. Yet, knowledge workers need to understand why the system gives certain recommendations [9]. Also, predictions and prescriptions are based

© The Author(s), under exclusive license to Springer Nature Switzerland AG 2024
G. Guizzardi et al. (Eds.): CAiSE 2024, LNCS 14663, pp. 195–211, 2024.
https://doi.org/10.1007/978-3-031-61057-8_12

on a metric, whose value needs to be predicted or optimized. It is the input of machine learning models that are trained before executing a case. This is insufficient for KiPs because knowledge workers' goals are defined and revised at run-time. These goals may change during run-time and can be more complex than pre-defined process outcomes. Therefore, they cannot be used for predictive process monitoring yet.

In prior work, we proposed a model-driven approach to derive decision support during the execution of knowledge-intensive processes [11]. During runtime, knowledge workers can specify process instance-specific goals that describe desired future execution states. The state space of the process model is analyzed to identify paths that align with them. Model-checking is used to filter the currently available actions according to their alignment with the specified goals. For now, this approach can not make sophisticated statements about different levels of suitability for different actions.

Based on these considerations, this paper now aims to combine model-driven decision support with predictive process monitoring, which allows knowledge workers to tailor recommendations according to their needs during the execution of knowledge-intensive process models. Predictive process monitoring techniques are well suited to assign costs to process execution sequences. At run-time, they can be combined with different goals to identify prospect paths in the state space and their cost. According to the knowledge worker's requirements, scores for the next actions can be calculated.

The approach in this paper allows knowledge workers to remain in charge of specifying their requirements toward their desired process outcomes. Yet, they can still profit from the knowledge obtained from predictive monitoring models for their recommendations. The approach is supported by a prototypical implementation and evaluated with user experiments.

Section 2 outlines the work related to this paper, while Sect. 3 elaborates the background for the presented approach. In Sect. 4, we elaborate our approach to define and compute suitable actions. Our work is evaluated in Sect. 5, before discussing and concluding it in Sect. 6.

2   Related Work

Related work includes literature about (i) KiPs and KiP models, (ii) goal modeling in KiPs, (iii) predictive and prescriptive process monitoring, and (iv) recommending next actions in KiPs.

Di Ciccio et al. characterize KiPs as goal-driven, data-aware, and multivariant [4]. Due to their complexity and tacit knowledge, KiPs must be modeled flexibly. Instead of defining procedures, KiPs emerge gradually at run-time, based on the decisions of well-informed knowledge workers. Swenson claims imperative modeling languages, such as BPMN, are unsuited for KiPs due to a lack of support for flexibility [13]. Therefore, new languages focus on flexibility by being more declarative and data-centric [4]. Di Ciccio et al. [4] and Steinau et al. [12] provide surveys on different modeling approaches.

In KiPs, decisions are made by knowledge workers regarding their case-specific goals [4]. Goal modeling is a relevant subject in the context of requirements engineering. The use of goal-oriented requirements language in the context of BPM is investigated by Amyot et al. [1]. They find that goal models are mostly used to specify requirements toward the process model rather than process instances. Burratin et al. use requirement models as a description of the influence of actions and goals on each other to derive information on the informativeness of process traces [3]. In prior work [11], we provided the means to model the goals of knowledge workers by specifying first-order logic formulas over possible future execution states. By using temporal logic, actions can be filtered whether they comply with the modeled goals. To this point, actions could not be recommended according to their suitability to reach the goal.

Predictive process monitoring aims to provide predictions on how the process continues for a running case based on machine learning on past case executions. Di Francescomarino and Ghidini [5] and Di Francescomarino et al. [6] provide an overview of the contemporary approaches. Prescriptive process monitoring approaches aim to derive recommendations from such predictions. An overview is presented by Kubrak et al. [9]. Next-event predictions can estimate the most likely next activity [6]. Weinzierl et al. use such predictions to recommend actions that are expected to improve the process performance [15]. Still, these predictions are based on a fixed value and do not support flexible goals.

Existing works tackle the topic of recommending next actions. Venero et al. [14] use Markov decision processes (MDP) to compute planning support by encoding the planning problem for reaching a goal as an MDP. Lo Bianco et al. [2] provide a formalism to incorporate MDPs and Petri nets to solve task assignment problems. For both approaches, the reward function of the MDP is optimized toward one specific goal and limits the flexibility for changing goals and cost measures during run-time.

Recommendations explicitly for knowledge-intensive processes were proposed by Ozturk Yurt et al. [16]. They propose guiding knowledge workers by providing a task prioritization based on a fixed mapping of the benefit of tasks for a specific context. Still, such contexts have to be defined during design time and can not depict knowledge workers' flexible goals. In a different approach, Khan et al. [8] propose the use of reinforcement learning to recommend next-best actions as decision support for knowledge-intensive processes. Yet, these predictions are based on a fixed value that does not depict knowledge workers' case-specific goals.

3   Background

To model KiPs as defined by Di Ciccio et al. [4], we use fragment-based Case Management (fCM) [7]. Furthermore, this chapter summarizes preceding work on modeling goals for KiPs and filtering compliant actions regarding a given goal.

3.1   Fragment-Based Case Management

The main concept of fCM is splitting the control flow of the process into multiple fragments. Knowledge workers can combine these fragments and add new ones at run-time. Their combination is limited by declarative data constraints. An fCM model consists of (i) a set of process fragments, (ii) a data class model, and (iii) a data object behavior model.

Fragments. The process fragments describe the process's activities $a \in \mathfrak{A}$, their connection via control flow, and their dependency on data objects. Fragments can be executed concurrently and arbitrarily often. Yet, activities can only be executed if they are control flow and data flow enabled, i.e., the data dependencies of at least one data input set need to be satisfied. The activity instance can create and update data objects.

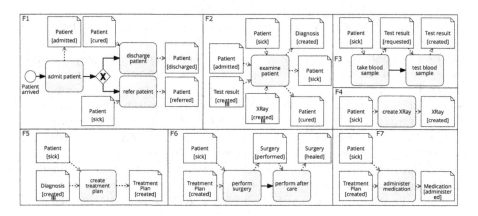

Fig. 1. Fragments for the hospital admission.

The simplified process of hospital admission is depicted by the fragments in Fig. 1. The process starts, once a patient enters the hospital by admitting them in fragment 1. In fragment 2, the admitted patient can be examined. The practitioners can determine whether the patient is sick or healthy. If the patient is sick, a diagnosis is made. For a sick patient, blood samples can be drawn and tested (cf. fragment 3) or X-rays can be created (cf. fragment 4). A set of X-rays and test results from blood samples can be used as an input in fragment 2 to examine the sick patient. For a set of created diagnoses, a treatment plan can be developed in fragment 5. Based on the treatment plan, surgeries may be performed (cf. fragment 6) and medication can be administered (cf. fragment 7). The patient can be examined again until finally cured. Once the patient is cured, they can be discharged (cf. fragment 1). Also, a sick patient can be referred to another medical facility at any point.

Data Model. The set of data classes $\mathfrak{C}$ can be described by a UML class diagram (cf. Fig. 2) describing the classes and their associations. A patient can have arbitrarily many diagnoses, test results, and X-rays. Treatment plans can exist for one patient and a non-empty set of diagnoses. Medicine and surgeries exist for a given treatment plan. The behavior of data objects, i.e., instances of data classes, is defined by state transition systems (cf. Fig. 3). For each data class $c \in \mathfrak{C}$, a set of data object states $\mathfrak{S}_c$ is defined. For instance, an object of the class *patient* can be in the state *admitted*. From thereon, it can change to *sick* or *cured*. A sick patient can remain sick, can be cured, or be referred to another health facility. Finally, a cured patient can be discharged.

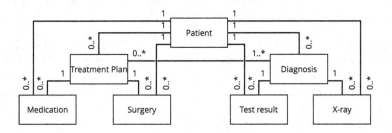

Fig. 2. Data classes for the hospital admission.

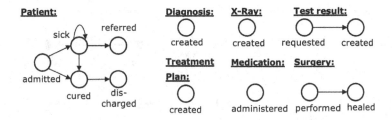

Fig. 3. Data behavior for the hospital admission.

Execution Semantics. The state of a case is a tuple $s = (O_s, L_s, A_s)$ of data objects O_s, their links L_s, and available actions A_s [11]. Each data object $o \in O_s$ belongs to a data class $c \in \mathfrak{C}$, is in a state $\mathfrak{s} \in \mathfrak{S}_c$, and has a unique identifier $id \in ID$. The set L_s contains the links among data objects. The set A_s holds all actions that are currently enabled. Each action $a \in A_s$ is an instance of one activity $\mathfrak{a} \in \mathfrak{A}$ as described in the fragments. It binds a subset of the data objects O_s in the current state s and writes another subset of data objects. The execution of an action a results in a new state s' with a new set of data objects $O_{s'}$, links $L_{s'}$, and available actions $A_{s'}$. In the hospital admission example, a state may hold an instance of *patient* in the state *sick* that is linked to a data object *X-ray* in the state *created*. This enables different actions. It is possible to examine the patient resulting either in a newly created *diagnosis*, or in the *patient* being *cured*. Also, practitioners may take a blood sample, create an X-ray, or refer the patient.

The state space of a process model holds all its states and state transitions. It is a directed graph $\mathcal{S} = (S, E)$ with nodes S representing case states and edges E representing state transitions inferred by executing actions.

A path in the state space represents a possible execution sequence of the case. It consists of a sequence of actions that can be performed according to the behavioral model and the sequence of case states that are reached subsequently.

Definition 1 (Execution Sequences). *Given a state space $\mathcal{S} = (S, E)$, an execution sequence $\sigma = (\sigma_s, \sigma_a)$ consists of a sequence of case states $\sigma_s = \langle s_1, ...s_n \rangle$, and a sequence of actions $\sigma_a = \langle a_1, ...a_{n-1} \rangle$, such that $\forall i \in \mathbb{N}^+, i < n : s_i \xrightarrow{a_i} s_{i+1}$. The set of all possible execution sequences is denoted by Σ.*

Figure 4 shows an excerpt of the state space for the hospital admission process. Due to the size, not all available actions are represented. Also, only the path starting in the initial state s_0 leading to the current state s_b is displayed, i.e., the past execution $\sigma_s = \langle s_0, ...s_a, s_b \rangle$. For the current state, multiple future paths are possible starting with executing any of the available actions, e.g., *create X-ray*, *take blood sample*, or *refer patient*.

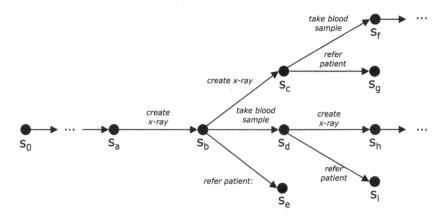

Fig. 4. Excerpt of the state space for the hospital admission process.

3.2 Filtering Actions According to Goal Models

In preliminary work, we already introduced a model-driven framework to model goals and use them for model checking [11]. During run-time, this allows for filtering actions that allow reaching the goal. The presented approach can be applied to settings in which a process model describes the allowed system behavior and where goal models can be specified that are within the scope of the process model.

Goals are defined to consist of objectives. An objective $\omega \in \Omega$ is defined as one of all possible first-order logical statements over any possible future case state $s = (O_s, L_s, A_s)$ [11]. Regarding the hospital admission example, a knowledge worker may specify the objective that it should be possible to discharge the patient. Also, there should exist at least three X-rays and up to two diagnoses for this patient. This objective ω_1 can be expressed as the following first-order logic expression over O_s, L_s, and A_s of a possible future state s.

$$\omega_1 \equiv \exists a \in A_s, o \in O_s : a.\mathfrak{a} = \text{"discharge patient"} \wedge o.c = patient \wedge o.\mathfrak{s} = sick$$
$$\{l = (o_i, o_j) \in L | o_i = o \wedge o_j.\mathfrak{c} = X\text{-}Ray\} \geq 3 \wedge$$
$$\{l = (o_i, o_j) \in L | o_i = o \wedge o_j.\mathfrak{c} = Diagnosis\} \leq 2$$

Two objectives ω_1 and ω_2 can be temporally ordered [11]. This means that given a path $\sigma = (\sigma_s, \sigma_a) \in \Sigma$ in the state space $\mathcal{S}$, one objective holds in one state of a path and the second holds in a later state of the same path. I.e., there exists a state $s_i \in \sigma_s$ where the ω_1 holds, and a state $s_j \in p_s$ where ω_2 holds, such that there is a path from s_i to s_j in the state space.

A goal $\gamma \in \Gamma$ is a partial order of temporally ordered objectives [11]. This partial order describes a set of possible sequences of objectives. To satisfy a goal, an execution of the process model must comply with any of these sequences.

With a goal model at hand, it is possible to analyze the state space of a process model [11]. The goal is translated into a model-checking problem expressed as a computation tree logic formula. In the current state of a case, knowledge workers can define their goals. For each enabled action, we check whether the action is suitable to reach the goal. To do so, the action is simulated, and a model checker can search the sub-graph of the state space to determine whether a path exists that satisfies the goal. If it exists, the action is suitable. With these results, actions can be filtered to provide *filter-based recommendations* for knowledge workers.

4 Action Scores

Based on our previous work [11], we use a process model and goal models to compute decision support. But in addition to just filtering goal-conforming actions, we now support knowledge workers in choosing the next action based on action scores. We propose to compute action scores as recommendations that depict how well-suited a certain action is to reach a set of modeled goals. Similar to Buratti et al. [3], we consider multiple goals to influence the relevance of a path. Required and optional goals can have different levels of influence. In the following, we elaborate on what makes an action suitable before defining how actions can be scored accordingly.

4.1 Scores and Suitable Actions

In the following, we elaborate on the rationale of what makes actions suitable. It is determined by the suitability of the paths that can reach the specified goals.

Suitability of Actions. An action is suitable if it is the start of at least one suitable path. An action can be considered more suitable if the paths to reaching the goals are themselves more suitable. For instance, this can be the case if there are more suitable paths starting with an action or a single path that is especially suitable compared to others.

In Fig. 5 for the current state s_b of the hospital admission, one set of action scores is calculated. A practitioner might have the goal to create at least three X-rays. However, executing additional actions is expensive. Then, an action is suitable if it allows for reaching the goal, for instance in the states s_c or s_h. For the current state s_b, these suitable actions are *create x-ray* and *take blood sample*. If executing the next action implies executing more actions before reaching the goal, it could be less suitable as depicted for taking the blood sample in Fig. 5. On the other hand, taking more blood samples allows for a new diagnosis. This could be beneficial to achieve other goals and allow for more flexibility in uncertain situations. This may come at a higher cost of the execution. There is a trade-off between (i) minimizing the costs of the execution paths to reach the goal and (ii) executing actions that add more context to the process execution and allow for more options in the future. With the presented approach, knowledge workers are supported in specifying their prioritization in regard to this trade-off.

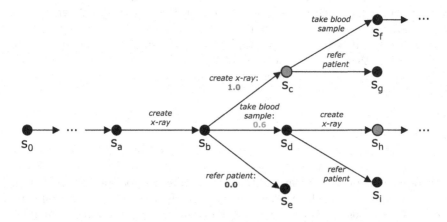

Fig. 5. Excerpt of state space for the hospital admission with recommendations.

Suitability of Paths. A path is considered suitable if it satisfies a set of required goals, like the path from s_0 to s_c or to s_h in Fig. 5. It is more suitable than another path if it satisfies a goal specification better. Different aspects play into this: A goal specification is a set of required goals that need to be satisfied. Additionally, there can be optional goals. Also, goals can be weighed. The path score is higher the more highly weighed goals are satisfied. Considering the hospital admission, an optional goal could be that there are at most three blood tests that were performed. It could also be weighed lower than the other required goals to indicate its lower importance.

A path is more suitable if it is less expensive. The costs of a path can be determined by using existing predictive process monitoring approaches. Those could, for example, determine the expected cycle time based on past executions. They would investigate the past execution of states $\langle s_0, ...s_a, s_b \rangle$. Analog to the prior work in the field of predictive process monitoring [5], the presented approach allows tracking the current execution of the process and using the running trace with concrete attribute values as an input to a machine learning model. Such a model is trained on an event log of historic process executions. Our approach has no additional demands than existing predictive process monitoring approaches.

Moreover, the path cost function can incorporate costs for the future execution of the case, that is the path from the current state to the goal-satisfying state, e.g., $\langle s_b, s_d, s_h \rangle$. Taking a blood sample before creating the X-ray requires more time. Therefore, this path is less suitable than $\langle s_b, s_c \rangle$. In the hospital setting, certain actions, such as performing surgery, might be more expensive in terms of time consumption. They should not be performed unnecessarily. A path cost function can assign a cost to each action of a path. It can incorporate costs for the involved data objects as well. Creating a treatment plan based on one diagnosis could be easier and faster than on multiple ones.

Path Prioritization. The set of goal-satisfying paths starting with one action determines its score. The calculation of action scores is domain and case-dependent. If the knowledge worker is uncertain and/or the execution context volatile, it may be beneficial to have many paths that satisfy the goals. On the other hand, a single especially suitable path starting with one action could be favored over a number of slightly less suitable actions.

In summary, an action is suitable if it is likely to lead to a state where the goals hold by having a cheap execution. However, the specifics of this trade-off are to be defined by the knowledge workers.

4.2 Calculating Action Scores

To calculate action scores as previously described, we define the input that knowledge workers must provide before using it to score actions.

Input. Based on the previously described aspects that make an action suitable, we define an input configuration. It specifies knowledge workers' highly case-specific requirements for action scores.

Definition 2 (Input Configuration). *Given a set of goals Γ and the set of paths Σ in a state space $\mathcal{S}$, the input configuration to compute score-based recommendations is the tuple $\mathcal{I} = (\Gamma_r, \Gamma_o, wf, cf, pf)$.*

- *$\Gamma_r \subseteq \Gamma$ is a set of required goals, and $\Gamma_r \neq \emptyset$.*

- $\Gamma_o \subseteq \Gamma$ is a set of optional goals, and $\Gamma_r \cap \Gamma_o = \emptyset$.
- $wf \colon \Gamma \to \mathbb{R}_0^+$ is a weight function for goals.
- $cf \colon (\Sigma \times \Sigma) \to \mathbb{R}^+$ is a path cost function that assigns a cost to a pair of the past execution $\sigma \in \Sigma$ and a possible future execution $\sigma' \in \Sigma$.
- $pf \colon 2^{\mathbb{R}^+} \to \mathbb{R}^+$ is a path prioritization function that derives a numeric score for a set of path scores.

For a situation where a patient is sick and three X-rays and two diagnoses exist, a practitioner in a hospital defines the input configuration $\mathcal{I}_1 = (\Gamma_{r_1}, \Gamma_{o1}, wf_1, cf_1, pf_1)$ with the required goal γ_1 and the optional goal γ_2. The weight function wf assigns a cost of 1.0 to γ_1 and 0.5 to γ_2.

The path cost function cf describes the costs of execution paths in the model's state space. The path consists of a sub-path σ from the initial state of the state space to the current case state and a sub-path σ' from the current case state to another state. Contemporary predictive process monitoring approaches [5] solely use the past execution σ to compute recommendations. Additionally, we can take each prospect path σ', into account for computing path scores. As defined in Definition 1, a path in the state space is a sequence of case states connected by actions. Therefore, the path costs can be calculated based on the states and the actions given in a path. This includes all data objects with their individual states and links to other data objects. Furthermore, all actions of the path can be considered. It needs to be mentioned that the provided definition of a state space only covers the abstract state of data objects. When implementing our approach in an information system, the information about the past execution can be recorded and used as input for the path cost function like in contemporary approaches. In our example, the cost function cf_1 assigns the average duration of an action as cost. Creating X-rays or treatment plans is laborious, but surgeries take especially long. However, the path cost function can also implement contemporary predictive process monitoring techniques. For instance, a machine-learning-based path cost function could encode implicit knowledge about the human resources that execute the process. Their labor costs are learned and predicted for the path resulting in an estimated path cost.

If the suitability of a set of paths Σ can be determined, knowledge workers may specify a path prioritization function pf. This function can, for instance, return the sum/average/maximum of all path scores. The function depends on the priorities of the knowledge workers. If the knowledge worker is interested in the cheapest path, the maximum can be used. If they want to keep their options open, the sum may be a good choice. The path prioritization can be used according to the current needs. In the hospital admission example, the practitioner might be certain about the future execution of the case and requires pf_1 to return the highest path score.

Score Computation. With the previously defined input, we can now look into the actual computation of path scores and action scores.

In previous work, we provided the means to check whether an action can be used to reach a defined goal [11]. That is the case if there exists a path starting in the current state that satisfies the goal. This can be checked by the goal-checking function $check\_goal$. It takes a path in the state space as input and evaluates whether a goal can be satisfied on this path as elaborated in Sect. 3.2.

Definition 3 (Required Goals Checking Function).
Let Σ be all paths of a state space S and Γ_r be a set of required goals. The required goals-checking function determines if the path σ satisfies all goals in Γ_r.

$$check\_required\_goals : \Sigma \times (2^{\Gamma} \setminus \emptyset) \to Boolean$$

$$check\_required\_goals(\sigma, \Gamma_r) = \bigwedge_{\gamma_i \in \Gamma_r} check\_goal(\sigma, \gamma_i)$$

For a given path, the set of required goals Γ_{r1} from the input configuration can be checked (cf. Definition 3). If all of those goals are satisfied by the path, it evaluates to true and the path is considered suitable. If a required goal is not satisfied, the function evaluates to false and the path is considered not suitable.

To compute an action score, not all paths from the state space should be considered. A potential suitable path starts in the initial state of the state space. It consists of the past execution σ of the case to the current state and of one future path σ'. Knowledge workers are interested in reaching their goals. Therefore, it is sufficient for a path to end in a state, where the goals hold, and it does not need additional actions afterward. We are only interested in minimal satisfying paths for computing action scores.

Definition 4 (Minimal Satisfying Paths).
Let Γ_r be a set of required goals. The set of minimal satisfying paths Σ_{min} contains all the minimal paths $\sigma + \sigma'$ to reach the required goals.

$$\Sigma_{min} = \{\sigma + \sigma' = (\langle s_1, ...s_n \rangle, \langle a_1, ...a_{n-1} \rangle) \in \Sigma \mid$$
$$check\_required\_goals((\langle s_1, ...s_n \rangle, \langle a_1, ...a_{n-1} \rangle), \Gamma_r) \wedge$$
$$\neg check\_required\_goals((\langle s_1, ...s_{n-1} \rangle, \langle a_1, ...a_{n-2} \rangle), \Gamma_r)\}$$

This set contains only those paths that satisfy at least the required goals. For each minimal satisfying path, its score is computed by summing up the weights of all satisfied goals divided by the path costs. The more high-weighted goals are satisfied, and the lower the cost, the higher the resulting path score.

Definition 5 (Path Score).
Given an input configuration $\mathcal{I} = (\Gamma_r, \Gamma_o, wf, cf, pf)$ with a set of required goals Γ_r and optional goals Γ_o, a path cost function cf, and a weight function wf for the goals, the function $score_\Sigma$ defines the score of a path $(\sigma + \sigma') \in \Sigma$.

$$score_\Sigma : (\Sigma \times \Sigma) \to \mathbb{R}_0^+,$$

$$score_\Sigma(\sigma, \sigma') = \frac{\sum_{\gamma_i \in \Gamma_r \cup \Gamma_o} \begin{cases} wf(\gamma_i), & if\ check\_goal(\sigma + \sigma', \gamma_i) \\ 0, & else \end{cases}}{cf(\sigma, \sigma')}$$

For example, a fictive path with the past execution σ_1 and the future execution σ_1' starts with the action *create X-Ray*. The path satisfies γ_1 and γ_2 and is assigned a cost of 6 h. Its score is calculated as:

$$score_\Sigma(\sigma_1, \sigma_1') = \frac{wf_1(\gamma_1) + wf_1(\gamma_2)}{cf_1(\sigma_1, \sigma_1')} = \frac{1.0 + 0.5}{6} = 0.25$$

All the path scores of all the minimal satisfying paths starting in a certain action can be combined into an action score. They are combined by using the path prioritization function *pf* as defined in Definition 6.

Definition 6 (Action Score).
Given an input configuration $\mathcal{I} = (\Gamma_r, \Gamma_o, wf, cf, pf)$ and the set of minimal satisfying paths, which start with the past execution σ and the future execution σ' starting with the action a $\Sigma_{min}^a = \{(\sigma, \sigma') \mid (\sigma + \sigma') \in \Sigma_{min} \wedge \sigma' = (\sigma_s, \langle a_1, ...a_n \rangle) \wedge a_1 = a\}$. The function $score_A$ defines the action score for all enabled actions A.

$$score_A : A \to \mathbb{R}_0^+,$$
$$score_A(a) = pf(\{score_\Sigma(\sigma, \sigma') \mid (\sigma + \sigma') \in \Sigma_{min}^a\})$$

In the example, a practitioner has defined the input configuration $\mathcal{I}_1$ for the current situation. As a result, the actions *create X-Ray*, *create treatment plan*, and *perform surgery* receive low scores, while *examine patient* does not comply with the goal and is not recommended. The highest score is assigned to *discharge patient* as it has the shortest path to comply with the goals. Other high scores are assigned to *take blood sample* as it allows satisfying the optional goal of having more blood samples. The computation of action scores may result in different scores for each situation. To produce comparable scores, they can be normalized. As a result, all action scores are within the interval from zero to one. If there exists no goal satisfying path starting with the action a, the score is zero.

To implement the computation of action scores for a current situation, the sub-graph of the state space must be searched, which has the current state as its root. Graph traversal algorithms can analyze it. We propose using a breadth-first search to find minimal satisfying paths efficiently. The state space can be computed ad hoc during the search according to the process model or in advance of the search. The latter requires the state space to be finite.

5   Evaluation

We provide a prototypical implementation that shows the technical feasibility of score-based recommendations. Additionally, user experiments indicate the value of recommending scores to knowledge workers during the process execution.

Prototype. We provide a prototype[1] extending prior work on filter-based recommendations [11]. It enables knowledge workers to model their input configuration during run-time. Goals are modeled using a form input. Knowledge workers can weigh a set of goals and combine them with a path cost function.

FCM models are formalized as colored Petri nets and can be executed in CPN Tools [7]. CPN Tools allows execution of the resulting Petri net and generating its state space, which can be used for analysis as discussed previously. The prototype compiles a user's input configurations into a state space query for the current execution state, which implements a breadth-first search returning action scores in accordance with the defined computation in Sect. 4.

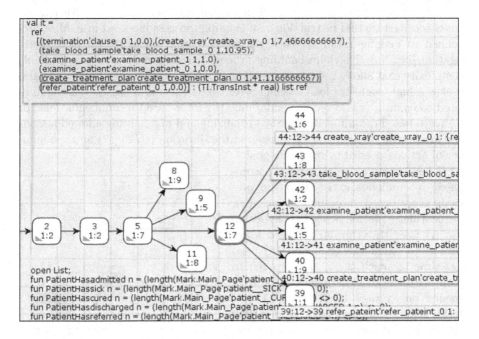

Fig. 6. Action scores computed by a state space query in CPN Tools.

Figure 6 displays an excerpt of the state space in CPN Tools. It returns the action scores for all next actions for the current execution state 12. As shown in the state space, there are six next actions possible to follow state 12. In the upper left of Fig. 6, for each action, the respective non-normalized score is shown. For referring a patient, the score is 0.0; hence, it should not be selected as the next action. The action score of taking blood samples is 10.95; hence, it is the better choice. The highest score (41.12) is assigned to creating a treatment plan, which should be conducted as the next action since it is the next best action.

---

[1] https://github.com/bptlab/fCM-query-generator.

208   A. Seidel et al.

User Experiments. In the authors previous work [11], user experiments showed that filter-based recommendations can be of assistance to knowledge workers. A group (a) was given no recommendations, while a group (b) was given filter-based recommendations. These users made no errors and needed fewer actions and less time to reach a goal.

In the following, we compare a third user group (c), which were recommended scores for their next actions, against the results from group (a) and (b). In total, we observed 22 computer science students and assigned them to three groups: (a) seven were given no recommendations; (b) seven were provided filter-based recommendations; (c) eight participants got scores as recommendations. The complete setup and the results are documented online[2].

The experiments were conducted in the same in-person setting. All participants received textual instructions, an example process modeled in fCM, a predefined goal configuration to reach, and an execution engine. In the prior investigation [11], a fictive claim handling process was chosen to have a controllable complexity that allows users to reach the goal without recommendations, yet also evokes a high cognitive load causing errors. The execution engine was manipulated to contain (a) no recommendations, (b) filter-based recommendations, or (c) score-based recommendations by visualizing and highlighting allowed actions and annotating their score. We measured the duration (cf. Fig. 7) and the number of actions needed to reach the goal.

When comparing the novel score-based recommendations (c) to the previous score-based recommendations (b), we postulate the following two hypotheses: (i) Users from group (c) need fewer actions to reach the goal, and (ii) need less time to reach the goal compared to group (b). In our experiments, group (b) needed on average 19.43 actions (sd = 1.13), while group (c) only needed 19.0 (sd = 0.0). Although not statistically significant, all users of group (c) found the optimal (shortest) path to reach their goal with exactly 19 actions. More participants or a different experimental setup is needed to confirm hypothesis (i) statistically. Considering hypothesis (ii), we

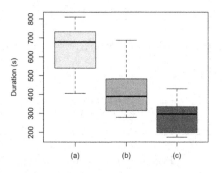

Fig. 7. Users' durations (a) without, with (b) filter-based, and (c) score-based recommendations.

observed that group (b) needed on average 422 s (sd = 145) and group (c) only 283 s (sd = 89). A t-test results in an effect of t(9.6) = 2.18 and a p-value of p < 0.03 confirming the hypothesis (ii) with statistical significance.

Still, the results are subject to some limitations. The experiments were conducted with a small number of computer science students. Their uniform background may introduce biases. The proposed approach focuses on knowledge

---

[2] https://github.com/bptlab/fCM-Engine/tree/master/user_study.

workers that define complex goals themselves. Also, goals are allowed to change during run-time. Yet, a rather simple goal and input configuration were predefined and they did not change during the experiment. The usefulness of score-based recommendations might be influenced by various factors as the complexity of goals and the domain, the experience of knowledge, or other external factors. Future experiments in more complex or real-world settings can provide more detailed and reliable results. Still, the results indicate the value of score-based recommendations for knowledge workers with case-specific goals.

6   Discussion and Conclusion

Knowledge workers act in complex and quickly changing contexts. This makes knowledge-intensive processes particularly hard to predict. We presented a novel framework for recommending actions to knowledge workers. An extensive input configuration allows knowledge workers to tune the framework to their personal needs during run-time by combining a KiP model with goal models and existing predictive process monitoring approaches to score the enabled actions. Given this input, the state space is analyzed and each enabled action is scored according to being more or less suited for reaching the goals.

Still, this model-based approach yields limitations: To apply the approach, the presence of an enacted process model is assumed but in many real-world use cases that might not be the case. Eliciting and enacting process models is especially challenging for unstructured knowledge-intensive processes. The proposed input configurations allow knowledge workers a high degree of freedom in defining their requirements toward recommendations. Yet, small changes can have a big influence on the result making the choice of the right configuration a complex task and adding cognitive load. But also with process and goal models at hand, a suitable execution sequence may not always exist, or the state space may be too large to find suitable paths within time and memory constraints. In fact, searching the state space is an undecidable problem. Therefore, smart heuristics, pruning strategies, and stopping criteria should be considered. In our definition, the case states only hold information about the abstract states of data objects and not continuous values like those used in most predictive process monitoring approaches. In future implementations, the concrete values of the past execution can be recorded and considered as well. Also, specifying input specifications is very complex. Knowledge workers can profit from domain-specific support in defining them. Nevertheless, our prototypical implementation shows the technical feasibility of the approach, and our user experiments indicate its value to knowledge workers. Future studies should apply and test the framework in the field in combination with existing and novel predictive process monitoring techniques.

In summary, our approach allows combining data-driven monitoring with model-based analysis to get the best of both worlds: Estimations based on the process history are guard-railed by the process and goal models. While machine learning algorithms may uncover tacit knowledge from data, knowledge workers are in charge of modeling process goals and input configurations for the running case. With this work, we notice the promising merit of combining the different research areas for mutual benefits.

References

1. Amyot, D., et al.: Combining goal modelling with business process modelling two decades of experience with the user requirements notation standard. Enterp. Model. Inf. Syst. Archit. Int. J. Concept. Model. **17** (2022)
2. Bianco, R.L., Dijkman, R.M., Nuijten, W., van Jaarsveld, W.: Action-evolution petri nets: a framework for modeling and solving dynamic task assignment problems. In: Di Francescomarino, C., Burattin, A., Janiesch, C., Sadiq, S. (eds.) Business Process Management. BPM 2023. LNCS, vol. 14159, pp. 216–231. Springer, Cham (2023). https://doi.org/10.1007/978-3-031-41620-0_13
3. Burattin, A., Guizzardi, G., Maggi, F.M., Montali, M.: Fifty shades of green: how informative is a compliant process trace? In: Giorgini, P., Weber, B. (eds.) CAiSE 2019. LNCS, vol. 11483, pp. 611–626. Springer, Cham (2019). https://doi.org/10.1007/978-3-030-21290-2_38
4. Ciccio, C.D., Marrella, A., Russo, A.: Knowledge-intensive processes: characteristics, requirements and analysis of contemporary approaches. J. Data Semant. **4**(1) (2015)
5. Francescomarino, C.D., Ghidini, C.: Predictive process monitoring. In: van der Aalst, W.M.P., Carmona, J. (eds.) Process Mining Handbook, Lecture Notes in Business Information Processing, vol. 448. Springer (2022)
6. Francescomarino, C.D., Ghidini, C., Maggi, F.M., Milani, F.: Predictive process monitoring methods: which one suits me best? . In: van der Aalst, W.M.P., Carmona, J. (eds.) Process Mining Handbook. LNBIP, vol. 448, pp. 320–346. Springer, Cham (2022). https://doi.org/10.1007/978-3-031-08848-3_10
7. Haarmann, S.: WICKR: A Joint Semantics for Flexible Processes and Data. Ph.D. thesis, Universität Potsdam (2022)
8. Khan, A., Ghose, A., Dam, H.: Decision support for knowledge intensive processes using RL based recommendations. In: Polyvyanyy, A., Wynn, M.T., Van Looy, A., Reichert, M. (eds.) BPM 2021. LNBIP, vol. 427, pp. 246–262. Springer, Cham (2021). https://doi.org/10.1007/978-3-030-85440-9_15
9. Kubrak, K., Milani, F., Nolte, A., Dumas, M.: Prescriptive process monitoring: quo vadis? PeerJ Comput. Sci. **8** (2022)
10. Pyöriä, P.: The concept of knowledge work revisited. J. Knowl. Manag. **9**(3) (2005)
11. Seidel, A., Haarmann, S., Weske, M.: Model-based decision support for knowledge-intensive processes. J. Intell. Inf. Syst. (2022)
12. Steinau, S., Marrella, A., Andrews, K., Leotta, F., Mecella, M., Reichert, M.: DALEC: a framework for the systematic evaluation of data-centric approaches to process management software. Softw. Syst. Model. **18**(4) (2019)
13. Swenson, K.: State of the art in case management (2013)
14. Venero, S.K., Schmerl, B., Montecchi, L., dos Reis, J.C., Rubira, C.M.F.: Automated planning for supporting knowledge-intensive processes. In: Nurcan, S., Reinhartz-Berger, I., Soffer, P., Zdravkovic, J. (eds.) BPMDS/EMMSAD -2020. LNBIP, vol. 387, pp. 101–116. Springer, Cham (2020). https://doi.org/10.1007/978-3-030-49418-6_7

15. Weinzierl, S., Dunzer, S., Zilker, S., Matzner, M.: Prescriptive business process monitoring for recommending next best actions. In: Fahland, D., Ghidini, C., Becker, J., Dumas, M. (eds.) BPM 2020. LNBIP, vol. 392, pp. 193–209. Springer, Cham (2020). https://doi.org/10.1007/978-3-030-58638-6_12
16. Yurt, Z.O., Eshuis, R., Wilbik, A., Vanderfeesten, I.T.P.: Guiding knowledge workers under dynamic contexts. In: Franch, X., Poels, G., Gailly, F., Snoeck, M. (eds.) Advanced Information Systems Engineering. CAiSE 2022. LNCS, vol. 13295, pp. 218–234. Springer, Cham (2022). https://doi.org/10.1007/978-3-031-07472-1_13

Prediction, Monitoring and Planning

Towards Learning the Optimal Sampling Strategy for Suffix Prediction in Predictive Monitoring

Efrén Rama-Maneiro[1]([⊠]) [iD], Fabio Patrizi[2] [iD], Juan Vidal[1] [iD], and Manuel Lama[1] [iD]

[1] Centro Singular de Investigación en Tecnoloxías Intelixentes (CiTIUS), Universidade de Santiago de Compostela, 15782 Santiago de Compostela, Spain
{efren.rama.maneiro,juan.vidal,manuel.lama}@usc.es
[2] DIAG Sapienza University of Rome, via Ariosto 25, 00185 Rome, Italy
patrizi@diag.uniroma1.it

Abstract. Predictive monitoring is a subfield of process mining which focuses on forecasting the evolution of an ongoing process case. A related main challenge is activity suffix prediction, the problem of predicting the sequence of future activities until a case ends. One aspect that has been neglected is the activity selection strategy during inference and its impact on the results. This paper introduces the "Deep Reinforcement Learning Predictor" (DOGE), a system which leverages Deep Reinforcement Learning to learn the ideal sampling strategy during training of the neural model. This approach not only simplifies the design of the neural network but also enhances inference speed by avoiding explorative sampling strategies. Through an extensive evaluation against established benchmarks, DOGE shows significant improvements in both performance and adaptability across diverse event log characteristics, highlighting the efficacy of reinforcement learning in predictive monitoring.

Keywords: Deep Reinforcement Learning · Neural Networks · Suffix Prediction · Predictive Monitoring · Process Mining

1 Introduction

Predictive monitoring is the subfield of *process mining* concerned with forecasting how an ongoing process case will unfold [13]. Many predictive problems have been defined in this context, such as forecasting the next activity, timestamp, or outcome of a case. This paper focuses on one of these problems, i.e., *activity suffix prediction*, which consists in predicting the entire sequence of activities that will occur until the end of the case, given the sequence of activities (or *prefix*) observed up to the current time point.

E. Rama-Maneiro—The work presented in this paper was carried out during a research stay in Sapienza Università di Roma.

Deep learning is emerging as a powerful tool for Predictive Monitoring, due to its power in handling sequential data and automating feature-extraction capabilities. Many neural network (NN) architectures have been employed, such as Convolutional NN (CNNs), Recurrent NN (RNNs), Generative Adversarial Networks (GANs), Graph NN (GNNs), Transformers [4,14,19,23,25].

These approaches typically consist in training a network to predict the next activity and then use a *sampling strategy* to iteratively produce the predicted suffix [6,23]. Recent studies in Natural Language Processing (NLP) [15] show that the decoding strategy used to generate sequences–in our case, of predicted activities– from the model plays an essential role w.r.t. performance. At the same time, studies in predictive monitoring [17] show that the performance on suffix prediction heavily depend on the sampling strategy, and that *beam search*, the strategy commonly used, is biased towards sequences shorter than typically observed in business processes. While limited to four strategies only and excluding alternative approaches with potentially better performance, such as *top-k* or *nucleus sampling* [15], this research suggests that the approach based on selecting a "promising" sampling strategy may not yield the best results.

We believe that the performance disparities across sampling strategies stem from the training methodology. Indeed, excluding those for GANs, these approaches rely on Maximum Likelihood Estimation (MLE), thus train the model to maximize next token's likelihood. Unfortunately, though, this is not synonymous with maximizing the likelihood of the *entire sequence of tokens*, which is our goal. To address this, we propose to learn, instead of pre-select, the most suitable sampling strategy, so that, at inference time, the most probable activity already corresponds to that maximizing the similarity between expected and predicted future activities. Besides avoiding pre-selection of a sampling strategy, a further benefit of our proposal is that it drops the need for hyperparameters' tuning, thus yielding an effective simplification in neural models' design.

In this paper, we use Reinforcement Learning (RL) to estimate the probability distribution of suffixes. RL, in our case, provides a more natural framework for taking into account the global properties of the sequence, rather than just focusing on local decisions at each timestep, as is the case for MLE-based approaches. In our setup, actions correspond to selecting the next activity, while rewards account for the similarity of the predicted suffix w.r.t. ground truth.

We implemented our approach in the DOGE system and performed an extensive evaluation against established benchmarks, which shows significant improvements in both performance and adaptability across diverse event log characteristics, thus highlighting the efficacy of RL in predictive monitoring.

2   Related Work

Many works in predictive monitoring concern forecasting control-flow aspects of business processes. Both [23] and [11] rely on LSTM to forecast next activity and activity suffix. In [23], the next activity of a suffix is selected as the most probable one (*argmax* sampling) while in [11] it is selected by *random sampling*, according to a predicted probability distribution. [10] builds upon the architecture of [23] but proposes to select the next activity during suffix prediction to guarantee compliance with a set of mined Linear-temporal logic (LTL) rules, and then employs beam search to select the most probable suffix. Also [26] builds upon [23] but the activity is predicted according to a given KPI, and the suffix is predicted according to compliance with a process model and target KPI maximization.

Other approaches focus on the effective encoding of event log information. In [6], roles are first learnt from resources using a role-discovery algorithm and, then, a single embedding representation is learnt by pre-training the network on the existence of role-activity pairs. The approach uses LSTMs to learn the predictive model and compares the sampling efficiency of suffixes using the *argmax* and *random* strategies. In [9], the whole prefix is encoded into a single representation through embeddings. Then, a FF-NN is trained to predict the next suffix identifier in a one-shot fashion. In [21] the prefixes of a Petri net process model are replaced in order to obtain its behavioral context and train an LSTM to predict the next sequence of attributes. The prediction is then the suffix from the training set that is most similar according to both pieces of information.

Finally, some approaches are based on novel architectures devised to address the suffix prediction problem. [24] presents an encoder-decoder LSTM trained as a GAN, with the discriminator trained to distinguish between fake suffixes from the generator and real suffixes from the training set. [12] compares multiple architectures for suffix prediction, such as LSTM, GAN Recurrent Autoencoders, or Transformers, concluding that no architecture outperforms the others.

RL was introduced as a tool for predictive monitoring only recently. [3] proposes an approach to recommend next activity and suffix based on KPI optimization. In the underlying Markov Decision Process (MDP), states incorporate the activity prefix, the current time and the KPI value, actions model the activities, and the reward is the KPI of interest. [1] tackles the same problem using Proximal Policy Optimization (PPO), which allows for dealing with a multigoal-oriented activity recommendation by adopting a reward function that balances the outcome of the recommended activity and goal satisfaction. [7] evaluates the performance of Deep Q-Networks for the prediction of next activity, next timestamp, remaining time, and activity suffix, with the reward capturing correctness of the agent's predictions at each timestep.

Despite the advancements in the field of predictive monitoring, a common theme in all approaches is the focus on learning and predicting individual activities in the suffix. This strategy, essentially a MLE approach, independently estimates the probability distribution of each activity in the suffix, possibly introducing errors that accumulate over the sequence. This exact phenomenon occurs, in fact, in the state-of-the-art approach most similar to ours, i.e. [7], which obtains comparable results in terms of next activity prediction but way worse w.r.t. to suffix prediction. Since they give the reward at each timestep, the agent does not learn to maximize the entire sequence but, instead, to predict each individual token. This problem could be avoided by using GANs as, e.g., in [24], but GANs can be very difficult to train due to mode collapse, where the generator produces limited diversity of suffixes, and to the need for tuning the loss functions so that the generator and discriminator learn at the same pace. Additionally, applying GANs to discrete outputs often requires workarounds, like the Gumbel-Softmax trick, due to the non-differentiability of *argmax* over discrete variables, which complicates the use of gradient-based learning approaches.

3 Preliminaries

The basis for any predictive monitoring approach is the *event log*, i.e., a set of process executions, named *traces*, consisting in a timestamp-ordered sequence of *events* (*e*). Each event includes, at least, the executed activity (*a*), the corresponding timestamp (*t*) and, optionally, a set of attributes (*d_i*). Our machine learning model aims to predict the remaining sequence of activities (*activity suffix*) given, as input a partial sequence of activities (*activity prefix*). Formally, let $\sigma = \langle e_1, \cdots, e_n, e_{end} \rangle$ be a trace, with e_{end} the *end-of-case* token. Then, the *k-event prefix* of σ is defined as $hd^k(\sigma) := \langle e_1, \cdots e_k \rangle$ and the *k-event suffix* of σ is defined as $tl^k(\sigma) := \langle e_{k+1}, \cdots, e_n, e_{end} \rangle$, with $k \in \{1, \ldots, n\}$.

Deep learning models for activity suffix prediction output a probability distribution $p(a_i)$ for each activity in the predicted suffix, rather than directly predicting an activity suffix. A sampling strategy λ is then used to select the predicted activity at each timestep from this distribution, where $\lambda(p(a_i)) = a$. The prediction process begins with the input activity prefix $hd^k(\sigma)$ and involves concatenating each predicted activity to create the complete trace. This iterative process ends when the end-of-case token e_{end} is predicted. However, as most deep learning models are trained using MLE, the resulting predicted probabilities are more aligned with predicting the next activity rather than the entire suffix, thus making the performance of the sampling strategy λ very sensitive to the characteristics of the event log, as noted in [6,18].

We aim at automatically approximating the predicted probability distribution $p(a_i)$, to make it as close as possible to that which would be produced using an optimal sampling strategy λ^*. This can be formalized as follows.

Definition 1 (Optimal   sampling   strategy   approxima-tion). *Let $p(a_i|a_1, \ldots, a_{i-1})$ be the predicted probability distribution of the next activity a_i, as returned by a predictive model trained with MLE. Let λ^* be the optimal sampling strategy for activity suffix prediction, from the universe of all possible sampling strategies $\Lambda = \{\lambda_1, \ldots, \lambda_n\}$, returning the optimal suffix, given an MLE-trained model. The objective of optimal sampling strategy approximation is to find a probability distribution $p^*(a_i|a_1, \ldots, a_{i-1})$ such that:*

$$\arg\max(p^*(a_i|a_1, \ldots, a_{i-1})) \approx \lambda^*(p(a_i|a_1, \ldots, a_{i-1})),$$

where $i \in [1, k]$, being k the length of the prefix plus the length of the predicted suffix so far.

So, for example, if the optimal suffix from an MLE-trained model is obtained by applying an unnormalized beam search sampling strategy, we aim to adjust the predicted probability distribution so that this suffix can be obtained by selecting always the activity with the highest probability. In the following sections we describe how RL helps in approximating λ^*.

3.1 Reinforcement Learning

Reinforcement learning [22] is a set of machine learning techniques where an agent learns how to interact with an environment to perform a certain task.

Definition 2 (Reinforcement Learning). *Let (S, A, P, R, γ) be a tuple where:*

- *S represents the set of all possible states the agent can be in.*
- *A is the set of all possible actions the agent can take.*
- *$P : S \times A \times S \rightarrow [0, 1]$ is the transition probability, indicating the likelihood of moving from one state to another given an action.*
- *$R : S \times A \times S \rightarrow \mathbb{R}$ represents the reward function, which provides a scalar feedback signal when transitioning from one state to another.*
- *$\gamma \in [0, 1]$ is the discount factor where a value closer to 0 gives more importance to immediate rewards, while a value closer to 1 makes it prioritize long-term rewards.*

The main objective in RL is to find an optimal policy $\Pi^* : S \rightarrow A$ that maximizes the expected cumulative discounted reward:

$$\Pi* = \max_{\Pi} E_{\Pi} \left[\sum_{t=0}^{\infty} \gamma^t R(s_t, a_t, s_{t+1}) \right]$$

where $s_t \in S$ is the state at time t, and $a_t \in A$ is the action taken at time t.

In our predictive monitoring approach, S is represented by the information contained in the prefix plus the predictions from the agent, A is the set of possible activities to predict at each timestep, R is 1 minus the edit distance between the predicted suffix and the ground truth, P is initially unknown, and γ is set to a default value commonly used in RL tasks (0.99). Thus, under the RL paradigm, the agent learns to predict the suffix by interacting with the prefix (predicting activities at each timestep), getting a reward, and adjusting the probabilities of the next activities to maximize the reward. Hence, the sampling strategy *is implicitly defined in the output probability distribution of the next activity.*

We rely on Proximal Policy Optimization (PPO) [20], a state-of-the-art RL algorithm, to learn the optimal policy for predicting activity suffixes. PPO optimizes the policy through gradient ascent. PPO employs two neural networks to guide the learning process: a policy network, which proposes actions based on the current state, and a value network, which estimates the expected reward from each state. This setup creates a feedback loop where the critic (value network) evaluates the decisions made by the actor (policy network), and the actor adjusts its policy based on this feedback, enhancing the predictive accuracy and reliability of the neural model. Furthermore, PPO incorporates exploration during the training phase by encouraging the selection of different next activities by sampling from the probability distribution of the policy network, which helps in discovering effective suffix prediction strategies and learning the optimal sampling strategy for a given event log. Finally, at inference time, PPO adopts a deterministic approach by selecting the next activity with the highest probability according to the policy network.

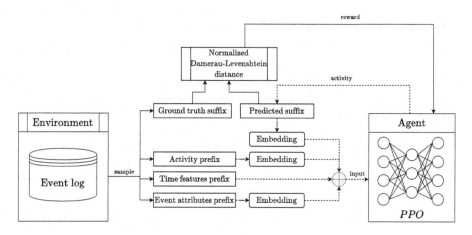

Fig. 1. Pipeline of DOGE. Dotted lines depict dataflow from each timestep, while solid lines represent dataflow executed once per episode.

4   Approach

In this section, we describe our reinforcement-learning based approach for activity suffix prediction, "Deep Reinforcement Learning Predictor" or "DOGE". In DOGE, the event log serves as the environment, each predicted activity suffix is considered an episode, every activity predicted represents a timestep, and the reward is the normalized Damerau-Levenshtein distance (NDL). DOGE is able to ingest the full information from the prefix while only predicting the activities from the suffix, emulating the workings of an encoder-decoder.

Figure 1 shows the two types of dataflow of DOGE during training: the ones that are executed once per episode —filled lines— and the ones that are executed for every action taken by the agent —dotted lines—. Thus, the operations of suffix sampling and edit distance calculation are done once per episode, while the policy network is executed for every action taken by the agent and the predicted suffix is accordingly updated.

Figure 2 shows how the observation matrix is created for the policy network in the case of a given event prefix. This matrix consists of four different pieces of information obtained from the event prefix sampled at the beginning of the episode: the sequence of activities; the sequence of times elapsed since the start of the case; the sequence of times between two consecutive events; and, for each attribute, its corresponding sequence of values. Each sequence of attributes and the sequence of activities are embedded using different embedding matrices, while the time features are standardized using z-score normalization. Furthermore, this prefix information is concatenated with the sequence of predicted activities by the agent so far. At each timestep —t_1, t_2, and t_3—, the predicted suffix is updated by appending the predicted activity to the end of the list. By separating the event prefix and the predicted suffix into different matrices, we ensure that the policy network does not "forget" the current prefix. To ensure that the dimensions of both matrices are the same, we simply pad with zeros both matrices before feeding them to the policy network.

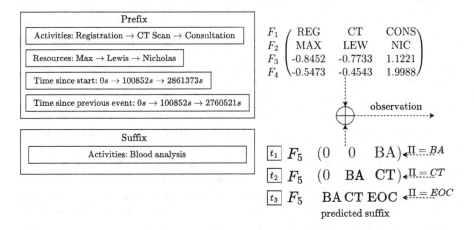

Fig. 2. Example of the observation encoding procedure. $\oplus$ denotes the concatenation operator.

Algorithm 1 shows the training procedure of DOGE. The process starts with the configuration of three key variables in line 1: the current number of activities predicted by the agent ($curr\_timesteps$), the best edit distance similarity achieved on the validation set ($best\_dl$), and the count of validation iterations without any improvement. The training loop in DOGE is determined by a fixed number of timesteps rather than epochs (line 2). This approach aligns with the *dynamic* nature of the learning procedure in reinforcement learning, where the agent continually interacts with the environment at each timestep. In contrast, supervised learning generally operates in a *static* manner, iterating over the entire dataset for each epoch. Therefore, looping over the full set of prefixes, as done in supervised learning, does not align with RL since the agent *learns from its interactions with the environment*, which is controlled by the MAX_TIMESTEPS variable. In line 3, a prefix (P) and its corresponding ground truth suffix (S_{gt}) are sampled from the training event log, that is, from the set of all possible prefixes and suffixes that can be obtained from the training event log. Note that this sampling is performed *with repetitions* so the same prefix could be sampled multiple times.

Line 4 initializes three essential variables: the predicted suffix (S_{pred}), a tensor (T) containing tuples of the input and the corresponding action taken at each timestep. The main training loop spans from lines 5 to 20. Line 5 stops the agent predictions if the end-of-case token (e_{end}) is predicted or if the sum of the length of the sampled prefix ($|P|$) and the length of the predicted suffix ($|S_{pred}|$) is greater than the maximum trace length from every trace of the event log ($|L_{max}|$).

The state tensor for the policy network is created in line 6. This tensor concatenates the embedded activity sequence of the prefix ($\pi_{AC}(P)$), the temporal features of the prefix ($\pi_{TI}(P)$), the sequence of attributes from the prefix ($\pi_{D_1}(P) \oplus \cdots \oplus \pi_{D_n}(P)$), and the activities predicted by the agent up to that point (S_{pred}) being the latter the only dynamic component updated with each prediction. In line 7, the policy network stochastically samples an action a_t from its probability distribution $\Pi(I_t)$. This allows the policy network to explore the space of possible suffixes, and to effectively learn a strategy that allows predicting a suffix that maximizes the reward. This strategy is going to the implictly available in the output probability distribution of the policy network. The sampled action is then appended to the predicted suffix S_{pred}, the tuple (I_t, a_t) is added to the trajectory tensor T (line 8), and the timestep counter is incremented by one (line 9).

Lines 10 to 18 detail the validation procedure, which is triggered whenever the total number of timesteps is divisible by the EVAL_FREQ variable. Contrary to conventional RL practices, in which the agent is evaluated in a subsample of the same environment used for training, the agent is evaluated on the entire validation set, which contains different traces from the training environment (line 11). During validation and testing the agent operates deterministically, selecting the most probable action always according to the policy network. This strategy ensures that the predicted suffix is always the same for any given prefix.

After the validation step, the algorithm assesses the performance of the current best policy against the best observed performance on the whole validation event. If the current policy achieves a better average NDL distance value (val_dl) than the best average value previously observed ($best\_dl$, in line 13), the algorithm updates the best observed value, resets the counter tracking the number of evaluations without improvement, and saves the current policy parameters (line 14). However, if there is no improvement in the NDL distance value, the counter tracking evaluations without improvement is incremented (line 16). If this counter exceeds a predefined patience threshold (line 17), the algorithm terminates early, returning the best observed policy parameters (line 18). This early stopping mechanism ensures computational efficiency and prevents potential overfitting.

After the validation and potential early stopping checks, the algorithm returns to the main training loop. Once an episode —i.e., a prediction of a suffix for a given prefix— is complete, the agent computes the reward based on

---

Algorithm 1: Training procedure of DOGE

Input: L_{train} - Training event log, L_{val} - Validation event log, L_{max} - Maximum trace length, Π - Policy network, MAX_TIMESTEPS - Maximum number of timesteps to train, PATIENCE - Number of evaluations without improvement before early stopping, EVAL_FREQ - Frequency of evaluations

Output: Trained policy network Π

1 $curr\_timesteps, best\_dl, eval\_without\_improving = 0, 0, 0;$
2 **while** $curr\_timesteps < MAX\_TIMESTEPS$ **do**
3 $\quad P, S_{gt} = \text{sample\_prefix}(L\_train);$
4 $\quad S_{pred}, T, action = <>, <>, \emptyset;$
5 $\quad$ **while** $action \neq e_{end}$ **and** $(|S_{pred}| + |P|) < L_{max}$ **do**
6 $\quad\quad I_t = \pi_{AC}(P) \oplus \pi_{TI}(P) \oplus \pi_{D_1}(P) \cdots \oplus \pi_{D_n}(P) \oplus S_{pred};$
7 $\quad\quad a_t = \text{sample}(\Pi(I_t));$
8 $\quad\quad \text{append}(S_{pred}, a_t); \text{append}(T, (I_t, a_t));$
9 $\quad\quad curr\_timesteps \mathrel{+}= 1;$
10 $\quad\quad$ **if** $curr\_timesteps \% EVAL\_FREQ == 0$ **then**
11 $\quad\quad\quad val\_dl = \text{evaluate}(\pi, L_{val});$
12 $\quad\quad\quad$ **if** $val\_dl > best\_dl$ **then**
13 $\quad\quad\quad\quad best\_dl = val\_dl; eval\_without\_improving = 0;$
14 $\quad\quad\quad\quad \text{save}(\Pi)$
15 $\quad\quad\quad$ **else**
16 $\quad\quad\quad\quad eval\_without\_improving\mathrel{+}= 1;$
17 $\quad\quad\quad$ **if** $eval\_without\_improving > PATIENCE$ **then**
18 $\quad\quad\quad\quad$ **return** $best(\Pi);$
19 $\quad r = \text{NDL}(S_{pred}, S_{gt});$
20 $\quad \Pi = \text{update\_policy\_with\_PPO}(\Pi, T, r);$

---

the NDL distance between the predicted and the ground truth suffixes (line 20). This reward serves as a feedback mechanism, guiding the learning of the agent. Finally, the policy network is updated using the PPO algorithm that takes into account all the elements stored in the trajectory list, the policy network and the reward. In this last step, the policy network adapts the predicted probability distribution at each timestep to maximize the expected reward for predicting the correct prefix sequence.

This allows the neural network to automatically learn the optimal probability distribution (or *implicit sampling strategy*) for predicting future suffixes given prefixes, during training itself. Traditional MLE models require manually selecting a fixed sampling strategy at inference time. Since the RL training process already learns this optimal predictive distribution, at inference time the model simply needs to select the most probable next activity per timestep. This is more efficient than having to apply an explorative sampling strategy like beam search used in traditional models.

5   Evaluation

5.1   Experimental Setup

We compared DOGE with 5 different state-of-the-art approaches [6,10,11,23,24] on 12 different event logs, whose characteristics are depicted in Table 1. The evaluation has been performed using the same methodology described in [18] under the same exact conditions: a 5-fold cross-validation is performed, splitting each training fold into an 80%-20% trace distribution to obtain a validation set, which is used to select the best-performing model. Furthermore, we take into account every possible size of prefixes, from $k = 1$ to the maximum trace length of the event log. We compare the approaches using the NDL edit distance so that the approaches can be comparable. In the case of [6], the approach can not be executed in the event logs "Sepsis" and "Nasa" due to them not having resources, which are mandatory to run the approach.

Table 1. Statistics of the event logs used in the evaluation. Time-related measures are shown in days.

Event log	Traces	Activities	Events	Avg. case length	Max. case length	Avg. event duration	Max. event duration	Avg. case duration	Max. case duration	Variants
BPI 2012	13087	36	262200	20.04	175	0.45	102.85	8.62	137.22	4366
BPI 2012 A	13087	10	60849	4.65	8	2.21	89.55	8.08	91.46	17
BPI 2012 C.	13087	23	164506	12.57	96	0.74	30.92	8.61	91.46	4336
BPI 2012 O	5015	7	31244	6.23	30	3.28	69.93	17.18	89.55	168
BPI 2012 W	9658	19	170107	17.61	156	0.7	102.85	11.69	137.22	2621
BPI 2012 W C.	9658	6	72413	7.5	74	1.75	30.92	11.4	91.04	2263
BPI 2013 C. P.	1487	7	6660	4.48	35	51.42	2254.84	178.88	2254.85	327
BPI 2013 I.	7554	13	65533	8.68	123	1.57	722.25	12.08	771.35	2278
Env. permit	1434	27	8577	5.98	25	1.09	268.97	5.41	275.84	116
Helpdesk	4580	14	21348	4.66	15	11.16	59.92	40.86	59.99	226
Nasa	2566	94	73638	28.7	50	0.00	0.00	0.00	0.00	2513
Sepsis	1049	16	15214	14.48	185	2.11	417.26	28.48	422.32	845

We implemented DOGE using the implementation of PPO available in stable-baselines3 [16] using its default hyperparameters, setting the embedding size of every categorical variable to 8. Note that no hyperparameter tuning has been performed. We opted for a feedforward policy network, as our experiments with Recurrent PPO [16] demonstrated significant instability and slowness during training (actually, our implementation is very similar to using PPO with frame stack in Atari games). DOGE has been trained using a validation set evaluating its performance in terms of NDL distance every quarter length of the training set (EVAL_FREQ in Algorithm 1). This makes the validation procedure dependant on the characteristics of the event log, instead of relying on fixed amount of timesteps. Furthermore, the number of fixed timesteps for training also varies according to the characteristics of the event log providing a training regimen that can dynamically adapt to it. This number is calculated as follows:

Definition 3 (Number of RL timesteps for training). *Let L_{train} be the training split of an event log L, L_{max} the maximum trace length of the event log, and $|AC|$ be the number of activities in the event log. Then, the number of timesteps to train the agent is calculated as:*

$$4 \cdot |hd^{1 \cdots L_{max}}(L_{train})| \cdot L_{max} \cdot (|AC| + 1)$$

where the expression $hd^{1 \cdots L_{max}}(L_{train})$ denotes the number of possible prefixes that can be obtained from the training split of the event log.

The aforementioned expression has been determined empirically, based on preliminary experiments to ensure optimal training duration and performane. The constant factor "4" ensures that the agent is given enough timesteps to learn the policy for any event log and while the other variables make the number of timesteps adaptable to the event log.

Finally, and also following the methodology of [18], we aid the discussion of the performance of DOGE using *Bayesian Statistical Tests*. These type of statistical tests are more powerful than the *Null Hypothesis Statistical Tests* commonly used in the literature because they are easier to interpret and they allow us to take into account the variance of the individual folds of the cross-validation experimentation. Thus, a two-stage comparison is performed: first, we rank the approaches according to a technique based in the Plackett-Luce model [5] and, then, according to that ranking, we perform a Hierarchical Bayesian model [8] to compare DOGE with the two best-performing approaches of the state-of-the-art. Also, for the statistical tests involving the approach of Camargo et al. [6], we exclude results from the "Nasa" and "Sepsis" event logs since the results are not available, and including them as *non-available* would penalize their approach.

5.2 Results

Table 2 shows the results for the DOGE evaluation. DOGE obtains the best result overall in 8 of the 12 tested event logs, the second best result in 3 event logs, and the third best in one event log. In general, DOGE comfortably surpasses the other approaches from the state-of-the-art, except in the event logs *BPI 2012 A*, *BPI 2012 Ω*, *Env permit*, and *Helpdesk*, whose differences with the best approach from the state of the art are 1.57%, 7.11%, 0.71%, and 1.21%. On the other hand, the biggest differences of DOGE with the other approaches from the state-of-the-art are in the *Sepsis*, *BPI 2013 I*, and *BPI 2012 W*, with a 10.68%, 9.36%, and 8.9% respectively.

Figure 3 illustrates the 5% and 95% credible intervals for each evaluated approach ordered by their ranking, along with the the corresponding probability of achieving the best ranking according to the bayesian Plackett-Luce ranking model. In the figure, non-overlapping pairs of approaches suggest statistical difference in terms of ranking. As shown in Fig. 3, DOGE achieves the highest overall ranking among all the evaluated methods. Figure 3 also highlights that our approach statistically outperforms all other state-of-the-art methods in terms of ranking. Note that statistical significance in this test only means that DOGE performs significantly better in terms of its *ranking* compared to other approaches.

The performance of DOGE was compared with Camargo (random) [6] and Evermann [11] using hierarchical Bayesian statistical tests. These tests provide the probability of approach A outperforming approach B ($A > B$), underperforming B ($A < B$), and being equivalent to B ($A = B$). The sum of probabilities for $A > B$ and $A = B$ is used to infer whether approach A is not worse than approach B (and vice versa). Two approaches are considered distinct if their edit distance is greater than 1% (*rope* value) [2], and an approach is deemed statistically different from another if the probability exceeds 95%. The statistical tables include results for each dataset as well as the overall result for one approach's superiority over another.

Table 2. Results of the 5-fold cross-validation for the activity suffix prediction task in terms of the Damerau-Levenshtein similarity. The best, second-best, and third-best results are highlighted in green, orange, and yellow, respectively. The "difference" columns shows the difference between DOGE and the second-best approach for a given event log.

Event log	Camargo/ argmax [6]	Camargo/ random [6]	Evermann [11]	Francesco-marino [10]	Tax [23]	Taymouri [24]	DOGE	Difference
BPI 2012	0.1851	0.3891	0.1986	0.1321	0.1409	0.1867	0.4061	0.017
BPI 2012 A	0.6536	0.6441	0.5847	0.2871	0.4597	0.5420	0.6379	-0.0157
BPI 2012 C.	0.2218	0.4495	0.2693	0.0883	0.1717	0.3557	0.4711	0.0216
BPI 2012 O	0.6845	0.6042	0.5544	0.4591	0.4972	0.5150	0.6134	-0.0711
BPI 2012 W	0.1941	0.3110	0.2800	0.1410	0.0975	0.2493	0.4000	0.089
BPI 2012 W C.	0.0501	0.3191	0.3372	0.1126	0.0789	0.3201	0.3829	0.0457
BPI 2013 C. P.	0.6641	0.5337	0.6416	0.5276	0.5824	0.4358	0.6933	0.0292
BPI 2013 I.	0.2607	0.5294	0.4730	0.3607	0.3336	0.2452	0.6230	0.0936
Env. permit	0.8440	0.7595	0.5713	0.3924	0.8163	0.4271	0.8369	-0.0071
Helpdesk	0.9110	0.8524	0.8354	0.4619	0.8695	0.6298	0.8989	-0.0121
Nasa	-	-	0.1218	0.0842	0.2320	0.4844	0.4981	0.0137
Sepsis	-	-	0.2693	0.0742	0.1158	0.3217	0.4285	0.1068

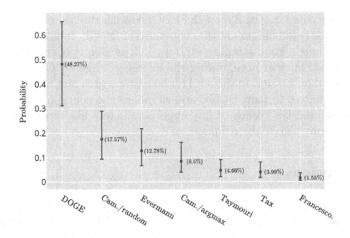

Fig. 3. Credible intervals —quantiles 5% and 95%— and probability of winning for each of the evaluated approaches, ordered by ranking.

Table 3. Hierarchical bayesian tests comparing DOGE (D) against Camargo (random). (C) [6] and Evermann (E) [11]. Statistical significant results (greater than 95%) are underlined.

	DOGE vs Camargo			DOGE vs Evermann		
	$D > C$	$D = C$	$D < C$	$D > E$	$D = E$	$D < E$
BPI 2012	96.86%	3.10%	0.04%	100%	0%	0%
BPI 2012 A	17.67%	57.07%	25.26%	99.95%	0.03%	0.02%
BPI 2012 C.	96.60%	3.26%	0.14%	100%	0%	0%
BPI 2012 O	57.58%	38.08%	4.33%	99.98%	0.01%	0.01%
BPI 2012 W	99.06%	0.64%	0.31%	99.99%	0.01%	0%
BPI 2012 W C	99.80%	0.16%	0.04%	99.80%	0.15%	0.05%
BPI 2013 C P	99.87%	0.09%	0.04%	99.27%	0.51%	0.22%
BPI 2013 I	99.95%	0.04%	0.01%	99.99%	0.01%	0%
Env permit	99.70%	0.22%	0.08%	99.99%	0.01%	0%
Helpdesk	99.99%	0.01%	0.00%	99.99%	0.01%	0%
NASA	–	–	–	99.99%	0.01%	0%
Sepsis	–	–	–	99.99%	0.01%	0%
Overall	99.4%	0	0.6%	99.96%	0%	0.04%

Table 3 shows the results from the hierarchical bayesian test that compares DOGE with Camargo (random) [6] and DOGE with Evermann [11]. DOGE demonstrates a clear advantage over the approach of Camargo et al. across a majority of datasets. As the approach from Camargo relies on a random sampling, whose performance is heavily dependant on the type of event log used, the strengths of DOGE in this area are clearly displayed. We can observe a similar effect when we compare the approach of DOGE with the one of Evermann [11]. Therefore, these results highlight the robustness of DOGE, indicating its capability to approximate a good sampling strategy independently of the characteristics of the event log. Furthermore, during the inference stage DOGE always selects the most probable activity, so the need for heuristic search methods such as beam search is eliminated. In fact, DOGE also simplifies the neural network design as it does not require the tuning of any hyperparameters like beam size, which is required in beam search algorithms.

6 Conclusions

In this paper we have introduced a novel RL-based approach for predictive monitoring, called *Deep Reinforcement Learning Predictor* (DOGE). The approach allows for learning an optimal activity sampling strategy for the activity suffix prediction task. DOGE overcomes the drawbacks of previous approaches based on Deep Learning, all of which require the selection of a sampling strategy beforehand and exhibit certain biases regarding the length of the predicted suffix, which significantly affects the quality of the returned predictions. Since DOGE does not require choosing a sampling strategy but instead learns it, design and implementation are greatly simplified and the approach is more general. In addition, DOGE turns out to be more efficient at inference time, in that, in contrast to other approaches, it directly generates the most probable suffix, instead of first producing a pool of candidate suffixes and then selecting the one that is best explained by the (fitted) sampling strategy. The approach has been fully implemented and evaluated against several benchmarks. Comparing the results with those obtained by previous techniques, DOGE clearly outperforms the others, especially in handling diverse event log features. For future work, we plan to explore the impact of other policy networks, such as RNN and GNN, and refine the input pre-processing phase. Furthermore, we plan to address the challenge of reward sparsity in DOGE by integrating knowledge from the process model, particularly for event logs with very long traces, to improve the agent's ability to correlate actions with rewards.

Acknowlegements. This work was supported by the Consellería de Educación, Universidade e Formación Profesional (ED431G-2019/04), the ERDF acknowledging CiTIUS as part of the Galician University System, and the Spanish Ministry of Science and Innovation (grants PDC2021-121072-C21, PID2020-112623GB-I00). It also received funding from the EU's Horizon 2020 program (grant No 952215) and utilized CESGA's supercomputer facilities. Fabio Patrizi was partially funded by MUR under the PNRR MUR project PE0000013-FAIR, the ERC Advanced Grant WhiteMech (No. 834228), and the Sapienza Project MARLeN.

References

1. Agarwal, P., Gupta, A., Sindhgatta, R., Dechu, S.: Goal-oriented next best activity recommendation using reinforcement learning. CoRR **abs/2205.03219** (2022)
2. Benavoli, A., Corani, G., Demšar, J., Zaffalon, M.: Time for a change: a tutorial for comparing multiple classifiers through Bayesian analysis. J. Mach. Learn. Res. **18**(77), 1–36 (2017)
3. Branchi, S., Di Francescomarino, C., Ghidini, C., Massimo, D., Ricci, F., Ronzani, M.: Learning to act: a reinforcement learning approach to recommend the best next activities. In: BPM Forum (2022)
4. Bukhsh, Z.A., Saeed, A., Dijkman, R.M.: Processtransformer: predictive business process monitoring with transformer network. CoRR **abs/2104.00721** (2021)
5. Calvo, B., Ceberio, J., Lozano, J.A.: Bayesian inference for algorithm ranking analysis. In: Proceedings of GECCO, ACM (2018)
6. Camargo, M., Dumas, M., González-Rojas, O.: Learning accurate LSTM models of business processes. In: Proceedings of BPM (2019)
7. Chiorrini, A., Diamantini, C., Mircoli, A., Potena, D.: A preliminary study on the application of reinforcement learning for predictive process monitoring. In: Process Mining Workshops - ICPM (2020)
8. Corani, G., Benavoli, A., Demsar, J., Mangili, F., Zaffalon, M.: Statistical comparison of classifiers through bayesian hierarchical modelling. Mach. Learn. **106**(11), 1817–1837 (2017)
9. Dalmas, B., Baranski, F., Cortinovis, D.: Predicting process activities and timestamps with entity-embeddings neural networks. In: Cherfi, S., Perini, A., Nurcan, S. (eds.) Research Challenges in Information Science. RCIS 2021. LNBIP, vol. 415, pp. 393–408. Springer, Cham (2021). https://doi.org/10.1007/978-3-030-75018-3_26
10. Di Francescomarino, C., Ghidini, C., Maggi, F.M., Petrucci, G., Yeshchenko, A.: An eye into the future: leveraging a-priori knowledge in predictive business process monitoring. In: Proceedings of BPM (2017)
11. Evermann, J., Rehse, J., Fettke, P.: Predicting process behaviour using deep learning. Decis. Support Syst. **100**, 129–140 (2017)
12. Ketykó, I., Mannhardt, F., Hassani, M., van Dongen, B.F.: What averages do not tell: predicting real life processes with sequential deep learning. In: The 37th ACM/SIGAPP Symposium on Applied Computing (2022)
13. Maggi, F.M., Di Francescomarino, C., Dumas, M., Ghidini, C.: Predictive monitoring of business processes. In: Proceedings of CAISE (2014)
14. Mauro, N.D., Appice, A., Basile, T.M.A.: Activity prediction of business process instances with inception CNN models. In: Proceedings of AI*IA (2019)
15. Meister, C., Wiher, G., Cotterell, R.: On decoding strategies for neural text generators. Trans. Assoc. Comput. Linguistics **10**, 997–1012 (2022)
16. Raffin, A., Hill, A., Gleave, A., Kanervisto, A., Ernestus, M., Dormann, N.: Stablebaselines3: reliable reinforcement learning implementations. J. Mach. Learn. Res. **22**(268), 1–8 (2021)
17. Rama-Maneiro, E., Monteagudo-Lago, P., Vidal, J.C., Lama, M.: Encoder-decoder model for suffix prediction in predictive monitoring. CoRR **abs/2211.16106** (2022)
18. Rama-Maneiro, E., Vidal, J.C., Lama, M.: Deep learning for predictive business process monitoring: review and benchmark. IEEE Trans. Serv. Comput. **16**(1), 739–756 (2023)

19. Rama-Maneiro, E., Vidal, J.C., Lama, M.: Embedding graph convolutional networks in recurrent neural networks for predictive monitoring. IEEE Trans. Knowl. Data Eng. **36**, 1–16 (2023)
20. Schulman, J., Wolski, F., Dhariwal, P., Radford, A., Klimov, O.: Proximal policy optimization algorithms. CoRR **abs/1707.06347** (2017)
21. Sun, X., Ying, Y., Yang, S., Shen, H.: Remaining activity sequence prediction for ongoing process instances. Int. J. Softw. Eng. Knowl. Eng. **31**(11&12), 1741–1760 (2021)
22. Sutton, R.S., Barto, A.G.: Reinforcement learning: an introduction. IEEE Trans. Neural Networks **9**(5), 1054–1054 (1998)
23. Tax, N., Verenich, I., Rosa, M.L., Dumas, M.: Predictive business process monitoring with LSTM neural networks. In: Proceedings of CAISE (2017)
24. Taymouri, F., Rosa, M.L., Erfani, S.M.: A deep adversarial model for suffix and remaining time prediction of event sequences. In: 2021 SIAM International Conference on Data Mining, pp. 522–530. SIAM (2021)
25. Taymouri, F., Rosa, M.L., Erfani, S.M., Bozorgi, Z.D., Verenich, I.: Predictive business process monitoring via generative adversarial nets: the case of next event prediction. In: Proceedings of BPM (2020)
26. Weinzierl, S., Dunzer, S., Zilker, S., Matzner, M.: Prescriptive business process monitoring for recommending next best actions. In: BPM Forum (2020)

HOEG: A New Approach for Object-Centric Predictive Process Monitoring

Tim K. Smit[ID], Hajo A. Reijers[ID], and Xixi Lu[✉][ID]

Utrecht University, Utrecht, The Netherlands
tksmit@protonmail.com, {h.a.reijers,x.lu}@uu.nl

Abstract. Predictive Process Monitoring focuses on predicting future states of ongoing process executions, such as forecasting the remaining time. Recent developments in Object-Centric Process Mining have enriched event data with objects and their explicit relations between events. To leverage this enriched data, we propose the Heterogeneous Object Event Graph encoding (HOEG), which integrates events and objects into a graph structure with diverse node types. It does so *without aggregating* object features, thus creating a more nuanced and informative representation. We then adopt a heterogeneous Graph Neural Network architecture, which incorporates these diverse object features in prediction tasks. We evaluate the performance and scalability of HOEG in predicting remaining time, benchmarking it against two established graph-based encodings and two baseline models. Our evaluation uses three Object-Centric Event Logs (OCELs), including one from a real-life process at a major Dutch financial institution. The results indicate that HOEG competes well with existing models and surpasses them when OCELs contain informative object attributes and event-object interactions.

Keywords: Object-Centric Process Mining · Graph Machine Learning · Predictive Process Monitoring · Heterogeneous Graph Neural Networks · Feature Encoding

1 Introduction

Predictive Process Monitoring (PPM) focuses on predicting the future status of ongoing process executions through historical event data. PPM techniques help to monitor ongoing process executions and offer timely interventions. Traditionally, PPM has relied on single-case event logs as the primary data source [14]. However, recent advancements in Object-Centric Process Mining (OCPM) have begun to enhance these event logs by incorporating objects and their interactions with events, providing a richer data context for training predictive models.

Early attempts in object-centric PPM have shown promising results [2,7, 9,12]. These studies have introduced novel methods of feature extraction and encoding from an object-centric perspective. Adams et al. [2] proposed event-level encoding using object-centric directly-follows graphs (OC-DFGs) [2], while

G. Guizzardi et al. (Eds.): CAiSE 2024, LNCS 14663, pp. 231–247, 2024.
https://doi.org/10.1007/978-3-031-61057-8_14

Berti et al. [4] focused on object-level encoding, leveraging object interactions via object graphs. Despite these advancements in handling multi-object data in OCELs, challenges remain in how to effectively encode object features and integrate them for prediction tasks.

To illustrate, consider a scenario involving process executions with object attributes `route length` and `urgency`. The challenge arises when these varying object attributes need to be integrated into an event-level encoding. For instance, including `route length` as an event feature can be problematic if it only applies to some events, potentially confusing the model due to missing values [7]. Similarly, encoding an object attribute like `urgency` as an event feature requires aggregating (e.g., averaging) the values across multiple objects, leading to information loss and less precise predictions, especially when there is significant variability in urgency levels [2,7]. Similar to event-level encoding, the object graph approach [4] requires aggregating events when encoding them at the object level. Such an aggregation leads to a loss of critical information.

This indicates a need for a more integrated approach that considers both event and object perspectives *natively*, without resorting to data manipulation techniques such as flattening or aggregating. To address this challenge, our research focuses on developing a general approach for encoding object-centric events, objects, and their attributes natively, aimed at enhancing prediction performance. We propose the Heterogeneous Object Event Graph encoding (HOEG[1]) that integrates events and objects into a graph with diverse node types without *aggregating* object attributes. More specifically, HOEG encodes different types of nodes to represent events and objects, creating a more intricate graph structure.

To assess the efficacy of HOEG, we measured the performance and runtime of HOEG. We compared these with two existing graph-based encodings and two baseline models in predicting the remaining time of a process. To allow for this assessment, we implemented a heterogeneous Graph Neural Network (GNN) architecture, adapted from a homogeneous counterpart, to optimize object information integration in our predictions. We conducted experiments using three object-centric event logs, including one from a real-life process in a major Dutch financial institution. Our results demonstrate that HOEG outperforms existing approaches when the OCEL contains informative object attributes and interactions. It performs similarly to the other approaches when object features or interactions are less informative.

Our contribution to the field of System Engineering lies in providing an advanced method for encoding event and object data in predictive tasks. The implementation of HOEG is specifically tailored for enhanced and native encoding and analysis, aiming to yield more accurate predictive models for OCELs. Such developments are essential for training more sophisticated and reliable models in complex information systems.

The remainder of this paper is organized as follows. First, we discuss related work and preliminaries in Sect. 2 and Sect. 3, respectively. Next, we introduce

---

[1] Open source implementation is found at https://github.com/TKForgeron/OCPPM.

our approach in Sect. 4, the evaluation in Sect. 5, and the results in Sect. 6. The discussion is presented in Sect. 7. Finally, we conclude the paper in Sect. 8.

2   Related Work

We discuss five related works that used OCELs for PPM tasks. Table 1 lists the related works, compared along six aspects of their encodings.

Both Gherissi et al. [9] and Rohrer et al. [12] followed a *non-native* approach, meaning they followed the idea of flattening an OCEL into a classical event log, by performing lossy data preprocessing techniques. Due to the flattening approach, the attributes of other objects are also not encoded. Interestingly, they also argued that OCELs allow for better predictions in PPM when compared to traditional event logs.

Three other approaches [2,4,7] propose to use OCEL-*native* feature extraction techniques. This means OCELs are *not flattened* along one object type during preprocessing but an object-centric case notion is used. Berti et al. [4] extract features per object, generating object vectors. As a consequence, their approach cannot be used for event-level prediction. In addition, due to this object-level view on OCELs, it cannot encode event-level features without losing information. On the contrary, Adams et al. [2] design their features on an event basis, enriching event vectors. However, they are unable to encode diverse object attributes and interactions without resorting to aggregations. Therefore, both works take a more methodical approach, describing a set of *aggregated* features for *event-object interactions* that can be applied to any OCEL, listed in Table 1 (Column 5).

Galanti et al. [7] followed the *native* approach and encoded OCELs at the event level while enabling the inclusion of object features. However, this method requires a predefined event vector structure, which consequently requires the *aggregation* of values or the *imputation* of missing values across all events. As a result, they do not support GNNs but only models that autofill missing values, like CatBoost.

Table 1. Characterization of encoding approaches in related PPM works on OCELs.

Approach	Encoding Granularity	Process Behavior Encoding	Event Attribute Encoding	Event-object Interaction Encoding	Object-object Interaction Encoding	Object Attribute Encoding
Non-native						
Rohrer et al. [12]	Event-level	One-hot	–	–	–	For one object type only
Gherissi et al. [9]	Event-level	One-hot	–	Event object type count	–	–
Native						
Galanti et al. [7]	Event-level	CatBoost algorithm	Categorical event attributes	Event object type count Aggregated activity-object relation	–	Aggregated & filled object attribute Aggregated previous object attribute
Berti et al. [4]	Object-level	–	–	Activity count Related events count	Object graph features	–
Adams et al. [2]	Event-level	OC-DFG data structure	Event-based features	Current total object count Previous object count Previous object type count Event objects Event object count Event object type count	–	–
HOEG						
This work	Event- and object-level	OC-DFG data structure	Event-based features	Directly encoded in the heterogeneous graph data structure	Direct encoding into graph structure possible	Directly encoded

Synthesizing, we observe information loss through *flattening* of OCELs, *aggregation* of object features, and *imputation* of missing values. These limitations are caused by the inherently complex structure of OCELs. When creating a feature vector per event (event-level granularity), this vector can refer to multiple objects with diverse attributes. To obtain an equal-size vector for each event, either none, a (manually) filled, or an aggregate of the object attributes (or other object-based features) may be taken into the vector. Similarly, when taking an object perspective, one creates a feature vector per object, trying to encode all events, leading to information loss [4]). In both perspectives, we experience a loss of information due to the unavailability of attributes or taking aggregates.

In this paper, we propose an encoding approach for GNN that captures object-centric event data without flattening the log, aggregating object features, or filling unavailable object features. The proposed encoding provides support for all six dimensions presented in Table 1. For a detailed explanation and discussion of each aspect listed in Table 1, we direct the reader to [13, p. 32].

3   Preliminaries

In this paper, we adapt the definitions of event log, object graph, process execution, and execution extraction that are introduced in [3]. For the sake of clarity and completeness, we provide a concise overview of these concepts in this section. Note that the definitions of event logs with objects are generic and also support the formalizations defined in [6].

Given a set X, we use $\sigma = \langle x_1, x_2, \cdots, x_n \rangle$ to refer to a sequence of length n over X. For an element $x \in X$ and a sequence $\sigma \in X^*$, we overload the notation $x \in \sigma$, expressing the occurrence of element x in the sequence $x \in \text{range}(\sigma)$.

To define event logs, we introduce the following universe: $\mathcal{E}$ denotes the universe of event identifiers, $\mathcal{D}$ denotes the universe of attributes and $\mathcal{V}$ denotes the universe of attribute values. In this paper, we are dealing with event data of different object types. Therefore, $\mathcal{T}$ defines the universe of types. There can be multiple instantiations of one type. We refer to each instantiation as an object. $\mathcal{O}$ defines the universe of objects. Each object is of one type $type : \mathcal{O} \to \mathcal{T}$. We define an event log that contains events and objects of different types, assigning each object to an event sequence.

Definition 1 (Event Log with Objects). *An event log $L = (E, O, \sigma, \pi_e, \pi_o)$ is a tuple where: $E \subseteq \mathcal{E}$ is a set of events; $O \subseteq \mathcal{O}$ is a set of objects; $\sigma : O \to E^*$ maps each object to an event sequence by overloading σ; $\pi_e : E \times \mathcal{D} \to \mathcal{V}$ maps event attributes onto values; $\pi_o : O \times \mathcal{D} \to \mathcal{V}$ maps object attributes onto values;*

For example, Table 2 shows an example of such an event log where the set of events $E = \{e_1, \cdots, e_{10}\}$ and the set of objects $O = \{o1, o2, i1, i2, i3, p1, p2, d1\}$. For instance, we have $\sigma(d1) = \langle e_9, e_{10} \rangle$, and $\pi_e(e1, \texttt{time}) = $"2023-01-30". Table 3 lists the object attributes, e.g., $\pi_o(o1, \texttt{Urgency}) = 1.0$.

Furthermore, we define the following two notations for $L = (E, O, \sigma, \pi_e, \pi_o)$: (1) $obj(e)$ denote the object(s) associated to event $e \in E$, i.e., $obj(e) = \{o \in O \mid e \in \sigma(o)\}$; (2) $conn_L$ defines the directly-follows relationships for all events and all objects, i.e., $conn_L = \cup_{o \in O} \cup_{1 \leq i < |\sigma(o)|} \{(e_i, e_{i+1}) \in E \times E \mid e_i, e_{i+1} \in \sigma(o)\}$.

Table 2. Events table of example log.

ID	Activity	Time	Resource	Order	Item	Package	Delivery
e1	Place order	2023-01-30	CloudServiceA	{o1}	{i1, i2}	{}	{}
e2	Pay order	2023-01-30	CloudServiceA	{o1}	{}	{}	{}
e3	Place order	2023-01-30	CloudServiceB	{o2}	{i3}	{}	{}
e4	Pay order	2023-01-30	CloudServiceB	{o2}	{}	{}	{}
e5	Pick item	2023-01-31	WarehouseTeamX	{o1}	{i1}	{}	{}
e6	Pick item	2023-01-31	WarehouseTeamX	{o2}	{i3}	{}	{}
e7	Pack item	2023-01-31	WarehouseTeamX	{o1}	{i1}	{p1}	{}
e8	Pack item	2023-01-31	WarehouseTeamX	{o2}	{i3}	{p2}	{}
e9	Ship package	2023-02-01	WarehouseTeamY	{o1, o2}	{i1, i3}	{p1, p2}	{d1}
e10	Confirm delivery	2023-02-02	PostalServiceP	{o1, o2}	{i1, i3}	{p1, p2}	{d1}

Table 3. Object tables per different object type in the example log.

ID	Urgency	ID	Discount	ID	Weight	Size	ID	Route length	No. stops
o1	1.0	i1	33.0	p1	3.5	medium	d1	short	5.0
o2	3.0	i2	0.0	p2	3.0	medium			
		i3	25.0						

We define the relationships between objects by defining the object graph of a log.

Definition 2 (Object Graph). *Let $L = (E, O, \sigma, \pi_e, \pi_o)$ be an event log. The object graph is an undirected graph $OG_L = (O, C_O)$ with the set of undirected edges $C_O = \{\{o_1, o_2\} \subseteq O \mid \exists e \in E : o_1, o_2 \in obj(e) \land o_1 \neq o_2\}$.*

Definition 3 (Process Execution). *Let $L = (E, O, \sigma, \pi_e, \pi_o)$ be an event log and $O' \subseteq O$ be a subset of objects that forms a connected subgraph in OG_L. The process execution of O' is a directed graph $p_{O'} = (E', D)$ where*

- *$E' = \{e \in E \mid O' \cap obj(e) \neq \varnothing\}$ are the nodes, and*
- *$D = conn_L \cap (E' \times E')$ are the edges.*

Given the object graph, we may extract each connected component (O', C'_O) of the graph and obtain the process execution $p_{O'} = (E', D')$.

Definition 4 (Connected Component Extraction). *Let $L = (E, O, \sigma, \pi_e, \pi_o)$ be an event log and $OG_L = (O, C_O)$ its object graph. Function $ext_{comp}(L) = \{p_{O'} \mid (O' \subseteq O) \land (O', C_O \cap (O' \times O'))$ is a connected component of $OG_L\}$ extracts process executions by connected components.*

Note that there are other extraction functions, for example, the leading type extraction defined in [3].

4   HOEG Approach

As discussed, to be able to encode OCELs *natively* both at event- and object-level, to leverage diverse object types and their features without aggregation or the need for imputing missing values, we present the HOEG approach in the following.

The HOEG approach incorporates both event-level and object-level perspectives into a graph using different node and edge types. In a heterogeneous graph, each node type may have its shape, equal to how OCELs contain data entities that can each have a different shape [8]. This enables HOEG to directly encode the complex relationships found in OCELs so that each relationship or attribute is left fully intact.

Definition 5 (HOEG). *Let $L = (E, O, \sigma, \pi_e, \pi_o)$ be an object-aware log and $P = \{p_{O_1}, \cdots, p_{O_k}\}$ the set of extracted process executions. For each execution $p_O = (E_O, D_O) \in P$, HOEG composes the related events and objects into a heterogeneous execution graph. We define each heterogeneous execution graph $HOEG \in \mathcal{HOEG}$ as the tuple $HOEG = (\mathcal{NT}, \mathcal{ET}, \mathcal{X}, \mathcal{A}, f_{ntflookup}, f_{etflookup}, f_{etalookup})$, with:*

- *$\mathcal{NT}$ is the set of node types in HOEG. Each node type $NT \in \mathcal{NT}$ represents a semantically distinct group of nodes. $\mathcal{NT}$ must include node type **event** and at least one object type, i.e., $|\mathcal{NT}| \geq 2$.*
- *$\mathcal{ET}$ is the set of edge types in HOEG. Each edge type $ET \in \mathcal{ET}$ describes a type of relationship between nodes via a semantic triple (**subject**, **predicate**, **object**), such that **subject**, **object** $\in \mathcal{NT}$ and **predicate** equals any word that describes the type of interaction the nodes have.*
- *$\mathcal{X}$ defines a set of feature matrices $\{X_1, \ldots, X_m\}$. For each node type $NT_i \in \mathcal{NT}$, there exists a feature matrix X_i, such that X_i is a matrix representing features associated with nodes of type NT_i. Optionally, for each edge type $ET_j \in \mathcal{ET}$, there may also be feature matrix $X_j \in \mathcal{X}$, such that X_j represents a matrix of edge features associated with edges of type ET_j, i.e., $|\mathcal{X}| \geq |\mathcal{NT}|$.*
- *$\mathcal{A}$ defines a set of adjacency matrices $\{A_1, \ldots, A_v\}$. For each edge type $ET_i \in \mathcal{ET}$, there exists an adjacency matrix $A_i \in \mathcal{A}$, such that A_i is a matrix representing connections between nodes based on edge type ET_i.*
- *Lookup functions $f_{ntflookup}$, $f_{etflookup}$, and $f_{etalookup}$ map node and edge types to their corresponding feature and adjacency matrices: (1) $f_{ntflookup} : \mathcal{NT} \to \mathcal{X}$; (2) $f_{etflookup} : \mathcal{ET} \rightarrowtail \mathcal{X}$; (3) $f_{etalookup} : \mathcal{ET} \to \mathcal{A}$.*

An OCEL that is encoded via HOEG can be expressed as the set $\mathcal{HOEG} = \{HOEG_1, \ldots, HOEG_k\}$, respectively.

As an example, consider a process execution (Execution A) of an Order-to-Cash process resulting in an example log listed in Table 2, and the referenced objects listed in Table 3. Figure 1, then, visualizes one HOEG instance.

HOEG in Fig. 1 uses connected components extraction (see Definition 4) to construct the OC-DFG that relates the events. Objects are connected to events via the references found in the OCEL (cf. Table 2). Let us express Fig. 1 in terms of Definition 5.

$$HOEG_{Execution_A} = (\mathcal{NT}, \mathcal{ET}, \mathcal{X}, \mathcal{A}, f_{ntflookup}, f_{etflookup}, f_{etalookup}), \text{ where:}$$

$$\mathcal{NT} = \{\texttt{event}, \texttt{order}, \texttt{item}, \texttt{package}, \texttt{delivery}\}$$

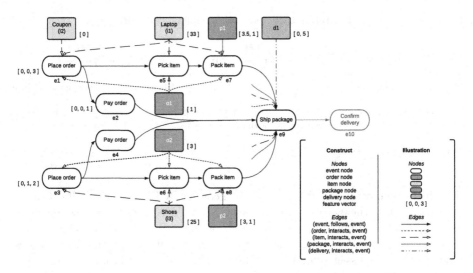

Fig. 1. Heterogeneous object event graph for Execution A (derived from Tables 2 and 3) of the running OTC example. *Note*: the trimmed (for readability) edges going out from *Ship package* (**e9**) are connected with objects **o1, o2, i1, i3, p1, p2**. Faded event node **e10** signifies future event *Confirm delivery*. Also note that for readability, not all edges are drawn.

$$\mathcal{ET} = \{(\texttt{event,follows,event}), (\texttt{order,interacts,event}),$$
$$(\texttt{item,interacts,event}), (\texttt{package,interacts,event}),$$
$$(\texttt{delivery,interacts,event})\}$$

For brevity and clarity, we represent only matrix dimensions of the elements in $\mathcal{X}$ and $\mathcal{A}$ paired with respective node and edge types.

The feature matrices $\mathcal{X}$ consist of:

- **event**: 3×9, encoding events $\{\texttt{e1}, \dots, \texttt{e9}\}$ with 3 features.
- **order**: 1×2, encoding objects $\{\texttt{o1, o2}\}$ with attribute **urgency**.
- **item**: 1×3, encoding objects $\{\texttt{i1, i2, i3}\}$ with attribute **discount**.
- **package**: 2×2, encoding objects $\{\texttt{p1, p2}\}$ with attributes **weight** and **size**.
- **delivery**: 2×1, encoding $\{\texttt{d1}\}$ with **route length** and **no. stops**.

The adjacency matrices $\mathcal{A}$:

- $(\texttt{event,follows,event}) : 2 \times 10$, encoding edges $\{(\texttt{e1, e2}), (\texttt{e1, e5}), \dots, (\texttt{e8, e9})\}$.
- $(\texttt{order,interacts,event}) : 2 \times 8$, encoding edges $\{(\texttt{o1, e1}), \dots, (\texttt{o2, e9})\}$.
- $(\texttt{item,interacts,event}) : 2 \times 9$, encoding edges $\{(\texttt{i1, e1}), \dots, (\texttt{i3, e9})\}$.
- $(\texttt{package,interacts,event}) : 2 \times 4$, encoding $\{(\texttt{p1, e7}), \dots, (\texttt{p2, e8})\}$.
- $(\texttt{delivery,interacts,event}) : 2 \times 1$, encoding $\{(\texttt{d1, e9})\}$.

This example shows that, in comparison with the Event Feature Graph (EFG) approach [2], HOEG distinctly encodes objects and their features explicitly. Conversely, EFG tends to either lose object information or aggregate object information into event features (e.g., **O1-O6** in [2]).

Table 4. Graph-based encoding technique configurations.

	EFG (Adams et al. [2])	HOEG (our approach)
Process Behavior Encoding	OC-DF graph structure	OC-DF graph structure enhanced with object nodes
Event Node Features	C2, P2, P5, O3 in [2] Numerically encoded event attributes	C2, P2, P5, O3 in [2] Numerically encoded event attributes
Object Type Node Features	N/A	A node type per object type with numerically encoded object attributes

Machine Learning on HOEG. When encoding OCELs using the HOEG approach, it enables the use of heterogeneous GNN architectures to perform machine learning tasks, as opposed to relying solely on homogeneous GNN architectures. In heterogeneous GNN architectures, we can define different edge relation types over which the message-passing mechanism transfers information during a forward pass of a neural network. Via linear projection, it can handle the different feature matrix dimensions. Through this, we can train on both event and object features simultaneously. The network learns how to best combine and transform the information from the different node types (edge types) to predict a certain target. Therefore, the HOEG approach supports a flexible and expressive encoding for OCEL while embracing the inherent structure of OCELs.

5 Evaluation

This section outlines the setup for evaluating the proposed HOEG. Firstly, we distinguish EFG as a graph-based encoding against which the HOEG is mainly compared. Their configuration is described. Secondly, GNN architecture design and hyperparameter tuning are discussed. Thirdly, evaluation methods are presented by which the graph-based feature encodings are compared and analyzed. Lastly, we explain the three OCELs used.

5.1 Feature Encodings

We compare HOEG to the state-of-the-art graph-based encoding technique for OCELs: the EFG by Adams et al. [2]. Other approaches discussed in Sect. 2 either do not support GNN natively or predict at the object level, making the results incomparable. Table 4 lists the configuration of both EFG and HOEG. It shows that HOEG complements EFG with diverse objects. Fundamentally, HOEG encodes the event nodes using the same features as EFG. Additionally, HOEG encodes each object type separately to include object attributes, also allowing more complex relations (event-object edges). We set *Remaining Time* (**P3** in [2]) as the prediction target for both EFG and HOEG. This is calculated by subtracting the timestamp of the last event in a process execution from the current timestamp. Using Z-score normalization, the target was standardized based on the training split, to mitigate information leakage.

Table 5. Hyperparameters used in the experiments.

Hyperparameter	Value(s)	Source(s)	Remark
Batch size	16		Dependent on available resources.
No. epochs	30	[2]	
Early stopping criterion	4		Dependent on available resources.
No. pre-message-passing layers	0	[2]	We use preprocessed features.
No. message-passing layers	2	[2,10]	k-Dimensional GNN
No. post-message-passing layers	1	[2]	
Drop-out rate	0.0	[15]	
Activation function	PReLU	[15]	
Optimizer	Adam	[2], [15]	Using default settings.
No. hidden dimensions	$\{8, 16, 24, 32, 48, 64, 128, 256\}$		Adams et al. [2] used 24.
Learning rate	$\{0.01, 0.001\}$	[2], [15]	You et al. [15] recommend 0.01, which is also used in [2].

5.2 Models and Hyperparameters

To leverage the multi-dimensional information contained in OCELs, we use graph-based deep learning models for each of the given scenarios to demonstrate how the graph-based models exploit their respective structures.

Though HOEG is agnostic of GNN layer choice, we employ k-dimensional GNN layers [10] in our architecture design. The message-passing layer captures higher-order graph structures at multiple scales. Higher-order graph structures refer to patterns or relationships that exist between groups of nodes in a graph, beyond merely the pairwise connections between individual nodes. This mechanism helps capture the state of an event in its process execution graph.

In Table 5, we outline the hyperparameters that are considered. Each row indicates the selected value or tunable value range. For the three experiments, we set nine hyperparameters to the recommended values via guidance from the literature. We choose the number of *hidden dimensions* (*hd*) and the *learning rate* (*lr*) to finetune in our first experiment to find the best value within a specified range, investigating the learning capability and stability of our approach.

5.3 Baselines and Evaluation Metrics

In addition to the EFG, three other baselines are used: (1) *Median*, which is used as a lower-bound, (2) *LightGBM*, and (3) EFG_{ss}. The *LightGBM* is a lightweight gradient booster model, which seems to be promising for PPM tasks [11]. Gradient boosting models require a tabular data structure with fixed-size dimensions. Therefore, the LightGBM baseline takes only a tabular version of the EFG as input data.

The EFG_{ss} is the baseline model where we replicate the EFG and GCN architecture [2] that uses subgraph sampling[2], which is a data augmentation technique. As this GNN baseline runs on a subgraphed EFG (configured equal to EFG in Table 4), it uses a global pooling operation to make (sub)graph-level predictions.

---

[2] The subgraph sampling is set to sample consecutive nodes of size four chronologically.

Table 6. Summary of the datasets used in the experiments.

OCEL	Events		Objects			Cases	Mean Object
		Attributes		Types	Attributes		Interactions per Event
BPI17	393, 931	3	74, 504	2	10	31, 509	1.35
OTC	22, 367	4	11, 484	3	1	8, 159	7.15
FI	695, 694	3	94, 148	3	14	31, 277	1.09

Finally, to evaluate the performance, the mean absolute error (MAE) and mean squared error (MSE) metrics are calculated. To evaluate the scalability of our approach, the model training time and prediction time are measured in seconds. The experiment is run on Intel Core i5-7500 with 48GB RAM and NVIDIA GeForce GTX 960 (4GB).

5.4   Object-Centric Datasets

We used three OCELs, listed in Table 6. The first OCEL, BPI17, concerns a loan application process [5]. Based on connected components extraction, a 56/14/30 split was taken as in [2]. The second OCEL, OTC, concerns an order management process. originally generated for demonstration purposes [1,8], now also used for PPM experiments [9,12]. Here, a 70/15/15 split was used, based on lead type (**item**) extraction because connected component extraction does not converge due to a high degree of object interaction (see Table 6).

The last OCEL, FI, is extracted from a real-life workflow management system (WfMS) operational at a large financial institution. The recorded process is part of the organization's Know Your Customer liabilities. These include customer identification, risk assessment, due diligence, and monitoring. The data contains actual events executed in the WfMS and objects enriched with intelligence from other systems. The WfMS supports standardization but allows room for deviations. Altogether, this results in a comprehensive global process model, when object-centric process discovery is applied. FI contains 94, 148 objects of three types that appear in sequential order throughout process executions: **signal**, **follow-up investigation**, and **complex follow-up investigation**. The three types are dossiers that progress in complexity, from a **signal** to a **complex follow-up investigation**. We extracted 695, 694 events recorded between January and May 2023. Events and objects were enriched with 3 and 14 attributes respectively. The OCEL includes complex process executions, that may start with events relating to a **signal** and end up with a series of **complex follow-up investigation** activities, while events are still being recorded relating to a **follow-up investigation** object. For model training, a 70/15/15 split was used, again based on connected components extraction.

6   Results

This section discusses the results obtained through three experiments. In the first, we experiment with different hyperparameter settings, producing one best-performing model per encoding. The second experiment compares model performance across the encodings. Third, we elaborate on the baseline experiment,

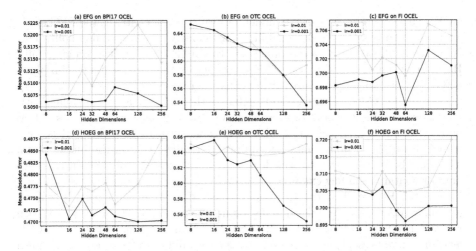

Fig. 2. Test MAE scores for EFG and HOEG per hyperparameter setting. *Note:* scales (y-axis) are not aligned, as we intend to compare hyperparameter settings within each encoding and dataset.

evaluating our models against different baselines. After this, interpretations are given that synthesize the experimental results into insights.

6.1 Hyperparameter Tuning Experiment

Figure 2 shows the effect of tuning *learning rate* and *hidden dimensions* simultaneously on the EFG-based and HOEG-based models. A first observation shows that the models are stable for both BPI17 and FI, as the MAE score range is relatively small. Performance on OTC seems to be more susceptible to model configuration.

In terms of hyperparameters, we generally observe that lower *learning rate* (0.001) scores better. Looking at *hidden dimensions*, 256 seems to work best for BPI17 and OTC, while *hidden dimensions* = 64 yields the lowest MAE on the FI OCEL for both encodings. Next to that, we observe a pattern for the OTC dataset suggesting that increasing model complexity improves the learning capacity for both EFG and HOEG.

6.2 Encoding Type Experiment

Figure 3 gives distributions of the model performance of all hyperparameter combinations per split (train, validation, test) for the three OCELs. To show statistical significance between EFG and HOEG performance (per split, $n = 16$), a t-test was done. In addition, the learning curves of the best models for both EFG and HOEG are plotted per dataset, providing insight into the training process and model performance during training.

For the BPI17 OCEL, the results show that HOEG performs significantly better than EFG in terms of MAE and learning capacity. The learning curve of

HOEG suggests relatively stable model performance. In contrast, the EFG curve exhibits some indications of instability, particularly on the training split. This is primarily attributed to a few outliers in the MAE scores on the training split. However, when considering the MAE scores across the three splits (violin plot), EFG's performance appears relatively consistent.

For the OTC OCEL, Fig. 3 shows that both models achieve a similar MAE and show a stable learning process. However, both models score a worse MAE on the validation and test set, see Fig. 3(c). This suggests that the models seem to overfit on the training data and do not generalize well on the unseen data. This may be because the dataset does not contain realistic object-centric event data or contains too few examples.

For the FI OCEL, Figs. 3(e) and (f) also show that both models achieve a similar MAE. The learning curves signify that our GNNs struggle to learn relevant complex patterns for predicting the remaining time. Though HOEG's learning curve presents itself as more stable, the validation loss is not going down by much throughout the epochs. This could be attributed to the additional

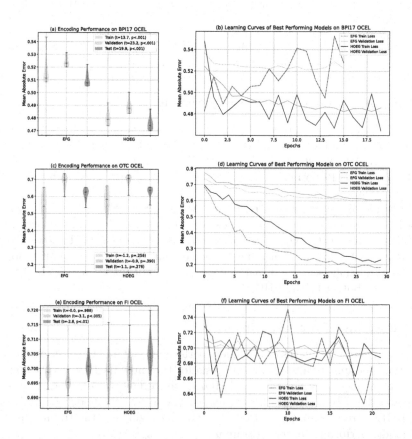

Fig. 3. Violin plot of the MAE score distribution over the hyperparameter settings per split (a, c, e). Training and validation loss learning curves of tuned models (b, d, f). BPI17: (a) and (b), OTC: (c) and (d), FI: (e) and (f).

data that HOEG includes compared to EFG (i.e., 14 object attributes). The violin plots show that EFG slightly outperforms HOEG on all hyperparameter configurations. Together with the learning curves, they suggest both models underfit this dataset.

The results of the second experiment are not conclusive about which encoding performs the best on OCEL logs for predicting the process remaining time. Looking at the learning curves, it might be suggested that HOEG trains in a more stable manner than EFG.

6.3   Baseline Experiment

We compare HOEG to three other baseline models: the Median, LightGBM, and EFG$_{ss}$ [2], in addition to EFG. By comparing the performance to the baseline models, the objective is to understand the relative impact of the results of the previous experiments. Note that these are not tuned, hence the traces in the validation split are assigned to the train split.

Table 7 lists the results. We observe that Median achieves the worst performance and the best scalability. While the EFG$_{ss}$-based GNN demonstrates superior performance in the case of BPI17, it ranks second to last among the models when applied to the other OCELs. LightGBM, then, strikes a balance between scalability and performance as it is the best scoring baseline on the OTC and FI OCELs.

Comparing this to EFG and HOEG, we notice that the EFG achieves the lowest score most frequently, meaning its predictions are closest to the actual values on average. Also, they do not deviate significantly from the true remaining

Table 7. Performance and scalability of HOEG and four baseline models. *Note*: the best-performing hyperparameter configurations are used for EFG and HOEG. Also, EFG$_{ss}$ is italicized for reasons mentioned in Sect. 7. Blank validation scores imply there was no model tuning.

OCEL	Model	Train MAE	Train MSE	Validation MAE	Validation MSE	Test MAE	Test MSE	Fitting Time (s)	Prediction Time (s)
BPI17	Median	0.7854	1.0802			0.7746	1.0472	**0.0042**	**0.0005**
	LightGBM	0.5282	**0.5730**			0.5282	0.5664	15.9230	0.8351
	EFG$_{ss}$	*0.4414*	*0.5481*	*0.4519*	*0.5627*	*0.4377*	*0.5322*	*547.1785*	*86.1564*
	EFG	0.5084	0.6010	0.5209	0.6211	0.5052	0.5855	122.0836	20.5225
	HOEG	**0.4739**	0.5745	**0.4836**	**0.5878**	**0.4700**	**0.5610**	536.0755	68.5030
OTC	Median	0.7379	0.9888			0.7175	0.8762	**0.0064**	**0.0021**
	LightGBM	0.5422	0.5021			0.6060	**0.5980**	1.9556	0.7211
	EFG$_{ss}$	*0.6359*	*0.7769*	*0.7338*	*1.0440*	*0.6585*	*0.7560*	*750.0486*	*150.5996*
	EFG	**0.1835**	**0.1601**	0.5985	0.8779	**0.5352**	0.6951	83.8779	6.6364
	HOEG	0.2163	0.1804	0.6069	**0.8723**	0.5505	0.6952	305.0114	25.1399
FI	Median	0.7673	1.2763			0.7702	1.2881	**0.0071**	**0.0005**
	LightGBM	0.7167	**0.8035**			0.7286	**0.8334**	15.8959	1.1631
	EFG$_{ss}$	*0.7250*	*1.0537*	*0.7222*	*1.0338*	*0.7310*	*1.0579*	*645.9569*	*749.5316*
	EFG	0.6928	0.9487	**0.6906**	**0.9328**	**0.6955**	0.9518	211.5477	21.3843
	HOEG	**0.6879**	0.9911	0.6919	0.9898	0.6961	1.0037	884.2844	82.1531

times compared to the other models. However, when considering test MAE and MSE scores, this edge is modest to negligible on OTC and FI, and HOEG more strongly outperforms EFG on the BPI17 OCEL.

7 Discussion

Performance and Scalability of HOEG. The results concerning the performance, in terms of minimizing prediction errors, seems inconclusive. The results of experiments 2 and 3 show that HOEG performs significantly better than EFG and LightGBM for BPI17 in terms of test MAE and MSE, see Fig. 3, but slightly worse than EFG on the OTC and FI logs, as listed in Table 7. One reason for these results would be the varying number of object features and event-object interactions in these three logs.

In terms of scalability, HOEG, as anticipated, requires more training and prediction time compared to EFG, attributed to its additional hidden dimensions. However, the training duration of HOEG is comparable to, and its prediction time is shorter than, EFG with subgraph sampling (EFG$_{ss}$), indicating its practical applicability.

Object Attributes and Interactions. The three OCELs exhibit varying numbers of informative object variables and event-object interactions, see Table 6. BPI17 has 10 object features with 1.35 object interactions per event on average. OTC only has one (dummy) object feature, while FI presents a lower degree of object interaction on average. These differences in object interaction levels set the stage for understanding the machine learning model performance across these datasets.

BPI17 is relatively structured, having only two object types and originating from a WfMS. Each event is always related to one application, and only the latter events in a trace are related to one or more offers. Regarding Table 7, this may be why the graph-based models learn so well in this scenario. Furthermore, BPI17 has well-defined object attributes. These two characteristics seem to be leveraged by HOEG, as indicated by it having the lowest test MAE and MSE (when disregarding EFG$_{ss}$ for reasons discussed later).

OTC has a high degree of object interaction, which was anticipated to favor HOEG's performance. Instead, we observe that EFG achieves a slightly lower MAE, and LightGBM outperforms HOEG in terms of MSE. Two factors may contribute to this unexpected outcome. Firstly, the questionable validity of event attributes such as weight and price in the OTC dataset poses challenges. From an ontological standpoint, these attributes might be better suited as object attributes for specific object types (e.g., **order**, **item**, or **package**). The current inclusion of these attributes as event attributes implies a leakage of unavailable object information into events. That is, all events have values for weight and price, while some events might not relate to an object of the type that these attributes would belong to in a more realistic setting. Secondly, OTC originally lacked object attributes. We might use this lack of object attributes and the questionable validity of event attributes to explain EFG slightly outperforming

HOEG. That is, where EFG might leverage `weight` and `price`, HOEG has to filter out the noise of the object IDs as object attributes.

FI, then, being extracted from an operational WfMS deployed in a highly complex process, has a lower level of both object interaction and process execution uniformity. HOEG seems to be surpassed by EFG by a negligible margin on MAE and was moderately outperformed by LightGBM in terms of test MSE. This might be explained by the process being extracted from a WfMS which is designed around a single case notion. This has led to different types of cases being forced into the same process, which might obscure the structuredness of process executions. This could result in a process that is difficult to predict. Furthermore, the vicinity of the MAE scores of Median and LightGBM might suggest a potentially limited predictive value of event and object attributes. That is, a naive predictor (Median), which does not learn from any attributes, approximates the performance of LightGBM which does learn complex patterns from attributes.

Therefore, HOEG is deemed promising *for scenarios characterized by extensive object interaction.* Moreover, when paired with informative object attributes, the increased number of edges in HOEG may facilitate the faster passage of object attribute information through nodes. This potentially enhances the overall learning capacity of HOEG-based models.

Subgraph Sampling. In Table 7, we observe that EFG_{ss}, which uses subgraph sampling, seems to perform better than HOEG and EFG for BPI17, but worse for OTC and FI.

We do note that this may not be a fair comparison. In essence, the subgraph sampling technique pools $k - 1$ previous events to augment the current event in the encoding. Reimplementing the subgraph sampling in [2], the technique excludes the first $k - 1$ events per trace from the predictions. Therefore, the performance of the model on these first $k - 1$ events is not included in the results. This implies that more samples are used for training and fewer samples are predicted.

Despite the potential performance improvement that may be achieved by using subgraph sampling (as listed in Table 7), its recommendation hinges on specific contextual factors. When scalability is a critical concern, subgraph sampling might not be advisable. That is, it requires the global pooling operation within the GNN architecture, which can be computationally expensive. Lastly, in high object interaction OCELs, subgraph sampling slices up relevant directly-follows edges, resulting in a series of unconnected events. For instance, in our illustrative Execution A (depicted in Fig. 1), taking a subgraph sample of size 4 produces many samples of events that are unconnected (e.g., $< e1, e2, e3, e4 >$).

Design Choices and Trade-offs. The current HOEG approach assumes that the object features are immutable, meaning the features of each object type do not change over time, which may be an interesting direction to explore. Moreover, in our configuration of HOEG, object-event relations were given a generic `interacts` qualifier in $\mathcal{ET}$ and its adjacency matrices $\mathcal{A}$. Nevertheless, if a future log format enables descriptors for these interaction relations (e.g., (order, createdby, event)), we can qualify these relations by configuring HOEG accordingly. This is supported already in our current definition of HOEG. Finally, the current (event, follows, event) edge type and its adjacency matrix in HOEG simply reflect the edges between the events in a process execution. As shown, HOEG accommodates different extraction techniques. It therefore also supports future, more refined extraction techniques.

8 Conclusion

In the evolving field of PPM, this study sought to develop a general approach for encoding object-centric event data including their objects, interactions, and features. This approach facilitates the encoding without the need for flattening events, filling unavailable object features, or aggregating objects and their features. Our efforts culminated in the creation of the HOEG approach.

Through three experiments performed on three datasets, we obtained insight into the efficacy of HOEG in terms of performance and scalability, particularly in predicting process remaining time. A key comparison was made with the EFG [2]. The results show that in scenarios involving well-structured object-centric processes, such as BPI17, HOEG-based GNNs perform better than EFG-based models. This result may suggest that HOEG is better suited for OCELs with abundant object interactions and well-defined attributes.

However, our study also revealed a trade-off in terms of scalability. HOEG-based models, with their more *native* structure and increased parameter count, tend to be less scalable than EFG-based models. Despite this, considering both performance and scalability, HOEG stands out as a promising approach for leveraging *native* data structures in OCELs, particularly for tasks like predicting the remaining time in processes.

Future work could explore various extensions of HOEG. Our study evaluated only one implementation, but others might include edge features or different heterogeneous GNN architectures. Additionally, the subgraph sampling technique might enhance model performance by more effectively capturing hierarchical patterns through pooling operations. Beyond our current focus, the HOEG approach offers flexibility to a variety of prediction tasks. Via HOEG one can train prediction models for different entities in the heterogeneous graph simultaneously, for instance, predicting for both events and objects, instead of creating a separate encoding as in [4]. This flexibility opens up intriguing possibilities for applications like outlier detection and seems worthy to be explored.

Acknowledgements. We thank Mike van Bussel for his invaluable contribution to this paper.

References

1. van der Aalst, W.M.P., Berti, A.: Discovering object-centric petri nets. Fundam. Inform. **175**(1–4), 1–40 (2020)

2. Adams, J.N., Park, G., Levich, S., Schuster, D., van der Aalst, W.M.P.: A framework for extracting and encoding features from object-centric event data. In: Troya, J., Medjahed, B., Piattini, M., Yao, L., Fernandez, P., Ruiz-Cortes, A. (eds.) Service-Oriented Computing. ICSOC 2022. LNCS, vol. 13740, pp. 36–53. Springer, Cham (2022). https://doi.org/10.1007/978-3-031-20984-0_3

3. Adams, J.N., Schuster, D., Schmitz, S., Schuh, G., van der Aalst, W.M.P.: Defining cases and variants for object-centric event data. In: ICPM, pp. 128–135. IEEE (2022)

4. Berti, A., Herforth, J., Qafari, M.S., van der Aalst, W.M.P.: Graph-based feature extraction on object-centric event logs. Int. J. Data Sci. Anal. (2023)

5. van Dongen, B.F.: Bpi challenge 2017 (2017)

6. Fahland, D.: Process mining over multiple behavioral dimensions with event knowledge graphs. In: van der Aalst, W.M.P., Carmona, J. (eds.) Process Mining Handbook. LNBIP, vol. 448, pp. 274–319. Springer, Cham (2022). https://doi.org/10.1007/978-3-031-08848-3_9

7. Galanti, R., de Leoni, M., Navarin, N., Marazzi, A.: Object-centric process predictive analytics. Expert Syst. Appl. **213**, 119–173 (2023)

8. Ghahfarokhi, A.F., Park, G., Berti, A., van der Aalst, W.M.P.: OCEL: a standard for object-centric event logs. In: Bellatreche, L., et al. (eds.) ADBIS 2021. CCIS, vol. 1450, pp. 169–175. Springer, Cham (2021). https://doi.org/10.1007/978-3-030-85082-1_16

9. Gherissi, W., Haddad, J.E., Grigori, D.: Object-centric predictive process monitoring. In: Troya, J., et al. (eds.) Service-Oriented Computing – ICSOC 2022 Workshops. ICSOC 2022. LNCS, vol. 13821, pp. 27–39. Springer, Cham (2023). https://doi.org/10.1007/978-3-031-26507-5_3

10. Morris, C., et al.: Weisfeiler and leman go neural: higher-order graph neural networks. In: AAAI, pp. 4602–4609 (2019)

11. Pourbafrani, M., Kar, S., Kaiser, S., van der Aalst, W.M.P.: Remaining time prediction for processes with inter-case dynamics. In: Munoz-Gama, J., Lu, X. (eds.) ICPM 2021. LNBIP, vol. 433, pp. 140–153. Springer, Cham (2022). https://doi.org/10.1007/978-3-030-98581-3_11

12. Rohrer, T., Ghahfarokhi, A.F., Behery, M., Lakemeyer, G., van der Aalst, W.M.P.: Predictive object-centric process monitoring. CoRR **abs/2207.10017** (2022)

13. Smit, T.K.: How object-centric is object-centric predictive process monitoring? (2023). https://studenttheses.uu.nl/handle/20.500.12932/45369

14. Teinemaa, I., Dumas, M., Rosa, M.L., Maggi, F.M.: Outcome-oriented predictive process monitoring: Review and benchmark. ACM Trans. Knowl. Discov. Data **13**(2), 17:1–17:57 (2019)

15. You, J., Ying, Z., Leskovec, J.: Design space for graph neural networks. In: NeurIPS (2020)

A Context-Aware Framework to Support Decision-Making in Production Planning

Simone Agostinelli$^{(\boxtimes)}$ (ID), Dario Benvenuti(ID), Angelo Casciani(ID),
Francesca De Luzi(ID), Matteo Marinacci(ID), Andrea Marrella(ID),
and Jacopo Rossi(ID)

Sapienza Universitá di Roma, Rome, Italy
{agostinelli,d.benvenuti,casciani,deluzi,marinacci,
marrella,j.rossi}@diag.uniroma1.it

Abstract. In the scope of Industry 4.0, this paper showcases the design
and implementation of a context-aware decision-making framework that
simulates the production planning of manufacturing activities by incorporating techniques from Process Mining, Business Process Simulation,
and Visual Analytics. The business case focuses on a manufacturing company specializing in sanitaryware production. The outcomes highlight the
potential of the proposed framework in automatically developing production planning simulations to enhance decision-making support.

Keywords: Business Process Simulation · Industry 4.0 · Process
Mining · Production Planning · Visual Analytics

1 Introduction

In the era of *Industry 4.0* (I4.0), we are witnessing the transformation of traditional working domains into new challenging cyber-physical environments characterized by the availability of a large variety of *Internet-of-Things* (IoT) devices
that monitor the evolution of several real-world objects of interest and produce
a massive amount of data and events, which can be referred as *Big Data*. In this
context, one of the primary objectives for companies is to leverage such data to
establish autonomous smart solutions that encompass the digitalization of the
entire *production process*, from the design to the testing phase [15].

This new industrial landscape calls for a change in *production planning* tools
[17]. Production planning describes in detail how the company's products will
be manufactured. It spells out the production process with its operational steps,
dependencies, required human and technological resources, and overall schedule.
Its goal is to design the most efficient way to make and deliver the company's
products at the desired level of quality to meet customers' demands (e.g., on-time
delivery) and organizational needs (e.g., reduced process cycle time).

To realize their full potential, production planning tools must take advantage
of the Big Data generated by the production process, relying on the new technologies fostered by I4.0 and adjusting automatically to the dynamic changes

G. Guizzardi et al. (Eds.): CAiSE 2024, LNCS 14663, pp. 248–264, 2024.
https://doi.org/10.1007/978-3-031-61057-8_15

in production [6]. However, the development of concrete solutions that integrate I4.0 with production planning is still in its infancy [6,17,22,24].

At the core of these envisioned solutions is a *digital model* that digitally mirrors the production process along its lifecycle [20]. A manual specification of the digital model is not achievable in practice because it would require considerable efforts for capturing the *context* within which the production process is operating. In production planning, context is a multi-faceted concept encompassing production-related information such as the time and cost associated with each production phase, the workforce availability, the warehouse capacity, the priority of planned orders, etc. [33]. Context may also relate to external factors that are not directly observable in the execution of the production process over time, such as market demand, competitive landscape, supplier relationships, etc.

Conversely, digital models should be automatically self-adaptable to the context and obtained by the collected production data associated to the ever-increasing variety of products the companies tend to manufacture. Although significant research has been made to automate the generation of digital models for enhancing their context-awareness, i.e., the ability to gather information about their context at any given time and to react to changes in the production environment [2], most approaches so far impose strong assumptions on the available data or cannot precisely specify the behavior of the production process [34]. Consequently, production planning activities and decisions are nowadays undertaken by expert users based on manual data collection and analysis techniques [9]. This is time-consuming, limits the degree of context-awareness to the experience and ability of the users involved in the production planning phase to capture up-to-date production-related data, and potentially leads to sub-optimal decisions that are poorly aligned with the production process requirements, as only a restricted subset of execution data and options are considered.

To mitigate this issue, in this exploratory paper, we present a context-aware framework that integrates some techniques from the I4.0 realm, namely *Process Mining*, *Business Process (BP) Simulation*, and *Visual Analytics*, to address two relevant research challenges for accelerating the automation of production planning tools by enhancing their degree of context-awareness, namely: (C1) the automated generation of up-to-date digital models of the production process from raw production data, and (C2) the elaboration of digital models for extracting insight-ready data to improve the quality of decision-making activities.

Specifically, *Process Mining* techniques [28] are used to analyze historical production data recorded in dedicated event logs to extract a digital model reflecting the production phases, their frequencies and temporal behaviour, and for creating accurate *simulation scenarios* of the company's production planning. Such scenarios are then executed through a *BP Simulation* tool [18]. BP Simulation involves accounting for the resources on hand and exploring ways to use them most effectively based on customer demand. Many potential production plans can be simulated to explore different strategies for optimizing the production process. Finally, *Visual Analytics* solutions provide interactive representations of the simulation results, thus allowing decision-makers to grasp essential patterns and trends for informed production planning. We explore the feasibility of our framework by realizing a specific instance for CER,[1] a leading I4.0 sanitary-ware company involved as a business case partner in the EU H2020 *DataCloud* project,[2] whose target is the development of novel solutions for covering the complete life-cycle of managing Big Data pipelines [21].

The rest of the paper is organized as follows. Section 2 discusses the state of the art on production planning in the context of I4.0. Section 3 details the design of the proposed framework. Section 4 describes the CER business case. Section 5 shows the implementation of our framework over the business case. Section 6 presents the lessons learned from applying the framework and discusses its limitations. Finally, Sect. 7 concludes the paper by outlining future works.

2   State of the Art

Production planning ensures that production occurs regularly and timely, satisfying a schedule made as part of a company's business strategy, to maximize profits and satisfy demand. It involves forecasting the quantities and types of products to be produced and, based on that, organizing the production process by defining the resources to be employed (materials, machinery, personnel) and the timelines for order completion. Such forecasting is based on various factors, including the quantity of confirmed or pending orders, the available machinery and personnel within the company, the seasonality of demand (if applicable, based on the product type), or customer-provided forecasts.

Production planning is mainly performed with the support of Manufacturing Execution Systems (MESs), Product Lifecycle Management Systems (PLMSs), and Discrete Event Simulation tools (DESs). In particular, DESs play a relevant role for I4.0-enabled factories equipped with smart sensors on machinery to collect production data. Such data can be leveraged by mature DESs, such as SIMIO[3], to create a digital production model and simulating the effect of potential changes on production before implementation [1,32].

However, these solutions face significant limitations. Specifically, they require a relevant effort performed by human experts to specify the potential production plans of a company manually. They typically rely on digital models developed during the design phase. Such models often represent outdated situations, and model obsolescence is a critical issue because it might lead to wrong decisions on production that can not be accurately predicted. In addition, creating and/or updating models requires a not negligible time, usually ranging from a few days to some weeks, depending on the production's complexity, making them inadequate to manage rapid changes in the production process [11]. In these circumstances, since the degree of context awareness is limited, the consequence is that decision-making is static, often relying on thresholds or alarms set at the design stages. On the other hand, I4.0-driven production is becoming highly

---

[1] The name of the company is not disclosed due to confidentiality constraints.

[2] https://cordis.europa.eu/project/id/101016835.

[3] https://www.simio.com/.

flexible, requiring an ever-increasing number of variants of a production plan to accurately perform decision-making by minimizing any imponderables [4].

While most of the recent literature on this field focused on investigating how production planning can be impacted by the capabilities offered by I4.0 [6,11, 17,22], in this paper we aim to take a step further by developing a context-aware framework that automatically creates a digital model of the production based on the most up-to-date production data (C1) and produces many production planning simulations to support the decision-making activity (C2). To sum up, our framework attempts increasing the degree of context-awareness in production planning tools, empowering the human expert role as a decision-maker.

In this direction, a couple of recent approaches investigate how to leverage Process Mining [13] and BP Simulation [16] to improve production planning outcomes. If compared with these approaches, which tend to employ Process Mining and BP Simulation in isolation, the rationale behind our framework is based on the idea that Process Mining allows not only to infer the causal relationships between production steps, but it may be used to estimate production parameters and support the generation of simulation models representing different production planning scenarios. The use of Process Mining to discover BP Simulation models is a deeply investigated topic in the Process Mining community [7,14,23], and enables us to develop production planning scenarios that are always up-to-date concerning the evolution of the production process. We finally notice that the use of simulation models is today considered highly relevant to improve the automation of production planning [1].

3   Framework Design

From a methodological perspective, the proposed framework has been conceptualized and designed for addressing the two research challenges (C1) and (C2) discussed in Sect. 1. The framework consists of 5 operational stages to be applied in sequence: *(i)* Event Log Extraction, *(ii)* Process Discovery and Parameters Estimation, *(iii)* Model Tuning and Context Management, *(iv)* BP Simulation, and *(v)* What-if Analysis, as shown in Fig. 1.

Event Log Extraction. Starting from the historical production data stored in the company's databases (DBs), e.g., those data keeping track of the evolution of production over the years, as well as incoming data related to new products to be manufactured, the first stage of the framework is to generate an *event log* that encapsulates all the information about the production phases involved in the end-to-end execution of the production process. Specifically, an event log is a collection of *traces*. A trace corresponds to the execution of one instance of the production process. Each trace contains a sequence of *events*, each related to a particular step of the production process. Events are associated with an activity label, a timestamp, and a trace identifier. The official IEEE standard for storing, exchanging and analysing event logs is XES[4] (eXtensible Event Stream).

---

[4] https://xes-standard.org/.

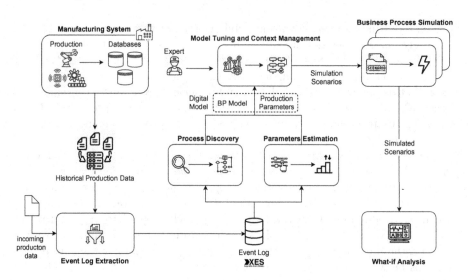

Fig. 1. Design of the framework.

Process Discovery and Parameters Estimation. Once the event log is obtained, well-established Process Mining techniques can be leveraged to reveal fact-based insights into how the production process transpires. Specifically, the objective of this stage is twofold: *(i)* learning the sequencing of production phases to reproduce the behaviour observed in the log; and then, *(ii)* extracting the relevant time and cost information associated with each production phase (e.g., the total and average time of the production process, processing time and cost of each phase, average arrival times between traces, waiting time, etc.), together with an estimation of the human and technological involvement (e.g., cost of the involved resources, human resource calendars, etc.). Thus, the output of this stage consists of defining a *digital model* of the production process, which includes two elements: *(i)* a *Business Process (BP) model* detailing the control flow of the production process to be emulated, and *(ii)* the estimated *production parameters*, that are passed to the next stage of the framework.

Model Tuning and Context Management. To build realistic simulation scenarios, the BP model can be customized by expert users to comply with the technological and physical limits of the current production process. This includes incorporating in the model those contextual information not directly observable in the execution of the production process (e.g., market demand, financial constraints, etc.), or removing complexities that may hinder the correct interpretation of the model developed. Through a proper customization of the production parameters computed in the previous stage, this stage enables us the generation of many *simulation scenarios* required to perform BP Simulation.

BP Simulation. It is the pivotal aspect of the framework. While traditional production planning requires a consistent involvement of human decision-makers to manually compute an optimal production strategy based on historical data, we rely on BP Simulation techniques to mimic the execution of the production process for specific product types. This allows us to automatically estimate the effectiveness of several potentially valid production plans that would require much human effort to be obtained manually. Once the computation of the multiple instances of the BP Simulation is completed, the results of the *simulated scenarios* are aggregated and visually presented to the decision-makers.

What-if Analysis. It is a well-known approach for estimating the impact of changes to a production process in terms of time and cost measures. This stage facilitates informed decision-making by providing visual insights into the potential consequences of adjustments to a production plan according to the simulated scenarios. It acts as a crucial component in the iterative refinement of production strategies, ensuring adaptability to the evolving production landscape.

The next section will delve into a real-world business case, serving as a basis for the application of the proposed framework.

4   Business Case Description

CER is a leading Italian company in the sanitaryware industry that targets innovating ceramic production by adopting advanced I4.0 automation technologies integrated with an IoT infrastructure to keep up with the ever-increasing demand for quality products.

CER experiences a continuous stream of purchase order requests, encompassing numerous ceramic-based sanitary items that need to be manufactured and delivered within a specific time frame. The CER production process relies on robotic arms to carry out the manufacturing phases. Specifically, starting from a CAD (Computer-Aided Design) 3D virtual prototype of a sanitary product, a *casting* phase generates its initial mould model, which is then manipulated by the subsequent steps of the production process (*drying, finishing, glazing* and *firing*) to obtain the final product as desired at design-time.

Given the high volume of daily requests, even if the company is equipped with some production lines to parallelize the manufacturing of different items, the reality is that it can only fulfill a limited number of production orders each day. This limitation arises from the manual intervention of expert decision-makers required to schedule the production and delivery of new orders, considering the production queue, the history of previously approved orders, the stock availability, etc. This activity involves variable factors such as the time needed to set up the production process for a new order and the non-fixed duration for a robotic arm to handle a ceramic artifact depending on the specific item being produced.

Figure 2 provides an example that describes the aforementioned issue. For instance, suppose that items of type 'X', 'Y' and 'Z' are part of an order with low priority and income. At the same time, imagine that CER receives a substantial order for item of type 'A' and decides to allocate it to the robotic arms that were scheduled to work on items of type 'X'. This decision incurs a fixed waiting

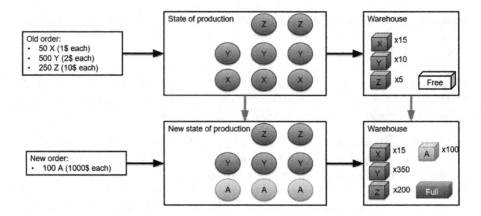

Fig. 2. An instance of CER's production process.

time as human operators need to switch mould stamps (*casting* step) and adjust the required parameters to set up the production process for the manufacturing of items of type 'A'. While items of type 'A' are being produced, items of type 'Y' and 'Z' from the original order are completed and stored in the warehouse, awaiting the completion of items of type 'X'. However, when the last piece of 'A' is finalized, the warehouse reaches its storage capacity. Consequently, the production of items of type 'X' can only be resumed once all items of type 'A' are shipped, resulting in an additional delay and causing CER to block its production process temporarily.

In the following section, we demonstrate how our framework can be instantiated to forecast the optimal timing for producing and delivering new orders automatically while meeting customer deadlines and minimizing the changes in the CER's production process. This is achieved by simulating different production plans and evaluating their insights through visual support, as explained in Sect. 5. The proposed framework aims to enable CER to optimize resource utilization in the medium term, including personnel and warehouse management.

5   Applying the Framework on the Business Case

CER receives constant purchase order requests, including numerous sanitary items that must be produced and delivered within a specific timeframe. Due to the high volume of daily requests, CER can only fulfill a limited number of orders each day since the production of new orders requires continuous updates to the production planning strategies, which is considered by CER a time-consuming and error-prone activity. To tackle this issue, in this section we explore the application of the framework proposed in Sect. 3 to support CER in automatically predicting the best production plan and meeting customers' demands more accurately and efficiently. In the following, we provide details on its implementation going through each stage outlined in Fig. 1.

The first stage of the framework is the **Event Log Extraction** that targets analyzing the three core relational databases (DBs) of the company, namely the Production DB, Warehouse DB, and Orders DB, together with the reception of a new order made by a customer. An order consists of essential details like the desired product types (e.g., washbasin of type 'A' and water closet of type 'X'), the number of items for each product type (e.g., 300 items of type 'A' and 500 of type 'X'), and an expected deadline for delivery. With this input at hand, the goal of this stage is to generate an *event log* reflecting the historical production data of the product types included in the order. In a nutshell, each *case* in the event log encapsulates the information about the manufacturing phases involved in the end-to-end execution of the production process for a single item belonging to an ordered product type (e.g., looking at the previous example, the event log will contain only data related to products of type 'A' or 'X'). The procedure to obtain the event log from the company's databases follows traditional event log extraction techniques [25], as thoroughly discussed in our previous paper [5]. The resulting event log is stored in the XES format.

Once the event log is obtained, the **Process Discovery and Parameters Estimation** stage comes into play with a twofold objective for defining the digital model of the CER production process:

- Initially, the *Inductive Miner* algorithm implemented in PM4PY[5] is executed to discover the BP model in BPMN (Business Process Modeling Notation) format[6]; even if the CER production process is relatively simple from a BP perspective, some of its steps require many iterations for specific product types. Thus, for different orders, the possibility exists that slightly different BP models are discovered from the log.
- Then, the event log is translated into a relational DB through the *RXES* schema [30]. We use it to feed a customized version of the Process Mining technique described in [8], which enables us to extract the relevant time and cost information associated with each manufacturing phase of the historical production of a product type included in the order, with an estimation of the human and technological involvement. When no historical information about a product type is available in the company's DBs (e.g., for novel products to be manufactured), we employ its default production parameters.

Finally, *(i)* the BP model detailing the control flow of the manufacturing phases to be emulated and *(ii)* the *production parameters* are passed to the next stage of the framework.

The **Model Tuning and Context Management** stage is employed to customize the behaviour of the BP model to make it compliant with the specific constraints of CER. Indeed, while some steps of the production process of CER involve robotic arms and machineries that can manipulate ceramic items associated with any kind of sanitary product (e.g., *drying, glazing,* and *firing*), other

---

[5] PM4PY is a suite of state-of-the-art Process Mining algorithms made available for Python language: https://pm4py.fit.fraunhofer.de/.

[6] ISO/IEC 19510:2013.

steps such as *casting* and *finishing* are constrained by technological and physical limits that must be considered in the BP model to build a realistic simulation scenario. These constraints represent an example of contextual information not available in process execution data but owned by CER domain experts that must be incorporated in the BP model before simulating the scenarios.

Concerning the *casting* step, the CER plant is equipped with N machineries configured with the specific mould stamp of the product the company will produce in a certain period. Switching mould stamps requires not only the direct and time-consuming involvement of human resources but even interrupts the working of some lines of the production process temporarily. To mitigate this issue, CER tends to produce sanitary items of a certain type in batches before changing the stamps. Consequently, based on the different product types in an order, the machineries available for the casting step must be wisely assigned to the different product types. For example, if an order includes only products of type 'A' or 'X', we may customize the BP model allocating $N/2$ casting machineries to 'A' and the others to 'X'. This is reflected by modeling two distinct BP activities for the casting phase in parallel branches, namely (for example) "*Casting_A*" and "*Casting_X*", each one associated with $N/2$ machineries. Another possible (more drastic) solution is to assign all the N casting machineries to 'A', meaning that products of type 'X' can start to be produced only after all products of type 'A' completed the casting phase. Further valid combinations can be implemented, enabling us to create many different BP models for simulating the production of an order following different strategies.

Similarly, the *finishing* step, which is required to remove defects in the ceramic items being produced, can be performed by one of the M dedicated machineries available in the CER's plant. In this case, the constraint is that $M/2$ are tailored for products of the kind "washbasin" and $M/2$ for products of the kind "water closet". Therefore, considering the previous order example, a possible customization is to parallelize the execution of the finishing step for the two product types in the order. Note that in the case of orders including, for example, only products of a specific type, the production process can utilize just $M/2$ finishing machineries, while the others would remain unused.

The point is that the BP model reflecting the CER's production process can be structured in many *variants* based on the nature of the order being received by combining the sequencing and the number of the *casting* and *finishing* phases. This task is performed automatically by a dedicated software component that generates suitable BP model variants considering their combination as realized in the historical production of orders of similar kind. Finally, once all the BP model variants are obtained, they are augmented with the production parameters computed in the previous stage to create the *simulation scenarios* required to perform **BP Simulation** in the next step of the framework.

Each simulation scenario is emulated independently using the simulation engine running behind BIMP.[7] In this work, we opted to use BIMP due to its wide range of simulation features and lightweight performance that align per-

---

[7] https://bimp.cs.ut.ee/simulator.

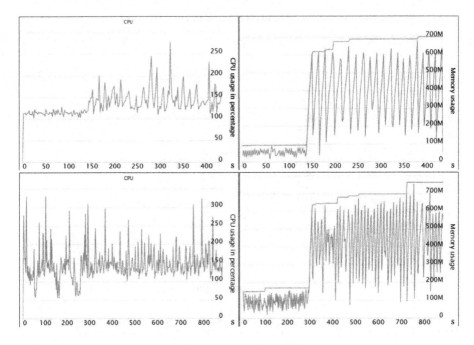

Fig. 3. Performance testing of the BP Simulation step.

fectly with our specific needs. The simulation of a single scenario configuration is repeated a fixed number of times (from 3 to 5, depending on the size and complexity of the order); this is a common practice to minimize the potential outliers that may arise from random factors during BP Simulation [18].

The negative side effect is that if, for example, 50 distinct simulation scenarios were generated for a specific order, repeating them 5 times each requires running 250 instances of the BP Simulation step, a time-intensive activity requiring several hours/days to be completed. To motivate this statement, we tested the performance of the BP Simulation step with two distinct simulation scenarios, one related to a (very simple) order (I) involving 100 items belonging to the product type 'A', and a second related to a (more complex) order (II) including 150 items for 'A' and 150 for 'X'. The test was conducted running one instance of the BP Simulation step for order (I) and one for order (II) on a PC equipped with an Intel Core i7-5820K CPU (6 physical cores) and 64 GB RAM, i.e., with a similar hardware configuration to the servers located in the CER's plant.

The results of the experiments are shown in Fig. 3. The two charts at the top of the figure are related to the CPU and RAM usage, expressed in MB (y-axis), of the BP Simulation of order (I), while the charts at the bottom are related to order (II). The x-axis indicates the time in *seconds* required to complete the execution of the BP Simulation step. Looking at the charts, it is evident that while there is a non-significant fluctuation of the CPU and RAM usage for the two simulations, the execution time required to complete the simulation for order

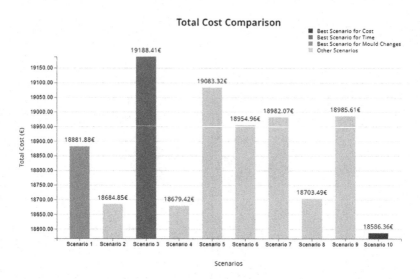

Fig. 4. The scenarios comparison page.

(II) was around 900 s, about twice as long as order (I). This means that executing (for example) 250 instances of the BP Simulation step for order (II) requires around 225000 s, i.e., 62.5 h (2.6 days), which is a time not acceptable for CER and very close to the current timing needed by the decision-makers to manually developing a production plan that accomplishes the order. A possible solution to improve performance scaling is to parallelize the elaboration of multiple instances of the BP Simulation step by relying on the distributed resources of the Cloud Computing. We discuss this solution in Sect. 6.

Once the computation of the multiple instances of the BP Simulation is completed, the results of the simulated scenarios are aggregated and visually presented to the decision-makers through the final stage of the framework. The **What-If Analysis** stage has been implemented through a *visual analytic tool* (cf. Figure 4) that offers a comprehensive range of visual comparisons among production scenarios. These comparisons focus on metrics such as total cost/time, and the total number of mould changes needed on machines required to implement the chosen production plan. Particular emphasis was put on the presentation of the top three scenarios for the aforementioned metrics. In general, the best scenario for cost, time, and mould changes depends on the configuration of the scenarios in terms of the quantity of production lines used to parallelize the manufacturing of different items, the order in which products are realized and the number of mould changes performed. Furthermore, this user interface provides the opportunity to delve into individual scenarios and get an overview of their relevant metrics.

Table 1. Result obtained from the survey administered after the pilot study.

	1	2	3	4	5
The visualization of the produced quantity of every item in an order over time helps the meeting of the deadline				3	5
The 2% reduction target for expired orders is realistic and achievable with this automated production planning				4 2	2
I am confident that the framework's usage will reduce the time for a new component to go into production by at least 5%				4	4
The visualization of the required mould changes helps in assessing the machine utilization					8
The chart depicting the mould changes over the machines properly assists the resource assignment (human resources for the mould change)				2	6

From a technological point, the development of the visual analytic tool follows a *User-Centered Design* (UCD)[8] approach, leveraging on the well-established front-end *Web stack* (HTML, CSS and JavaScript) to ensure that the implementation process does not require any additional local installation of dependencies or frameworks. This aspect holds great significance as it minimizes the effort required by CER to seamlessly integrate the tool into their existing information system. Moreover, this tool implements interactive charts for the scenarios comparison and KPIs visualization.

To this end, we conducted a pilot study involving 8 employees of CER, namely 1 *plant manager*, 2 *production managers*, and 5 *domain experts*. The pilot study consisted of asking each user to evaluate the results of the simulation scenarios produced by the framework for order (II). The task was to use the What-If Analysis tool to identify and interpret the metrics of the best production scenario in terms of the total time required to fulfill the order. Users were preliminary instructed about the features of the framework through a short training session.

At the end of the task, each user was asked to fill out a survey consisting of 5 statements evaluated with a 5-point numerical scale from 1 ("strongly disagree") to 5 ("strongly agree"). The survey was built to investigate the (estimated) level of fulfillment of the KPIs declared by CER in the context of the DataCloud project. Table 1 highlights the total number of users who selected a specific mark for every KPI. Even if this study can be considered preliminary, it confirms the positive feelings of the users in exploring the framework for generating and evaluating valid production plans toward fulfilling the CER's KPIs.

A screen-cast showing the framework in action is available at: https://tinyurl.com/3xuphns4, where each implemented stage has been encapsulated into Docker[9] containers [10].

---

[8] ISO 13407:1999.
[9] https://www.docker.com/.

6   Lessons Learned

Implementing the proposed framework for CER has demonstrated its ability to transform production data into digital models to simulate the effects of potential changes in the production process (C1), and improve predictive order forecasts, enabling more accurate decision-making (C2).

To make the computation of the BP Simulation more efficient, the solution we envisioned in the DataCloud project is to parallelize the elaboration of multiple instances of the BP Simulation step by relying on the distributed resources available in the Cloud Computing, which can provide a twofold advantage in terms of performance scaling:

- *horizontal scaling*, obtained by distributing the workload of the BP Simulation across multiple servers. For example, distributing the execution of the BP Simulation step on 8 servers in the Cloud will allow us to decrease the computation to 7.8 h (we assume the distributed servers provide at least the same hardware performance as the PC used for the test), thus enabling short-term outcomes of BP Simulation.
- *vertical scaling*, obtained by relying on servers providing more or faster CPUs, memory, or I/O resources than the ones available in the plant.

However, it is worth noticing that cloud resources are billed based on usage time. While employing more servers may reduce the duration of multiple runs of the BP Simulation step, it does not guarantee a proportional reduction in costs. This consideration is particularly critical for manufacturing companies where cost implications hold primary importance.

Despite the positive outcomes and advancements achieved through the implementation of the framework, there are certain limitations to acknowledge: *(i)* the effectiveness of the framework heavily relies on the quality and availability of historical production data. Incomplete or inaccurate data may lead to suboptimal predictions and recommendations. Therefore, ensuring data quality and integrity is crucial for maximizing the benefits of the framework [26]; *(ii)* our framework enables production planning tools to become automatically "aware" of the contextual information recorded in process execution data, while further contextual information not strictly related to the execution of the production process must be incorporated (if needed) by expert users into the BP model during the Model Tuning and Context Management stage; *(iii)* the complexity and variability of production scenarios make it challenging to generate realistic simulation models employing mainstream approaches to BP Simulation, which treat resources as undifferentiated entities grouped into resource pools. We have shown an example of this issue in Sect. 5 and the ad-hoc solution we found for properly combining the *casting* and *finishing* phases in a BP model. However, this limitation calls for novel BP Simulation techniques to capture the full complexity of manufacturing operations.

We believe the realized framework can be easily adapted to further business cases belonging to the manufacturing domain, as it utilizes state-of-the-art techniques and tools for its enactment.

7   Conclusions and Future Works

In this paper, we designed and implemented a *context-aware framework* to simulate the production planning of a manufacturing company. Specifically, by leveraging historical and incoming data of production, our framework enables predicting the optimal timing for fulfilling new requests and meeting customers' time requirements based on different simulated scenarios. By relying on the capabilities of *Process Mining, BP Simulation*, and *Visual Analytics*, we analyze and extract valuable insights from historical production data towards building a proactive approach to support decision-making for production planning, allowing for the simulation of different production scenarios before their execution.

As an immediate future work, we will conduct an extensive user evaluation of the proposed framework to measure the effective achievement of the KPIs outlined in Sect. 5 with a larger sample of users. In addition, we would like to assess not only the entire framework's effectiveness, including the accuracy of simulation scenarios and their alignment with real-world outcomes but also a comparative analysis with respect to alternative tools or approaches to production planning providing concrete performance metrics or objective measures.

This work could play a crucial role in the context of AI-augmented Business Process Management Systems (ABPMSs), that is, an emerging class of process-aware information systems empowered by AI technology for autonomously unfolding and adapting their execution flow [12]. Indeed, we envision extending this work in two different directions. Firstly, since the prominence and versatility of Large Language Models (LLMs) [27,31] have reached unprecedented heights, an additional future work could be to embed LLMs (i.e., GPT-4 and Llama 2) into the What-if Analysis stage to assist decision-makers in the selection of the optimal simulated scenario. Secondly, we envision leveraging the concept of *process framing* [19] to predict new possible production scenarios that break the boundaries imposed by the current production constraints, thus deviating from what is expected. Framing aims at capturing the boundaries within which the executions of one or more simulation scenarios of interest should be confined to proactively identify situations where failures may occur.

Besides ABPMSs, further research directions include expanding the scope of the framework to support object-centric event data (OCED) [3], thus enabling the shift from traditional event logs represented in XES format. In this way, each event may refer to any number of product objects, possibly of different types, instead of a single case identifier. To this end, object-centric Process Mining (OCPM) [29] techniques can be employed to take such data as input and allow for multi-perspective BP models to realize more realistic simulation models.

Last but not least, incorporating also real-time data streams, enables dynamic and adaptive production planning. Additionally, exploring advanced machine learning techniques can further enhance the accuracy and predictive capabilities of the framework.

Acknowledgments. This work is supported by the H2020 project DataCloud (Grant 101016835), the Sapienza projects DISPIPE and FOND-AIBPM, the PRIN 2022 project MOTOWN and the PNRR MUR project PE0000013-FAIR.

References

1. Abdelmegid, M.A., González, V.A., O'Sullivan, M., Walker, C.G., Poshdar, M., Alarcón, L.F.: Exploring the links between simulation modelling and construction production planning and control: a case study on the last planner system. Prod. Plan. Control **34**(5), 459–476 (2023)
2. Abowd, G.D., Dey, A.K., Brown, P.J., Davies, N., Smith, M., Steggles, P.: Towards a better understanding of context and context-awareness. In: Gellersen, H.-W. (ed.) HUC 1999. LNCS, vol. 1707, pp. 304–307. Springer, Heidelberg (1999). https://doi.org/10.1007/3-540-48157-5_29
3. Adams, J.N., Schuster, D., Schmitz, S., Schuh, G., van der Aalst, W.M.P.: Defining cases and variants for object-centric event data. In: 4th International Conference on Process Mining (ICPM), pp. 128–135 (2022)
4. Altaf, M.S., Bouferguene, A., Liu, H., Al-Hussein, M., Yu, H.: Integrated production planning and control system for a panelized home prefabrication facility using simulation and RFID. Autom. Constr. **85**, 369–383 (2018)
5. Benvenuti, D., Falleroni, L., Marrella, A., Perales, F.: An interactive approach to support event log generation for data pipeline discovery. In: 46th IEEE Annual Computers, Software, and Applications Conference, COMPSAC, pp. 1172–1177 (2022)
6. Bueno, A., Godinho Filho, M., Frank, A.G.: Smart production planning and control in the industry 4.0 context: a systematic literature review. Comput. Ind. Eng. **149** (2020)
7. Camargo, M., Dumas, M., González-Rojas, O.: Automated discovery of business process simulation models from event logs. Decis. Support Syst. **134**, 113284 (2020)
8. Camargo, M., Dumas, M., González-Rojas, O.: Learning accurate business process simulation models from event logs via automated process discovery and deep learning. In: 34th International Conference on Advanced Information Systems Engineering (CAiSE), pp. 55–71. Springer (2022). https://doi.org/10.1007/978-3-031-07472-1_4
9. Chapela-Campa, D., Dumas, M.: From process mining to augmented process execution. Softw. Syst. Model. 1–10 (2023)
10. De Benedictis, M., Lioy, A.: Integrity verification of docker containers for a lightweight cloud environment. Futur. Gener. Comput. Syst. **97**, 236–246 (2019)
11. Deuse, J., Wöstmann, R., Weßkamp, V., Wagstyl, D., Rieger, C.: Digital Work in Smart Production Systems: Changes and Challenges in Manufacturing Planning and Operations. In: Shajek, A., Hartmann, E.A. (eds.) New Digital Work, pp. 31–50. Springer, Cham (2023). https://doi.org/10.1007/978-3-031-26490-0_3
12. Dumas, M., et al.: AI-augmented business process management systems: a research manifesto. ACM Trans. Manag. Inf. Syst. **14**(1), 1–19 (2023)
13. ER, M., Arsad, N., Astuti, H.M., Kusumawardani, R.P., Utami, R.A.: Analysis of production planning in a global manufacturing company with process mining. J. Enterp. Inf. Manag. **31**(2), 317–337 (2018)
14. Estrada-Torres, B., Camargo, M., Dumas, M., García-Bañuelos, L., Mahdy, I., Yerokhin, M.: Discovering business process simulation models in the presence of multitasking and availability constraints. Data Knowl. Eng. **134**, 101897 (2021)

15. Ivanov, D., Dolgui, A.: A digital supply chain twin for managing the disruption risks and resilience in the era of industry 4.0. Prod. Plan. Control **32**(9), 775–788 (2021)
16. Langer, A., Ortmeier, C., Martin, N.L., Abraham, T., Herrmann, C.: Combining Process Mining And Simulation In Production Planning (2021). ESSN: 2701-6277
17. Luo, D., Thevenin, S., Dolgui, A.: A state-of-the-art on production planning in industry 4.0. Int. J. Prod. Res. 1–31 (2022)
18. Martin, N., Depaire, B., Caris, A.: The use of process mining in business process simulation model construction: structuring the field. Bus. Inf. Syst. Eng. **58**, 73–87 (2016)
19. Montali, M. Constraints for process framing in AI-augmented BPM. In: Cabanillas, C., Garmann-Johnsen, N.F., Koschmider, A. (eds.) Business Process Management Workshops. BPM 2022. LNBIP, vol. 460, pp. 5–12. Springer, Cham (2023). https://doi.org/10.1007/978-3-031-25383-6_1
20. Negri, E., Berardi, S., Fumagalli, L., Macchi, M.: MES-integrated digital twin frameworks. J. Manuf. Syst. **56**, 58–71 (2020)
21. Roman, D., et al.: Big data pipelines on the computing continuum: tapping the dark data. Computer **55**(11), 74–84 (2022)
22. Rossit, D.A., Tohmé, F., Frutos, M.: Industry 4.0: smart scheduling. Int. J. Prod. Res. **57**(12), 3802–3813 (2019)
23. Rozinat, A., Mans, R.S., Song, M., van der Aalst, W.M.P.: Discovering simulation models. Inf. Syst. **34**(3), 305–327 (2009)
24. Saad, S.M., Bahadori, R., Bhovar, C., Zhang, H.: Industry 4.0 and lean manufacturing – a systematic review of the state-of-the-art literature and key recommendations for future research. Int. J. Lean Six Sigma (2023)
25. Stein Dani, V., et al.: Towards understanding the role of the human in event log extraction. In: Marrella, A., Weber, B. (eds.) BPM 2021. LNBIP, vol. 436, pp. 86–98. Springer, Cham (2022). https://doi.org/10.1007/978-3-030-94343-1_7
26. Ter Hofstede, Arthur H.M., et al.: Process-data quality: the true frontier of process mining. J. Data Inf. Qual. **15**(3) Article 29, 21 (2023). https://doi.org/10.1145/3613247
27. van der Aa, H., Carmona, J., Leopold, H., Mendling, J., Padró, L.: Challenges and opportunities of applying natural language processing in business process management. In: 27th Int. Conference on Computational Linguistics, COLING 2018, pp. 2791–2801. Association for Computational Linguistics (2018)
28. van der Aalst W.M.P.: Data Science in Action. In: Process Mining, pp. 3–23. Springer, Heidelberg (2016). https://doi.org/10.1007/978-3-662-49851-4_1
29. van der Aalst, W.M.P.: Toward more realistic simulation models using object-centric process mining. In: 37th International Conference on Modelling and Simulation, ECMS 2023, Florence, Italy, 20–23 June 2023, pp. 5–13 (2023)
30. van Dongen, B.F., Shabani, S.: Relational XES: data management for process mining. In: CAiSE Forum, vol. 2015, pp. 169–176 (2015)
31. Vidgof, M., Bachhofner, S., Mendling, J.: Large language models for business process management: opportunities and challenges. In: Di Francescomarino, C., Burattin, A., Janiesch, C., Sadiq, S. (eds.) Business Process Management Forum. BPM 2023. LNBIP, vol. 490, pp. 107–123. Springer, Cham (2023). https://doi.org/10.1007/978-3-031-41623-1_7
32. Vieira, M., Barbosa-Póvoa, A.P., Moniz, S., Pinto-Varela, T.: Simulation-optimization approach for the decision-support on the planning and scheduling of automated assembly lines. In: 13th APCA International Conference on Automatic Control and Soft Computing (CONTROLO), pp. 265–269. IEEE (2018)

33. Ye, Y., Hu, T., Nassehi, A., Ji, S., Ni, H.: Context-aware manufacturing system design using machine learning. J. Manuf. Syst. **65**, 59–69 (2022)
34. Zhu, L., Lugaresi, G., Matta, A.: Automated generation of digital models for production lines through state reconstruction. In: 2023 IEEE 19th International Conference on Automation Science and Engineering (CASE), pp. 1–8 (2023)

Data Preparation, Sharing, and Architecture

Implementation Patterns for Zone Architectures in Enterprise-Grade Data Lakes

Corinna Giebler[1]([✉]) [iD], Christoph Gröger[1], Eva Hoos[1], Holger Schwarz[2], and Bernhard Mitschang[2]

[1] Robert Bosch GmbH, 70469 Stuttgart, Germany
{corinna.giebler,christoph.groeger,eva.hoos}@de.bosch.com
[2] IPVS, University of Stuttgart, 70569 Stuttgart, Germany
{holger.schwarz,bernhard.mitschang}@ipvs.uni-stuttgart.de

Abstract. In industry practice, zone models have been established as data lake architectures of choice to enable the reuse of data preparation, data modeling, and analytical results across the entire platform. However, when implementing a zone-based data lake, developers and architects find themselves lacking guidance, leading to costly, complex, and potentially single-case-only solutions. This paper addresses this challenge: Based on a comprehensive literature review and practical experiences from a large-scale enterprise context, we identify different groups of implementation approaches for zone models. We then derive nine systematic implementation patterns for zone-based data lake architectures. We evaluate the applicability and benefit of these patterns using three real-world case studies from different business contexts. Our assessment shows how the developed patterns support an effective and standardized implementation process of a zone-based data lake in enterprises.

Keywords: Data Lake · Data Zone Model · Data Lake Architecture · Patterns · Industry Case · Case Study

1 Introduction

The increasing digitalization in various domains provides enterprises with new chances and challenges. Digitalization initiatives like Industry 4.0 [1] as well as the rise of artificial intelligence in e.g. manufacturing [2] necessitate large amounts of data and thus the continuous data collection across the entire enterprise. This data may be production data gathered through sensors in machines and production lines, or data on customer satisfaction from social networks. Similar trends can be observed in connected homes, connected cars, eHealth, and others. To manage these heterogeneous data for analytics and AI, data lakes emerged as a scalable storage solution [3]. In this work, a data lake is defined broadly [3]: It is a scalable data management platform for data of any structure (structured, semi-structured, unstructured) that stores data in raw format for analytics. This way, no information is changed or lost when compared to the source systems. Data thus can be used very flexibly, i.e., without the need for predefined use cases. A

G. Guizzardi et al. (Eds.): CAiSE 2024, LNCS 14663, pp. 267–283, 2024.
https://doi.org/10.1007/978-3-031-61057-8_16

data lake can also include pre-processed data to improve efficiency. It comprises data storage, tooling for data transformation, and metadata management e.g., a data catalog. This broad definition also covers data lakehouses as a specific variant of data lakes. The concepts in this paper are also valid for other data management platforms that use zone architectures.

To manage both raw and pre-processed data in the data lake, data zone models arose as data lake architecture [4, 5], referred to as zone-based (data lake) architecture in the following. A zone-based architecture defines a set of zones, each of which is associated with different characteristics that data in this zone have. These characteristics typically refer to the processing degree of data (e.g., raw, consolidated, aggregated), but may also address the degree of applied governance (e.g., quality assured) [6]. They thus allow the reuse of data integration, data transformation, data models, and even analytical results across use cases in addition to the data themselves, reducing the effort needed for data preparation, which was estimated at around 80% of time needed by data analysts [7]. As a result, zone-based architectures are widely accepted for the implementation of enterprise-grade data lakes, e.g., by IBM [8] and Zaloni [9].

However, when it comes to transferring these conceptual architectures into a technical implementation of a zone-based data lake, various questions and challenges arose in our yearslong practical work with data lake teams from various domains and several analytical projects at a globally active manufacturer. For example, technology and platform architects are faced with the decisions which and how many storage systems to use or how to divide zones within the system. The lack of guidelines and best practices leads to massive overhead during development and a potential need to refactor the implemented data lake during operation. In this paper, we thus support the implementation for zone-based data lake architectures through the following contributions:

- We discuss existing approaches to the implementation of data lakes with focus on zone architecture implementation to identify implementation possibilities.
- We derive nine patterns for the implementation of zone-based data lake architectures from both literature and industry experience in a large-scale enterprise context. These patterns are organized in three categories: zone structure patterns, zone storage patterns, and zone data flow patterns.
- We showcase the application of these patterns in three separate case studies in a real-world business to assess their applicability and benefit.

The remainder of this paper is structured as follows: Sect. 2 discusses related work that focuses on data lake implementation with special focus on zone models. From the insights gained in this discussion, implementation patterns for zone data lake architectures are derived and discussed in Sect. 3. Section 4 contains the evaluation of the patterns for the implementation of data lakes in industry practice. Finally, Sect. 5 concludes the paper and gives a short outlook on future work.

2 Related Work: Implementation of Zone-Based Architectures and Other Data Lake Aspects

There are various zone models available in literature, e.g., Sharma's data lake reference architecture [9], Madsen's data architecture [10], Gorelik's zone model [11], Ravat's data lake functional architecture [4]. Because these zone models are quite varied and without any systematic derivation based on practical requirements, we developed the zone reference model in our previous work [6], which combines insights from research and practical scenarios. All zone models have in common that they aim to increase the reuse of data and transformations by making data available in various states along the transformation pipeline, e.g., in a raw, consolidated, and use-case specific state [6]. Only the data zones model presented by Zikopoulos et al. [8] provides unspecific hints towards its technical implementation, in this case using HDFS[1], Db2[2], and Apache Hive[3], among others. However, there is no systematic approach or discussion for the implementation and it remains unclear how to adapt to a different scenario. This means that when trying to implement any of the given zone models, including the zone reference model, developers receive little to no support from these works on how to systematically implement a zone-based data lake architecture.

Aside from what was mentioned so far, some additional works advice the usage of a zone model in data lakes (e.g., [12]), but no detailed discussion is given. In addition, there exist works that include implementations of zone architectures, e.g., by Martínez-Prieto et al. [13], but these focus on specific domains and concrete use cases rather than on a generally applicable approach.

Beyond the implementation of zone data lake architectures, data lake literature offers different approaches for the implementation of data lakes overall. Depending on the work, different aspects of data lakes are covered [14], where zone models fall in the aspect of data organization. This aspect is of central importance to the implementation, as it influences a variety of other aspects, such as data storage and data modeling. It is thus recommended to detail the data organization aspect at an early stage in the data lake development process and refer to it when discussing other aspects [14].

From the aspects related to data organization, three are of main interest when it comes to the implementation of zone-based architectures: infrastructure, data storage, and data flow. This is because these aspects refer to the physical setup of components and their interactions. As the aspects of infrastructure and data storage are closely linked in literature, we will discuss them as one in the following.

For *infrastructure/data storage* implementations, two alternatives can be found in literature, namely multiple storage system architectures and single storage system architectures [15]. James Dixon, the inventor of the data lake concept, proposed the usage of multiple storage systems in his blog post "Data Lakes Revisited" [16]. According to him, the best tool should be used to manage data, e.g., an analytic database for analytic purposes. Judging by this, data are managed according to their intended usage. Other sources share the idea of multiple storage systems for data lake implementation (e.g.,

---

[1] https://hadoop.apache.org/docs/current/hadoop-project-dist/hadoop-hdfs/HdfsDesign.html.

[2] www.ibm.com/analytics/db2.

[3] hive.apache.org/.

[8, 17]). However, especially papers on concrete data lakes make use of a single storage system for their data lake, typically Hadoop (e.g., [13, 18]). In literature, there is no discussion of the benefits and shortcomings of these two alternatives.

In the area of *data flow* implementations, various works propose the lambda architecture [19] as a basis of the data lake (e.g., [3, 18]). Here, data arrive as a data stream and are both processed in real-time, as well as stored persistently for batch processing. The real-time processing fills the gap between two lengthy batch processing cycles, allowing results to always be up-to-date. We encountered no other alternatives for the data lake architecture that equally supports batch and stream processing.

However, when researching for data flow architectures in the context of zone-based architectures, we encountered architectures that focus on how to incorporate stream processing into a zone-based architecture, such as [6, 8]. Here, two alternatives are presented in literature: 1) a streaming zone and 2) a zone-based architecture for streaming. The streaming zone is a dedicated zone that exists in parallel to the rest of the zone-based architecture (e.g., in [8]). While the rest of the data are processed in batches throughout the remaining zones, all stream processing is handled in this disjoint zone. In the zone-based architecture for streaming, multiple zones are applied to the processing of the data stream (e.g., in [6]). The data stream proceeds through the zone-based architecture and is processed zone by zone, just like the batch data are. Intermediate results of the stream processing are available to end users. Again, there is no comparative discussion available on the two alternatives.

Overall, while literature provides pointers towards data lake architectures, but these are lacking detail, discussion, and differentiation. Only few works about the implementation of zone-based architectures are available, which neither offer insights into their capabilities, nor into the implications of the chosen implementation. Thus, no comprehensive or systematic guidance is that allows developers to understand and compare different options for the implementation of a zone-based data lake architecture.

3   Implementation Patterns for Zone Architectures

To address the gap highlighted in Sect. 2, we introduce the implementation patterns for zone-based data lake architectures. The aim of these patterns is to offer insight into the different implementation options, and to identify benefits and potential shortcomings. The origin of these patterns is twofold: As a first step, we conducted an extensive literature study across more than 100 sources from both research and practice with regards to data lake architectures and data lake implementations[4]. To identify relevant work, we used search terms of interest (data lake implementation, zone model/architecture, data lake storage etc.) in various scientific databases and search engines, such as ResearchGate and Google Scholar. From this initial set, we continued our research following the snowballing methodology [20]. The reviewed works are of conceptual and/or technical nature and focus on storage architecture, metadata management, processing architectures, and more [4, 5, 8, 13, 18, 21–25]. In a second step, we refined and expanded upon the insights from literature using experiences made in real-world case studies on

---

[4] For a full list of references see here: https://t1p.de/tlln0.

the implementation of various data lakes in industry practice at a large, globally active manufacturer. More detail on the specifics of this industry case can be found in our previous work [26]. From both literature review and practical insights, we identified three different groups of zone implementation patterns:

1. Zone structure patterns describe how zone are represented in the data lake, i.e., whether they are represented by namespaces, folders or other internal structures, or through metadata.
2. Zone storage patterns describe how zones refer to the underlying data storage, e.g., whether a zone spans multiple storage systems.
3. Zone data flow patterns describe how especially streaming data are handled in the zone-based architecture, i.e., whether a streaming-specific zone is used.

Each of these groups is associated with two or more implementation patterns, resulting in nine implementation patterns overall. At the time of writing this paper, this set of patterns covers the data lake architectures found in the literature and in practice. However, it is possible that further patterns and even categories will be added in the future. The following subsections detail on the different patterns in each of these groups by first listing the design of the pattern before discussing advantages and shortcomings.

3.1 Zone Structure Patterns

The zone structure represents how zones are delimited within the data lake. With its help it can be determined to which zone a data object belongs. We have derived three patterns for zone structure: *Structure through Systems, Structure through Containers*, and *Structure through Metadata*. In practice, mixed forms are also conceivable.

We use four criteria to compare these patterns: the separation of the zones within the system (how well are the zones separated from each other), the centrality of the structure (is the structure managed at a central location), the complexity of the resulting system, and the latency of the processing pipeline. An overview of the comparison of the individual patterns is shown in Table 1.

Structure Through Systems. In this pattern, each individual zone is delimited by the systems used to implement it. This means that each system only contains data from a single zone. For example, there is one RDBMS for the Landing Zone and one separate system for the Raw Zone. Other systems may also be used, such as the Hadoop Distributed File System (HDFS) or NoSQL databases. The usage of this pattern does not mean that each zone is implemented in only one system. Rather, multiple systems can be used to implement a single zone. At the same time, one system can be used in multiple zones, but in multiple separate instances or installations. Each system instance is assigned to exactly one zone. This pattern is derived from the Data Zones Model of Zikopoulos et al. [8]. Here, zones are distinguished from each other based on the systems used to implement them. For example, the Deep Analytic Zone is defined through the usage of systems that enable more complex and advanced analytics than Hadoop [8].

The advantage of this pattern is that by using separate systems and instances, the zones are clearly separated from each other. Whenever data are accessed, it is clear to which zone they belong. One of the disadvantages of this pattern, however, is that there is no central location where zone membership is managed. If data are found via a data catalog, for example, only the storage location provides information about the zone to which the data belong. This pattern has a large number of different systems and system instances, which increases the complexity and administrative effort of the data lake. In addition, whenever data are prepared for a new zone, they must be transferred from one system to another. This leads to high latencies in the processing pipeline. This pattern is best used when each zone has unique requirements towards data management and data processing that can only be covered by differing technologies.

Table 1. Comparison of the Zone Structure Patterns (+ = better in comparison, − = worse in comparison).

Pattern	Separation	Centrality	Complexity	Latency
Structure through Systems	+	−	−	−
Structure through Containers	+	−	+	+
Structure through Metadata	−	+	+	+

Structure Through Containers. To separate zones by containers, internal structuring methods of the employed systems are used to represent zones, such as database namespaces in RDBMS or folders in HDFS. In contrast to the pattern *Structure through Systems*, multiple zones can be implemented on the same system or system instance. In this case, each used system has an internal structure representing the respective zone, e.g., HDFS and RDBMS storing a part of the Raw Zone. This pattern can be found for example in the AIRPORTS DL [13], where zones are represented by folders in HDFS.

Advantages of this pattern are that zones are clearly separated within the storage systems. Also, this pattern is significantly less complex than the *Structure through Systems* pattern and there are fewer cross-system data transfers. This reduces the latency of the processing pipeline. While multiple systems can be involved, the complexity is still lower than in the *Structure through Systems* pattern, as the number of involved systems is typically lower. However, a disadvantage of this pattern is that again there is no centralized zone management. In particular, this means here that subsets of zones that span multiple systems are isolated from each other. For example, the Raw Zone in HDFS exists completely separate from the Raw Zone in RDBMS. This pattern is especially beneficial in data lakes that consist of only one system.

Structure Through Metadata. The last zone structure pattern focuses on the representation of zones through metadata. This means that for each piece of data in the data lake an additional piece of metadata exists that describes which zone the data belongs to, such as a tag. Metadata are managed in a central metadata repository that is separate from the data lake storage. Please note that even when not using this pattern, metadata management is a crucial component of a data lake and needs to be considered [27]. This pattern only refers to whether zones are distinguished from each other using metadata. Like the pattern *Structure through Containers*, zones can span across multiple systems, however there is no further separation of zones within the systems. In literature, this pattern can be found in the metadata model HANDLE [22].

The advantage of this pattern lies in the central management of the zone information. All data of a single zone can be kept together virtually to prevent isolation. Complexity and latency of the processing pipeline are similar to those of the *Structure through Containers* pattern. A disadvantage is, however, that there is no separation of zones within the systems themselves. If data are accessed directly instead of through their metadata, it is thus impossible to tell which zone the data belong to. This pattern is best used in a scenario, where data are typically found and accessed through metadata rather than on the systems directly.

As already mentioned, combinations of these patterns are also possible. For example, the patterns *Structure through Containers* and *Structure through Metadata* could be used in combination by having zones both represented through internal structures like database namespaces and folders as well as through metadata. Thus, the advantages of both patterns are combined and the disadvantages are circumvented. However, this also means that the zone membership is defined in two different places, which may result in inconsistencies. This is a disadvantage that the patterns do not have in isolation.

3.2 Zone Storage Patterns

The second kind of implementation patterns for zone architectures are the zone storage patterns. These patterns describe how the data storage architecture interacts with a zone-based architecture. This includes the number of storage systems used in the implementation, as well as the distribution of data across systems. Literature provides two alternatives, namely single storage architectures (e.g., [13, 18]) and polyglot architectures, i.e., architectures consisting of multiple systems (e.g., [8, 28]). However, no details or discussions can be found. Construction guidelines as well as benefits and shortcomings of the different approaches remain unclear. This section thus presents four implementation patterns, which are derived from concrete data lake implementations as well as other works on data lake architectures. The patterns are: *Single Storage, Polyglot – Data-Oriented, Polyglot – Usage-Oriented*, and *Polyglot – Best Fit*.

For the discussion of these patterns, we use the following criteria: management functionality (how well can the stored data be managed), the complexity of the resulting system, the latency of the processing pipeline, and the redundancy in the data storage. The results of this comparison are summarized in Table 2. The presented zone storage patterns also provide a rough guideline for their implementation.

Single Storage. In this pattern, the entire zone-based architecture is implemented using a single data storage system. In existing literature, the system commonly used is HDFS, for example in [13]. Although HDFS and the Hadoop ecosystem are the most commonly used tools for a single storage data lake, the pattern itself is not limited to their use. Other possible alternatives to implement a single storage data lake are RDMBS, MongoDB[5], Neo4J[6], or other scalable storage systems.

---

[5] https://www.mongodb.com/.
[6] https://neo4j.com/.

The main advantage of this pattern is its low number of systems. Data do not have to be transferred between systems once they have entered the data lake, and maintaining the single system is relatively simple. Since only one storage system is used, data do not have to be held redundantly, but instead views or references can be used to reflect the different processing stages across zones. Since no data transfer is required between systems, the latency of the resulting system is rather low as well. The shortcoming of this pattern is the lack in management functionality. Since all data are stored in the same system, the management functionality is limited to the capabilities of this system. For example, relational data are stored without key constraints in MongoDB, or videos have to be stored as binary blobs in RDBMS. This makes queries on these data potentially slower and less efficient, and the required governance can potentially not be applied due to missing functionality. Oftentimes, this issue is addressed by adding further systems from the same ecosystem, such as Hive or Impala[7] for Hadoop. While this does improve the management functionality with regards to accessing data, the actual storage of data still does not differentiate between different management requirements. This pattern cannot be combined with the zone structure pattern *Structure through Systems*, since only one single system and instance are used here. It is beneficial in data lakes that only handle one type of data, e.g., data lakes specialized in managing IoT data.

Table 2. Comparison of the Zone Storage Patterns (+ = better in comparison, − = worse in comparison, 0 = neutral).

Pattern	Management Functionality	Complexity	Latency	Redundancy
Single Storage	−	+	+	+
Data-Oriented	+	0	0	0
Usage-Oriented	+	0	0	0
Best Fit	+	−	0	0

Polyglot Patterns. The Single Storage pattern is contrasted with polyglot patterns, in which multiple storage systems are used to implement the zone-based architecture. Since literature gives no guidance on how such a polyglot data lake could be implemented, three zone storage patterns for polyglot implementation with different orientations derived from existing data lake implementations are defined below. All polyglot zone storage patterns can be combined with any zone structure pattern. An example for a polyglot storage setup is available in [8].

Polyglot – Data-Oriented. The first polyglot pattern is the *Data-Oriented* pattern. In this pattern, the data lake is built on multiple storage systems that support different properties of data, such as structured, unstructured, relational, or strongly interconnected. Data are then stored in the system that aligns best with their properties, e.g., structured relational data in a RDBMS and strongly connected data in a graph database. If these properties change, for example because semi-structured data are brought into a structured format,

---

[7] https://impala.apache.org/.

data are transferred from one storage system into the other. While this pattern is not usage-focused, data may be brought into a specific format targeted at a use case, like multidimensional cubes.

An advantage of this pattern is its good management functionality when it comes to supporting data properties. The weaknesses of the pattern lie in its complexity, as each zone is implemented using a potentially very large number of storage systems. Furthermore, as data may be transferred between storage systems depending on their characteristics, this pattern typically results in a tradeoff between keeping data redundantly or using virtualization with higher latencies in data access. This pattern is best used in cases where data are complex and can only be properly represented in specific storage technologies, e.g., graphs. Furthermore, it should only be used when the usage of the data aligns with the capabilities of the used technologies.

Polyglot – Usage-Oriented. The second of the polyglot patterns is the *Usage-Oriented* pattern. It focuses on managing data according to their intended usage and not their properties. As long as the storage of the data is usage independent, data are stored in a single storage system, similar to the described *Single Storage* pattern. In the zone reference model [6] this use-case-independent part consists of the Landing Zone, the Raw Zone, and the Harmonized Zone. All other zones are use-case-dependent. In the *Usage-Oriented* pattern, data in these zones are stored in storage systems that best support their intended use. For example, sensor data are stored in time series databases to enable time-oriented queries. This also means that multiple versions of the same data are available in multiple systems if they are used in various ways.

This pattern has the advantage of good management functionality when it comes to querying and using data. Since the use-case-independent part is realized with a single storage system, this part of the zone-based architecture has low complexity and a short latency in the processing pipeline. This is particularly advantageous because the use-case-independent part of the data lake typically contains the bulk of the data, as data is only transferred to the use-case-dependent part in a demand-based manner. Since there is no transfer between systems in this use-case-independent part, the resulting redundancy is also low. The disadvantages of this pattern lie in the use-case-dependent part. Here, the complexity is high because more interfaces are needed to transfer data to the correct systems when moving from one zone to another. Again, data redundancy and latency can be reduced at the cost of each other. Opposed to the *Data-Oriented* pattern, this pattern should be used when different use cases have specific requirements for the data used, e.g. relational tables are needed for specific tools, but data can be adapted to be managed in different technologies.

Polyglot – Best Fit. The final of the zone storage patterns is the *Best Fit* pattern. This pattern combines the *Data-Oriented* and the *Usage-Oriented* patterns, which means that data are distributed among different systems according to their characteristics and intended use. For example, in the Raw Zone, data may be split according to their properties (relational data in relational databases, highly interconnected data in a graph database), while in zones with use case dependency (e.g., the delivery zone), data are stored according to both usage and properties. This means that data are moved between systems as their properties or intended use change, e.g., when moving to another zone. In addition, data are replicated across multiple systems depending on their intended use.

For example, customer data may be stored in a relational database for operational use, in a dimensional data store for reporting, and in a graph database to identify connections between customers and the products they purchase. The number of data storage systems and processing tools used is unlimited in this pattern.

Table 3. Comparison of the Zone Data Flow Patterns (+ = better in comparison, − = worse in comparison).

Pattern	Intermediate Results Available	Complexity	Latency
Streaming Zone	−	+	+
Zone-Based Architecture for Streaming	+	−	−

One advantage of this pattern is optimal management functionality, as data are always stored in the system that best supports its characteristics and intended use. However, this pattern also comes with very high complexity due to the large number of systems used. In addition, data are replicated across storage systems, resulting in high redundancy. Just like with the other polyglot patterns, redundancy and latency can be reduced at the cost of the other. This pattern is best used in cases where both use cases and data management have very specific requirements. It is also possible to implement some zones data-oriented and others usage-oriented with this pattern.

3.3 Zone Data Flow Patterns

The last type of implementation patterns for zone-based architectures are zone data flow patterns. They describe how the different modes of data movement (data at rest and data streams) are implemented in a zone-based architecture. Two alternatives exist in the literature for implementing data flow in zone-based architectures: a single streaming zone and a zone-based architecture for data stream processing. However, as with previous patterns, there is neither a detailed description of the patterns, nor a comparison of the alternatives. Thus, the following sections discuss both patterns in more detail.

Several criteria are used for this purpose, namely: whether intermediate results of data stream processing are available (such as cleansed data or the combination of multiple streams), the complexity of the overall system, and the latency of the pipeline. The evaluation of these patterns is shown in Table 3.

Streaming Zone. In this pattern, the zone-based architecture used includes a single separate zone for stream processing that exists alongside the tiered zone-based architecture for batch processing. The incoming data stream is processed in this zone and is not made accessible until it is fully processed. In Fig. 1, such a single dataflow zone is shown alongside the zone-based architecture for batch processing. An instance of this pattern can for example be found in the work of Zikopoulos et al. [8].

The advantages of this pattern are its low complexity and a fast pipeline. Data are only transferred into a single stream processing system and can be fully processed as soon as they arrive. The disadvantage of the pattern is the lack of accessibility to intermediate processing steps. Since the data stream is processed in one pass, only the raw data stream or the finished result stream is available. This pattern should be used when near-real time analyses are required on the streaming data.

Table 4. Pattern Application Summary.

Pattern	Best When	Cannot be Combined with
Structure through Systems Structure through Containers Structure through Metadata	Separate data management requirements per zone Only one (or few) systems Data access through metadata	Single Storage
Single Storage Data-Oriented Usage-Oriented Best Fit	All data share management requirements Complex data Specific needs per use case; data can be adapted Specific requirements for both management and usage	Structure through Systems, other Zone Storage Patterns Other Zone Storage Patterns Other Zone Storage Patterns Other Zone Storage Patterns
Streaming Zone Zone-Based Architecture for Streaming	Real-time analytics required Intermediate results on streaming data required	Zone-Based Architecture for Streaming Streaming Zone

Zone-Based Architecture for Streaming. The alternative to the *Streaming Zone* pattern is the usage of a zone-based architecture for stream processing. This pattern can be found in the work of Ravat and Zhao [4, 29]. In this pattern, there is no differentiation between batch data and streaming data, both are processed using the same zones. While batch data are stored persistently in the different zones, streaming data can be accessed via interfaces in the respective processing degree in each zone. The pattern also offers the possibility to persist the intermediate results of the stream processing for later use.

This pattern has the advantage that all intermediate processing levels of the data stream are accessible. The disadvantages lie in the data transfer between the different zones. This leads to high complexity. In addition, transferring data from one zone to another increases the overall latency in the processing pipeline, which, for many streaming applications, is not acceptable. In some cases however, the availability of intermediate results may outweigh the additional latency. This pattern should only be used when near-real time results are not required.

Table 4 summarizes all patterns with respect to their appropriate application and the possibilities for combination.

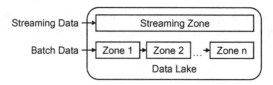

Fig. 1. The Streaming Zone Pattern

4 Pattern Evaluation

This section focuses on the evaluation of the derived patterns. As mentioned before, implementing a zone-based data lake architecture proves a challenging task in practice due to the lack of guidance in available works on zone models. However, only with a physical implementation of a zone-based architecture can organizations leverage its benefits, e.g. reusability of data and transformations. To show how the derived patterns support and guide developing teams, this section evaluates them in three ways: 1) Applicability, i.e. can the patterns successfully be applied in the development process of a data lake in practice, 2) Effectivity, i.e. can developers understand their options and choose the most appropriate pattern easily, and 3) Efficiency, i.e. how does the use of the derived patterns affect cost, time, and resources. To this end, we applied the patterns in three separate real-world case studies in different business contexts from industry practice. Section 4.1 describes the used case studies, while Sect. 4.2 gives insights into how the patterns were applied in the data lake implementation process. Section 4.3 summarizes the results of this evaluation. The case studies described below offer a qualitative evaluation to show applicability and the helpfulness of the patterns, with some initial quantitative results regarding efficiency and effectiveness.

4.1 Case Studies

Each of the investigated case studies centers around the implementation of a data lake focused on different analytical needs at a large, globally active manufacturing enterprise. Data in these data lakes comes from a wide variety of source systems and is used by many different business departments. The zone reference model [6] is used as zone model for all three data lakes as it is the zone model of choice at the enterprise, though the provided patterns can be applied with any zone model. The following paragraphs summarize the three case studies, with Table 5 giving a structured overview:

I. *Relational Enterprise Data Lake.* Since many analytical applications in the enterprise rely on structured data from relational operational systems, such as ERP or CRM systems, the central IT department hosts a data lake dedicated to the integration and provisioning of these data. Data are mainly used for dashboarding and reporting by a variety of business divisions. All zones of the zone model are available in this data lake.

II. *Cloud-Based Data Lake.* To take advantage of the opportunities provided by cloud environments, an initiative for a data lake based on cloud technologies was started in the enterprise. In this data lake setup, raw data from both on-premise and cloud systems are ingested into the Landing Zone and Raw Zone on a central cloud subscription before being distributed to subscriptions owned by various business departments, realizing the remaining zones. Data are largely used for dashboarding and reporting, but AI-based use cases are on the rise.

III. *Data Lake for Sustainability Analytics.* With the EU Corporate Sustainability Reporting Directive (CSRD) making it necessary to provide detailed insights into a company's sustainability, the observed enterprise set up a data lake dedicated to sustainability analytics. Data from a wide variety of systems, both traditional operational systems and semi-structured/unstructured sensor measurements, are integrated to provide reporting on e.g. employee wages, energy consumption, or produced waste. All zones are available in this data lake.

Table 5. Case Study Overview.

	I. Relational Enterprise Data Lake	II. Cloud-based Data Lake	III. Data Lake for Sustainability Analytics
Used Data Types	Structured	Structured, semi-structured	Structured, semi-structured, unstructured
Use Cases	Reporting, Dashboarding	Reporting, Dashboarding, AI	Reporting, Dashboarding
Source Systems	Relational operational systems on-premise	Operational and analytical systems on-premise and cloud	Operational systems on-premise, sensor measurements
Employed Zones	All	Landing Zone, Raw Zone in central subscription, other zones owned by business departments	All

The developed zone implementation patterns were applied in all three cases and discussed with platform architects and product owners to determine the applicability, effectiveness, and efficiency of the patterns.

4.2 Pattern Application

This section details on how the patterns were applied in the different case studies.

Zone Structure Pattern. As mentioned above, the zone reference model is used in all three case studies due to its systematic approach. In this zone model, there are no specific data management requirements per zone. Instead, data are expected to easily move between zones as they are prepared for consumption. Thus, the *Structure through Systems* pattern was ruled out in all three cases as it complicates data transfer between zones. All three data lakes include a data catalog and the possibility to create containers (namespaces in the relational systems and folders in file systems). Users in all three cases may find data through the catalog or on the systems directly. Thus, we decided to combine the patterns *Structure through Containers* and *Structure for Metadata* to have both a strong separation within the systems as well as a central zone management. To mitigate the problem of potential inconsistencies between the two, the zone tag in the metadata catalog is derived from the namespace/folder name the data is in.

Zone Storage Pattern. For the zone storage patterns, each of the three data lakes has different requirements and focus. In the relational enterprise data lake (I), only structured data are ingested and used in relational form. Referring back to Table 4, this proposes the *Single Storage* pattern, as all data have the same management requirements. In the cloud-based data lake (II), all zones despite the Landing and Raw Zone are owned by business department. Thus, only these first two zones can be designed by the central data lake team. To keep the complexity low, it was decided to go with the *Single Storage* pattern again, but coupled with a thorough evaluation of different storage systems to ensure that all data could be managed appropriately. Because all zones after the Raw Zone are designed by the business teams based on their intended use of data, this overall results in a *Usage-Oriented* implementation. Finally, in the case of the sustainability analytics data lake (III), it quickly became clear that the data handled have a wide variety of management requirements. Some data comes from relational systems, others from sensor measurements, resulting in a wide range of data volumes and data quality. This means that the *Single Storage* pattern is not applicable, but a *Data-Oriented* approach is necessary. At the same time, a wide variety of users is accessing the data in the data lake with many tools, requiring it to be available in different forms for analysis. This speaks for the *Usage-Oriented* pattern. As a result, it was decided to go with the *Best Fit* pattern, where the Landing, Raw, and Harmonized Zone consist of two different storage systems: A relational system for structured data and HDFS for semi-structured and unstructured data. In the remaining use-case-dependent zones, data are then stored based on their intended usage.

Zone Data Flow Patterns: While streaming data could be consumed in any of the case studies, only case III ingests streaming data as of now. As some use cases require real time data in their dashboards, it was decided to use the *Streaming Zone* pattern to avoid unnecessary latencies. In parallel, streaming data are also persisted in the batch-based zones of the data lake for later analysis.

4.3   Evaluation Results

Section 4.2 demonstrates the *applicability* of the developed patterns in practice. In all three cases, it was possible to systematically select a pattern that fits the requirements of the data lake. The patterns were easy to understand and the resulting architecture could quickly be documented and comprehended.

To evaluate the *effectivity* of the patterns, we carried out qualitative interviews with the architects of the developing teams per data lake implementation. They confirmed that the patterns allowed them to understand the different options for implementation and their implications on complexity or functionality. This was a great benefit especially for the architects of the sustainability analytics data lake (III), who faced a complex context for their data lake setup. Using the patterns, they could match their case to different implementation options and reuse existing knowledge. Additionally, the different aspects of zone-based architectures (structure, storage, data flow) were highlighted to prevent them from being overlooked.

For *efficiency*, we compared the implementation of the case studies using the patterns to a data lake implementation without any such guidance. It showed that the usage of the patterns reduced both the number of resources needed as well as the time required to formulate the technology architecture: In a separate, comparable implementation without patterns, a team of five architects worked out the data lake architecture over the course of multiple months. Using the patterns in the three considered cases, on average a team of two architects and a few weeks of time were sufficient.

Both the relational and the cloud-based data lake have been successfully serving a large number of use cases for more than two years now: Between them, they manage over 650 TB from 170 sources and serve more than 200 use cases and applications. The sustainability analytics data lake is currently being finalized.

5   Conclusion

In this work, we investigated possibilities to implement zone architecture in industry practice. While various works discuss different zone models as well as their potential benefits, to the best of our knowledge there exist no works on their actual implementation. We thus derived nine implementation patterns for zones in three categories (zone structure patterns, zone storage patterns, and zone data flow patterns) to aid developing teams in their implementation decisions. We applied the derived patterns in three data lake implementations in the real-world business of a large manufacturer. This showed that the patterns were not only applicable, but also provided overview, structure, and understanding for the different implementation options. They thus provided a helpful basis for the implementation of a zone-based data lake architecture.

Future areas of research are patterns for the remaining aspects of data lakes in relation to zone-based architectures, for example in data modeling or data processes.

References

1. Wang, S., Wan, J., Li, D., Zhang, C.: Implementing smart factory of industrie 4.0: an outlook. Int. J. Distrib. Sens. Netw.Distrib. Sens. Netw. **12**, 3159805 (2016)
2. Kim, S.W., Kong, J.H., Lee, S.W., Lee, S.: Recent advances of artificial intelligence in manufacturing industrial sectors: a review. Int. J. Precis. Eng. Manuf. **23**, 111–129 (2022)
3. Mathis, C.: Data lakes. Datenbank-Spektrum **17**, 289–293 (2017)
4. Ravat, F., Zhao, Y.: Data lakes: trends and perspectives. In: Hartmann, S., Küng, J., Chakravarthy, S., Anderst-Kotsis, G., Tjoa, A., Khalil, I. (eds.) DEXA 2019. LNCS, vol. 11706, pp. 304–313. Springer, Cham (2019). https://doi.org/10.1007/978-3-030-27615-7_23
5. Sawadogo, P., Darmont, J.: On data lake architectures and metadata management. J. Intell. Inf. Syst.Intell. Inf. Syst. **56**, 97–120 (2021)

6. Giebler, C., Gröger, C., Hoos, E., Schwarz, H., Mitschang, B.: A zone reference model for enterprise-grade data lake management. In: Proceedings of the 24th IEEE Enterprise Computing Conference (2020)

7. Hellerstein, J.M., Heer, J., Kandel, S.: Self-service data preparation: research to practice. IEEE Data Eng. Bull. **41**, 23–34 (2018)

8. Zikopoulos, P., DeRoos, D., Bienko, C., Buglio, R., Andrews, M.: Big data beyond the hype (2015)

9. Sharma, B.: Architecting data lakes - data management architectures for advanced business use cases (2018)

10. Madsen, M.: How to build an enterprise data lake: important considerations before jumping in (2015)

11. Gorelik, A.: The Enterprise Big Data Lake (2016)

12. Russom, P.: Data lakes - purposes, practices, patterns, and platforms. TDWI. Q1 (2017)

13. Martínez-Prieto, M.A., Bregon, A., García-Miranda, I., Álvarez-Esteban, P.C., Díaz, F., Scarlatti, D.: Integrating flight-related information into a (big) data lake. In: Proceedings of the 36th IEEE/AIAA Digital Avionics Systems Conference (2017)

14. Giebler, C., Gröger, C., Hoos, E., Eichler, R., Schwarz, H., Mitschang, B.: The data lake architecture framework: a foundation for building a comprehensive data lake architecture. In: Proceedings der 19. Fachtagung Datenbanksysteme für Business, Technologie und Web (2021)

15. Giebler, C., Gröger, C., Hoos, E., Schwarz, H., Mitschang, B.: Leveraging the data lake: current state and challenges. In: Ordonez, C., Song, I.Y., Anderst-Kotsis, G., Tjoa, A., Khalil, I. (eds.) DaWaK 2019. LNCS, vol. 11708, pp. 179–188. Springer, Cham (2019). https://doi.org/10.1007/978-3-030-27520-4_13

16. Dixon, J.: Data lakes revisited. https://jamesdixon.wordpress.com/2014/09/25/data-lakes-revisited/. Accessed 27 Oct 2023

17. Gröger, C., Hoos, E.: Ganzheitliches metadatenmanagement im data lake: anforderungen, IT-werkzeuge und herausforderungen in der praxis. In: Proceedings der 18. Fachtagung Datenbanksysteme für Business, Technologie und Web (2019)

18. Munshi, A.A., Mohamed, Y.A.-R.I.: Data lake lambda architecture for smart grids big data analytics. IEEE Access **6**, 40463–40471 (2018)

19. Marz, N., Warren, J.: Big Data - Principles and Best Practices of Scalable Real-Time Data Systems (2015)

20. Wohlin, C.: Guidelines for snowballing in systematic literature studies and a replication in software engineering. In: Proceedings of the 18th International Conference on Evaluation and Assessment in Software Engineering (2014)

21. Ravat, F., Zhao, Y.: Metadata management for data lakes. In: Welzer, T., et al. (eds.) ADBIS 2019. CCIS, vol. 1064, pp. 37–44. Springer, Cham (2019). https://doi.org/10.1007/978-3-030-30278-8_5

22. Eichler, R., Giebler, C., Gröger, C., Schwarz, H., Mitschang, B.: HANDLE - a generic metadata model for data lakes. In: Song, M., Song, I.Y., Kotsis, G., Tjoa, A.M., Khalil, I. (eds.) DaWaK 2020. LNCS, vol. 12393, pp. 73–88. Springer, Cham (2020). https://doi.org/10.1007/978-3-030-59065-9_7

23. Sawadogo, P.N., Scholly, É., Favre, C., Ferey, É., Loudcher, S., Darmont, J.: Metadata systems for data lakes: models and features. In: Welzer, T., et al. (eds.) ADBIS 2019. CCIS, vol. 1064, pp. 440–451. Springer, Cham (2019). https://doi.org/10.1007/978-3-030-30278-8_43

24. Jarke, M., Quix, C.: On warehouses, lakes, and spaces: the changing role of conceptual modeling for data integration. In: Cabot, J., Gómez, C., Pastor, O., Sancho, M., Teniente, E. (eds.) Conceptual Modeling Perspectives. Springer, Cham (2017). https://doi.org/10.1007/978-3-319-67271-7_16

25. Hai, R., Geisler, S., Quix, C.: Constance: an intelligent data lake system. In: Proceedings of the 2016 International Conference on Management of Data (2016)
26. Giebler, C., Gröger, C., Hoos, E., Schwarz, H., Mitschang, B.: Modeling data lakes with data vault: Practical experiences, assessment, and lessons learned. In: Laender, A., Pernici, B., Lim, E.P., de Oliveira, J. (eds.) ER 2019. LNCS, vol. 11788, pp. 63–77. Springer, Cham (2019). https://doi.org/10.1007/978-3-030-33223-5_7
27. Walker, C., Alrehamy, H.: Personal data lake with data gravity pull. In: Proceedings of the 2015 IEEE Fifth International Conference on Big Data and Cloud Computing (2015)
28. Dixon, J.: Pentaho, hadoop, and data lakes. https://jamesdixon.wordpress.com/2010/10/14/pentaho-hadoop-and-data-lakes/. Accessed 27 Oct 2023
29. Zhao, Y., Megdiche, I., Ravat, F., Dang, V.: A zone-based data lake architecture for IoT, small and big data. In: Proceedings of the 25th International Database Engineering & Applications Symposium (2021)

Improving Understandability and Control in Data Preparation: A Human-Centered Approach

Emanuele Pucci⬤, Camilla Sancricca$^{(\boxtimes)}$⬤, Salvatore Andolina⬤,
Cinzia Cappiello⬤, Maristella Matera⬤, and Anna Barberio

Politecnico di Milano, Piazza Leonardo da Vinci 32, 20133 Milan, Italy
{emanuele.pucci,camilla.sancricca,salvatore.andolina,cinzia.cappiello,
maristella.matera,anna.barberio}@polimi.it

Abstract. Data preparation is the process of normalizing, cleaning, transforming, and combining data prior to processing or analysis. It is crucial for obtaining valuable results from data analysis. However, designing the most effective data preparation pipeline is often one of the biggest challenges for data analysts, consuming up to 70–80% of their time. The work illustrated in this paper is the first step toward designing a framework that simplifies the selection and validation of data preparation tasks. It proposes an environment with diverse levels of assistance and autonomy, accommodating varying data analysts' skills and expertise. The requirements for the design of this new framework were elicited through in-depth interviews and think-aloud sessions involving a sample of data analysts, which highlighted understandability, explainability, and continuous learning as fundamental factors. The paper discusses alternatives to enhance these factors, also considering strategies that adopt Large Language Models.

Keywords: Data preparation · Human-centered Design · Explainability

1 Introduction

A data-driven culture is becoming widespread, bringing a wide range of benefits but also risks [22]. While the benefits relate to more efficient decision processes and industrial productivity, the risks may include a potential disengagement of human beings in crucial aspects of decision-making, as well as a lack of control on and transparency of these decisions.

The significance of Data Quality (DQ) also becomes paramount. High-quality data is the cornerstone of any effective Artificial Intelligence (AI)/Machine Learning (ML) system, ensuring the reliability and validity of outcomes. Managing data analysis pipelines becomes relevant, and this activity can also benefit from an increased understanding and control of data and DQ improvement actions by the stakeholders involved.

G. Guizzardi et al. (Eds.): CAiSE 2024, LNCS 14663, pp. 284–299, 2024.
https://doi.org/10.1007/978-3-031-61057-8_17

In addressing the final user's understanding and control, Explainable Artificial Intelligence (XAI) aims to develop methods that enable stakeholders, including those without expertise in AI, to comprehend the behaviour of AI and ML models and the rationale behind their outcomes [23]. Despite its growth, XAI has however faced criticism for its technocentric view, which often overlooks the needs of the final non-expert users [11].

All these considerations, in general, highlight the need for the integration of human factors in the data science process, to achieve more effective, transparent, and trustworthy systems [11]. In an attempt to fill this gap, this paper illustrates a human-centered approach to designing an environment to support the definition and management of data-analysis pipelines and a solution that represents knowledge of system and user characteristics to increase analytics-model transparency and enhance explainability.

Specifically, the proposed solution focuses on *data preparation*, the most challenging and time-consuming phase in the data-analysis pipeline, striving to design an environment that not only supports users with recommendations on the most effective DQ methods but also provides explanations and gathers feedback for continuous learning.

Our proposed approach adopts Miller's broader definition of explanation, which considers it as "an answer to a why question" [23]. We emphasize the need to extend comprehensible explanations to non-technical users of AI-powered systems by tailoring explanations to their needs, skills, and expertise and letting them understand and better control the data preparation process. It is crucial to enhance *understandability for control and discovery*, intended to make a model understandable by end-users [31], and let them control the model and discover new knowledge. To study these aspects, we employed a human-centered requirement elicitation methodology involving users with different backgrounds and expertise. This approach was instrumental in uncovering pitfalls and challenges.

This paper, in particular, discusses the impact of this human-centered analysis on identifying solutions to improve users' understanding and control within the data preparation process [31]. It also illustrates how the analysis has driven the extension of a data preparation platform, now equipped to explain the recommended DQ improvement actions and gather user feedback to foster continuous evolution and refinement of the system.

The paper is organized as follows. Section 2 introduces a framework for data preparation that was the starting point for our human-centered analysis. Section 3 illustrates the human-centered process of determining requirements for understandability and control in a self-service data-analysis environment, and distills relevant design implications for redesigning the data preparation platform. Section 4 describes how the requirements deriving from the user studies guided the re-design of the initial platform to respond to the identified needs for understandability and control. Section 5 then highlights the novelty of our approach by contextualizing it in the related work panorama. Finally, Sect. 6 draws our conclusions and outlines our future work.

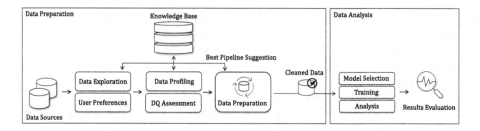

Fig. 1. The initial architecture of the data preparation framework

2   A Framework for Supporting Data Preparation

The starting point of the work discussed in this paper is a framework supporting the definition of data preparation pipelines [28], which we then re-designed
thanks to the insights gained through the human-centered analysis.

Figure 1 illustrates the initial high-level architecture of the framework. A
traditional data-science pipeline comprises two main steps: *Data Preparation*, to
collect and process data to guarantee a certain level of DQ, and *Data Analysis*.
The framework, in particular, focuses on Data Preparation by providing: *(i)*
data exploration, data profiling, and DQ assessment functionality to make users
aware of errors and/or anomalies; *(ii)* recommendations of the data preparation
tasks and the order with which they have to be performed, to achieve better
analysis results.

The platform relies on a *Knowledge Base* (KB) representing the information needed to recommend the most appropriate pipeline for a specific analysis
context determined by the combination of the dataset profile and the type on
analysis (*e.g.*, ML algorithm) to be executed. The *KB* contains data such as the
association between the *DQ dimensions* with their corresponding *data preparation* (*i.e.*, improvement) methods, the list of considered *ML models*, the *profiles*
of the data sources analyzed in previous experiments, and the results of such
experiments, which are fundamental to support the generation of recommendations. In particular, we run two types of experiments [28]. The first one evaluated
the impact of DQ errors on the accuracy of the results and identified the DQ
dimensions to be prioritized in a specific context (*i.e.*, dataset profile and ML
method). For each *DQ dimension*, the second experiment identified the top-
k *preparation actions* to be applied in the considered context. Thanks to this
knowledge, the platform has been enriched with a classification algorithm able
to suggest the proper preparation strategies.

The process enabled by this environment begins with the upload of the considered *Data Sources*. The users can then inspect the data through the *Data
Exploration* engine and specify a set of *Users Preferences*. For example, the users
can select the type of the desired ML model to run on the data (if known) or a
subset of the most relevant dataset's features (if known) to filter the data and
consider only the significant values. Once collected, data can be inspected via
the *Data Profiling* phase to extract metadata. This phase allows users to check

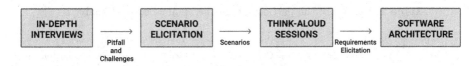

Fig. 2. Human-centered Process

the dataset's content, providing basic statistics and interactive visualizations on value distributions, correlations, or missing values. The *DQ Assessment* assesses the level of several DQ aspects (*e.g.*, completeness, accuracy, consistency) and reveals the presence of DQ issues that might compromise data analysis results.

At this point, the KB is queried to extract *(i)* the ranking that suggests the order in which the DQ dimensions should be improved and *(ii)* for each DQ dimension, a recommendation about the best improvement technique to apply. Note that the ranking considers both the relevance of the DQ dimensions to the analysis context set by the user, and the current level of DQ.

The *Data Preparation* phase allows users to design and execute a data preparation pipeline. This phase provides the pipeline of suggested preparation actions with the possibility of executing them. Users are free to follow the suggestions; they can change the execution order of the suggested actions and/or substitute them by selecting other options from the available ones. Once the data preparation pipeline is defined, the included tasks are executed, and the cleaned dataset is available for download.

3 Human-Centered Analysis

The framework described in the previous section was equipped with a basic interaction paradigm that allowed the users to view the results of the different data preparation steps and select limited configuration options. Starting from that, we focused on enhancing the users' understanding of DQ issues and control of the data preparation pipeline configuration. Therefore, we identified requirements for a data preparation tool by involving users in a human-centered approach. In particular, we adopted a scenario-based need elicitation, since it facilitates the understanding of the stakeholders' operational context [9]. Then we run three different think-aloud sessions to dig deeper into their expectations for such a tool and come up with a conceptual framework. As represented in Fig. 2, and detailed in the following, the study followed different steps that in total involved 8 participants (see Table 1 for the participants' profile).

3.1 Interviews

The first step consisted in 5 **in-depth interviews** with technical and non-technical participants (P1, P2, P3, P4, P5). This phase helped us identify the potential target of the tool and common pitfalls during data analysis activities.

Table 1. Profiles of the participants in the human-centered analysis

	Type	Age	Role	Background	Analysis Goal & Approach
P1	Tech	26	Data Analyst	Computer Science	Identify possible targeted customers manually checking datasets on excel
P2	Tech	26	PhD Student in Computer Science	Computer Science	Omomorphic encryption, process encrypted data through ML models without decripting them
P3	Tech	27	PhD Student in Computer Science	Computer Science	Studying green-impact of cities applying non-supervised clustering on spatial data
P4	Not-Tech	39	Post-Doctoral in Architecture	Architecture	Measure green-impact of cities through manual checks and compute metrics/indicators on spatial data
P5	Not-Tech	30	PhD Student in Architecture	Architecture	Designing green-impact solutions to generate recommendations on cities' morphology
P6	Tech	27	PhD Student in Computer Science	Computer Science	Monitor the evolution of natural disasters analyzing social-media, geographic data and time series
P7	Tech	38	Data Analyst	Telecommunication	Creation and release of machine learning models to analyze data, mainly time series and images
P8	Not-Tech	26	PhD Student in Computer Science	Design	Event log analysis, text analysis and data visualization to study the duration of processes in courts

As detailed in Table 2, after a brief introduction and a session where demographic data were gathered, the questions addressed the **workflow of activities performed by each participant**, and the **interventions** the participants would need with regards to the challenges they encounter every day during their work activities. In the final part of the interview, participants were asked to interact with a mockup of the tool presented in Sect. 2. The goal was to solicit further discussion and uncover additional desiderata, needs, and design opportunities based on the interaction with a concrete prototype. As illustrated in Fig. 3, the main offered functionality was *Data Preparation*, for suggesting a pipeline of actions. Here, users can *(1)* focus on one DQ dimension at a time, visualizing the action that can improve it; *(2)* drag the preferred data preparation action and drop it in the pipeline box; *(3) apply modifications* so that the data preparation pipeline is executed, and the dataset preview is updated; *(4)* go back if the output is not as expected; *(5)* download the cleaned dataset.

3.2 Scenarios

Two researchers independently analyzed the interview results to extract the recurring themes. They then defined two scenarios (leveraging the analysis results) that would be used to contextualize the subsequent user-based sessions [27]. A joint session followed individual analyses to establish a unified agreement on these scenarios, as outlined below.

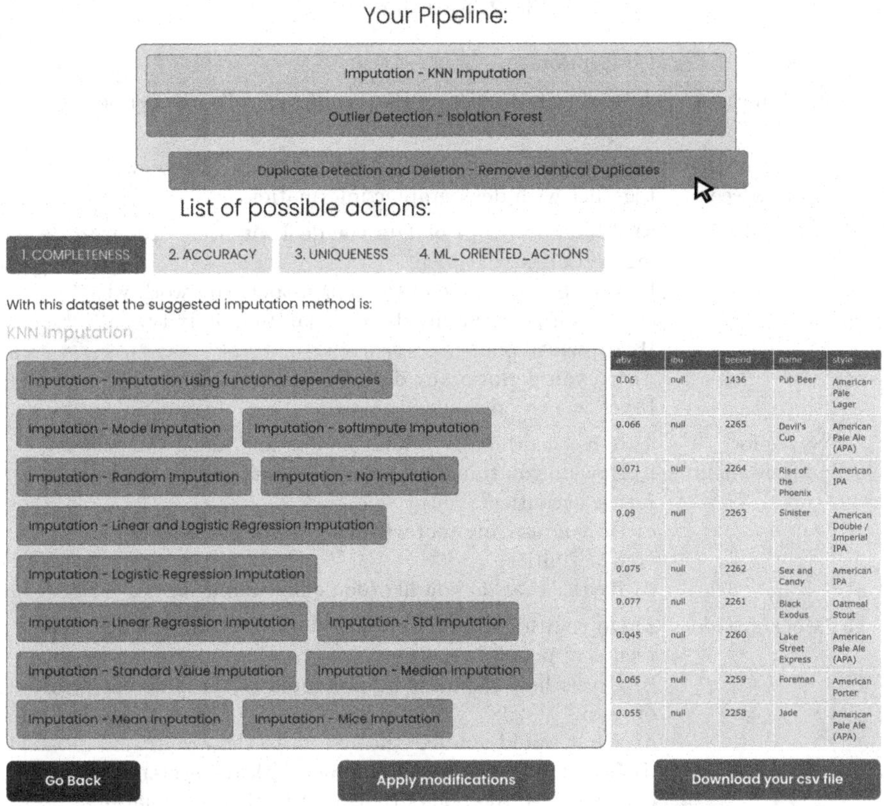

Fig. 3. Data preparation functionality of the tool's mockup

Non-tech/Scenario1. Claudio, an architect with experience as a data analyst, efficiently extracts actionable insights from diverse data sources in city performance evaluation. He navigates through various formats and meticulously inspects each field to identify meaningful performance indicators. Depending on the data type and structure, the analysis can take from a few hours to some days (he usually checks data manually). First, *he has to understand the reality represented by the data.* He would use an interface to upload different types of datasets easily, transform them if necessary, and *explore them to get an immediate answer to his questions.* Then, he goes on with the analysis. He looks for the *most-recommended type of analysis* to perform with the data he is dealing with. Still, before selecting a certain option, he wants to understand the operation's impact through a preview. He also asks for the possibility to *set thresholds* or *exclude records* (or vice versa, to apply the action only to certain elements). Before accepting or refusing suggestions, he would like to know which actions people before him performed in a similar situation.

Table 2. First interview

	Step	Description
1	Introduction	A brief introduction of the researcher with an overview of the project where this study is situated
2	Profile of the interviewee	Information about the background of the interviewee together with demographic information
3	Workflow	a) What is the type of data you deal with during your working activities? b) Which is the type of tasks or models you work with? c) Do you perform any data preparation activity? If yes, which one? d) Do you perform any data transformation activity? If yes, which one?
4	Space for improvement	a) Is it something you don't understand along the process? b) How do you think technology can help during data preparation activities? c) Do you use any tool which supports you during your activities? d) If yes, what do you like/don't like about it?
5	Mockup video	a) Do you think the tool is good for both technical and non-technical people? b) If yes, how should it be presented to the different types of users? c) What would you like the system to show you? d) How would you like to interact with the system? e) Which are the points that need further explanations?

Tech/Scenario2. Emily, a data scientist, examines large amounts of data for various purposes, such as market analysis, statistical analysis, correlation discovery, and recommendations. She uses ML models on datasets with different data types. Emily has to address several DQ issues, such as data errors, varying formats, duplicates, and missing values, and she often deals with unstructured data. She needs a tool to easily *change data formats* and detect problems during conversion. She spends most of her time exploring the data and seeks quicker ways to *gather information, anticipate problems,* and visualize the data. Emily also considers exploring the dataset and correcting errors using *natural language* to expedite the analysis. When the analysis type is not specified, she tries different algorithms and wants *suggestions on the type of analysis* based on data properties. During data preparation, she often lacks clarity on the transformations being performed. She needs *guidance to understand the impact* of each transformation and wants *recommendations* based on similar contexts. Emily also requires support in *merging* datasets and effectively communicating analysis results in a modality that is understandable even to non-experts.

3.3   Think-Aloud Sessions

The final user-centered activity was a think-aloud session, in which the researchers asked the participants to imagine being involved in the designed scenarios and express their opinions and desiderata. This activity was useful in deepening the analysis of the identified process and of the prototype shown to the users during the interviews, as well as understanding limitations and further developments. This time, we selected three expert users (two technical, P6 and P7, and one non-technical, P8), and focused on the developed mockup to gather information about i) the **functions** they could benefit from during their analyses, ii) the **support** they would like to receive from the tool, and, more in general, iii) any potential problems and future directions for the tool development.

3.4   Results and Conceptual Framework

A thematic analysis of the integrated data gathered through the initial interviews, the scenarios analysis, and the think-aloud sessions helped us synthesize the main problems faced by the participants:

- **Data exploration and understanding:** users are interested in a tool that not only helps them prepare the dataset but also supports them in the **exploration** and **comprehension** of the same data (***P3:*** *"The dataset study is the most time-consuming and effort-intense part of my work routine"*).
- **Guidance:** the users asked to be guided through suggestions about the errors to solve, the actions to apply, and possible analyses to perform (***P5:*** *"If we can use this tool to get connection among data, we can see what is behind and relationships among them."*).
- **Interaction:** other than visual support, *e.g.*, based on the adoption of graphic visualizations, the users asked for a tool they can **converse** in natural language (***P8:*** *"I would appreciate the possibility to ask and receive information in natural language."*).
- **Understandability:** before applying the recommended actions, the users want to simulate the transformation actions' effects, understand the reason for a specific suggestion, and eventually undertake an action. In this context, the **social dimension** is also essential: being able to compare their analysis context with previous ones, and know what other colleagues did in similar situations can enhance their awareness in making decisions (***P4:*** *"Sometimes I find references of previous actions or choices, and I have no idea what they are about."*). Moreover, **the language** used is very important, especially when stakeholders for the same system come from different backgrounds. The same terminology might represent different concepts when used in different disciplines. (***P6:*** *"There is a need for a shared vocabulary for tech and non-tech users."*). For example, the term *accuracy* is interpreted as *the number of correctly predicted data points out of all the data points (error rate)* when working with AI models, as *the extent to which data are correct, reliable and certified* [32] when working with data preparation, and not understood at

all by a naive data analyst performing simple actions. **Semantic of words** in different contexts and how to ease their comprehension is an interesting aspect to be further investigated.

- **Control granularity:** the users asked for the possibility of not applying the recommended actions to the entire dataset and setting thresholds for specific features (***P5:*** *"I would like to be able to set some kind of limit under which the operations suggested won't be performed"*).

4   The Human-Centered Solution

The identified challenges underwent a more detailed analysis and discussion, specifically delineating the requirements for designing an architecture closely aligned with the users' needs and emphasizing enhanced understanding and control. This phase was crucial in translating abstract challenges into concrete, actionable specifications, ensuring that the resulting architecture would effectively address the users' concerns. It resulted in the following requirements:

R1 Users must be able to **explore** a data set interactively to **understand** the data, both at the schema and instance level. They must be enabled to specify the analysis **goal**, selecting from a set of options. Natural language emerged as a possible interaction paradigm.

R2 Besides providing **warnings** about data errors and quality problems, the system should highlight the data features that can contribute better to reaching the user's goal if specified.

R3 Besides offering default strategies, the system must enable users to select, define, or **customize** metrics that are relevant to the analysis, set threshold values, and generate a notification if the identified metrics go below the configured thresholds.

R4 Users must be able to apply **data preparation** actions either to the whole dataset or to a subset of data.

R5 The system has to **simulate** the effect of the data preparation action the users want to apply.

R6 The system has to provide **suggestions** on the data preparation actions, the type of analysis to perform, also considering what past users have done in similar contexts.

R7.1 The system has to provide **tips** as a guide for using the tool and allow non-experts to **understand** the process and the analysis results by **explaining** the generated suggestions.

R7.2 Any explanation should be provided only if requested by the users and not by default. Moreover, explanations should **adapt** to the users' skills using different terminology for different users' expertise.

As illustrated in Fig. 4 and detailed in the following, these requirements led to the introduction of new modules, namely an interactive *User Interface* and a *Generative AI Explainer*, to: *i)* offer recommendations and explanations designed for users with different levels of expertise; *ii)* allow the users to intervene and

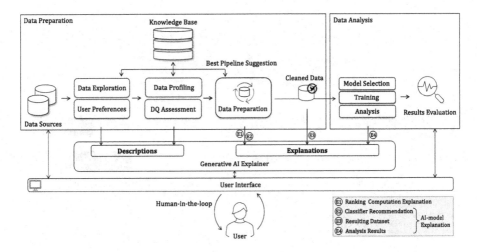

Fig. 4. The extended architecture

control the definition of the data preparation process; *iii)* enable the platform to employ users' interventions and feedback to learn how to improve the recommendations.

4.1 Modeling Explanations

The insights gathered from the users led us to identify three types of explanations that can contribute to achieving understandability and control: *descriptions*, *AI-model explanations*, and *computation explanations*.

A *description* provides information and definitions about an object, process, or concept. It can add context to a specific topic, describe theoretical concepts, or explain how a simple computation is performed. In contrast, it does not explain the results of black-box analysis algorithms. In our platform, descriptions are referred to, for example, data summaries, statistical analysis, additional details on generated visualizations, or the elucidation of specific DQ problems. Descriptions are built starting from the results of the exploration, profiling, and DQ assessment phases and, therefore, concern the input data.

An *explanation* represents the ability to clarify the reason behind a certain action or decision the system makes. An *AI-model explanation* refers to the execution of an ML algorithm and aims to clarify the most important features for which a prediction is generated, *e.g.*, the reason behind the outcome of our platform's classification algorithms. Then, a *computation explanation* gives details on the output of any other algorithm of which the user might be unaware, *e.g.*, how the system computes the DQ dimensions ranking.

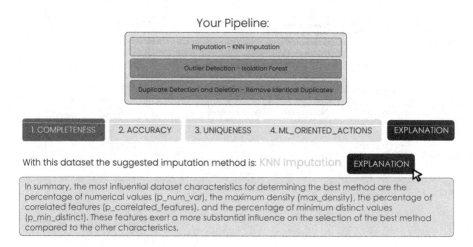

Fig. 5. Data preparation functionality of the tool's mockup with explanations

4.2 Generating the Explanations

The information embedded in our KB and the output of the different phases become the input of the *Generative AI Explainer*, which provides the explanations through text and interactive visualizations. In particular, as described in the previous section, descriptions are based on the insights gathered from the data profiling and quality assessment. We relied on LIME (Local Interpretable Model-Agnostic Explanations) [26] for the AI-model explanations, while the computation explanations were based on the KB content.

The generation of textual descriptions and explanations is supported by an external Large Language Model (LLM) library that takes as input the platform's results and knowledge and describes them using natural language, which is more understandable for the users. Within this objective, several contributions have already demonstrated the potential of LLMs in the generation of detailed natural language explanations [19,29].

Explanations are generated *on demand, i.e.*, only if the user asks for them. Also, the explanations' narrative may vary depending on the user profile; the terminology varies along with the users' expertise to improve the clarity and effectiveness of explanations. For this reason, all users receive the same description/explanation at first. Then, depending on their specific skills and needs, users can ask for a simplified version or additional details.

4.3 New Interactive Data Preparation Process

The provision of explanations, the interactive data exploration, and the control offered on configuring the data preparation pipeline, all required the definition of a new interactive process.

In comparison with the previous version of the platform, the user can now interact with the *DQ Assessment* module to specify further information to compute the DQ metrics *(R3)* (*e.g.*, by adding dependencies rules between features or allowed value ranges useful to detect outliers). For each function in the Data Profiling and DQ Assessment phase, the user can ask for *descriptions (R1, R2)* that are provided through text and interactive visualizations. Textual descriptions are mainly related to data summaries, theoretical concepts, or simple computations (*e.g.*, how correlations are computed or how a DQ metric is assessed). Interactive visualizations focus on interactive plots displaying value distributions, missing values, and correlations. The user could also request a textual data summary by selecting a specific plot area.

AI-model and Computation explanations are provided in the *Data Preparation* and *Data Analysis* phases. In the *Data Preparation* phase *(R6, R7)*, the ranking of the best sequence of DQ dimensions to be improved is complemented by: *i)* a *computation explanation (E1)* clarifying how the ranking is computed, and ii) an *AI-model explanation (E2)*, explaining why the classifier has recommended specific data preparation actions. Figure 5 shows an *AI-model explanation (E2)* provided through the new UI of the tool. Note that the user can still customize the pipeline *(R4)* before executing it.

To facilitate the choice and to further clarify why a certain technique is suggested, the system also provides samples of the results to show immediately and concretely the effect of the proposed data improvement actions *(R5)*. It is worth noting that, in case the data preparation task is based on ML, clarifications on the resulting dataset could also be provided by a second *AI-model explanation (E3)*. Once the process is completed, the system saves the user's actions in the KB to store the data provenance and feed a learning module that can support future users facing similar contexts *(R6)*. After the *Data Preparation* phase, the user can continue with the *Data Analysis* and validate the obtained results with the support of proper *AI-model explanations (E4)*.

As highlighted by the mapping between the new platform's functionalities and the requirements defined in Sect. 4, the redesigned solution attempts to satisfy all the identified users' needs.

5 Related Work

With the recent spread of data analysis applications, we are witnessing an increased number of tools that help users explore, manipulate, and analyze data. For data exploration and profiling, which is the process of examining and creating useful summaries of data, relevant contributions propose the adoption of interactive visualizations [14,15,24]. Some relevant contributions focus on supporting non-expert users in the design of data preparation pipelines, providing automation of several preprocessing activities (*e.g.*, [1]). With the aim of maximizing the analysis results, other tools extract suggestions on relevant data preparation actions to apply through the computation of potential data issues [12] or through the execution of learning algorithms [2]. Other contributions [5,7,20,34] use past knowledge to generate recommendations.

Table 3. Coverage of the defined requirements on related work

		[1]	[2]	[3]	[5]	[7]	[8]	[12]	[14]	[15]	[16]	[18]	[20]	[21]	[24]	[25]	[30]	[34]
Explore/ understand	R1							X		X	X	X			X	X	X	
Warnings/ alerts	R2				X			X		X				X	X			
Customize metrics	R3						X											
Prepare	R4	X	X	X			X		X			X	X	X			X	
Simulate	R5								X									
Suggest	R6				X	X		X	X			X	X					X
Explain	R7			X							X	X				X		

It should be noted that data cleaning is not a fully automated process since many tasks take advantage of human intervention. This is why the implementation of human-centered approaches to data cleaning is gaining momentum, for example, to inspect provenance information [25], or to combine data cleaning and explainability [3, 16]. Interactive solutions are proposed to enable users to participate in the cleaning process through the definition of constraints [8], interactive views [30], iterative processes [21], or making use of user feedback [18].

As summarized in Table 3, the literature only partially covers the requirements identified through our studies (see Sect. 4). For example, the users' need for better data understanding *(R1)* is the primary focus of [12, 15, 24, 25, 30], while need for interactivity *(R1)* is partially covered by [16, 18]. However, these works focus only on specific problems, and they are not adaptive to different types of users and needs. The need for warnings about possible DQ problems *(R2)* is treated in [5, 12, 15, 21, 24]. Customization needs *(R3)* are covered only by [8], which, however, not allows users to customize the data cleaning pipeline directly. The majority of the analyzed works propose tools for data preparation *(R4)*, minimizing human effort [1–3, 8, 14, 18, 20, 21, 30]. However, most of them automatize the data preparation pipeline, and do not allow the user to customize the data preparation interventions.

Moreover, the need to simulate the results *(R5)* of an action before its application is covered only by one work [14]. Supporting the data cleaning process with recommendations *(R6)* is the goal of the works presented in [5, 7, 12, 14, 18, 20, 34], which in most cases provide suggestions based on what other users have done in the past. However, the problem is making the user understand the recommended actions. Transparency and explainability *(R7)* are treated in [3, 16, 18, 25]. However, these works explain only fully automated data cleaning pipelines or define explanations for specific aspects. Providing explanations adapted to the users' expertise is still a challenge.

If we focus on requirements elicitation in XAI, few proposals present methods to obtain requirements and evaluate existing explanation techniques through human-centered approaches (*e.g.*, [4,10,13]). In [17], the authors interpret user needs for explainability as potential questions they might ask the system and then develop a "bank of questions" by interviewing 20 UX-design practitioners working on AI products. The approach described in [33] is the first attempt to use a scenario-based design to elicit XAI requirements, followed by [6], which discusses how user scenarios can help identify end users' or experts' requirements for appropriate explanations in decision making for fraudulent cases in banking.

6 Conclusions

This work is a contribution toward the design of a human-centered data-analysis platform. In this paper, we focus on the data preparation stage and propose an architecture designed based on requirements collected through a human-centered analysis. Despite the increased attention to integrating human factors in requirement elicitation for explainable systems, the requirements highlighted by our study are still uncovered or only partially covered. The predominant emphasis in data-analysis pipelines is still on technical features and automation aspects. Moreover, while research increasingly recognizes the need for transparency and explanations, a comprehensive solution for a human-centered data preparation pipeline enhancing understandability and control is still lacking.

Our work addresses these limitations with two fundamental contributions. *First*, we proposed a conceptual framework obtained through a human-centered approach and designed an environment that can support the analysis of the dataset and the selection of DQ improvement actions thanks to adequate descriptions. *Second*, we worked on that environment and defined a solution to support data analysis by recommending actions and providing different types of explanations. As a result, we improved transparency and user control to facilitate more informed decision-making processes. We also showed how the identified strategy is made concrete in a platform for data preparation.

We are working on the KB design as a property graph database. Moreover, to let the system evolve and learn, we aim to enrich the KB with data derived from users' profiles, goals, and past actions (*i.e.*, provenance). This data will be available as soon as the system starts to be used.

Future work will improve the current prototype to address the identified limitations. In particular, we will:

- Integrate additional methods for data preparation and enhance the generation of interactive recommendations and explanations.
- Study further applications of LLMs beyond formulating explanations and descriptions of data preparation tasks, such as algorithm training, source documentation selection, configuration, and testing.
- Run additional user studies with a larger number of participants with a diversified background, to generalize the achieved results for the definition of models for explainability in the data analysis domain. We will also equip the prototype with auditing mechanisms to collect feedback and determine users' satisfaction with the proposed approach.

References

1. Aguilar, L., Dao, D., Gan, S., Gurel, et al.: Ease. ML: a lifecycle management system for MLDev and MLOps. In: Proceedings of Innovative Data Systems Research (2021)
2. Berti-Équille, L.: Active reinforcement learning for data preparation: Learn2Clean with human-in-the-loop. In: Proceedings of CIDR 2020 (2020). www.cidrdb.org
3. Berti-Équille, L., Comignani, U.: Explaining automated data cleaning with CleanEX. In: Proceedings of XAI 2021 (2021)
4. Chazette, L., Schneider, K.: Explainability as a non-functional requirement: challenges and recommendations. Requirements Eng. 25(4), 493–514 (2020)
5. Chu, X., et al.: KATARA: a data cleaning system powered by knowledge bases and crowdsourcing. In: Sellis, T.K., Davidson, S.B., Ives, Z.G. (eds.) Proceedings of SIGMOD 2015, pp. 1247–1261. ACM (2015)
6. Cirqueira, D., Nedbal, D., Helfert, M., Bezbradica, M.: Scenario-based requirements elicitation for user-centric explainable AI. In: Holzinger, A., Kieseberg, P., Tjoa, A.M., Weippl, E. (eds.) CD-MAKE 2020. LNCS, vol. 12279, pp. 321–341. Springer, Cham (2020). https://doi.org/10.1007/978-3-030-57321-8_18
7. Corrales, D.C., Ledezma, A., Corrales, J.C.: A case-based reasoning system for recommendation of data cleaning algorithms in classification and regression tasks. Appl. Soft Comput. 90, 106180 (2020)
8. Cui, Q., et al.: HoloCleanX: a multi-source heterogeneous data cleaning solution based on lakehouse. In: Traina, A., Wang, H., Zhang, Y., Siuly, S., Zhou, R., Chen, L. (eds.) HIS 2022. LNCS, vol. 13705, pp. 165–176. Springer, Cham (2022). https://doi.org/10.1007/978-3-031-20627-6_16
9. Dick, J., Hull, E., Jackson, K.: Requirements engineering in the problem domain. In: Dick, J., Hull, E., Jackson, K. (eds.) Requirements Engineering, pp. 113–134. Springer, Cham (2017). https://doi.org/10.1007/978-3-319-61073-3_5
10. Eiband, M., Schneider, H., Bilandzic, M., Fazekas-Con, J., Haug, M., Hussmann, H.: Bringing transparency design into practice. In: Proceedings of IUI 2018, pp. 211–223 (2018)
11. Garibay, O.O., et al.: Six human-centered artificial intelligence grand challenges. Int. J. Hum.-Comput. Interact. 39(3), 391–437 (2023). https://doi.org/10.1080/10447318.2022.2153320
12. Gupta, N., et al.: Data quality toolkit: Automatic assessment of data quality and remediation for machine learning datasets. CoRR abs/2108.05935 (2021)
13. Hall, M., et al.: A systematic method to understand requirements for explainable AI (XAI) systems. In: Proceedings of XAI 2019, Macau, China (2019)
14. Heer, J.: Agency plus automation: designing artificial intelligence into interactive systems. Proc. Natl. Acad. Sci. 116(6), 1844–1850 (2019)
15. Issa, O., Bonifati, A., Toumani, F.: INCA: inconsistency-aware data profiling and querying. In: Proceedings of SIGMOD 2021, pp. 2745–2749 (2021)
16. Kim, Y., Lee, K., Oh, U.: Understanding interactive and explainable feedback for supporting non-experts with data preparation for building a deep learning model. Int. J. Adv. Smart Convergence 9(2), 90–104 (2020)
17. Liao, Q.V., Gruen, D., Miller, S.: Questioning the AI: informing design practices for explainable AI user experiences. In: Proceedings of CHI 2020, pp. 1–15 (2020)
18. Luo, Y., Chai, C., Qin, X., Tang, N., Li, G.: Interactive cleaning for progressive visualization through composite questions. In: Proceedings of ICDE 2020, pp. 733–744 (2020)

19. MacNeil, S., Tran, A., Mogil, D., Bernstein, S., Ross, E., Huang, Z.: Generating diverse code explanations using the GPT-3 large language model. In: Vahrenhold, J., Fisler, K., Hauswirth, M., Franklin, D. (eds.) ICER 2022: ACM Conference on International Computing Education Research, Lugano and Virtual Event Switzerland, 7–11 August 2022, vol. 2, pp. 37–39. ACM (2022). https://doi.org/10.1145/3501709.3544280

20. Mahdavi, M., Abedjan, Z.: Semi-supervised data cleaning with Raha and Baran. In: 11th Conference on Innovative Data Systems Research, CIDR 2021, Virtual Event, 11–15 January 2021, Online Proceedings (2021). www.cidrdb.org

21. Martin, N., Martinez-Millana, A., Valdivieso, B., Fernández-Llatas, C.: Interactive data cleaning for process mining: a case study of an outpatient clinic's appointment system. In: Di Francescomarino, C., Dijkman, R., Zdun, U. (eds.) BPM 2019. LNBIP, vol. 362, pp. 532–544. Springer, Cham (2019). https://doi.org/10.1007/978-3-030-37453-2_43

22. McGregor, S., Paeth, K., Lam, K.: Indexing AI risks with incidents, issues, and variants. arXiv preprint arXiv:2211.10384 (2022)

23. Miller, T.: Explanation in artificial intelligence: insights from the social sciences. Artif. Intell. **267**, 1–38 (2019)

24. Papenbrock, T., Bergmann, T., Finke, M., Zwiener, J., Naumann, F.: Data profiling with metanome. Proc. VLDB Endow. **8**(12), 1860–1863 (2015)

25. Parulian, N.N., Ludäscher, B.: DCM explorer: a tool to support transparent data cleaning through provenance exploration. In: Proceedings of Theory and Practice of Provenance 2022, pp. 1–6 (2022)

26. Ribeiro, M.T., Singh, S., Guestrin, C.: "Why should i trust you?": explaining the predictions of any classifier. In: Proceedings of KDD 2016, KDD 2016, pp. 1135–1144. ACM (2016)

27. Rosson, M.B., Carroll, J.M.: Scenario-based design. In: The Human-Computer Interaction Handbook, pp. 1067–1086. CRC Press (2007)

28. Sancricca, C., Cappiello, C.: Supporting the design of data preparation pipelines. In: Proceedings of the SEBD 2022. CEUR Workshop Proceedings, vol. 3194, pp. 149–158. CEUR-WS.org (2022)

29. Sarsa, S., Denny, P., Hellas, A., Leinonen, J.: Automatic generation of programming exercises and code explanations using large language models. In: Vahrenhold, J., Fisler, K., Hauswirth, M., Franklin, D. (eds.) ICER 2022: ACM Conference on International Computing Education Research, Lugano and Virtual Event, Switzerland, 7–11 August 2022, vol. 1, pp. 27–43. ACM (2022). https://doi.org/10.1145/3501385.3543957

30. Shimizu, T., Omori, H., Yoshikawa, M.: Toward a view-based data cleaning architecture. arXiv preprint arXiv:1910.11040 (2019)

31. Vilone, G., Longo, L.: Notions of explainability and evaluation approaches for explainable artificial intelligence. Inf. Fusion **76**, 89–106 (2021)

32. Wang, R.Y., Strong, D.M.: Beyond accuracy: what data quality means to data consumers. J. Manag. Inf. Syst. **12**(4), 5–33 (1996)

33. Wolf, C.T.: Explainability scenarios: towards scenario-based XAI design. In: Proceedings of IUI 2019, pp. 252–257 (2019)

34. Yan, C., He, Y.: Auto-suggest: learning-to-recommend data preparation steps using data science notebooks. In: Proceedings of SIGMOD 2020, pp. 1539–1554 (2020)

Data Friction: Physics-Inspired Metaphor to Evaluate the Technical Difficulties in Trustworthy Data Sharing

Matteo Falconi[1]([✉]), Giacomo Lombardo[1], Pierluigi Plebani[1],
and Sebastian Werner[2]

[1] Politecnico di Milano, Milan, Italy
{matteo.falconi,pierluigi.plebani}@polimi.it,
giacomo.lombardo@mail.polimi.it
[2] Information Systems Engineering, Technische Universität Berlin, Berlin, Germany
werner@tu-berlin.de

Abstract. Data sharing between organizations is becoming an ever-increasing necessity. Data sharing allows organizations to improve business processes that depend on what happens in other organizations, just as having data from other organizations can enrich data analysis models. However, even though data is seen as the new oil, it does not move like oil. There are several technical and organizational factors that make data sharing difficult.

In this work, inspired by the definition of friction in physics, we want to provide a first friction model that is able to capture the elements that hinder data sharing. The proposed model hypothesizes that through the adoption of data mesh in conjunction with a service-oriented sharing approach, we can utilize this model to reduce and reuse the effort for sharing data.

Keywords: Federated Data Sharing · Modeling Data Friction

1 Introduction

Although companies recognize data as an important asset, and it is proven that sharing this resource can improve the business, data sharing is often hindered by technical and organizational aspects [9]. In fact, every organization would like to have access to other organizations' data, there is a certain distrust in sharing their own data. Among the main problems, there is the fear of losing control over critical information and the costs of making the sharing process compatible with current regulations (for example, GDPR for the personal information of European citizens). From a technical point of view, data sharing implies the definition of data governance policies that make access to data safe, limited only to the data to which a potential consumer has the right to access, and efficient in both construction and maintenance of the technological elements necessary

G. Guizzardi et al. (Eds.): CAiSE 2024, LNCS 14663, pp. 300–315, 2024.
https://doi.org/10.1007/978-3-031-61057-8_18

for data sharing. There is therefore a growing need to have solutions capable of guaranteeing sovereignty over one's data, i.e., full control over them even when they are shared with other organisations [2].

In this context, the adoption of data mesh [4] as an approach for managing data for analytics purposes is proving useful for efficiently managing data within an organization [10]. However, when you intend to expand data sharing to other organizations you need to have a data sharing process in place that ensures controlled and observable access to the data. Control refers to the fact that sharing is limited to only the data that the specific consumer has the right to access. Observability refers to the need to know what happens when data leaves the organization and is no longer directly managed. The combination of these two elements enables the creation of trustworthy data sharing, and the effort required to create them somehow opposes data sharing. Taking inspiration from what happens in physics, we can say that there is a force that opposes the movement of data and which can be equated to the concept of friction. Then, the following research question is defined: *How can we evaluate data frictions in data sharing in a fair and manageable way?*

To answer this question, this work starts from the assumption that the organizations involved in data sharing belong to the same federation. This allows us to guarantee that some rules are shared and adopted by all participants. On this basis, a data sharing process is proposed in a federated context that allows the definition of friction. As in physics, this friction is based on two components, static and dynamic, which are linked to the effort necessary to build the data sharing system, modeled as data pipelines, and to perform data sharing also including the effects of the network and observability mechanisms.

The remainder of this paper is organized as follows: First, we present related work in Sect. 2, followed by the introduction of the problem of federated data meshes (Sect. 3). Then, we present the trustworthy data friction model in Sect. 4, before presenting a preliminary validation in Sect. 5 and concluding in Sect. 6.

2   Related Work

Coined by Paul Edwards [6], the term *Data Friction* refers to 'the costs in time, energy, and attention required simply to collect, check, store, move, receive, and access data". Similarly to what happens in physics, *Data Friction* occurs at the interface of two "surfaces", two points where data moves. Data Friction restricts and impedes the natural movement of data and requires cost and effort to overcome and it emerges when data, primarily due to low levels of data governance and curation, is not properly collected and managed.

From a technology perspective, the main driver of data friction is the lack of a proper data-sharing infrastructure and data management practices [1]. It has been observed [14] that the technological advances that have facilitated data collection have also hindered the sharing and reuse of data in the scientific community due to a lack of licensing and standards. Unified models and platforms to support data sharing are often lacking, even within the same domain [12].

Focusing on the platforms, in centralized data architectures such as data lakes, oftentimes, the absence of data and metadata standards, as well as poor data curation, lead to high friction when sharing and using data [3]. To address these challenges, Dehghani proposes the data mesh paradigm [3,4] as a new approach for organizations to build their data architectures. The Data Mesh paradigm argues that re-organizing data according to business domains and decentralizing data ownership, moving data closer to sources and consumers can reduce the frictions that hamper value-generation in centralized data architectures. Of course, this is only possible if adequate data governance policies are enforced to ensure high data quality and standardization across the business domains of the organization.

Although data mesh can reduce the effort in sharing the data inside an organization, some problems remain when organizations want to share this data [8]. The goal of this paper is to deal with these problems by extending the idea of the *data product*, which is central in the data mesh approach, in a different setting inspired by the data spaces ecosystems that are characterizing the European arena [15]. In fact, while a data product is designed to be managed and consumed internally by an organization, the situation changes when it is assumed that the data product can be shared with external organizations. In this case, the adoption of a service oriented approach allows to offer data products as services. Exploiting the well established service orientation principles defined by Erl [7], a data product is designed to be consumed by a class of consumers which are interested in different aspects of the data that is managed in that product. Although this could facilitate the initial engagement between the data provider and consumer, unlike the usual service provisioning, the data that can be shared must be properly tailored with respect to the real needs and rights that the consumer has. In this sense, the added effort of exposing the right data to the right consumer affects the data friction as it is defined in this paper.

3   Federated Data Sharing Model

Based on the work of Jussen et al. [11], data sharing is defined as the domain-independent process of giving third parties access to data sets of others within the framework of the agreement between the involved parties. In our setting, we assume that two parties are involved: a data provider that wants to share the data and a data consumer that is interested in these data. It might happen that the data provider shares the same data with different data consumers, thus, a specific data sharing process is required to manage the relationship between the data provider and each of the data consumers. Five main steps constitute this process (see left of Fig. 1):

- Dataset preparation: data are collected and organized by the data provider.
- Data sharing agreement: data consumer and data provider, according to a negotiation process, which is out of the scope of this paper, agree on which data are actually shared, as well as, the format (e.g., JSON, CSV) and the possible mandatory transformations (e.g., anonymization).

Fig. 1. Federated data sharing process (left) and FDP architecture (right).

- Planning of the data trading process: the requirements dictated by the agreement are translated into technical elements that ensure that only the agreed data are exchanged.
- Data exchange: here, the actual data movement occurs from the data provider to the data consumer.
- Feedback to the data provider and data consumer: assuming that the data exchange is partially or fully observable (e.g., through a monitoring system), data about how the data exchange occurred and to which extent the agreement has been respected are collected.

Based on the steps above, in this section, we introduce the approach adopted to implement a trustworthy data sharing process assuming that: (i) the data sharing occurs in a federated setting; (ii) data mesh approach is used as a foundation of the data sharing; (iii) data mesh is extended to support cross-organizational data sharing; (iv) blockchain is adopted as the mechanism to attest the correctness of the data exchange.

To better introduce the aspects related to the data sharing and to better motivate the proposed approach to improve the effectiveness of data sharing, we refer to a common scenario in the healthcare domain: hospitals that want to share data about their patients with other hospitals in the realm of a multi-centric clinical trial [5]. Conducting a clinical trial requires both properly anonymized individual data and already aggregated data from the two hospitals. The patient data will be used by the other hospital for further aggregation or by the medical center for research purposes. Data sharing is, therefore, a major component of a successful clinical trial. When the multi-centric clinical trial is set up a set of rules is identified and the participating hospitals must adhere with. This is a sort of federation. Possible rules could refer to how to collect data, who has the right to read the data, the format, and whether the data are anonymized or not. In particular, we assume that an hospital of this network is willing to share a dataset of its patients with the other hospitals. Each of these hospitals could be interested in all the patients, in a portion of them, in a data set organized in a specific format, or a subset of data obtained by aggregation.

Data Preparation: Starting from the successful use of the data mesh approach, the data preparation is related to generating the *data product* is well supported in organizations. However, the data mesh focuses mainly on data management within an organization without considering the possibility of sharing data externally. Here, we extend the concept of data mesh to a federated perspective. In particular, our attention focuses on the extension of the data product model by proposing the so-called *Federated Data Product (FDP)* (see right of Fig. 1). In order to support the data governance policies, an FDP has the capability to run code, store data, and to enforce policies. Not all capabilities must be included if not needed by the governance policies.

An FDP is, therefore, an architectural element designed for sharing the data it contains. Inspired by the principles of service orientation [7], this element must also be loosely coupled and reusable. About the former principle, it is expected that the lifecycle of the FDP is as much as possible independent of its consumer. About the latter, the logic encapsulated by the service is associated with a context that is sufficiently agnostic to any one usage scenario so as to be considered reusable by different consumers.

Therefore, the design and creation of a FDP must be targeted to a consumer type and not by a particular consumer. In this way, the same FDP can be used for different consumers. At the same time, each consumer may have particular needs, or data governance policies may restrict the amount or the level of data aggregation depending on the type of consumer.

Referring to the example, an FDP could be the list of patients whose data has been collected in a clinical trial within a hospital. This FDP contains different data types, e.g., biographical, and clinical. This does not mean that all this data can be visible to everyone, but rather, visibility must be consumer-dependent. For example, a particular doctor from another hospital can have visibility into the entire data set as long as it is anonymized. Or, the ethics committee of another hospital that is studying the possibility of using this data for another clinical trial has access to a subset of the data, always subject to anonymization.

Data Sharing Agreement: Here the producer and consumer must decide what part of the data product is allowed, needed, and wanted. Consumer identification, processing purposes, and data quality guarantees can be negotiated here.

Adapting to these needs can be seen as a series of transformations on the output of the FDP. The execution costs of these transformations could and should be divided between the consumer and producer. Hence, part of the agreement must clearly describe transformations and the resources both parties are willing to provide. Here, we should offer both parties the capability to judge the potential friction an exchange might cause and, thus, how much effort in terms of resources, implementation and execution capacity is needed for that exchange.

Data Trading Process Plan: The specific agreement between a provider and consumer can stipulate mandatory or desired transformations executed in a pipeline between the FDP port and the customer. During the data trading process, the specificities of this pipeline are defined (e.g., how and where to execute). Naturally, this concrete specification presents several Data Frictions, e.g., in the volume of data to transport across the network. Besides the execution plan, the data provider must be able to verify and observe the correct execution of the pipeline. These observations must be accessible to the provider and must be trustworthy.

Between the implicit decision on where to perform each part of the data sharing pipeline and the decision on when to move data across the network, observing that execution also becomes crucial explicit friction. Hence, the earlier the data is moved across the network, the more steps need to be observed to ensure that the consumer receives only the agreed data in an agreed format. On the other hand, the later data is moved, the more computing and storage resources the provider must use. The decision of when to move data is influenced by resource availability, projected data volume, technical capabilities, implementation capacity, and the reliability of approaches to processing data without leaking confidential information. We can address the first part by carefully modeling the friction between each decision point. For the second part, we must rely on best-effort approaches, i.e., combining blockchain properties with infrastructure and process observation approaches and modeling the cost of interacting with these technologies. This paper presents a concrete model to evaluate these frictions, which can be used to find a fair or acceptable distribution.

Data Exchange: Once the execution plan is defined, the pipeline and accompanying components for observation and potentially needed identity or policy enforcement are deployed and started. How this happens depends strongly on the used resources and implementations provided by both the consumer and producer. One can envision sharing access to Kubernetes namespaces across networks, sharing prepared VMs, or deploying serverless functions that react based on consumption events. Similarly, the transformation itself could be custom Python code or transformations defined in a workflow engine such as Kubeflow or Apache Spark. For this paper, the automatic management of the execution across the resources of two organizations is out of scope.

Feedback: Once a data exchange is completed or has sufficiently been used, both the consumer and provider may want or need to review the interactions of the data exchange. This feedback of the exchange has several goals. It allows both parties to review data movement decisions, which may inform future exchanges. A more crucial goal is related to the partially personal or confidential data exchange; here, providers are obligated to report all processing and used procedures. Similarly, customers may want to validate that the data was provided truly from raw sources, e.g., sensor measurements.

These needs imply the transfer of observation data as evidence between the consumer and provider after a data exchange and the retention of such data for the legal reporting periods or alternatively means to prove correctness even without the original logging data. To that end, we can either enable contractual means to provide access to that data after the exchange or utilize public repositories to store relevant evidence. However, as this evidence can also become crucial in disputes, we must ensure that the access can not be revoked later and that publicly shared evidence is verifiable and self-contained. We envision an evidence-based infrastructure as part of the FDP connected to immutable distributed storage solutions, such as IPFS. Combined with distributed ledgers, it can function as a verifiable public repository.

Table 1. Reference table for the notation

Symbol	Description	Symbol	Description
d	Data object	$\overrightarrow{p}^{\,k}_{x+1}$	Part of p_k deployed by the consumer
c	Capability	$\widehat{p_x}^{\,k}$	Deployment configuration x of $\widehat{p}^{\,k}$
C	Set of capabilities implemented by the provider	$E^I(c)$	Implementation effort of c
C'	Set of capabilities already executed on the same data	$E^I_{\widehat{p_x}^{\,k}}$	Implementation effort of $\widehat{p_x}^{\,k}$
c_t	Transmission capability	$E^E(c,d)$	Execution effort of c on d
c_o	Observability capability	$E^E_{\widehat{p_x}^{\,k}}$	Execution effort of $\widehat{p_x}^{\,k}$
$\overleftarrow{C} \subseteq C$	Set of c that must be deployed by the provider	$e(c)$	Unitary execution effort of c
$\overrightarrow{C} \subseteq C$	Set of c that must be deployed by the consumer	$sizeof(d)$	Size of the data object d
p^k	Data pipeline between provider and consumer k	$\mu^I_{\widehat{p_x}^{\,k}}$	Implementation friction of $\widehat{p_x}^{\,k}$
$\overleftarrow{p}^{\,k}_x$	Part of p_k deployed by the provider	$\mu^E_{\widehat{p_x}^{\,k}}$	Execution friction of $\widehat{p_x}^{\,k}$

4   Evaluating Data Friction

In physics, friction F is the force that opposes the movement of an element when it scrapes a certain surface. Therefore, to move the element it is necessary to apply a force F_{apply} that is greater than the force that friction generates. This is represented by the equation:

$$F_{apply} > F \text{ where } F = \mu \cdot N$$

N is the force that opposes the movement (usually associated with the gravity of an element) and μ is a coefficient that takes into account the material of the involved surfaces.

In case of data friction, naming d_{fdp} the data exposed by an FDP and d_{cons} the data that is requested by the consumer, the forces that oppose to the movement are related to the effort that is required to transform and observe the data from the original format and content as it is created by the data provider, to the format and content as required by the user. Like in physics, where there are static and dynamic friction, also in our case, we have two components of the data friction: (i) the *static friction* F_S related to the effort E^I required to *implement* the pipeline that performs the transformation required, and (ii) the *dynamic friction* F_D related to the effort E^E in *moving* data from the provider to the consumer:

$$F_S = \mu^I \cdot E^I \qquad F_D = \mu^E \cdot E^E$$

As discussed in the next paragraphs, the higher the reuse of transformation and observation capabilities, the lower the coefficient of static friction μ^I. Similarly, the higher the amount of transformation applied to the same data, the lower the coefficient of the dynamic friction μ^E. This is because of the adoption of a data mesh approach, where the same FDP can be offered to different consumers and several of them could require one or more common transformation capabilities in the related pipelines.

The computation of F_S and F_D can be used during the agreement phase to make (i) the data provider aware of the effort that should be put in place to implement the pipeline, and (ii) the data consumer aware of the effort required to move and observe the data from the provider side.

This value can be used to enrich the description of an FDP and it can be included in the set of metadata used to classify the FDP in a data catalog.

As a guideline for the rest of this section, Table 1 lists all the elements used to introduce the proposed approach to quantify F_S and F_D.

Data Transformation Capability. A transformation is carried out by a *capability*, that is represented by a function c that receives a data object d_{in} as input and returns as output a data object d_{out} that has undergone a certain transformation: $d_{out} = c(d_{in})$. For instance, a transformation could be converting the data object from *.csv* to *.json* format or anonymizing a data set.

The set of capabilities required for a data exchange must be first *implemented* by the data provider, and then *executed* on the data object d_{in} to produce the d_{out}. The implementation phase consists of the realization of a software script or program that is able to perform the required transformation (e.g., using Spark or Airflow). As a basic assumption, the data provider is in charge of the implementation of the capabilities to ensure the proper control on the way in which the data is offered to avoid possible data leakage. In fact, the consumer has only the role of consuming the data produced by the set of transformations.

The execution phase, as the name suggests, consists of the execution of the implemented program on the data object, thus applying the transformation $c(d)$ on the data object. Each capability can be implemented only once, but they can be executed multiple times, e.g. if in the future another data consumer will request a data object in *.json* format, the hospital on focus in our example scenario will not need to implement again the script, but will only need to execute it on the new data object required for the exchange. On this basis, we define C as the set of capabilities that a provider has already implemented. If a new capability will be required, this set will increase.

Data Pipeline. A data pipeline p concerns an *ordered sequence* of data transformations supported by a related set of capabilities, thus:

$$p = \{c_1, \ldots, c_n\}$$

The order is related to the execution of the capabilities, thus, c_i will be executed before c_j, if $i < j$.[1] Referring to our case study, a possible pipeline could be: data filtering, anonymization, conversion to *.json* format.

---

[1] For the sake of simplicity, only sequential pipelines are considered. In the case of branches or loops, their execution traces can be considered as pipeline variants, but this is out of the scope for this work.

Considering the set of capabilities already implemented by the provider C, therefore $p - C$ indicates the set of capabilities that are defined in the pipeline that are required to be implemented by the data provider.

From a functional standpoint, a pipeline can be also represented as a function with respect to the data object on which the pipeline operates. In fact, by leveraging the composition operator (represented with $\circ$), the result of the transformations applied to d_{fdp} is:

$$d_{cons} = c_n \circ \ldots \circ c_1(d_{fdp}) = p(d_{fdp}).$$

Thus a pipeline is the tool that allows the data provider to ensure that the data offered through an FDP is exposed to the consumer as agreed in terms of format and content. For the sake of clarity, we indicate as p^k the pipeline used to transform the data offered by an FDP according to the agreement reached with a given consumer k, thus $d_k = p^k(d_{fdp})$. As several consumers might be interested in the data offered by the same FDP, this notation makes it possible to distinguish the related pipelines.

Once the FDP is created, we assume that $C = \emptyset$ as no capabilities have been implemented at that time by the provider. Every time a new pipeline is requested due to the arrival of a new customer, this set is updated as follows:

$$C = C \cup (p^k \cap C)$$

In fact, $p^k \cap C$ indicates the capabilities required in the pipeline but not yet implemented. Assuming that they will be implemented by the provider, C will include these new capabilities. As a result, C evolves during the time and the capabilities required to be implemented for a given pipeline depend on the history of that FDP.

For instance, in our reference scenario, we can have an agreement with a medical research center that results in a pipeline $p^1 = \{filter,\ anonymize,\ convert\}$, while the pipeline required to expose data to another hospital is $p^2 = \{anonymize,\ convert,\ compress\}$. Thus, starting with $C = 0$, with the definition of p^1 and the related implementations, we have $C = \{filter,\ anonymize,\ convert\}$, Then, when p^2 comes into play, so that $p^2 \cap C = \{compress\}$ which will set $C = \{filter,\ anonymize,\ convert,\ compress\}$.

Data Pipeline Deployment. While the implementation of a capability is under the responsibility of the provider, a peculiar aspect of the proposed approach concerns the possibility to deploy this capability on resources at provider or consumer side. The decision on where to deploy can sometimes be forced by the nature of the transformation (e.g., it is reasonable that an anonymization can be performed only at the provider side) or the availability of the resources.

More formally, being C the set of capabilities implemented by the provider, $\overleftarrow{C} \subseteq C$ and $\overrightarrow{C} \subseteq C$, respectively, indicate the capabilities that must be deployed only at the data provider side and at the data consumer side. These constraints are set during the agreement phase, where the provider and the consumer consider their available resources and the nature of the transformations. Once the

$\overleftarrow{C}$ and $\overrightarrow{C}$ are defined, considering a pipeline p^k, it might exist an index x so that:

$$\forall c_i \in p^k,\ 1 \leq i \leq x : c_i \in \overleftarrow{C} \quad \text{and} \quad \forall c_j \in p^k,\ x < j \leq n : c_j \in \overrightarrow{C}$$

In this way, a pipeline p^k can be seen as $p_x^k = \overleftarrow{p}_x^k, \overrightarrow{p}_{x+1}^k$. In other words, the pipeline can be divided into two sub-pipelines: the first, composed of x capabilities, deployed on the provider side ($\overleftarrow{p}_x^k$), while the second, composed of $n - x$ capabilities deployed on the consumer side ($\overrightarrow{p}_{x+1}^k$). In case the index x does not exist, the pipeline is meant to be deployed entirely at provider side. It is also possible that more than one x can be found for a given pipeline. This generates, from p^k, a series of different configurations $\{p_x^k\}$.

In general, if $\overleftarrow{C} = \emptyset$ and $\overrightarrow{C} = \emptyset$, then there are $n + 1$ possible configurations. Otherwise, the number of possible configurations is given by the formula $1 + |p^k| - |p^k \cap \overleftarrow{C}| - |p^k \cap \overrightarrow{C}|$.

The ability to divide the pipeline gives the opportunity to understand when the transmission from the provider to the consumer occurs. This data transmission affects the friction as it is a fundamental component of the effort required to move the data. To capture the effect of the network, a specific *transmission capability* c_t is introduced in the pipeline. Similarly, we must consider the observability of the part of the pipeline running on the customer side to ensure the trustworthiness and verifiability requirements of the data provider. For this, we introduce the *observability capability* c_o, which must be executed at the end of the pipeline. Thus, given a pipeline p_x^k configuration, then the correspondent deployable configuration is:

$$\widehat{p}_x = \overleftarrow{p}_x, c_t, \overrightarrow{p}_{x+1}, c_o$$

As said, considering the constraints expressed by $\overleftarrow{C}$ and $\overrightarrow{C}$, there could be different configurations. During the agreement phase, the consumer and the provider have the objective of identifying which is the best alternative. For example, consider $p^1 = \{filter, anonymize, convert\}$, where $\overleftarrow{C} = \{anonymize\}$, the only possible pipeline deployable configuration will be $\widehat{p_2}^1 = \{filter, anonymize, c_t, convert, c_o\}$.

The goal of the data friction is to compute, for a given deployable configuration, which is the effort that must be put in place in order to move the data from the initial FDP to the destination after applying all the transformations and the network transmission. *This effort is a combination of implementation effort and execution effort.*

Implementation Effort. Given a deployable configuration $\widehat{p_x}^k$, the implementation effort required to implement the pipeline is defined as the sum of the effort to implement the composing capabilities, thus:

$$E_{\widehat{p_x}^k}^I = \sum_{c_i \in \widehat{p_x}^k\ C} E^I(c_i)$$

where $E^I(c_i)$ is defined as the amount of work required by the provider to implement a capability. The implementation effort depends only on the complexity of the capability: a complex capability will require more effort to be implemented with respect to a simpler capability. An estimate of the implementation effort required by a capability can be obtained by applying software cost estimation models such as SLIM, COCOMO [13] or, as used in our validation the lines of code. As some of the capabilities could be already in C because of previous implementations, then the implementation effort does not count their effect.

As said, the implementation effort corresponds to the **static friction**. Only for aesthetic reasons, to make it aligned with the formulation of the static friction in physics, the static friction coefficient $\mu_{\widehat{p_x}^k}^I$ is introduced and defined as the ratio between the number of capabilities of $\widehat{p_x}^k$ that have already been implemented at the beginning of the implementation phase and the total amount of capabilities in the data pipeline, thus

$$\mu_{\widehat{p_x}^k}^I = \frac{\sum_{c_i \in \widehat{p_x}^k \backslash C} E^I(c)}{\sum_{c_i \in \widehat{p_x}^k} E^I(c)}, \quad 0 \leq \mu_{\widehat{p_x}^k}^I \leq 1 \text{ , so that, } E_{\widehat{p_x}^k}^I = \mu_{\widehat{p_x}^k}^I \cdot \sum_{c_i \in \widehat{p_x}^k} E^I(c_i)$$

The formula is inversely proportional between the number of capabilities already implemented and the value of implementation friction, as the more capabilities have been already implemented, the lower the resulting implementation friction will be.

On this basis, the static effort does not only depend on the deployment configuration, but also on the history of the customers that are attached to the same FDP because of the evolution of C as previously discussed. Thus, if a consumer is lucky, it can select an FDP and agrees on a pipeline where all the capabilities are included in C so that $\mu_{\widehat{p_x}^k}^I$ is 0 and the corresponding effort E^I, thus the static friction, will be 0.

Execution Effort. Similarly to the implementation effort, the execution effort is defined as

$$E_{\widehat{p_x}^k}^E(d_{fdp}) = \sum_{c_i \in \widehat{p_x}^k} E^E(c_i, d)$$

With respect to the implementation effort, the execution effort of a capability $E^E(c_i, d)$ does not depend only on the complexity of the capability, but it might also depend on the size of the data object d on which the capability is executed. For this reason, in case this dependency occurs:

$$E^E(c_i, d) = u(c_i) \cdot sizeof(d) \text{ otherwise } E^E(c_i) = u(c_i)$$

where $u(c_i)$ is *unitary effort* $e(c)$ as the effort required to execute the capability c on a single data item of the data object d. The value of the unitary effort $u(c_i)$ can be estimated experimentally or based on existing benchmarks and at this stage we assume it is linearly dependent on the size of the data.

For instance, the execution effort of the transmission capability $E^E(c_t, d)$ is the effort required to transmit a single data item of the data object. The bigger the data object size, the higher the effort to transmit it. While the execution effort for the observability capability $E^E(c_o)$ is the effort required to observe all capabilities in $\overrightarrow{p}^k$. Thus, this effort is always proportional to the number of capabilities running not on the provider side.

As per the implementation effort, also for the execution effort the reuse deeply affects the friction. In fact, given a pipeline $\widehat{p}_x$, if some of the capabilities are shared with other pipelines, it might be possible that those capabilities have been already executed with the same data as input, thus producing the same data as output. Assuming that sort of caching mechanism is possible[2], C' indicates the set of capabilities that have been executed.

For example, if the hospital has its data already filtered from a previous request, then only the capabilities for anonymization, transmission, and conversion have to be executed to complete the data sharing process.

On this basis, we introduced the coefficient of execution friction $\mu^E_{\widehat{p}_x^k}$ as the ratio between the amount of capabilities of $\widehat{p}_x^k$ that have already been executed and the total amount of capabilities in the pipeline that must be executed. Thus:

$$\mu^E_{\widehat{p}_x^k} = \frac{\sum_{c_i \in \widehat{p}_x^k \setminus C'} E^E(c)}{\sum_{c_i \in \widehat{p}_x^k} E^E(c)}, \quad 0 \leq \mu^E_{\widehat{p}_x^k} \leq 1$$

Based on this coefficient, the **execution friction** can be expressed as:

$$E^E_{\widehat{p}_x^k} = \mu^E \cdot \sum_{c_i \in \widehat{p}_x^k} E^E(c_i)$$

5 Validation

Assumptions and Setup: In this section, we present a preliminary validation of the model based on the running example. The goal of this validation is to prove the feasibility of the method and to show how it can be adopted. As, to the best of our knowledge, our approach is the first one that proposes a systematic way to measure the friction, comparisons with other approaches are not possible at this time. The validation is being performed on a synthetic dataset of patient data, that is stored as a *.csv* file that contains 124,150 rows of patient data with a total size of 36 MB. The implementation and execution of the data friction model are not bound to the utilization of certain software. For our validation, the capabilities will be implemented in Apache Airflow. All experiments are performed on a MacBook Pro with 16 GB of RAM and an Intel chip.

To estimate the effort and friction in this example, we define the metrics to calculate the efforts as: (i) for capability implementation as the lines of code

---

[2] At this stage, only a binary situation is considered. A more articulated analysis that considers the possibility that only a subset of data have been considered will be investigated, as well as the definition of the caching policies.

Fig. 2. Example Pipelines

Capability	$E^I(c)(LoC)$	$E^E(c)(s)$
get	16	9.01
subset	8	2.07
filter	8	0.44
anonymize	12	0.27
convert	12	0.28
Σ	56	12.07

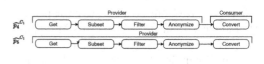

Fig. 3. $E^I(c)$ and $E^E(c)$ of the capabilities (left) and deployment conf. (right) of p^{C_1}.

(LoC) required and (ii) for the execution effort as the execution time in AirFlow. Consequently, the implementation effort is expressed as a pure number, while the execution effort in seconds.

While LoC may not be the most accurate in a real-world scenario because the complexity of some capabilities depends on many factors, this metric can provide a first fair estimate of the implementation effort. Similarly, for the execution effort, more complex metrics could be used.

To estimate c_t, we assume a network bandwidth of 5 MB/s, thus $u(c_t) = 0.2$ s/MB. About c_o, we utilize verifiable credentials stored on a blockchain (Ethereum) and IPFS and the execution effort depends on the size in IPFS and transaction cost. In our implementation, each generated credential is ~36 KB, and ~48310 in gas costs. For this evaluation, we only consider the time to transfer of all observation credentials to the provider assuming the same bandwidth as above.

Validation: In a multi-centric clinical trial, a hospital needs to exchange data about its patients with a medical center (C_1) and the other hospital (C_2) that takes part in the clinical trial. We assume that the hospital and the two data consumers have already agreed on the pipelines defined in Fig. 2 where the first to be considered is p^{C_1}, while the second is p^{C_2}.

Starting with p^{C_1} for its capabilities, the left of Fig. 3 reports the implementation effort $E^I(c)$ required measured as Line of Codes (LoC) and the execution effort $E^E(c)$ as the time needed to execute on Apache Airflow.[3]

Assuming that $c_4 \in \overleftarrow{C}$, i.e., the capability $c_4 = anonymize$ must be executed at the provider side, thus there are only two possible deployment configurations: $\widehat{p_4}^{C_1}$, and $\widehat{p_5}^{C_1}$, (see the right of Fig. 3).

Since p^{C_1} is the first pipeline to be implemented and executed the $C_P = \varnothing$. As result, both the implementation and execution friction coefficients for

---

[3] For the sake of brevity, instead of reporting the values of $u(c)$ for all the capabilities, which have to be multiplied by the size of the data, the resulting $E^E(c)$ is reported.

Capability	$E^I(c)(LoC)$	$E^E(c)(s)$
get	16	8.42
filter	8	2.33
aggregate	8	0.36
convert	15	0.49
Σ	47	11.60

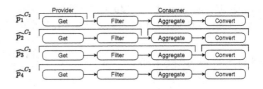

Fig. 4. $E^I(c)$ and $E^E(c)$ of the capabilities (left) and deployment conf. (right) of p^{C_2}.

Table 2. E^E for c_t and c_o in p^{C_1}

Dep. config.	Output size	$E^E(c_t)$	$E^E(c_o)$
$\widehat{p_4}^{C_1}$	205 KB (from c_4)	0.04	0.01
$\widehat{p_5}^{C_1}$	477 KB (from c_5)	0.09	0.0

Table 3. E^E for c_t and c_o in p^{C_2}

Dep. config.	Output size	$E^E(c_t)$	$E^E(c_o)$
$\widehat{p_1}^{C_2}$	3.9 MB (from c_1)	3.9	0.02
$\widehat{p_2}^{C_2}$	101 KB (from c_2)	0.101	0.01
$\widehat{p_3}^{C_2}$	94 B (from c_3)	≈ 0	≈ 0
$\widehat{p_4}^{C_2}$	539 B (from c_4)	≈ 0	≈ 0

each deployment configuration, i.e., $\mu^I_{\widehat{p_4}^{C_1}}, \mu^I_{\widehat{p_5}^{C_1}}, \mu^E_{\widehat{p_4}^{C_1}}, \mu^E_{\widehat{p_5}^{C_1}}$, will be 1. The resulting implementation friction, i.e., the static friction, will be the same for both configurations as they are composed of the same capabilities:

$$E^I_{\widehat{p_4}^{C_1}} = E^I_{\widehat{p_5}^{C_1}} = 1 \cdot 56 = 56 \text{ LoC}$$

As a consequence, the choice of the deployment configuration depends on the execution effort that depends on the amount of data to be transmitted by c_t, and the effort related to the observation measured by c_o, as reported in Table 2. For the deployment configuration $\widehat{p_5}^{C_1}$ the value of c_o is zero because all the capabilities are executed at provider side. Applying the execution friction formula, we obtain that $\widehat{p_4}^{C_1}$ requires less execution effort ($E^E_{\widehat{p_4}^{C_1}} = 1 \cdot (12.07\,\text{s} + 0.04\,\text{s} + 0.01\,\text{s}) = 12.12\,\text{s}$) than $\widehat{p_5}^{C_1}$ ($E^E_{\widehat{p_5}^{C_1}} = 1 \cdot (12.07\,\text{s} + 0.09\,\text{s} + 0.0\,\text{s}) = 12.16\,\text{s}$).

Moving to the data pipeline p^{C_2}, the implementation and execution effort of its four capabilities are reported in Fig. 4 (left). For the capabilities in common with the other pipeline, the values of $E^I(c)$ are equal to the previous case, while the $E^E(c)$ are different due to the different amounts of data.

Assuming that $c_1 \in \overleftarrow{C}$, thus the only capability required to be executed at the provider side is $c_1 = get$, the resulting possible deployment configurations are represented at the right of Fig. 4.

Since the pipeline p^{C_2} happens after the pipeline p^{C_1}, then the set C is no longer empty, but $C = \{get, subset, anonymize, convert\}$. Thus, the provider only has to implement the $aggregate$ and $convert$ capabilities, thus

$$\mu^I_{\widehat{p_1}^{C_2}} = \mu^I_{\widehat{p_2}^{C_2}} = \mu^I_{\widehat{p_3}^{C_2}} = \mu^I_{\widehat{p_4}^{C_2}} = \frac{8 + 15 \text{ LoC}}{47 \text{ LoC}} = 0.489$$

and the related $E^I = 23$ LoC. About the dynamic friction, assuming that the *get* task has been already executed, the $\mu^E_{\widehat{p_x}C_2}$ coefficient will be

$$\mu^E_{\widehat{p_1}C_2} = \mu^E_{\widehat{p_2}C_2} = \mu^E_{\widehat{p_3}C_2} = \mu^E_{\widehat{p_4}C_2} = \frac{2.33 \text{ s} + 0.36 \text{ s} + 0.49 \text{ s}}{11.6 \text{ s}} = \frac{3.18 \text{ s}}{11.6 \text{ s}} = 0.027$$

so that, based on the efforts reported in Table 3, the fourth and fifth configurations are preferable:

$$E^E_{\widehat{p_1}C_2} = 0.027 \cdot (3.18 \text{ s} + 3.9 \text{ s} + 0.02 \text{ s}) = 0.191 \text{ s}$$
$$E^E_{\widehat{p_2}C_2} = 0.027 \cdot (3.18 \text{ s} + 0.101 \text{ s} + 0.01 \text{ s}) = 0.088 \text{ s}$$
$$E^E_{\widehat{p_3}C_2} = E^E_{\widehat{p_4}C_2} = 0.027 \cdot (3.18 \text{ s}) = 0.085 \text{ s}$$

It is important to underline that the values expressed by E^I and E^E are only intended to provide an estimate of the effort necessary to share data that can be relevant in the design phase and not of accurate performance values. For example, the approach is useful when you are looking for a service that provides data in a federation, or you are thinking about offering a data service to a potential set of customers.

6   Conclusions

Despite the growing importance of inter-organizational data sharing, several factors obstacle the flow of data. To measure these obstacles, this paper has proposed a physics-inspired data friction model. The model distinguishes between static and dynamic friction, which influence different stages of the sharing process. The proposed model can provide a useful framework, especially in a data mesh-driven ecosystem to evaluate the effort required to expose or to consume a data product.

While this initial work focuses on linear pipelines, future research should explore the cost and other friction factors like carbon and address the contractual complexities of reusing pipelines. We also plan further validation in a broader European context and incorporate larger datasets from diverse inter-organizational data-sharing scenarios. Preliminary validation indicates the model's ability to guide data providers in evaluating different data sharing deployments, considering both data transport and trustworthy observability. Further, a more systematic validation in terms of acceptance of the method will be conducted to also improve the significance of the approach. In this direction, we plan to build a supporting tool able to guide the data provider in the execution of the steps required by the method.

Acknowledgements. Funded by the European Union (TEADAL, 101070186). Views and opinions expressed are, however, those of the author(s) only and do not necessarily reflect those of the European Union. Neither the European Union nor the granting authority can be held responsible for them.

References

1. Bates, J.: The politics of data friction. J. Doc. **74**(2), 412–429 (2018)
2. Dalmolen, S., Bastiaansen, H., Kollenstart, M., Punter, M.: Infrastructural sovereignty over agreement and transaction data ('metadata') in an open network-model for multilateral sharing of sensitive data. In: 40th International Conference on Information Systems, ICIS 2019. Association for Information Systems (2020)
3. Dehghani, Z.: Data Mesh. O'Reilly Media, Inc. (2022)
4. Dehghani, Z., Fowler, M.: How to move beyond a monolithic data lake to a distributed data mesh (2019). https://martinfowler.com/articles/data-monolith-to-mesh.html
5. D'Amore, J.D., et al.: Clinical data sharing improves quality measurement and patient safety. J. Am. Med. Inform. Assoc. **28**(7), 1534–1542 (2021). https://doi.org/10.1093/jamia/ocab039
6. Edwards, P.N.: A Vast Machine: Computer Models, Climate Data, and the Politics of Global Warming. MIT Press, Cambridge (2010)
7. Erl, T.: Service-Oriented Architecture: Concepts, Technology, and Design. Prentice Hall Professional Technical Reference, Upper Saddle River (2005)
8. Falconi, M., Plebani, P.: Adopting data mesh principles to boost data sharing for clinical trials. In: ICDH 2023, pp. 298–306 (2023)
9. Gelhaar, J., Gürpinar, T., Henke, M., Otto, B.: Towards a taxonomy of incentive mechanisms for data sharing in data ecosystems. In: PACIS, p. 121 (2021)
10. Goedegebuure, A., et al.: Data mesh: a systematic gray literature review (2023)
11. Jussen, I., Schweihoff, J., Dahms, V., Möller, F., Otto, B.: Data sharing fundamentals: characteristics and definition. In: Proceedings of the 56th Hawaii International Conference on System Sciences (HICSS), Maui, Hawaii, USA (2023)
12. Leonelli, S., et al.: Making open data work for plant scientists. J. Exp. Bot. **64**(14), 4109–4117 (2013)
13. Leung, H., Fan, Z.: Software cost estimation. In: Handbook of Software Engineering and Knowledge Engineering: Volume II: Emerging Technologies, pp. 307–324. World Scientific (2002)
14. Murray-Rust, P.: Open data in science. Nat. Precedings 1 (2008)
15. Otto, B.: A federated infrastructure for European data spaces. Commun. ACM **65**(4), 44–45 (2022)

Requirements

Assuring Runtime Quality Requirements for AI-Based Components

Dan Chen[1], Jingwei Yang[1($\boxtimes$)], Shuwei Huang[2], and Lin Liu[2]

[1] BNU-HKBU United International College, Zhuhai, China
{chendan,jingweiyang}@uic.edu.cn
[2] Tsinghua University, Beijing, China
hsw22@mails.tsinghua.edu.cn, linliu@tsinghua.edu.cn

Abstract. As Artificial Intelligence makes astonishing progress, various AI-embedded applications are being built to unleash their potential. However, all technologies come with their inherent limitations in dealing with unanticipated situations, making it difficult to assure the satisfaction of critical qualities at runtime. This is partly due to the challenge of specifying requirements for quality-critical AI-based components. We argue that for a deployed AI model whose accuracy cannot be validated at runtime, an accuracy-centric specification method is not good enough to support AI application engineering practice. To address this fundamental issue, requirements engineering techniques can help, especially an NFRs-based approach has been proposed for mitigating the impacts of two types of errors caused by uncertainties, so that critical qualities can be assured in the specification of AI-based components. We have implemented our strategy by a combined use of requirements analysis techniques, including modelling goals as in goal-oriented RE and modelling of environment and problems as in problem-oriented RE. We have showcased its application on a Facial Recognition Payment (FRP) system. This work could help create a runtime engineering shield for AI-based components and move forward its application in quality essential scenarios.

Keywords: AI-based Component · Non-function Requirements · Quality Assurance · Requirements Specification · Uncertainty

1 Introduction

Recently, AI technologies have experienced unprecedented advances in systems and algorithms research and have influenced various research areas [1]. However, despite the enormous effort devoted to AI theoretical and applied research, the technologies of AI still possess their own limitations, including difficulties in dealing with uncertainties [2]. The uncertainties can be ascribed to many reasons, originating from the changing environment to the black-box nature of various AI models. Hence, they were questioned due to unpredictable [3] and unexplainable [4]. Such technological limitations bring up a common engineering challenge to build AI into product functions or features, which

G. Guizzardi et al. (Eds.): CAiSE 2024, LNCS 14663, pp. 319–335, 2024.
https://doi.org/10.1007/978-3-031-61057-8_19

is the quality assurance process of these AI-based components [5]. To tackle this issue, much research effort has been spent on AI model calibration and uncertainty estimation [6], and also on identifying uncertainties in a given domain, safety-driven modeling and analysis, and formal verification or quantitative evaluation approaches. However, a generally applicable methodology to ensure the satisfaction of critical qualities for a given domain, such as the safety and reliability of AI-based components at runtime, is not in place yet. On the other hand, driven by the potential social or economic interests, products with AI-based component(s) have been released to the mass market. As a result of inadequate methodological engineering guidance, the technological limitations of AI have been exposed and magnified over time in various application domains. For example, digital addiction is caused by inappropriate use of predictive analytics [7], and catastrophic accidents take place with Autopilot navigating in an unanticipated scenario [8]. As stated in [9], *"the rush to deploy AI-enabled systems just increased the urgency of making progress on how to model, analyze, and safeguard against the inherent uncertainty of our systems"*.

From a Requirements Engineering (RE) perspective, given that the primary focus of RE lies in system analysis conducted before the commencement of system construction, RE has emerged as the most challenging endeavor within the context of building an AI-based system, and the uncertainty introduced by AI is a key contributory factor underlying this challenge [10]. To analyze the intrinsic uncertainty of AI during the RE phase, a possible method is to apply the obstacle analysis within the KAOS [11], while treating the AI uncertainty as obstacles to system goals. However, a requirements analysis and modeling technique that has been customized to address AI's uncertainty with a wholistic view is still in need [5]. Ishikawa et al. [12] investigated the influence of AI uncertainty on goal-oriented requirements analysis (GORE) techniques, with a focus on decision-making during the requirements analysis. In [13], the ramifications of AI uncertainty on arguments were explored, and potential support through Goal Structuring Notation (GSN) was introduced in response to these impacts. In addition, there have been some studies on training data uncertainty for AI-based systems [14, 15]. These studies either proposed conceptual high-level ideas that have not been materialized, or failed to emphasize the aspect of quality assurance when dealing with uncertainty. So far, there has not been sufficient intellectual support from the RE community on approaches to mitigating the impacts of uncertainty within AI-based components, to achieve an acceptable level of quality assurance and meet the pragmatic needs of the end-users and stakeholders. Hence, in this work, we choose to analyze AI uncertainty with the quality aspects of the system that AI models are built into and try to address uncertainty with a global view so that all critical qualities are satisfied at the system level at the same time.

The structure of this paper is organized as follows: Sect. 2 briefs on different methods to deal with uncertainty in AI, from the perspectives of AI model, quality assurance, requirements engineering, and obstacle analysis. Section 3 presents the context, rationale, and procedure of our proposed Non-Functional Requirements (NFRs)-based approach to mitigating the impact of uncertainties within the specification of AI-based components. Section 4 illustrates our approach with a Facial Recognition Component in a Mobile Banking App. Section 5 concludes this work and discusses its limitation and potential future extension.

2 Related Work

2.1 Uncertainties in AI

In the AI domain, there are two primary categories of uncertainties: 1) aleatoric uncertainty which is also known as statistical uncertainty, due to inherently random effects, and 2) epistemic uncertainty which is due to inadequate knowledge [16]. More specifically, uncertainty associated with the accuracy of the AI model can be categorized into data uncertainty (as aleatoric uncertainty) and model uncertainty (as epistemic uncertainty) [6]. Data uncertainty is caused by the inherent characteristics of the training data, while model uncertainty is caused by several primary factors listed in Table 1. The above-mentioned uncertainties can serve to quantify the level of confidence or trust in the AI model's prediction and are usually measured through probability [6, 17]. From an engineering perspective, uncertainty is related to *"the feasibility of performance and the extent of value to be delivered"* [12]. In this regard, uncertainty may reside in the requirements and implementation of AI-based systems, and may even exhibit in their operational environments [12]. In this work, we focus on the uncertainty in the requirements specification, which is primarily caused by Factors 3 and 4 in Table 1 i.e., mismatches between historical training data and actual run-time data.

Table 1. The primary factors that induce model uncertainty [6]

Primary factors contributing to model uncertainty
Factor 1 – Errors in the training procedure of the model
Factor 2 – Errors in the structure of the model
Factor 3 – Lacking of knowledge because of unknown data
Factor 4 – Lacking of knowledge because of inadequate coverage of the training data set

Handling uncertainties effectively after the model is deployed in its operational environment is particularly imperative for AI-based applications with critical quality requirements, because systems incorporating AI components may exhibit a substantial error margin attributable to the inherent uncertainty [9], which can constitute a catastrophe for these quality-critical systems, such as autonomous navigation systems. To date, numerous researchers have dedicated their efforts to tackling uncertainty in AI models at run time. For example, a collection of studies has focused on addressing the uncertainty in AI from the perspective of algorithms [6, 18], we refer to these methods as *"inside-out"* approaches. In this regard, uncertainty prediction is the primary approach to address uncertainty issues, which mainly encompasses uncertainty estimation and model calibration [18]. Many approaches for uncertainty estimation/quantification have been proposed to imbue AI models with self-awareness regarding their prediction confidence, such as Single Deterministic Methods, Bayesian Methods, and Ensemble Methods [6]. On the other hand, there are several types of uncertainty calibration methods that have been presented as well, such as Post-processing methods, and Regularization methods. However, the incorporation of these methods into real-world mission/safety-critical applications remains markedly restricted. Challenges include that the uncertainty linked to a single decision is hard to be assessed, the absence of a standardized evaluation protocol, the susceptibility of certain methods to the training dataset, and more [6].

Other related research endeavors address uncertainty from the perspective of software engineering (SE), which we refer as *"outside-in"* approaches, which tackle uncertainty from an engineering standpoint. For example, Ishikawa et al. [12] emphasized that addressing AI model uncertainty during the requirements analysis is pivotal in ensuring the success of AI-based systems. They proposed to tackle uncertainty issues of the AI model with an emphasis on the area of decision-making of design. In [13], Ishikawa et al. proposed some guidelines through GSN to facilitate employing arguments for AI-based systems given the uncertain nature of AI. Additionally, there has been research focused on addressing uncertainty related to training data for AI-based systems. For example, a framework was presented by Dey et al. [14, 15] delineating a process for data requirements engineering and assessing data uncertainty in the context of AI-based safety-critical systems. Another relevant research thread is SE of self-adaptive systems [19], which includes the exploration of methods dealing with uncertainties in problem definition, system design, and run-time execution. However, there is still a huge gap between the above-mentioned methods and the engineering of general AI-based components with runtime critical qualities.

2.2 Quality Assurance of AI-Based Components

The limitations of AI technologies give rise to a common engineering challenge to most AI-based projects, regarding the quality assurance of AI-based components. It has become one of the most difficult engineering problems related to the application of AI technologies, especially, in scenarios where some critical qualities of the systems must be guaranteed, such as safety, and has recently attracted attention in the research communities of AI and software engineering. In terms of safety assurance, traditionally, there are four common types of methods for enhancing engineering safety, including inherently safe design, safety reserves, safe fail, and procedural safeguards [20]. Within the AI context, Dey et al. [5] have surveyed the safety approaches for machine learning-based systems. The survey was conducted from the software engineering perspective and has mapped existing work into the layers of requirements, design, and verification. Dey et al. concluded that among all three layers of work, the requirements layer has received the least attention, which is alarming. It is imperative to clearly define *"what to verify"*, *"against which metrics to verify"*, and *"what are the qualitative and quantitative targets"*, before conducting any subsequent quality assurance activities, in the phases of design, verification & validation, and maintenance. That is, having clear and complete requirements specifications is the prerequisite to properly conducting the quality assurance process.

Kuwajima et al. [21] explored the unresolved engineering challenges associated with the development of safety-critical AI-based systems. The authors argue that the crucial approach to employing an AI model within safety-critical systems requires the partitioning of the training process of AI models into distinct phases, including requirements specification, design, and verification, and they found that the biggest challenge in measuring the quality of AI-based systems lies in the requirements specification. Meanwhile, Kuwajima et al. pointed out that the quality of the AI-based system holds greater significance than that of the AI model itself, especially once the AI model approaches maximum accuracy, and highlighted that the adoption of supplementary security analysis methods is imperative to mitigate model uncertainties.

Additionally, Siebert et al. [22] highlighted the necessity for guidelines tailored to quality models applicable to AI-based software systems. The authors developed a specific quality model relevant to a particular industrial use case. Their model covers different dimensions of AI-based systems, including model, data, system, infrastructure, and environment. Nakamichi et al. [23] proposed a methodology to ensure the quality of the development process for AI-based software, by extending the traditional quality model ISO/IEC 25010. A recent study conducted by Ali et al. [24] helps gain insights into quality models regarding AI-based systems, software, and components, indicating that there is no work addressing quality models at the AI component level.

2.3 Requirements Specification of AI-Based Components

The inherent uncertainty in AI applications requires new software requirements specification techniques to fully meet the demands imposed by AI-based systems. For instance, among existing RE approaches and techniques, it has been well discussed how to specify testable and measurable requirements for software systems. Roberson et al. have elaborated on the needs and methods to derive and formulate testable requirements, a.k.a., fit criteria, based on the original requirements and their corresponding rationale [25]. However, this type of method cannot be directly applied to specify requirements for AI-based components because of the limitations discussed in Sect. 2.1, due to uncertainties within AI.

Over the past few years, there has been a burgeoning interest in research on requirements specification for AI. Berry et al. [26] discussed the requirements specification for AI-based systems, and emphasized the utilization of measures, criteria to establish acceptable thresholds for these measures, and a contextual comprehension of the AI to assess its performance. Ahmad et al. presented a framework "RE4HCAI", which is designed for the extraction and modeling of requirements for AI systems with a human-centered focus [27]. Their work touched upon the area of requirements for errors and failure, and the authors proposed the inclusion of error sources, error risks, error types, and methods for error mitigation. However, in terms of mitigating errors, the authors only suggested that *"(user shall) provide suggestions"* and *"to allow user to fix"*, lacking specific solutions tailored to address errors specifically attributable to uncertainty. Maalej et al. [28] presented six aspects that demand tailoring within the AI landscape, one of which is regarding specifying quality requirements precisely and quantifiably. The authors advocate for the utilization of acceptable quality levels, such as " > 90%", rather than fixed metrics, to achieve consensus on exact values for quality criteria within responsible AI systems.

In the context of requirements specification for AI components, Rahimi et al. [29] introduced a method aimed at enhancing the specification of unambiguous requirements, such as the definition of "pedestrians", for AI components by developing a web-based benchmark. Hu et al. [30] proposed a method for specifying and testing the robustness requirements of AI components grounded in human perception. On the other hand, several attempts have been made to analyze and specify data requirements for AI-based systems [14, 15], and to analyze and specify certain NFRs for AI [30].

Another relevant research thread is requirements modeling techniques for AI, and a recent extensive review, encompassing 43 studies published between 2010 and mid-2021, was conducted pertaining to the RE for AI (RE4AI) field by Ahmad et al. [31, 32], and UML, GORE, and Domain Specific Models have been found as the favored approaches for requirements modeling for AI. This study also shows that the primary emphasis within the RE4AI literature pertained to data requirements and explainability, and no research was identified regarding error addressing during the RE phase [31, 32]. However, according to another recent survey involving industry professionals [33], a desire was expressed by the practitioners to understand the methods for handling errors and specifying their sources during the RE phase, and meanwhile, the significance of both identifying errors and establishing their connection to user needs is also underscored in industrial guidelines.

In summary, the existing literature pertaining to the requirements specification for AI-based systems has endeavored to tackle diverse issues from a multitude of perspectives. However, these proposed methods consistently suffer from the following limitations: 1) They are "*inside-out*" methods and do not address uncertainties at the runtime, but only focus on certain aspects of AI models, e.g., training data. 2) They are too high level and not elaborated enough to provide pragmatic support or guidance toward engineering practice. Moreover, recent works in RE focused on specifying requirements for AI models or processes, instead of treating AI-based components as black-boxes at first. Such a tendency might distract the focus of a specification from "what" to "how" and might eliminate the opportunities for creativity by making upfront design decisions. Overall speaking, there is little systematic work addressing uncertainties in the specification of the AI-based components to ensure runtime critical qualities.

2.4 Obstacle Analysis

Risk analysis constitutes a vital component of the RE phase, which is employed to recognize scenarios capable of inducing failures of the systems [34, 35]. Within the context of goal-oriented RE, "*obstacle analysis is a goal-oriented form of risk analysis*" [35], which can be subdivided into three steps: 1) Identifying as many obstacles as possible; 2) Assessing obstacles' likelihood and consequences severity; 3) Identifying solutions to the obstacles and incorporating them as new goals [35]. KAOS-based [11] obstacle analysis framework, as a mainstream technique for obstacle analysis, has been employed in various application scenarios. For example, obstacle analysis within KAOS has been used to identify contingency requirements for an unpiloted aerial vehicle [36], and a KAOS-based Goal-Obstacle analysis has been conducted to facilitate the specification of system scalability requirements [37]. Overall, the elimination of obstacles has been validated as a necessary pre-condition for the achievement of system goals.

In the engineering process of AI-based systems, uncertainties in data and AI models can be viewed as obstacles for the AI model to make the right prediction. In this regard, these uncertainties can be treated as obstacles for the AI-based system to fulfill its goals. Hence, the rationale and methodology of obstacle analysis [35] can be referred to when dealing with errors caused by uncertainties in AI-based components. For example, DiMatteo et al. analyzed the consequence severity of false positive and false negative errors in the context of monitoring the inattention of the responsible human in an autonomous vehicle [38]. Provost et al. emphasized the cost of false positive and false negative errors is unlikely to be equal, and presented an Expected Value framework that can be used to calculate the impact of the above two types of errors, in which the calculation of the probabilities and costs of the errors are involved [39].

3 Making Uncertainty Certain by NFR

3.1 The Context

The subsequent discussion is expanded upon the specification of AI-based components, rather than the AI model itself, i.e., the AI model is treated as a black-box. We will focus on the satisfaction of critical qualities at runtime, rather than over a period of time, because the current research in self-learning/adaptation of AI is making great progress in dealing with the latter case. To simplify the discussion, we will focus on the scenarios in which the AI-based component functions as a classifier, i.e., the output from the AI-based component would be a finite set. This assumption, however, does not restrict the type of AI technologies under consideration. For example, deep learning models can be used for classification, whose use case is included in our discussion.

3.2 The Rationale

$\mathcal{E}$ Describes the properties of the environment, $\mathcal{S}$ is *"an optative description of a condition over the shared phenomena at the interface between the machine and the environment"* [40]. $\mathcal{R}$ describes the properties that the environment will exhibit after a machine is installed in the environment whose behavior satisfies $\mathcal{S}$, as shown in Fig. 1 (a). That is, $\mathcal{E}, \mathcal{S} \vdash \mathcal{R}$. However, due to the uncertainties that reside in the machine, i.e., the AI-based component, $\mathcal{S}$ cannot be fully specified. Hence, $\mathcal{R}$ inherits the genetic uncertainties associated with $\mathcal{S}$, making it difficult to use as a reference for quality assurance purposes.

This issue asks for serious consideration for AI-based components because the users must rely on the accuracy of the components to achieve their goals. Naturally, a specification is created centering around the accuracy of the AI-based components, which eventually is drilled down to the accuracy of the AI model. We refer to these types of specification methods as *"accuracy-centric"* ones. However, in the application context, it is uncertain if the accuracy of a pre-trained AI model will remain true. In addition, at runtime, it is not realistic to validate the correctness or accuracy of the AI model. (Note that a probability of a prediction is still yet to be validated.) Hence, a specification based on the accuracy of an AI model (Fig. 1. (b)) is not able to deliver a complete assurance on critical qualities. For example, Fig. 1 (c) shows a specification of Alipay's Facial Recognition Component (FRC), which is modeled with KAOS, **i***, and Problem

Frames (PFs) using RE-Tools [41]. The users are granted the ability to complete their transactions through facial recognition within FRC. This is a security-critical scenario, because an error produced by the AI-based (a.k.a., facial recognition) component may give rise to undesirable consequences, i.e., unauthorized charges. According to [42], their facial recognition component boasts an accuracy rate of 99.99% which is acquired from statistics of historical data and training results, and its implication is that for future unknown application scenarios, especially for those that have not been seen before, there is little guarantee that the above-mentioned accuracy rate would always hold, same for the specification built upon that. Hence, when it comes to building AI into applications, we shall recognize the possibility that the AI models, consequently the AI-based components, may fail and produce False Positive and False Negative results [27], and the fact that it remains unknown when, where, and how it would fail.

In quality-non-critical application scenarios, the above-discussed issue may not be a huge concern. For example, most users can tolerate some errors when using a voice recognition feature of a virtual assistant, such as Siri. When Siri fails to correctly recognize users' voice input, users may choose to switch to other input methods, such as the keyboard. However, in other application scenarios, some critical quality of AI-based components must be guaranteed. For example, the obstacle detection component of an Autonomous Driving system must function properly to guarantee the safety of the driver, passengers, the vehicle itself, and others on the road. In this case, other safety measures must be established to work with the obstacle detection component together to achieve safety at the system level.

As discussed above, because of uncertainties, an "*inside-out*" approach that produces an accuracy-centric specification, cannot assure the fulfillment of critical qualities in AI-based components. Intuitively to try with the other way around, an "*outside-in*" approach may be worthy of some exploration, that is to use various critical qualities to "contain" the ambiguous behavioral boundary of AI-based component. In Siri's case, other non-AI-based input methods are used as an alternative mechanism, to ensure the accessibility of other subsequent virtual assistance functions (shown in Fig. 2 (a)). We could use $\mathcal{A}$ to represent the properties of the alternative mechanism, and because it is a regular, non-AI-based component, $\mathcal{A}$ can be clearly defined using the traditional requirements specification techniques such as PFs [40], i* [43], KAOS [11], NFR framework [44], UML [45], without any ambiguity. Hence, when applying $\mathcal{A}$ on top of the specification of the AI-based component $\mathcal{S}$, that is $\mathcal{E}, \mathcal{S}'' \vdash \mathcal{R}$, where $\mathcal{S}'' = \mathcal{S} \bigcap \mathcal{A}$, it can help assure the accessibility of the system. Similarly, in the case of Autonomous Driving, some auxiliary safe measures shall be adopted, to establish a "Safe Zone $\mathcal{Q}$", within the native domain of the AI-based component $\mathcal{S}$, as shown in Fig. 2 (b). When $\mathcal{Q}$ is properly specified without ambiguity, its application on top of $\mathcal{S}$ can help assure the safety of the system, that is $\mathcal{E}, \mathcal{S}''' \vdash \mathcal{R}$, where $\mathcal{S}''' = \mathcal{S} \bigcap \mathcal{Q}$.

To generalize, for an AI-based system that comes with some critical NFRs, these NFRs can be used as constraints on top of the domain of the AI-based component. As shown in Fig. 2 (c), $\mathcal{E}, \mathcal{S}^* \vdash \mathcal{R}$, where $\mathcal{S}^* = \mathcal{S} \bigcap \mathcal{C}_1 \bigcap \mathcal{C}_2 \bigcap \dots \bigcap \mathcal{C}_n$. Since each $\mathcal{C}_i$ is specified as a precise constraint to satisfy a critical NFR, $\mathcal{S}^*$ will consequently satisfy all required critical NFRs. In this manner, the uncertainties with the AI-based component are mitigated and all of the system-level critical NFRs are assured.

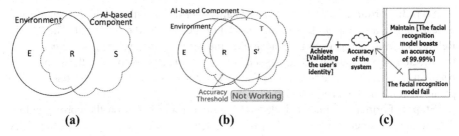

Fig. 1. (a) $\mathcal{E}, S_{ai} \vdash R_{ai}$ (b) $\mathcal{E}, S'_{c=T} \vdash R_{ai}$ (c) Rationalization of goals for AI components

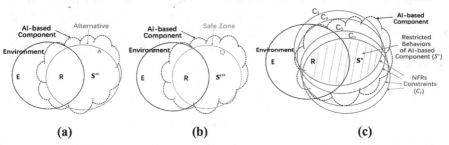

Fig. 2. (a) $\mathcal{E}, S'' \vdash R, S'' = S \bigcap A$ (b) $\mathcal{E}, S''' \vdash R, S''' = S \bigcap Q$ (c) $\mathcal{E}, S^* \vdash R, S^* = S \bigcap C_1 \bigcap C_2 \bigcap \ldots \bigcap C_n$

3.3 An NFRs-Based Approach

So far, we have acknowledged the following facts and observations:

1) The AI-based component that aims at solving classification tasks will surely produce four types of results, including True Positive, True Negative, False Positive (Type I Error), and False Negative (Type II Error) [27].
2) When enforcing critical NFR constraints on top of an AI-based component, the domain properties of the component will surely satisfy these critical NFRs.

Based on the above and the rationale of obstacle analysis [35], an NFRs-based approach to mitigating the impact of uncertainties within the specification of AI-based components is proposed as follows (Fig. 3):

Step 1: Based on the domain context and the acquired user requirements, identify as many system NFRs (both critical and non-critical ones) to be achieved for the AI-based component as possible. Analyze the influence of false decisions (Type–I - False Accept and Type –II - False Reject) of the AI model on these NFRs. Then analyze stakeholders' different tolerance for Type I and Type II errors, which becomes to rationale for a trade-off between conflicting NFRs. Contribution relationships from **i*** framework can be used to represent different influence types [43].

Step 2: Based on the domain knowledge, decompose each affected NFR to system-level constraints $(C_1, C_2, \ldots, C_i)$ that will be further specified formally and built into the AI-based component, by using modeling techniques such as KAOS, **i***, PFs. We recommend using Robertsons' fit criteria as the form of these constraints [25].

Step 3: Correlate each decomposed quality constraint with problem domains and data streams within the problem frame model of the AI-based component. The "Topic Reference" dash line is used to indicate the link between the system requirements and the affected NFRs, and the "Data Association" dash line is used to show the association between the decomposed constraints from Step 2 and the corresponding data stream parameters within the problem frame.

Step 4: Formally define each decomposed constraint based on the corresponding data stream parameters in the problem frame, denoted as $C'_1, C'_2, \ldots, C'_i$ in Fig. 3. A "Dependency" line is used to show this dependency relationship. We recommend using KAOS to formally define the constraints.

Step 5: Formulate the specification of the AI-based component by enforcing all formal constraints with the trade-off rationale identified in Step 1. Because in this case, the system behavior space becomes $S^* = S \cap C'_1 \cap C'_2 \cap \ldots \cap C'_n$, as discussed in Sect. 3.2, the uncertainties with the AI-based component are mitigated and all involved critical NFRs are guaranteed as well.

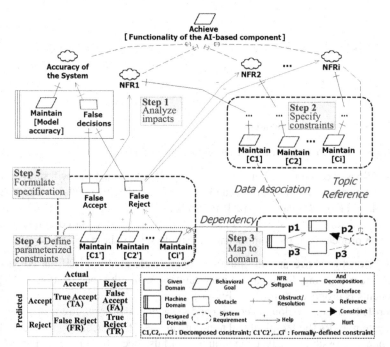

Fig. 3. An NFRs-based approach to mitigating the impact of uncertainties within the specification of AI-based components.

4 A Running Example for the Approach

In this section, the aforementioned Facial Recognition Component (FRC) is used as an example to illustrate our proposed approach. Figure 4 shows a partial use case of a Mobile Banking App (MBA), in which the *"Facial Recognition"* use case will be implemented as an AI-based component.

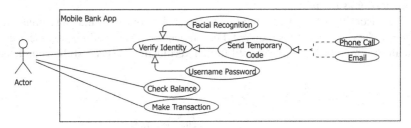

Fig. 4. The domain context of a Mobile Banking App.

Some example requirements of the FRC are given as follows:
"The FRC shall have good performance and the facial recognition process should be expeditious."

"The FRC shall allow users to freely switch between the following methods to verify their identities: 1) Automated verification with facial recognition through facing scanning; 2) Manual verification with their password; 3) Secondary verification using a temporary code sent via pre-registered phone or email."

"The FRC must be accurate and secure, and shall guarantee that the transaction is executed by the user in person."

Our proposed approach is executed step-by-step as follows:

Step 1: By studying the domain context, related NFRs are identified as follows:

(1) **NFR1**: Performance – the facial recognition process shall be expeditious.
(2) **NFR2**: Accessibility – the system shall be accessible to users.
(3) **NFR3**: Security – the system shall be secure.
(4) **NFR4**: Accuracy – the system shall exhibit a high degree of accuracy.

As shown in Fig. 5, NFR4 Accuracy is directly fulfilled by the facial recognition AI model at the operational level. As discussed in Sect. 3.2, we would anticipate Type I False Accept and Type II False Reject errors from the AI model. In the use case of completing a transaction, a Type I error will hurt NFR3 Security, and a Type II error will hurt NFR1 Performance and NFR2 Accessibility. In the business context of the FRC, False Accept poses significant risk and is not acceptable. Comparatively, the adverse consequences of False Reject are relatively moderate and can be tolerated to some extent. Hence, the satisfaction of NFR3 Security shall be prioritized over that of NFR1 Performance and NFR2 Accessibility. Similarly, because the impact of Type II False Reject errors on NFR2 Accessibility (*Hurt*) is more severe than on NFR1 Performance (*Some-*), the satisfaction of NFR2 Accessibility shall be prioritized over that of NFR1 Performance.

Step 2: NFR 1, 2, and 3 are written into fit criteria as follows:

(1) **C**1 : Performance – The facial recognition process shall be completed within 2 s.
(2) **C**2 : Accessibility – When facial recognition fails or is timed out, the system shall prompt the user with an option to switch to a secondary verification method. Available options include using a password, or a temporary verification code sent via a pre-registered phone number or email.
(3) **C**3.1 : Security – At the initial setup of the facial recognition feature or when making large transactions or conducting transactions with high frequency, a secondary verification is required.
(4) **C**3.2 : Security – If the user exhibits abnormal behaviors while making a transaction, a secondary verification is required. For a failed secondary verification, the account shall be temporarily protected until further verification is successfully completed.

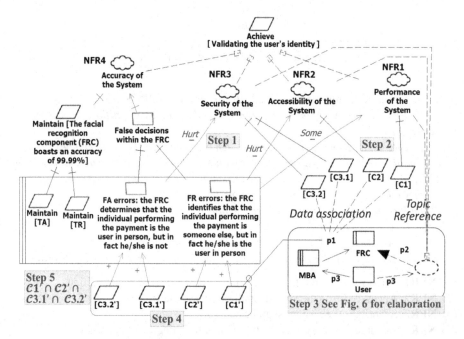

Fig. 5. An illustration of the application of our approach on FRC.

Step 3: Each decomposed quality constraint is associated with corresponding the data streams in the problem frame of the AI-based component (Fig. 6). Based on such referencing and data association, business-level fit criteria can be contextualized into operational-level constraints in Step 4.

Step 4: Formally define each decomposed constraint (**C1, C2, C3.1, C3.2**) based on the data stream parameters, specifically, p1, p4, p7, and p10, in the problem frame. Some parameters and domains are defined as follows: *s: FacialRecognitionSystem, u: User, ta: TransactionAmount, tf: TransactionFrequency, duo: SecondaryVerification, vc: VerificationCode, pn: PhoneNumber, e: Email, pw: Password, td: TimeofDay, tz: TimeZone, ip: IP.*

(1) $C1'$: Performance – ∀ s, u: Recognition(s, u) ∧ s.response_time ≤ 2 s ⟹ timeOut = False

(2) $C2'$: Accessibility – ∀ s, vc, e, pn, pw, u: Recognition(s, u) ∧(s.timeout = True ∨ s.state = "Reject") ⟹ TriggerAlternative(s, vc, e, pn, pw)

(3) $C3.1'$: Security – ∀ s, ta, tf, duo, vc, pn, e, pw, u: u.type = "new" ∨ ta ≥ u.transactionAverage() ∨ tf ≥ u.frequencyAverage() ⟹ Require(s, duo, vc, pn) ∨ Require(s, duo, vc, e) ∨ Require(s, duo, pw)

(4) $C3.2.1'$: Security – ∀ s, duo, td, tz, ip, vc, e, pn, pw, u: u.type = "existing" ∧ (td ∉ u.activityPattern() ∨ u.mostFrequent (tz) = False ∨ ip ∉ u.topIP(2)) ⟹ Require(s, duo, vc, pn) ∨ Require(s, duo, vc, e) ∨ Require(s, duo, pw)

(5) $C3.2.2'$: Security – ∀ s, duo, u: u.type = "existing" ∧ duo.state = "Failed" ⟹ s.state = "Reject" ∧ u.type = "suspended_temp"

Step 5: Enforcing all the formally defined constraints by applying $\mathcal{S}^* = \mathcal{S} \cap C1' \cap C2' \cap C3.1' \cap C3.2'$. According to Step 1, NFR Security has higher priority over NFR Performance and Accessibility, that is $C3.1' \cap C3.2'$ shall be prioritized over $C1'$ and $C2'$, and $C2'$ shall be prioritized over $C1'$.

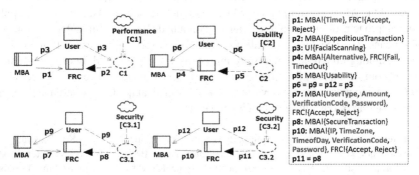

Fig. 6. Correlating problem domains, data streams (p*i*), with each quality constraint C*i*.

Hence, the NFRs of the mobile banking application shall be specified as follows:

(1) **Security-1**: [*Priority-high*], ∀ s, duo, ta, tf, td, tz, ip, vc, e, pn, pw, u: u.type = "new" ∨ (u.type = "existing" ∧ (ta ≥ u.transactionAverage() ∨ tf ≥ u.frequencyAverage()∨ td ∉ u.activityPattern() ∨ u.mostFrequent (tz) = False ∨ ip ∉ u.topIP(2))) ⟹ Require(s, duo, vc, pn) ∨ Require(s, duo, vc, e) ∨ Require(s, duo, pw)

   Security-2: [*Priority-high*] – ∀ s, duo, u: u.type = "existing" ∧ duo.state = "Failed" ⟹ s.state = "Reject" ∧ u.type = "suspended_temp".

(2) **Accessibility**: [*Priority-medium*], ∀ s, vc, e, pn, pw, u: Recognition(s, u) ∧(s.timeout = True ∨ s.state = "Reject") ⟹ TriggerAlternative(s, vc, e, pn, pw)

(3) **Performance**: [*Priority-low*], ∀ s, u: Recognition(s, u) ∧ s.response_time ≤ 2 s ⟹ s.timeOut = False

5 Conclusion and Discussion

In this paper, an NFRs-based approach to mitigating the impacts of uncertainty in AI-based components in quality-critical scenarios has been proposed. We also illustrated how to use our proposed approach to specify requirements for a real-world AI-based component – a Facial Recognition Component, with a combination of various RE techniques, including KAOS, i*, and PFs. To the best of our knowledge, we are among the first to link Type I and Type II errors of AI-based components for NFRs analysis and prioritization, and to address uncertainties at the runtime for quality assurance of the AI-based system.

Our proposed approach is geared towards AI-based components used as classifiers, which stands out as one of the foremost AI tasks that have attracted considerable attention from participation in the industry [33]. However, it could also be applicable to the AI-based components that are intended to address non-classification tasks, such as regression problems, as long as the quality quantification of the regression output is specified with discrete values, e.g., a numeric threshold. Hence, it would be interesting to explore and see if our approach could be applied in scenarios of a similar nature.

The limitation of our approach is that it can assure the runtime satisfaction of critical qualities of the AI-based component, while AI models remain as black-boxes. By applying our approach, the uncertainties can be contained, but not eliminated completely, which means AI's behaviors are still uncertain, but at least all the critical qualities are assured. Although the requirements are inherently incomplete [46], in order to achieve sufficient completeness of the requirements while accepting the existence of uncertainty, studying how to maximize the power of AI with all critical qualities assured at the same time will be one of our future research endeavors.

Acknowledgments. This study was supported by the Guangdong Provincial Key Laboratory of Interdisciplinary Research and Application for Data Science, BNU-HKBU United International College (project code 2022B1212010006) and the National Key R&D Program of China, Tsinghua University (project code 2021YFC2701702).

References

1. AITopics. https://aitopics.org/. Accessed 23 Nov 2023
2. Association for uncertainty in Artificial Intelligence. https://www.auai.org/. Accessed 23 Nov 2023
3. Yampolskiy RV.: Unpredictability of AI. arXiv preprint arXiv:1905.13053v1 (2019)
4. Yampolskiy, R.V.: Unexplainability and incomprehensibility of artificial intelligence. arXiv preprint arXiv:1907.03869v1 (2019)
5. Dey, S., Lee, S.W.: Multilayered review of safety approaches for machine learning-based systems in the days of AI. J. Syst. Softw. **176**, 110941 (2021)
6. Gawlikowski, J., Tassi, C.R.N., Ali, M., Lee, J., Humt, M., Feng, J., et al.: A survey of uncertainty in deep neural networks. Artif. Intell. Rev. **56**(Suppl 1), 1513–1589 (2023)
7. Yang, J., Liu, L.: What users think about predictive analytics? A survey on NFRs. In: 2020 IEEE 28th International Requirements Engineering Conference (RE), pp. 340–345 (2020)

8. NHTSA Office of Defects Investigation #PE 16–007, https://static.nhtsa.gov/odi/inv/2016/INCLA-PE16007-7876.PDF. Accessed 23 Nov 2023

9. Ozkaya, I.: What is really different in engineering AI-enabled systems? IEEE Softw. **37**(4), 3–6 (2020)

10. Ishikawa, F., Yoshioka, N.: How do engineers perceive difficulties in engineering of machine-learning systems? - questionnaire survey. In: 2019 IEEE/ACM Joint 7th International Workshop on Conducting Empirical Studies in Industry (CESI) and 6th International Workshop on Software Engineering Research and Industrial Practice (SER&IP), pp. 2–9. IEEE, Canada (2019)

11. Van Lamsweerde, A.: Goal-oriented requirements engineering: a guided tour. In: Proceedings Fifth IEEE International Symposium on Requirements Engineering, pp. 249–262. IEEE, Toronto, Canada (2001)

12. Ishikawa, F., Matsuno, Y.: Evidence-driven requirements engineering for uncertainty of machine learning-based systems. In 2020 IEEE 28th International Requirements Engineering Conference (RE), pp. 346–351. IEEE, Zurich (2020)

13. Ishikawa, F., Matsuno, Y.: Continuous argument engineering: tackling uncertainty in machine learning based systems. In: Gallina, B., Skavhaug, A., Schoitsch, E., Bitsch, F. (eds.) Computer Safety, Reliability, and Security. SAFECOMP 2018. LNCS, vol. 11094, pp. 14–21. Springer, Cham (2018). https://doi.org/10.1007/978-3-319-99229-7_2

14. Dey, S.: Evidence-driven data requirements engineering and data uncertainty assessment of machine learning-based safety-critical systems. In: 2022 IEEE 30th International Requirements Engineering Conference (RE), pp. 219–224. IEEE, Melbourne (2022)

15. Dey, S., Lee, S. W.: A Multi-layered collaborative framework for evidence-driven data requirements engineering for machine learning-based safety-critical systems. In: Proceedings of the 38th ACM/SIGAPP Symposium on Applied Computing (SAC 2023), pp. 1404–1413. ACM, New York (2023). https://doi.org/10.1145/3555776.3577647

16. Hüllermeier, E., Waegeman, W.: Aleatoric and epistemic uncertainty in machine learning: an introduction to concepts and methods. Mach. Learn. **110**(3), 457–506 (2021)

17. Hong, Y., et al.: Statistical perspectives on reliability of artificial intelligence systems. Qual. Eng. **35**(1), 56–78 (2023)

18. Mohseni, S., Wang, H., Xiao, C., Yu, Z., Wang, Z., Yadawa, J.: Taxonomy of machine learning safety: a survey and primer. ACM Comput. Surv. **55**(8), 157:1–157:38 (2022)

19. Weyns, D.: Software engineering of self-adaptive systems. In: Cha, S., Taylor, R., Kang, K. (eds.) Handbook of Software Engineering, pp. 399–443. Springer, Cham (2019). https://doi.org/10.1007/978-3-030-00262-6_11

20. Möller, N., Hansson, S.O.: Principles of engineering safety: risk and uncertainty reduction. Reliab. Eng. Syst. Saf. **93**(6), 798–805 (2008)

21. Kuwajima, H., Yasuoka, H., Nakae, T.: Engineering problems in machine learning systems. Mach. Learn. **109**(5), 1103–1126 (2020). https://doi.org/10.1007/s10994-020-05872-w

22. Siebert, J., et al.: Towards guidelines for assessing qualities of machine learning systems. In: Shepperd, M., Brito e Abreu, F., Rodrigues da Silva, A., Pérez-Castillo, R. (eds.) Quality of Information and Communications Technology. QUATIC 2020. Communications in Computer and Information Science, vol. 1266, pp. 17–31. Springer, Cham (2020). https://doi.org/10.1007/978-3-030-58793-2_2

23. Nakamichi, K., et al.: Requirements-driven method to determine quality characteristics and measurements for machine learning software and its evaluation. In: 2020 IEEE 28th International Requirements Engineering Conference (RE), pp. 260–270, IEEE, Switzerland (2020)

24. Ali, M.A., Yap, N.K., Ghani, A.A.A., Zulzalil, H., Admodisastro, N.I., Najafabadi, A.A.: A systematic mapping of quality models for AI systems, software and components. Appl. Sci. **12**(17), 8700 (2022)

25. Robertson, S., Robertson, J.: Mastering the Requirements Process: Getting Requirements Right. 3rd eds. Addison-Wesley Professional (2012)
26. Berry, D.M.: Requirements engineering for artificial intelligence: what is a requirements specification for an artificial intelligence?. In: Gervasi, V., Vogelsang, A. (eds.) Requirements Engineering: Foundation for Software Quality. REFSQ 2022. LNCS, vol. 13216, pp. 19–25. Springer, Cham (2022). https://doi.org/10.1007/978-3-030-98464-9_2
27. Ahmad, K., Abdelrazek, M., Arora, C., Baniya, A.A., Bano, M., Grundy, J.: Requirements engineering framework for human-centered artificial intelligence software systems. Appl. Soft Comput. **143**(C), 110455 (2023)
28. Maalej, W., Pham, Y.D., Chazette, L.: Tailoring requirements engineering for responsible AI. Computer **56**(4), 18–27 (2023). https://doi.org/10.1109/MC.2023.3243182
29. Rahimi, M., Guo, J. L., Kokaly, S., Chechik, M.: Toward requirements specification for machine-learned components. In 2019 IEEE 27th International Requirements Engineering Conference Workshops (REW), pp. 241–244. IEEE, Korea (2019)
30. Hu, B.C., Salay, R., Czarnecki, K., Rahimi, M., Selim, G., Chechik, M.: Towards requirements specification for machine-learned perception based on human performance. In: 2020 IEEE Seventh International Workshop on Artificial Intelligence for Requirements Engineering (AIRE), pp. 48–51. IEEE, Zurich, Switzerland (2020)
31. Ahmad, K., Bano, M., Abdelrazek, M., Arora, C., Grundy, J.: What's up with requirements engineering for artificial intelligence systems?. In 2021 IEEE 29th International Requirements Engineering Conference (RE), pp. 1–12. IEEE, USA (2021)
32. Ahmad, K., Abdelrazek, M., Arora, C., Bano, M., Grundy, J.: Requirements engineering for artificial intelligence systems: a systematic mapping study. Inf. Softw. Technol. **158**, 107176 (2023)
33. Ahmad, K., Abdelrazek, M., Arora, C., Bano, M., Grundy, J.: Requirements practices and gaps when engineering human-centered artificial intelligence systems. Appl. Soft Comput. **143**, 110421 (2023)
34. Aydemir, F. B., Giorgini, P., Mylopoulos, J.: Multi-objective risk analysis with goal models. In: 2016 IEEE Tenth International Conference on Research Challenges in Information Science (RCIS), pp. 1–10. IEEE, France (2016)
35. Cailliau, A., Van Lamsweerde, A.: Handling knowledge uncertainty in risk-based requirements engineering. In: 2015 IEEE 23rd International Requirements Engineering Conference (RE), pp. 106–115. IEEE, Canada (2015)
36. Lutz, R., Patterson-Hine, A., Nelson, S., Frost, C.R., Tal, D., Harris, R.: Using obstacle analysis to identify contingency requirements on an unpiloted aerial vehicle. Requirements Eng. **12**, 41–54 (2007)
37. Duboc, L., Letier, E., Rosenblum, D.S.: Systematic elaboration of scalability requirements through goal-obstacle analysis. IEEE Trans. Software Eng. **39**(1), 119–140 (2012)
38. DiMatteo, J., Berry, D.M., Czarnecki, K.: Requirements for monitoring inattention of the responsible human in an autonomous vehicle: the recall and precision tradeoff. In: REFSQ Workshops (2020)
39. Provost, F., Fawcett, T.: Data science for Business: What you need to know about Data Mining and Data-Analytic Thinking. Inc, O'Reilly Media (2013)
40. Jackson, M.: Problem Frames: Analyzing and Structuring Software Development Problems. Addison-Wesley, USA (2000)
41. Supakkul, S., Chung, L.: The RE-Tools: a multi-notational requirements modeling toolkit. In: 2012 20th IEEE International Requirements Engineering Conference (RE), pp. 333–334. IEEE, Chicago, IL, USA (2012)
42. Alipay documentation center. https://opendocs.alipay.com/open/20180402104715814204/intro. Accessed 6 Dec 2023

43. Yu, E.S.: Towards modelling and reasoning support for early-phase requirements engineering. In: Proceedings of ISRE'97: 3rd IEEE International Symposium on Requirements Engineering, pp. 226–235. IEEE, USA (1997)
44. Chung, L., Nixon, B.A., Yu, E., Mylopoulos, J.: Non-Functional Requirements in Software Engineering. Springer, New York (2012)
45. Rumbaugh, J., Jacobson, I., Booch, G.: The Unified Modeling Language Reference Manual. Addison-Wesley, UK (1998)
46. Arango, G., Freeman, P.: Application of artificial intelligence. ACM SIGSOFT Soft. Eng. Notes 13(1), 32–38 (1988)

Designing Military Command and Control Systems as System of Systems – An Analysis of Stakeholder Needs and Challenges

Jan Lundberg[1,2]([✉]) [iD], Janis Stirna[2] [iD], and Kent Andersson[1] [iD]

[1] Swedish Defence University, Drottning Kristinas väg 37, 114 28 Stockholm, Sweden
jan.lundberg@dsv.su.se

[2] Department of Computer and Systems Sciences, Stockholm University, Borgarfjordsgatan 12, 164 55 Kista, Sweden

Abstract. In the context of capability development and to respond to the influence of new technology, a conceptual framework to support the integration of new technology in military command and control systems (C2-systems) is being developed. It focuses on the need to support multi-domain operations (MDO), which requires speed, flexibility, and precision. This paper presents a study of stakeholder needs and goal analysis for future C2-systems. The work is part of a Design Science Research project aiming to design a conceptual framework, with models and methods, that will help designers to evaluate and better understand the potential of a C2 System of Systems (SoS). The current state of the project is that of problem explication with preliminary findings suggesting the categorization of the core issues into three themes. These are (1) new technology, stakeholders highlighting both the opportunities and adjustments necessitated by technological advancements, (2) capability development, stakeholders critically examining and questioning the existing development strategies, and (3) leadership, organization, and culture, emphasizing the necessity of decisive leadership in this domain. The study proposes a shift in the prevailing method of capability development to apply a more comprehensive and holistic approach, aimed at adjusting to the ever-changing technological landscape in military operations.

Keywords: Stakeholders · command- and control systems (C2-systems) · capability development · System of Systems (SoS)

1 Introduction

The war in Ukraine has compelled western nations to boost their military capabilities and leverage emerging technologies. Notably, advancements in automation, machine learning, and artificial intelligence (AI) are spearheading these transformative developments. However, the effective integration of new technologies into MDO[1], which

---

[1] Multi-domain operations (MDO) involve coordinating sensors, effectors, and units across multiple domains, like air, land, sea, and space, to handle a complex operational environment.

© The Author(s), under exclusive license to Springer Nature Switzerland AG 2024
G. Guizzardi et al. (Eds.): CAiSE 2024, LNCS 14663, pp. 336–351, 2024.
https://doi.org/10.1007/978-3-031-61057-8_20

primarily requires efficiency, adaptability, and compatibility, poses a significant challenge. Moreover, future defense forces must manage a combination of new and legacy systems and methodologies, that requires seamless integration to achieve the desired level of functionality and capability [1].

Capability is a central concept in the defense sector. This is evident from the plethora of definitions and related concepts found in military theory [2]. Having a holistic approach, your authors adhere to the NATO Architecture Framework [3] (NAF) definition - *the ability to achieve a desired effect under specified standards and conditions.* This definition is compatible with several approaches to analyze capability as a system discussed further in [4]. In the context of capability development, a paradigm shift is needed. As legacy, operational, systems coexist with emerging ones, a holistic and comprehensive approach to the System of Systems (SoS) framework is required. Merely procuring new technical systems falls short of evolving a potent and effective military force. In the past, there has been a tendency to focus on technology as the main driver of military capability development. This approach fails to address the larger picture of how armed forces use technologies and organize themselves. As they strive to upgrade existing military systems with new technology, a deeper understanding of the development process is necessary. A broader and more integrated approach to capability enhancement is essential, focusing on the complete SoS. This approach should address not only technological needs but also the organizational, methodical, and cultural impacts of adopting new technologies. In addressing these challenges, developers must prioritize integration and connectivity of subsystems in a SoS over their individual performance. In military terms, the capacity of a sensor to share data with a weapon may outweigh its technical performance, and similarly, a weapons capacity to receive and act to sensor data can be more crucial than its range or penetration capability. This principle of reasoning extends further to method- and organizational integration [5, 6].

In the wake of this swift, technological progress, adaptability, and agility are likely to be valued more than stability. In this study your authors depart from a view that technical solutions should be regarded as temporary rather than fixed, despite the challenges this presents. The ability for continual adaptation is crucial, meaning the ability for change should be integrated in the organization, its methods, and its leadership [5].

Currently, there is a gap in research that fittingly explains the relationship between information systems (IS), methodologies, processes, and organizational evolution within the context of a C2 System of Systems framework. For example, the existing enterprise architecture frameworks provide languages for modeling system designs and high-level guidance how to use the language, but they do not offer holistic support for creating and maintain SoS. The absence of a comprehensive approach increases the risk of creating misaligned systems and dysfunctional SoS. Several development approaches have been subject to critique for their biased emphasis on the technical aspects of IT systems, overlooking more comprehensive elements. As a result, the human and organizational aspects were neglected [6, 7].

To address these challenges the overall goal of our research-project is to develop a conceptual framework to support the integration of new technology in military C2-sytems. The goal of this study is *to capture and analyze stakeholder needs and goals for the envisioned framework.*

The rest of the paper is structured as follows. Section 2 presents the background, related work, and the research gap. Section 3 explains the research methodology; Sect. 4 presents findings, and Sect. 5 discusses and interprets those results to identify requirements on the artefact. Section 6 presents conclusions and future work.

2 Background and Related Work

2.1 The Role of New Technology

Many nations today are actively enhancing their warfighting potential by embracing the concept of MDO [8]. However, synchronized across domains operations that creates joint effects capabilities are difficult due to their complex nature.

AI is part of this evolutionary shift, as there is great potential in this technology enhancing capabilities such as intelligence and C2 functions [9]. The expansion of AI has resulted in various advanced models, supporting different processes, e.g., military decision-making processes. One example comes from the targeting process[2] of the US XVIII Airborne Corps, where AI predominantly plays a role in detecting targets [10]. As we look ahead, the application of AI is expected to extend into further phases of the targeting process and to other aspects of military operations. Still, technological development for military operations presents a complex endeavor. It is nearly impossible to foresee a military system potential until it has been implemented in the field. In this context, the ongoing war in Ukraine has emerged as an unprecedented platform for the evaluation and experimentation of AI-supported technology, such as loitering munitions [11]. NATO highlights the critical role of adopting new technologies, especially AI, with potential for military use in areas like surveillance, cyber security, and more [12]. Despite those potentials, some challenges must be addressed. One is that military AI-supported C2-systems must be thrusted by operators, and this is difficult when many AI applications lack necessary transparency [13].

2.2 Shifting Paradigms in Military Capability Management

Capability development, where new technologies will play a prominent role, requires a comprehensive and systematic approach that considers both the technical and social dimensions. Yet, the current approaches regarding military capability development, tend to favor technical elements while overlooking the need for multidisciplinary considerations. This condition poses a problem towards a comprehensive and effective capability development process.

A variety of methods for predicting technological trends, to support capability development, exist. Each suited for different purposes [14], for example quantitative assessment methods [15, 16] and qualitative approaches [17]. Relying on historical technology trends and estimations regarding future technologies, can be misleading. Consequently, it is crucial to evaluate new technologies and systems within scenarios that reflect a future context. This kind of evaluation could help analyzing the capabilities of current

---

[2] Targeting entails the identification and selection of entities such as military units, objects, or structures for engagement during military operations.

military assets and the potential capability enhancements from new technologies. Also, assessing new technology in a forward-thinking context could uncover opportunities for collaboration among different systems or for replacing old systems with new ones [14].

Accordingly, further investigation is needed to highlight the intricacy and unpredictability of capability development [18]. While there have been some contributions in capability management for digital businesses configuring capabilities according to situational context, c.f. [19], the focus has not been on large and complex SoS. When capability development lacks a holistic approach, there is a significant risk of creating IS, organizations, and processes that are less than optimal or even a waste of time and resources. A potential way forward to address these challenges should involve the adoption of incremental capability development. This approach requires building upon existing capabilities while simultaneously concentrating on the overall SoS capability requirements and architectures, rather than focusing on detailed technical specifications of the individual systems [20].

Another aspect originates from the assumption that the initial capability requirements are consistently incorrect and challenging to formulate. This comes from the absence of a clearly defined starting point or the challenge in identifying one, due to the swift evolution of technology. This approach also underlines the needs for broader, holistic aspects of development [21].

In accordance with Baxter and Sommerville [22] the imperative to adopt a socio-technical framework for system development is acknowledged, but not yet widely implemented in practical settings.

2.3 Military Command and Control (C2)

The domain of Military C2 has been explored through diverse narratives. Brehmer [23] argue that to understand C2, the first step is to recognize C2 as a human-centric activity designed to solve military challenges. Additionally, it is important to understand that C2 operates within a system influenced by its own structure, comprising not only the technological interfaces but also the personnel, their organizational hierarchy, and the strategies they deploy. The central argument is that C2 should be interpreted as an activity conducted by the entire system, rather than solely attributed to the actions of the commander. This perspective shifts the assessment focus to the effectiveness of the system rather than examining individual components. Consequently, evaluating, understanding, or designing C2-systems effectiveness calls for a holistic approach towards the C2-system. Brehmer also outlines the functional components of C2-system as; 1) Collection: an activity of accumulating data from sensors, evaluations etc. 2) Sensemaking: a process that transforms data into a coherent context, guiding decision-making, and 3) Planning: The formulation of directives based on insights drawn from sensemaking. These three components imply a cyclic and responsive mechanism within the C2-systems, emphasizing the need for an iterative approach. Furthermore, this approach suggests that technological advancements in these functions could streamline the C2 process, enhancing its speed and precision [23]. Consequently, system-wide analysis and design play a crucial role in creating efficient C2 artifacts.

Emerging technologies influence and improve C2-systems. AI holds substantial potential in information management, crucial for to empower situational awareness and for to support decision-making. The integration of AI in C2-systems is assessed to *"likely be able to avoid many shortcomings inherent to human strategic decision-making during the fog of war."* [24]. Experiences from Ukraine indicates that most targets are identified and localized by sensor-based platforms such as drones [25]. To link this sensor information to the best effector, and to do this as fast as possible, AI enables this information to be processed and analyzed [26]. As a result, a C2-system that effectively connects drones and artillery can reduce the time from detecting targets to effect from up to half-an-hour to minutes [27]. However, the integration of new technology, particularly in the C2 domain, presents ethical dilemmas, when this technology makes it possible to execute a task without human intervention. This accentuates the importance of operators to understand the actions undertaken by AI-enhanced systems [28].

An initial overarching conclusion is that future military C2-systems will consist of a diverse array of manual and automated technical systems and processes, with humans needing to retain sufficient control to maintain accountability. The objective is to execute the decision-making process and enhance its accuracy. Consequently, it becomes important for methods, and organizations to undergo a transformation, applying a more dynamic and resilient nature [6].

3 Method

This paper is part of a research project following the framework of Design Science research (DSR) [29]. The envisioned design artefact is a conceptual framework, with models and methods, that would help designers to evaluate and better understand the potential of a SoS, and how the different sub-systems influence a SoS. The scope of this paper is problem explication and requirements analysis. To this end, the main research question is, *what are the problems experienced by stakeholders of a practice and why are they important.* This task is not just about pinpointing an issue, but also understanding its depth, context, significance and justify the value of a solution, as suggested in [30]. This holistic understanding assures that the coming design artifact, the solution, is relevant, transparent, and effective. To understand the problem more accurately, engaging various stakeholder groups is beneficial since they might offer diverse perspectives and insights thus solidifying relevance of the envisioned design artefact. Hence, comprehending the needs and expectations of stakeholders is fundamental to ensuring the successful outcome of system development [31]. By merging input from these groups, the researcher can achieve a more in-depth understanding of the problem [32]. The research strategy for this stage of research is that of a case study to capture a broad view of stakeholders. The method for data collection is semi-structured interviews and the method for data analysis is thematic analysis [32].

The interviews were conducted in the form of one-to-one interviews [33] and telephone interviews. A semi-structured approach was adopted due to its effectiveness in facilitating in-depth exploration of thoughts and reasoning [33]. The selection of one-to-one interviews as the primary approach is driven by the need to achieve depth, maintain flexibility, and avoid potential biases associated with group settings (stakeholders) [33]. The stakeholders involved, from high-ranking officers to designers and researchers, possess specialized knowledge that often requires detailed exploration, which one-to-one interviews can provide. One-to-one interviews also allows for a flexible approach to the interview process, thereby enabling a more precise exploration into emergent areas of interest that arise during the interviews [34].

The interviews were audio recorded and lasted between 45 and 78 min. To obtain a more precise understanding of the problem, it is advantageous to involve various stakeholder groups as they can provide diverse perspectives and insights on the issue. By integrating input from these groups, the researcher can attain a more thorough comprehension of the problem [35]. The stakeholders chosen to be respondents represent problem owners, specifically military commanders, experts and designers involved in acquisition processes, and researchers in relevant technology areas. Of the stakeholders, three were categorized as problem owners, two as researchers, and eight as experts and designers.

Prior to the interviews, everyone was notified that the data would be assessed and used strictly for academic research purposes. When interviews where the prime method for data collection, preserving the anonymity of participants in interviews are important. According to Cohen et al. anonymity is achieved when a participant cannot be identified [36]. Participants were therefore assigned with an index, A-M, instead of detailed personal information. The complete interview guide, including questions directed towards problem owners, experts and designers, and researchers can be found in [37]. The data were first transcribed[3] and then analyzed by using a six-step thematic analysis method, c.f. [32]. NVivo tool was used to support the coding and identifying themes. Upon evaluation of the findings, every stakeholder was consulted. Most had no additional contributions, and only two provided minor feedback that did not impact the analysis or the outlined artifact goals.

4 Findings

In total, 13 individuals (see Table 1) were interviewed, resulting in more than 13 h recorded interviews. Overall, the challenges and opportunities presented by new technology and capability development have a significant impact on the participants in this survey. Each participant expressed frustration with these challenges, particularly with the integration of new technology into military structures and how the implementation of new technology results in an increased capability. The most common word in the data is *holistic*, in the meaning of the importance to consider the whole rather than detailed entities. Thematic analysis made it possible to code the data and to cluster it in three

---

[3] The automatic service by Amberscript was used (www.amberscript.com/en/).

themes. A detailed description of the coding schema and the connection of codes to themes and goals is found in [37]. The three themes are described in the following of this section.

Table 1. Participants

Participant/Rank/Position	Years of experience[4]	Group	Length of interview (min)/in-person (P) or telephone (T)
A/BG[5]//Higher tactical level	20	Problem owner	58/P
B/Colonel/Tactical level	4	Problem owner	58/P
C[6]/Colonel /Higher tactical level	8	Problem owner	72/P
D/ BG /Swedish defense materiel admin	10	Expert & designer	52/P
E/ BG /Swedish defense materiel admin	15	Expert & designer	53/T
F/Colonel/Army headquarter	20	Expert & designer	61/P
G/Civilian/Army headquarter	3	Expert & designer	61/T
H/LTC[7]/Swedish defense materiel admin	15	Expert & designer	45/P
I/LTC/SWE Military Headquarters	15	Expert & designer	53/P
J/LTC/Land Warfare Centre	21	Expert & designer	78/P
K/Civilian/ Swedish defense materiel admin	30	Expert & designer	78/P
L/Civilian/SWE Military Headquarters[8]	20	Researcher	72/P
M/Civilian/ Defense Research Agency	18	Researcher	61/T

---

[4] Refers to experience of *capability development*, not necessarily related to the current position.
[5] Brigadier-General.
[6] Previous experience as brigade commander.
[7] Lieutenant colonel.
[8] Attached to Swedish Defence Research Agency (www.foi.se).

Theme 1 - New Technology
The data indicates that there is a broad understanding of differing aspects of new technology. Both, opportunities, and challenges. Almost every interviewee underlined the opportunities that come with new technology, and the need to assess the potential impact.

"It creates the conditions for me to be able to tackle a complex problem, perhaps with the support of the systems in a different way." Participant A.

One participant discussed the possibilities of disseminating information early on in a planning process, and hereby significantly shortening the planning- and decision-making process. Some suggested that new technology could help use older systems in another way.

"New technology, new transmission, and new types of software and applications enable us to use old technology in a completely new way." Participant D.

Some participants also mentioned the high expectation of new technology, which indicates a mental readiness for change.

"One could say that the expectations are high regarding the impact." Participant L.

Several participants underscored the difficulties associated with integrating new technologies into military structures and procedures. One challenge is foreseeing the future operational landscape, another is to predict the technology development and future emergent technologies. Consequently, some participants debated the relevance of formulating procurement strategies that often stretch across multiple decades.

"Can we aim for a ten, or twenty-year horizon? Or is it naive to believe that it's possible?" Participant G.

Regarding autonomous systems or platforms, the data indicates the interviewees understand that there is an ethical challenge, and that this area must be developed synchronously with operational methods and organizations. This is also considered as a possible hindrance when those questions are difficult and time consuming.

"How much command can be given to a machine, and how much is controlled by a human? We tend to always get stuck at the initial stage of the question, which is that it is dangerous for machines to do things." Participant D.

Another challenge will most likely be to terminate old technical systems, old methods, and old organizations. One participant underlined his experience of individuals reverting to old behaviors instead of implementing new capabilities that would work more efficiently, despite having systems that could aid in applying our doctrines.

Theme 2 - Capability Development
Every participant communicated opinions regarding capability development. How it works, how it should work, and the main challenges. The most expressed opinion was

the need for a holistic approach in capability development. The participants argued that the opposite, to focus on single systems, single functions, or only on technology and not on methods and organizations, will result in inadequate systems, organizations, and methods. Some participants highlighted the need to always think jointly, i.e., to explore the synergies between all domains (air, land, sea, cyber).

"One does not develop with the intent of integrating a system or systems." Participant B.

"We have just bought vehicles that the new radios cannot be installed in." Participant J.

As the second quote indicate, missing the holistic approach could also result in a situation where different parts of the SoS are sub-optimized. In this example, a new and accurate vehicle was procured, but when the new high-end radio was to be integrated, it resulted in increased cost and efforts to integrate the two systems. This could have been avoided by adopting a holistic approach at the beginning of the design process. In this context, some participants underlined the need to be able to assess the level of holism. Some participants also highlighted the socio-technical aspect in early design phases and expressed the importance of a broad analysis when identifying requirements, i.e., the need to focus not only on technical requirements.

Regarding the skills and abilities of the personnel working with capability requirement or the operators, using the systems, some participants underlined increased competence requirements for individuals. An engineer must not only design and construct technical systems, but he or she must also understand the context where the technical system will be delivered and how it is to be used. Similarly, the operator must have sufficient understanding of technology to be able to define requirements.

Regarding methods for capability development, some major threads are identified. There is a common understanding that a well-defined context is to be identified and described early in the process. The first step in doing this could be to describe and define the military problem. This means that designers must address the question, *what problem should be solved?* It is our perception that it is important to describe this problem holistically and on a high enough level. The context should also describe the expected opponent and its abilities and must require estimations regarding the expected technology development speed.

"Experiences from Ukraine also show how fast everything happens." Participant I.

However, a well-defined context can also hinder the free thought. One participant raised this as a risk and expressed a need for both, i.e., a well-defined context, but also at occasionally a broader context where designers can experiment with new technology and find new ways to solve the military problem.

When it comes to development strategies, the overwhelming part affirms to incremental development (step-by-step or piece-by-piece), with the whole SoS in sight. The use of this strategy means that different parts of the SoS, could be upgraded or exchanged when the functionality becomes obsolete. This includes operational methods and the organization.

"We need to be in constant development and continually take incremental steps - because we need to be, to express it operationally, operationally relevant over time." Participant F.

One participant highlighted the need of a de-centralization of the capability development method. The motivation is to come closer to users, and thereby to possibly speed-up the tempo of development while avoiding irrelevant solutions.

Theme 3 – Leadership, Organization, and Culture
One participant questioned the selection process of high-ranking officers and argued that most officers lack the right competence and suggested a coaching system to enhance knowledge and expertise. The selection and coaching of commanders at different levels is crucial for capability development since commanders finally decide the capability requirements and design of future military forces. Therefore, commanders must have a broad understanding of technology and systems of systems. With a deeper understanding and knowledge, commanders will find it easier to devote to a personal commitment, and this is crucial to achieve change and capability development.

"Without a personal commitment from commanders, I believe it will be difficult to achieve acceptance and change in a rather conservative officer corp." Participant B.

Most participants confirm that emerging technology will change methods and organizations inside the operational units. However, one participant highlighted the need for a stable development organization. This will most likely be needed when experimenting with many different variables.

The cultural aspect is a vital element when it comes to capability development. For many years, due to budget shortages, a culture where administration was the prime focus, emerged. This approach probably served well then, but nowadays, in an era in which we need enhanced capability, it is counterproductive. However, as one participant expressed it, to influence a rather conservative officer corps with its spirit and ethos, is challenging and time consuming.

5   Discussion and Analysis

All participants responded to the questions regarding capability in relation to emerging technologies. In addition, eight individuals diverged from the given questions, and presented their vision for the future of capability development. This vision is connected to the previous themes and serve as a concentrated perception regarding how future capability development must be conducted. It should be considered as the stakeholders' broad strategic direction for improving the process of capability development. One part of this vision is, as mentioned before, *a holistic approach* (G1 in Table 2). Military capability development must avoid platform-centric acquisition. The current acquisition system, that is optimized to develop and purchase platforms, often connected to long term and expensive industrial contract, should be replaced with an acquisition system that emphases integration, a common force design and a SoS approach. This would ensure that every part of a system in a larger SoS is connected, both regarding technical communications, methods, and organizations. The designers must also analyze the principle of having a *holistic perspective* and decide how to apply this in a design process. Some participants highlighted the socio-technical aspect, in early design phases, and expressed the importance of a broad analysis. There is no exact answer of how to conduct this analysis, because in one situation, holistic could mean to levitate in organization-levels, e.g., focus on brigade- or divisional level instead of platoon- or company level. In another situation, this could mean to focus on a specific function, e.g., C2 or intelligence[9]. This leads to the conclusion that instead of purchasing a platform, for example, a howitzer, one must *adopt the approach of acquiring, or strengthen, an entire function* consisting of several different technical and socio-technical systems. In this context it is also important to be able to *simulate and to evaluate the impact of new technologies on the C2-system's total capability* (G2) and to *identify the interdependencies between sub-systems* (G5).

Another part incudes how to manage and handle new technology. An improved method for capability development must be able to detect nuances, pick up on influences regarding technological development, and *assess the impact of new technology.* (G3) The motive is to initiate studies, experimentation, and, if possible, immediate implementation. An example of this is drones. Both in Nagorno-Karabakh and in Ukraine [26, 27], drones emerged to some extent as disruptive technologies. However, drones have been studied by many western countries for decades, and it should not have been a surprise that this technology can deliver significant effect on the battlefield. Nevertheless, the focus has been on studies rather than a large-scale acquisition and implementation, despite the availability of products to acquire.

The stakeholders also indicated that an improved method for capability development must have the ability to *coordinate and synchronize several development lines continuously and in parallel.* (G6) One example could be optical and electro-optical sights that are designed for main battle tanks (MTB) and combat vehicles (CV). It is now possible to integrate algorithms in those sights that supports identification and engagement of drones. However, the current plan for upgrading the MTB/CV was designed and financed five years ago, and at that time this function was not available. Another example is the plan to upgrade the current battle management system (BMS), where the financing and details often are agreed upon with the industry, years in advance.

Information systems (IS) is an area where the speed of development is especially challenging. Today there is operational, deep learning-supported, decision tools that would enhance the decision-cycle within several functions, e.g., situational awareness, intelligence, etc. [38, 39]. But the current acquisition-cycle, with long lead times, makes it nearly impossible to succeed. An improved method must establish teams or constellations that overcome those obstacles. Another improvement regarding methods would be to *involve the operational and tactical aspects and requirements early in the process,* (G8 and G9) briefly mentioned in Theme 2. This could enable an approach that underscores the question - *how can this new technology make it possible to solve the tactical task in a different way?* Instead of trying to solve the task in the same way as before, but better.

---

[9] NATO warfighting functions - Command and Control, Movement and Maneuver, Intelligence, Fires, Sustainment, Protection.

Another activity that would speed up the development tempo, and ensure that relevant systems are designed, is to establish merged teams from universities, industry partners, research agencies, and the defense materiel procurement administration. If this was established, basic research in several areas could be decentralized. One participant suggested a comprehensive process where proposals that support capability enhancement can come from anyone. Anyone should be allowed to submit those proposals if the capability development is likely to benefit.

Several participants argued for de-centralization to reduce the gap and not to have too many separate decision-makers before making final decisions at a higher level.

One participant argued that capability development should be described as a circular process, *where multiple development lines and development principles operate simultaneously.* There is no defined start and no clear end, only version management of individual parts or whole SoSs. A clear example of this can be when the entire BMS is replaced at the same time, or over a short period. The development lines are mentioned earlier, and involve the parallel development of multiple technical systems, while the organization and method are also being developed. Development strategies can be iterative or incremental model, or continuous, because at the same time, these lines must be able to *handle disruptive development* (G7) and do so quickly. To utilize new technologies as efficiently as possible, a *structured implementation* (G7) is required, even if it must be done quickly. It is important to be able to *handle the integration* (G4) of legacy and new technical systems and methods, and to realize this, some form of enhanced *controller function* (G4) is needed. This function should not control capability development except when it comes to the integration of technology, methods, and organization. Here, the *potential impact must be evaluated* (G2), as well as how the disruptive technology affects tactics, organization, and training. A feedback loop is also needed to improve and develop the artifact itself, and this must occur after each iteration. (G11).

Often, designers let the technical possibilities dictate the requirements, without analyzing the context regarding their physical or organizational environment. This can lead to IS being perceived as poorly designed. An example is when IS are integrated into combat vehicles and are equipped with a mouse and scroll keys. These are extremely difficult to use when the vehicle is in motion due to vibrations and shaking.

The *focus on the whole system* of systems, and ambition to *identify and explore synergies cross domain* (G10), results in two conclusions that will have implications of the capability strategy. The first is that regardless of strategy, when focusing on a system of systems, a major part of developing technical systems will be about IP-based systems. Every sensor, effector, or BMS depend on IP-standards. The second conclusion is that designing a SoS must *focus on integration* (G4) from the very beginning of the design process. Otherwise, large investments of time and money are needed in getting technology, method, and organization to harmonize and work together. Both conclusions indicate that designers of military systems of systems must adopt and learn from adjacent IS-developments strategies.

From this analysis, the goals of the artefact have been summarized in Table 2.

Table 2. Artefact goals

Goal	Description
G1	Be able to be levering from a high system level to a lower, i.e., adopting a holistic approach where all part of a system in a SoS are analyzed. (Methods, technology, doctrine, etc.)
G2	Be able to evaluate holistic, i.e., a multi-dimensional evaluation method/model within the artefact that assesses not just technology, but also processes, organizational, human factors, and interoperability. This method/model must use specific criteria for each dimension and provide an aggregate score for the overall SoS
G3	Stakeholders must be able to use the artefact to simulate the impact of new technology. For commanders, with purpose to estimate mission outcomes, and for designer and researchers to identify interoperability requirements for new and existing systems
G4	Be able to integrate earlier version and interact with higher and lower level. (Method, technical systems, organizations, etc.) Note that this function (controller function) should not control capability development except when it comes to the integration of technology, methods, and organization
G5	Be able to analyze capability relationships, i.e., integrate a capability dependency tool in the artefact that underlines the interdependencies between technology, processes, and organizational elements in the SoS, highlighting areas of strength and potential vulnerabilities
G6	Be able to handle both incremental, and disruptive development, consequently, the artefact must be able to work continuous in two different time cycles. In this function, the artefact must also identify and describe a successful incremental and disruptive integration/strategy, e.g., integration of a new subsystem within (time), or ability to adapt to a new warfare technology within (time)
G7	Be able to integrate disruptive technology structurally, i.e., establish a method/model within the artefact for integrating disruptive technologies. This method/model must describe assessment criteria, such as the technology maturity level, potential impact on current C2 SoS capability, and suggest changes to processes and organization
G8	Be able to handle un-specified capability requirements and be functional even if the context is open and not specified in detail, to enable *free thought* and herby identify new approaches to a military problem
G9	Be able to perform a comprehensive risk/opportunity assessment, i.e., establish a method/model within the artefact for conducting comprehensive risk and opportunity assessments that account for new technology integration and process– and organizational changes
G10	Be able to evaluates the synergies between different domains within a SoS (air, land, sea, cyber), i.e., establish a method/model within the artefact that could measure how changes in one domain has effect on other domains. This function should also suggest recommendations to enhance cross-domain effects
G11	Be able to provide continually feedback and improvements, i.e., establish a method/model within the artefact that after a simulation cycle, debrief and evaluate the execution, and that this feeds into the next iteration of the development of the artefact

6 Conclusions and Future Work

This study applied a design science research approach on the design of military command and control systems in a context of rapidly growing societal and technological complexity. The findings have produced an enhanced view of problems, experienced by stakeholders in the domain. Why these problems are important to address has also been analyzed. This will make it easier to describe the requirements of the artefact, a conceptual framework for designing C2-systems as SoS, and as a result, contribute to understanding the integration of new technology in military systems.

The results of the interviews went beyond just explicating the problem. All stakeholders had a clear view of how the envisioned framework, consisting of methods or models, should work to be able to handle technological development. These stakeholder needs elicited and analyzed in this study and presented as a set of artefact goals (Table 2). The goals as well as the themes and their supporting empirical sources will serve as input for the next step in the DSR process, namely, the definition of requirements, as suggested in [35]. The goal of that step will be to identify and describe an artefact that meets the artefact goals identified here. Particularly, understanding how technology affects the overall performance. Your authors will concentrate on this topic in order to deepen the understanding of how enhancing the ability to understand and evaluate new technology, particularly within a military setting, can reveal more, yet unknown, advantages than previously acknowledged.

References

1. Brose, C.: The Kill Chain: Defending America in the Future of High-Tech Warfare. Hachette Books, New York (2020)
2. Andersson, K., Lundberg, J., Stirna, J.: Emerging technology calls for a systemic view on military capability. In: Poels, G., Van Riel, J., Fernandes Calhau, R. (eds.) CEUR-WS.org, Vienna (2023)
3. NATO, NATO ARCHITECTURE FRAMEWORK Version 4 Acknowledgments for NAFv4 Publication (2020)
4. Andersson, K., Lundberg, J., Stirna, J.: Emerging technology calls for a systemic view on military capability (2023)
5. Pasmore, B.: Leading Continuous Change: Navigating Churn in the Real World, 1st edn. Berrett-Koehler Publishers, Oakland (2015)
6. Lundberg, J.: Towards a conceptual framework for system of systems. In: CEUR Workshop Proceedings (2023)
7. Avison, D.: Information Systems Development, 4th edn. McGraw-Hill Education, New York (2006)
8. Department of the Army, 'FM 3–0 Operations' (2022)
9. Cirincione, G.H., Verma, D.: Federated machine learning for multi-domain operations at the tactical edge. In: Pham, T. (ed.) Artificial Intelligence and Machine Learning for Multi-Domain Operations Applications, SPIE, p. 73 (2019). https://doi.org/10.1117/12.2526661
10. Pfaff, C.A., Lowrance, C.J., Washburn, B.M., Carey, B.A.: Trusting AI: Integrating Artificial Intelligence into the Army's Professional Expert Knowledge. US Army War College Press (2023). https://press.armywarcollege.edu/cgi/viewcontent.cgi?article=1955&context=monographs. Accessed 07 Sep 2023
11. Greene, T.: Ukraine has become the world's testing ground for military robots. https://thenextweb.com/news/ukraine-has-become-worlds-testing-ground-for-military-robots. Accessed 10 Oct 2023
12. NATO Science & Technology Organization, 'Science & Technology Trends 2023–2043 - Across the Physical, Biological, and Information Domains VOLUME 1: Overview (2023)
13. Svenmarck, P., Luotsinen, L., Nilsson, M., Schubert, J.: Possibilities and challenges for artificial intelligence in military applications (2018)

14. Suojanen, M., Kuikka, V., Nikkarila, J.P., Nurmi, J.: An example of scenario-based evaluation of military capability areas: an impact assessment of alternative systems on operations. In: 9th Annual IEEE International Systems Conference, SysCon 2015 - Proceedings, pp. 601–607 (2015). https://doi.org/10.1109/SYSCON.2015.7116817

15. Urwin, E.N., et al.: Scenario-based design and evaluation for capability. In: 2010 5th International Conference on System of Systems Engineering, SoSE 2010 (2010). https://doi.org/10.1109/SYSOSE.2010.5544073

16. Biltgen, P.T., Mavris, D.N.: Capability-based quantitative technology evaluation for systems-of-systems. In: 2007 IEEE International Conference on System of Systems Engineering, SOSE (2007). https://doi.org/10.1109/SYSOSE.2007.4304300

17. Giegerich, B., et al.: Military capabilities in Europe: a framework for assessing the qualitative dimension. The International Institute for Strategic Studies (2022)

18. Liwång, H., Andersson, K.E., Bang, M., Malmio, I., Tärnholm, T.: How can systemic perspectives on defence capability development be strengthened? Def. Stud. 23(3), 399–420 (2023). https://doi.org/10.1080/14702436.2023.2239722

19. Sandkuhl, K., Stirna, J.: Capability Management in Digital Enterprises. Springer, Cham (2018)

20. Moran, S.: System of systems development for the DoD - tailoring acquisition reform for emerging needs (2008)

21. Keating, C., et al.: System of systems engineering. EMJ – Eng. Manag. J. 15(3), 36–45 (2003). https://doi.org/10.1080/10429247.2003.11415214

22. Baxter, G., Sommerville, I.: Socio-technical systems: from design methods to systems engineering. Interact. Comput. 23(1), 4–17 (2011). https://doi.org/10.1016/j.intcom.2010.07.003

23. Brehmer, B.: Command and control as design (2010). http://www.dodccrp.org/events/15th_iccrts_2010/papers/182.pdf. Accessed 13 Aug 2023

24. Johnson, J.: Artificial intelligence & future warfare: implications for international security. Def. Secur. Anal. 35(2), 147–169 (2019). https://doi.org/10.1080/14751798.2019.1600800

25. Joshi, S.: The war in Ukraine shows how technology is changing the battlefield. https://www.economist.com/, https://www.economist.com/special-report/2023/07/03/the-war-in-ukraine-shows-how-technology-is-changing-the-battlefield. Accessed 26 Nov 2023

26. Wilmot, M.: AI on the Battlefield: Lessons from Ukraine. Wavell Room. https://wavellroom.com/2023/09/07/ai-on-the-battlefield-lessons-from-ukraine/. Accessed 26 Nov 2023

27. Kunertova, D.: Drones have boots: learning from Russia's war in Ukraine. Contemp Secur Policy 44(4), 576–591 (2023). https://doi.org/10.1080/13523260.2023.2262792

28. Lange, D.S., Verbancsics, P., Gutzwiller, R.S., Reeder, J., Sarles, C.: Command and control of teams of autonomous systems. In: Calinescu, R., Garlan, D. (eds.) Large-Scale Complex IT Systems. Development, Operation and Management. Monterey Workshop 2012. Lecture Notes in Computer Science, vol. 7539, pp. 81–93. Springer, Berlin (2012). https://doi.org/10.1007/978-3-642-34059-8_4

29. Hevner, M.: Park, and ram, 'design science in information systems research.' MIS Q. 28(1), 75 (2004). https://doi.org/10.2307/25148625

30. Peffers, K., Tuunanen, T., Rothenberger, M.A., Chatterjee, S.: A design science research methodology for information systems research. J. Manag. Inf. Syst. 24(3), 45–77 (2007). https://doi.org/10.2753/MIS0742-1222240302

31. Sommerville, I., et al.: Software Engeneering, 9th edn. Addison-Wesley, Boston (2011)

32. Braun, V., Clarke, V.: Using thematic analysis in psychology. Qual. Res. Psychol. 3(2), 77–101 (2006). https://doi.org/10.1191/1478088706qp063oa

33. Denscombe, M.: The Good Research Guide - for Small-Scale Social Research Projects, 4th edn. Open University Press, Maidenhead (2010)

34. Edwards, R., Holland, J.: What is Qualitative Interviewing? What is Qualitative Interviewing? (2013). https://doi.org/10.5040/9781472545244

35. Johannesson, P., Perjons, E.: An Introduction to Design Science (2014). https://doi.org/10. 1007/978-3-319-10632-8

36. Cohen, L., Manion, L., Morrison, K.: Research Methods in Education, vol. 8 (2018)

37. Lundberg, J., Stirna, J., Andersson, K.: Operationalizing military insights: a report on C2 System development, Stockholm (2024). https://www.researchgate.net/publication/379084 821_Operationalizing_military_insights_A_report_on_C2_System_development

38. Abu Zitar, R., Al-Betar, M., Ryalat, M., Kassaymeh, S.: A review of UAV visual detection and tracking methods (2022). https://hal.science/hal-04108638. Accessed 07 Dec 2023

39. Swett, B.A., Hahn, E.N., Llorens, A.J.: Designing robots for the battlefield: state of the art. Robot., AI, Human.: Sci., Ethics Policy., 131–146 (2021). https://doi.org/10.1007/978-3-030-54173-6_11/FIGURES/7

Improving Requirement Traceability by Leveraging Video Game Simulations in Search-Based Software Engineering

Javier Verón[1]([✉]), Raúl Lapeña[1], Carlos Cetina[1], Óscar Pastor[2], and Francisca Pérez[1]

[1] SVIT Research Group, Universidad San Jorge, Zaragoza, Spain
{jveron,rlapena,ccetina,mfperez}@usj.es
[2] PROS Research Center, Universidad Politecnica de Valencia, Valencia, Spain
opastor@dsic.upv.es

Abstract. Video games pose different challenges during development and maintenance than classic software. For example, common and widespread assets, that are typically created as part of video game development are Non-Player Characters (NPCs). NPCs contribute to different aspects such as storytelling and user experience, and they are typically controlled by the CPU. We theorize that a reproduction of the actions of NPCs within the game (i.e., simulations) holds key information for Game Software Engineering (GSE) tasks such as Traceability Link Recovery (TLR). This paper presents our approach for supporting TLR in GSE by leveraging video game simulations. Simulation data from NPCs is used to reduce the search space. Since the reduced search space might still be too large for manual inspection, an evolutionary TLR procedure evolves a population of code fragments. As a result, a ranking of code fragments that map the requirement to the code is obtained. We evaluate our approach in Kromaia, a commercial video game released on PC and PlayStation 4. We compare our approach against a baseline that does not incorporate simulations by means of a statistical analysis. Our approach reduces the search space by 99.21% on average, and significantly outperforms the baseline with large differences in all performance indicators. A focus group with professional developers has confirmed the acceptance of our approach. Our work provides a new direction in TLR, which is an essential task in not only GSE but also in classic software engineering.

Keywords: Traceability Links Recovery · Video Games · Search-Based Software Engineering · Topic Modeling

1 Introduction

Video games are complex products where art and software are combined during the development process to conform the final product. Due to their nature

Partially supported by MINECO under the Project VARIATIVA (PID2021-128695OB-I00), by Gobierno de Aragón (Research Group S05_20D), and by Centro para el Desarrollo Tecnológico y la Innovación (CDTI) (Reference: SAV-20221011).

and the software artifacts that compose them, video games present challenges that differ from those of classic software, leading to important differences between Game Software Engineering and Classic Software Engineering [1,10]. Our hypothesis is that it is possible to leverage the particularities and specific domain assets of video games to provide semi-automated support and solutions for Game Software Engineering tasks.

To that extent, we have set our sight on one of the most common and widespread assets of video games: non-player characters (NPCs). NPCs are non-playable entities and elements (typically controlled by the CPU) that are created as part of the video game development process. Some examples of NPCs in video games are: the generals of the enemy troops in a Real-Time Strategy (RTS), or the rival drivers in a racing game.

It is important to note that NPCs are not created with the intention of performing Game Software Engineering (GSE) tasks on the game. Nonetheless, NPCs often have pre-programmed behaviors to allow for CPU control. We theorize that it is possible to observe NPC behaviors within the game (i.e., simulations) to reproduce and even generate knowledge that enables automated support and solutions for GSE tasks (e.g., testing the implementation of a specific requirement, or the solution to a known bug in the game). Specifically, we put the focus on Traceability Link Recovery (TLR). TLR is a software engineering task that deals with automated identification and comprehension of dependencies and relationships between software artifacts [20]. Establishing and maintaining traceability links has proven to be a time-consuming, error-prone, and labor-intensive task [20].

In this paper, we propose a novel approach that leverages the information provided by NPC simulations to provide semi-automated support for TLR between the main artifacts of GSE: the requirements and the code of a video game. To do this, the NPC's scenarios are reproduced to obtain simulation data, which is then used to reduce the search space to a subset of code that represents the scenario (and in turn contains the requirement). Since the reduced search space might still be too large for manual inspection, an evolutionary TLR procedure along with the requirement evolves a population of code fragments. The output is a ranking of code fragments that serve as candidate solutions towards the mapping of the requirement to the code.

We evaluate the performance of our approach considering an industrial case study, which belongs to a commercial video game, Kromaia. Kromaia is a video game about flying and shooting with a spaceship in a three-dimensional space. It was released on PC, PlayStation and has been translated to eight different languages. In addition, we compare our results with those of a baseline that does not incorporate simulations within the TLR process by means of a statistical analysis and an effect size measure. Finally, we carried out a focus group interview with the aim of acquiring qualitative data and feedback about the obtained results. Hence, the contributions of this paper are threefold:

- We investigate the use of NPC simulations within the TLR process in an industrial case study. To the best of our knowledge, this is the first effort in the literature. This is relevant because TLR is an essential software maintenance and evolution task [4].

- We experimentally demonstrate that NPC simulations reduced the search space (by 99.21% on average). This enables our approach to significantly outperform the traceability results of the baseline with large differences in all performance indicators (by 23.23% in recall, 18.34% in precision, and 22.87% in F-measure).
- We provide evidence that software engineers prefer the results of our approach using simulations over the results of the baseline even though they have not used simulations for TLR before. In fact, software engineers valued very positively both the use and the usefulness of simulations to find requirements in other video game genres and more complex problems (e.g., fighting games).

In the remainder of the paper, Sect. 2 presents the background for our work. Section 3 presents our approach, and Sect. 4 describes the evaluation. Section 5 presents the results, and Sect. 6 discusses the outcomes of our work. Section 7 presents the threats to the validity. Section 8 reviews the related work. Finally, Sect. 9 concludes the paper.

2   Background

The case study we use to evaluate TLR with NPCs is the commercial video game Kromaia. Kromaia is a commercial video game programmed in C++, where the human player (i.e., the user) moves a spaceship in a three-dimensional space and fights different enemy elements through a collection of levels. In each level, the player must make the spaceship fly from an initial point to a destination point multiple times without being destroyed. The spaces where this action is carried out include: a scene or architecture with asteroids to avoid while flying, different improvements for the player's spaceship, and NPCs acting as enemies of the player (which will try to destroy the player's spaceship and have to be fought with projectiles that the player's spaceship can fire).

Video games can be defined as a series of requirements that define the multiple mechanics, dynamics, and situations in the gameplay. An example of a requirement of this nature in Kromaia is "When the human unit is damaged its armor level decreases and the interface shows the information". Developers often need to trace these requirements to fix errors or change some behaviors.

Kromaia, like most video games, has a significant amount of source code: a total of 145915 lines. Traceability between requirements and lines of code in a case like Kromaia would require approximately one hour per requirement. A game like Kromaia usually needs to trace five or more requirements every day. Thus, tracing the regular number of requirements in a regular working week would take 25 h of work, which is impossible for a small studio to bear.

3   Our Approach

Figure 1 shows an overview of our approach. Our approach starts from a require-ment that needs to be traced to the code of the game. Software engineers build a scenario for simulation that contains the requirement and use NPCs to repro-duce the scenario. The simulation gathers data, registering the code that was executed to fulfill the scenario. The simulation data is used to filter the entirety of the code of the game, thus reducing the search space to a subset of code that represents the simulated scenario, which in turn contains the requirement. For the requirement "When the human unit is damaged its armor level decreases and the interface shows the information", a scenario must be built with a single NPC that damages the human unit. This action decreases the armor level and triggers the logic to display the change in the armor level information on the graphical user interface. The logic meeting this requirement is executed and reg-istered. Thus, this registered code constitutes the reduced search space instead of the entire source code.

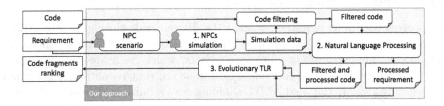

Fig. 1. Approach overview

Since the code search space for the scenario can still be too large for manual inspection, the filtered code is then processed via Natural Language Processing (NLP) techniques. Afterwards, the filtered and processed code is fed into an evo-lutionary TLR procedure along with the requirement, which is also processed via NLP techniques. The evolutionary TLR procedure generates, evaluates, and evolves a population of code fragments, converging into a ranking of code frag-ments that constitutes the final output of the approach. Each code fragment serves as a candidate solution towards the traceability of the requirement.

The ranking of code fragments is sorted according to the parameters of the TLR fitness function, which is used within the evolutionary TLR procedure. Video game software engineers can use the ranking as a starting point to deter-mine and document the traceability, validating or enhancing the top solutions according to their knowledge of the video game.

3.1   NPC-Based Simulations

Non-player characters (NPCs) are video game entities that simulate human play-ers when performing specific actions in the game through various artificial intel-ligence algorithms created by the developers. NPCs are developed and included in a game and accompany the player during the game, antagonize the player, or simply populate the world recreated in the video game.

Nonetheless, NPCs and their simulation capabilities are embedded within the architecture of the game. Our rationale is that leveraging NPC-based simulations can support software engineering tasks in the game. Specifically, we aim to reproduce particular requirements with these simulations and capture the code executed to fulfill these requirements. This approach intends to identify code fragments associated with each requirement, thus reducing the search space.

To achieve this, the developers of the game set a scenario within the game, using its architecture and NPCs. The NPCs perform the actions defined in each requirement, substituting the human player when necessary. We register the executed code, creating filtered code documents for the requirements that must be traced. The filtered code documents are used as the search space for an evolutionary algorithm that performs the traceability procedure on the requirements.

3.2   Natural Language Processing

We process the input requirements and the filtered code through Natural Language Processing (NLP) techniques. This processing step serves as a means of unifying the language of the software artifacts, which facilitates the TLR process. The techniques in use are syntactical analysis, root reduction, and human NLP. Figure 2 shows the used NLP techniques on a requirement in our approach.

1 **Syntactical Analysis:** SA techniques analyze the specific roles of each word in a sentence, determining their grammatical function. These techniques filter words that fulfill specific grammatical roles in a requirement, discarding those that do not have semantic value (such as articles or adverbs).

2 **Root Reduction:** The technique known as lemmatizing reduces words to their semantic roots (lemmas), thus avoiding verb tenses, noun plurals, and several other word forms that can negatively interfere with the TLR process.

3 **Human NLP:** Human NLP is often carried out through domain term extraction or stopword removal. Our approach searches the requirements for domain terms provided by software engineers and adds the domain terms found to the processed artifact. On the other hand, stopwords are filtered out after root reduction, using a list of stopwords that is also provided by the software engineers.

3.3   Evolutionary TLR

Figure 3 shows an overview of the Evolutionary Algorithm that generates, evaluates, and evolves a population of code fragments, converging into a ranking of potential solutions towards the input requirement. The algorithm takes both the filtered and processed code, and the processed requirement as input, and iterates over a population of code fragments, modifying them using genetic operations

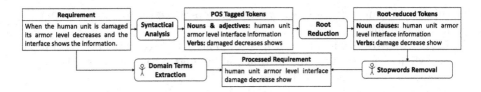

Fig. 2. Natural Language Processing Techniques

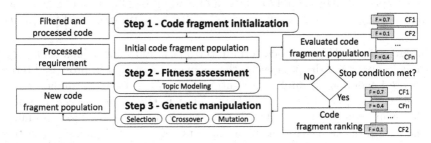

Fig. 3. Evolutionary algorithm

until a final ranking is produced as output. More precisely, the algorithm runs in three steps:

1. **Initialization:** The algorithm generates a population of code fragments that serves as input for the algorithm. To generate the population, parts of the code documents are extracted randomly and then added to a collection of code fragments, which are linked to the code documents they belong to.
2. **Fitness function:** This step assesses each of the candidate code fragments produced, ranking them according to a fitness function. Our approach uses Topic Modeling as fitness function because it obtained the best results when performing Feature Location, a similar Information Retrieval task to the one at hand [22].
   To do this, we utilize Latent Dirichlet Allocation (LDA) [7] since it is one of the most popular topic modeling methods [17]. LDA is an unsupervised probabilistic technique for estimating a topic distribution over a text corpus made up of a set of documents, where each document is a set of terms. As a result, a probability distribution is obtained for each document, indicating the likelihood that it expresses each topic. In addition, a probability distribution is obtained for each topic identified by LDA, indicating the likelihood of a term from the corpus being assigned to the topic.
   LDA inputs include: the documents (D), the number of topics (K), and a set of hyper-parameters. The hyper-parameters of any LDA implementation are: k, which is the number of topics that should be extracted from the data; α, which influences the topic distributions per document. A lower α value results in fewer topics per document; and β, which affects the distribution of terms per topic. A lower β value results in fewer terms per topic, which in

turn implies an increase in the number of topics needed to describe a particular document.

LDA outputs include: ϕ, which is the matrix that contains the term-topic probability distribution; and θ, which is the matrix that contains the topic-document probability distribution.

To assess the relevance of each code fragment with regard to the provided requirement (i.e., query), we use LDA. Given the terms for the query Q and the outputs of LDA (ϕ and θ), the conditional probability P of Q given a document D_i is computed as follows [5]: $Sim(Q, D_i) = P(Q|D_i) = \prod_{q_k \in Q} P(q_k|D_i)$ where q_k is the kth processed term in the query, and D_i is a document (i.e., a code fragment) of the population that is made up of a set of processed terms. Figure 4 shows an example of the fitness assessment for each candidate code fragment (i.e., individual) from the population. Given the processed terms of the requirement (query) and each code fragment (represented as a column in the matrix of the figure), the figure depicts how a value is assigned per term in each code fragment of the population (values in the cells of the matrix) by using the LDA outputs (the ϕ and θ matrices). For example, the conditional probability for the processed term *human* given the code fragment CF_n, that is, $P(human|CF_n) = 0.39$ (as can be seen in the shaded cell in the matrix of Fig. 4). Using the values of the matrix, the fitness value is obtained for each code fragment as shown in the vector of Fig. 4. The highest fitness value in the vector of the figure is 0.41, which belongs to CF_2.

3. **Genetic manipulation:** Finally, if the solution does not converge, this step generates a new population of code fragments through genetic manipulation. The generation of new code fragments, based on existing ones, is done by applying a set of three genetic operations (selection, crossover, and mutation), which are taken from the literature [6]:

The **selection operation** picks candidates from the population as input for the rest of the operations. Candidates with high fitness values have higher probabilities of being chosen as parents for the next generation. The **crossover operation** enables the creation of a new individual by combining genetic material from two parent code fragments. The **mutation operation** imitates mutations that randomly occur in nature when new individuals are born, by adding or removing code lines from the fragment.

Step 2 (fitness assessment) and Step 3 (genetic manipulation) are repeated until the solution converges to a certain stop condition (e.g., number of iterations). When this occurs, the evolutionary algorithm provides a code fragment ranking, ordered according to the values determined by the fitness function.

Similarly to other works that retrieve text from an initial query using LDA or other information retrieval techniques, the results depend on the quality of the queries [5], which is typically improved through an iterative refinement process [16]. Therefore, even when irrelevant code fragments are obtained in the ranking, the results can be considered as a starting point for the iterative refine-

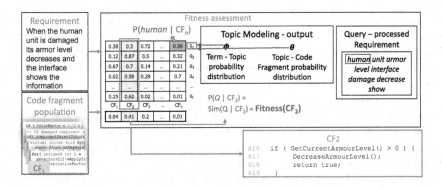

Fig. 4. Example of the fitness assessment of code fragments

ment process. From there, software engineers can either manually modify the proposed ones or modify the requirement to automatically obtain different code fragments for the solution.

4 Evaluation

4.1 Research Questions

From our work, several research questions arise:

RQ₁ *Does the inclusion of simulations influence the traceability search space in Game Software Engineering?*

RQ₂ *What is the performance in terms of solution quality of the traceability results in Game Software Engineering for our approach using simulations and a state-of-the-art technique?*

RQ₃ *Are the differences in performance between our approach using simulations and the baseline significant?*

RQ₄ *How much do the simulations influence the quality of the solution compared to the baseline?*

4.2 Experimental Setup

The inputs to build the test cases are the requirements and the code. These test cases are then employed to perform TLR in both our approach and the baseline. The baseline is similar to our approach and it also uses topic modeling as a fitness function (as described in Sect. 3.3), but, unlike our approach, it does not integrate simulations into the TLR process and it does not reduce the search space. Finally, a measurements report is obtained after comparing the approved traceability that is provided as input (used as oracle) with the results of the baseline and our approach.

The case study that we used in the evaluation is Kromaia, a commercial video game which code has been provided by our industrial partner, Kraken Empire[1]. Kromaia is made up of 145915 lines of code. In total, 18 requirements with their corresponding oracles and simulation scenarios were provided by the company. The provided requirements were selected and provided by the developers, who considered those requirements as being a representative collection in terms of maintenance. The approved traceability for each requirement (i.e., oracle) is the set of code lines (i.e., code fragment) that correspond to the full coverage for a requirement in the traceability search space. The code fragment that corresponds to each requirement has between 1 and 43 code lines.

As a result of comparing the approved traceability with the results of the baseline and our approach, a measurements report is obtained to answer each research question as follows.

Answering RQ$_1$: To determine whether the inclusion of simulations influences the traceability search space in GSE, the evaluation starts by taking the inputs of the case study (requirements, code, and simulation scenarios and approved traceability) to obtain the set of methods that are called during the simulations scenarios for each test case. This set of methods will conform the traceability search space for each test case. Afterwards, it is possible to assess whether the size of the traceability search space has been reduced, and if so, by how much.

In addition, the traceability search space is compared to the approved traceability to determine whether the traceability search space limits the quality of the solution by excluding code lines that are in the approved traceability.

Answering RQ$_2$: To determine the performance in terms of solution quality for each test case in our approach and the baseline, we compare the code fragment that achieves the highest fitness score in our approach and in the baseline against its respective oracle (i.e., ground truth) to calculate a confusion matrix.

A confusion matrix is a table that is often used to describe the performance of a classification model, comparing a set of test data (the solutions provided by the approach) against a set of known true values (the solutions from the oracle). In our case, the solutions obtained by the approach are code fragments, which are composed of a subset of code lines that are part of the original code. Since the granularity is at the level of code lines, the presence or absence of each code line is considered as a classification. The confusion matrix distinguishes between the predicted values (i.e., solution of the approach) and the real values (i.e., solution of the oracle), classifying them into four categories: (1) True Positive (TP), values that are predicted as true and are true in the real scenario; (2) False Positive (FP), values that are predicted as true but are false in the real scenario; (3) True Negative (TN), values that are predicted as false and are false in the real scenario; and (4) False Negative (FN), values that are predicted as false but are true in the real scenario.

From the values in the confusion matrix, it is possible to derive a series of performance measurements. Specifically, we report three performance measure-

---

[1] https://www.krakenempire.com/.

ments that are widely accepted by the software engineering community [25]: recall, precision, and F-measure. Recall ($\frac{TP}{TP+FN}$) measures the number of elements of the solution that are correctly retrieved by the proposed solution (how many code lines from the oracle are present in the retrieved code fragment). Precision ($\frac{TP}{TP+FP}$) measures the number of elements from the solution that are correct according to the ground truth, i.e., the oracle (how many code lines from the retrieved fragment appear in the oracle). Finally, F-measure ($2 * \frac{Precision*Recall}{Precision+Recall}$) corresponds to the harmonic mean of precision and recall.

For each requirement in both the baseline and the approach, we executed 30 independent runs (as suggested by Arcuri and Fraser [3]): 18 (requirements) × 2 (baseline and approach) × 30 repetitions, for a total of 1080 independent runs.

Answering RQ₃: To determine whether the differences in performance between our approach and the baseline are significant, the results must be properly compared and analyzed using statistical methods. With the aim of providing formal evidence that the differences do in fact have an impact on the performance measurements, we follow the guidelines presented in [2]. The statistical test that must be followed depends on the properties of the data, and it is accepted by the research community that a *p-value* under 0.05 implies statistical significance [2]. For each performance measure a *p-value* is recorded.

Answering RQ₄: To determine how much the performance is influenced by using our approach compared to the baseline, it is important to assess whether our approach is statistically better than the baseline, and if so, to measure by how much. To do this, we use Cliff's delta [11], which is an ordinal statistic that describes the frequency with which an observation from one group is higher than an observation from another group compared to the reverse situation. It can be interpreted as the degree to which two distributions overlap, with values ranging from −1 to 1. For instance, when comparing distributions of the treatment and the control, a value of 0 means no difference between the two distributions, a value of −1 means that all of the samples in the distribution of the treatment are lower than all of the samples in the distribution of the control, and a value of 1 means the opposite. In addition, threshold values can be defined [24] for the interpretation of Cliff's delta effect size as *negligible* ($|d| < 0.147$), *small* ($|d| < 0.33$), *medium* ($|d| < 0.474$), and *large* ($|d| \geq 0.474$). A Cliff's delta value is recorded for each pair-wise comparison between our approach and the baseline for each performance measure.

4.3   Implementation Details

For the development of our approach and the baseline, we used Eclipse with Java. For the NLP operations used in both our approach and the baseline, we used the OpenNLP Toolkit [14].

Topic Modeling was implemented using the Collapsed Gibbs Sampling (CGS) for LDA because it requires less computational time [27], and it was previously used for locating features in source code [5].

Since the focus of this paper is not to tune the values to improve the performance of our approach when applied to a specific problem, we used default values from the literature [6,13,22]. As suggested by Arcuri and Fraser [3], default values are sufficient to measure the performance of search-based software engineering algorithms.

For the evaluation, we used an Asus ROG Strix G15 G512LW-HN038 laptop with an Intel(R) Core(TM) i7-10750H processor, 16GB RAM, an NVIDIA® GeForce® RTX 2070 graphics card, and Windows 11 (64-bit). The oracle was provided directly by the developers of the video game.

The CSV files used as input in the statistical analysis as well as an open-source implementation of the approach are available here: https://github.com/VeronLinks/simulations-ss-tlr.

5   Results

5.1   Research Question 1

After obtaining the set of methods that are called during simulation scenarios for each test case, the traceability search space has been reduced from 145915 code lines to an average of 1157 code lines. Afterwards, the traceability search space is checked to determine whether any of the code lines that are included in the oracle have been omitted. If no code line has been omitted, the quality of the solution of our approach is not limited after reducing the search space.

RQ_1 **Answer:** The inclusion of simulations has been shown to significantly reduce the search space for TLR in GSE by 99.21% on average. We have found that the inclusion of simulations does not limit the quality of the solution.

5.2   Research Question 2

Table 1 shows the mean values and standard deviations of recall, precision, and F-measure for our approach and the baseline. As the values show, our approach outperforms the baseline in all performance measurements.

Table 1. Mean values and standard deviations for recall, precision, and the F-measure

	Recall ± (σ)	Precision ± (σ)	F-measure ± (σ)
Our work	65.58 ± 24.32	76.36 ± 14.90	67.65 ± 15.43
Baseline	42.35 ± 25.71	58.02 ± 8.35	44.78 ± 16.84

RQ_2 **Answer:** The results reveal that our approach outperforms the baseline in the three performance measurements. Hence, the inclusion of simulations improves the quality of the traceability results in GSE when using a state-of-the-art technique by 23.23% in recall, 18.34% in precision, and 22.87% in F-measure.

5.3   Research Question 3

The *p-values* obtained for our approach are 0.0037 for recall, 9.4×10^{-6} for precision, and 4.1×10^{-5} for F-measure.

RQ$_3$ Answer: Since the Quade test *p-values* are smaller than the 0.05 statistical significance threshold for all performance measurements, we can state that there are significant differences in performance between our approach and the baseline for TLR in GSE.

5.4   Research Question 4

With regard to how much the simulations influence the quality of the solution compared to the baseline, the obtained Cliff's Delta values of the three reported performance measurements are large, being 0.5 for recall, 0.7623 for precision, and 0.6512 for F-measure.

RQ$_4$ Answer: From the effect size analysis of the Cliff's Delta values that are obtained when our approach is compared to the baseline, we can conclude that there is a large influence on the quality of the solution for all performance measurements with our approach using simulations for TLR in GSE.

6   Discussion

Industrial video games feature many requirements involving multiple methods, but they also bring opportunities to TLR. Simulations, scarce in traditional software, are common in video games due to NPCs being created during the development. By analyzing the results, the noise that the simulations remove by reducing the search space helps the evolutionary TLR procedure to work significantly better than when using the complete code.

At least in the case study that was used in this work, there is no limitation in the quality of the solution (recall) when the reduced traceability search space is obtained. Nevertheless, our approach should be replicated with case studies from other domains before assuring the generalization of the results. Nevertheless, our results suggest that leveraging video game simulations for TLR is promising.

Our focus group, consisting of five software engineers in the field of GSE, included one with 15 years of video game development experience, two with six years, and two with two years of experience. This focus group dealt with the following open questions: (1) What do you think of the results of the approaches?; (2) How do you feel about locating requirements in video games using simulations?; (3) How do you imagine locating requirements using simulations in video games of other genres and in more complex video games?

The software engineers valued very positively the results of our approach using simulations, and stated that they preferred our approach using simulations because the results were far superior to the results of the baseline. Although none of the five engineers had thought of or used simulations for TLR before, they agreed on the relevance of simulations for TLR in video games. In their opinion, the idea of using simulations for TLR is promising, and they would use simulations for TLR in video games on a daily basis.

The engineers imagined using our approach in another of their video games since they could also use simulations of NPCs to find requirements that give them trouble. In addition, the engineers confirmed that our approach using simulations can be used for other video game genres and more complex problems.

7   Threats to Validity

In this section, we acknowledge the limitations of our approach using the classification of threats to validity proposed by Wohlin et al. [26]:

Conclusion Validity: To minimize this threat, we have based our work on research questions. In addition, the requirements and code used in our approach were taken from an existing commercial video game. None of the authors of this work were involved in the creation of the game or in the generation of the data, which was provided by the developers of the game.

Internal Validity: To minimize this threat, we have used the same NLP techniques on all of the software artifacts and followed the same evaluation process for all evaluated approaches. In addition, the available test cases represent a broad scope of different scenarios within the case study in an accurate manner.

Construct Validity: To minimize this threat, our evaluation was performed using three measurements that are widely accepted and utilized in the state-of-the-art literature: precision, recall, and F-measure. Moreover, we have used the same software artifacts for all of the approaches, representing the same scenarios, so that cause and effect are equally represented among them.

External Validity: This threat is concerned with generalization. All of the artifacts under study in our work (requirements and code) are frequently used in video games development. In addition, TLR is a common practice in all kinds of video game development scenarios and the real-world case study used in our research represents the industrial scene of video game developments well. Moreover, we defined our approach independently of the case study, and then applied it to the case study. Hence, our approach can potentially work in any video game scenario where requirements and code are available. Nevertheless, our results should be replicated with other case studies before ensuring their external validity.

8   Related Work

After reviewing a traceability survey that contains works from 1999 to 2011 [8], we used the same query presented in the survey, and we found 11 more works between 2012 and November 2023. For example, Dekhtyar et al. [12] assess the accuracy of provided Requirements Traceability Matrix (RTM) by means of an assessment committee composed of three to five different trace recovery methods, such as Probabilistic Information Retrieval (ProbIR). Parvathy et al. [21] propose automating the computation of traceability by looking at the correlation between documents. Gethers et al. [15] propose the Relational Topic Model for TLR and combine different orthogonal IR-based methods for improving recovery accuracy. These three approaches require additional information sources beyond source code, such as RTM, design documents, and domain models that support traceability. However, in the development of commercial video games, creating or synchronizing these artifacts is often neglected. Therefore, approaches like this work that focus on searching for solutions in terms of code fragments in the source code are necessary in this context. Lapeña et al. [18,19] leverage an already existing feature of the software artifacts to improve TLR using BPMN models and leveraging on execution traces. None of these works use simulations to reduce the search space.

We also performed a manual search and we only found three studies on locating artifacts in video games for GSE. Two of the three studies focus on bug location using simulations, but neither reduces the search space as we propose. Blasco et al. [6] focus on TLR for video games and use an evolutionary algorithm for obtaining a code fragment from the source code that realizes a requirement specified in a natural language. Casamayor et al. [9] use simulations in video games and leverage the existence of NPCs in video games to remove any additional cost for the developers, as we do, but they do not use these simulations to reduce the search space. Prasetya et al. [23] present an agent-based automated testing framework for locating bugs in video games.

The rationale behind using simulations is that video game bugs are not always related to code malfunction, making traditional testing and bug location inefficient. Video games bugs include other aspects related to design, such as balancing certain values. Testing and bug location in video games need to be reactive and able to interpret their environment to determine what actions to take. This rationale differs from the rationale behind using simulations in this work. We leverage these simulations for performing automated and precise executions of the program, and registering the executed code. Thus, the search space for TLR can be reduced with the goal of improving the quality of the results.

9   Conclusion

In this work, we have focused on GSE and TLR. GSE is a very novel field of work that deals with the challenge of developing and maintaining the software of video games, whereas TLR is a key support activity for the development, management, and maintenance of software. Video games not only bring challenges to TLR, but they also provide opportunities such as the information that can be extracted from the simulations of NPCs, which are created as part of the video game.

This information had not yet been exploited for either reducing the search space or for TLR. We have filled this gap, and we have shown that the search space can be reduced and that TLR can be significantly improved by leveraging video game simulations in a commercial video game. Specifically, compared to the baseline, the search space was reduced by 99.21% on average, and our approach improved the results with large differences (by 23.23% in recall, 18.34% in precision, and 22.87% in F-measure). A focus group has demonstrated that software engineers prefer the results of our approach using simulations over the results of the baseline. The software engineers have also highlighted the usefulness of simulations to find requirements in other video game genres and more complex problems (e.g., fighting games).

Our work opens a new direction in TLR, which is an essential task in both GSE and in classic software engineering. Other essential maintenance tasks such as bug location (our future work) can also benefit from the use of simulations.

References

1. Ampatzoglou, A., Stamelos, I.: Software engineering research for computer games: a systematic review. Inf. Softw. Technol. **52**(9), 888–901 (2010)
2. Arcuri, A., Briand, L.: A hitchhiker's guide to statistical tests for assessing randomized algorithms in software engineering. Softw. Test. Verif. Reliab. **24**(3), 219–250 (2014). https://doi.org/10.1002/stvr.1486
3. Arcuri, A., Fraser, G.: Parameter tuning or default values? An empirical investigation in search-based software engineering. Empir. Softw. Eng. **18**(3), 594–623 (2013). https://doi.org/10.1007/s10664-013-9249-9
4. Ballarín, M., Arcega, L., Pelechano, V., Cetina, C.: On the influence of architectural languages on requirements traceability. Softw. Pract. Exp. **53**(3), 704–728 (2023). https://doi.org/10.1002/spe.3166, https://onlinelibrary.wiley.com/doi/abs/10.1002/spe.3166
5. Biggers, L.R., Bocovich, C., Capshaw, R., Eddy, B.P., Etzkorn, L.H., Kraft, N.A.: Configuring latent Dirichlet allocation based feature location. Empir. Softw. Engg. **19**(3), 465–500 (2014)
6. Blasco, D., Cetina, C., Pastor, Ó.: A fine-grained requirement traceability evolutionary algorithm: Kromaia, a commercial video game case study. Inf. Softw. Technol. **119**, 106235 (2020)
7. Blei, D.M., Ng, A.Y., Jordan, M.I.: Latent Dirichlet allocation. J. Mach. Learn. Res. **3** (2003). https://doi.org/10.1162/jmlr.2003.3.4-5.993
8. Borg, M., Runeson, P., Ardö, A.: Recovering from a decade: a systematic mapping of information retrieval approaches to software traceability. Empir. Softw. Eng. **19**, 1565–1616 (2014)
9. Casamayor, R., Arcega, L., Pérez, F., Cetina, C.: Bug localization in game software engineering: evolving simulations to locate bugs in software models of video games. In: Proceedings of the 25th International Conference on Model Driven Engineering Languages and Systems, pp. 356–366 (2022)
10. Chueca, J., Verón, J., Font, J., Pérez, F., Cetina, C.: The consolidation of game software engineering: a systematic literature review of software engineering for industry-scale computer games. Inf. Softw. Technol. (2023)
11. Cliff, N.: Ordinal Methods for Behavioral Data Analysis. Lawrence Erlbaum Associates, Inc. (1996)
12. Dekhtyar, A., Hayes, J.H., Sundaram, S., Holbrook, A., Dekhtyar, O.: Technique integration for requirements assessment. In: 15th IEEE International Requirements Engineering Conference (RE 2007), pp. 141–150. IEEE (2007)

13. Font, J., Arcega, L., Haugen, Ø., Cetina, C.: Achieving feature location in families of models through the use of search-based software engineering. IEEE Trans. Evol. Comput. 1 (2017)
14. Foundation, T.A.S.: Apache OpenNLP: toolkit for the processing of natural language text (2020). https://opennlp.apache.org/
15. Gethers, M., Oliveto, R., Poshyvanyk, D., Lucia, A.D.: On integrating orthogonal information retrieval methods to improve traceability recovery. In: IEEE 27th International Conference on Software Maintenance, ICSM 2011, Williamsburg, VA, USA, 25–30 September 2011, pp. 133–142 (2011)
16. Hill, E., Pollock, L., Vijay-Shanker, K.: Automatically capturing source code context of NL-queries for software maintenance and reuse. In: Proceedings of the 31st International Conference on Software Engineering, ICSE 2009, pp. 232–242 (2009)
17. Jelodar, H., Wang, Y., Yuan, C., Feng, X.: Latent Dirichlet allocation (LDA) and topic modeling: models, applications, a survey. Multimed. Tools Appl. **78**, 15169–15211 (2019). https://doi.org/10.1007/s11042-018-6894-4
18. Lapeña, R., Pérez, F., Cetina, C., Pastor, Ó.: Leveraging BPMN particularities to improve traceability links recovery among requirements and BPMN models. Requirements Eng. 1–26 (2022)
19. Lapeña, R., Pérez, F., Pastor, Ó., Cetina, C.: Leveraging execution traces to enhance traceability links recovery in BPMN models. Inf. Softw. Technol. **146**, 106873 (2022)
20. Oliveto, R., Gethers, M., Poshyvanyk, D., De Lucia, A.: On the equivalence of information retrieval methods for automated traceability link recovery. In: IEEE 18th International Conference on Program Comprehension, pp. 68–71 (2010)
21. Parvathy, A.G., Vasudevan, B.G., Balakrishnan, R.: A comparative study of document correlation techniques for traceability analysis. In: International Conference on Enterprise Information Systems, vol. 3, pp. 64–69. SCITEPRESS (2008)
22. Pérez, F., Lapeña, R., Marcén, A.C., Cetina, C.: Topic modeling for feature location in software models: studying both code generation and interpreted models. Inf. Softw. Technol. **140**, 106676 (2021)
23. Prasetya, I., Pastor Ricós, F., Kifetew, F.M., Prandi, D., et al.: An agent-based approach to automated game testing: an experience report. In: Proceedings of the 13th International Workshop on Automating Test Case Design, Selection and Evaluation, pp. 1–8 (2022)
24. Romano, J., Kromrey, J.D., Coraggio, J., Skowronek, J.: Appropriate statistics for ordinal level data: should we really be using T-test and Cohen'sd for evaluating group differences on the NSSE and other surveys. In: Annual Meeting of the Florida Association of Institutional Research, pp. 1–33 (2006)
25. Salton, G., McGill, M.J.: Introduction to Modern Information Retrieval. McGraw-Hill Inc., New York (1986)
26. Wohlin, C., Runeson, P., Höst, M., Ohlsson, M.C., Regnell, B., Wesslén, A.: Experimentation in Software Engineering. Springer, Heidelberg (2012). https://doi.org/10.1007/978-3-642-29044-2
27. Xuan-Hieu Phan, C.T.N.: Jgibblda. a java implementation of latent Dirichlet allocation (LDA) using Gibbs sampling for parameter estimation and inference (2020)

Process and Decision Mining

From Loss of Interest to Denial: A Study on the Terminators of Process Mining Initiatives

Vinicius Stein Dani[1](✉), Henrik Leopold[2], Jan Martijn E. M. van der Werf[1], Iris Beerepoot[1], and Hajo A. Reijers[1]

[1] Utrecht University, Princetonplein 5, 3584 CC Utrecht, The Netherlands
{v.steindani,j.m.e.m.vanderwerf,i.m.beerepoot,h.a.reijers}@uu.nl
[2] Kühne Logistics University, Großer Grasbrook 17, 20457 Hamburg, Germany
henrik.leopold@the-klu.org

Abstract. Process mining has been used to obtain insights into work processes in various industries. While there is plenty of evidence that process mining has helped a number of organizations to improve their processes, there are also a few studies indicating that it did not happen in other cases. An obvious yet frequently overlooked challenge in that context is that organizations actually need to take action based on the insights process mining tools and techniques provide. In practice, analysts typically use process mining insights to recommend actions, which then need to be performed and implemented, for example, by process owners or management. If, however, recommended actions are not performed, the insights will not help organizations to progress into process improvement either. Recognizing this, we use this paper to develop a better understanding of the extent to which recommended actions are actually performed, as well as the causes hampering the progress from recommended to performed actions. To this end, we combine a systematic literature review involving 57 papers with 17 semi-structured interviews of process mining experts. Based on our analysis, we discover specific causes why organizations do not perform recommended actions. These findings are crucial for both researchers and organizations to develop measures to anticipate and mitigate these causes.

Keywords: Process mining · Insights to action · Process improvement · Obstacles

1 Introduction

Process mining is used to obtain insights into work processes in organizations. It has been successfully employed in various industries including manufacturing [7], finance [35], and healthcare [40]. Among others, process mining techniques support discovering, analyzing, and improving processes [1,46]. While there is plenty of evidence that process mining can effectively help organizations improve their

© The Author(s), under exclusive license to Springer Nature Switzerland AG 2024
G. Guizzardi et al. (Eds.): CAiSE 2024, LNCS 14663, pp. 371–386, 2024.
https://doi.org/10.1007/978-3-031-61057-8_22

processes [5,28], there are also a few studies indicating that it was not successful in other cases [38,55].

Taking a closer look at scholarly work on process mining endeavors, we observe that it is often concerned with proposing process mining techniques to obtain specific *insights*. Recent examples include the work from Lashkevich et al. [31], who propose an approach providing insights into the causes of wait times and their impact. Another example is the work by Bozorgi et al. [10], who propose a prescriptive monitoring method that decides which process instances are worth intervening to obtain a desired outcome. What these and many other techniques have in common is that they require humans to take *action*. In practice, analysts typically use the insights to *recommend* actions, which then need to be *performed*, for example, by process owners or management. If, however, recommended actions are not performed, the insights will also not help organizations to improve their processes.

Recognizing this, we argue that we need to develop a better understanding of the extent to which recommended actions are performed, as well as actually the causes hampering the progress from recommended to performed actions. While existing work has studied the relation between process mining insights and actions on a general level [53], the distinction between recommended and performed actions has not been made. As a result, there is also no understanding of when or why recommended actions are not being followed up by performed actions. In this work, we address this research gap by posing the following two research questions:

RQ1. To what extent are recommended actions also performed?
RQ2. What are the causes for certain recommended actions not resulting in performed actions?

To answer these research questions, we combine a systematic literature review and semi-structured interviews. We analyzed a total of 57 papers, as well as 17 transcripts from semi-structured interviews with process mining experts. In this way, we cross-validate and corroborate our findings, enhancing reliability and validity of our research. We identify five specific causes why organizations do not perform recommended actions. These findings are crucial for researchers and organizations to develop strategies to anticipate and mitigate these causes.

The remainder of this paper is organized as follows. Section 2 discusses the background and related work. Section 3 introduces our methodology and research method. Section 4 presents the identified causes hampering the progress of recommended to performed actions, while Sect. 5 discusses the high-level relation of the identified causes to process mining projects. Finally, Sect. 6 concludes the paper.

2   Background and Related Work

In this section, we introduce the background and related work of our research. We first provide a brief overview of process mining and process mining methodologies. We then highlight the research gap.

Process mining is a set of specialized data analysis techniques. It leverages so-called event logs to provide insights into the execution of work processes [1]. Among others, it allows organizations to automatically discover as-is processes and to detect violations against rules and regulations. To support the application of process mining in organization, different process mining methodologies have been proposed and adopted. Two widely known process mining methodologies are Process Diagnostics [9] and PM^2 [15]. Although these methodologies highlight the importance of progressing process mining insights into process improvement, they also acknowledge that this is an aspect they consider out of scope. That is, because they primarily focus on analytical techniques rather than the practical implementation of the acquired insights. According to Emamjome et al. [16], this lack of practical implementation of the acquired process mining insights has hindered process mining in delivering the promised outcomes, despite the growing adoption of process mining.

However, several studies also investigate the application of process mining and the associated challenges. In [38], the authors analyze reports of process mining case studies to identify critical success factors. In [66], the authors use semi-structured interviews to investigate the challenges regarding process mining analysis. They identified a set of over twenty challenges highlighting the need for enhanced support for acquiring process mining insights. Similarly, the authors in [55] used interviews with process mining experts to derive challenges organizations face when progressing process mining insights to process improvement. Finally, the authors in [53] have also analyzed which type of insights lead to what type of actions in the organizations. They introduce the notion of an *intervention space* to conceptualize what aspects of an organisation (e.g., the process itself or its underlying IT infrastructure) are affected by improvement actions.

What is currently still missing is an understanding of when and why certain actions triggered by process mining insights are only recommended but not performed. Insights into this phenomenon can serve as a basis for augmenting process mining methodologies. What is more, it can support organizations proactively mitigating issues that can potentially lead to the termination of their process mining initiatives.

3   Methodology and Research Methods

To answer our research questions, we conducted a systematic literature review and a series of semi-structured interviews with process mining experts to provide an integrated overview of literature and practice. Figure 1 presents an overview of our methodology composed by three main stages. First, we conducted a *data collection* (cf. Sect. 3.1) on two data sources: a systematic literature review and a series of semi-structured interviews. Second, we conducted a *data analysis* (cf., Sect. 3.2) on the data acquired from both the literature and the interviews. Third, we *synthesized* our findings (cf., Sect. 3.3) from both data sources into one to derive an integrated view of literature and practice.

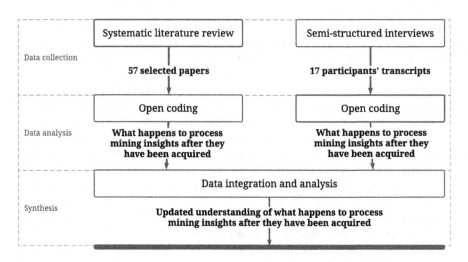

Fig. 1. Methodology overview

3.1 Data Collection

Our data collection consists of two steps. First, inspired by [29,43], we conducted a systematic literature review. Then, based on [8,11], we conducted a series of semi-structured interviews.

Systematic Literature Review. We conducted a systematic literature review by defining a review protocol that encompasses the research questions and the definition of the search string, search engines, and the papers selection criteria [29,43]. Then, we applied the search string to the search engines, followed by the paper selection by applying our selection criteria. These stages were collaboratively conducted by several authors, discussing and resolving disagreements altogether in order to mitigate threats to validity regarding reproducibility.

Because we wanted to obtain insights into the application of process mining, we were particularly interested in case studies. Hence, we defined our search string as "(process mining) AND ('case study' OR 'case studies') AND (application OR apply OR applied)". To decide on the search engines to be used, we investigated other systematic literature reviews in the process mining field [51,64] and adopted the following search engines: ACM Digital Library, IEEE Xplore, Science Direct, Scopus, and Web of Science. We defined the following selection criteria: i) the paper is about the use of process mining in a case study; ii) the paper mentions what happens to process mining insights; iii) the paper is either from accounting, business, computer or decision or social sciences, healthcare, or management; iv) the paper is published either in conference proceedings or a journal; v) the paper is written in English. The final set of selected papers amounts to 57 peer-reviewed papers, which together provide an overview of the extent to which recommended actions are also performed from the literature perspective.

Semi-structured Interviews. We conducted a series of semi-structured interviews with process mining experts as our target population and defined the interview protocol based on [8,11]. We invited participants via email, reinforcing the invitation via LinkedIn. In total, 17 experts averaging seven years of experience in process mining were interviewed. The interviewed experts included process mining specialists, business analysts, managers, transformation consultants, and product owners. Over 64% of the participants pursued their PhDs in the process mining field, on top of their years in industry. The interviewees are from four continents, and 82% of them are from organizations with over one thousand employees. They have used different process mining tools including Celonis, ARIS Process Mining, UiPath Process Mining, SAP Signavio, and Fluxicon Disco. The interviews took on average 54 min.

We asked participants about their role regarding process mining in their organization, and we asked them to share some examples of process mining initiatives that they had worked on. We wanted to see how recommended and performed actions would naturally emerge from the interviews. Therefore, we did not directly ask the interview participants what the recommended and performed actions were, nor which were the causes of a process mining project termination. For each example shared by the interviewees, we asked what happened to process mining insights after they had been acquired. The final set of collected interview transcripts together provides an overview of the extent to which recommended actions are also performed from the practitioners' perspective.

3.2 Data Analysis

Based on [49], we conducted separate open codings on the data acquired from both the literature and the interviews. To do so, our qualitative coding process was composed of three main stages: i) getting acquainted with the data by reading it and taking broad notes, ii) re-reading the data and generating codes, and iii) reviewing the codes to merge semantically similar ones into categories. We coded each of the selected research papers and interview transcripts whenever it discussed a recommended (R) or performed (P) action or a cause for not performing the recommended action. Then, we categorized the actions into different types of process mining insights, such as data quality, wait time, etc. This categorization allowed us to (1) identify specific instances where recommended actions did not materialize into actual process improvement and (2) determine their causes.

3.3 Synthesis

To provide an integrated view of literature and practice about the extent to which recommended actions are also performed and the causes for certain recommended actions not resulting in performed actions, we integrated the data from the systematic literature review with data from the interviews. Doing so allowed us to quantify the frequency of actions, resulting in an overview of recommended and performed actions across different process mining insights, as reported in the literature and interviews. Interestingly, the literature does not report on the causes for not performing recommended actions. Thus, we drew on the interviews to derive those causes.

4   Findings

In this section, we present the results of our study. Section 4.1 first provides an overview of the extent to which recommended actions are performed (RQ1). Sections 4.2 through 4.6 then elaborate on the reasons why recommended actions are not performed (RQ2).

4.1   Overview

In Table 1, we provide an overview of the extent to which recommended actions are performed. We grouped the reported actions into five types of insights that are typically acquired during process mining initiatives [53]:

- *Data quality*: Data quality refers to issues such as incomplete or inconsistent data. Several studies discuss that data quality is the starting point for recommended and performed actions [3,65].
- *Wait time*: Wait time refers to insights indicating that waiting in the process leads to delays. As examples consider waiting for a resource to become available or waiting for a process participant to finish their task [4,63].
- *Rework*: Process mining insights related to rework refer to, for example, an activity that is repeated unnecessarily [13,48].
- *Discovered process*: In many cases, the discovered process is already an insight for the stakeholders. This is the case when, for example, the organization does not have their processes documented [21,41].
- *Compliance*: Process mining insights related to compliance refer to, for example, a mismatch between the documented process and its execution [25,34].

The top part of Table 1 shows the results based on the literature, the bottom part shows the results from the interviews. It illustrates that literature and interviews provide different viewpoints. Many papers report on recommended actions without discussing whether the recommendations were implemented or not. At the same time, case studies tend to report on successful process mining projects rather than unsuccessful ones. The interviews, by contrast, often discuss why actions were not performed and the particular reasons for that.

In the subsequent sections, we take a closer look at this phenomenon and discuss which are the causes that prevent organizations moving from recommended to performed actions. We refer to these causes as *terminators*. And because the terminators differ considerably depending on the insight that led to a recommended action in the first place, we use the five types of insights that are typically acquired during process mining initiatives.

Table 1. Recommended (R) and performed (P) actions across the frequently reported process mining insights from literature and interviews

Data source	Process mining insights									
	Data quality		Wait time		Rework		Discovered process		Compliance	
	R	P	R	P	R	P	R	P	R	P
Literature	[17] [62]	[3] [50] [65]	[4] [18] [27] [39] [47] [60] [63]	[4] [48] [52] [65]	[6] [22] [45] [57] [62] [63]	[2] [4] [13] [27] [32] [48]	[3] [14] [24] [30] [33] [34] [56] [61] [63]	[12] [19] [21] [23] [34] [41] [44] [59]	[19] [20] [25] [34] [37] [48] [61]	[22] [26] [34] [42] [50]

2⊟——⊟3   7⊟——⊟4   6⊟——⊟6   9⊟——⊟8   7⊟——⊟5

Total literature support number for recommended or performed actions

Interview	I5 I9 I16	I12 I15	I8 I12 I17	I2 I3 I5 I6	I4 I17	I4 I6 I11 I15	I12 I13 I16	I3 I5 I8 I9 I11	I15	I2 I6 I14 I15

3⊟——⊟2   3⊟——⊟4   2⊟——⊟4   3⊟——⊟5   1⊟——⊟4

Total interviews support number for recommended or performed actions

4.2 Data Quality

In many studies, insights related to data quality were acquired during the process mining initiative. Recommended actions include conducting a follow-up investigation to understand the root-cause of the data quality issues or adjusting the information system to start recording the end time of specific activities for further process analysis [3,62]. However, these actions are not always performed. We identified two terminators related to the insight *data quality* that are causing such initiatives to stagnate.

Laborious Data Preparation. Interviewee I15 reported on identifying late payments related to an order-to-cash process, initially aiming to review the overall standardization of the process. However, they needed to restart the project because of low data quality for further analysis. The event log was re-extracted, and the project went through another round. However, this iterative process of data preparation and event log re-extraction was taking too long, and the project was eventually stopped. Similarly, Interviewee I16 reported on a procure-to-pay process where they learned that *"the ERP system users were not following the* *predefined steps in the system"*. However, the *"organization lost interest in using process mining when they learned about the different levels of granularity in their data, and the work they would need to put to it to be able to extract an event log suitable for process mining"*. Again, *laborious* data preparation of the data was considered as the terminator here. Interviewee I9 reported on a similar project, where the suggestion to track customers with bad payment records was not acted upon because it required data integration from different systems. This was perceived as too complex and resource-intensive. Interviewee I5 discussed a project where the automation rate needed to be added to an existing dashboard. However, because the required *data was not fully accessible*, and to make it accessible would be too *laborious*, the project was terminated.

Loss of Interest. Interviewee I5 reported about the *lost of interest* in the process mining initiative being the cause for the initiative to be terminated. The interviewee mentioned that the stakeholders *"were not sure what to ask for. They had the idea that it would be good to use process mining, but they could not specify what they wanted"*; on top of that, there were more important projects to deal with. In the end, the stakeholders ended up *losing interest* in the initiative, and *"at some point, we just had to stop the project"*.

4.3   Wait Time

Process mining initiatives may also culminate in insights related to long wait times that lead to delays, triggering different recommended and performed actions [4,63]. Below, we present the terminators we identified related to *wait time*.

Lack of Expertise. Interviewee I12 referred to an eye surgery process where the department was *"eager about taking action on the acquired insights"*, and *"they were keen on improving things"*. One of the acquired insights was related to a high wait time before surgery. In this case, however, the project was halted before any improvements could be made because the process analyst of the project switched jobs. With the departure of this employee the organization *lost their expert* in process mining which hampered the continuity of the project.

Lack of Incentive. Interviewee I17 referred to a femur surgery process where they found a high length of stay in the hospital before surgery. After discussing this with the stakeholders, no action was taken because of the way the "fee for services" is established. In some countries, doctors and hospitals can earn more money by asking for more exams or for more days in the hospital. As such, there was *no financial incentive* to implement the recommended action. On the contrary, implementing the action would result in decreased income for the doctors and hospital.

Denial. Interviewee I8 described a process mining study about a financial support request procedure, uncovering excessive delays due to long-lasting checks. The proposed solution would streamline the process by automating several steps. Despite the clear benefits of the proposed solution, *"there were two managers* *that simply ignored the insights and recommendations, pushing their own solution, and nothing was done regarding the acquired process mining insights".*

4.4 Rework

Process mining insights related to rework can trigger different actions [13,48]. We identified one process mining project terminator connected to *rework*.

Lack of Incentive. Interviewee I17 reported on a case about a consultation with physicians, where they identified a high amount of unnecessary repeated activity. The interviewee learned that the repeated activities were related to unnecessary exams. After inquiring with the stakeholders about this issue, no action was taken because both the hospital and the physicians were financially benefiting from this behavior because of the funding scheme of hospitals. Again, there is *no incentive* for the stakeholders to implement the action, as it would affect them negatively. According to the interviewee, *"in some cases, discussing the issues with higher-level management staff in a hospital can help reduce bad practices, but this is rare, especially in public hospitals. In private hospitals, addressing bad practices is somewhat easier".*

4.5 Discovered Process

The discovered process is also reported as an insight, as it can bring awareness and trigger different actions as, for example, identifying improvement opportunities or improving communication with stakeholders [21,41]. Below, we present the terminators we identified for the insight *discovered process*.

Denial. Interviewee I13 reported on a case where they were working on a ticketing system handling outstanding payments of a big financial institution. The process mining analysis revealed that clients with outstanding payments were not properly charged. However, no action was taken because *"the stakeholder preferred to say that they do not believe process mining results rather than to admit they were wrong and taking the responsibility, disregarding the fact that they were losing a lot of money".* Another situation in which the insights were *denied* by those involved was mentioned by interviewee I12 that reported on a process mining initiative in a hospital related to a Gastroenterology process. The interviewee explained that the department was reluctant to take any actions based on the acquired process mining insights, that the staff were not enthusiastic either, and that they kept *denying* the acquired insights. As a result, the project was terminated.

Loss of Interest. Interviewee I13 reported on an occasion related to a credit analysis process where the manager, after learning that the problem was not in their department, *lost interest* in the findings and decided to halt the project without sharing the insights.

Lack of Expertise. Interviewee I4 referred to a meter-to-cash process of an energy provider, where the organization had a threshold to decide when to conduct a manual check on the energy consumption of a customer. With process mining, they learned this threshold should be readjusted because in 80% of the cases where a manual check was conducted, no deviation from the calculated consumption was detected. However, no action was taken because the organization *did not have the expertise* to make the required changes in the system and did not want to invest in a consultant.

4.6   Compliance

Literature reports on different process mining insights related to compliance, along with the corresponding triggered recommended and performed actions [25, 34]. Below, we present the terminator for performed actions we identified for the insight *compliance*.

Lack of Incentive. Interviewee I14 reported on the handling of a service request process. The interviewee identified *"strangely equalized service delivery time"*. In other words, service delivery time could take any amount of minutes when the service time took more than 10 min; otherwise, it was always set to 10 min. Despite the large potential impact on customer satisfaction, the project was shut down after the presentation of the findings.

5   Discussion

In the previous section, we reported on a total of five different *terminators*, i.e. causes why organizations were not progressing from recommended to performed actions. Below, we present our contributions, recommendations, and research limitations.

5.1   Contributions

The terminators identified in this study can be organized into three main dimensions: causes related to the analyzed process *data*, causes related to the process mining *project* itself, and causes related to the acquired *insights*. Figure 2 provides an overview of the relation between the different causes and the three dimensions. As indicated by the layout, the three main dimensions are in a temporal order. Below, we discuss each dimension and its related project termination causes in detail.

Data. Aspects related to data are also often responsible for a process mining initiative not moving forward. According to interviewees, process mining initiatives have been called off because of inaccessible data, low data quality, or complex data, making data preparation a laborious effort. As we know from the literature, many different event log generation [54] and event data preprocessing [36] tasks require proper expertise to be performed in order to generate an event log and improve the quality of the data for process mining purposes.

Project. A project can be terminated because there are other projects with higher priority in the backlog of the organization, diminishing the incentive for

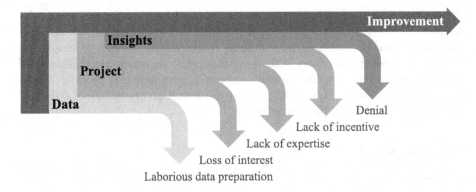

Fig. 2. Causes for certain recommended actions not resulting in performed actions. These causes can stem from the data, the project itself, or the acquired process mining insights

the project continuity, or because sponsors of the initiative may lose interest in the project for different reasons. Other causes for the termination of a process mining project may be the existence of an alternative solution that is pushed top-down into the organization, stagnation regarding technical knowledge from the staff, complacency with not following good practices, and the departure of key employees from the organization, which are related to lack of incentive, loss of interest, and lack of expertise.

Insights. There are also causes for the termination of a process mining initiative linked directly to the acquired insights. In some cases, there is a strong denial of the acquired insights. This can be a problem by itself or lead to the concealment of the acquired insights in an attempt to not undergo scrutiny of one's work or because the acquired insights are actually related to mediocre work from another department in the organization. Another aspect that can lead to the termination of a project is reluctance to take any actions based on the insights, which can be because of disbelief in the acquired insights.

5.2   Recommendations

Reflecting on the identified terminators, we derive two conjectures. First, data preparation for process mining remains (too) laborious for organizations. Although efforts have been made in the area of event data preprocessing and data quality improvement [36,58], data quality remains a major challenge and a dominant factor in the termination of process mining initiatives. Organizations require the research community and technology vendors to pay more attention to the standardization of data and the provision of guidance for extraction and preprocessing.

Second, we need to rethink approaches to process improvement based on process mining insights. Our examples have shown that the employees to whom the process mining insights are presented are either (1) not the ones with the mandate to make changes to the process, or (2) not the ones who benefit from the changes. To follow up on the insights, it is insufficient to involve local, functional managers. Managers with decision-making power on end-to-end processes are required. Moreover, there needs to be a (financial) incentive for stakeholders to implement actions, or else projects are easily terminated. If process mining initiatives are to have a significant positive impact on an organization, the right management level needs to be involved.

5.3 Limitations

Our work is subject to limitations, such as generalizability, because it is a qualitative study in its essence. To mitigate this, we integrated and analyzed data from different sources (i.e., literature and interviews). We also worked on mitigating the researcher bias by jointly building the data collection and analysis protocols and jointly conducting, reviewing, and discussing the coding effort related to the data analysis phase, and conducting the synthesis phase of our research methodology. To mitigate participant bias, we made sure not to share the interview questions previously with the participants and not interview direct colleagues, reducing the chance for the participants to change their answers or behavior to favor the researcher.

Against the acknowledgement of and countermeasures to mitigate these limitations, and in the context of progressing process mining insights into process improvement, we are confident that our results appropriately reflect the realm of recommended and performed actions and, especially, the causes behind certain recommended actions not resulting in performed actions, leading to process mining project termination.

6   Conclusion

In this work, we investigated to what extent recommended actions are also performed, and the causes for certain recommended actions not resulting in performed actions. We identified five causes that can potentially lead to the termination of a process mining initiative because recommended actions were not performed, and these causes are related to three main dimensions: the data, the process mining project itself, and the acquired process mining insights. With this understanding, we contribute to the body of knowledge regarding progressing process mining insights into process improvement.

With the understanding of the causes hampering progress to process improvement from process mining insights presented in this work, we aim to provide a basis for augmenting existing process mining methodologies. Therefore, we plan to incorporate our findings into a comprehensive proposal for enhancing process mining methodologies. We highlight the fact that process mining can bring value to organizations, but not without any further effort. Awareness of the causes we unveil with this work can be critical to moving beyond process mining insights.

In future work, we aim to steer our focus towards the process improvement initiatives in more detail. Specifically, we intend to investigate the link between process improvement initiatives that are triggered by tools and techniques other than process mining and the relations between process improvement initiatives that are triggered by insights from process mining and by insights from other methods. Our goal is to develop a broader understanding of the factors that drive process improvement initiatives in order to enhance the effectiveness of process mining-driven process improvement initiatives.

Acknowledgements. Part of this research was funded by NWO (Netherlands Organisation for Scientific Research) project number 16672.

References

1. van der Aalst, W.M.P.: Process Mining: Discovery, Conformance and Enhancement of Business Processes. Springer, Heidelberg (2011). https://doi.org/10.1007/978-3-642-19345-3
2. van der Aalst, W.M.P., et al.: business process mining: an industrial application. information systems, pp. 713–732 (2007)
3. Agostinelli, S., Covino, F., D'Agnese, G., Crea, C.D., Leotta, F., Marrella, A.: Supporting governance in healthcare through process mining: a case study. IEEE Access **8**, 186012–186025 (2020)
4. Aksu, Ü., Reijers, H.A.: How business process benchmarks enable organizations to improve performance. In: EDOC. IEEE (2020)
5. Badakhshan, P., Wurm, B., Grisold, T., Geyer-Klingeberg, J., Mendling, J., vom Brocke, J.: Creating business value with process mining. TJSIS **31**, 101745 (2022)
6. Bahaweres, R.B., Amna, H., Nurnaningsih, D.: Improving purchase to pay process efficiency with RPA using fuzzy miner algorithm in process mining. In: International Conference on Decision Aid Sciences and Applications. IEEE (2022)
7. Bernardi, M.L., Cimitile, M., Di Francescomarino, C., Maggi, F.M.: Do activity lifecycles affect the validity of a business rule in a business process? IS **62**, 42–59 (2016)
8. Boyce, C., Neale, P.: Conducting in-Depth Interviews: A Guide for Designing and Conducting In-Depth Interviews for Evaluation Input. Pathfinder International (2006)
9. Bozkaya, M., Gabriels, J., van der Werf, J.M.: Process diagnostics: a method based on process mining. In: eKNOW, pp. 22–27 (2009)
10. Bozorgi, Z.D., Dumas, M., Rosa, M.L., Polyvyanyy, A., Shoush, M., Teinemaa, I.: Learning when to treat business processes: prescriptive process monitoring with causal inference and reinforcement learning. In: Indulska, M., Reinhartz-Berger, I., Cetina, C., Pastor, O. (eds.) CAiSE 2023. LNCS, vol. 13901, pp. 364–380. Springer, Cham (2023). https://doi.org/10.1007/978-3-031-34560-9_22
11. Bryman, A.: Social Research Methods. Oxford University Press, Oxford (2016)
12. Cardenas, I.P., Espinoza, M., Armas-Aguirre, J., Aguirre-Mayorga, H.: Security of the information model on process mining: case study of the surgery block. In: CONIITI (2021)
13. Dees, M., de Leoni, M., van der Aalst, W.M.P., Reijers, H.A.: What if process predictions are not followed by good recommendations? In: BPM Industry Forum, pp. 61–72 (2019)

14. Delias, P., Nguyen, G.T.: Prototyping a business process improvement plan. An evidence-based approach. IS **101**, 101812 (2021)
15. van Eck, M.L., Lu, X., Leemans, S.J.J., van der Aalst, W.M.P.: PM^2: a process mining project methodology. In: Zdravkovic, J., Kirikova, M., Johannesson, P. (eds.) CAiSE 2015. LNCS, vol. 9097, pp. 297–313. Springer, Cham (2015). https://doi.org/10.1007/978-3-319-19069-3_19
16. Emamjome, F., Andrews, R., ter Hofstede, A.H.M.: A case study lens on process mining in practice. In: Panetto, H., Debruyne, C., Hepp, M., Lewis, D., Ardagna, C.A., Meersman, R. (eds.) OTM 2019. LNCS, vol. 11877, pp. 127–145. Springer, Cham (2019). https://doi.org/10.1007/978-3-030-33246-4_8
17. Erdogan, T.G., Tarhan, A.: A goal-driven evaluation method based on process mining for healthcare processes. Appl. Sci. **8**, 894 (2018)
18. Esiefarienrhe, B.M., Omolewa, I.D.: Application of process mining to medical billing using L∗ life cycle model. In: ICECET (2021)
19. Fleig, C., Augenstein, D., Mädche, A.: Process mining for business process standardization in ERP implementation projects - an SAP S/4 HANA case study from manufacturing. In: BPM (2018)
20. Gerke, K., Petruch, K., Tamm, G.: Optimization of service delivery through continual process improvement: a case study. In: INFORMATIK, pp. 94–107 (2010)
21. Goel, K., Leemans, S.J.J., Wynn, M.T., ter Hofstede, A.H.M., Barnes, J.: Improving PhD student journeys: insights from an Australian higher education institution. In: BPM Industry Forum, pp. 27–38. CEUR-WS.org (2021)
22. Gupta, M., Serebrenik, A., Jalote, P.: Improving software maintenance using process mining and predictive analytics. In: ICSME (2017)
23. Huang, C., Cai, H., Li, Y., Du, J., Bu, F., Jiang, L.: A process mining based service composition approach for mobile information systems. MIS 1–13 (2017)
24. van Hulzen, G., Martin, N., Depaire, B., Souverijns, G.: Supporting capacity management decisions in healthcare using data-driven process simulation. J. Biomed. Inform. **129**, 104060 (2022)
25. Jans, M., Alles, M., Vasarhelyi, M.: The case for process mining in auditing: sources of value added and areas of application. JAIS **14**, 1–20 (2013)
26. Jans, M., van der Werf, J.M., Lybaert, N., Vanhoof, K.: A business process mining application for internal transaction fraud mitigation. ESA **38**, 13351–13359 (2011)
27. Kedem-Yemini, S., Mamon, N.S., Mashiah, G.: An analysis of cargo release services with process mining: a case study in a logistics company. In: IEOM (2018)
28. Kipping, G., et al.: How to leverage process mining in organizations - towards process mining capabilities. In: Di Ciccio, C., Dijkman, R., del Río Ortega, A., Rinderle-Ma, S. (eds.) BPM 2022. LNCS, vol. 13420, pp. 40–46. Springer, Cham (2022). https://doi.org/10.1007/978-3-031-16103-2_5
29. Kitchenham, B., Charters, S.: Guidelines for performing systematic literature reviews in software engineering. Technical report, EBSE (2007)
30. Kudo, M., Nogayama, T., Ishida, A., Abe, M.: Business process analysis and real-world application scenarios. In: SITIS (2013)
31. Lashkevich, K., Milani, F., Chapela-Campa, D., Suvorau, I., Dumas, M.: Why am i waiting? Data-driven analysis of waiting times in business processes. In: Indulska, M., Reinhartz-Berger, I., Cetina, C., Pastor, O. (eds.) CAiSE 2023. LNCS, vol. 13901, pp. 174–190. Springer, Cham (2023). https://doi.org/10.1007/978-3-031-34560-9_11
32. Lee, C.K.H., Choy, K.L., Ho, G.T.S., Lam, C.H.Y.: A slippery genetic algorithm-based process mining system for achieving better quality assurance in the garment industry. ESA **46**, 236–248 (2016)

33. Leemans, M., van der Aalst, W.M.P., van den Brand, M.G.J., Schiffelers, R.R.H., Lensink, L.: Software process analysis methodology – a methodology based on lessons learned in embracing legacy software. In: ICSME (2018)

34. Leemans, S.J.J., Poppe, E., Wynn, M.T.: Directly follows-based process mining: exploration and a case study. In: ICPM (2019)

35. de Leoni, M., van der Aalst, W.M.P.: Data-aware process mining: discovering decisions in processes using alignments. In: ACM SAC, p. 1454-1461 (2013)

36. Liu, Y., Dani, V.S., Beerepoot, I., Lu, X.: Turning logs into lumber: preprocessing tasks in process mining. In: De Smedt, J., Soffer, P. (eds.) ICPM 2023. LNBIP, vol. 503, pp. 98–109. Springer, Cham (2024). https://doi.org/10.1007/978-3-031-56107-8_8

37. Mahendrawathi, E., Zayin, S.O., Pamungkas, F.J.: ERP post implementation review with process mining: a case of procurement process. PCS **124**, 216–223 (2017)

38. Mamudu, A., Bandara, W., Wynn, M., Leemans, S.: A process mining success factors model. In: Di Ciccio, C., Dijkman, R., del Río Ortega, A., Rinderle-Ma, S. (eds.) BPM 2022. LNCS, vol. 13420, pp. 143–160. Springer, Cham (2022). https://doi.org/10.1007/978-3-031-16103-2_12

39. Meincheim, A., dos Santos Garcia, C., Nievola, J.C., Scalabrin, E.E.: Combining process mining with trace clustering: manufacturing shop floor process - an applied case. In: TAI (2017)

40. Munoz-Gama, J., et al.: Process mining for healthcare: characteristics and challenges. J. Biomed. Inform. **127**, 103994 (2022)

41. Partington, A., Wynn, M., Suriadi, S., Ouyang, C., Karnon, J.: Process mining for clinical processes. Trans. Manag. Inf. Syst. **5**, 1–18 (2015)

42. Peters, E.M.L., Dedene, G., Poelmans, J.: Understanding service quality and customer churn by process discovery for a multi-national banking contact center. In: ICDM Workshops (2013)

43. Petersen, K., Feldt, R., Mujtaba, S., Mattsson, M.: Systematic mapping studies in software engineering. In: EASE (2008)

44. Polyvyanyy, A., Pika, A., Wynn, M.T., ter Hofstede, A.H.: A systematic approach for discovering causal dependencies between observations and incidents in the health and safety domain. Saf. Sci. **118**, 345–354 (2019)

45. Ramires, F., Sampaio, P.: Process mining and lean six sigma: a novel approach to analyze the supply chain quality of a hospital. IJLSS **13**, 594–621 (2021)

46. Reinkemeyer, L.: Process mining in action. In: Process Mining in Action: Principles, Use Cases and Outlook (2020)

47. Rismanchian, F., Kassani, S.H., Shavarani, S.M., Lee, Y.H.: A data-driven approach to support the understanding and improvement of patients' journeys: a case study using electronic health records of an emergency department. VH **26**, 18–27 (2023)

48. Rubin, V.A., Mitsyuk, A.A., Lomazova, I.A., van der Aalst, W.M.P.: Process mining can be applied to software too! In: ESEM (2014)

49. Saldana, J.: The Coding Manual for Qualitative Researchers. SAGE (2015)

50. Samalikova, J., Kusters, R., Trienekens, J., Weijters, T., Siemons, P.: Toward objective software process information: experiences from a case study. SQJ **19**, 101–120 (2010)

51. dos Santos Garcia, C., et al.: Process mining techniques and applications - a systematic mapping study. ESA **133**, 260–295 (2019)

52. Smit, K., , and, J.M.: Process mining in the rail industry: a qualitative analysis of success factors and remaining challenges. In: HTSS (2019)

53. Stein Dani, V., Leopold, H., van der Werf, J.M.E.M., Beerepoot, I., Reijers, H.A.: From process mining insights to process improvement: all talk and no action? In: Sellami, M., Vidal, M.E., van Dongen, B., Gaaloul, W., Panetto, H. (eds.) CoopIS 2023. LNCS, vol. 14353, pp. 275–292. Springer, Cham (2023). https://doi.org/10.1007/978-3-031-46846-9_15

54. Stein Dani, V., et al.: Towards understanding the role of the human in event log extraction. In: Marrella, A., Weber, B. (eds.) BPM 2021. LNBIP, vol. 436, pp. 86–98. Springer, Cham (2022). https://doi.org/10.1007/978-3-030-94343-1_7

55. Stein Dani, V., Leopold, H., van der Werf, J.M.E.M., Reijers, H.A.: Progressing from process mining insights to process improvement: challenges and recommendations. In: Proper, H.A., Pufahl, L., Karastoyanova, D., van Sinderen, M., Moreira, J. (eds.) EDOC 2023. LNCS, vol. 14367, pp. 152–168. Springer, Cham (2023). https://doi.org/10.1007/978-3-031-46587-1_9

56. Stuit, M., Wortmann, H.: Discovery and analysis of e-mail-driven business processes. Inf. Syst. **37**, 142–168 (2012)

57. Tawakkal, I., Kurniati, A.P., Wisudiawan, G.A.A.: Implementing heuristic miner for information system audit based on DSS01 COBIT5. In: IC3INA (2016)

58. Ter Hofstede, A.H.M., et al.: Process-data quality: the true frontier of process mining. JDIQ **15**, 1–21 (2023)

59. Toth, K., Machalik, K., Fogarassy, G., Vathy-Fogarassy, A.: Applicability of process mining in the exploration of healthcare sequences. In: NC (2017)

60. Trinkenreich, B., Santos, G., Confort, V., Santoro, F.: Toward using business process intelligence to support incident management metrics selection and service improvement. In: SEKE (2015)

61. Wang, Y., Caron, F., Vanthienen, J., Huang, L., Guo, Y.: Acquiring logistics process intelligence: methodology and application for a Chinese bulk port. ESA **41**, 195–209 (2014)

62. Weerdt, J.D., Schupp, A., Vanderloock, A., Baesens, B.: Process mining for the multi-faceted analysis of business processes - a case study in a financial services organization. CI **64**, 57–67 (2013)

63. Zerbino, P., Aloini, D., Dulmin, R., Mininno, V.: Towards analytics-enabled efficiency improvements in maritime transportation: a case study in a mediterranean port. Sustainability **11**, 4473 (2019)

64. Zerbino, P., Stefanini, A., Aloini, D.: Process science in action: a literature review on process mining in business management. TFSC **172**, 121021 (2021)

65. Zhou, Z., Wang, Y., Li, L.: Process mining based modeling and analysis of workflows in clinical care - a case study in a Chicago outpatient clinic. In: ICNSC (2014)

66. Zimmermann, L., Zerbato, F., Weber, B.: What makes life for process mining analysts difficult? a reflection of challenges. SoSyM 1–29 (2023)

Variants of Variants: Context-Based Variant Analysis for Process Mining

Christoffer Rubensson[1,3]([envelope]) [ID], Jan Mendling[1,2,3] [ID], and Matthias Weidlich[1] [ID]

[1] Humboldt-Universität zu Berlin, Berlin, Germany
{christoffer.rubensson,jan.mendling,matthias.weidlich}@hu-berlin.de
[2] Wirtschaftsuniversität Wien, Vienna, Austria
[3] Weizenbaum Institute, Berlin, Germany

Abstract. An essential aspect of analyzing processes with process mining is the notion of variants. Analysts can make better decisions and improve processes by understanding variants based on event data. Conventional variant analysis methods, however, focus primarily on variation based on event sequences only, which means they cannot effectively capture the complexity and contextual specificity of real-world process variation in other dimensions. In addition, the few methods that allow for a multifaceted analysis presume process variants as already predefined entities rather than customizable to specific target use cases. To overcome this limitation, we reconceptualize variant analysis at the level of variant extraction and propose an approach that maps process instances to equivalence classes over a set of properties utilizing an unsupervised binary mapping technique. The approach was implemented as a Python application, allowing analysts to define various variant types flexibly. We validate the approach by creating domain-specific variants with real-world event data representing pathways of sepsis patients from a hospital. The evaluation demonstrates that it can handle domain-specific process variation more effectively than conventional variant analysis methods.

Keywords: Process mining · Process variants · Variant analysis · Feature engineering · Healthcare

1 Introduction

Process mining helps to understand real-life processes by discovering process models from event data. A key challenge in this context is appropriately capturing the variation of different instances of the process. Process instances that are grouped based on common characteristics are often referred to as process variants [28]. We refer to corresponding process mining techniques as *variant analysis techniques*. By comparing variants, analysts can enhance both the understanding of a business process, e.g., by detecting anomalous behavior [12] or performance problems [13] in certain types of cases. Such insights might be the source of inspiration for process improvements. In this way, understanding the variability of processes is a critical factor for reducing process complexity and leveraging the quality of automatic discovery algorithms [4].

Process mining research has defined a plethora of techniques for analyzing process variants [28]. On the one hand, most of these techniques are based on variants as unique sequences of process activities only, while some extensions towards multi-perspective [9,21] or object-centric event logs [3] have been proposed recently. On the other hand, research on process improvement emphasizes the need for a more multifaceted analysis of the variant definition [8,23,29,30]. This would require process variants to be defined based on process properties regarding, e.g., contextual process information as well. We observe that current variant analysis techniques do not meet this requirement comprehensively.

To address this research problem, we propose an approach that defines a process variant as an equivalence class over a set of properties using a pattern-based feature generation method. Specifically, the properties are sets of patterns that, combined with an unsupervised binary mapping function, can be utilized to create unique binary sequences for each event sequence in an event log. We demonstrate the approach as a proof of concept implemented in Python, which we use for evaluation in a use case with real-world event data from a hospital describing clinical pathways of sepsis patients.

The paper proceeds as follows. Section 2 describes the problem exemplified by a typical healthcare process, from which we identify three requirements for a variant analysis method. Section 3 specifies our variant analysis approach. Section 4 presents an evaluation of our approach using a sepsis healthcare process. Section 5 concludes this paper.

2   Background

This section discusses the concept of process variants in process mining. First, we illustrate the problem of variant analysis exemplified by a healthcare process (Sect. 2.1). Then, we define general requirements for extracting various variant types from event data (Sect. 2.2). Finally, we analyze to which extent related work meets these requirements (Sect. 2.3).

2.1   Problem Statement

Variation is a general challenge for the effective management of business processes. A high degree of process variation often implies a high process complexity associated with complexity costs and performance issues [4]. Classic techniques like *Six Sigma* have focused on reducing variation in organizational processes [25]. Measures to reduce variation are also referred to as process standardization efforts, with demonstrated improvements of process performance [19,24].

The increasing availability of event logs permits the data-driven analysis of process variants [11]. Various process mining techniques have been developed to support such variant analysis. The key focus of these techniques are similarities and differences of event sequences [28]. A challenge in this context are complex

Table 1. An excerpt from the *sepsis* log [17].

Case	Event attributes				Case attributes		
	Activity	Timestamp	Lactic acid	Leucocytes	Age	SIRS (≥2 criterion satisfied)	Infection Suspected
P	ER Registration	2014-04-22 09:39			20	FALSE	FALSE
	ER Triage	2014-04-22 10:04					
	ER Sepsis Triage	2014-04-22 11:01					
MCA	ER Registration	2014-01-14 22:14			85	TRUE	TRUE
	ER Triage	2014-01-14 22:33					
	ER Sepsis Triage	2014-01-14 22:34					
	Leucocytes	2014-01-14 22:43		6.5			
	CRP	2014-01-14 22:43					
MMA	ER Registration	2014-12-14 16:14			75	TRUE	FALSE
	ER Triage	2014-12-14 16:21					
	CRP	2014-12-14 16:48					
	Leucocytes	2014-12-14 16:48		19.0			
	LacticAcid	2014-12-14 17:10	4.7				
	ER Sepsis Triage	2014-12-14 17:21					
	IV Liquid	2014-12-14 17:21					
	IV Antibiotics	2014-12-14 17:21					

processes with high variability [9,10,12]. Once every process instance defines a unique event sequence, many techniques fail to provide any insight at all.

These observations have strong practical implications. Consider the event log of a sepsis process [17] and an excerpt shown in Table 1. The sepsis log describes the clinical pathways of sepsis patients in a hospital. The log is commonly used and considered challenging because of its high variability. Sepsis processes have also been analyzed based on data from other hospitals with several thousand deviations from the predefined clinical pathway [22], emphasizing variation as a general issue of such processes.

Clinical professionals are interested in the combinations of attributes (and their values) and activities that lead to a successful treatment. A range of practical guidelines have been proposed to improve diagnosis and treatment. These include SIRS[1] and (q)SOFA[2], which comprise sets of criteria to assess the condition of a patient [26,27]. From these and related research, it is known that, e.g., age, gender, and type of infection have to be considered [22]. As a consequence, clinical professionals might select different treatment paths and vary the speed of action or the dose of medication.

The analysis of process variants is considered a major step towards understanding the causes of this variability and their impact [11]. Considering the cases shown in Table 1, we observe that the 20-year-old patient did not meet SIRS (≥ 2 criteria not satisfied), and no infection was suspected. From these criteria, the

---

[1] SIRS = Systemic Inflammatory Response Syndrome.
[2] (q)SOFA = (quick) Sequential [Sepsis-related] Organ Failure Assessment.

case looks less critical, which may explain the slow pace of examination (>1 h) with no subsequent treatment or sampling. In contrast, the 85-year-old patient showed critical symptoms and was treated fast with sample drawing within one hour. The 75-year-old patient looks a bit less critical, but sample results alert for a quick application of treatments. A classical process variant analysis would focus on the event sequences and their differences. Yet, it would ignore the fact that the event sequences are not the cause but the consequence of specific conditions. Event sequences could also be identical with variations in pace and differences in case attributes. Hence, variant analysis requires a joint understanding of event sequences and the attributes providing contextual information.

2.2   Requirements

Variant analysis at the level of variant extraction is a transformation task where a given set of process instances is mapped onto a set of variations. To address the problem above, an analyst must also be able to create use-case-specific properties on which the transformation process is based. For this purpose, we have identified three requirements based on previous literature: (R1) an analyst should be able to define a set of domain-specific properties; (R2) the variants should be a partition of the log based on these properties; and (R3) the sequence information should be preserved.

The first requirement highlights the need for a higher degree of variant customization to enable analysts to target specific business use cases (cf. [23]). In addition, a process variant may not only be based on structure, i.e., the sequence of events but comprise further dimensions of process behavior and context [16]. Similarly, the contextual dimension is relevant in terms of multiple dimensions regarding organizational and environmental factors of processes [7]. For instance, an analyst interested in why some customers in an order-to-cash process are returning their products could define a variant based on specific activities (event attribute), product type ordered (case attribute), and according to address (case attribute). Restricting the variation to the frequency of unique activity sequences bears the risk of omitting relevant properties.

R1 (Properties). Process variants should be based on a set of domain-relevant features that allow for the extraction of different types of variants not limited to a structural dimension.

The second requirement relates to the capability of comparing different process cohorts; thus, extracting variants has to consider similar attribute values and respective grouping of instances [28]. This implies that cohorts must be non-overlapping. The number of separate cohorts may range from comparing sets of two [9,21] or multiple variants [13].

R2 (Partitioning). There should be a surjective function that maps process instances onto disjoint sets of classified instances representing equivalence classes with the same properties.

Finally, an analyst compares variants to understand the variability of the same business process [5, 8]. Therefore, maintaining the sequence information is essential to understand how certain instances behave differently.

R3 (Sequence). Each classified instance should maintain the information regarding the sequence structure.

2.3 Related Work

Taymouri et al. [28] provided a comprehensive review of variant analysis methods in process mining. Almost all methods exclusively consider control flow [28, p. 12], such that R1 is not addressed. Similarly, most methods focus on the analysis rather than the construction of variants. In the following, we discuss proposals that consider R1 at least partially.

Nguyen et al. [21] use differential perspective graphs to compare sets of attributes of two variants and abstraction levels (event-, fragment-, or case level). Their approach allows for a multi-perspective property analysis without changing the structure of the sequences, thus addressing R1 and R3. However, the approach does not partition the data: it is assumed that two separate event logs are available, thus not addressing R2.

Table 2. Related work.

Authors	R1	R2	R3
Nguyen et al. [21]	+	−	+
Cremerius et al. [9]	+	−	+
Adams et al. [3]	+/−	+	+
Bose et al. [6]	−	+	+/−
Our approach	+	+	+

Cremerius et al. [9] propose a variant analysis approach that considers different data types (categorical and continuous) for comparing variants using statistical testing. The authors specify two types of variant comparison mechanisms that compare variation from either the perspective of a specific activity (*activity data variant comparison*) or from the perspective of the transition between activities (*data flow variant comparison*) [9, p. 3257]. However, variants need to be created by manually splitting the event data before analysis rather than as a result of a mapping based on their attributes, thus not addressing R2.

Adams et al. [3] is one of few works that handle the challenges with variant analysis in object-centric event logs. In their graph-based approach, they first extract process executions as connected sub-graphs by considering the co-dependencies of objects and events. Then, a hashing technique is applied to derive equivalence classes based on *an* attribute and graph isomorphism. Even though the structural equivalence between the instances cannot be entirely guaranteed because of the challenges with isomorphism, the authors apply different methods to improve the accuracy of the equivalence classes (cf. [3, p. 132]). In that regard, the approach satisfies both R2 and R3. However, R1 is only partially met. Although the approach allows for potentially selecting any attribute to define variants, process executions are still grouped based on the structural properties of the chosen attribute, i.e., variants are equal with respect to the structural similarities of attribute value occurrences.

Lastly, Bose & van der Aalst [6] propose a framework to extract signature patterns from traditional event logs using methods from feature engineering. The aim is to investigate behavioral differences in the data, with an emphasis on faulty and fraudulent behavior. This approach does not explicitly focus on variant analysis. However, it integrates concepts from feature engineering that are relevant for R2.

Table 2 relates existing approaches to the requirements we identified. Similar to [3], we also form variants by grouping process instances onto equivalence classes while preserving control-flow information. However, our work distinguishes itself by allowing analysts to customize variants based on a combination of multiple event attributes and features, not limited to their structural qualities. In this regard, our work is closer to [9,21], as they, too, provide a multi-perspective examination of variants. Nevertheless, unlike [9,21], who assume that variants are given or must be manually created before analysis, we instead focus on the extraction of variants as an outcome of the analysis. Moreover, our approach allows for the creation of both control-flow and context-based variants without compromising the structural qualities of the event sequences by applying principles from feature engineering. Hence, our work addresses all three requirements.

3   Context-Based Process Variants

To meet the requirements outlined in the previous section, we propose a general approach to variant analysis at the level of variant extraction. We make use of concepts from feature engineering as it involves the definition of patterns used to transform instances and form equivalence classes. Specifically, the approach takes event sequences from a traditional event log as input and groups them based on properties, which are defined by an analyst, using an unsupervised binary mapping function. Below, we first define a basic model (Sect. 3.1), before we turn to variants (Sect. 3.2) and their construction (Sect. 3.3).

3.1   Event Log and Event Sequences

We assume a conventional event log, as illustrated in Table 1 above. An event log is a record of partially ordered events, often stored in the eXtensible Event Stream format (*XES*) [1] or as a table. Each event comprises at least three attributes: a *timestamp*, an *activity*, and a *case*. The timestamp indicates the execution time and is often used to order the event data. The activity indicates the type of execution. As events are atomic, one event could refer to *an* activity but also to a phase of some activity in its lifecycle, e.g., to the start or to the completion. Finally, assuming a one-case notion, a case refers to a process execution to which multiple events are related. For example, in a healthcare log, a case often refers to a patient; in an order-to-delivery log, a case could be a customer order.

A real-life log often includes a range of further attributes, which provides analysts with more details about the process and its context. As previously seen in Table 1, the attributes are tied to the events but could refer to different abstraction levels, such as the event itself (event attributes), or the complete case (case attributes). In a healthcare log, with each case referring to a patient, event attributes could include measurements taken in the clinical process, whereas case attributes could store patient data that cannot change during a process, such as demographics.

We formalize the above model based on [2, pp. 14–16]. Let $\mathcal{U}_{ev}$ be the universe of events, let $\mathcal{U}_{att}$ be the universe of event attribute labels, let $\mathcal{U}_{val}$ be the universe of all values, and let $\mathcal{U}_{map} = \mathcal{U}_{att} \nrightarrow \mathcal{U}_{val}$ be the universe of attribute-value mappings. Based thereon, we capture an event log as follows:

Definition 1 (Event Log). *An event log is a tuple* $L = (E, \#, \prec)$ *where*

- $E \subseteq \mathcal{U}_{ev}$ *is a set of events,*
- $\# \in E \to \mathcal{U}_{map}$ *is a function assigning attribute-value mappings to events,*
- $\prec \subseteq E \times E$ *is a strict total order over events.*

As a short-hand, we define $\#_{att}(e) = \#(e)(att)$ to refer to the value of attribute $att \in \text{dom}(\#(e))$ of an event $e \in E$. We further assume that a log L contains at least the following attributes: an event id $\#_{eid}$, a case id $\#_{case}$, an activity type $\#_{activity}$, and a timestamp $\#_{time}$, and that no event $e \in L$ has empty values for the former three attributes, i.e., $\#_{case}(e), \#_{activity}(e), \#_{eid}(e)$ are set to values of the respective domain. If events contain timestamps, the timestamps shall be consistent with the defined order, i.e., for any pair of events $e_1, e_2 \in E$, it holds that $\#_{time}(e_1) < \#_{time}(e_2) \Rightarrow e_1 \prec e_2$.

Based on an event log, we can extract process instances to be used as input for variant extraction. We define a process instance as a sequence of events that correlate with the same case, and formalize it based on [2, p. 16] as follows:

Definition 2 (Event Sequence). *Given a log* $L = (E, \#, \prec)$, *an event sequence* $\sigma \in E^*$ *is a non-empty, finite sequence of events* $\sigma = \langle e_1, \ldots, e_n \rangle$, *where all events* $e_i, e_j, 1 \leq i < j \leq n$ *respect the order of the log,* $e_i \prec e_j$, *and refer to the same case, i.e.,* $\#_{case}(e_i) = \#_{case}(e_j)$. *By* $\mathcal{E}(L)$, *we denote the set of all event sequences of* L. *Function* $\#^* \in E^* \to \mathcal{U}_{map}$ *assigns attribute-value mappings to event sequences.*

The assignment of an attribute-value mapping further enables the derivation of representative values for the event sequence-based on event attributes. With the short-hand $\#^*_{att}(\sigma) = \#^*(\sigma)(att)$, an example would be the case duration as calculated from the timestamps of events, i.e., $\#^*_{dur}(\sigma) = \#_{time}(e_n) - \#_{time}(e_1)$ with $\sigma = \langle e_1, \ldots, e_n \rangle$.

3.2 Properties and Variants

Process variants are groups of instances with the same characteristics [28]. Following the ideas of pattern-based feature generation [14], patterns may be constructed from items that reflect the features (attribute values) in some dataset.

Based thereon, we can classify instances in a dataset by determining whether or not they satisfy a pattern. For example, for an event log where each instance denotes a patient, a pattern may check if an attribute capturing *age* is "≥ 50". Also, we could extend the pattern, thereby enforcing constraints on the values of additional attributes, e.g., $p = \{age \geq 50,\ diagnosis = "heart\,failure\,type\ 2"\}$.

Let $\mathcal{U}_{pred}$ be a universe of atomic predicates over the event attribute labels $\mathcal{U}_{att}$, i.e., each predicate is of the form $(a\ \psi\ u)$ with $a \in \mathcal{U}_{att}$ being an attribute label, $u \in \text{dom}(a) \subseteq \mathcal{U}_{val}$ being a value of the respective domain, and ψ being a comparison operator. Then, we define a property and its semantics as:

Definition 3 (Property). *Given a log $L = (E, \#, \prec)$, a property $p \subseteq \mathcal{U}_{pred}$ is a set of predicates. An event sequence $\sigma \in \mathcal{E}(L)$ satisfies property p, denoted by $\sigma \models p$, if for any predicate $(a\ \psi\ u) \in p$, it holds that:*

- *$a \in \text{dom}(\#^*)$ (attribute of event sequence) implies $\#_a^*(\sigma)\ \psi\ u$, and*
- *$a \in \text{dom}(\#)$ (attribute of event) implies that $\#_a(e_i)\ \psi\ u$ for some event e_i of $\sigma = \langle e_1, \ldots, e_n \rangle$, $1 \leq i \leq n$.*

Once an analyst has selected a set of properties, these can be used to partition the event sequences of an event log. We define the resulting process variants as equivalence classes that are induced by a set of properties. Following [15, pp. 52–53], we define variants as the sets of event sequences that are defined by the equivalence relation that is induced by the properties.

Definition 4 (Variant). *Given a log $L = (E, \#, \prec)$ and a set of properties P, let $\sim_P \subseteq \mathcal{E}(L) \times \mathcal{E}(L)$ denote the equivalence relation over event sequences induced by P, i.e., $\sigma \sim_P \sigma'$, if and only if for all $p \in P$, it holds that $\sigma \models p \Leftrightarrow \sigma' \models p$. Then, a variant $V \subseteq \mathcal{E}(L)$ is a set of event sequences that form an equivalence class, i.e., $V = \{\sigma, \sigma' \in \mathcal{E}(L) \mid \sigma \sim_P \sigma'\}$, also denoted by $[\sigma]$ for some $\sigma \in V$.*

Note that the definition implies that: (i) any event sequence of a log is indeed part of a variant, and (ii) all variants are non-overlapping in terms of their event sequences. Put differently, the event sequences are partitioned into variants.

The above conceptualization of variants enables the creation of context-based variants, but covers traditional notions of variants based on the control flow.

Lemma 1 (Activity Sequence Variants). *For a log $L = (E, \#, \prec)$, there exists a set of properties P that yields a set of variants $\{V_1, \ldots, V_m\}$ of L that are induced by the sequence of activities of events, i.e., for all $\sigma = \langle e_1, \ldots, e_n \rangle$ and $\sigma' = \langle e_1', \ldots, e_m' \rangle$, it holds that:*

- *$\sigma' \in [\sigma]$ implies that $\#_{activity}(e_i) = \#_{activity}(e_j)$ for all $1 \leq i \leq n$ and $1 \leq j \leq m$, and*
- *$\sigma' \notin [\sigma]$ implies that there exists $\#_{activity}(e_i) \neq \#_{activity}(e_j)$ for some $1 \leq i \leq n$ and $1 \leq j \leq m$.*

Proof. We show the result by constructing the required properties. Let $\sigma = \langle e_1, \ldots, e_n \rangle \in \mathcal{E}(L)$ be an event sequence. We define an attribute *seq* for it as the sequence of activities of its events, $\#^*_{seq}(\sigma) = \langle \#_{activity}(e_1), \ldots, \#_{activity}(e_n) \rangle$. Then, we define a set of properties as $P = \bigcup_{\sigma \in \mathcal{E}(L)} \{\{(seq = \#^*_{seq}(\sigma))\}\}$, i.e., each property contains only a single predicate that requires the attribute *seq* to be equal to one of the sequences of activities of events, as observed in an event sequence of the log. This set of properties induces variants that meet the above requirements. □

3.3 Variant Extraction

Given a set of event sequences of an event log, we want to transform them into a representation that enables direct classification of the variants induced by a set of properties. In pattern-based feature generation [14], attributes for a set of instances are referred to as the original feature space, which is then transformed into a pattern feature space. These two feature spaces differ in size, as the original feature space reflects the elements of the original dataset, and the pattern feature space reflects the number of patterns selected. Specifically, we adopt an unsupervised binary mapping function ϕ, which is the most common pattern-based feature generation [14, pp. 262–263]. In our setting, it corresponds to a one-hot encoding that is formulated as a function $\phi : \mathcal{E}(L) \rightarrow \{0, 1\}$ that maps event sequences to Boolean values, encoding whether they satisfy a particular property. For example, consider the property $p = \{age \geq 50, diagnosis = \text{"}heart\,failure\,type\,2\text{"}\}$ stated above. Any event sequence σ that represents a patient of 50 years of age or older, who was also diagnosed with heart failure of type 2 would be assigned a value of 1 ($\phi(\sigma) = 1$) for property p.

We realize the above idea through the following definition of a mapping function that, given a set of user-defined properties, yields the encoding per event sequence. The formalization is based on [14, pp. 262–263].

Definition 5 (Mapping Function). *Given a log* $L = (E, \#, \prec)$ *and a set of properties* $P = \{p_1, \ldots, p_m\}$, *a mapping function* $\phi : \mathcal{E}(L) \rightarrow \{0, 1\}^*$ *assigns a Boolean feature vector to an event sequence. It is defined as* $\phi(\sigma) = (\phi_1(\sigma), \ldots, \phi_m(\sigma))$, *where* $\phi_i(\sigma)$ *is the feature value of property* p_i, $1 \leq i \leq m$:

$$\phi_i(\sigma) = \begin{cases} 1, & if \sigma \models p_i \\ 0, & otherwise. \end{cases}$$

We note that the dimensionality of the obtained encoding corresponds to the number of properties and, hence, is independent of the properties of the log.

To this end, the model described in this section addresses all requirements R1-3 defined in Sect. 2.2. An analyst can define properties based on both event and case attributes included in an event log to create variants of different types (R1). The log can then be partitioned over this same set of properties to form equivalence classes (R2) without compromising the structural information of each event sequence (R3).

4   Evaluation

In this section, we first present a demonstrator of our approach as a Python application (Sect. 4.1). Then, we evaluate the approach by applying the application to a real-world healthcare log (Sect. 4.2). We end with a brief discussion (Sect. 4.3).

4.1   Implementation

We implemented our approach as a Python application, which is available at GitHub[3]. The application allows the user to apply an event log and define properties over some attributes in the log that are used to calculate unique variants. For this purpose, various packages were used, such as *pandas*[4] and *numpy*[5] for data processing, *pm4py*[6] for process mining techniques, and *scikit-learn*[7] for the feature generation and binary mapping. After successful execution, the application exports an event log extended with variants (both *.csv* and an *.xes* formats), an instance log with the transformation calculations (*.csv*), and a summary of the properties (*.txt*).

The application can be executed in a command-line interface or a Jupyter notebook[8] by running the main script *ve_main.py*. The program then operates in five stages. First, the user imports an event log (*.xes*). Secondly, the properties are defined. This is done iteratively by typing in the preferable property of a set of options. The options available depend on the attribute and data type for that attribute in the iteration. Third, the program uses the properties to create a new table in which each row refers to an instance with all necessary attributes. An instance is defined as a case by default but can be manually changed to denote a different type of instance. Fourth, the program executes a one-hot-encoding procedure to transform the instance table onto a binary space. Each unique binary sequence per instance is assigned a decimal number to identify a unique variation. Finally, the classifications are integrated as a new column into the original event log and exported as a new log together with the calculations, and the properties defined. The exported data can be used for further analysis. Analysts can create various variants for the same event log by replaying the program.

4.2   Evaluation Based on Sepsis-Log

For evaluation purposes, we turn to the *sepsis log* [17]. This log is commonly used for evaluation purposes because it is considered challenging due to its high variability. The sepsis log describes the clinical pathways of sepsis patients in a

---

[3] https://github.com/rubenssohn/VARIANT_EXTRACTION (accessed: 2024-03-23).
[4] https://pandas.pydata.org (accessed: 2024-03-23).
[5] https://numpy.org (accessed: 2024-03-23).
[6] https://pm4py.fit.fraunhofer.de (accessed: 2024-03-23).
[7] https://scikit-learn.org (accessed: 2024-03-23).
[8] https://jupyter.org (accessed: 2024-03-23).

Table 3. Summary statistics of eight variant types from the *sepsis log*.

Variant Type	Sequence		Demographics		Clinical guidelines			
	V1	V2	V3	V4	V5	V6	V7	V8
#Variants, total	846	841	15	3	2	15	20	4
#Cases per Variant								
-Mean	1.2	1.2	70	350	525	70	52.5	262.5
-Max	35	35	155	433	853	421	378	983
-Min	1	1	11	223	197	1	1	7
Most prevalent variant								
- Age (median)	50	50	90	85	75	80	82.5	80
- Case duration, in days (median)	0.01	0.01	6.59	6.78	6.33	17.12	17.96	12.23
- Case length, #events (median)	3	3	14	14	14	18.5	20.5	31
Least prevalent variant								
- Age (median)	35	50	20	45	70	70	70	75
- Case duration, in days (median)	4.73	5.18	0.05	3.01	0.09	0.06	0.06	5.10
- Case length, #events (median)	15	23	5	12	6	5.5	5.5	13
Cases	1,050							
Activities	16							

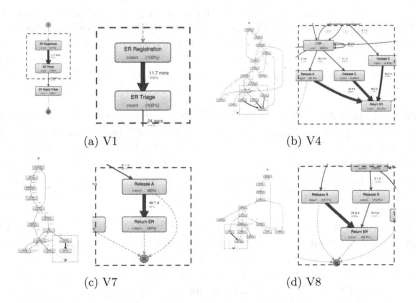

(a) V1 (b) V4

(c) V7 (d) V8

Fig. 1. Directly follows graphs of the most prevalent variants from four different variant types (V1, V4, V7, V8) created with Disco (Filter: Activities 100%, 5%; Performance statistics: Median duration (days), and case coverage (% of variant). Each subfigure shows the full model (left) and a possible bottleneck (right).

hospital and comprises 1,050 cases, 15,214 events, 16 activity types, and 32 data attributes. The attributes include patient demographics, clinical test results, checklist information, and activity performer (hospital unit).

We extracted eight variant types: two based on event sequences (V1–2), two based on demographics (V3–4), and four based on clinical guidelines (V5–8). All variant types were extracted using our application, except for V1, which originates from *Disco*[9]. Table 3 depicts a statistics summary and comprises for each variant type: (1) the total number of variants; (2) the mean, maximum, and minimum number of cases per variant; and information about the median age, the median case duration in days, and the median number of events in a case for (3) the most prevalent variant (MPV) and (4) the least prevalent variant (LPV). MPV refers to the variant that satisfies all properties or the *highest* property value. For sequence variants, MPV instead refers to the variant with most cases. The LPV is the opposite of MPV. The results are described in the following.

Variant Types 1–2 (Sequence-Based). The first two variant types, V1 and V2, are based on the differences in event sequences. The minor statistical differences between V1 and V2 are due to how events with identical timestamps are handled. Compared to *Disco*, our approach orders events based on activity type alphabetically when timestamps are equal.

The amount of variants is very high for both types, 846 for V1 and 841 for V2, and most variants only consist of one single case. Considering the MPV and LPV for both types, we can see that the median age of the patients is 50. Only the LPV for V1 is an exception at 35. The median case duration and median case length are lower for both MPVs than their respective LPV. The analytical insights for further investigation are limited because of the high number of variants with a low number of cases per variation.

Variant Types 3–4 (Demographic-Based). The second two variant types, V3 and V4, are based on patient age. Illness severity and management complexity tend to increase with age [20]. V3 was created based on the age groups with a five-year interval already existing in the log. V4 was created by defining three age groups: patients below < 60 years, the *elderly* ≥ 60, and the *very elderly* ≥ 80. The two last groups are linked to a significant increase in management complexity (cf., [20]).

The number of variants is considerably lower for both V3 (15 variants) and V4 (3 variants) compared to the sequence-based variants. The median case lengths for both the MPVs and LPVs are also relatively low (below 15 events); however, the case durations for the MPVs are higher (>6 days). Since the MPVs comprise the oldest patients, this might indicate an increased need for recovery or re-emission for this demographic group.

Variant Types 5–8 (Clinical Guideline-Based). The first three guideline-based variant types, V5–V7, are based on the clinical guidelines SIRS, whereas V8

---

[9] https://fluxicon.com/disco (accessed: 2024-03-23).

simulates the qSOFA guideline (see Sect. 2.1). In short, SIRS is a four-criteria checklist (e.g., elevated heart rate) to diagnose sepsis patients. Sepsis is suspected when at least two criteria are satisfied [27]. V5 was created solely based on whether the minimum of two criteria for SIRS was met. V6 considers all criteria separately. V7 extends V6 with the additional criteria of whether an organ dysfunction was present, as this may significantly impact treatment [27].

Furthermore, qSOFA is a simplified assessment for quick and repeated identification of poor outcomes of sepsis patients without the need for laboratory testing [27]. It usually includes tests of blood pressure, respiratory rate, and mental state [27, p. 9]. Because of log limitations, we adapted this guideline for V8 to be based on the presence of *hypotensia* (low blood pressure) and *hypoxie* (low bodily oxygen saturation).

Similar to V3 and V4, there is a reduction in the number of variants compared to the sequence variants, with 2 variants for V5, 15 for V6, 20 for V7, and 4 for V8. The statistical outcomes are also similar to the demographic-based types. Noticeably, the case durations and case lengths for MPV of V6-8 are longer/higher compared to V5. For V6–7, this might indicate increased process complexity for patients satisfying increasingly more SIRS criteria. For V8, the adapted qSOFA may provide an alternative to SIRS despite the adaptations. Furthermore, the minimum number of cases per variant is much lower for V6–8 than for V5, indicating a less balanced case distribution for these variant types.

Process Discovery. Figure 1 illustrates directly-follows graphs of the MPV of variant types V1, V4, V7, and V8 to highlight bottlenecks discovered with *Disco* (see footnote 9) (filter: 100% activities, 5% paths). The graphs also depict the median duration (in days) and the case coverage for a variant (in %) for each directly-follows relation. As previously discussed, the sequence-based variant V1 does not provide sufficient analytical insights to analyze sepsis patients. Here, the median duration of 11.7 min between registration and triage could be considered a normality rather than a bottleneck. In contrast, V4 shows a bottleneck between the release and return to hospital with a median duration between 35.2 and 48.4 days, depending on which ward[10] the patient was discharged from (A, C, or D). As the MPV of V4 comprises the *very elderly* patients, this aligns with empirical evidence [20]. Furthermore, 62.1% of patients in this variant were released from ward A. By further investigating the same bottleneck present in the guideline-based variant types V7-8, we may assume that it represents patients of critical sepsis.

4.3 Discussion

The results of the evaluation can be reflected along the following lines. Overall, our approach can effectively and flexibly create various variants, such as

---

[10] The sepsis-log comprises five activities ("Release A-E") referring to a specific discharge type [18, p. 75]. We assume that the discharge activities are associated with a ward (A-E), as this is the case for most activities (cf., [18, p. 75]).

control-flow-based and context-based variation. We have applied our approach with a layman's understanding of basic medical concepts and were able to separate behavior and critical characteristics of the sepsis log, which are obfuscated when using classical sequence variant techniques. The feature generation approach with binary mapping makes the creation of variants simple and fast and can utilize different attribute types. The evaluation confirms that our approach satisfies all three requirements defined in Sect. 2.2. Mind that our approach addressed variant analysis at the level of variant extraction. Therefore, it offers capabilities that are complementary to other specific variant analysis methods, such as described in [9,21]. Similarly, feature engineering comprises many algorithms with varying complexity, many of which could extend this approach, e.g., to analyze more complex data or to include a feature relevance analysis.

The current evaluation setup has limitations regarding the effectiveness of our approach. To strengthen external validity, we need additional evaluation scenarios involving domain experts to assess their understanding and utilization of the concepts defined in this paper. Furthermore, we suggest conducting evaluations in diverse settings with varying contextual factors, such as knowledge intensity or process complexity. This would further facilitate the understanding of the effectiveness and utility of our approach.

5   Conclusion and Future Work

This paper addresses the need for flexible and context-based solutions for variant analysis in process mining. For this purpose, we reconceptualized variant analysis at the level of variant extraction. We proposed an approach based on feature engineering principles to partition a traditional event log over pre-defined properties. We implemented the approach in Python and applied it to real-life data. Specifically, we created and compared eight variant types to understand the clinical pathways of sepsis patients in a hospital. The variant types were created using event sequence information, demographics, and clinical guidelines. The approach was proven effective compared to conventional variant analysis methods for exploring context-based variants, as it simply and flexibly handles context-based variation. It can also extract conventional control-flow-based variants. For future work, we want to extend the approach to include more complex event data types, such as object-centric event logs and event networks, and incorporate a dynamic user interface that simplifies the property definition. Another interesting future work direction would be investigating different feature generation algorithms. So far, we have applied our approach to one specific case. We aim to study its application in different contexts in future research.

Acknowledgments. The research of the authors was supported by the Einstein Foundation Berlin under grant EPP-2019-524, by the German Federal Ministry of Education and Research under grant 16DII133, and by Deutsche Forschungsgemeinschaft under grant ME 3711/2-1.

Disclosure of Interests. The authors have no competing interests to declare that are relevant to the content of this article.

References

1. IEEE standard for eXtensible Event Stream (XES) for achieving interoperability in event logs and event streams. IEEE Std 1849-2016, pp. 1–50 (2016)
2. van der Aalst, W.M.P.: Process mining: a 360 degree overview. In: van der Aalst, W.M.P., Carmona, J. (eds.) Process Mining Handbook. LNBIP, vol. 448, pp. 3–34. Springer, Cham (2022). https://doi.org/10.1007/978-3-031-08848-3_1
3. Adams, J.N., Schuster, D., Schmitz, S., Schuh, G., van der Aalst, W.M.P.: Defining cases and variants for object-centric event data. In: Burattin, A., Polyvyanyy, A., Weber, B. (eds.) 4th International Conference on Process Mining, ICPM 2022, Bolzano, Italy, 23–28 October 2022, pp. 128–135. IEEE (2022)
4. Augusto, A., Mendling, J., Vidgof, M., Wurm, B.: The connection between process complexity of event sequences and models discovered by process mining. Inf. Sci. **598**, 196–215 (2022)
5. Bolt, A., de Leoni, M., van der Aalst, W.M.P.: Process variant comparison: using event logs to detect differences in behavior and business rules. Inf. Syst. **74**(Part 1), 53–66 (2018)
6. Bose, R.P.J.C., van der Aalst, W.M.P.: Discovering signature patterns from event logs. In: IEEE Symposium on Computational Intelligence and Data Mining, CIDM 2013, Singapore, 16–19 April 2013, pp. 111–118. IEEE (2013)
7. vom Brocke, J., Zelt, S., Schmiedel, T.: On the role of context in business process management. Int. J. Inf. Manag. **36**(3), 486–495 (2016)
8. Cognini, R., Corradini, F., Gnesi, S., Polini, A., Re, B.: Business process flexibility - a systematic literature review with a software systems perspective. Inf. Syst. Front. **20**(2), 343–371 (2018)
9. Cremerius, J., Patzlaff, H., Rahn, V.X., Leopold, H.: Data-based process variant analysis. In: Bui, T.X. (ed.) 56th Hawaii International Conference on System Sciences, HICSS 2023, Maui, Hawaii, USA, 3–6 January 2023, pp. 3255–3264. ScholarSpace (2023)
10. Cremerius, J., Pufahl, L., Klessascheck, F., Weske, M.: Event log generation in MIMIC-IV research paper. In: Montali, M., Senderovich, A., Weidlich, M. (eds.) ICPM 2022. LNBIP, vol. 468, pp. 302–314. Springer, Cham (2023). https://doi.org/10.1007/978-3-031-27815-0_22
11. Dumas, M., Rosa, M.L., Mendling, J., Reijers, H.A.: Fundamentals of Business Process Management, 2nd edn. Springer, Heidelberg (2018). https://doi.org/10.1007/978-3-662-56509-4
12. Huang, Z., Dong, W., Duan, H., Li, H.: Similarity measure between patient traces for clinical pathway analysis: problem, method, and applications. IEEE J. Biomed. Health Inform. **18**(1), 4–14 (2014)
13. Ingh, L.V.D., Eshuis, R., Gelper, S.: Assessing performance of mined business process variants. Enterp. Inf. Syst. **15**(5), 676–693 (2021)
14. Jia, Y., Bailey, J., Kotagiri, R., Leckie, C.: Pattern-based feature generation. In: Dong, G., Liu, H. (eds.) Feature Engineering for Machine Learning and Data Analytics, 1 edn. CRC Press (2018)
15. Krantz, S.G.: Handbook of Logic and Proof Techniques for Computer Science, 1st edn. Birkhäuser Boston, Boston (2002)

16. Lu, R., Sadiq, S.: On the discovery of preferred work practice through business process variants. In: Parent, C., Schewe, K.-D., Storey, V.C., Thalheim, B. (eds.) ER 2007. LNCS, vol. 4801, pp. 165–180. Springer, Heidelberg (2007). https://doi.org/10.1007/978-3-540-75563-0_13

17. Mannhardt, F.: Sepsis cases - event log (2016). https://doi.org/10.4121/uuid:915d2bfb-7e84-49ad-a286-dc35f063a460. Accessed 23 Mar 2024

18. Mannhardt, F., Blinde, D.: Analyzing the trajectories of patients with sepsis using process mining. In: Joint Proceedings of the Radar tracks at the 18th International Working Conference on Business Process Modeling, Development and Support (BPMDS), and the 22nd International Working Conference on Evaluation and Modeling Methods for Systems Analysis and Development (EMMSAD), and the 8th International Workshop on Enterprise Modeling and Information Systems Architectures (EMISA) co-located with the 29th International Conference on Advanced Information Systems Engineering 2017 (CAiSE 2017), Essen, Germany, 12–13 June 2017. CEUR Workshop Proceedings, vol. 1859, pp. 72–80 (2017)

19. Münstermann, B., Eckhardt, A., Weitzel, T.: The performance impact of business process standardization: an empirical evaluation of the recruitment process. Bus. Process. Manag. J. 16(1), 29–56 (2010)

20. Nasa, P., Juneja, D., Singh, O.: Severe sepsis and septic shock in the elderly: an overview. World J. Crit. Care Med. 1(1), 23–30 (2012)

21. Nguyen, H., Dumas, M., La Rosa, M., ter Hofstede, A.H.M.: Multi-perspective comparison of business process variants based on event logs. In: Trujillo, J.C., et al. (eds.) ER 2018. LNCS, vol. 11157, pp. 449–459. Springer, Cham (2018). https://doi.org/10.1007/978-3-030-00847-5_32

22. Quintano Neira, R.A., et al.: Analysis and optimization of a sepsis clinical pathway using process mining. In: Di Francescomarino, C., Dijkman, R., Zdun, U. (eds.) BPM 2019. LNBIP, vol. 362, pp. 459–470. Springer, Cham (2019). https://doi.org/10.1007/978-3-030-37453-2_37

23. Rosa, M.L., van der Aalst, W.M.P., Dumas, M., Milani, F.: Business process variability modeling: a survey. ACM Comput. Surv. 50(1), 2:1–2:45 (2017)

24. Schäfermeyer, M., Rosenkranz, C., Holten, R.: The impact of business process complexity on business process standardization: an empirical study. Bus. Inf. Syst. Eng. 4, 261–270 (2012)

25. Schroeder, R.G., Linderman, K., Liedtke, C., Choo, A.S.: Six sigma: definition and underlying theory. J. Oper. Manag. 26(4), 536–554 (2008)

26. Seymour, C.W., et al.: Assessment of clinical criteria for sepsis: for the third international consensus definitions for sepsis and septic shock (Sepsis-3). JAMA 315(8), 762–774 (2016)

27. Singer, M., et al.: The third international consensus definitions for sepsis and septic shock (Sepsis-3). JAMA 315(8), 801–810 (2016)

28. Taymouri, F., Rosa, M.L., Dumas, M., Maggi, F.M.: Business process variant analysis: survey and classification. Knowl. Based Syst. 211, 106557 (2021)

29. Wurm, B., Goel, K., Bandara, W., Rosemann, M.: Design patterns for business process individualization. In: Hildebrandt, T., van Dongen, B.F., Röglinger, M., Mendling, J. (eds.) BPM 2019. LNCS, vol. 11675, pp. 370–385. Springer, Cham (2019). https://doi.org/10.1007/978-3-030-26619-6_24

30. Wurm, B., Mendling, J.: A theoretical model for business process standardization. In: Fahland, D., Ghidini, C., Becker, J., Dumas, M. (eds.) BPM 2020. LNBIP, vol. 392, pp. 281–296. Springer, Cham (2020). https://doi.org/10.1007/978-3-030-58638-6_17

Towards a Comprehensive Evaluation of Decision Rules and Decision Mining Algorithms Beyond Accuracy

Beate Wais[1]([✉]) [ID] and Stefanie Rinderle-Ma[2] [ID]

[1] Faculty of Computer Science, Research Group Workflow Systems and Technology;
UniVie Doctoral School Computer Science DoCS, University of Vienna,
Vienna, Austria
beate.wais@univie.ac.at
[2] TUM School of Computation, Information and Technology,
Technical University of Munich, Garching, Germany
stefanie.rinderle-ma@tum.de

Abstract. Decision mining algorithms discover decision points and the corresponding decision rules in business processes. So far, the evaluation of decision mining algorithms has focused on performance (e.g., accuracy), neglecting the impact of other criteria, e.g., understandability or consistency of the discovered decision model. However, performance alone cannot reflect if the discovered decision rules produce value to the user by providing insights into the process. Providing metrics to comprehensively evaluate the decision model and decision rules can lead to more meaningful insights and assessment of decision mining algorithms. In this paper, we examine the ability of different criteria from software engineering, explainable AI, and process mining that go beyond performance to evaluate decision mining results and propose metrics to measure these criteria. To evaluate the proposed metrics, they are applied to different decision algorithms on two synthetic and one real-life dataset. The results are compared to the findings of a user study to check whether they align with user perception. As a result, we suggest four metrics that enable a comprehensive evaluation of decision mining results and a more in-depth comparison of different decision mining algorithms. In addition, guidelines for formulating decision rules are presented.

Keywords: Process Mining · Decision Mining · Evaluation · Metrics · User Study · Explainability

1 Introduction

An important part of process discovery is decision mining, which provides algorithms to discover decision points in processes and the underlying decision rules guarding that decision based on event logs [22]. The discovered decision points and rules can enhance transparency by capturing the underlying logic of decisions and allowing users to understand the decisions in a process, i.e., *"making implicit decision information explicit"* [18]. Process and decision mining are

© The Author(s), under exclusive license to Springer Nature Switzerland AG 2024
G. Guizzardi et al. (Eds.): CAiSE 2024, LNCS 14663, pp. 403–419, 2024.
https://doi.org/10.1007/978-3-031-61057-8_24

increasingly gaining traction as transparency and standardization become crucial across different domains [9,18]. Decision mining enables domain experts to detect potential deviations from underlying business logic (e.g., regulations) or discover changes in the process [30], as well as evaluate if these deviations and changes are intentional or due to errors (cf. [36]). This ability, in turn, can lead to fewer errors or a decrease in time until an error is detected, thereby minimizing the negative impact of an error. Decision mining algorithms[1] have been evaluated using common sense so far (see [3,6,31]) or concerning performance, e.g., accuracy and fitness [20,23,29]. Related fields such as rule induction also use performance-based criteria, e.g., coverage or error rates to evaluate results, cf. [4]. Similarly, in process mining, methods to evaluate process discovery algorithms include criteria such as fitness or precision [27]. While high performance is necessary, it is not sufficient to achieve valuable decision mining results. By valuable, we refer to the ability to accomplish the intended goal, e.g., to provide a profound understanding of process decisions and enable the user to take action.

Imagine a logistics use case where temperature-sensitive cargo is moved to a destination, where the cargo is unloaded and transferred to the customer. During transportation, the temperature is measured. As the destination is reached, it is checked if the temperature exceeds 25 degrees more than three times. If so, the goods are not OK ('NOK') and must be discarded. Otherwise, they will be transferred to the customer. The discovered decision rule could look like ①: IF $temperature.count(>= 26.0) >= 4.0$ THEN Discard Goods.

Another decision mining algorithm might discover the following decision rule ②: If $temperature\_quantile\_q\_0.8 > 25.90$ AND $temperature\_change\_quantiles\_f\_agg\_var\_isabs\_True\_qh\_1.0\_ql\_0.6\_ <= 27.67$ THEN Discard Goods. Rules ① and ② describe the same logic, which might not be visible at first sight. The second version is more complex, as the decision attributes are engineered, including more complex names and statements. Therefore, although the performance, measured using accuracy, is the same, the second version might provide less insight into the process. Insufficient insight might lead to a misinterpretation of the decision rules and, in turn, result in unfavorable business decisions. In the example, one could derive from ② to discard the goods for any temperature measurement above 25.90 degrees, which can result in either unnecessarily discarded goods or a violation of food safety regulations. This example shows that accuracy, or any performance-related metric, alone is insufficient to evaluate decision mining results. Having metrics to measure the performance and the ability to provide valuable insights can help decide which algorithm to apply for a specific use case.

Measuring criteria beyond performance-related criteria is also a goal of explainability in AI (XAI). XAI generates explanations for black-box models, thereby providing more information to the users. The extent of explainability achieved by the provided explanations can be measured using different metrics. Mostly, the understandability of the generated explanation, as well as how accu-

---

[1] Note that the result of a decision mining algorithm comprises the decision model as well as the textual decision rules stemming from the decision model.

rately the explanation fits the underlying model, are evaluated; see [24,37] for a general overview and [32] for explainability metrics with regards to predictive process monitoring. The criteria used in XAI can be a start to evaluating decision mining results. However, further criteria may be of interest. Software engineering and process mining domains provide additional criteria beyond performance-related criteria and might be valuable in evaluating decision mining results.

Therefore, this work aims to discover which criteria are suitable to evaluate decision mining results in addition to performance-based criteria by addressing the following research questions. **RQ1:** Which non-performance related criteria are relevant in the context of decision mining? **RQ2:** How to measure non-performance related criteria in decision mining? **RQ3:** How to achieve decision mining results that enable users to make informed decisions?

To answer RQ1-RQ2, software engineering, XAI, and process mining literature is analyzed to find suitable criteria in Sect. 2. Section 3 proposes metrics to evaluate these criteria regarding decision mining results. The metrics are applied to different data sets and compared to user perception in Sect. 4, followed by proposing guidelines ($\mapsto$ RQ3). A conclusion is given in Sect. 5.

2   Literature Review on Evaluation Criteria

Evaluating decision mining results should encompass performance-based and non-performance-based criteria to ensure a comprehensive evaluation. In this section, we look at literature from the domains of software engineering (SE), XAI, process mining (PM), and business process quality (QoBP) to analyze which criteria are used to evaluate methods and created artifacts. The literature analysis is not exhaustive. However, it provides comprehensive criteria covering many aspects of decision mining results.

We start by discussing SE literature as there exists an abundance of criteria to evaluate different aspects of created software, e.g., [19], and because SE criteria have already been applied to process modeling research. [34], for example, analyze how SE quality metrics can be applied to process modeling and [11] in the context of business processes in general. A concept in the SE domain related to decision mining is *useful transparency*. It refers to the goal of *"enabling stakeholders to make decisions based on the provided information and act upon them"*, capturing the challenge to get from information being available to information being useful [12]. The authors suggest that *information quality* is essential in achieving useful transparency. The information quality criteria used in [12] are initially defined by [14] and encompass 16 criteria including consistency, free-of-error, and understandability. Other information and data quality frameworks[2] such as the literature review on data quality in [10] often contain similar and overlapping criteria. The first conclusion is that data and information quality criteria provide a reasonable basis for our goal of comprehensive evaluation in decision mining.

---

[2] Data and information are distinct concepts; data consists of the raw data points and requires some interpretation to become information [10]. However, the quality criteria are strongly overlapping.

Data quality in decision mining can be analyzed at multiple levels. Firstly, the underlying data, i.e., *event logs*, can be evaluated as the quality of the event logs affects the quality of decision mining results. We consider event logs as out of scope for this work and instead refer to [2]. Secondly, the *decision model* as primary decision mining result can be evaluated. Thirdly, the textual *decision rules*, which are generated using the decision model and presented to the user, can be examined. We select data quality dimensions relevant to decision mining and address the quality of the decision model and decision rules. The 16 information quality criteria provided in [14] are used as basis and compared to quality criteria from literature in SE [10], XAI [24], PM [16], and QoBP [11]. The results are summarized in Table 1 and discussed in the following. The last column indicates whether the criterion refers to the quality of the event log, the decision model, or the decision rule. All criteria will be analyzed, and the criteria relevant to decision mining are highlighted in grey.

Table 1. Quality criteria in literature.

Information Quality [14]	Data Quality [10]	XAI [24]	Qualitative PM Criteria [16]	QoBP, Input/ Output [11]	Level
Accessibility	Accessibility			Accessibility	L(og)
Appropriate Amount of Information				Amount of Data	L
Believability				Believability	R(ule)
Completeness	Completeness	Fidelity (Completeness)	Quality (Completeness)	Completeness	M(odel)
Concise Representation		Interpretablity (Parsimony)	Quality (Conciceness)		R
Consistent Representation	Concistency	Interpretability (Clarity)	Quality (Concistency)		R, M
Ease of Manipulation					N/A
Free-of-Error	Accuracy, Validity, Reliability	Fidelity (Soundness)	Quality (Correctness)	Accuracy	M
Interpretability		Interpretability	Understandability (Readability)		R
Objectivity				Objectivity	L
Relevancy	Relevancy			Relevancy	R
Reputation				Reputation	L
Security				Security	L
Timeliness	Timeliness, Currentness			Timeliness	L, M
Understandability		Interpretability (Parsimony)	Understandability (Complexity)		R
Value-Added			Usability	Value-Added	R

XAI research provides criteria relating to explainability as discussed in Sect. 1. In XAI, explainability consists of two main criteria: understandability of the generated explanation and model fidelity, i.e., how well the explanations represent the underlying model. The two criteria can be further split into clarity, parsimony, completeness, and soundness. Understandability is relevant for decision mining. Model fidelity is relevant for non-transparent methods, e.g., neural networks. Typically, inherently transparent decision trees are used in decision mining, and a proxy model is unnecessary to generate an explanation. However, in the context of the correctness of the discovered decision model, the sub-criteria completeness and soundness are relevant.

Qualitative criteria to evaluate PM results are explored by [16]. PM artifacts are usually examined concerning three qualitative aspects, i.e., understandability, quality, and usability. Understandability and quality can be further split into sub-dimensions, overlapping with criteria named in [14], e.g., completeness and conciseness. Usability is defined as being beneficial to the user, which aligns with the criteria "Value-Added' in [14]'. Dimensions of QoBP have been defined based on SE quality criteria [11]. The Input/Output quality aspect is relevant to this work, as decision models and rules could be seen as output. These have substantial overlap with [14].

Table 1 shows the mapping of criteria from XAI, PM, and QoBP onto information quality criteria. All criteria correspond or overlap with information quality dimensions. The terms used in literature are inconsistent, e.g., interpretability and understandability are sometimes synonymous and sometimes seen as different concepts. "Believability" refers to the extent to which the presented rule is credible. It is important for the presented decision rule to be accepted as credible to be useful to users. The extent to which all necessary data values are included is described by the "Completeness" criterion. This questions whether the decision model covers all cases and data ranges. Rules should be represented as simple as possible, captured by "Concise Representation". "Consistent Representation" can refer to the rule format, but also if the model is free of contradiction. Both interpretations are potentially relevant to evaluating decision mining results. The criterion "Ease of Manipulation" captures the ability to change information. In decision mining, this applies to cases where a user feedback mechanism exists, which is generally not the case; therefore, this criterion is not included in this paper, however it might be of interest in future work. "Free-of-Error" refers to the correctness, i.e., in decision mining to the correctness of the discovered decision model and decision rules and therefore relates to performance-based criteria such as accuracy. "Interpretability" refers to the extent to which appropriate language, symbols, units, and definitions are used, which relates to attributes and conditions used in the textual rules in decision mining. The degree to which a rule meets the expectations and requirements of a user relates to "Relevancy". The extent to which data is sufficiently up-to-date is captured by "Timeliness". This can refer to the log data and the decision model if it is updated regularly to incorporate changes. This criterion is relevant for online decision mining. As up to now, only one online decision mining algorithm exists, see [30], this criterion is not included in the analysis presented here. The extent to which a user easily comprehends a rule is described by the criterion "Understandability", which relates to the complexity of a decision rule. Note that in the definition by [14] "Interpretability" and "Understandability" cover different aspects, the first one describing the comprehensibility of the contained variable names, symbols, etc., whereas the second term covers the comprehensibility of the overall rule, which are related but not identical issues. "Value-Added" can be equated to the overall goal of decision mining, i.e., providing not just information but useful information. In total, the following criteria have been defined as relevant for decision mining, i.e., "Believability","Completeness", "Conciseness", "Consistency", "Free of Error", "Interpretability', "Relevancy", "Understandability"' and "Value-Added". The following section will analyze existing metrics and, if necessary, propose new metrics to quantify the specified criteria.

3   Metrics in Decision Mining

Metrics to assess non-performance-based criteria enable evaluating decision mining results and comparing different decision mining algorithms. Data and information quality criteria can be used as proxy measurements to measure overall achieved quality. This relates to a functionally grounded evaluation strategy [5]. This section contains an analysis of related literature and a proposition of metrics to measure the defined criteria in decision mining.

Information and data quality frameworks such as [8,10,35] propose metrics for measuring quality criteria. The literature on information quality often refers to databases, web pages, and search engines. Therefore, some metrics are too broad or too specific for the context of decision mining. [10] give an overview of data quality frameworks and related measurements for, e.g., completeness, which is calculated by dividing all available items by the number of expected items, i.e., missing values in a database. Information quality regarding search engines can be assessed by a mix of quantitative metrics such as consistency using the number of style guide deviations and user surveys for, e.g., comprehensiveness or clarity [15]. Searching for missing values in a database and looking at web page style guides do not apply to decision mining.

Looking at XAI literature such as [24,37], different measures for explainability dimensions are defined. Understandability[3], for example, is measured using parsimony, i.e., the complexity of explanations. Parsimony is calculated using the number of different attributes (e.g., control flow or event attributes). Another metric is the effective complexity, which calculates the dependency of a prediction on specific attributes. For explainable predictive process monitoring, [32] discusses evaluation metrics. Parsimony and functional complexity are used to

---

[3] Please note that the terms interpretability and understandability are often used interchangeably in the literature. However, interpretability in our context refers to the attribute names, not the overall understanding of the decision rule, building on the definition by [14]. Therefore, we use the term understandability, even if the related work uses the term interpretability.

evaluate the understandability of predictions. Functional complexity measures the model complexity, similar to effective complexity, by permutating the possible values for each attribute and measuring the change in predictions.

Based on the literature analysis, we propose six metrics covering the criteria defined in Sect. 2, see Table 2: Accuracy (Free-of-Error), Model Completeness (Completeness), Effective Complexity (Conciseness), Interpretability (Interpretability), Parsimony (Understandability), and Remine Consistency (Consistency). The possible value range for all metrics is $[0, 1]$; higher values indicate "better", e.g., more accurate or less complex, results. Criteria "Believability", "Relevancy" and "Value-Added" do not have an associated metric. 'Believability" and "Relevancy" require a user survey to be evaluated appropriately, as they are inherently subjective dimensions. The criterion "Value-Added" refers to the overall benefit of the decision mining results, which depends on the use case and requires a different evaluation strategy, see [5].

Table 2. Metrics and covered criteria.

Metric	Covered Criterion
Accuracy	Free-of-Error
Model Completeness	Completeness
Effective Complexity	Conciseness
Interpretability	Interpretability
Parsimony	Understandability
Remine Consistency	Consistency

Accuracy evaluates if the discovered decision rule can classify instances correctly. The following definition is used:

$$Accuracy := \frac{Number\ of\ correctly\ classified\ instances}{Total\ number\ of\ instances}$$

Accuracy is used to evaluate the criterion "Free-of-Error". A rule is assumed to be correct, i.e. free-of-error, if the accuracy is high. There still might be cases where the accuracy is high, but the rule is incorrect, for example, due to noisy data or overfitting. A second, broader, performance-based metric is added for the evaluation, the *F1 Score*, which considers precision and recall [33].

Completeness can refer to different aspects and is used differently in literature, e.g. [10]. For decision mining, completeness can be defined as all possible classes, i.e., paths, are covered by the decision model and can be measured by:

$$Model\_Completeness := \frac{Number\ of\ classes\ in\ decision\ model}{Total\ number\ of\ classes}$$

Effective Complexity - EC is defined by [26] as the minimum number of attributes that can meet an expected performance measure; lower values indicate simple and less complex models. Similarly, [32] use functional complexity to measure understandability. Functional complexity is calculated by permutating attributes of an explanation, measuring the resulting prediction changes using the Hamming Distance. We adapt these definitions and calculate the effective complexity for decision mining by looking at the contained conditions in a decision rule and measuring the change in results if one condition is dropped at a time, using the Hamming Distance, see Algorithm 1.

Algorithm 1. Effective Complexity in Decision Mining

Input: Decision Rule R,Output: Effective Complexity
1: Change = 0, Split rule R in Conditions C, delimiter: "AND","OR"
2: **for** c in C **do**
3:     Make new rule r without c, make prediction p with r
4:     Calculate Normalized Hamming Distance(p, original prediction)
5:     Change += Hamming Distance
6: **end for**
7: EffectiveComplexity = 1-(Change/#Conditions)

Effective complexity relates to the criterion "Conciseness", as higher values indicate that the results are considerably altered if a condition is removed, and therefore, the rule only contains necessary conditions.

Interpretability for decision rules covers the comprehensibility of attribute names, symbols, and used units, as defined in Sect. 2. A new metric is proposed that evaluates the interpretability of each used attribute by considering if the attribute name contains special characters and can be found in the dictionary, i.e., if it is an understandable word[4]. Note that this definition also includes syntactic accuracy, which leads to classifying a word as not understandable if there are spelling mistakes, for example; this is reasonable as spelling mistakes can make it more difficult to comprehend names and conditions. The overall length of the rule is also taken into account, as longer rules make it more difficult to interpret the contained attributes and conditions. Units are not included, as this strongly depends on the underlying data, i.e., if the units are part of the log. The calculation can be seen in Eq. 1.

$$SpecialChars = 1 - \frac{\#Special\ Characters}{\#Characters}$$

$$NonWords = 1 - \frac{\#Words\ not\ in\ Dictionary}{\#Words\ in\ Rule}$$

$$Interpretability = \frac{1}{Length(Rule)} * x + SpecialChars * y + NonWords * z$$

$$(1)$$

---

[4] Which languages are checked can be changed. Currently, English and German dictionaries are used.

The three conditions are scaled to 1 using weights, x, y, z, with $x + y + z = 1$ and $x, y, z \in [0, 1]$. The weights are optimized using the results of the pre-test user study, see Sect. 4. Interpretability is in itself a subjective value and depends on many different components. Therefore, this metric is only intended as an approximation but cannot represent the true value of interpretability.

Parsimony is often used to evaluate the understandability of an explanation, e.g., [37]. It measures the complexity of an explanation or, in this case, a decision rule. The less complex an explanation is, the more understandable it is for humans [25]. Parsimony can be defined as the number of attributes part of an explanation [13,32]. We extend that definition by considering the number of relational conditions in a decision rule. Relational conditions are defined as conditions where the relationship between two or more attributes is relevant, e.g., `temperature1` < `temperature2` instead of `age` > 40, which adds to the complexity. Weights x and y, with $x + y = 1$ and $x, y \in [0, 1]$, are optimized using the pre-test results from Sect. 4.

$$Parsimony = \frac{1}{\#Attributes} * x + (1 - \frac{\#RelationalConditions}{\#Conditions}) * y \quad (2)$$

Remine Consistency - RC is the degree to which the decision rule stays consistent when the decision model is re-discovered on the same input data, thereby measuring the "Consistency". In literature, consistency can relate to consistency regarding a format, i.e., the proportion of items consistent with a format [10] or consistency regarding the model as used here. For decision mining, the following metric is implemented:

$$Consistency := 1 - \frac{LevenshteinDistance(Rule, ReminedRule)}{Length(Rule)} \quad (3)$$

The extent of change in a decision rule is measured using the Levenshtein distance, which calculates the least changes required to change one string into another. A high remine consistency can indicate that the model cannot accurately represent the underlying logic, therefore describing "Free-of-Error" as well, as the model changes even though the input data stays the same. Remaining refers to mining decision rules on the exact same input data with the same algorithm. This can, in future work, be expanded to investigate the change that occurs when different algorithms are used. In the following sections, the proposed metrics are applied to different data sets and compared to the results of a user study.

4   Experimental Analysis and User Study

The metrics proposed in Sect. 3 have been implemented using Python. Accuracy and F1 Score are calculated using existing libraries. The metrics are then applied to nine decision rules in the experimental analysis. To validate the metrics, a user study was conducted, and the results were compared. The source code, datasets, user study questionnaire as well as full results are available online[5].

4.1 Experimental Analysis

We start with a short description of the evaluation data sets.

Use Case I - Logistics is based on the running example (cf. Sect. 1). In addition to the rules ① and ② mentionied in Sect. 1, a third rule for Use Case I is extracted ③:

IF *temperature_intervall1_max* > 25.5 AND *temperature_intervall2_max* > 25.5 AND *temperature_intervall4_max* > 25.5 THEN Discard Goods.

Use Case II - Manufacturing is an example from the manufacturing domain, where a workpiece is produced and manually measured. The measurements are compared to the tolerances in the engineering drawing to check if the workpiece is "OK" or "Scrap". One of the discovered decision rule is ④:

IF *measurement1* > 9.5 AND *measurement1* <= 20.0 AND *measurement2* <= 70.5 AND *measurement0* > 19.5 AND *measurement0* <= 80.5 AND *measurement2* > 29.5 THEN Put in OK pile.

Use Case III - Manufacturing contains data from a real-life manufacturing process [7]. Workpieces are produced, and the workpiece's diameter is subsequently measured using the workpiece silhouette. This takes a couple of seconds but can be inaccurate. Therefore, the workpieces are transferred to a second measuring machine to measure more attributes, e.g., surface quality and flatness, resulting in more precise results. This step takes a couple of minutes. Therefore, the goal is to filter most workpieces using the first measuring step and only continue to the next step with workpieces that are likely to be "OK". An exemplary discovered decision rule looks like ⑦:

IF *diameter_intervall2_percentchange* > 0.16 THEN Discard Goods

We compare existing decision mining algorithms *BDT*, *EDT-TS*, *EDT*, and *BranchMiner*. *BDT* uses a standard decision mining algorithm without including attribute engineering methods [28]. *EDT-TS* can work with time series data and might lead to more insightful decision rules when time series data is involved [29]. EDT-TS works by applying different attribute engineering methods and can be further divided by which attributes are produced. i.e., if the time series data is split into intervals (I), calculations are applied on the whole time series (G), or pattern-based attributes (P) are engineered. *EDT* [28] and *BranchMiner* [21] are decision mining algorithms that can include relational conditions by generating new attributes. For each use case, three different algorithms were applied according to the data, i.e., Use Case 1 contains time series data; therefore, EDT-TS was applied with different attribute engineering methods. The metrics proposed in Sect. 3 are calculated for each result. In addition, a combined metric (**Interpretability&Parsimony–I&P**) is calculated, as these two metrics show a high correlation.

---

[5] https://github.com/bscheibel/dm_eval.

Table 3. Results from the experimental analysis.

Rule	Use Case	Algorithm	Accuracy	F1 Score	I&P	Effect. Complexity (EC)	Remine Consistency (RC)
①	I	EDT-TS (P)	1.00	1.00	0.82	1.00	1.00
②	I	EDT-TS (G)	0.99	0.99	0.67	0.21	1.00
③	I	EDT-TS (I)	0.70	0.70	0.75	0.50	0.23
④	II	BDT	1.00	1.00	0.80	0.08	1.00
⑤	II	EDT	1.00	1.00	0.65	0.08	0.71
⑥	II	BranchMiner	0.99	0.97	0.68	0.08	1.00
⑦	III	EDT-TS (I)	0.91	0.84	0.84	1.00	1.00
⑧	III	BDT	0.45	0.47	0.78	0.29	0.00
⑨	III	EDT-TS (P)	0.09	0.01	0.65	0.00	0.60

Table 3 shows the results for all use cases. Rule ① has high accuracy, "I&P", "EC" and "RC" values. Rule ② has almost the same accuracy, but "I&P" and "EC" are considerably lower. The low "EC" value indicates that the rule is not as concise as possible. The lower value in "I&P" is probably due to complex variable names that hinder an intuitive understanding. Rule ③ is lower in accuracy; the "I&P" value lies between rules ① and ②. The rule contains a list of interval features, which are readable but more complex than ① due to multiple conditions, which are not as intuitive. The "EC" is also lower, indicating that not all conditions are essential. The low "RC" hints that the rule does not entirely cover all necessary conditions; therefore, ③ contains redundant conditions, but not all necessary conditions are discovered. Therefore, the first rule is the most suitable for this use case. For Use Case II, rule ④ has redundant conditions; the "EC" is very low as several conditions are part of the rule. The "I&P" value is high, as the conditions are simple. Rules ⑤ and ⑥ both include a mix of relational conditions and constant values, which lead to lower "I&P" values. The "EC" value is the same for all three rules, as they all contain the same number of conditions and all three lead to accurate results. The difference only lies in the interpretability and parsimony. The lower "RC" value of ⑤ can be due to changing relational conditions in each remaining process. Rule ⑦ has high overall values; "I&P" is at 0.84 as the rule consists of one condition with a complex attribute name. Rule ⑧ has similar high "I&P" values but a much lower accuracy. This also shows that interpretability is not sufficient for evaluation of decision rules, as in this case, the rule is easy to understand but not accurate. This also shows up in the low "RC" values, as the rule is different each time, but does not contain the accurate result. Rule ⑨ has overall low to medium values for all metrics as this rule contains multiple conditions that are not accurate and change within each remining. This leads to the conclusion that ⑦ is the most suitable rule for use case III.

4.2   User Study

To evaluate the validity of the proposed metrics regarding user perception, a **user study** was conducted. The user study is used to analyze if metrics and user perception correlate, and the metrics enable an assessment of the user's perceived benefits of the textual decision rules. The user study is based on a questionnaire adapted from [17] and contains four sections. First, an introduction to decision mining and general questions are presented. Then, each section covers one use case, including a description of the use case and three decision rule versions, including the rules mentioned in Sect. 1. For each rule presented, the participants had to rate the rules according to the criteria, using a scale from 1(strongly disagree) to 5(strongly agree). In addition, a possibility for comments was provided.

Selection of Participants. In total, 20 participants filled in the questionnaire. 7 participants were part of the pre-test. According to the pre-test feedback, the phrasing of questions was adapted, and a clear definition of the criteria was added. In the main phase of the user study, 13 participants, consisting of master's students, PhD students, and post-docs, filled out the questionnaire. Several considerations guided the selection of participants. Firstly, practical feasibility was a key factor, as procuring sufficient participants for a comprehensive user study was challenging. Secondly, the chosen population has similar education and background as data analysts in companies, so they are suitable for evaluation. Thirdly, the user study was intentionally focused on this population rather than spreading resources and efforts across numerous demographic groups. This enables future comparative analyses with other demographic groups. Examples of potentially relevant stakeholder groups for use cases II and III include shop-floor workers and supervisors.

The full results can be seen online[6]. Figure 1 shows the correlation between the calculated metrics and the user study results. Most metrics strongly correlate with multiple aspects of user perception, while the "Completeness" metric does not correlate with any aspect. Looking at Fig. 1, several insights about the validity of metrics regarding user perception can be gained. The performance of the decision rule does not correlate with perceived understandability or interpretability. The metrics parsimony and interpretability correspond to the user perception of understandability and interpretability and other aspects, i.e., if the interpretability value is high, the rule was rated as concise, consistent, complete, relevant, and believable. Most metrics correlate with multiple aspects of user perception. "I&P" has higher correlations than these metrics independently.

Analyzing the strongest correlation for each aspect of the user study, "I&P" best represents understandability, interpretability, relevance, believability, and consistency, with a correlation between 0.7 and 0.89, indicating a strong correlation. Perceived conciseness is best matched by "EC", exhibiting a correlation of 0.89. Lastly, "RC" best describes completeness with a correlation of 0.57.

Comparing the results with the intended purposes of the metrics defined in Sect. 3, parsimony and interpretability metrics do correlate highly with perceived understandability and interpretability, especially when looking at the combined metric "I&P". However, "RC" does not correlate strongly with consistency but rather with completeness. "RC" measures how much the textual rule changes

---

[6] https://github.com/bscheibel/dm_eval.

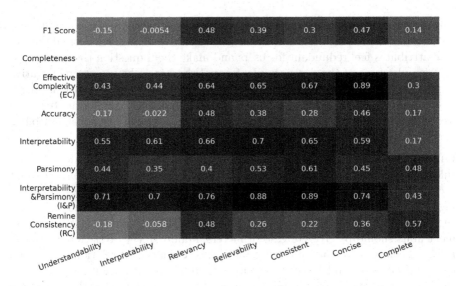

Fig. 1. Correlation between metrics (y-axis) and user perception (x-axis).

when the model is newly discovered on the same input data; high values indicate that only slight changes occur with remining, indicating that the model contains all necessary conditions. The metric "Completeness" is not informative in this case, as completeness equaled 1 in all cases. It might be interesting for future work when more complex decision rules are analyzed. "EC" accurately depicts conciseness. High "EC" values indicate more straightforward rules, i.e., fewer conditions in a rule, making the contained conditions more impactful.

The criteria relevancy and believability had no associated metrics, as we argued that these are subjective. However, these also strongly correlate with "I&P". The results show that "Interpretability& Parsimony" is the most informative metric, indicating that understandability and interpretability are essential for the user, i.e., if the user does not understand the decision rule, all other criteria cannot be evaluated adequately. We can, therefore, conclude that four metrics, "Interpretability& Parsimony", "Effective Complexity", "Remine Consistency"', and a performance-based metric, might be used to draw more meaningful conclusions about decision mining results. Therefore, we suggest including these four key metrics when analyzing decision mining results or selecting a suitable algorithm. The analysis shows that the metrics presented in the literature do not cover all aspects sufficiently. Specifically, the aspects covered by the interpretability metric and "RC" are not part of XAI metrics. In addition, "EC" was significantly changed compared to XAI.

In addition to the quantitative results, the comments have been analyzed. The following points were mentioned: A description of used attributes should be added, especially if engineered attributes are used. Users were confused about the measurement units, particularly if multiple values were part of one decision rule. If attributes are split into intervals, an explanation is needed, i.e., how many intervals exist, how many data points are contained in each interval, which intervals are relevant, etc. Showing intervals as intervals, e.g., $10 <= x <= 20$, and not a combination of conditions, i.e., $x >= 10 \ AND \ x <= 20$ is desired. Duplicate attributes feel redundant for users and make them question the correctness and completeness of the decision rule. Special characters have a strong negative impact on interpretability and understandability. Relational conditions might best represent the underlying business logic (i.e., attribute1 $<=$ attribute2), but users mentioned it is hard to understand. However, a mix of relational attributes and constant values was especially hard to understand.

Guidelines: Based on the study insights, the following guidelines for decision rule discovery and representation are proposed: (I) Additional information about the used attributes should be included as part of the decision rule, e.g., explaining the attribute name or usage of intervals. (II) Engineered attribute names should be kept as simple as possible and should be explained. (III) Measurement units should be given (e.g., centimeters, minutes). (IV) Relational decision rules are complex to read and understand. A combination of relational rules and constant values should be avoided without explaining the attributes in depth. (V) Parsimony and interpretability can be the first indicators to check decision rules, as these are the essential preconditions for the user to benefit from the rule. (VI) Effective complexity can be used to check the decision rules concerning redundant conditions. (VII) Remine consistency allows for an additional "sanity check" for the decision model as it allows for an assessment of completeness.

5   Conclusion

This work analyzes metrics to evaluate decision mining results comprehensively. One of the main findings is that performance-based metrics do not automatically relate to valuable decision rules. Another main finding is that understandability and interpretability are essential for all other criteria and can be seen as a first indicator. Furthermore, additional information about the variable names and used units, especially when using engineering attributes or intervals, is essential for understandability. In general, four metrics, "Interpretability&Parsimony", "Effective Complexity", "Remine Consistency" and a performance-based metric, can benefit a comprehensive evaluation of decision mining results.

Limitations and Threats to Validity: So far, only decision rules including two classes and presented in an "IF-THEN" format have been studied. However, decision rules can include more than two classes and be visualized in tree or table form. A more extensive, quantitative evaluation should be part of future work, focusing on more aspects, e.g., the impact of the different formats. Furthermore, the user study only contained limited participants with similar backgrounds. Therefore, future work will include comparing different stakeholder groups to ensure the generalizability of the results. This can also be used to investigate the impact of domain knowledge, for example, the use of abbreviations. Moreover, quality metrics for process event logs are considered out-of-scope for this paper. However, the guidelines for log creation [1,2] can be additionally followed to achieve valuable results.

In future work, we want to address the limitations and expand the evaluation metrics to runtime decision mining with the related challenges of data storage and outdated data.

Acknowledgements. This work has been partly supported and funded by the Austrian Research Promotion Agency (FFG) via the Austrian Competence Center for Digital Production (CDP) under the contract number 881843. and the Deutsche Forschungsgemeinschaft (DFG, German Research Foundation) – project number 514769482.

References

1. van der Aalst, W.M.P.: Extracting event data from databases to unleash process mining. In: BPM - Driving Innovation in a Digital World, pp. 105–128 (2015)
2. Andrews, R., van Dun, C.G.J., Wynn, M.T., Kratsch, W., Röglinger, M.K.E., ter Hofstede, A.H.M.: Quality-informed semi-automated event log generation for process mining. Deci. Support Syst. **132**, 113265 (2020)
3. Bazhenova, E., Haarmann, S., Ihde, S., Solti, A., Weske, M.: Discovery of fuzzy DMN decision models from event logs. In: CAiSE, pp. 629–647 (2017)
4. Dean, P., Famili, A.: Comparative performance of rule quality measures in an induction system. Appl. Intell. **7**(2), 113–124 (1997)
5. Doshi-Velez, F., Kim, B.: Towards A Rigorous Science of Interpretable Machine Learning (2017)
6. Dunkl, R., Rinderle-Ma, S., Grossmann, W., Anton Fröschl, K.: A method for analyzing time series data in process mining: application and extension of decision point analysis. In: Nurcan, S., Pimenidis, E. (eds.) CAiSE 2014. LNBIP, vol. 204, pp. 68–84. Springer, Cham (2015). https://doi.org/10.1007/978-3-319-19270-3_5
7. Ehrendorfer, M., Mangler, J., Rinderle-Ma, S.: Assessing the impact of context data on process outcomes during runtime. In: ICSOC, pp. 3–18 (2021)
8. Ehrlinger, L., Wöß, W.: A survey of data quality measurement and monitoring tools. Front. Big Data **5**, 850611 (2022)
9. Guidotti, R., Monreale, A., Ruggieri, S., Turini, F., Giannotti, F., Pedreschi, D.: A survey of methods for explaining black box models. ACM Comput. Surv. **51**(5), 93:1–93:42 (2018)
10. Hassenstein, M.J., Vanella, P.: Data quality-concepts and problems. Encyclopedia **2**(1), 498–510 (2022)
11. Heravizadeh, M., Mendling, J., Rosemann, M.: Dimensions of business processes quality (QoBP). In: Ardagna, D., Mecella, M., Yang, J. (eds.) BPM 2008. LNBIP, vol. 17, pp. 80–91. Springer, Heidelberg (2009). https://doi.org/10.1007/978-3-642-00328-8_8
12. Hosseini, M., Shahri, A., Phalp, K., Ali, R.: Four reference models for transparency requirements in information systems. Requirements Eng. **23**(2), 251–275 (2018)
13. Islam, S.R., Eberle, W., Ghafoor, S.K.: Towards quantification of explainability in explainable artificial intelligence methods (2019)
14. Kahn, B., Strong, D., Wang, R.: Information quality benchmarks: product and service performance. Commun. ACM **45**, 184–192 (2002)
15. Knight, S.A.: Developing a framework for assessing information quality on the world wide web. informing science: Int. J. Emerg. Transdisc. **8** (2005)

16. Koorn, J.J., et al.: Bringing rigor to the qualitative evaluation of process mining findings: an analysis and a proposal. In: Process Mining, pp. 120–127 (2021)
17. Lee, Y.W., Strong, D.M., Kahn, B.K., Wang, R.Y.: AIMQ: a methodology for information quality assessment. Inf. Manage. **40**(2), 133–146 (2002)
18. Leewis, S., Berkhout, M., Smit, K.: Future challenges in decision mining at governmental institutions. In: AMCIS 2020 Proceedings, vol. 6 (2020)
19. Leite, J.C.S.D.P., Cappelli, C.: Software transparency. Bus. Inf. Syst. Eng. **2**(3), 127–139 (2010)
20. de Leoni, M., van der Aalst, W.M.P.: Data-aware process mining: discovering decisions in processes using alignments. In: Symposium on Applied Computing, p. 1454 (2013)
21. de Leoni, M., Dumas, M., García-Bañuelos, L.: Discovering branching conditions from business process execution logs. In: Cortellessa, V., Varró, D. (eds.) FASE 2013. LNCS, vol. 7793, pp. 114–129. Springer, Heidelberg (2013). https://doi.org/10.1007/978-3-642-37057-1_9
22. de Leoni, M., Mannhardt, F.: Decision discovery in business processes. In: Encyclopedia of Big Data Technologies, pp. 1–12 (2018)
23. Mannhardt, F., de Leoni, M., Reijers, H.A., van der Aalst, W.M.P.: Decision mining revisited - discovering overlapping rules. In: Nurcan, S., Soffer, P., Bajec, M., Eder, J. (eds.) CAiSE 2016. LNCS, vol. 9694, pp. 377–392. Springer, Cham (2016). https://doi.org/10.1007/978-3-319-39696-5_23
24. Markus, A.F., Kors, J.A., Rijnbeek, P.R.: The role of explainability in creating trustworthy artificial intelligence for health care: a comprehensive survey of the terminology, design choices, and evaluation strategies. J. Biomed. Inform. **113**, 103655 (2021)
25. Miller, G.A.: The magical number seven, plus or minus two: some limits on our capacity for processing information. Psychol. Rev. **63**, 81–97 (1956)
26. Nguyen, A.p., Martínez, M.R.: On quantitative aspects of model interpretability (2020)
27. Rozinat, A.: Towards an evaluation framework for process mining algorithms. In: BPM reports, vol. 0706. BPMcenter. org, Eindhoven (2007)
28. Scheibel, B., Rinderle-Ma, S.: Comparing decision mining approaches with regard to the meaningfulness of their results. arXiv:2109.07335 [cs] (2021)
29. Scheibel, B., Rinderle-Ma, S.: Decision mining with time series data based on automatic feature generation. In: Advanced Information Systems Engineering, pp. 3–18 (2022)
30. Scheibel, B., Rinderle-Ma, S.: Online decision mining and monitoring in process-aware information systems. In: Ralyté, J., Chakravarthy, S., Mohania, M., Jeusfeld, M.A., Karlapalem, K. (eds.) ER 2022. LNCS, vol. 13607, pp. 271–280. Springer, Cham (2022). https://doi.org/10.1007/978-3-031-17995-2_19
31. De Smedt, J., Hasić, F., vanden Broucke, S.K.L.M., Vanthienen, J.: Towards a holistic discovery of decisions in process-aware information systems. In: Carmona, J., Engels, G., Kumar, A. (eds.) BPM 2017. LNCS, vol. 10445, pp. 183–199. Springer, Cham (2017). https://doi.org/10.1007/978-3-319-65000-5_11
32. Stevens, A., De Smedt, J.: Explainability in process outcome prediction: guidelines to obtain interpretable and faithful models (2022)
33. Ting, K.M.: Precision and recall. In: Encyclopedia of Machine Learning, p. 781. Springer (2010)
34. Vanderfeesten, I., Cardoso, J., Mendling, J., Reijers, H., van der Aalst, W.M.P.: Quality Metrics for Business Process Models. IEEE Trans. Softw. Eng. (2007)

35. Wang, R.Y., Strong, D.M.: Beyond accuracy: what data quality means to data consumers. J. Manag. Inf. Syst. **12**(4), 5–33 (1996)
36. Weller, A.: Transparency: motivations and challenges. In: Samek, W., Montavon, G., Vedaldi, A., Hansen, L.K., Müller, K.-R. (eds.) Explainable AI: Interpreting, Explaining and Visualizing Deep Learning. LNCS (LNAI), vol. 11700, pp. 23–40. Springer, Cham (2019). https://doi.org/10.1007/978-3-030-28954-6_2
37. Zhou, J., Gandomi, A.H., Chen, F., Holzinger, A.: Evaluating the quality of machine learning explanations: a survey on methods and metrics. Electronics **10**(5), 593 (2021)

Event and Process Discovery

Making Sense of Temporal Event Data: A Framework for Comparing Techniques for the Discovery of Discriminative Temporal Patterns

Chiara Di Francescomarino[1,2] , Ivan Donadello[3(✉)] , Chiara Ghidini[1,3] ,
Fabrizio Maria Maggi[3] , Williams Rizzi[2,3] , and Sergio Tessaris[3]

[1] Fondazione Bruno Kessler, Trento, Italy
[2] University of Trento, Trento, Italy
[3] Free University of Bozen-Bolzano, Bolzano, Italy
ivan.donadello@unibz.it

Abstract. Extracting knowledge from complex data in an explicit formalization is one of the main challenges in creating human understandable descriptions of data, and in bringing humans in the loop when analyzing it. Recent developments in Process Mining and Machine Learning have brought about several approaches for the extraction of an important form of knowledge: the one that discriminates between two classes of temporal event data using temporal logic patterns. In this exploratory paper, we introduce a framework for analyzing and comparing these different approaches. In particular, the framework is used to test three different state-of-the-art approaches, namely binary discovery, Deviance Mining and explanation-based techniques. While the specific results could be affected by the considered implementations, the evaluation framework is general and enables the comparison of any methods for extracting temporal logic knowledge from temporal event data.

Keywords: Linear Temporal Logic · Process Mining · Temporal Data · Deviance Mining · Discriminative Patterns

1 Introduction

Making sense of data, and extracting the knowledge it contains in explicit formalizations, such as the one provided by conceptual or formal models, is an important step in creating human understandable descriptions of data, and in bringing humans in the loop when analyzing it.

A specific form of knowledge extraction that is gaining more and more importance is the one that aims at investigating, in a comparative manner, the difference (or *discrimination*) between different datasets by characterizing this difference through appropriate patterns. This task, which can be considered a special instance of "contrast pattern mining" [9], is of particular importance when dealing with complex problems and complex domains in the real world, since the

G. Guizzardi et al. (Eds.): CAiSE 2024, LNCS 14663, pp. 423–439, 2024.
https://doi.org/10.1007/978-3-031-61057-8_25

detection of differences between process executions with positive and negative outcomes can be crucial to support appropriate decisions based on data.

Consider for instance a process analyst within a hospital aiming at analyzing the procedures for the treatment of fractures, whose executions are logged in an Information System in the form of traces. The analyst aims at understanding the difference between traces in which the patient recovers slowly and the (desired) ones in which the patient recovers quickly. This analysis could, for example, provide insights on specific patients' characteristics (e.g., their area of residence, or their age), or control-flow patterns characterizing the slow-recovery traces w.r.t. the fast-recovery ones.

In this paper, we focus on the latter case, i.e., on the identification of *temporal patterns* that represent the difference (in terms of control-flow) between two classes (sets) of *temporal event data* (a.k.a. execution traces). We call the two classes of data $\mathcal{L}^+$ and $\mathcal{L}^-$, and we use the DECLARE process modeling language [22] (see Sect. 4.1), as the language to express those patterns. We use DECLARE as it is one of the reference languages used to describe *temporal patterns* (or temporal constraints) between activities, and it also comes with a clear semantics based on Linear Temporal Logic over finite traces (LTL_f) [6].

Let us assume that a process analyst has classified execution traces in two classes $\mathcal{L}^+$ and $\mathcal{L}^-$ that exhibit different characteristics to investigate (e.g., different recovery times as in the example above). The techniques that the analyst can use to identify DECLARE patterns that represent the differences between $\mathcal{L}^+$ and $\mathcal{L}^-$ are manifold. Nonetheless the sets of specific patterns returned in output by these techniques can greatly differ. This leaves the question of how we can characterize and compare these outputs, and ultimately how we can help process analysts to choose the approach that is more suited to their needs.

In this paper, we make a first attempt to answer this question and aim at providing an evaluation framework enabling the comparison of techniques for the discovery of discriminative temporal patterns, whose output can be expressed in LTL_f, using: (i) metrics based on deterministic finite-state automata (DFA) for computing logical relationships among models, and (ii) metrics based on the compliance of execution traces to models (Sect. 6). To demonstrate the framework, we instantiate it using three techniques stemming from different approaches, namely *binary discovery*, *Deviance Mining*, and *feature-based explainers*, also detailed in Sect. 5. While being born in different ways, relying on different techniques, and extracting different types of knowledge from the same data, they all have in common the goal of describing the differences between $\mathcal{L}^+$ and $\mathcal{L}^-$ with the DECLARE language. These approaches may, for instance, discover in the example above that patients recovering slowly correspond to patients who do not perform rehabilitation after surgery. Specifically, the techniques we take into consideration can be described as follows:

1. *binary discovery* aims at discovering process models that characterize the behaviors contained in $\mathcal{L}^+$, while enabling to discard as much as possible the behaviors contained in $\mathcal{L}^-$ [5,25].
2. *Deviance Mining* identifies only the constraints that discriminate between $\mathcal{L}^+$ and $\mathcal{L}^-$ [2,23]. Therefore, it enables us to understand aspects where the two

sets differ (e.g., the mandatory presence of a particular ordering between two events in $\mathcal{L}^+$ that is never present in $\mathcal{L}^-$).

3. *feature-based explainers* of a binary classification model trained to predict if a trace belongs to $\mathcal{L}^+$ or $\mathcal{L}^-$ describe why a certain prediction is given, not only for a single trace but also for the entire quadrants of the confusion matrix associated to the classification model [24].

Thus, we neither aim at providing yet another technique for the discovery of discriminative patterns, nor strive for evaluating or surveying techniques (as in [28]). We rather aim at proposing a framework (method and metrics) to compare different LTL$_f$-based techniques for the discovery of discriminative temporal patterns. The specific evaluation reported in Sect. 7 is meant to compare the three specific techniques described above, and represents the first available study in the literature aimed at understanding their differences and similarities. While the specific results could be affected by the considered implementations, the evaluation framework is general and enables the comparison of any methods that aim at extracting knowledge that can be rewritten in LTL$_f$.

2   Motivating Example

A hospital carries out the procedures for the treatment of fractures, whose executions are logged in its Information System. Every process instance starts with the patient examination (doExamin). For each X-ray exam (doXRay), a checkRisk activity must be performed before it. Activities doRepositioning, applyCast and doSurgery require that doXRay occurs before they are executed. After every execution of applyCast, eventually removeCast must be executed. At the end of the process the rehabilitation may, or may not be performed (doRehab). The head of the orthopaedic ward of the hospital is interested in identifying the best therapy for the ward's patients, helping them recover fast. To this aim, the head of the ward needs to understand the discrimination between two distinct trace classes by characterizing the slow-recovery ($\mathcal{L}^-$) w.r.t. the fast-recovery ($\mathcal{L}^+$) ones. A resulting list of temporal logic patterns will give suggestions on how to intervene so to match the behavior of the desired (fast-recovery) traces. In

Table 1. Trace distribution in terms of DECLARE patterns.

DECLARE pattern	Description	Fast-recovery trace %	Slow-recovery trace %
RESPONSE (doSurgery, doRehab)	doSurgery is eventually followed by doRehab	100%	40%
EXISTENCE2 (doX-Ray)	doX-Ray is performed at least twice	90%	5%
CHAIN SUCCESSION (doExamin,doSurgery)	doExamin and doSurgery are executed one immediately after the other	90%	20%

the context of a scenario like this, the fast-recovery ($\mathcal{L}^+$) and the slow-recovery traces ($\mathcal{L}^-$) are provided by a process analyst to process analysis tools that output two process models (expressed using the DECLARE language) representing the behavior of the two classes of traces. The tools can be implemented by using (i) a DECLARE discovery technique; (ii) a deviance miner, i.e., a classifier in combination with a rule extractor (such as RipperK), or (iii) a classifier in combination with a feature-based explainer. By assuming a distribution of the traces as reported in Table 1, the process analyst aims at comparing the models returned by the three approaches.

3   Related Work

This section is organized in three parts: in the first part, we report about existing approaches for the discovery of declarative models that learn from execution traces partitioned into a positive and a negative set, in the second part, we describe Deviance Mining techniques applied to temporal event data, while the last part focuses on explanation-based techniques for temporal event data.

The information contained in a set of negative traces is used in declarative process discovery approaches, e.g., [1,4,5,14]. While the works in [1,4,14] mainly rely on the principles of the Inductive Constraint Logic algorithm, in [5,15,25], process discovery is considered as a binary classification task.

The main works related to business process Deviance Mining can be classified into two main families: the ones using delta-analysis can be used to (manually) identify differences between the models discovered from deviant and non-deviant traces, e.g., [26], and those based on classification techniques [2,3,16,20,23,27]. Among the works in this latter group, some use the frequency of individual activities [20,27] to train a classifier, others [3] leverage sequential pattern mining to discover sequential features to be used in the training phase. In [2,23], the authors evaluate the impact of different sequential and declarative patterns and their combination to train a classifier, while, in [16], discriminative mining is used to discover discriminative patterns that, although not necessarily very frequent, clearly discriminate between deviant and non-deviant traces. A benchmark collecting all these works, evaluating and comparing them in terms of different feature types and classifiers is presented in [28].

Concerning explainability approaches, only few - and extremely recent - works have applied explainability techniques to temporal event data - especially in the field of Predictive Process Monitoring [18] (PPM). A framework to equip PPM systems with explanations intelligible by the actors of a business process is proposed in [11]. The framework is based on post-hoc techniques. In [24], post-hoc techniques have been used to characterize the quadrants of the confusion matrix associated to a predictive model and to identify the features leading to wrong predictions, with the final goal of improving the prediction accuracy of the predictive model. An approach leveraging Bayesian Networks to capture dependencies between the features used to train a predictive model and a prediction provided by the model on the next activity that will be executed in a business process is presented in [21].

None of the above works provides a framework to compare approaches for the discovery of discriminative patterns from temporal event data.

4 Preliminaries

In this section, we provide preliminary concepts used in remainder of the paper.

4.1 The DECLARE Language

As a formal basis for specifying temporal patterns, we use a formalization based on Linear Temporal Logic over finite traces (LTL_f) [6]. This logic is at the basis of the well-known DECLARE [22] constraint-based process modeling language.

A DECLARE model fixes a set of activities $\mathcal{A}$, and a set of constraints over such activities D, formalized using LTL_f rules. The overall model is then formalized as the conjunction of the LTL_f rules of its constraints. Among all possible LTL_f rules, DECLARE selects some predefined templates. Each DECLARE template is a rule with placeholders to be substituted by concrete activities. For example, constraint RESPONSE (doSurgery, doRehab) is an instantiation of RESPONSE template and indicates that every occurrence of activity doSurgery must be eventually followed by an occurrence of doRehab.

4.2 Encoding Traces Using LTL_f Temporal Patterns

In order to explain discrepancies between the set of *positive* traces ($\mathcal{L}^+$) and the set of *negative* traces ($\mathcal{L}^-$) contained in a set of traces $\mathcal{L}$ (a.k.a. event log), the traces need to be transformed into numerical feature vectors, which can then be used to train a classifier. To this aim, we use the encoding presented in [2,23], where each element of the feature vector corresponds to the LTL_f temporal pattern derived from a DECLARE constraint and has value:

- 0, if the corresponding DECLARE constraint is violated in the trace;
- 1, if the corresponding DECLARE constraint is satisfied in the trace.

The event log is then transformed into a matrix of numerical values where each row corresponds to a trace and each column corresponds to a feature. For instance, given the trace $\langle a, b, c, a, b, c, d, a, b \rangle$:

- constraint RESPONSE (a, c) is violated, since the third occurrence of a leads to a violation (is not eventually followed by c) and is encoded as 0;
- constraint RESPONSE (a, b) is satisfied and is encoded as 1.

To select the DECLARE constraints to be used for building the feature vectors, the first step is to discover a list of constraints from the event log. To this aim, frequent activity sets (i.e., pairs of activities occurring frequently together in the same trace according to a user-defined percentage threshold) are extracted separately from $\mathcal{L}^+$ and $\mathcal{L}^-$ and a list of candidate constraints is generated by instantiating DECLARE templates with all the possible permutations of each frequent set. Each candidate is then checked separately over $\mathcal{L}^+$ and $\mathcal{L}^-$ (depending on whether it is derived from an activity set discovered from $\mathcal{L}^+$ or $\mathcal{L}^-$) to verify if it is satisfied in a percentage of traces that is above a given *support* threshold.

The number of patterns generated from the discovery is, generally, still too large to use all of them to build the feature vectors. Therefore, it becomes important to remove the ones that are less discriminative and, therefore, do not give much value for training the explanatory model. To this aim, the temporal patterns discovered in the previous step are selected by first ranking them according to the Fisher score [13]. Following the ranking, patterns are selected until every trace satisfies at least a fixed number of patterns (*coverage* threshold). A pattern is only chosen if it is satisfied in at least one of the traces not totally covered yet.

5   Discovery of Discriminative Temporal Patterns

In this section, we introduce the three approaches for the discovery of discriminative temporal patterns from temporal event data we compare in this paper, which are also summarized in Fig. 1. We remind the reader that, although we demonstrate the presented comparison framework by instantiating it using these approaches, the framework is easily applicable to other methods that extract LTL_f-based temporal knowledge. We selected these approaches because they represent the most recent advances in the discovery of discriminative temporal patterns and because the code needed to implement them and running the experiments was publicly available. In particular, for *binary discovery*, we use the approach presented in [5], for *Deviance Mining*, we use the encoding presented in [2,23] in combination with a white-box classifier, and for *feature-based explainers*, we use SHapley Additive explanations (SHAP) [17] in combination with a gray-box classifier. Note that each of these approaches returns a single DECLARE model $\mathcal{M}^+$ describing the class of positive traces $\mathcal{L}^+$. To obtain the negative model $\mathcal{M}^-$, we simply flip the labels in the traces of the log and run each approache as is.

5.1   Discovery as a Binary Supervised Task

Differently from traditional process discovery approaches that discover models from an unlabeled event log, a recent stream of works [5,15,25] treats model discovery as a binary supervised task that learns from execution traces partitioned into two sets according to some business or domain-related criterion.

In this paper, we use the NEGDIS approach presented in [5] to discover, given two input sets of positive $(\mathcal{L}^+)$ and negative $(\mathcal{L}^-)$ traces, a DECLARE model accepting all positive traces and rejecting as much as possible the negative ones. NEGDIS can be seen as a two-step procedure: in the first step, a solution space is built; in the second step, solutions are selected from the solution space by leveraging an optimization algorithm.In order to build the solution space, a set

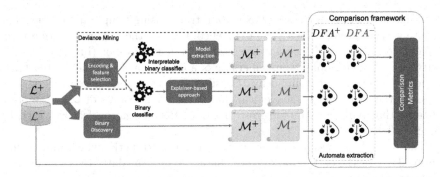

Fig. 1. The proposed framework.

C of candidate constraints is identified. Each candidate constraint is a constraint in $D[\mathcal{A}]$ (i.e., the set of DECLARE constraints instantiated over the alphabet of activities $\mathcal{A}$) that accepts all positive traces and rejects at least one negative trace. To build C, NEGDIS constructs a *compatibles* set ($compatibles(D[\mathcal{A}], \mathcal{L}^+)$), i.e., the set of constraints that accept all traces in $\mathcal{L}^+$.

Then, it defines the *sheriffs* function ($sheriffs(t)$) to associate to any trace t in $\mathcal{L}^-$ the constraints of *compatibles* that reject t. Then, $C = \bigcup_{t \in \mathcal{L}^-} sheriffs(t)$ is the set of all the constraints in $D[\mathcal{A}]$ accepting all positive traces and rejecting at least one negative trace. The solution space is therefore:

$$\mathcal{Z} = \{\mathcal{M} \in 2^C \mid \forall t \in \mathcal{L}^- \ t \not\models \mathcal{M} \ or \ sheriffs(t) = \emptyset\}.$$

The second step of NEGDIS uses an optimization strategy to identify the "best" solutions; in [5], two different criteria are taken into account: *generality* (or conversely, *specificity*), and *simplicity*. NEGDIS uses a (incomplete) model closure operator to take into account redundancy among constraints. If the user is interested in the most general models, then NEGDIS optimizes w.r.t. subset inclusion; while in the other case it uses just the cardinality as the objective function. In our motivating example, NEGDIS would discover a model containing RESPONSE (doSurgery, doRehab). This constraint is discovered because is satisfied in 100% of the fast-recovery traces and violated in a relatively high number of slow-recovery traces. Note that, although EXISTENCE2(doXRay) discriminates better between traces in $\mathcal{L}^+$ and traces in $\mathcal{L}^-$ (i.e., satisfies less negative traces), NEGDIS provides a model satisfying all positive traces.

5.2 Combining LTL$_f$ Encoding and Deviance Mining Techniques

Business process Deviance Mining [19,28] is a branch of process mining which aims at analyzing event logs in order to discover and characterize business process deviances. The purpose is to discover a descriptive and informative model distinguishing the "good" traces from the deviant ones.

The LTL$_f$ encoding (described in Subsect. 4.2) of the positive ($\mathcal{L}^+$) and negative ($\mathcal{L}^-$) logs can be used together with Deviance Mining techniques to explain the differences between classes of execution traces using temporal patterns. The feature vectors produced with the LTL_f encoding and the feature selection technique, introduced in Subsect. 4.2, are used to train a white-box (binary) classifier that is used to determine the membership of a trace to a class. Then, a DECLARE model $\mathcal{M}$ is extracted from such a classifier to have a logical characterization of one of the two classes. This logical characterization is a set of LTL_f temporal patterns that will be extracted from the most discriminating features used by the classifier.

The white-box classifier we use in this paper is RipperK, which implements a procedure for the extraction of rules characterizing the data. Every single rule r is a conjunction of features implying a class C, $r : c_1 \wedge c_2 \wedge \ldots \wedge c_m \rightarrow C$. In our case, every feature c_i is a DECLARE constraint and $C \in \{0, 1\}$. Therefore, a DECLARE model $\mathcal{M}$ can be extracted from each rule r by considering its left side. RipperK extracts rules in an iterative manner. In particular it:

1. discovers from a training (labeled) dataset a single rule with the highest information gain (in the first iteration the rule is a single feature, in the following ones a conjunction of features);
2. removes the samples covered by the discovered rule;
3. repeats steps 1) and 2) until a stopping criterion is met, e.g., the information gain cannot be improved.

Notice that RipperK produces a disjunction of different rules, i.e., a set of different DECLARE models characterizing a class. To extract a single DECLARE model from RipperK, we select the rule with highest discriminating power. In our motivating example, RipperK would discover a model containing EXISTENCE2 (doXRay). This constraint is discovered because it is the one that best discriminates between fast- and slow-recovery traces (i.e., it is satisfied in 90% of the traces in $\mathcal{L}^+$ and violated in 95% of the ones in $\mathcal{L}^-$).

5.3   Combining LTL_f Encoding and Explanation-Based Techniques

Black-box approaches in Machine Learning motivate the adoption of explainers providing an explanation of their outcomes. Current literature distinguishes two techniques for explainers: post-hoc and ante-hoc techniques [12]. While the former generate the explanations while testing the trained model, the latter integrate explanations while training the data. In this paper, we use SHAP, which falls into the former branch, and is widely recognized to be the most effective explainer available nowadays [17]. The goal of SHAP is to explain the prediction of an instance x by computing the contribution of each feature to the prediction. The SHAP explanation method computes Shapley values from game theory, thus showing the relative impact of each feature on the output of the Machine Learning model by comparing the relative effect of the inputs against the average.

The LTL_f encoding discussed above can also be leveraged with post-hoc feature-based explainers as SHAP in order to characterize positive and negative traces in terms of temporal descriptions. The feature-based explainer takes as input a classifier (trained with the LTL$_f$ encoding) and a trace, whose class we want to predict, encoded in terms of temporal patterns, and returns as output a vector of *explanations*. Each explanation contains a feature-value pair and a score value ranging between −1 and 1, which represents the impact of the feature-value pair on the classification. A positive value means that the feature-value pair influences the classifier towards the prediction, while a negative value means that the feature-value pair influences the classifier towards the opposite class. The absolute value of the score denotes the strength of the impact of the feature-value pair towards the predicted class or towards the opposite class. In each vector returned by the feature-based explainer (for a given trace), explanations are filtered out based on an *importance threshold*, so as to keep only the feature-value pairs influencing the most the predictions.

As we want to characterize classes of temporal event data using explanations, and explainers provide a set of explanations for each trace separately, we leverage an abstraction mechanism to provide global explanations valid for all traces belonging to a certain class. In particular, we use Association Rule Mining to identify which explanations are the most frequently provided together by the explainer. Using a *frequency threshold*, we extract the set of feature-value pairs frequently provided together for traces belonging to a given class. The sets of feature-value pairs are cleaned in order to remove intra-set redundancies and subsumptions among LTL$_f$ temporal patterns.

We finally use a ranking based on the Fisher score in order to extract the set of feature-value pairs with the highest score, i.e., the set that discriminates best between traces belonging to one class and traces belonging to the other class. If two or more sets of feature-value pairs get the same score at the top of the ranking, then the strongest set of feature-value pairs, i.e., the set that subsumes the others, is selected. In our motivating example, the explainer would discover a model containing RESPONSE (doSurgery,doRehab), EXISTENCE2 (doXRay) and CHAIN SUCCESSION (doExamin,doSurgery). These constraints are discovered since they all represent features discriminating between fast- and slow-recovery traces.

6   The Proposed Framework

We now introduce the proposed framework (see Fig. 1) for comparing the (LTL$_f$-based) temporal patterns returned by different approaches such as the ones described in the previous section. Each approach A explains the temporal event data recorded in an event log $\mathcal{L}$ in terms of a set of LTL$_f$ patterns, i.e., in terms of a model $\mathcal{M}_A$. We aim at comparing the models returned by the approaches both (i) in terms of the language they describe by identifying the logical relationships between them (*model relationship metrics*); and (ii) in terms of their ability to explain the temporal data from which they have been generated, i.e., in terms of their ability to accept the traces of one class and discard the traces in the opposite class (*compliance metrics*). To be able to compute these two groups of metrics, the framework transforms each model $\mathcal{M}_A$ into its corresponding DFA $DFA[\mathcal{M}_A]$ using the algorithm presented in [7].

6.1 Model Relationship Metrics

The aim of this group of metrics is identifying the logical relationships between two models $\mathcal{M}_{A_1}$ and $\mathcal{M}_{A_2}$, i.e., (i) whether they describe exactly the same behavior (*trace equivalence*), corresponding to logical equivalence (if the automata representing the two models are deterministic and minimized they are equivalent if they are exactly the same); (ii) whether the behavior described by one of the two models subsumes the behavior described by the other model (*subsumption*), corresponding to logical implication (if the automata representing the two models are deterministic and minimized, this is verified by checking that their intersection is equal to one of the two original automata); and (iii) whether they describe completely different behaviors (*empty intersection*). To this aim, we transform each model $\mathcal{M}_A$ into its corresponding automaton $DFA[\mathcal{M}_A]$. Given $DFA[\mathcal{M}_{A_1}]$ and $DFA[\mathcal{M}_{A_2}]$, the two automata generated starting from $\mathcal{M}_{A_1}$ and $\mathcal{M}_{A_2}$, we identify their logical relationships by using the following metrics:

Trace equivalence ($\equiv$): boolean metric indicating whether the two automata are equivalent, i.e., whether they accept the same set of traces.
Subsumption ($\supseteq$): boolean metric indicating whether the first automaton subsumes the second one, i.e., $DFA[\mathcal{M}_{A_1}] \supseteq DFA[\mathcal{M}_{A_2}]$;
Empty intersection ($\cap = \emptyset$): boolean metric indicating whether the automata intersection accepts no traces, i.e., $(DFA[\mathcal{M}_{A_1}] \cap DFA[\mathcal{M}_{A_2}]) = \emptyset$.

In our motivating example, the models discovered by NG, DvM and E are not equivalent (the models are all different), they do not subsume each other, and they never have empty intersection (they do not contradict each other).

6.2 Compliance Metrics

The compliance metrics aim at measuring the ability of a model $\mathcal{M}_A$ to accept one class of traces and to discard the traces in the other one. To this aim, given a log $\mathcal{L}$ and a model $\mathcal{M}_A$, we define the *acceptance accuracy* as the metric that measures the percentage of traces of $\mathcal{L}$ accepted by $DFA[\mathcal{M}_A]$:

$$acc(DFA[\mathcal{M}_A], \mathcal{L}) = \frac{|\mathcal{S}(DFA[\mathcal{M}_A], \mathcal{L})|}{|\mathcal{L}|}$$

where $\mathcal{S}(DFA[\mathcal{M}_A], \mathcal{L})$ is the set of traces in $\mathcal{L}$ accepted by $DFA[\mathcal{M}_A]$.

As each approach A returns both a positive and a negative model explaining $\mathcal{L}^+$ and $\mathcal{L}^-$, respectively, we are interested in studying the accuracy of the four combinations of models and logs. A good model will show high accuracy with the log with the same polarity and low accuracy with the log with the opposite polarity. For instance, in our motivating example, $acc(\mathcal{M}_{\text{NG}}^+/\mathcal{L}^+)$ is 90%, since 90% of the traces in $\mathcal{L}^+$ satisfy $\mathcal{M}_{\text{NG}}^+$, while $acc(\mathcal{M}_{\text{NG}}^+/\mathcal{L}^-)$ is 5%. For DvM, $acc(\mathcal{M}_{\text{DvM}}^+/\mathcal{L}^+)$ is 100%, while $acc(\mathcal{M}_{\text{DvM}}^+/\mathcal{L}^-)$ is 40%.

7   Evaluation

We demonstrate the proposed framework by providing real-life logs as input to the approaches described in Sect. 5: (i) NEGDIS (NG); (ii) the technique based on Deviance Mining (DvM), which uses RipperK as white-box classifier; and (iii) the technique based on explainers (E), which uses Random Forest (RF) as (gray-box) classifier and SHAP for building the explanations. The aim of our experiments is to compare these approaches based on the following desiderata:

D1 the acceptance accuracy of models with logs with the same polarity should be maximized and the one with logs with the opposite polarity minimized;
D2 discrepancies between positive and negative models should be maximized.

The term polarity here indicates whether a class of traces is positive or negative, e.g., a fast or slow recovery in our motivating example. In addition, we check the hypothesis (H) that different models with the same polarity are able to characterize the log (with the same polarity) in a similar manner, i.e., the intersection automaton of two models with the same polarity should not be empty and should have high acceptance accuracy with the log with that polarity.

7.1   Experimental Settings

In our experiments, the optimization strategy we used to run the NG approach is *simplicity*. For both the Deviance Mining DvM and the explainer-based E approaches, we preprocessed the logs by encoding the traces using the LTL$_f$ encoding and the feature selection technique, introduced in Section *Preliminaries*. We used a *coverage threshold* of 20 and grid search for hyperparameter tuning.

In the E technique, we selected the top 10 feature-value pairs for which the explainer returned a positive value, i.e., the top 10 features (the *importance threshold*) contributing towards the prediction provided by the RF. In the Association Rule Mining algorithm, we set the *frequency threshold*, for the extraction of the sets of feature-value pairs, to 2, i.e., all the sets of feature-value pairs that are satisfied by at least two traces are scored based on the Fisher score. The experiment source code, the datasets and the discovered models are available at https://github.com/ivanDonadello/MakingSenseTemporalEventData.

7.2   Datasets

We now describe the datasets used for our experiments.

The ***Sepsis Single Constraint Labeling (SCL)*** dataset was obtained from a real-life log (the *Sepsis* event log https://data.4tu.nl/articles/Sepsis_Cases_-_Event_Log/12707639) containing execution traces pertaining to the treatment of sepsis cases in a hospital. The criterion chosen for dividing the traces into positive and negative traces (*labeling*) is based on the trace compliance with a single DECLARE constraint.[1] Using this criterion, the whole log $\mathcal{L}$ is

---

[1] The constraint(s) are identified using the discovery tool available in the process mining toolkit RuM available at https://rulemining.org/.

split into parts of similar sizes, i.e., a positive log $\mathcal{L}^+$ including the traces of $\mathcal{L}$ satisfying the constraint ($\sim 54\%$) and a negative one $\mathcal{L}^-$ including the traces of $\mathcal{L}$ violating the constraint ($\sim 46\%$).

The *Sepsis Multiple Constraints Labeling (MCL)* dataset relies on the same *Sepsis* event log used to create SCL, but has a more complex labeling w.r.t. the previous dataset. Here, the positive log contains traces that jointly satisfy multiple constraints.[2] Using this criterion, the log is split into positive traces ($\mathcal{L}^+$) satisfying (all) the constraints ($\sim 35\%$) and negative traces ($\mathcal{L}^-$) that violate at least one of the selected constraints ($\sim 65\%$).

The *Sepsis Patient Return, Sepsis IC and Sepsis Release (Sepsis Rel.)* datasets (provided in [29]) rely on the *Sepsis* dataset with three different labelings:

- *Sepsis Return dataset*: in the positive log $\mathcal{L}^+$, the patient returns to the Emergency Room within 28 days from the discharge ($\sim 14\%$);
- *Sepsis IC dataset*: in the positive log $\mathcal{L}^+$, the patient is (eventually) admitted to intensive care ($\sim 14\%$);
- *Sepsis Release dataset*: in the positive log $\mathcal{L}^+$, the patient is discharged from the hospital on the basis of a reason different from *Release A*, i.e., the most common release type ($\sim 86\%$).

The *BPIC 2011* dataset has been published in relation to the Business Process Intelligence Challenge (BPIC) in 2011. This event log refers to traces from the Gynaecology department of a Dutch academic hospital. Each trace records procedures and treatments applied to a given patient. In the positive log $\mathcal{L}^+$, patients are more than 60 years old ($\sim 51\%$). This labeling investigates whether treatments are different according to the age of the patient.

The *BPIC 2017* dataset refers to the execution history of a loan application process in a Dutch financial institution. Each trace stores the events related to a particular loan application. The labeling (provided in [29]) is based on whether a loan application is accepted or not. The accepted applications in the positive log $\mathcal{L}^+$ are $\sim 41\%$ of the traces.

The *Dreyers Foundation* dataset, provided in [8], documents the application grant process of the Dreyers Foundation that supports budding lawyers and architects. The application requests are traced through an information system and the log also collects the early stages of deployment and the testing phase of the system. The labeling [25] classifies the executions based on whether they were reset due to a system failure ($\mathcal{L}^+$, $\sim 43\%$) or not.

The *Production* dataset contains traces of a manufacturing process. Each trace stores information about the activities, workers and/or machines involved in the production process of an item. The labeling (provided in [29]) is based on whether, in a trace, there are rejected work orders ($\mathcal{L}^+$, $\sim 53\%$) or not.

---

[2] The constraint(s) are identified using the discovery tool available in the process mining toolkit RuM available at https://rulemining.org/.

Table 2. Acceptance accuracy (denoted as $\mathcal{M}/\mathcal{L}$) of all the considered models and datasets. $|\mathcal{M}|$ indicates the cardinality of a model.

Dataset	Appr.	$|\mathcal{M}^+|$	$|\mathcal{M}^-|$	$\mathcal{M}^+/\mathcal{L}^+$	$\mathcal{M}^+/\mathcal{L}^-$	$\mathcal{M}^-/\mathcal{L}^+$	$\mathcal{M}^-/\mathcal{L}^-$	Dataset	Appr.	$|\mathcal{M}^+|$	$|\mathcal{M}^-|$	$\mathcal{M}^+/\mathcal{L}^+$	$\mathcal{M}^+/\mathcal{L}^-$	$\mathcal{M}^-/\mathcal{L}^+$	$\mathcal{M}^-/\mathcal{L}^-$
Sepsis SCL	E	2	3	96.3	0	0	97.72	Sepsis IC	E	5	1	91.59	4.30	35.51	100
Sepsis SCL	NG	1	1	100	0	0	100	Sepsis IC	NG	3	2	100	0	98.13	100
Sepsis SCL	DvM	1	1	100	0	0	100	Sepsis IC	DvM	2	1	75.70	2.52	34.58	99.70
Sepsis MCL	E	8	2	100	6.6	0.82	57.77	Sepsis Rel.	E	5	1	100	27.03	0.15	50.45
Sepsis MCL	NG	4	5	100	0	98.64	100	Sepsis Rel.	NG	2	18	100	0	87.78	100
Sepsis MCL	DvM	5	1	78.26	0	0	47.36	Sepsis Rel.	DvM	3	1	99.85	27.03	0.15	50.45
BPIC 2011	E	6	2	93.15	68.37	6.85	31.63	Dreyers	E	1	1	98.98	0	1.02	100
BPIC 2011	NG	76	63	100	34.01	35.96	100	Dreyers	NG	8	12	100	1.44	38.41	100
BPIC 2011	DvM	3	1	52.40	25.85	26.03	26.87	Dreyers	DvM	1	1	98.98	0	1.02	100
BPIC 2017	E	4	4	100	0	0	100	Production	E	2	1	86.32	30.10	13.68	69.90
BPIC 2017	NG	1	1	100	0	0	100	Production	NG	25	22	100	48.54	51.28	100
BPIC 2017	DvM	1	1	100	0	0	100	Production	DvM	1	1	86.32	30.10	13.68	69.9
Sepsis Return	E	4	1	65.77	46.65	20.72	31.74								
Sepsis Return	NG	27	3	100	76.01	97.30	100								
Sepsis Return	DvM	3	1	44.14	31.59	30.63	43.07								

7.3 Results

In this section, we first assess the three considered approaches on desideratum $D1$ (Table 2), desideratum $D2$, and hypothesis H (Table 3)[3] using the two datasets with a DECLARE-based labeling (*Sepsis SCL* and *Sepsis MCL*). Then, we provide an overall evaluation of the techniques on desideratum $D1$ based on all the 9 considered datasets (Table 2).

Sepsis SCL is a dataset with a single constraint discriminating between $\mathcal{L}^+$ and $\mathcal{L}^-$. This discrepancy is captured by all the discovered models. This is witnessed by the high acceptance accuracy of the models with the log with the same polarity (Table 2) and by the acceptance accuracy of the models with the log with the opposite polarity equal to 0. The explainer-based models contain also some noisy constraints that make these models slightly less accurate than the others, but still very accurate. For all the other discovered models, the additional constraints mined do not introduce noise as their acceptance accuracy with the log with the same polarity is 100% and the one with the log with the opposite polarity is 0. Desideratum $D1$ is therefore satisfied. Desideratum $D2$ is also met as different models with different polarities are inconsistent (see the intersection column in Table 3a). Concerning hypothesis H, the models with the same polarity have their intersections not empty and recognize almost all the traces in the log with same polarity and no traces in the log with the opposite polarity. So, even if the automata are not equivalent (i.e., they recognize different languages), they well reflect the behavior of the logs. Also in this case, models with the same polarities share common behaviors. In particular, for both polarities, the models derived with NG and DvM are equivalent and include the ones derived using E.

---

[3] For space limitations, we report this analysis only for the logs with a DECLARE-based labeling.

The positive log $\mathcal{L}^+$ in *Sepsis MCL* contains the traces that satisfy the conjunction of multiple constraints (e.g., $c_1 \wedge c_2 \wedge \ldots \wedge c_M$) instead of a single controlled constraint. As shown in Table 2, all the tested approaches are able to characterize $\mathcal{L}^+$. This is witnessed by the high acceptance accuracy of the positive models with $\mathcal{L}^+$ and by the low acceptance accuracy of the negative models with $\mathcal{L}^-$. On the other hand, the traces in the negative log $\mathcal{L}^-$ satisfy the negation of the conjunction used to characterize $\mathcal{L}^+$, i.e., $\neg c_1 \vee \neg c_2 \vee \ldots \vee \neg c_M$. This justifies the low accuracy of $\mathcal{M}_{\mathrm{DvM}}^-$ and $\mathcal{M}_{\mathrm{E}}^-$ reported in Table 2. Indeed, both $\mathcal{M}_{\mathrm{DvM}}^-$ and $\mathcal{M}_{\mathrm{E}}^-$, which aim at capturing the differences of the negative class w.r.t. the positive one, are unable to capture all these alternative patterns in a unique DECLARE model. This would rather require a disjunction of alternative DECLARE models. The result is that both DvM and E are forced to choose among these alternative models the one that best discriminates between the two classes. This negatively affects the effectiveness of these approaches. Differently from DvM and E, NG produces a negative model with a high accuracy with $\mathcal{L}^-$, which is counterbalanced by a high accuracy also with $\mathcal{L}^+$. This means that NG discovers a set of constraints from $\mathcal{L}^-$ that describe well the negative traces but are not able to effectively discard the positive ones. This is due to the fact that NEGDIS, by construction, aims at discovering a model that favor the satisfaction of all traces in $\mathcal{L}^-$ w.r.t. discarding traces in $\mathcal{L}^+$. The above discussion shows that desideratum $D1$ is only met for the positive models that manage to discover the behavior of the positive logs, which is characterized by a conjunction of constraints. Instead, the behavior of the negative logs is challenging to be discovered since it is characterized by a disjunction of constraints. This difficulty is confirmed by the results shown in Table 3, where almost all the pairs of models have non-empty intersections (even the ones with opposite polarities) and the inclusion criterion is never satisfied (even for models with the same polarity). This means that desideratum $D2$ is not met, and that, concerning hypothesis H, the discovered models, in this case, show diverse behaviors. Nevertheless, the approach that provides the best discrimination and that better explains the temporal event data in this case is E.

From the results in Table 2, we notice that, independently of the dataset, NG generates models that have a high acceptance accuracy with the logs with the same polarity, but, in many cases, also high accuracy with the logs with the opposite polarity. Instead, DvM and E guarantee a lower accuracy of the models with the logs with the opposite polarity. These results show that NG characterizes well the behaviors available in $\mathcal{L}^+$ and $\mathcal{L}^-$, but it is not able to generate models that are able to discriminate between the two behaviors. Generally speaking, desideratum $D1$ can be, therefore, more easily met by using DvM and E.

From the user point of view, we can say that, although DECLARE does not guarantee perfect results in terms of accuracy, this language has the advantage to be designed for being easily understandable for humans [10] and, for this reason, it is still a viable solution to represent discriminative temporal patterns. From the point of view of understandability, we can also notice that, in general, DvM and E generate smaller (and, therefore, more understandable) models.

Table 3. Model relationship metrics and acceptance accuracy of the model intersections for *Sepsis SCL* and *Sepsis MCL*.

(a) *Sepsis SCL* dataset.

$\mathcal{M}_{A_1}$	$\mathcal{M}_{A_2}$	≡	⊆	⊇	∩=∅	$acc(\cap,\mathcal{L}^+)$	$acc(\cap,\mathcal{L}^-)$
$\mathcal{M}_{BG}^+$	$\mathcal{M}_{E}^+$	False	False	True	False	96.3	0
$\mathcal{M}_{BG}^+$	$\mathcal{M}_{DvM}^+$	True	True	True	False	100	0
$\mathcal{M}_{E}^+$	$\mathcal{M}_{DvM}^+$	False	True	False	False	96.3	0
$\mathcal{M}_{BG}^+$	$\mathcal{M}_{E}^-$	False	False	False	True	0	0
$\mathcal{M}_{BG}^+$	$\mathcal{M}_{DvM}^-$	False	False	False	True	0	0
$\mathcal{M}_{E}^+$	$\mathcal{M}_{DvM}^-$	False	False	False	True	0	0
$\mathcal{M}_{BG}^-$	$\mathcal{M}_{E}^+$	False	False	False	True	0	0
$\mathcal{M}_{BG}^-$	$\mathcal{M}_{DvM}^+$	False	False	False	True	0	0
$\mathcal{M}_{E}^-$	$\mathcal{M}_{DvM}^+$	False	False	False	True	0	0
$\mathcal{M}_{BG}^-$	$\mathcal{M}_{E}^-$	False	False	True	False	0	97.72
$\mathcal{M}_{BG}^-$	$\mathcal{M}_{DvM}^-$	True	True	True	False	0	100
$\mathcal{M}_{E}^-$	$\mathcal{M}_{DvM}^-$	False	True	False	False	0	97.72

(b) *Sepsis MCL* dataset.

$\mathcal{M}_{A_1}$	$\mathcal{M}_{A_2}$	≡	⊆	⊇	∩=∅	$acc(\cap,\mathcal{L}^+)$	$acc(\cap,\mathcal{L}^-)$
$\mathcal{M}_{BG}^+$	$\mathcal{M}_{E}^+$	False	False	False	False	100	0
$\mathcal{M}_{BG}^+$	$\mathcal{M}_{DvM}^+$	False	False	False	False	78.26	0
$\mathcal{M}_{E}^+$	$\mathcal{M}_{DvM}^+$	False	False	False	False	78.26	0
$\mathcal{M}_{BG}^+$	$\mathcal{M}_{E}^-$	False	False	False	False	0.82	0
$\mathcal{M}_{BG}^+$	$\mathcal{M}_{DvM}^-$	False	False	False	False	0	0
$\mathcal{M}_{E}^+$	$\mathcal{M}_{DvM}^-$	False	False	False	True	0	0
$\mathcal{M}_{BG}^-$	$\mathcal{M}_{E}^+$	False	False	False	False	98.64	6.6
$\mathcal{M}_{BG}^-$	$\mathcal{M}_{DvM}^+$	False	False	False	False	77.17	0
$\mathcal{M}_{E}^-$	$\mathcal{M}_{DvM}^+$	False	False	False	False	0.82	0
$\mathcal{M}_{BG}^-$	$\mathcal{M}_{E}^-$	False	False	False	False	0.82	57.77
$\mathcal{M}_{BG}^-$	$\mathcal{M}_{DvM}^-$	False	False	False	False	0	47.36
$\mathcal{M}_{E}^-$	$\mathcal{M}_{DvM}^-$	False	False	False	False	0	21.26

8   Conclusion

This paper presents an evaluation framework enabling the comparison of state-of-the-art implementations of three approaches : (i) *binary discovery* of DECLARE models; (ii) *Deviance Mining*; (iii) *explainers*.

Our experiments show that, in case the discrepancies between the two classes cannot be explained using DECLARE, the tested *binary discovery* technique may return models that contain behaviors that are not supposed to be captured. The models generalize too much and are not able to discriminate one class of traces from the other. On the other hand, the tested *Deviance Mining* technique characterizes very precisely the discrepancies between the two classes, but the discovered constraints may not cover all the traces of the class to be characterized. The technique based on *explainers* has the potential of understanding the characteristics of the execution traces that correlate (or not) with the two classes. This method seems to guarantee the best (although not optimal) description of the two classes of traces.

One limitation of the tested techniques is that the behavior of a log that is characterized by a disjunction of constraints is challenging to be discovered using the DECLARE language. Nonetheless, when a log is characterized by a pure disjunction of DECLARE constraints, it is possible to characterize the log with the opposite polarity, and, by negating the discovered model, we can effectively characterize the original log. This solution becomes, however, unfeasible when a log is characterized by a mix of conjunctions and disjunctions. We finally highlight that, although the obtained results are not generalizable to all methods for extracting temporal logic knowledge from temporal event data, the same framework can be used to test any of these methods. In addition, the paper represents the first study aimed at understanding differences and similarities of the most recent techniques developed in the context of the three categories of approaches *binary discovery*, *Deviance Mining*, and *feature-based explainers*.

References

1. Bellodi, E., Riguzzi, F., Lamma, E.: Statistical relational learning for workflow mining. Intell. Data Anal. **20**(3), 515–541 (2016)
2. Bergami, G., Di Francescomarino, C., Ghidini, C., Maggi, F.M., Puura, J.: Exploring business process deviance with sequential and declarative patterns. CoRR **abs/2111.12454** (2021). https://arxiv.org/abs/2111.12454
3. Bose, R.P.J.C., van der Aalst, W.M.P.: Discovering signature patterns from event logs. In: CIDM, pp. 111–118. IEEE (2013)
4. Chesani, F., Lamma, E., Mello, P., Montali, M., Riguzzi, F., Storari, S.: Exploiting inductive logic programming techniques for declarative process mining. Trans. Petri Nets Other Models Concurrency (ToPNoC) **5460** (2009)
5. Chesani, F., et al.: Process discovery on deviant traces and other stranger things. IEEE Trans. Knowl. Data Eng. **35**(11), 11784–11800 (2023)
6. De Giacomo, G., Vardi, M.Y.: Linear temporal logic and linear dynamic logic on finite traces. In: Proc. of IJCAI. AAAI Press (2013)
7. De Giacomo, G., Vardi, M.Y.: Synthesis for LTL and LDL on finite traces. In: IJCAI, vol. 15, pp. 1558–1564 (2015)
8. Debois, S., Slaats, T.: The analysis of a real life declarative process. In: SSCI. pp. 1374–1382. IEEE (2015)
9. Dong, G., Bailey, J.: Overview of contrast data mining as a field and preview of an upcoming book. In: Proceedings of the IEEE 11th International Conference on Data Mining Workshops, pp. 1141–1146. ICDMW 2011, IEEE Computer Society (2011)
10. Fahland, D., et al.: Declarative versus imperative process modeling languages: the issue of understandability. In: Halpin, T., et al. (eds.) BPMDS/EMMSAD -2009. LNBIP, vol. 29, pp. 353–366. Springer, Heidelberg (2009). https://doi.org/10.1007/978-3-642-01862-6_29
11. Galanti, R., Coma-Puig, B., de Leoni, M., Carmona, J., Navarin, N.: Explainable predictive process monitoring. CoRR **abs/2008.01807** (2020). https://arxiv.org/abs/2008.01807
12. Gilpin, L.H., Bau, D., Yuan, B.Z., Bajwa, A., Specter, M.A., Kagal, L.: Explaining explanations: an overview of interpretability of machine learning. In: DSAA, pp. 80–89. IEEE (2018)
13. He, X., Cai, D., Niyogi, P.: Laplacian score for feature selection. In: NIPS, pp. 507–514 (2005)
14. Lamma, E., Mello, P., Riguzzi, F., Storari, S.: Applying inductive logic programming to process mining. In: Blockeel, H., Ramon, J., Shavlik, J., Tadepalli, P. (eds.) ILP 2007. LNCS (LNAI), vol. 4894, pp. 132–146. Springer, Heidelberg (2008). https://doi.org/10.1007/978-3-540-78469-2_16
15. de León, H.P., Nardelli, L., Carmona, J., vanden Broucke, S.K.L.M.: Incorporating negative information to process discovery of complex systems. Inf. Sci. **422**, 480–496 (2018)
16. Lo, D., Khoo, S., Liu, C.: Efficient mining of iterative patterns for software specification discovery. In: KDD, pp. 460–469. ACM (2007)
17. Lundberg, S.M., Lee, S.: A unified approach to interpreting model predictions. In: NIPS, pp. 4765–4774 (2017)
18. Maggi, F.M., Di Francescomarino, C., Dumas, M., Ghidini, C.: Predictive monitoring of business processes. In: Quix, C., et al. (eds.) CAiSE 2014. LNCS, vol. 8484, pp. 457–472. Springer, Cham (2014). https://doi.org/10.1007/978-3-319-07881-6_31

19. Nguyen, H., Dumas, M., La Rosa, M., Maggi, F.M., Suriadi, S.: Mining business process deviance: a quest for accuracy. In: Meersman, R., et al. (eds.) OTM 2014. LNCS, vol. 8841, pp. 436–445. Springer, Heidelberg (2014). https://doi.org/10. 1007/978-3-662-45563-0_25

20. Partington, A., Wynn, M.T., Suriadi, S., Ouyang, C., Karnon, J.: Process mining for clinical processes: A comparative analysis of four Australian hospitals. ACM Trans. Manage. Inf. Syst. 5(4), 19:1–19:18 (2015)

21. Pauwels, S., Calders, T.: Bayesian network based predictions of business processes. In: Fahland, D., Ghidini, C., Becker, J., Dumas, M. (eds.) BPM 2020. LNBIP, vol. 392, pp. 159–175. Springer, Cham (2020). https://doi.org/10.1007/978-3-030-58638-6_10

22. Pesic, M., Schonenberg, H., van der Aalst, W.M.P.: DECLARE: full support for loosely-structured processes. In: Procedings of EDOC. IEEE Computer Society (2007)

23. Richetti, P.H.P., Jazbik, L.S., Baião, F., Campos, M.L.M.: Deviance mining with treatment learning and declare-based encoding of event logs. Expert Syst. Appl. 187, 115962 (2022)

24. Rizzi, W., Di Francescomarino, C., Maggi, F.M.: Explainability in predictive process monitoring: when understanding helps improving. In: Fahland, D., Ghidini, C., Becker, J., Dumas, M. (eds.) BPM 2020. LNBIP, vol. 392, pp. 141–158. Springer, Cham (2020). https://doi.org/10.1007/978-3-030-58638-6_9

25. Slaats, T., Debois, S., Back, C.O.: Weighing the pros and cons: process discovery with negative examples. In: Polyvyanyy, A., Wynn, M.T., Van Looy, A., Reichert, M. (eds.) BPM 2021. LNCS, vol. 12875, pp. 47–64. Springer, Cham (2021). https://doi.org/10.1007/978-3-030-85469-0_6

26. Suriadi, S., Mans, R.S., Wynn, M.T., Partington, A., Karnon, J.: Measuring patient flow variations: a cross-organisational process mining approach. In: Ouyang, C., Jung, J.-Y. (eds.) AP-BPM 2014. LNBIP, vol. 181, pp. 43–58. Springer, Cham (2014). https://doi.org/10.1007/978-3-319-08222-6_4

27. Suriadi, S., Wynn, M.T., Ouyang, C., ter Hofstede, A.H.M., van Dijk, N.J.: Understanding process behaviours in a large insurance company in Australia: a case study. In: Salinesi, C., Norrie, M.C., Pastor, Ó. (eds.) CAiSE 2013. LNCS, vol. 7908, pp. 449–464. Springer, Heidelberg (2013). https://doi.org/10.1007/978-3-642-38709-8_29

28. Taymouri, F., La Rosa, M., Dumas, M., Maggi, F.M.: Business process variant analysis: survey and classification. Knowl. Based Syst. 211, 106557 (2021)

29. Teinemaa, I., Dumas, M., Rosa, M.L., Maggi, F.M.: Outcome-oriented predictive process monitoring: review and benchmark. ACM Trans. Knowl. Discov. Data 13(2), 17:1–17:57 (2019)

Improving Simplicity by Discovering Nested Groups in Declarative Models

Vlad Paul Cosma[1]([✉])[ID], Axel Kjeld Fjelrad Christfort[1][ID],
Thomas T. Hildebrandt[1][ID], Xixi Lu[2][ID], Hajo A. Reijers[2][ID], and Tijs Slaats[1][ID]

[1] Department of Computer Science, University of Copenhagen,
Copenhagen, Denmark
{vco,axel,slaats}@di.ku.dk
[2] Information and Computing Sciences, Utrecht University, Utrecht, Netherlands
hilde@di.ku.dk, {x.lu,h.a.reijers}@uu.nl

Abstract. Discovering simple, understandable and yet accurate process models is a well-known issue for models mined from real-life event logs. In this paper, we consider algorithms for automatically computing nested groups of activities in declarative process languages, concretely Dynamic Condition Response (DCR) Graphs, to reduce complexity while preserving accuracy. The DCR Graphs notation is, on the one hand, supported by the very accurate DisCoveR process mining algorithm, and on the other hand, by mature design and execution tools used in industrial processes and enterprise information management systems. We evaluate our approach by applying the DisCoveR miner to a large benchmark of real-life and synthetic event logs, measuring the size, density, separability, and constraint variability of mined models with and without grouping of activities. In earlier work, these measures have been shown to have a significant effect on the intrinsic cognitive load for users of declarative models, in particular DCR Graphs. We also evaluate the effect of prioritizing in particular the grouping of activities that model mutual exclusive choices. Our evaluation confirms that grouping of activities in general lowers the complexity on 3 of the 4 measures, while prioritizing choices in some cases makes the improvement slightly smaller.

Keywords: Process Discovery · Declarative · Simplicity · Choices · Nested Groups · DCR Graphs

1 Introduction

Process Discovery has been one of the most prominent tasks in Process Mining, allowing to automatically reconstruct the process from event data. Process discovery has been applied in many domains such as healthcare and financing and is the foundation for enhanced process analysis. Most existing discovery techniques focus on the imperative approach, tailoring towards structured, simple processes. When the process is more flexible and complex, these techniques tend to discover spaghetti models. By explicitly modelling the constraints between

© The Author(s), under exclusive license to Springer Nature Switzerland AG 2024
G. Guizzardi et al. (Eds.): CAiSE 2024, LNCS 14663, pp. 440–455, 2024.
https://doi.org/10.1007/978-3-031-61057-8_26

activities, declarative process languages such as Declare [1] and Dynamic Condition Response (DCR) Graphs [2–4] have been shown to represent processes with a high degree of flexibility more succinctly than imperative process languages. The DisCoveR [5] process mining algorithm produces DCR Graphs, and through experiments on public logs and in particular, winning the 2021 and 2023 Process Discovery Contest (PDC), has been shown to produce highly accurate models. However, some more restrictive constructs, such as mutual exclusive choices, require many constraints to be modelled, which may lead to models that are difficult for users to comprehend.

In the present paper, we address this shortcoming by utilizing the extension of DCR Graphs with nested groups of activities [6] to automatically reduce the number of visual elements in the model. A constraint for a group of activities is in essence just a short-hand for having the constraint for all activities in the group. In particular, the short-hand maintains the semantics of the model and, as a result, its accuracy. By being just a syntactic short-hand, nested groups of activities are different from hierarchies of sub-processes, which typically introduce a new notion of state for a sub-process. As an example, consider the commonly encountered choice pattern, i.e. a group of activities of which only one can be executed. This is modelled in a DCR graph by a so-called exclusion constraint between any pair of activities in the group in each direction, also including a constraint from any activity to itself. That is, a choice between a group of N activities requires N^2 constraints. In   Fig. 1 we see the quadratic relation reduction on the DCR Graph mined from the Business Process Intelligence Challenge 2017 Offers (BPIC17o) event log [7]. The use of a group allows to replace N^2 exclusions constraints between the mutually exclusive activities O_Refused, O_Cancelled and O_Accepted by a single self-exclusion on the choice group Choice1.

Andaloussi et al. [8] have shown that such a large reduction in the number of relations has a significant impact on the comprehensibility of DCR Graphs in terms of perceived difficulty, answer correctness, and answer time. In particular they proposed 4 simplicity measures for DCR Graphs capturing size, density, separability, and constraint variability and showed that these were accurate predictors for the intrinsic cognitive load and therefore understandability of models. We evaluate our approach on these measures by mining models for a large set of public event logs and show that we achieve on average a 42% reduction in size, a 65% reduction in density, a 5% increase in separability, in exchange for a 22% increase in constraint variability. While the first three of these results are linked to an increase in simplicity, the latter may be interpreted as a decrease in simplicity. However, as we will discuss in more detail in Sect. 5, the increase in constraint variability is a direct consequence of the reduction in size and we posit that together these results indicate a significant increase in the expected understandability of the mined models.

Our algorithm and experiments are available as an open source python implementation[1] extending the pm4py library [9], where we provide the original Dis-

---

[1] https://github.com/paul-cvp/pm4py-dcr.

CoveR miner together with DCR execution semantics and model import and export capabilities which are compatible with the DCRSolutions design tool[2].

As such, our contributions include (1) two novel algorithms for discovering nested groups of activities in DCR graphs in Sect. 3, (2) a thorough evaluation of these algorithms on an exhaustive set of public event logs in Sect. 4, and (3) the first application of the simplicity measures proposed in [8] to real models leading to important insights regarding the interplay between these measures discussed in Sect. 5, and in particular (4) an improved DisCoveR miner that provides simpler models without sacrificing accuracy. Finally, it is worth noting, that the use of nested groups to reduce the number of edges in a graph can be applied to any graph model, such as e.g. Declare and Petri Net models.

2   Preliminaries

2.1   Dynamic Condition Response Graphs with Nested Groups

Below we give the definition of Dynamic Condition Response (DCR) graphs with nested groups of activities as introduced in [3,4,6] but simplified to the graphs discovered by the DisCoveR process miner, that is, graphs where each activity is represented by a unique node in the graph and we only have the original four relations between nodes as introduced in [2].

Definition 1. *A DCR Graph G with nested groups of activities is given by a tuple $(A, M, R, A_G, \rhd)$ where*

(i) $AG = A \uplus A_G$ *is a finite set of* activities A *and* activity groups A_G,
(ii) $M = (Ex, Re, In) \in \mathcal{P}(A) \times \mathcal{P}(A) \times \mathcal{P}(A)$ *is the* marking,
(iii) $R = \{\rightarrow\!\bullet, \bullet\!\rightarrow, \rightarrow+, \rightarrow\%\}$ *are the four basic relations, i.e.*
(iv) $\rightarrow\!\bullet \subseteq AG \times AG$, *is the* condition *relation,*
(v) $\bullet\!\rightarrow \subseteq AG \times AG$, *is the* response *relation,*
(vi) $\rightarrow+, \rightarrow\% \subseteq AG \times AG$ *are* include *and* exclude *relations respectively,*
(vii) $\rhd: AG \rightarrow A_G$ *is a* grouping *function,*

We write $>$ for $\rhd^+$ (the transitive closure of $\rhd$) and require that it is irreflexive. We write $\geq$ for reflexive closure of $>$ and $\leq$ for the inverse of $\geq$.

Compared to the original DCR Graphs [2], DCR Graphs with nested groups allow also groups as nodes of the graph, and the grouping function $\rhd$ defines a partial order $\geq$ on groups and activities, determining which group an activity or group belongs to (if any). As already explained in the introduction, the idea of DCR Graphs with nested groups is, that a relation from/to a group is a concise way of expressing a relation from/to all members of the group. As shown in [6] and formalized in Definition 2 below, a DCR Graph G with nested groups of activities can be mapped to a semantically equivalent standard, flat DCR Graph $G^\flat$, by replacing a relation from/to a group by a relation from/to all the members of the group and removing the group.

---

[2] Freely available for academic use at https://dcrsolutions.net.

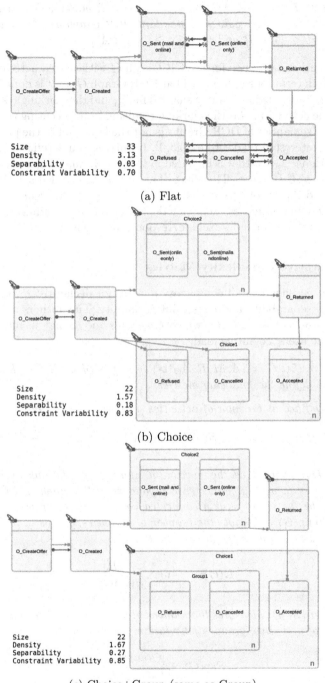

(a) Flat

(b) Choice

(c) Choice+Group (same as Group)

Fig. 1. DCR Graphs of the BPIC17 Offer log.

Definition 2. *Let $G = (A, M, R, A_G, \rhd)$ be a DCR graph with nested groups of activities. We define the equivalent standard DCR Graph as $G^\flat = (A, M, R_{\leq \geq})$, where $R_{\leq \geq} = \{\phi^\flat \mid \phi \in R \text{ and } \phi^\flat =\leq \phi \geq \cap(A \times A)\}$.*

The execution semantics for a DCR Graph G with nested activity groups is then defined in terms of the standard flat DCR Graph $G^\flat$ as it is done in [6]. That is, an activity is enabled in G if it is enabled in $G^\flat$, and the marking resulting from executing the activity in G is the marking resulting from executing the activity in $G^\flat$. Since the semantics of DCR Graphs is not the key point of the present paper, we refer the interested reader to e.g. [3,4]. Intuitively, an activity a is enabled if every condition $a' \rightarrow\!\bullet^\flat a$ that is included in the present marking is also previously executed, i.e. $a' \in In \cap Ex$. The effect of executing an enabled activity is to add the activity to the set of executed activities in the marking, remove it from the set Re of pending activities, and include/exclude/make pending the activities that the activity has include/exclude/response relations to.

2.2 Declarative Complexity Metrics

The work in [8] introduces 4 complexity metrics for declarative process models: size, density, separability and constraint variability. The authors also provide a qualitative study of the metrics which correlates the change in metrics with a change in the users' cognitive load.

Definition 3. *Let $G = (A, M, R, A_G, \rhd)$ be a nested DCR Graph with $AG = A \uplus A_G$. We define the following metrics:*

Size (S): *Defined as the sum of activities, groups and relations:*

$$S(G) = |AG| + |R| \tag{1}$$

Density (D): *Defined as the maximum number of relations over the number of activities in weakly connected components of the graph. Let $Comp(G) = \{c_1, \ldots, c_n\}$ be the set of weakly connected components of graph G, then for a given $c \in Comp(G)$ we denote the number of activities/groups in the component c as AG_c and the number of relations as R_c.*

$$D(G) = \max_{c \in Comp(G)} \left| \frac{R_c}{AG_c} \right| \tag{2}$$

Separability (Sep): *Measures the number of weakly connected components over the number of activities, groups and relations in the model:*

$$Sep(G) = \frac{|Comp(G)|}{|AG| + |R|} \tag{3}$$

Constraint Variability (CV): *Related to Shannon entropy, it is defined as the maximum entropy over different relation types in the components of the model.*

Let R_c be the set of different types of relations within a component c and R_c^r be the relation of type $r \in R$ in component c. Then the relative frequency is:

$$p(c, r) = \begin{cases} \frac{|R_r^c|}{|R_c|} & \text{if } |R_c| > 0 \\ 0 & \text{otherwise} \end{cases} \tag{4}$$

Now we can define constraint (or relation) variability as:

$$CV(G) = \max_{c \in \{c' | c' \in Comp(G) \wedge |R_{c'}| > 0\}} \left\{ - \sum_{r \in R_c} p(c, r) \cdot \log_{|R|} p(c, r) \right\} \tag{5}$$

An increase in size, density and constraint variability relates to an increase in the users' cognitive load. Separability is inversely correlated, a decrease in separability relates to an increase in cognitive load.

Example: Based on the BPIC17 Offer log [7] we consider the mined flat DCR Graph and the semantically equivalent DCR Graphs with choices and nested groups in Fig. 1. The nested graphs have a significant reduction in the number of relations while remaining behaviourally equivalent. Observe that the Choice graph in Fig. 1b can still be improved by reducing the two condition relations to O_Refused and O_Cancelled. In Fig. 1c the greatest relation reduction comes at the expense of adding 3 activity groups Choice1, Choice2 and Group1 to the graph. The declarative complexity metrics on the flat and fully grouped process model show this reduction. The flat model 1a has a size of 33, density of 3.13, separability of 0.03 and a constraint variability of 0.70. The grouped model 1a has improvements on size 22 (33%), density 1.67 (46%), and separability 0.27 (25%), and a worsening for constraint variability 0.85 (−21%). Observe that between Fig. 1b and 1c size stays the same as the number of removed relations is the same as the added nested groups, but density will change because it is a ratio of the two.

3   Discovering Nested Groups in DCR Graphs

Starting from a flat DCR Graph we provide a Choice algorithm to group maximal subsets of activities that are all connected by exclusion relations and replacing the exclusion relations by a single self-exclusion for the group, and a greedy algorithm Group for groups of activities that all share a relation and replace the individual relations by a single relation for the group. Both algorithms are easily seen from the definition to preserve the trace semantics.

3.1   Choice

Choices in a DCR Graph are represented as a set of activities that, when executed, mutually exclude each other and themselves. We now define the mutual exclusion sub-graph $G_\#$ as we are only interested in self excluding activities and the exclusion relations between them.

Algorithm 1. choice($G_\#$)

```
1: cliques = enumerate_all_cliques(G_#)
2: cliques = sort(cliques, key = length, reverse = True)          ▷ Largest clique first
3: used = set.empty()
4: ▷= map.empty()
5: A_G = set.empty()
6: for clique ∈ cliques do
7:     if clique ∪ used = ∅ and length(clique) > 1 then      ▷ Check that the activities inside the
       clique have not been already used
8:         a_g = id()
9:         A_G = A_G ∪ {a_g}
10:        ▷ (a_g) = clique                                   ▷ Update the nesting map
11:        used = used ∪ clique                               ▷ Update the used activities set
12:    end if
13: end for
14: return (A_G, ▷)                    ▷ Return the set of choice group activities, and the nesting map
```

Definition 4. *Let $G = (A, M, R)$ be a DCR Graph. Let $G_\# = (A_\#, \#)$ be the mutual exclusion sub-graph of G where: $A_\# = \{a | (a, a) \in \text{→%}\}$, and*

$$\# = \{(a, a') | a \in A_\#, a' \in A_\#, (a, a') \in \text{→%}, (a', a) \in \text{→%}\}.$$

Note that the mutual exclusion relation $\#$ is an undirected edge. Now we define Algorithm 1 that takes the mutual exclusion sub-graph $G_\#$ and finds the optimal grouping of connected activities. The equivalent problem from graph theory is that of finding all cliques with a size greater than 1. In the worst case, time complexity is known to be exponential in the number of nodes.

To update the flat DCR Graph we first add the resulting cliques as choice activity groups. Then we remove all exclusions →% between the grouped activities together with their self excludes, add a self-exclude relation to the activity group and move any shared relations by all individual activities to point in/out of the choice group. For each choice group with activities clique added we thus reduce the number of visual exclusions by $|\text{clique}|^2 - 1$. For each further relation the grouped activities share one get further reduction of $|\text{clique}| - 1$ relations. An example can be seen in Fig. 1b, where the two activities grouped inside Choice2 leads to the removal of $2^2 - 1 = 3$ exclusion relations and two condition relations.

3.2   Group

We here explore another approach, finding all groups that reduce the relations of the graph with regard to a metric. The metric scores candidate groups higher when the relation reduction is also higher.

In order to do this we propose the efficient greedy algorithm as seen in Algorithm 4. The algorithm works on an encoded DCR graph, which can be obtained from a flat DCR graph with Algorithm 2. This encoding simply represents a graph as the sets of all incoming and outgoing relations for each activity, allowing for easy computation of shared relations by intersection. It does, however, split each

Algorithm 2. encode(G)

```
1: (A, M, R) = G
2: enc = map.empty()
3: for a ∈ A do
4:     enc(a) = {b, out, r.type)| →∈ R, (a, b) = r ∈→}
5:     enc(a) = enc(a) ∪ {(b, in, r.type)| →∈ R, (b, a) = r ∈→}
6: end for
7: return enc
```

Algorithm 3. decode(enc)

```
1: AG = enc.keys
2: →• = { (b, ag)|ag ∈ AG.((b, in, condition) ∈ enc(ag) }
3: •→ = { (ag, b)|ag ∈ AG.((b, out, response) ∈ enc(ag) }
4: →% = { (ag, b)|ag ∈ AG.((b, out, exclude) ∈ enc(ag) }
5: →+ = { (ag, b)|ag ∈ AG.((b, out, include) ∈ enc(ag) }
6: return (AG, (AG, ∅, ∅), (→•, •→, →+, →%))
```

relation into each of its start and end points, and as such it requires slight book-keeping to keep consistent under alteration as can be seen in lines 26–29 of the algorithm.

Algorithm 4 works by computing the intersection of the encoded relations for each pair of activities as the candidate groups. We then choose the best group with regards to the size metric, *e.g.* number of relations removed, and add it to the encoding by moving all the shared relations onto the group from the individual activities and updating ▷. For each found group, we apply this method recursively to find further nested groups. The method is then repeated on the remaining un-grouped activities until no further groups can be found that improve the metric.

Finally, we decode the resulting encoding with Algorithm 3, which when joined with the found groups A_G and the group function ▷, yield exactly a DCR Graph with nested groups as per Definition 1.

4   Evaluation

Data Sets: To evaluate the Choice and Group algorithms, we used the same real-world event logs from [10] on which imperative miners have been evaluated. In addition, we used BPIC 2017 [11] and the Offer subset (BPIC17o) [7], BPIC 2019 [12] and Dreyers [13] logs. An overview of the results for these logs is provided in Table 2. To show that the reduction works also on noisy logs, we extended our evaluation to synthetically generated logs from the 2019–2023 PDC[3]. From the PDC data sets, we only use the training logs. In total we use 21 publicly available data sets, 16 real world logs and 5 synthetic ones. Note

---

[3] https://www.tf-pm.org/competitions-awards/discovery-contest.

Algorithm 4. group(enc, A = enc.keys)

1: $\triangleright$ = map.empty()
2: $A_G = \emptyset$
3: **while** True **do**
4:     cands = map.empty()
5:     **for** $a, t \in A$ **do** $\triangleright$ Find all candidate groupings by intersection
6:         $\rightarrow_s$ = enc(a) $\cap$ enc(t)
7:         cands($\rightarrow_s$) = cands($\rightarrow_s$) $\cup$ $\{a, t\}$
8:     **end for**
9: $\triangleright$ Choose the best one by the given score
10:     $\rightarrow_b$, best_score = max(cands.keys, metric($\rightarrow_s$))
11:     **if** best_score = 0 **then** $\triangleright$ Return if no improvement can be made
12:         **break**
13:     **end if**
14:
15:     a_g = id()
16:     $A_G = A_G \cup \{a_g\}$
17:
18:     **if** nested **then** $\triangleright$ if this grouping is nested
19:         Update($\triangleright$) $\triangleright$ then $\triangleright$ needs to point to the parent grouping
20:     **end if** $\triangleright$ this is left as an implementation detail
21:
22:     enc(a_g) = $\rightarrow_b$ $\triangleright$ add shared relations to the grouping
23:     **for** $a \in$ cands($\rightarrow_b$) **do**
24:         $\triangleright$ (a) = a_g
25:         enc(a) = enc(a)\ $\rightarrow_b$ $\triangleright$ remove shared relations from each grouped activity
26:         **for** (b, $direction$, $type$) $\in \rightarrow_b$ **do** $\triangleright$ redirect other ends of shared relations
27:             enc(b) = enc(b) \ $\{(a, \mathbf{flip}(direction), type)\}$
28:             enc(b) = enc(b) $\cup$ $\{(a_g, \mathbf{flip}(direction), type)\}$
29:         **end for**
30:     **end for**
31:
32:     (enc$'$, A'_G, $\triangleright'$) = nest(enc, cands($\rightarrow_b$)) $\triangleright$ Recursively find nested groupings
33:     $A_G = A_G \cup A'_G$
34:     enc = enc'
35:     $\triangleright$ = $\triangleright \circ \triangleright'$
36:     $A = A \setminus$ cands($\rightarrow_b$) $\triangleright$ Remove already grouped events from further consideration
37: **end while**
38: **return** (enc, A_G, $\triangleright$)

---

that the 5 PDC data sets are collections of logs, we therefore average the metrics across each collection such that they are equally weighted in the overall aggregated *results*.

Setup: Starting from the event log we use DisCoveR to mine a perfectly fitting flat DCR Graph. We then derive three models from the flat one: (1) a Choice based grouping as defined in Sect. 3.1, (2) Group, the greedy algorithm from Sect. 3.2, and (3) a Choice+Group approach where we first find Choices and then further Group the model by the greedy relation reduction. By Definition 2 the derived models are also perfectly fitting DCR Graphs.

Metrics: We calculate the Size, Density, Separability and Constraint Variability to evaluate the process models derived from the mined flat DCR Graph. All 3 algorithms achieve the relation reduction at the cost of adding activity groups.

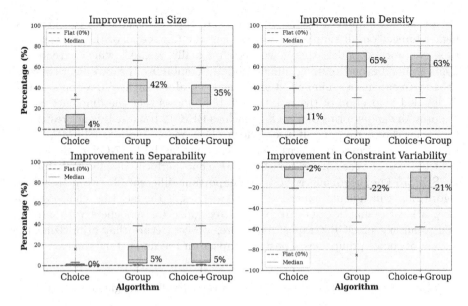

Fig. 2. Boxplot of metrics as percentage improvements (negative percentages indicate deterioration)

Results: The results for the real-life logs are also shown in Table 2 and our full evaluation results are available online[4]. In Fig. 2 we show the percentage changes compared to the flat DCR Graph as box plots for each metric and algorithm combination. The flat DCR Graph is shown as a dashed red line at 0%. Overall the `Group` algorithm performs best, achieving a 42% median improvement on Size, 65% improvement on Density, 5% improvement on Separability, and a −22% worsening of Constraint Variability. Note that the scale on the constraint variability box plot is between 0% and −100%. The improvement trend in size, density and separability correlates with a decrease in the users' cognitive load [8]. Constraint variability is the only metric where our approaches perform worse. This is an expected outcome as the ratio between the total number of relations and the individual relations tends to even out.

5 Discussion

5.1 Interpretation

Comparison of Algorithms. The intuition behind the relation reduction can be seen in Table 1. We observe visually that the models have less overlapping relations, or relations that have to cross over other activities. By understanding the concept of groups, users looking at the discovered models will spend less time following relations back and forth between the connected activity pairs.

---

[4] https://github.com/paul-cvp/all-complexity-results.

As can be seen in our results, the general `Group` algorithm has a considerably higher impact on all simplicity metrics than the `Choice` algorithm. `Group` also runs on process models that have been manually created, which extends its applicability beyond refining mined models. Combining the two algorithms as `Choice+Group` has a similar effect on the metrics, albeit slightly lower on average. A detailed inspection of the results in Table 1 shows that the difference is not uniform. `Group` performs best on logs such as BPIC12 because it is not restricted by a prior choice grouping. It also performs best on logs, such as RTFMP, where there are no discovered choices. For others, such as BPIC17-Offer, all derived models from `Choice`, `Group` and `Choice+Group` perform equally well. Finally for SEPSIS `Choice+Group` is best. An important difference between these two algorithms, which is not expressed by the metrics, is the fact that choice groups have a clear semantics and are easy to recognize for modellers with a basic understanding of DCR Graphs. Therefore, we conjecture that prioritizing the finding of choice groups has a positive impact on the understandability.

Table 1. Results for a subset of the logs (best results highlighted in **bold**)

Datasets	Flat	Choice	Group	Choice+Group
BPIC12	S: 156(0%) D: 5.50(0%) Sep: 0.01(0%) CV: 0.59(0%)	S: 134(14%) D: 4.15(24%) Sep: 0.01(0%) CV: 0.66(-10%)	S: **91(41%)** D: 1.96(64%) Sep: **0.05(4%)** CV: 0.78(-31%)	S: 101(35%) D: **1.91(65%)** Sep: 0.04(3%) CV: 0.77(-29%)
RTFMP	S: 33(0%) D: 2.00(0%) Sep: 0.03(0%) CV: 0.77(0%)	S: 33(0%) D: 2.00(0%) Sep: 0.03(0%) CV: 0.77(0%)	S: 30(9%) D: 1.40(30%) Sep: **0.27(24%)** CV: 1.00(-29%)	S: 30(9%) D: 1.40(30%) Sep: **0.27(24%)** CV: 1.00(-29%)
BPIC17o	S: 33(0%) D: 3.13(0%) Sep: 0.03(0%) CV: 0.70(0%)	S: **22(33%)** D: **1.57(49%)** Sep: 0.18(15%) CV: 0.83(-17%)	S: **22(33%)** D: 1.67(46%) Sep: **0.27(25%)** CV: 0.85(-21%)	S: **22(33%)** D: 1.67(46%) Sep: **0.27(25%)** CV: 0.85(-21%)
SEPSIS	S: 107(0%) D: 6.00(0%) Sep: 0.02(0%) CV: 0.90(0%)	S: 76(28%) D: 3.63(39%) Sep: 0.03(1%) CV: 1.00(-10%)	S: 54(49%) D: 2.07(46%) Sep: 0.15(13%) CV: 0.96(-6%)	S: **51(65%)** D: **1.47(75%)** Sep: **0.18(16%)** CV: 0.97(-7%)

Table 2. Algorithm and metrics from real world event logs

Log name	Algorithm	|AG|	|R|	S	D	Sep	CV	Log name	Algorithm	|AG|	|R|	S	D	Sep	CV
BPIC12	Flat	24	132	156	5.50	0.01	0.59	BPIC15_5f	Flat	74	573	647	7.74	0.00	0.79
	Choice	26	108	134	4.15	0.01	0.66		Choice	82	546	628	7.11	0.01	0.82
	Group	32	59	91	1.96	0.05	0.78		Group	114	240	354	2.19	0.03	0.98
	Choice+Group	36	65	101	1.91	0.04	0.77		Choice+Group	117	347	464	3.19	0.03	0.95
BPIC13_cp	Flat	4	4	8	1.00	0.13	0.81	BPIC17	Flat	26	119	145	4.58	0.01	0.74
	Choice	4	4	8	1.00	0.13	0.81		Choice	27	108	135	4.00	0.01	0.76
	Group	5	3	8	0.50	0.38	0.00		Group	40	67	107	1.78	0.03	0.83
	Choice+Group	5	3	8	0.50	0.38	0.00		Choice+Group	40	70	110	1.79	0.02	0.83
BPIC13_i	Flat	4	6	10	1.50	0.10	1.00	BPIC17-Offer	Flat	8	25	33	3.13	0.03	0.71
	Choice	4	6	10	1.50	0.10	1.00		Choice	10	12	22	1.57	0.18	0.83
	Group	6	3	9	1.00	0.44	1.00		Group	11	11	22	1.67	0.27	0.86
	Choice+Group	6	3	9	1.00	0.44	1.00		Choice+Group	11	11	22	1.67	0.27	0.86
BPIC14_f	Flat	9	27	36	3.00	0.03	1.00	BPIC17_f	Flat	18	64	82	3.56	0.01	0.86
	Choice	9	27	36	3.00	0.03	1.00		Choice	19	61	80	3.33	0.03	0.86
	Group	11	8	19	1.60	0.37	1.00		Group	25	49	74	2.00	0.03	0.88
	Choice+Group	11	8	19	1.60	0.37	1.00		Choice+Group	25	48	73	1.96	0.03	0.86
BPIC15_1f	Flat	70	475	545	6.79	0.00	0.82	BPIC19	Flat	42	599	641	14.26	0.00	0.32
	Choice	81	437	518	5.88	0.02	0.86		Choice	45	504	549	11.20	0.00	0.36
	Group	112	237	349	2.24	0.03	1.00		Group	69	218	287	3.25	0.01	0.48
	Choice+Group	107	309	416	3.20	0.04	1.00		Choice+Group	76	215	291	2.95	0.01	0.49
BPIC15_2f	Flat	82	902	984	11.00	0.00	0.64	Dreyers	Flat	33	268	301	8.12	0.00	0.53
	Choice	90	875	965	10.24	0.01	0.65		Choice	33	268	301	8.12	0.00	0.53
	Group	133	379	512	2.95	0.02	0.72		Group	52	109	161	2.38	0.04	0.67
	Choice+Group	148	429	577	3.19	0.03	1.00		Choice+Group	65	112	177	1.95	0.05	0.66
BPIC15_3f	Flat	62	699	761	11.27	0.00	0.50	RTFMP	Flat	11	22	33	2.00	0.03	0.77
	Choice	71	659	730	9.65	0.01	0.51		Choice	11	22	33	2.00	0.03	0.77
	Group	97	202	299	2.27	0.05	0.92		Group	14	16	30	1.40	0.27	1.00
	Choice+Group	108	390	498	4.18	0.03	0.52		Choice+Group	14	16	30	1.40	0.27	1.00
BPIC15_4f	Flat	65	522	587	8.03	0.00	0.82	SEPSIS	Flat	16	91	107	6.00	0.02	0.91
	Choice	70	500	570	7.32	0.01	0.83		Choice	17	59	76	3.63	0.03	1.00
	Group	103	202	305	2.12	0.05	1.00		Group	22	32	54	2.07	0.15	0.96
	Choice+Group	110	245	355	2.52	0.05	1.00		Choice+Group	24	27	51	1.47	0.18	0.98

Constraint Variability and Multi-perspective Measures: On all evaluated event logs we see that an improvement on the first three measures implies a worsening in constraint variability. A possible explanation for this is that DisCoveR tends to find an unbalanced set of relations where conditions and exclusions are more common. This reduces the constraint variability of the flat model. Since the Choice algorithm reduces exclusions, and the Group algorithm prioritizes reducing the most relations, exclusions and conditions are more likely to be grouped than the other relations. As a result, the constraint variability of the grouped model increases. We can see this in Fig. 1: consider the response relation •→ between O_CreateOffer and O_Created, relative frequency $p(G, \bullet\to)$ is $1/25$ in the flat graph and $1/11$ in the grouped one.

This insight into the correlated increase in constraint variability strengthens the claim from the original study that a combination of measures is necessary "to provide a multi-perspective view of users' cognitive load when engaging with declarative process models." [8]. It remains an open question whether or not it is possible to improve on all 4 metrics simultaneously via algorithmic means.

5.2   Metric Validity

Our experimental results show an improvement in 3 out of the 4 metrics that were selected. This is a reassuring result, which provides positive support for the effectiveness of our proposal.

The question remains on whether the metrics themselves provide a valid and decisive assessment for our particular proposal. The original metrics are specifically tuned to DCR Graphs, but do not take groups as a visual element into account. It cannot be entirely ruled out, therefore, that the groups themselves introduce additional cognitive load, which is not covered by the metrics.

What is reassuring is that previous studies have found that hierarchy does not introduce additional cognitive load in declarative processes [14,15]; neither do groupings for BPMN models [16]. Therefore, one possible use of our findings is to use groups to create hierarchies in DCR Graphs and hide relations within the groups, only making them visible on-demand. It seems very plausible that this will reduce any cognitive load, which is worthwhile to investigate further.

6   Related Work

The main work done within declarative process discovery has been on Declare models, DCR graphs, and Log Skeletons [17]. Declare Miner [18] and MINER-ful [19] discover Declare models. All existing DCR miners [5,20,21] discover flat DCR Graphs. Our work is built on the DisCoveR miner as it outputs the most accurate DCR Graphs [5]. Zugal et al. [14] and Haisjackl et al. [15] found that introducing hierarchical sub-processes in declarative process models does not lead to any significant change in cognitive load. Turetken et al. [16] showed that groupings have no measurable effect on cognitive load for BPMN models. However, unlike our approach, the use of BPMN groupings in [16] does not decrease the number of visual elements in a model. Smirnov et al. [22] systematically catalog business process model abstraction techniques and show their value through use cases.

Discovering hierarchies or sub-processes is well studied for imperative process model notations [23–27]. Here the use of the word "hierarchy" denotes different levels of event abstraction, which in contrast to our use of groups changes the semantics (and accuracy) of the model. In the context of fuzzy mining, a hierarchy is based on metrics from the event log and relates to how a directly follows graph can be simplified by removing less frequent nodes and edges [28]. In the context of multi-level event logs, mining hierarchical process models [29] means discovering hierarchies in logs where each part can be mined with its own miner resulting in a combination of several process model notations, including Declare. FlexHMiner [30] is a miner for hierarchical process models that discovers sub-processes based on three different methods, using domain knowledge, random clustering, and a flat tree, with the domain knowledge approach being on average the highest-scoring one. Prime Miner [31] was the only other work that explicitly mines choices. Several complexity metrics have been used for imperative models as a proxy for simplicity [10,32,33]. Augusto et al. [33] review complexity metrics on a similarly large set of event logs, and indeed find a correlation between the metrics and the quality of process models mined with imperative miners. They investigate how pre-processing event logs before mining can improve the results. A similar approach is taken for Declare in [34].

7 Conclusion

We provided the first evaluation of automatic grouping of activities in order to reduce the complexity of mined declarative models and used the complexity metrics proposed in [8] on a set of 16 real-life and 5 synthetic logs. The result is a likely significant reduction in cognitive load for model users. For future work, a user-centered evaluation study seems desirable to corroborate and expand our current, metric-based evaluation. As mentioned in our discussion, the inclusion of groupings may introduce cognitive load not taken into account by the used metrics. By involving users it can be tested whether this effect materializes or not. Additionally, it would be worth investigating how the reduction of cognitive load through groupings ties to the expertise level of users, i.e., beginners/intermediate/experts, which may have important ramifications for tailoring tool support and instruction materials. Finally, it seems worthwhile to evaluate the use of activity groups for Declare models.

References

1. Pesic, M., Schonenberg, H., Van der Aalst, W.M.: Declare: full support for loosely-structured processes. In: 11th IEEE International Enterprise Distributed Object Computing Conference (EDOC 2007). IEEE, pp. 287–287 (2007)
2. Hildebrandt, T.T., Mukkamala, R.R.: Declarative event-based workflow as distributed dynamic condition response graphs In: PLACES, pp. 59–73 (2010)
3. Mukkamala, R.R.: A formal model for declarative workflows: Dynamic condition response graphs, Ph.D. dissertation, IT University of Copenhagen (2012)
4. Slaats, T.: Flexible process notations for cross-organizational case management systems. Ph.D. dissertation, IT University of Copenhagen (2015)
5. Back, C.O., Slaats, T., Hildebrandt, T.T., Marquard, M.: Discover: accurate and efficient discovery of declarative process models. Int. J. Softw. Tools Technol. Transfer (2021)
6. Hildebrandt, T., Mukkamala, R.R., Slaats, T.: Nested dynamic condition response graphs. In: Arbab, F., Sirjani, M. (eds.) FSEN 2011. LNCS, vol. 7141, pp. 343–350. Springer, Heidelberg (2012). https://doi.org/10.1007/978-3-642-29320-7_23
7. van Dongen, B.F.: Bpi challenge 2017 - offer log. https://doi.org/10.4121/12705737.v2
8. Abbad-Andaloussi, A., Burattin, A., Slaats, T., Kindler, E., Weber, B.: Complexity in declarative process models: metrics and multi-modal assessment of cognitive load. Expert Syst. Appl. **233**, 120924 (2023)
9. Berti, A., Van Zelst, S.J., van der Aalst, W.: Process mining for python (pm4py): bridging the gap between process-and data science, *arXiv preprint* arXiv:1905.06169 (2019)

10. Augusto, A.: Automated discovery of process models from event logs: review and benchmark. IEEE Trans. Knowl. Data Eng. **31**(4), 686–705 (2019)
11. van Dongen, B.F.: Bpi challenge 2017 (2017). https://data.4tu.nl/articles/_/ 12696884/1
12. van Dongen, B.F.: Bpi challenge (2019). https://doi.org/10.4121/UUID: D06AFF4B-79F0-45E6-8EC8-E19730C248F1
13. Debois, S., Slaats, T.: The analysis of a real life declarative process. In: IEEE Symposium Series on Computational Intelligence, SSCI 2015, Cape Town, South Africa, December 7-10, 2015, pp. 1374–1382 . IEEE (2015)
14. Zugal, S., Soffer, P., Haisjackl, C., Pinggera, J., Reichert, M., Weber, B.: Investigating expressiveness and understandability of hierarchy in declarative business process models. Softw. Syst. Model. **14**, 1081–1103 (2015)
15. Haisjackl, C., et al.: Understanding declare models: strategies, pitfalls, empirical results. Softw. Syst. Model. **15**(2), 325–352 (2016)
16. Turetken, O., Dikici, A., Vanderfeesten, I., Rompen, T., Demirors, O.: The influence of using collapsed sub-processes and groups on the understandability of business process models. Bus. Inf. Syst. Eng. **62**, 121–141 (2020)
17. Verbeek, H.: The log skeleton visualizer in prom 6.9: the winning contribution to the process discovery contest 2019. Int. J. Softw. Tools Technol. Transfer **24**(4), 549–561 (2022)
18. Maggi, F.M., Di Ciccio, C., Di Francescomarino, C., Kala, T.: Parallel algorithms for the automated discovery of declarative process models. Inf. Syst. **74**, 136–152 (2018)
19. Ciccio, C.D., Mecella, M.: On the discovery of declarative control flows for artful processes. ACM Trans. Manage. Inf. Syst. (TMIS) **5**(4), 1–37 (2015)
20. Nekrasaite, V., Parli, A.T., Back, C.O., Slaats, T.: Discovering responsibilities with dynamic condition response graphs. In: Giorgini, P., Weber, B. (eds.) CAiSE 2019. LNCS, vol. 11483, pp. 595–610. Springer, Cham (2019). https://doi.org/10.1007/ 978-3-030-21290-2_37
21. Debois, S., Hildebrandt, T.T., Laursen, P.H., Ulrik, K.R.: Declarative process mining for DCR graphs. In: Proceedings of SAC, pp. 759–764 (2017)
22. Smirnov, S., Reijers, H.A., Weske, M., Nugteren, T.: Business process model abstraction: a definition, catalog, and survey. Distrib. Parallel Databases **30**, 63–99 (2012)
23. Jagadeesh Chandra Bose, R.P., van der Aalst, W.M.P.: Abstractions in process mining: a taxonomy of patterns. In: Dayal, U., Eder, J., Koehler, J., Reijers, H.A. (eds.) BPM 2009. LNCS, vol. 5701, pp. 159–175. Springer, Heidelberg (2009). https://doi.org/10.1007/978-3-642-03848-8_12
24. Tax, N., Dalmas, B., Sidorova, N., van der Aalst, W.M., Norre, S.: Interest-driven discovery of local process models. Inf. Syst. **77** (2018)
25. Mannhardt, F., de Leoni, M., Reijers, H.A., van der Aalst, W.M.P., Toussaint, P.J.: From low-level events to activities - a pattern-based approach. In: La Rosa, M., Loos, P., Pastor, O. (eds.) BPM 2016. LNCS, vol. 9850, pp. 125–141. Springer, Cham (2016). https://doi.org/10.1007/978-3-319-45348-4_8
26. Leemans, M., Van Der Aalst, W.M., Van Den Brand, M.G.: Recursion aware modeling and discovery for hierarchical software event log analysis. In: 2018 IEEE 25th International Conference on Software Analysis, Evolution and Reengineering (SANER), pp. 185–196. IEEE (2018)
27. Conforti, R., Dumas, M., García-Bañuelos, L., La Rosa, M.: BPMN miner: automated discovery of BPMN process models with hierarchical structure. Inf. Syst. **56**, 284–303 (2016)

28. Bose, R.P.J.C., Verbeek, E.H.M.W., van der Aalst, W.M.P.: Discovering hierarchical process models using ProM. In: Nurcan, S. (ed.) CAiSE Forum 2011. LNBIP, vol. 107, pp. 33–48. Springer, Heidelberg (2012). https://doi.org/10.1007/978-3-642-29749-6_3

29. Leemans, S.J., Goel, K., van Zelst, S.J.: Using multi-level information in hierarchical process mining: Balancing behavioural quality and model complexity. In: 2020 2nd International Conference on Process Mining (ICPM), pp. 137–144 (2020)

30. Lu, X., Gal, A., Reijers, H.A.: Discovering hierarchical processes using flexible activity trees for event abstraction. In: 2020 2nd International Conference on Process Mining (ICPM), pp. 145–152. IEEE (2020)

31. Bergenthum, R.: Prime miner-process discovery using prime event structures. In: 2019 International Conference on Process Mining (ICPM), pp. 41–48. IEEE (2019)

32. Mendling, J.: Metrics for Process Models: Empirical Foundations of Verification, Error Prediction, and Guidelines for Correctness, vol. 6. Springer, Heidelberg (2008)

33. Augusto, A., Mendling, J., Vidgof, M., Wurm, B.: The connection between process complexity of event sequences and models discovered by process mining. Inf. Sci. **598**, 196–215 (2022)

34. Richetti, P.H.P., Baião, F.A., Santoro, F.M.: Declarative process mining: reducing discovered models complexity by pre-processing event logs. In: Sadiq, S., Soffer, P., Völzer, H. (eds.) BPM 2014. LNCS, vol. 8659, pp. 400–407. Springer, Cham (2014). https://doi.org/10.1007/978-3-319-10172-9_28

Discovering Two-Level Business Process Models from User Interface Event Logs

Irene Barba[1]([✉])(ID), Carmelo Del Valle[1](ID), Andrés Jiménez-Ramírez[1](ID),
Barbara Weber[2](ID), and Manfred Reichert[3](ID)

[1] Departamento de Lenguajes y Sistemas Informáticos, University of Seville,
Seville, Spain
{irenebr,carmelo,ajramirez}@us.es
[2] Institut for Computer Science, University of St. Gallen, St. Gallen, Switzerland
barbara.weber@unisg.ch
[3] Institute of Databases and Information Systems, Ulm University, Ulm, Germany
manfred.reichert@uni-ulm.de

Abstract. The widespread adoption of Robotic Process Automation
(RPA) to automate repetitive tasks has surged, utilizing front-end interfaces to replicate human actions. Task mining is integral to the RPA lifecycle, capturing and analyzing fine-grained user interactions. As opposed
to traditional process mining, which focuses on business processes, task
mining relies on low-level events from user interface (UI) logs. Bridging
the gap between task mining and process mining, this paper introduces
a novel approach to generate two-level process models from UI logs. This
method addresses challenges related to granularity and screen ambiguities by considering two levels of abstraction. It identifies each activity
at the screen level for a comprehensive overview and delves into fine-
grained user actions for a deeper understanding. This dual-level model
aids in resolving ambiguities in inferred user intention, offering labeled
activities for enhanced understandability. The proposed method was validated using synthetically generated UI event logs for an example with
real-world characteristics. The research highlights the importance of contextual information in UI event logs and provides a solution to effectively
map low-level UI interactions to higher-level user activities for meaningful analysis and automation.

Keywords: Robotic process automation · Hierarchical business
process models · Event abstraction · Process discovery

1 Introduction

Robotic Process Automation (RPA) has received attention for automating repetitive tasks by mimicking human actions through front-end interfaces [9,16,18].
Task mining, crucial in the RPA lifecycle [1], captures fine-grained user interactions using UI event logs. In contrast to traditional process mining focusing on
end-to-end business processes (BPs), task mining relies on low-level UI events

G. Guizzardi et al. (Eds.): CAiSE 2024, LNCS 14663, pp. 456–472, 2024.
https://doi.org/10.1007/978-3-031-61057-8_27

like mouse clicks and keystrokes, allowing for detailed insights and the identification of automation candidates [12]. However, the abundance of fine-grained event data poses challenges in obtaining a holistic understanding of BPs, which is indispensable for any process automation, requiring manual inspection of models for accurate automation. Abstracting low-level UI interactions to higher-level user activities is crucial for meaningful analysis and automation [2]. Different process stakeholders may prioritize varying levels of detail. Moreover, in processes with complex user interfaces, ambiguity can arise from similar sequences of low-level events leading to different outcomes. Incorporating multiple granularity levels can resolve such ambiguities, providing a nuanced understanding of user intentions and enhancing user-friendliness and adaptability in the analysis [8]. Such an integration would allow bridging the gap between task mining (with its focus on understanding how tasks are performed) and process mining (with its focus on obtaining an end-to-end view of a BPs).

Existing process mining literature (e.g., [24, 27, 30]) predominantly focuses on BP abstraction, with some works emphasizing event log abstraction through clustering or hierarchical representation (e.g., [10, 20, 21, 28]). Notably, these works overlook UI event logs, which pose an additional challenge due to the importance of event context, specifically the user screen and its information. In this regard, the same screen may be used for different purposes (e.g., the same screen is used for both opening and closing a case). Hence, *ambiguity* regarding user intentions [22] might exist, which may be better inferred, for example, after checking subsequent user actions (e.g., the button pushed). In this context, providing semantics to activities that aid in inferring the intention behind is vital for enhancing model understandability.

This paper introduces a method to generate two-level process models from UI event logs, where each event is associated with a screenshot [16]. Although a screen-level analysis of the log may produce useful models for a general understanding of the process —serving as an analytical level, e.g., to assess the suitability of the process to be automated— it may not reveal further concrete details that might be required at a functional level (e.g., to design and implement the automation effectively). For this, the current approach operates at two abstraction levels. At the higher level, each screen serves as a proxy for an activity, providing a comprehensive overview of the process model and capturing the flow between screens, which is particularly valuable in RPA processes. For the lower level of abstraction, standard process mining is applied individually for each screen, considering all relevant low-level events. This granular analysis addresses ambiguities in inferred user intentions. To improve clarity, providing meaningful names to all activities in the generated models is proposed.

The current work builds on our prior work on discovering flat models from UI event logs [16] by discovering two-level process models instead of flat ones, offering a more detailed view of process behavior. These two-level models overcome activity ambiguity issues seen in [16], where similar screens led to the incorrect identification of distinct activities. This proposal also adds labels to activities, improving model interpretation.

Therefore, the primary research question (PRQ) addressed in this paper is: *Can the proposed approach improve the analysis phase of an RPA project?*

The paper is structured as follows: Sect. 2 provides a succinct overview of related works. Section 3 provides insights into the process of generating an event log along a running example. Section 4 outlines our proposed methodology. Experimental results are presented in Sect. 5. The paper concludes in Sect. 6.

2   Related Work

This section presents related work on (1) event abstraction, (2) routine segmentation, (3) BP model discovery from UI event logs, and (4) hierarchical BP model discovery.

[30] investigates approaches to handle event logs with different granularity levels in the context of process mining. Usually, the granularity level is fixed during log preprocessing using event abstraction techniques [11,24,29], abstracting data based on factors like temporal proximity. Furthermore, there exist proposals for event abstraction that explore hierarchical clustering for events or event classes [13,14,25]. These hierarchical clustering methods rely on various techniques, including event correlation, predictive clustering trees, and spatial proximity of events within the log. In contrast, our method utilizes an image-similarity clustering algorithm, ensuring that events with similar screenshots are assigned to the same screen ID [16].

In the context of RPA, dealing with segmentation in the management of UI event logs has been identified as a significant challenge [4,19]. Addressing this challenge, studies such as [5] have delved into routine segmentation. This involves automatically analyzing which user actions contribute to which routines inside a UI event log and cluster such user actions into well-bounded routine traces. In the proposed approach we consider separating the stream of user actions into different cases (i.e., into different routine traces), ensuring that each event in the log is associated with a unique case identifier necessary for the subsequent process mining tasks. This is performed by considering a predefined sequence of events that delineate the start and the end of the cases [16]. However, unlike [5], we do not analyze the particular routine associated with each case since this is not required for the proposed approach. It is important to note that we are focusing on scenarios where a UI event log documents numerous executions of diverse routines, with certain user actions recurring across these routines.

In the realm of discovering BP models from UI event logs, the approach presented in [16] associates each activity with one screen during process mining, creating process models at the screen level (cf. Sect. 3.3). Such approach is then used as our baseline for addressing research question 1 in Sect. 5. Additionally, [9] proposes a methodology for RPA task selection based on UI event logs and process mining, whereas [26] incorporates large language models for task grouping, activity labeling, and connector recommendation. However, none of these works considers more than one level of hierarchy in the discovery of process models from UI event logs.

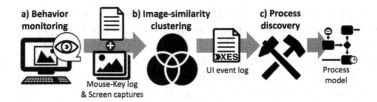

Fig. 1. Overview of the framework for process model discovery (adapted from [16]).

[28] focuses on the discovery of hierarchical BPMN models from logs that contain basic information such as caseID, task name, start time, and end time. [28] detects multi-instance models and builds a hierarchy tree of events and uses heuristic miner for the discovery of the sub-models. Similarly, [10] obtains BPMN models with sub-processes and multi-instances, but the logs need to contain certain data attributes (e.g., primary and foreign keys) to discover event dependencies, not being observable in many logs. In a related way, [21] proposes FlexHMiner, which is based on activity trees to define the components (activities or sub-processes) of the (sub)processes. FlexHMiner achieves better results if domain knowledge is provided, as explained in Sects. 3.3 and 5.4. [21] further allows for randomly grouping components of (sub)processes. Finally, [20] defines Hierarchical Petri Nets (HPNs) and proposes an approach to discover HPNs from event logs with lifecycle information, enabling the detection of nesting activity relations. Unlike these works, the proposed approach starts from UI event logs and considers the particularities of this kind of logs (e.g., image-similarity of screenshots) as valuable information for generating the process model.

3   Event Log Generation for a Running Example

As running example we consider a business context in which a process with three variants needs to be executed to manage client requests (see [7] for the related BPMN model): (1) the client requests unsubscription; after checking that she is up to date with payments, the unsubscription is performed (the client is notified by e-mail); (2) the client requests unsubscription; after checking that she is not up to date with payments, the unsubscription is not performed (the client is notified by e-mail); and (3) the client requests billing information related to her last payment receipt; this receipt is sent to her by e-mail.

Although the process is not real, it simulates a realistic situation based on our experience and previous RPA work. The chosen scenario presents a common challenge in real-world scenarios: the screens have an $n : m$ relationship with business activities, meaning the same screen is used for different goals. This introduces ambiguity in inferred user intentions (cf. Sect. 1). If we model screens as activities [16], the resulting model may depict distinct goals represented by the same activity (screen). To be more precise, within this context, we define a process activity as *ambiguous* if it can be utilized for different purposes, i.e., if the user's intention for it is varied. When screens are used as process activities, the same meaning of *ambiguity* is applied to the screens. For instance, in the example [7], the same screen, "S5", is linked to business activities "Get Client Information" and "Delete Client", leading to potential confusion and compromising the quality of the model. To gain comprehensive insights into process execution, it is crucial to analyze the actions within each screen, focusing on user interactions.

Regarding the running example, we presume that the input UI event log is clean [16], i.e., all log traces represent sequences of events related to the considered process variants. This suggests, for instance, that if the worker checks her email, we can infer that it is necessary for managing the ongoing case.

To address the analysis of this process, the framework described in [16] can be used (cf. Fig. 1). Unlike similar frameworks for process mining in RPA [3,12,16] considers the information in the screen valuable. At a glance, it consists of three main phases, i.e., (a) behavior monitoring of the users executing the process (cf. Sect. 3.1), (b) image-similarity clustering of the behavior to infer similar activities and cases (cf. Sect. 3.2), and (c) process model discovery to represent the observed behavior with a BP model (cf. Sect. 3.3).

Initially, we build upon our prior work [16] for steps (a) and (b), and subsequently extend step (c) to handle ambiguities, meaningful labels, and multiple granularity levels when discovering the process model.

3.1   Behavior Monitoring

The BP is supported by an IT system. As suggested by different authors [3,16, 19], recording the user interactions while the user is executing the BP might be more efficient, comprehensive, and less error-prone than conducting traditional interviews with the users. For this, a monitoring tool (cf. Fig. 1a) can be used to record the events produced by the user on the graphical user interface. Several tools are available for such respect [3,19] that produce UI event logs. To be more precise, we consider UI event logs containing the following attributes per event:

- *timestamp*: time at which the action took place.
- *actionType*: action performed by the user. For this attribute, we consider values Click, Keystroke, and RightClick. This categorization aligns with common distinctions in literature, where actions are frequently classified into mouse and keyboard inputs [2].
- *UIElementID*: id related to the UI element the action is performed on, e.g., Button1.
- *UIElementContent*: data contained within the element of the UI on which the action is performed, e.g., 'Send Form'.
- *softApp*: application used for the action, e.g., 'Excel sheet 1'.
- *inputValue*: the data or information provided by a user as input to a system or application, e.g., text the user writes into a text field.
- *screenShot*: image of the screen (and its content) at the moment the event took place (related to the UI Hierarchy attribute [2]).

timestamp	actionType	UIElementID	UIElementContent	UIElementContentHF	softApp	inputValue	screenShot	caseID	screenID	ActivityID
9225	Click	Button3	See cases	See cases	CMS		sc1.png	1	S1	CMS-S1-Click-Button3-See cases
9226	Click	TextBox3			CLI		sc2.png	1	S2	CLI-S2-Click-TextBox3-
9227	Keystroke	TextBox3			CLI	Irene	sc3.png	1	S2	CLI-S2-Keystroke-TextBox3-
9228	Click	Button1	Open	Open	CLI		sc4.png	1	S2	CLI-S2-Click-Button1-Open
9229	Right Click	Button2	Carmelo Romero		CLI		sc18.png	3	S5	CLI-S5-Right Click-Button2-
9230	Click	Button2	Payments	Payments	CLI		sc5.png	1	S3	CLI-S5-Right Click-Button2-Payments
9231	Click	Button3	See cases	See cases	CMS		sc6.png	2	S1	CMS-S1-Click-Button3-See cases
9232	Click	TextBox3			CLI		sc7.png	2	S2	CLI-S2-Click-TextBox3-
9233	Keystroke	TextBox3			CLI	Manfred	sc8.png	2	S2	CLI-S2-Keystroke-TextBox3-
9234	Click	Button1	Open	Open	CLI		sc9.png	2	S2	CLI-S2-Click-Button1-Open
9235	Click	TextBox2			MAIL		sc10.png	2	S4	MAIL-S4-Click-TextBox2-
9236	Keystroke	TextBox2			MAIL	manfred.reichert @uni-ulm.de	sc11.png	2	S4	MAIL-S4-Keystroke-TextBox2-
9237	Click	TextBox1			MAIL			2	S4	MAIL-S4-Click-TextBox1-
9238	Keystroke	TextBox1			MAIL	Dear Manfred....	sc12.png	2	S4	MAIL-S4-Keystroke-TextBox1-
9239	Click	Button2	Payments	Payments	CLI		sc13.png	2	S3	CLI-S5-Right Click-Button2-Payments
9240	Click	Button3	See cases	See cases	CMS		sc14.png	3	S1	CMS-S1-Click-Button3-See cases
9241	Click	TextBox3			CLI		sc15.png	3	S2	CLI-S2-Click-TextBox3-
9242	Keystroke	TextBox3			CLI	Carmelo	sc16.png	3	S2	CLI-S2-Keystroke-TextBox3-
9243	Click	Button1	Open	Open	CLI		sc17.png	3	S2	CLI-S2-Click-Button1-Open
9244	Right Click	Button2	Irene Lingard		CLI		sc18.png	3	S5	CLI-S5-Right Click-Button2-

Fig. 2. Example of Extended UI Event Log.

Based on this, we generated an entire dataset, i.e., an event log —aligned with the proposal presented in [2]— simulating the execution of the process with its different variants.[1]

3.2 Image-Similarity Clustering

Before applying process discovery algorithms, the previous log may include case IDs —identifying different instances of the process—, and activity IDs —identifying different activities. To facilitate this distinction, we leverage the *screenID* attribute, as introduced in [16]. Two events share the same screenID if their screenshots exhibit *similarity*. At a glance, to calculate the screenID (1) all screenshots are hashed into an array of bits (aka. fingerprint), (2) the hashes are clustered using a similarity function called Hamming distance [15] (i.e., counting the number of bits two hashes differ), and then (3) two screenshots are considered similar if they are in the same cluster. In [16], this screenID was used to identify the activities, which means that each low-level event was related to a higher-level group. Altogether, the considered UI event log attributes can be grouped [18,24] in process-related attributes (*timestamp, caseID, screenID*), context attributes (*actionType, softApp, screenShot, UIElementID, UIElementContent*), and data attributes (*inputValue*). Figure 2 shows an example UI event log related to 3 cases of the process detailed in [7]. The 3 cases were collected by monitoring the behavior and adding the derived attributes, i.e., it is a subset of the generated dataset. Note that the highlighted columns (i.e., *UIElementContentHF* and *ActivityID*) are also included as part of the proposed approach (cf. Sect. 4.1).

---

[1] The dataset and the related mockups of the IT system are available in [7].

3.3   Process Model Discovery

For applying a process mining algorithm to the UI event log², the activity and case columns need to be identified. The model discovered from the UI event log, considering *screenIDs* as activities, shows the flow between screens, but is missing the detailed actions performed on them and lacking of semantics in the activities. This approach (denoted as *FlatScreen* from now on) is used as one of the baselines (cf. Sect. 4.2) and considered in the evaluation (cf. Sect. 5). A more recent approach [21] allows discovering models with a hierarchical representation, which effectively bridges the gap between low-level operational details and high-level process insights. However, the efficacy of this approach significantly depends on the incorporation of business knowledge for the meaningful grouping of low-level activities. [21] further allows for randomly grouping components of (sub)processes. This approach (denoted as *RandomHier* from now on) is also used as one of the baselines (cf. Sect. 4.2) and considered in the evaluation (cf. Sect. 5). In conclusion, although hierarchical mining offers a more comprehensive perspective, it poses the following challenges:

1. The absence of business knowledge can significantly hinder the ability to group low-level activities in a meaningful way. This knowledge is crucial for understanding and accurately representing the relationships within the process as well as for properly dealing with ambiguity.
2. When event logs lack descriptive labels, the process model might not truly reflect the underlying process. Descriptive labels are essential for providing context and clarity, enabling the hierarchical model to capture the process accurately.

4   From UI Event Logs to Two-Level BP Models

As mentioned, improving the analysis phase of an RPA project involves tackling distinct challenges. These encompass dealing with (1) low-level events from front-end user interfaces to create a multi-granular and easily understandable model, and (2) resolving ambiguities in inferred user intentions. To tackle these challenges, we propose a method for uncovering two-level BP models from UI event logs. Our approach comprises following key steps:

1. Generating extended UI event logs (cf. Sect. 4.1). This step entails enriching the properties of each event by incorporating additional information necessary for subsequent stages.
2. Discovering hierarchical BP models (cf. Sect. 4.2). This step outlines the process of uncovering two-level BP models from the extended UI event log. It elucidates how activities at various granularity levels are labeled to enhance understandability.

---

² We consider using Inductive Miner due to its ability to guarantee sound process models and its balance to capture essential process behavior while maintaining model simplicity [17].

Algorithm 1. Generating Extended UI Event Logs

1: **procedure** EXTENDUILOG(**Input:** UIEventLog, **Output:** Modified UIEventLog)
2:    $addAttributes(UIEventLog, "UIElementContentHF", "ActivityID")$
3:    $freqThreshold \leftarrow calculateFreqThres(UIElementContent, UIEventLog)$
4:    **for each** entry e in UIEventLog **do**
5:        **if** frequency$(e.UIElementContent, UIEventLog) \geq freqThreshold$ **then**
6:            $valueUIElementContentHF \leftarrow e.UIElementContent$
7:        **else**
8:            $valueUIElementContentHF \leftarrow \emptyset$
9:        **end if**
10:       $valueActivityID \leftarrow concatenate(e.softApp, e.screenID, e.actionType,$
          $e.UIElementID, valueUIElementContentHF)$
11:       $extend(UIEventLog, e, valueUIElementContentHF, valueActivityID)$
12:    **end for**
13: **end procedure**

4.1   Generating Extended UI Event Logs

Before delving into the discovery of two-level BP models, several preparatory steps are essential including the extension of the UI event log (cf. Algorithm 1). Specifically, the creation of a distinct identifier for user actions, denoted as *ActivityID* attribute, shall represent the activities at the most fine-grained level (Line 2 of Algorithm 1). This identifier serves a dual purpose—supporting process discovery at the user action level and providing semantics to activities in the discovered model.

To formulate the user action ID, we must identify relevant properties within the log while ignoring irrelevant ones. As stated in [2], a user action is defined by both the performed action (i.e., the *actionType* attribute) and the target object the action is executed on. In the considered event log, this target object can be unambiguously identified by attributes *UIElementID*, *softApp*, and *screenID*. While these attributes suffice for identifying user actions, adding semantics to related activities in discovered models can benefit from including the *UIElementContent* attribute. Specifically, the contents of *UIElementContent* serve a dual role in describing user actions. When it involves elements associated with the consistent labeling of UI components (e.g., button labels like "See cases" or "Open"), its content becomes essential for conveying meaning. In such cases, this content frequently occurs in the log. Conversely, when *UIElementContent* contains data-dependent elements (e.g., names or surnames), its contribution to action descriptions is minimal, with infrequent occurrences. To selectively consider the content crucial for describing user actions, a new attribute, *UIElementContentHF*, is introduced (Line 2 of Algorithm 1). This attribute replicates the value of *UIElementContent* only when its frequency in the UI event log exceeds a threshold calculated from the input data, otherwise it remains empty (Lines 3–9 of Algorithm 1). This inclusion is based on the consideration that the content is relevant for providing semantics to the associated user action. Altogether, the new attribute *ActivityID* is computed by concatenating the values

---

Algorithm 2. Discovering Two-level BP Models

1: **procedure** DISCOVERHIERMODELS(**Input:** Extended *UIEventLog*, **Output:**
    Two-level BP Model *hierModel*)
2:     *screens* ← *getDifferentScreens(UIEventLog)*
3:     **for each** *screen* in *screens* **do**
4:         *newLabelScreen* ← *generateLabelScreen(UIEventLog, screen)*
5:         *replace(UIEventLog, screen, newLabelScreen)*
6:     **end for**
7:     *highLevelModel* ← *discover(UIEventLog, "ScreenID")*
8:     *hierModel* ← *createTwoLevelModelHL(highLevelModel)*
9:     **for each** *highLevelAct* in *highLevelModel* **do**
10:         *filteredLog* ← *filterLog(UIEventLog, highLevelAct)*
11:         *lowLevelModel* ← *discover(filteredLog, "ActivityID")*
12:         *replaceLabels(lowLevelModel)*
13:         *addSubprocess(hierModel, highLevelAct, lowLevelModel)*
14:     **end for**
15: **end procedure**

---

from *softApp*, *screenID*, *actionType*, *UIElementID*, and *UIElementContentHF*
(Line 10 of Algorithm 1), see Fig. 2 for examples. Subsequently, the event infor-
mation is expanded by incorporating the previously computed values for both
UIElementContentHF and *ActivityID* (Line 11 of Algorithm 1).

When we generate the fine-grained model by applying process mining directly
to the extended UI event log using *ActivityID* as the activity ID, this results in a
model resolving ambiguity, but lacking semantics. However, the model discovered
when considering *screenID* as activity ID is more coarse-grained, but presents
ambiguity issues and lacks label semantics.

4.2 Discovering Two-Level BP Models

This section delineates the procedure for discovering two-level BP models from
the expanded UI event log (cf. Algorithm 2). These models, unlike flat models
that can be directly learned from the raw UI event log, enable the analysis of
the process at two levels of granularity while assigning semantics to the different
activities they encompass to improve understandability.

In the realm of RPA, processes typically entail a sequence of steps or actions
executed across various screens or interfaces. Consequently, we find it fitting to
construct the process model by treating each screen as an individual activity.
To achieve this, first, for the sake of understandability, we label each *screenID*
as follows (Lines 2–6 in Algorithm 2): for every sequence of events sharing the
same *screenID* within the same case, we take the last one with a non-empty value
of *UIElementContentHF*, as it reflects one of the possible goals of the process
behind the screen. The set of values obtained for the complete log can be used
to define the semantics of the screen. Therefore, we concatenate these values
and use them as the label of the screen. Additionally, we add at the beginning
the *appName* to each group of *UIElementContentHF* values associated with

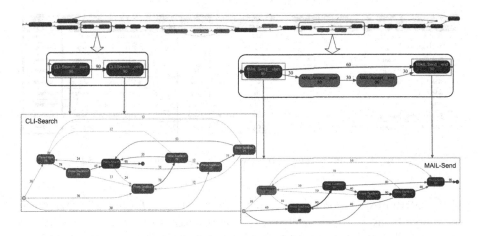

Fig. 3. Two-level model that is discovered for the running example, showcasing subprocesses associated with screens "CLI-Search" and "MAIL-Send".

the same application. In case several screens have the same label, we follow the approach presented in [24] and use other attributes to disambiguate the different classes obtained. If multiple screens still have the same label, we use the *UIElementID* attribute of the same event as the *UIElementContentHF* value, which is more screen-specific. Finally, if there are still several screens with the same label, we add the *screenID* value to resolve the ambiguity.

Then, we suggest process mining on an extended UI event log, where the screen ID is treated as the activity ID to unveil a high-level model (Line 7 in Algorithm 2) that shows the flow between screens.

While the preceding step yields a high-level model depicting the flow between screens, the diverse roles within a process entail varying user interests at different levels of detail. Operational teams, for instance, may demand detailed insights at lower granularity levels, facilitating a nuanced understanding of specific user interactions and finer subprocesses. Additionally, ambiguity in inferred user actions might arise from distinct activities with different aims, but being identified as the same activity due to screen similarities.

To tackle both multigranularity and ambiguity, we suggest creating distinct event logs for each screen, exclusively containing the events relevant to that specific screen (Line 10 in Algorithm 2). Subsequently, process mining is applied to the filtered logs, considering attribute *ActivityID* as the activity ID, to unveil the subprocess related to each screen (Lines 11–13 in Algorithm 2).

When labeling the activities in the resulting model, attributes *softApp* and *screenID* are irrelevant as user actions linked to the same screen ID share identical values in these attributes, i.e., these values do not contribute to identify the user actions performed during screen processing. On the contrary, the content of the *actionType* attribute is highly relevant for adding semantics to the user action. Similarly, the *UIElementContentHF* attribute is appropriate for giving semantics to the user action when it contains content (cf. Sect. 4.1). However,

timestamp	actionType	UIElementID	UIElementContent	UIElementContentHF	softApp	inputValue	screenShot	caseID	screenID	ActivityID	ActivityLabel
9226	Click	TextBox3			CLI		sc2.png	1	S2	CLI-S2-Click-TextBox3-	Press-TextBox3
9227	Keystroke	TextBox3			CLI	Irene	sc3.png	1	S2	CLI-S2-Keystroke-TextBox3-	Write-TextBox3
9228	Click	Button1	Open	Open	CLI		sc4.png	1	S2	CLI-S2-Click-Button1-Open	Press-Open
9232	Click	TextBox3			CLI		sc7.png	2	S2	CLI-S2-Click-TextBox3-	Press-TextBox3
9233	Keystroke	TextBox3			CLI	Manfred	sc8.png	2	S2	CLI-S2-Keystroke-TextBox3-	Write-TextBox3
9234	Click	Button1	Open	Open	CLI		sc9.png	2	S2	CLI-S2-Click-Button1-Open	Press-Open
9241	Click	TextBox3			CLI		sc15.png	3	S2	CLI-S2-Click-TextBox3-	Press-TextBox3
9242	Keystroke	TextBox3			CLI	Carmelo	sc16.png	3	S2	CLI-S2-Keystroke-TextBox3-	Write-TextBox3
9243	Click	Button1	Open	Open	CLI		sc17.png	3	S2	CLI-S2-Click-Button1-Open	Press-Open

Fig. 4. Labels given to some user actions related to screen S2.

as this attribute may be empty in some events, the *UIElementID* attribute is considered being a proper substitute for composing the user action name in such situations. Therefore, to name each user action, we propose concatenating the content of the *actionType* and *UIElementContentHF* attributes when *UIElementContentHF* is not empty. Conversely, if *UIElementContentHF* is empty, concatenation involves the *actionType* and *UIElementID* attributes. To improve the clarity of user action labels, we suggest replacing the identifier used for action types (Line 11 in Algorithm 2). Given that the values of this attribute are {Click, Keystroke, RightClick} (consistent with most related works [2]), we find it more descriptive to use the term "Press" in place of "Click" and the term "Write" instead of "Keystroke." Therefore, in the post-composition phase, such replacement is performed to enhance clarity. Figure 4 illustrates the labels assigned to some user actions associated with screen *S2*.

In Fig. 3, which shows the two-level model discovered for the running example when considering the UI event log as input and using the proposed approach (denoted as *ScreenHier* from now on), the high-level model and the labels generated for the high-level activities can be observed. It also contains the models of the subprocesses associated to screens "CLI-Search" and "MAIL-Send". We opted for these screens as illustrations as they represent the two subprocesses with the highest control-flow complexity and size.

Note that with some small adaptations the proposed approach can also be used in combination with FlexHMiner [21] by providing domain knowledge in such a way that user actions are grouped by *screenID* (approach denoted as *KnowScreenHier* from now on). However, FlexHMiner cannot independently discover the models aligned with the previously provided motivation; instead, its functionality is embedded within the framework detailed in this article.

5   Evaluation

As motivated in Sect. 1, this work addresses the following Primary Research Question (PRQ): *Can the proposed approach improve the analysis phase of an RPA project?* This inquiry can be tested by comparing the quality and understandability of process models generated from UI event logs with existing approaches against those produced using the proposed approach. To answer the PRQ, the evaluation explores the following Research Questions (RQs):

(**RQ1**): Do the models that can be generated with the proposed approach describe the process behind an UI event log better than other proposals for generating flat models in the area of RPA?

(**RQ2**): Do the models that can be generated with the proposed approach describe the process behind an UI event log better than other proposals for generating hierarchical models in the area of process mining?

5.1 Case Selection

We assess our approach by applying it to the BP exemplified in Sect. 3. This example is well-suited for evaluation as both the model directly derived by applying process mining to the raw UI event log level and the model obtained by considering *screenIDs* as activity IDs [16] are inadequate for comprehending the underlying process within the UI event log. Moreover, an $n : m$ relationship exists between activities and screen IDs (see [7]), posing a challenge in generating process models from UI event logs (cf. Sect. 1).

5.2 Experiment Design

As explained in Sect. 4.2, the proposed approach gives rise to *ScreenHier* and *KnowScreenHier* (cf. Sect. 4.2)–both discovering two-level models with activity names that carry semantic meaning.

To address RQ1, we compare the results obtained with the proposed approach with those obtained with *FlatScreen* (cf. Sect. 3.3). *FlatScreen* is the most closely related proposal in literature for generating process models from UI event logs in the context of RPA. In the model obtained with *FlatScreen*, the activity names lack semantics.

Regarding RQ2, we assess the results of the proposed approach against those obtained with *RandomHier* (cf. Sect. 3.3). We chose this approach as baseline as it is the most comparable proposal in literature for generating hierarchical process models from event logs. *RandomHier* discovers a hierarchical model by using FlexHMiner[3] [21] in ProM[4], where activities are randomly grouped based on user actions as activity IDs. The resulting model also suffers from a lack of semantics in its activity names.

As response variables for both RQ1 and RQ2 we consider quality and understandability of the generated models. For evaluating the quality of a model M concerning a log L we consider the following quality measures [21]:

- Fitness $Fi(M, L) \in [0, 1]$: represents the proportion of events in the event log that are correctly captured by the model.

---

[3] It is accessible at github.com/xxlu/prom-FlexHMiner.
[4] http://www.promtools.org/.

- Precision $Pr(M, L) \in [0, 1]$: measures the proportion of activities modeled by process discovery that actually belong to the underlying process.
- F1-score $F1(M, L) \in [0, 1]$ (F-measure [20]): is the harmonic mean of fitness and precision: $F1(M, L) = 2 * \frac{Fi(L,M)*Pr(L,M)}{Fi(L,M)+Pr(L,M)}$.
- Generalization $Ge(M, L) \in [0, 1]$: evaluates how well the discovered model generalizes to new instances or variants of the process that were not present in the original event log. We adopt the same methodology as described in [6, 21]. Specifically, we partition the log into $k = 3$ subsets: L is randomly divided into L_1, L_2, and L_3. Subsequently, $Ge(L, M) = \frac{1}{3} \sum_{1 \leq i \leq 3} 2 * \frac{Fi(L_i,M_i)*Pr(L,M_i)}{Fi(L_i,M_i)+Pr(L,M_i)}$ with M_i corresponding to L_i.

The evaluation of understandability of a model is intricately linked to its complexity. For this study, following [6, 21], we assess complexity using both the control-flow complexity $CFC(M)$ and the size (i.e., number of nodes) $Size(M)$ of a model as response variables.

For the proposals that generate hierarchical models, the values of the response variables are computed as the mean values of the individual measurements for each subprocess within the hierarchical model and the root process.

For the 4 aforementioned approaches, the Inductive Miner algorithm with a 0.2 path filtering threshold is employed for mining the log.

5.3   Dataset

The experiments involve a synthetic UI event log tailored to the selected case[5], created through a method supported by specialized tools [23]. This log encapsulates diverse variations witnessed during the execution of business activities in the running example [7] with corresponding mockups (see [7]). To be more specific, we generate an UI event log comprising 90 cases (30 for each process variant). Each case encompasses an average of 32.73 events (min=23, max=41), featuring 13 distinct screenIDs and 39 unique activityIDs.

5.4   Results

Table 1 shows the values that are obtained for each response variable when considering the aforementioned approaches.

Concerning RQ1 our results show that both newly proposed approaches, i.e., *ScreenHier* and *KnowScreenHier*, exhibit substantial improvement over one of the baselines (i.e., *FlatScreen*) when focusing on both quality and complexity metrics. This enhancement is attributed to hierarchical models usually delivering better results than flat models for these metrics.

Concerning RQ2, *ScreenHier* and *KnowScreenHier* outperform *RandomHier* in general when focusing on quality and complexity metrics. This superiority arises from the consideration of screens for grouping user actions, as proposed

---

[5] Available at: [7].

Table 1. Values that are obtained for the response variables.

Approach	$\overline{Fi}$	$\overline{Pr}$	$\overline{F1}$	$\overline{Ge}$	$\overline{CFC}$	$\overline{Size}$
FlatScreen	0.571	0.605	0.588	0.595	28.00	52.00
RandomHier	0.964	0.674	0.765	0.809	9.40	31.00
ScreenHier	0.967	**0.839**	**0.885**	**0.888**	5.14	**13.64**
KnowScreenHier	**0.997**	0.813	0.870	0.885	**4.21**	14.43

in this work, leading to two-level models that surpass random grouping. Metrics combining precision and fitness (i.e., F1-score and generalization) also favor *KnowScreenHier* over *RandomHier*.

Additionally, although not empirically demonstrated in this study, providing semantics to activities, as done in *ScreenHier* and *KnowScreenHier*, is likely to further improve the comprehension of the generated models.

5.5   Threats to Validity and Limitations

Concerning *construct validity*, we assert that the conducted experiments align well with the intended objective of assessing the efficacy of the proposed approach in enhancing the analysis phase of an RPA project. The chosen response variables and the generated UI event log are deemed appropriate for addressing research questions *RQ1* and *RQ2*. Nevertheless, additional response variables and cases could be defined to broaden the analysis performed. Regarding *external validity*, we believe that the study findings can be generalized to scenarios adhering to the outlined assumptions in Sect. 3. Though the proposed approach is described along the running example, its applicability extends to other scenarios that present similar characteristics. The running example encapsulates typical characteristics frequently encountered in common legacy system scenarios. Additionally, the attributes considered for each event in the UI event log align seamlessly with other significant works in the RPA field [2,18,24].

The UI event log in our experiments was synthetically generated from realistic screenshots, introducing potential bias as it simulates expected behavior rather than precisely reflecting real-world scenarios. However, the tool used for screenshot generation has been validated in previous research, closely replicating events and screenshots from the original log. Additionally, the tool's configurability enables the consideration of various generated configurations, helping to mitigate this potential bias. Additionally, we acknowledge the limitation of analyzing results related to only one process scenario. Evaluating the proposed approach in diverse process scenarios of increasing complexity, preferably real ones, would contribute to a more comprehensive understanding of the proposed approach. Moreover, we consider partially evaluating the understandability of the generated models through analyzing their complexity. Nevertheless, we recognize the importance of conducting controlled experiments involving real users to achieve a more comprehensive evaluation of model understandability. Furthermore, to generate the two-level models, we have considered FlexHMiner [21], although there are other options that could be investigated.

6 Summary and Outlook

This paper presents a novel method for extracting two-level BP models from UI event logs. The approach works at two levels: for a comprehensive overview it captures activities at the screen level and delves into detailed user actions for deeper insights. This dual-level model not only support multi-granularity, but helps addressing ambiguities in inferred user intention and improves clarity with labeled activities. The method was validated using synthetically generated UI event logs, demonstrating that the proposed approach yields improved models in terms of both quality and complexity. For future work, we aim to evaluate our approach using real-world scenarios. Additionally, we plan to explore incorporating more levels of granularity in the discovered models and consider UI event logs with supplementary information, such as database logs.

Acknowledgement. This research was supported by the EQUAVEL project PID2022-137646OB-C31 funded by MICIU/AEI/10.13039/501100011033 and by FEDER, UE. ChatGPT was utilized to assist shortening parts of the paper.

References

1. van der Aalst, W.M.: On the pareto principle in process mining, task mining, and robotic process automation. In: DATA, pp. 5–12 (2020)
2. Abb, L., Rehse, J.R.: A reference data model for process-related user interaction logs. In: Di Ciccio, C., Dijkman, R., del Rio Ortega, A., Rinderle-Ma, S. (eds.) Business Process Management. BPM 2022. LNCS, vol. 13420, pp. 57–74. Springer, Cham (2022). https://doi.org/10.1007/978-3-031-16103-2_7
3. Agostinelli, S., Lupia, M., Marrella, A., Mecella, M.: Reactive synthesis of software robots in RPA from user interface logs. Comput. Ind. **142**, 103721 (2022)
4. Agostinelli, S., Marrella, A., Mecella, M.: Research challenges for intelligent robotic process automation. In: Di Francescomarino, C., Dijkman, R., Zdun, U. (eds.) BPM 2019. LNBIP, vol. 362, pp. 12–18. Springer, Cham (2019). https://doi.org/10.1007/978-3-030-37453-2_2
5. Agostinelli, S., Marrella, A., Mecella, M.: Exploring the challenge of automated segmentation in robotic process automation. In: Cherfi, S., Perini, A., Nurcan, S. (eds.) RCIS 2021. LNBIP, vol. 415, pp. 38–54. Springer, Cham (2021). https://doi.org/10.1007/978-3-030-75018-3_3
6. Augusto, A., et al.: Automated discovery of process models from event logs: review and benchmark. IEEE Trans. Knowl. Data Eng. **31**(4), 686–705 (2018)
7. Barba, I., Del Valle, C., Jimenez-Ramirez, A., Weber, B., Reichert, M.: Example of a business process with three process variants: mockups and log (2024). https://doi.org/10.5281/zenodo.10730799
8. Beerepoot, I., et al.: The biggest business process management problems to solve before we die. Comput. Ind. **146**, 103837 (2023)

9. Choi, D., R'bigui, H., Cho, C.: Candidate digital tasks selection methodology for automation with robotic process automation. Sustainability **13**(16), 8980 (2021)
10. Conforti, R., Dumas, M., García-Bañuelos, L., La Rosa, M.: BPMN miner: automated discovery of BPMN process models with hierarchical structure. Inf. Syst. **56**, 284–303 (2016)
11. Dogan, O., de Leoni, M.: Parallelism-based session creation to identify high-level activities in event log abstraction. In: De Smedt, J., Soffer, P. (eds.) Process Mining Workshops. ICPM 2023. LNBIP, vol. 503, pp. 58–69. Springer, Cham (2024). https://doi.org/10.1007/978-3-031-56107-8_5
12. Dumas, M., La Rosa, M., Leno, V., Polyvyanyy, A., Maggi, F.M.: Robotic process mining. Process Min. Handb. 468–491 (2022)
13. Folino, F., Guarascio, M., Pontieri, L.: Mining multi-variant process models from low-level logs. In: Abramowicz, W. (ed.) BIS 2015. LNBIP, vol. 208, pp. 165–177. Springer, Cham (2015). https://doi.org/10.1007/978-3-319-19027-3_14
14. Günther, C.W., Rozinat, A., van der Aalst, W.M.P.: Activity mining by global trace segmentation. In: Rinderle-Ma, S., Sadiq, S., Leymann, F. (eds.) BPM 2009. LNBIP, vol. 43, pp. 128–139. Springer, Heidelberg (2010). https://doi.org/10.1007/978-3-642-12186-9_13
15. Gusfield, D.: Algorithms on stings, trees, and sequences: computer science and computational biology. ACM SIGACT News **28**(4), 41–60 (1997)
16. Jimenez-Ramirez, A., Reijers, H.A., Barba, I., Del Valle, C.: A method to improve the early stages of the robotic process automation lifecycle. In: Giorgini, P., Weber, B. (eds.) CAiSE 2019. LNCS, vol. 11483, pp. 446–461. Springer, Cham (2019). https://doi.org/10.1007/978-3-030-21290-2_28
17. Leemans, S.J.J., Fahland, D., van der Aalst, W.M.P.: Discovering block-structured process models from event logs - a constructive approach. In: Colom, J.-M., Desel, J. (eds.) PETRI NETS 2013. LNCS, vol. 7927, pp. 311–329. Springer, Heidelberg (2013). https://doi.org/10.1007/978-3-642-38697-8_17
18. Leno, V., Augusto, A., Dumas, M., La Rosa, M., Maggi, F.M., Polyvyanyy, A.: Identifying candidate routines for robotic process automation from unsegmented UI logs. In: ICPM, pp. 153–160 (2020)
19. Leno, V., Polyvyanyy, A., Dumas, M., La Rosa, M., Maggi, F.M.: Robotic process mining: vision and challenges. Bus. Inf. Syst. Eng. **63**, 301–314 (2021)
20. Liu, C., Cheng, L., Zeng, Q., Wen, L.: Formal modeling and discovery of hierarchical business processes: a petri net-based approach. IEEE Trans. Syst. Man Cybern. Syst. (2023)
21. Lu, X., Gal, A., Reijers, H.A.: Discovering hierarchical processes using flexible activity trees for event abstraction. In: Proceedings of the ICPM, pp. 145–152. IEEE (2020)
22. Macías, J.A.: Intelligent assistance in authoring dynamically generated web interfaces. World Wide Web **11**, 253–286 (2008)
23. Martínez Rojas, A., Jiménez Ramírez, A., González Enríquez, J., Reijers, H.A.: A tool-supported method to generate user interface logs. In: Proceedings of the HICSS, pp. 5472–5481 (2023)
24. Rebmann, A., van der Aa, H.: Unsupervised task recognition from user interaction streams. In: Indulska, M., Reinhartz-Berger, I., Cetina, C., Pastor, O. (eds.) Advanced Information Systems Engineering. CAiSE 2023. LNCS, vol. 13901, pp. 141–157. Springer, Cham (2023). https://doi.org/10.1007/978-3-031-34560-9_9
25. Rehse, J.-R., Fettke, P.: Clustering business process activities for identifying reference model components. In: Daniel, F., Sheng, Q.Z., Motahari, H. (eds.) BPM

2018. LNBIP, vol. 342, pp. 5–17. Springer, Cham (2019). https://doi.org/10.1007/978-3-030-11641-5_1

26. Sani, M.F., Sroka, M., Burattin, A.: LLMS and process mining: challenges in RPA task grouping, labelling and connector recommendation. In: De Smedt, J., Soffer, P. (eds.) Process Mining Workshops. ICPM 2023. LNBIP, vol. 503, pp. 379–391. Springer, Cham (2024). https://doi.org/10.1007/978-3-031-56107-8_29

27. Seiger, R., Franceschetti, M., Weber, B.: An interactive method for detection of process activity executions from IoT data. Futur. Internet **15**(2), 77 (2023)

28. Wang, Y., Wen, L., Yan, Z., Sun, B., Wang, J.: Discovering BPMN models with sub-processes and multi-instance markers. In: Debruyne, C., et al. (eds.) OTM 2015. LNCS, vol. 9415, pp. 185–201. Springer, Cham (2015). https://doi.org/10.1007/978-3-319-26148-5_11

29. van Zelst, S.J., Mannhardt, F., de Leoni, M., Koschmider, A.: Event abstraction in process mining: literature review and taxonomy. Granul. Comput. **6**(3), 719–736 (2021)

30. Zerbato, F., Seiger, R., Di Federico, G., Burattin, A., Weber, B.: Granularity in process mining: can we fix it? In: CEUR Workshop Proceedings, vol. 2938, pp. 40–44 (2021)

Session Trust, Security and Risk

The Power of Many: Securing Organisational Identity Through Distributed Key Management

Mariia Bakhtina[1]([✉])[ID], Jan Kvapil[2][ID], Petr Švenda[2][ID],
and Raimundas Matulevičius[1][ID]

[1] University of Tartu, Tartu, Estonia
{bakhtina,rma}@ut.ee
[2] Masaryk University, Brno, Czech Republic
kvapil@mail.muni.cz, svenda@fi.muni.cz

Abstract. Organisational Digital Identity (ODI) often relies on the credentials and keys being controlled by a single person-representative. Moreover, some Information Systems (IS) outsource the key management to a third-party controller. Both the centralisation and outsourcing of the keys threaten data integrity within the IS, allegedly provided by a trusted organisation. Also, outsourcing the control prevents an organisation from cryptographically enforcing custom policies, e.g. time-based, regarding the data originating from it. To address this, we propose a Distributed Key Management System (DKMS) that eliminates the risks associated with centralised control over an organisation's identity and allows organisation-enforceable policies. The DKMS employs threshold signatures to directly involve multiple organisation's representatives (e.g. employees, IS components, and external custodians) in data signing on its behalf. The threshold signature creation and, therefore, the custom signing policy inclusion, is fully backwards compatible with commonly used signing schemes, such as RSA or ECDSA. The feasibility of the proposed system is shown in an example data exchange system, X-Road. The implementation confirms the ability of the design to achieve distributed control over the ODI during the operational key phase. Excluding a network delay, the implementation introduces less than 200 ms overhead compared to the built-in signing solution.

Keywords: organisational digital identity · key management · security · zero trust · distributed control · threshold signatures

1 Introduction

Organisational Digital Identity (ODI)[1] defines an organisation and its attributes for other entities through credentials. It enables trust between business partners and ensures the authenticity and confidentiality of cross-organisational data

---

[1] If not specified otherwise, we also use *identity* to refer to ODI.

G. Guizzardi et al. (Eds.): CAiSE 2024, LNCS 14663, pp. 475–491, 2024.
https://doi.org/10.1007/978-3-031-61057-8_28

exchanges [31]. ODI commonly relies on centrally managed credentials and keys used in Public Key Infrastructure (PKI). A centralised management introduces a single point of failure [7] in the system. As an alternative, decentralised Identity Management (IdM) based on distributed ledgers has been proposed [7]. Decentralised ODI enhances security and identity control. However, this approach requires a new governance framework and a shift of the participants to a new infrastructure. This process is time-consuming and may require legislative updates, especially in information systems used in e-governance like X-Road [22] and Gaia-X [1]. Moreover, the decentralised trust and IdM address external threats, while internal actors contribute significantly to data breaches through privilege misuse [29]. Thus, centralised control by internal actors is an open issue which threatens the authenticity of messages sent on behalf of ODI.

Regardless of the identity and trust model, organisations may use digital wallets or hardware security modules as a part of their Information System (IS) to store their identity's certificates and key material, with policies defining access rights [12]. Proprietary solutions like OpenID [2] control internal authorisation, determining who can initiate cross-organisational data exchange on behalf of ODI. Meanwhile, some organisations prefer external trusted partners to manage their identity and key materials [12,19,28], removing access control from their IS, but this raises concerns about potential compromise or misuse. Based on [7,12], we recognise the need for a more secure yet backwards compatible identity model, which would allow enforcing security through custom access policies (under what conditions are ODI-related cryptographic keys accessible/used) for information systems that rely on a centrally issued ODI.

We see a lack of attention from the Information Systems Engineering (ISE) community to the cryptographic measures used in IdM, which aims to protect ODI from insider threats. Thus, state-of-the-art cryptographic measures are researched mainly by cryptographers and the formal security analysis community. Meanwhile, the IdM's characteristics are primarily driven by the business needs and the goals of IS users. In this paper, we bridge the gap between formal security research and research of ISE, showing how the former addresses the latter's challenges. Assuming centrally issued PKI-based credentials, we aim to eliminate centralised usage of identity by embracing the zero trust paradigm [9]. While key management enables digital identity per se, this paper considers the following research question: *how to secure a centrally issued organisational digital identity through key management mechanisms for achieving zero trust?*

In this paper, we follow the design science research method [13]. We review the knowledge base of cryptographic and business mechanisms which help secure ODI with a focus on key management. As a result, we design an artefact of Distributed Key Management System (DKMS) that secures a centrally issued ODI. The DKMS uses partial custody and threshold signatures to secure ODI in cross-organisational data exchange through zero trust principles. The proposed system ensures that messages signed on behalf of ODI originate from the organisation and are not created by a single trusted ODI custodian or a company representative. The DKMS design application and utility are evaluated through implementation for the X-Road data exchange system.

2 Background

To provide new services, multiple organisations may connect their systems to form a new information system. Securing such a system requires identifying the individual organisations to allow authenticity and integrity of the shared data. Data exchange systems enable secure interoperable cross-organisation data exchange between separately built information systems in e-governance and other industries [2,17,18]. The examples of commercial, worldwide used systems are X-Road [22], UXP [10], and Dawex Data Exchange Platform, European Gaia-X [1]; while Dutch NLX [30] and Australian Secure Data Exchange application are national. Yet, they operate securely under the assumption of already established trust between collaborating entities and their digital identities.

Digital identity enables participants of the data exchange systems to confirm the authenticity of involved entities. Credentials associated with identities are the documents enabling the verification, with issuance procedures determined by a trust model. While the procedures of issuing credentials in decentralised and centralised identity models vary [7], PKI stays essentially the same. Thus, the key management is equally relevant regardless of the trust and identity model. Both the internal and external trusted representatives that manage the keys may become malicious. To mitigate this threat, the organisation should control every single data exchange attempt made on its behalf. Such a mitigation strategy [9] of avoiding the need for trust is the key component of the Zero Trust (ZT) architecture [25]. Among the key components of ZT architecture is the policy decision point that enforces control over access to resources based on the defined policies and is supported by PKI and identity management, on which this work is focused.

2.1 Targeted System Characteristics

As zero trust is a maturing strategy, little research has been done to map which of the existing security mechanisms can help secure ODI with respect to it. To study the security of an ODI and Identity Management (IdM) system, we consider characteristics targeted by identity and key management mechanisms. The need for the characteristics depends on the scenario. Through the literature review, we gathered a set of non-functional characteristics that affect ODI's security. In [5], we describe the literature procedure and provide a mapping of system characteristics with reviewed in Sect. 2.2 mechanisms.

The following business-oriented characteristics may be targeted, primarily reflecting the trust among the individual business entities. *Trustlessness* is a part of the zero trust paradigm and refers to the ability of the system to operate without relying on the honest behaviour of internal or external entities [19,25].

To react to the dishonest behaviour, the IdM system may target to deliver *traceability* that refers to the ability to know who did what, when, and how [11,12]. The more proactive approach to secure the system against internal attacks is *privilege escalation prevention*, which aims to restrict users from gaining unauthorised access. In this research, we consider privilege escalation as a result of both privilege escalation attacks and privilege misuse. Another way of enabling zero trust is *decentralisation*, which refers to distributing the responsibility for managing ODI and its keys across multiple entities to enhance security, resilience, and user control. As a result, the organisation can differentiate between *multiple users* of the ODI. Another business-demanded aspect of its system's security is *availability*, which is the ability to deliver its value continuously. System availability [12] is crucial both in the everyday data exchange and in the case of extraordinary trigger events – e.g. a loss of access to the keys or if an employee that is involved in the ODI management leaves or becomes malicious. Finally, the *usability* refers to the feasibility and convenience of the identity and key management. Usability encompasses the backwards compatibility of the proposed design with the existing infrastructure. Besides, usability defines whether the end-users will use the ODI following the defined interaction set-up with ODI [12,19,28].

2.2   Review of Key Management Mechanisms

Assuming ODI relies on PKI, key management is an enabler of digital identity per se and ensures the security of IdM systems. The key management includes pre-operational, operational, post-operational and destroyed phases [8]. IdM is involved in the four stages: (i) generation and distribution of asymmetric key pairs (i.e. private and public keys) for the key generation during the pre-operational phase; (ii) the key registration and the public key certification during the pre-operational phase; and (iii) storage, usage and backup of keys during the operational phase. The certification is crucial for establishing trust within the system as it enables verification of the exchanged data integrity. Our research aims to comply with the existing verification process to remain IdM backwards compatible. Thus, we exclude the second stage from our analysis. Figure 1 depicts artefacts used for key management that are discussed in this section.

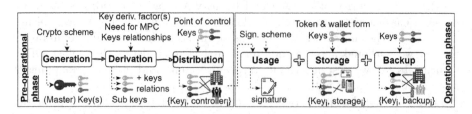

Fig. 1. Key management phases: stages, parameters and artefacts.

Here, we overview the cryptographic and business mechanisms found through the literature review, details of which can be found in [5]. The paper focuses on asymmetric cryptographic schemes that provide digital signatures.

Pre-operational Key Phase

Key Generation. To use any of the existing signature schemes, a (master) key pair needs to be generated. The signature schemes differ by key and signature size and mathematical structure, computational efficiency and security assumptions. Regardless of the scheme, the key pair creation process involves a cryptographically secure pseudorandom number generator that needs to be seeded. At the expense of security, the seed can also be derived from a user-provided input, such as a password (using a password-based key derivation function). To improve trustlessness and resilience and not rely on a single factor, the multi-factor key derivation function [20] can be utilised. Also, there are protocols for Distributed Key Generation (DKG), such as FROST [16], where multiple parties collaboratively generate secret shares of a key in a distributed manner. DKGs have a major benefit over the previous methods – the key never exists in a complete form at a single location. Finally, once generated, the master (public) key can have a certificate issued to bind it to a particular entity.

Sub-keys Derivation. Data can be signed either directly by the master private key or by sub-keys derived from it. Bitcoin Improvement Proposal No. 32 (BIP32) [23] defines deterministic key derivation, where sub-keys are obtained by a *path* from the master key. The path is also needed for the signature verification algorithm. The deterministic derivation is specified only for certain schemes based on elliptic curves (as in Bitcoin) or lattices [4]. Another option is threshold signature, where at least a threshold of K signers out of all N need to collaborate to form a valid signature. As a result, an attacker would need to compromise at least K signers to forge a valid signature. As mentioned previously, key shares can be derived using DKGs (e.g. FROST [16]) or generated and distributed by a trusted dealer (e.g. as in RSA-based threshold signature schemes [27]).

Key Distribution. The key distribution phase defines a point of control over the ODI's keys and their delivery to controllers. The point of control is driven by the level of custody over the keys. Non-custodial (i.e. self-custodial) approach [15] enables more control but more overhead, as the ODI owner is also the controller responsible for securing the keys. An opposite approach is full outsourcing of the control (i.e. custody) [19], which removes overhead from the ODI owner but disable control. Custodial ODI directly conflicts with the ZT strategy as it puts complete trust in a third-party custodian. The custodian manages the keys and can conduct any operations on behalf of the organisation. Thus, none of the approaches address trustlessness, resilience, or protection from privilege escalation and enable multiple conditional users using internal organisational access control.

Operational Key Phase

Key Storage. The keys are stored on tokens that generate, protect and manage them. The token can be a software application installed on a general device, e.g. the one that requests the signature, or a full-fledged external device such as a Hardware Security Module (HSM). The dedicated device can be a USB token, a smart card (e.g. JavaCard) or a trusted platform module built into an end-consumer device. Another device relevant for storing keys is a hardware wallet. Finally, deterministically derived keys do not require storage, as they can be generated on the spot – needing at least the threshold number of factors in the case of DKGs. The form of a token affects ODI's portability and usability.

Key Usage. The key usage is split into data signing and signature verification algorithms. For a single signer and a single pre-generated key, the key should be available either explicitly (e.g. for software tokens) or through a signing interface as with dedicated signing devices. If the master key is derived, the appropriate number of valid factors must be provided to derive the signing key. If BIP32 deterministic derivation is used, the path from the master key to the child key is also needed. Threshold schemes involving multiple signers improve recoverability and, thus, resilience – any quorum of more than the threshold of signers can create a signature using there key shares. Replacing a single ODI controller with a threshold group of K-out-of-N protects against privilege escalation. Most threshold signatures do not disclose which signers have participated in the signing. Thus, threshold signatures may help hide signers' identities from the verifier. However, all signers are accountable for N-out-of-N threshold groups. Also, elaborate policies, like signing only during a specific time range (such as working hours), can be enforced through automated signer applications. Threshold groups can also be nested – e.g. top-level 3-out-of-3 group with two shares residing with individual representatives and the last share being an employee auto-signer that signs if another K-out-of-N employee group also provides a signature. Thereby, the ODI owner can trace back to who of the key shareholders participated in the signature creation or mandate policies.

Key Backup. To enable recovery of lost keys, an identity holder should back up the secret key elsewhere than the storage used during regular key operations. Such backup storage can be an additional HSM, a trusted execution environment for key backup [28] or a third-party custody of the keys. The latter carries the risks of identity theft through privilege escalation [28]. For enhanced security, an identity holder may employ multiparty computation and Shamir's Secret Sharing, distributing key shares among multiple custodians [28]. For multiparty computation, keys should be generated with DKG, while secret sharing requires the distribution of later-derived parts of a single key. A defined minimum threshold of custodians must provide their key shares to the identity holder to recover the backed-up key [28].

To sum up, we identified mechanisms that help secure keys and signatures and, thus, ODI itself. The commonly used approaches of key management can address the problem of centralisation or bring zero trust in a targeted manner, while none of them addresses the problem on their own. In this paper, we address this research gap by proposing a distributed key management system that can bring ZT and decentralisation through the combination of reviewed mechanisms.

3   Design of a Distributed Key Management System

In this section, we present a design of a Distributed Key Management System (DKMS) for ODI as depicted in Fig. 2. It enables zero trust within the organisation's information system and is compatible with any trust model. The design assumes that the identity's credentials rely on PKI and, thus, prescribes a selection of cryptographic and business mechanisms for each stage of the key lifecycle. The design aims to eliminate the centralisation of control over ODI throughout the lifetime of keys. It increases the set of representatives or custodians to enable partial custody of ODI.

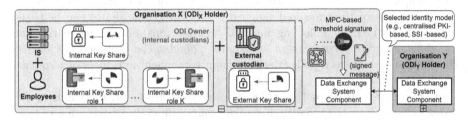

Fig. 2. DKMS for organisational digital identity in cross-organisational data exchange.

To bring zero trust into ODI management, we propose a combination of the reviewed self-custodian and custodian control, namely, *partial custody*. An IS with centralised control over ODI is prone to a single point of failure [24] due to a strong assumption on a single fully trusted entity for signing messages on behalf of an organisation. If the entity is compromised or its administrator becomes malicious, the IS cannot assure the authenticity and, thus, integrity, of the provided information. The partial custody brings decentralisation of control and storage of keys for signing or recovery. Ergo, the system can operate with reduced trust in each single entity. The distribution of the keys eliminates the single point of failure since multiple key controllers would need to cooperate to compromise the system's security. By that, partial custody boosts the overall security posture of an IS and mitigates the risks associated with centralised control of keys. DKMS allows trustlessness, improves recoverability and resilience, supports traceability, and may enable the prevention of privilege misuse.

To achieve zero trust through partial custody in DKMS, the decentralisation of control over keys may be introduced in one of two steps – during key generation or distribution. First, the keys can be initially generated in a decentralised manner. It refers to a decentralised ODI through self-sovereign identity principles usage and decentralised key generation for all the entities involved in the

ODI management and data exchange (e.g. like it was proposed in [7]). Second, if there should be one centrally generated master key, decentralisation can be introduced in the step of distributing the keys (e.g. through distributed key generation or key shares derivation) so that the derived sub-keys are used for the operational phase.

Regardless of the phase during which key shares are generated and distributed to semi-trusted custodians, an organisation can derive multiple keys to enable distributed key storage and threshold signature creation. Semi-trusted custodians can be internal entities (IS components or employees) and external service providers (i.e. external custodians). When new employees come, and old ones leave, the distributed key generation re-sharing can be performed while keeping the (certified) public key the same.

For the point of control during keys distribution, we use *partial custody* achieved through *threshold signatures*, where internal entities (e.g. employees' roles and an information system component) and an external custodial are the contributors to the signing of messages on behalf of an ODI. Users' keys are the key shares for the threshold signature. Access to these shares can be based on the user's identity following internal organisation policy. Each entity can use *different token forms* to store its share. Thereby, the proposed DKMS has threshold signatures as a policy decision point component in respect of zero trust architecture [25].

In this paper, we show that threshold signature allows organisations to distribute control over the identity. First, key shares allow the distribution of trust among the organisational parties – employees and IS components – which are primary representatives of the organisation and the initiators of messages. Second, it helps maintain access control in case of employee turnover in an organisation. Finally, a threshold of K shares protects the ODI and organisation against a compromise of up to $K - 1$ signing parties.

Additionally, DKMS brings access policies enforcement. In a centralised trust model, the external key controllers need to be trusted with complying to the access policies. With threshold signatures, the organisation can implement these access policies by assigning shares to individual internal IS components that are then responsible for enforcing the policies. For example, an IS can include a component that signs only at a specified time range and another that verifies the requester's IP address. Compliance with the access policy is enforceable by the organisation and does not require any changes on the verifying side.

For zero trust secure ODI, we propose distributing control over ODI between internal and external custodians so that multiple parties compose a group for signing messages. For example, an organisation can generate N key shares based on a certified ODI master key, where one share is given to an IS (i.e. automatic or policy-based signer), one – to an external custodian who represents the data exchange system, and others are distributed among employees of different roles who can initiate or validate the messages, e.g. semi-automatically. Signing a message requires the participation of K-out-of-N parties, where K ≤ N, (e.g. an IS, external custodian and any employee). Additionally, the second layer of threshold signature by employees of different roles or physical identities may be set up if needed to form a tree-like signing structure. In the end, the derived key shares and threshold signature on behalf of an organisation ensure that the valid signature is created based on the definition by an organisation group of ODI representatives. For internal entities, either software or hardware modules for storing key shares may be selected.

The proposed system should be applied when (i) organisational identity relies on public key infrastructure; (ii) organisation uses digital identity for cross-organisational IS (e.g. through data exchange systems for connecting standalone ISs); (iii) organisation want to remove a single point of control over its identity; (iv) multiple organisation representatives can contribute to the signing.

4   DKMS Design Evaluation

4.1   X-Road Use Case

X-Road is a distributed data exchange system between Information Systems (ISs) within the trusted network [21]. X-Road relies on PKI to ensure trust between members of the network. Members are organisations with their ISs used for operations by internal users (e.g. employees) and external users (e.g. customers). For cross-organisational data exchange, a component called *Security Server* (SS) serves as an intermediary [21]. Let us consider Member-Client and Member-Provider as X-Road Members with set-up SSs. The Client requests data from the Provider. The SSs are the components which are responsible for the PKI-verified message exchange. The Client's SS signs the data requests on behalf of the Client. The Provider's SS verifies the Client's signature in the received request and signs the response on behalf of the Provider. Finally, the response signature is verified by the Client's SS. Additionally, SS logs the data exchange so that a third party can check the Member's request or response signature if a proof is needed (e.g. in a court) [21]. In the current set-up, the X-Road is oriented toward protecting the confidentiality and integrity of the data exchange messages delivered via the public Internet. Meanwhile, all the entities inside the network are fully trusted (including SSs) based on the PKI certificates, and SS is not necessarily managed by the organisation that uses it.

Thus, we aim to eliminate the delegation of an ODI to a single SS component and enable the zero trust principle to manage identity and improve security. The following goals should be achieved: G_1. Member's ODI cryptomaterial is not in the sole control of one entity. G_2. Member can trace back the internal initiator of the message sent on Member's behalf through X-Road. G_3. Member can define the access of internal entities to operations on its behalf. G_4. The system is backwards compatible. G_5. No single entity can create a valid signature.

Table 1 maps X-Road characteristics (Sect. 2.1), which can be achieved using the reviewed key management mechanisms (Sect. 2.2). The mapping highlights the key phase and the mechanisms, the implementation of which primarily affects the respective system characteristics. An empty cell in the table refers to no direct effect or the lack of evidence which would confirm the impact.

Table 1. Mapping of system characteristics and mechanisms targeting them.

System characteristic	X-Road Related targeted goals	Pre operational phase — Key gener. (Crypto scheme)	Pre operational phase — Key derivation (Factors for key deriv.)	Pre operational phase — Key derivation (Enabled MPC sign.)	Pre operational phase — Key distribution (Point of control)	Operational phase — Key storage (Token form)	Operational phase — Key storage (Wallet form)	Operational phase — Key storage (Keys relationship)	Operational phase — Key usage (Sign.& verif. algorithm)
Decentralisation	G1				+				
Trustlessness	G1				+			+	
Portability	G1					+	+		
Multiple users	G1,G2,G5		+	+					
Traceability	G2			+					+
Usability	G4	+			+	+			+
Prevent. priv. misuse	G3		+	+				+	

To achieve our goals, we propose targeting specific system characteristics. For G_1, we aim for decentralisation, trustlessness, portability, and support for multiple users. We focus on multiple-user support and traceability for G_2 and G_5. For G_3, we emphasise preventing privilege escalation. Altogether, the stated goals aim to protect the integrity of the data exchanges within the trusted network by assuring message authenticity and proof of origin.

4.2 System Design

We set up the distributed key management system in X-Road, as depicted in Fig. 3, to evaluate its feasibility. White classes depict current X-Road entities, green classes represent the added DKMS components, and dark grey represents services used to implement the DKMS for X-Road. Currently, each Member has a fully trusted custodian, represented by a Security Server (SS). SS is responsible for ODI's key management and message signing on the organisation's behalf. The key can be either managed by an external service provider or by a Member itself. To eliminate the centralised management, we use threshold signatures to increase the number of key controllers from one to N, where at least $K \leq N$ controllers are needed to create a valid signature. Each controller can validate different policy rules for using its key.

In the X-Road use-case, we propose to share the Member's identity key material between the three key share controllers which already participate in the process of message exchange: (i) Member's information system used for creating a message; (ii) Client's employee making a data request so to ensure that the request comes from Clients' identity; (iii) Security Server (SS) used by a Member for the message exchange. For multiparty threshold signatures, we use an open-source threshold signing platform. The employees may store their key

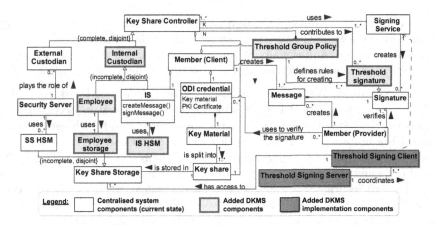

Fig. 3. DKMS for organisational digital identity in X-Road (N – the size of a group, K – threshold number of controllers contributing to a signature, K ≤ N). (Color figure online)

share on a cryptographic smartcard, while the external custodial (represented by an SS) and Member's IS may use Hardware Security Modules (HSMs) as key share storage. The threshold signing scheme [27] ensures full backward compatibility with the latest X-Road version 7.0.0. The selected scheme requires a trusted dealer for generating and dealing with the individual key shares [27]. We chose the Member's appointed representative (e.g. administrator) to be a dealer for ODI keys; as such, it has control over whom the individual shares are available. After the shares are generated, the dealer must securely delete the private parameters used during the generation of the shares. Figure 3 depicts the design of the DKMS for the Client's side only. Such implementation assures the integrity of data requests sent on behalf of the Client's ODI. The analogous DKMS can also be implemented at the Provider to ensure the authenticity of the response to the Client's request.

4.3   DKMS for X-Road Implementation

In the DKMS proof of concept implementation[2], we connect the threshold signing platform to X-Road to achieve the proposed design through the supported cryptographic interface PKCS #11 protocol. The chosen threshold signature scheme is compatible with the current scheme, Rivest-Shamir-Adleman (RSA), used in X-Road. The threshold signing platform includes a coordination server and the clients (signing service). The threshold signing server can be deployed either by the Member or by its SS, and clients must be accessible to the signing parties.

---

[2] The repository with the proof of concept implementations is available at https://github.com/crocs-muni/xroad-threshold-signatures.

To evaluate the quality of the developed proof of concept, first, we conduct the qualitative assessment to check the meeting of the targeted goals and system characteristics. Additionally, we do the quantitative assessment of time for message signing and transfer, compared to other common signing tokens.

Testing Scenario. We consider the following two-member X-Road scenario to validate that the proposed DKMS achieves the goals stated in Sect. 4.1. One Member is a governmental data repository provider (e.g. a health agency), and another is a hospital. The hospital (Client) has an information system IS_C. The client uses Security Server SS_C for the data exchange in X-Road. The health board (Provider) has an information system IS_P that stores health-related data. Provider uses Security Server SS_P for the data exchange. IS_C has a user interface for internal usage by three roles: employees who can be doctors, receptionists, and interns who are practising students from the medical school. Interns work in the hospital for a short time during their practice time and leave the hospital afterwards. Interns only have a temporary need to use the system.

Setup. The Client's ODI key material should be distributed between IS_C, SS_C, and employees' roles. Thus, there should be at least five shares, where each role representative holds the same key share. To allow excluding some of the key shares, we propose to derive more than one key share for interns so that after their practice time passes, the interns' key share is defined as 'deprecated' (signing service does not allow to use it anymore) and other pre-generated key shares are made available to the next round of new interns. In particular, we have chosen a 3-out-of-5 threshold signing group.

Goals Achievement. During the operational phase, the keys used to create a signature on behalf of ODI are distributed among at least three entities – SS, IS, and some employees (G_1). The set-up threshold group policy used by the signing service guarantees that key share controllers from the threshold group all participate in the signature creation. Thus, Members can partially trace back the entities (to the level of roles) who initiated the message (G_2). An ODI representative who defines a threshold group policy can define among which internal entities key shares are distributed, how the shares are derived, and how to deprecate access. Thus, the signing service using the threshold group policy controls that only the active key shares can be used for the signature creation (G_3). The implementation uses an RSA-based threshold signature signing scheme that is backwards compatible with the standard RSA verification algorithm (G_4). The set-up threshold group policy used by a signing service guarantees that IS, SS and employee contributed to the signature creation (G_5). As a result, the proposed DKMS for X-Road allows us to satisfy the stated goals and enables distribution control over Member's ODI during the operational phase of keys.

System Assessment. For time measurements, the previously described testing scenario with Client's IS_C, SS_C and Provider's IS_P, SS_P is used. All the components are running on a single device as various virtual machines. The Provider uses X-Road's built-in software token (SoftToken) in SS_P, and the Client uses a 3-out-of-5 threshold signing group. The group's coordination server is deployed to

Table 2. Round Trip Time (RTT) comparison for Client-Provider data exchange (the Provider uses SoftToken, and the Client's signing token varies; the mean is across 1000 measurements, SoftToken is used as a baseline).

Client's token:	SoftToken	SoftHSM	YubiKey 5	TPM NTC 7.2.3.1	*this work*
mean RTT	82 ms	75 ms	216 ms	260 ms	276 ms
mean slowdown	1.0×	0.92×	2.65×	3.18×	3.38×

IS_C and connected through PKCS#11 protocol to SS_C. The signing applications are individual running processes that automatically sign any incoming requests. This local deployment allows us to measure the system's throughput with a negligible network delay. In a real-world deployment, the timing would also be affected by the network requests within the signing group. At the expense of implementation changes in X-Road, the request to SS_C could be partially signed to avoid extra network requests within the group. The Round Trip Time (RTT) measurement starts with the IS_C requesting data from the IS_P and stops when the response is received. The mean RTT over 1000 measurements is in Table 2. Also, we have done the exact measurements for the Client using SoftToken, test hardware security module implemented in software (SoftHSM), Yubikey (5C NFC) and a Trusted Platform Module (TPM NTC 7.2.3.1). Using SoftTokens on both the Client's and Provider's side is a baseline measurement. Excluding a network delay, the tested DKMS introduces less than 200 ms overhead compared to the centralised signing solution. Even less overhead (10–60 ms) is seen compared to commercial hardware security modules, such as TPM NTC or YubiKey.

The main limitation of the presented implementation of DKMS for X-Road is relying on a trusted central party (dealer) during the pre-operational phase. Thus, our system design assumes trust in an organisation representative responsible for key generation, certification and key shares distribution. Hence, the presented proof of concept is prone to a single point of failure in the pre-operational key phase when the identity's keys are generated, and the threshold group policy and threshold signing service are not enabled. At the expense of backwards compatibility, using distributed key generation would lift this limitation.

5   Discussion

5.1   Related Work

For managing the keys related to ODI, multiple access control models can be used (e.g. role-based, attribute-based, and discretionary [26]). But to the best of our knowledge, none of the traditional access control models considers the control over keys in view of the zero trust paradigm and the context of cross-organisational data exchange. The closest to our research focus is the architecture vision for the data exchange platform Simpl [2]. There, the authors review three Identity Management (IdM) models: centralised based on PKI [2], hybrid based on PKI and extensions for verifiable credentials [2], and self-sovereign identity with a distributed ledger [2,3,7]. However, the three models differ in the procedure of trust establishment between the organisations, leaving out of scope users who act on behalf of an organisation. Identification of such physical entities is proposed to be handled as a separate task through proprietary identification solutions (e.g. Microsoft Single sign-on, OpenID) [2], internal access control systems, or employee's wallet (digital or smart cards). Therefore, in this paper, the proposed DKMS bridged two IdM systems – (i) for end-users of organisational IS and ODI, and (ii) for ODIs and cross-organisational data exchange. As a result, the novelty of the proposed DKMS is in its ability to enforce organisational identity policies for the system users through threshold signature, performed in opt-in and backward-compatible way directly applicable to existing information systems. The solution cryptographically guarantees compliance with the policies and, thus, enables zero trust within the IS.

5.2   Limitation

The paper does not consider the legal implications of the proposed design. The proposed DKMS allows the usage of smart cards and personal devices as hardware security modules for key shares. Thus, signatures created by physical custodians can be legally binding in such a way. The reason for such a conclusion is that the same technology is used in Smart-ID[3], an electronic authentication tool used for governmental services in Estonia. As Smart-ID is a qualified signature creation device, the generated signatures are legally binding. However, using a threshold K < N eliminates the non-repudiation nature of digital signatures, which could have legal consequences.

The implementation of the proposed DKMS may vary – employees' active approval involvement may be required or semi-automated – depending on the organisation's internal policy. Waiting on the employee's approval is a limitation on one hand, but complies with the four-eyes security principle on the other.

Integrating the proposed DKMS adds overhead for the operator of the threshold signing platform and the individual clients' signing application. Optionally, storing the signing shares on dedicated tokens, such as JavaCards, improves the security, but brings additional financial costs.

6   Conclusion

This paper has investigated how organisations can secure their digital identity (ODI) from abuse by a centralised controller during cross-organisational data exchange. The theoretical contribution of the paper is a key management system for information systems which enables cryptographically assured access policies enforcement that brings zero trust to the control over organisational identity. The practical contribution includes proof-of-concept implementation of the proposed

---

[3] https://www.id.ee/en/article/smart-id/.

design for the X-Road data exchange system and the library for RSA-threshold implementation[4]. In this study, we have reached several insights.

The existing methods for managing organisational identity either assume complete trust in the selected internal or external entities for operating on behalf of the organisation [2,26] or require extensive infrastructural changes to avoid centralisation if self-sovereign identity ecosystems [2,7] are used. As an alternative, this paper proposes a Distributed Key Management System (DKMS) that allows partial custody by employing threshold signatures to distribute control over the identity between multiple semi-trusted entities. The system ensures the authenticity of the messages sent on behalf of an organisation and removes centralisation. The performance results show that threshold signatures are comparable to state-of-the-art key management solutions.

The implementation of DKMS demonstrates that the system design helps to achieve decentralisation and traceability of signed message origin, as well as the ability to involve multiple ODI users whose access rights can be controlled to prevent privilege escalation. Moreover, the proposed system is backwards-compatible without major changes for all the parties involved in the message exchange. Though the system evaluation is done using RSA threshold signature, the approach applies to other signature schemes with existing threshold variants, e.g. ECDSA [14]. Thus, the approach can be generalised to other data exchange systems, where ODI is verified through Public Key Infrastructure (PKI), e.g. Dutch NLX [30]. Even if the system is not prone to a single point of failure but lacks zero trust, the proposed DKMS enable ODI usage policy enforcement that can cryptographically guarantee the authenticity of the data exchanges.

Finally, though the study has been conducted in the context of the problem of centrally issued PKI certificates and certificate-based key management, the review of mechanism and system characteristics is agnostic to the trust model. Thus, the proposed DKMS design can be used for self-sovereign identity-based organisational digital identity where verifiable credentials are issued through a distributed ledger but based on the decentralised public key infrastructure [6].

Acknowledgements. We would like to thank reviewers for helpful comments contributing to significant paper improvements. This paper is supported by the European Union under Grant Agreement No. 101087529.

References

1. Gaia-X: A Federated Secure Data Infrastructure. https://gaia-x.eu/
2. Preparatory work in view of the procurement of an open source cloud-to-edge middleware platform. Technical report, European Commission (2022)
3. Abraham, A., Koch, K., More, S., Ramacher, S., Stopar, M.: Privacy-preserving eID derivation to self-sovereign identity systems with offline revocation. In: IEEE TrustCom 2021, pp. 506–513 (2021)
4. Alkeilani Alkadri, N., et al.: Deterministic wallets in a quantum world. In: CCS 2020, pp. 1017–1031. ACM (2020). https://doi.org/10.1145/3372297.3423361

---

[4] https://github.com/crocs-muni/pretzel

5. Bakhtina, M., Kvapil, J., Svenda, P., Matulevicius, R.: Review of key management mechanisms (2024). https://doi.org/10.5281/zenodo.10886209
6. Bakhtina, M., Leung, K.L., Matulevičius, R., Awad, A., Švenda, P.: A decentralised public key infrastructure for X-Road. In: ARES 2023. ACM (2023)
7. Bakhtina, M., Matulevičius, R., Awad, A., Kivimäki, P.: On the shift to decentralised identity management in distributed data exchange systems. In: SAC 2023, pp. 864–873. ACM (2023). https://doi.org/10.1145/3555776.3577678
8. Barker, E.: NIST SP 800-57. Recommendation for key management (2016)
9. Buck, C., Olenberger, C., Schweizer, A., Völter, F., Eymann, T.: Never trust, always verify: a multivocal literature review on current knowledge and research gaps of zero-trust. Comput. Secur. **110**, 102436 (2021)
10. Cybernetica: Unified eXchange Platform (UXP). https://cyber.ee/
11. Das, P., Erwig, A., Faust, S., Loss, J., Riahi, S.: The exact security of BIP32 wallets. In: CCS 2021, pp. 1020–1042. ACM (2021)
12. Guthoff, C., Anell, S., Hainzinger, J., Dabrowski, A., Krombholz, K.: Perceptions of distributed ledger technology key management - an interview study with finance professionals. In: IEEE SP 2023, pp. 588–605 (2023)
13. Hevner, A.R., March, S.T., Park, J., Ram, S.: Design science in information systems research. MIS Q. **28**(1), 75–105 (2004)
14. Johnson, D., Menezes, A., Vanstone, S.A.: The elliptic curve digital signature algorithm (ECDSA). Int. J. Inf. Secur. **1**(1), 36–63 (2001)
15. Kersic, V., Vidovic, U., Vrecko, A., Domajnko, M., Turkanovic, M.: Orchestrating digital wallets for on- and off-chain decentralized identity management. IEEE Access **11**, 78135–78151 (2023). https://doi.org/10.1109/ACCESS.2023.3299047
16. Komlo, C., Goldberg, I.: FROST: flexible round-optimized Schnorr threshold signatures. In: Dunkelman, O., Jacobson, M.J., Jr., O'Flynn, C. (eds.) SAC 2020. LNCS, vol. 12804, pp. 34–65. Springer, Cham (2021). https://doi.org/10.1007/978-3-030-81652-0_2
17. Krimmer, R., Dedovic, S., Schmidt, C., Corici, A.A.: Developing cross-border e-governance: exploring interoperability and cross-border integration. In: Edelmann, N., et al. (eds.) ePart 2021. LNCS, vol. 12849, pp. 107–124. Springer, Cham (2021)
18. McBride, K., Kamalanathan, S., Valdma, S.M., Toomere, T., Freudenthal, M.: Digital government interoperability and data exchange platforms: insights from a twenty country comparative study. In: ICEGOV 2022, pp. 90–97. ACM (2022)
19. Nair, V., Song, D.: Decentralizing custodial wallets with MFKDF. In: IEEE ICBC 2023, pp. 1–9 (2023). https://doi.org/10.1109/ICBC56567.2023.10174998
20. Nair, V., Song, D.: Multi-factor key derivation function (MFKDF) for fast, flexible, secure, & practical key management (2023)
21. NIIS: X-Road Documentation. https://docs.x-road.global/
22. NIIS: X-ROAD®. https://x-road.global/
23. Wuille, P.: BIP 0032. Hierarchical Deterministic Wallets. https://github.com/bitcoin/bips/blob/master/bip-0032.mediawiki
24. Preukschat, A., Reed, D.: Self-Sovereign Identity. Manning Publications, Shelter Island (2021)
25. Rose, S., Borchert, O., Mitchell, S., Connelly, S.: NIST SP 800-207. Zero trust architecture (2020)
26. Sarfaraz, A., Chakrabortty, R.K., Essam, D.L.: AccessChain: an access control framework to protect data access in blockchain enabled supply chain. FGCS **148**, 380–394 (2023). https://doi.org/10.1016/j.future.2023.06.009

27. Shoup, V.: Practical threshold signatures. In: Preneel, B. (ed.) EUROCRYPT 2000. LNCS, vol. 1807, pp. 207–220. Springer, Heidelberg (2000). https://doi.org/10.1007/3-540-45539-6_15
28. Soltani, R., Nguyen, U.T., An, A.: Decentralized and privacy-preserving key management model. In: ISNCC 2020, pp. 1–7 (2020)
29. Verizon Business: 2023 data breach investigations report (2023)
30. VNG Realisatie: NLX: Documentation. https://docs.fsc.nlx.io/
31. Windley, P.J.: Learning Digital Identity: Design, Deploy, and Manage Identity Architectures. O'Reilly Media, Incorporated (2023)

Configuring and Validating Multi-aspect Risk Knowledge for Industry 4.0 Information Systems

Stefan Biffl[1,2,3](✉) , Sebastian Kropatschek[1,3] , Kristof Meixner[1] ,
David Hoffmann[4] , and Arndt Lüder[3,4]

[1] Institute of Information Systems Engineering, Technische Universität Wien,
Wien, Austria
{stefan.biffl,sebastian.kropatschek,kristof.meixner}@tuwien.ac.at
[2] CDL-SQI, Technische Universität Wien, Wien, Austria
[3] Austrian Center for Digital Production, Wien, Austria
[4] Institute of Factory Automation, Otto-von-Guericke U, Magdeburg, Germany
{david.hoffmann,arndt.luder}@ovgu.de

Abstract. Industry 4.0 information systems support production stake-holders in configuring and debugging increasingly flexible Cyber-Physical Production Systems (CPPSs), such as automated car plants. A Failure Mode and Effects Analysis (FMEA) aims at mitigating production risks by analyzing the main causes of risks in production, such as defective products. However, a FMEA provides limited guidance on (i) validating risk knowledge and (ii) reducing risk knowledge complexity regarding CPPS engineering artifacts. This paper introduces the *Multi-aspect FMEA Configuration Management (MFCM)* approach (i) to design and validate a multi-aspect CPPS risk knowledge graph and (ii) to focus on required graph parts, adapting *conditioned backward program slicing*. This small graph serves as a foundation for answering stakeholder questions on production risks and causes with data from validated sources. We evaluated MFCM in a feasibility study on a real-world welding line. Results indicate that MFCM is effective for *production process slicing* of multi-aspect risk knowledge required to analyze a production condition.

Keywords: Industry 4.0 · cyber-physical production system engineering · configuration management · DIN 60812 · multi-aspect IS engineering

1 Introduction

Industry 4.0 (I4.0) Information Systems (ISs) facilitate production planning, configuration, and analysis in increasingly flexible Cyber-Physical Production Systems (CPPSs) [16], e.g., for automating welding lines that join car parts [15].

© The Author(s), under exclusive license to Springer Nature Switzerland AG 2024
G. Guizzardi et al. (Eds.): CAiSE 2024, LNCS 14663, pp. 492–508, 2024.
https://doi.org/10.1007/978-3-031-61057-8_29

When starting production on a new CPPS configuration, undesired behavior due to unexpected sub-system and process interaction [11] often leads to avoidable waste, resource consumption, and production delay that may cost a manufacturer millions of Euros per year for a single welding line [6]. Key stakeholder questions concern *debugging industrial production* by exploring causes of insufficient production quality or throughput towards monitoring production effects, i.e., process post-conditions, on CPPS engineering and operation data [13]. Answering these questions requires dealing with the complexity of heterogeneous multi-aspect CPPS engineering artifacts in a typically large production system [7].

A *Failure Mode and Effects Analysis (FMEA)* [2] aims at risk mitigation from human and system failures as required by EU directives.[1] Modeling the risk of a CPPS configuration in an FMEA requires the combined knowledge of various domain experts [5,20] on CPPS dependencies regarding their core knowledge and related domains. CPPS engineering provides operational goals, interdisciplinary engineering models, ISs, and sufficient data to evaluate goal achievement or deviation [7]. Engineering models define complete dependencies among the different disciplines [3] as a foundation to design valid FMEA configurations. However, the FMEA standard does not consider (i) validating FMEA configurations with the engineering models and artifacts of CPPS configurations and (ii) reducing the complexity of tracing risk knowledge to CPPS engineering artifacts. Domain experts' local, often isolated, views make it hard to validate FMEA completeness, e.g., regarding interdisciplinary CPPS dependencies, such as the impact of high welding temperature on welding process quality.

Goal. This paper aims for well-defined and validated FMEA configurations in CPPS engineering by (i) eliciting stakeholder questions on effects and risks for a production scope, (ii) designing a risk knowledge model from FMEA modules, which encapsulate an expert's core knowledge in relation to other disciplines, and (iii) validating to what extent the concepts used in system risk conditions are correctly represented in the local stakeholder views of a multi-aspect CPPS model [7] and the associated data sources from engineering and operation [6]. These measures target designing I4.0 ISs with data from validated sources.

Encapsulating stakeholder knowledge in FMEA modules shall facilitate (i) separating the concerns between stakeholders, (ii) combining modules to inform an IS, and (iii) validating data sources required to answer stakeholder questions. For reducing the complexity of debugging production, with the main domain concepts product, process, and resources (PPR) [1], we apply the principles of *software program slicing* [12] to multi-aspect risk knowledge models, leading to *production process slicing* that shall result in a small knowledge graph linked to the data required to analyze conditions of main causes for a production effect.

Building on the Production Asset Network (PAN) [6], we introduce the *Multi-aspect FMEA Configuration Management (MFCM) meta-model* to represent the required production knowledge. We evaluate the MFCM meta-model in a feasibility study on a real-world production line for *welding car body parts*, following

---

[1] EU Directive on Machinery: http://data.europa.eu/eli/dir/2006/42/oj.

the preliminary MFCM method to configure and validate a multi-aspect risk knowledge model. We compare MFCM's effectiveness to a traditional approach.

The remainder of this work is structured as follows. Sections 2 and 3 summarize related work and present the research question and approach. Section 4 describes an illustrative use case. Section 5 introduces the MFCM meta-model. Section 6 reports on a feasibility study of MFCM with real-world industry data. Sections 7 and 8 discuss the results and limitations, conclude, and outline future work.

2 Related Work

This section summarizes work on risk knowledge management and on slicing.

Risk Management in I4.0 CPPS Engineering. The *Failure Mode and Effects Analysis (FMEA)* (DIN EN 60812) [2] aims at risk analysis and mitigation in systems engineering and operation. Best-practice approaches, e.g., *Ishikawa 6M* [2, 5], provide a good starting point with risk concerns on the system level, e.g., business, production quality, or safety, and the detail level, e.g., risk of components on local safety and production functions. FMEA applications in safety-critical environments [21] and manufacturing [22] emphasize the importance of analyzing the main causes of risks, which requires combining FMEA knowledge with domain knowledge on Product-Process-Resource (PPR) dependencies [1].

Okazaki *et al.* [17] combine a production system and an FMEA ontology to design an FMEA from basic engineering models in SysML. Yet, their production domain aspects remain on a basic system level, lacking production debugging capabilities that require detailed knowledge on domain interaction effects. This work shall consider the required expertise on functional dependencies of a CPPS configuration, including component knowledge to explain a production effect.

Salah *et al.* [20] combine the traditional FMEA with component dependency information and weighting potential problems for risk management to evaluate the economic consequences of failures. Still, they assume complete information in the assessment team, not reflecting on implicit information from several engineering domains. This work shall collect, integrate, and validate contributions from several engineering domains for incremental assessment team design.

Arevalo *et al.* [5] consider the automated evaluation of context-free FMEA conditions with run-time data to report operational problems to users. However, their approach does not consider a method for creating the FMEA models. This work shall introduce an approach to formalize the collection of multi-view, multi-step FMEA models, which can provide input to Arevalo's approach [5].

In summary, best-practice approaches to CPPS risk management [5,17,20] combine FMEA conditions, typically rules in a formal or natural language, with more or less formalized and detailed domain knowledge, and possibly production run-time data. Razouk and Kern [18] report on considerable inconsistencies in FMEA conditions regarding the concepts used and the relationships between conditions, making data analysis harder and the FMEA less useful. These inconsistencies require sufficient validation of FMEA conditions.

Efficiently designing and validating I4.0 ISs requires sound stakeholder questions on production scenarios with semantically well-defined production effect conditions [21]. Current approaches [5,17,18,20] provide limited guidance on (i) domain knowledge to explain a production effect, (ii) FMEA configurations for a CPPS configuration, (iii) combining sub-system risk knowledge, (iv) data specification and validation for risk analysis, and (v) risk knowledge reuse.

Our recent work [6] considers the concept validation of pre-/post-conditions in test cases with domain models, which seems well applicable to FMEA conditions. Therefore, this work shall build on (i) multi-aspect production risk knowledge that represents stakeholder concerns in Cause+Effect Networks (CENs) [6] as conditions of production causes and effects; (ii) detailed production domain knowledge [1] on technical dependencies; and (iii) run-time data access to evaluate risk conditions during operation for concept validation in FMEA conditions.

Software program slicing [12,23] facilitates debugging code by excluding irrelevant code regarding a program result. To reduce the complexity of managing the multi-aspect knowledge in CPPS engineering, we propose *production process slicing* for the outcome of a production process, e.g., process quality, to reduce the scope of model and artifact parts for analysis and answering stakeholder questions. This is similar to software program slicing, as the transformation of material, energy, and information in production [1] is comparable to the transformation of data in a simulation program. *Static backward program slicing* [12] is comparable to slicing a multi-aspect production model regarding a production post-condition and the main domain concepts, tracing across multi-aspect models (cf. Fig. 4). *Conditioned slicing* [12] is defined by a slicing point/criterion, e.g., a production outcome and condition, and conditions regarding a more specific production case, e.g., a fulfilled pre-condition (cf. Fig. 5). Therefore, this work shall build on software program slicing principles to design and validate a meta-model, the MFCM model, which reflects backtracking results. These results shall be used for answering stakeholder questions on the data structure to identify sources of production defect conditions, e.g., bad welding quality.

3   Research Approach

We followed *Design Science* [10] to address the limitations identified in Sects. 1 and 2 and improve capabilities for representing, configuring, and validating stakeholder risk knowledge on production effects. We reviewed the literature on validation in CPPS engineering and quality assurance [15,16,22]. We conducted stakeholder focus workshops in two companies with 16 engineers from 6 domains and 7 researchers. We focused on eliciting (i) production effects and dependencies between the production assets, and ISs, (ii) the required knowledge, and (iii) gaps in risk knowledge representation. From these inputs, we derived the following research question (RQ) and requirements for MFCM.

RQ. *What is an effective meta-model to combine (1) the CPPS engineering and operation model with (2) the FMEA model required to analyze a production effect?* To address this RQ, we designed the *Multi-aspect FMEA Configuration Management (MFCM)* meta-model and a preliminary method for designing and validating risk knowledge for an I4.0 IS. For answering stakeholder questions on a production effect, e.g., insufficient welding quality, the I4.0 IS requires the representation of multi-aspect risk knowledge. We assume (1) the CPPS engineering and operation model to represent the multi-aspect production domain model required to describe a production effect; and (2) the FMEA model to describe and configure FMEA conditions of a production effect for validation and analysis with run-time data. As the CPPS engineering model may be large, slicing principles [12] shall focus the model considered for analysis of a production effect.

For the evaluation, we conducted a feasibility study on the use case *welding of car body parts*. The study aimed at a proof of concept [10] for (i) conducting a preliminary MFCM method with domain experts [9]; (ii) configuring and validating multi-aspect risk knowledge from CPPS design and ramp-up artifacts as a MFCM meta-model instance; and (iii) using the MFCM model to answer stakeholder questions on a production effect. Further, we evaluated the meta-model in comparison to a traditional FMEA knowledge representation in CPPS engineering regarding the following requirements (Rx.y).

R1. Technical Contributions Required for a Production Effect. MFCM shall facilitate the translation from stakeholder questions on production effects to required technical CPPS contributions, as a basis for *production process slicing*. MFCM shall facilitate representing (i) the production contributions in a process to describe a production effect; (ii) the input products and pre-processing contributions for describing cause conditions in processes preceding that process; (iii) the CPPS and human resource contributions for describing cause conditions in process resources; and (iv) the variability of the reconfiguration space.

R2. FMEA configuration capabilities. MFCM shall facilitate (i) configuring an FMEA model to represent the required dependencies and risk conditions from several stakeholders for a production effect; (ii) representing risk knowledge of stakeholders in FMEA modules, which can be efficiently combined into a larger FMEA knowledge graph; and (iii) validating for the production effect and cause conditions in the FMEA the availability and quality of data in CPPS engineering models and artifacts that represent design and run-time data sources, as a basis for *conditioned production process slicing*.

4   Illustrative Use Case for Evaluation

This section introduces the use case *welding of car body parts* to illustrate requirements for MFCM during CPPS engineering, ramp-up, and operation. We abstracted the use case from a domain analysis at a large European automotive manufacturing company that focused on product quality issues with robot cells for welding car parts during ramp-up and operation. Core stakeholders in car production are the Order Manager (OM), the Quality Manager (QM), and the Production System Engineers (PSEngs). OMs are interested in economically operating the CPPS to fulfill customer orders on time with sufficient throughput and quality. The QM ensures product quality based on CPPS functions. PSEngs ensure correct CPPS functionality and stability.

For instance, in a typical welding line, optical control systems ensure the welding spot quality, often utilizing cameras (cf. Fig. 1, variant A). The camera's picture quality may suffer from high welding temperature, leading to false positives in the inspection system and invalid measurement. Thus, a common stakeholder concern is understanding (i) the camera's impact on the throughput for different temperature levels, and (ii) mitigation options for this impact.

Fig. 1. CPPS variants A, B for welding car body parts, and variability model.

Figure 1 illustrates a CPPS for positioning and welding car parts focusing on geometric accuracy for sufficient stiffness to fulfill safety standards. Shortening the production cycle time (OM concern) led to higher production temperature and a high error rate of the quality control using the LCD camera's pictures (QM concern). Hence, the camera was replaced by a LIDAR[2] system that creates correct pictures even at high production temperature (PSEng concern). To represent the knowledge on valid CPPS configuration structures, Fig. 1 illustrates a part of an exemplary feature model [4] to represent a welding cell family with pre-processing steps and resource variants for quality control.[3]

This work focuses on stakeholder questions to an I4.0 IS on causes of effects towards production condition monitoring on CPPS engineering and operation data, motivated by the OM questions to improve throughput: *Q1 (QM): Why is the welding issue rate high?* and *Q2 (PSEng): When is the error rate of the quality control system high?* The result shall be an IS dashboard for production monitoring and data analysis of selected machine parameters to assess the production conditions' risk level with an impact on production throughput.

Traditional best-practice approach to risk analysis in CPPS engineering is *Natural language FMEA without modules*. In the use case context, the QM applied the DIN EN 60812 [2, 22] to the welding cell by designing Ishikawa 6M diagrams and by deriving a network of production cause-and-effect conditions in

---

[2] LIght Detection And Ranging (LIDAR): https://en.wikipedia.org/wiki/Lidar.
[3] For larger CPPS variability models, see https://github.com/tuw-qse/eipse.

natural language [18]. This network was useful for understanding the overall production process of the work cell. However, the approach (i) used heterogeneous natural language concepts on system and local detail levels, (ii) did not consistently consider PPR concepts, and (iii) did not validate the FMEA concepts with technical reality of the CPPS. Therefore, the FMEA suffered from semantic mismatches, did not represent important cause concepts, and contained superfluous causes from historic projects. This hindered finding main causes that concerned several production steps or sub-systems in different parts of the CPPS.

5 Solution Approach

This section introduces the *Multi-aspect FMEA Configuration Management (MFCM)* meta-model and considerations on the application method and graphic positioning. MFCM shall facilitate providing partial FMEA and domain models for focused data analysis on selected production effects to answer stakeholder questions in an Industry 4.0 Information System.

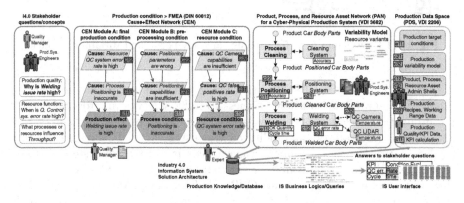

Fig. 2. *Multi-aspect FMEA Configuration Management* approach, based on [6]. (Color figure online)

Solution Overview. Figure 2 provides an overview of the MFCM approach. The MFCM aims at linking previously isolated stakeholder questions (orange elements) regarding concepts in FMEA conditions, represented in a CEN (violet elements) with CEN modules, with CPPS model data, represented in a PAN (blue elements) or in engineering artifacts and data from a Production Data Space (PDS) (pink elements). This way, quality managers can trace production conditions in an FMEA configuration, such as welding issues, to PAN assets and properties and to stakeholder production data views (cf. Fig. 2, violet, green, and orange tags with matching link IDs; dashed lines). By integrating these disparate models, quality managers validate (i) an FMEA's configuration plausibility and correctness against engineering data, and (ii) the availability of data in the PDS to evaluate the FMEA conditions for a PAN scope, which builds the foundation for conditioned production process slicing. Graph queries on the CEN knowledge graph can efficiently report missing links from FMEA conditions to the PAN or PDS [6]. After a successful validation of an FMEA configuration, IT experts that support stakeholders shall design an I4.0 IS building on the MFCM knowledge graph and CPPS engineering and operation data to answer stakeholder questions, e.g., by informing Artificial Intelligence (AI) data analytics.

MFCM Meta-model. The MFCM meta-model, illustrated in Fig. 3, builds on the *Production Test Scenario Validation (PTSV)* meta-model [6]. PTSV focuses on validating conditions of production test scenarios, without considering FMEA risk knowledge or modular design of a CEN. Integrating *PTSV* meta-model elements and the validation of FMEA effects with domain models and artifacts [6] facilitates designing the production knowledge base for an I4.0 IS.

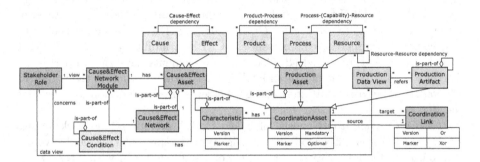

Fig. 3. MFCM meta-model, based on the PTSV meta-model [6] (in UML). (Color figure online)

Stakeholder (cf. Fig. 3, orange elements). The *Stakeholder Role* includes the QM, systems engineer, mechanical and software engineers. A stakeholder question concerns *CEN conditions*. A stakeholder can represent his FMEA knowledge in *CEN Modules*, supporting the separation of concerns between stakeholders.

Cause+Effect Network (CEN), the FMEA model (Fig. 3, violet elements). A *CEN* [6] is a graph that has nodes for production *Causes* and *Effects*, inherited from a *Cause & Effect Asset* that has *CEN Conditions*, e.g., *welding quality is high*, and inherits *Characteristics*, such as *Failure Mode* and *Risk Priority Number (RPN)*, from the *Coordination Asset*. *Cause-Effect dependencies* represent edges between causes and effects. Thus a CEN can represent an FMEA model [5,17–20]. *Cause & Effect Assets* concern conditions and refer via *CEN-to-PPR dependencies*, which are realized by *Coordination Links*, to *Production Assets*. *CEN Modules* define CEN graphs of a stakeholder. They share *Cause & Effect Assets* as interfaces. They can be combined into a CEN to inform an IS.

Production Asset Network (PAN), the CPPS model (Fig. 3, blue elements). A *PAN* [6] contains the production assets, i.e., PPR assets, and relationships to represent the production domain model for CPPS engineering and operation for describing a production effect. They can be related to the *Production Data Views* via *PPR-to-PDS-dependencies*, realized as *Coordination Links*.

Production Data Space (PDS), the CPPS artifacts (Fig. 3, pink elements). The *PDS* [6] provides *Production Data Views* that group *Production Artifacts*, representing CPPS engineering and operation data sources, e.g., CAD drawings or production log data, providing data on PAN assets, e.g., robots, to evaluate a CEN condition. A *Stakeholder Role* relates to *Production Data Views* that concern a particular CPPS aspect, e.g., mechanical engineering of a robot.

Coordination of and Between CEN, PAN, PDS (Fig. 3, green elements). *Coordination Assets* enable organizing the CEN and PAN/PDS domain sub-models. *Characteristics* are inherited, e.g., to the CEN or PAN asset classes,. Coordination assets can be *mandatory* and *optional* to represent partial variability in the CPPS reconfiguration space. *Coordination Links* link assets, e.g., CEN-to-PAN or CEN-to-PDS links, for validation and evaluation of CEN conditions with PDS data (cf. Fig. 5). *Or* and *xor* properties complement the *Coordination Asset* properties to represent the CPPS variability in a state-of-the-art model, e.g., a feature model [4]. Coordination elements have the properties (i) *Version*, to identify elements of an FMEA/CPPS configuration in time, and (ii) *Marker*, to label assets of interest, e.g., elements of a production process slice (cf. Fig. 4).

FMEA Configurations consist of linked FMEA modules. This work models FMEA modules as CEN modules (cf. Fig. 2) that represent stakeholder views, e.g., on a production process or resource, or its sub-systems, with internal and external dependencies that connect related CEN modules, forming a CEN to explain a set of production effects. FMEA modules shall facilitate the efficient reconfiguration of the FMEA, e.g., to validate the change of CPPS resources for improving production capabilities.

Variability models represent the configuration space of flexible CPPSs for production reconfiguration as commonalities and variability [4]. This work builds on the *de facto* standard *feature models* to structure variability and represent valid combinations of production processes and resources. Figure 1 shows on the right-hand side a feature model for the production resources of a positioning and welding process with the *alternative/xor* features LCD and LIDAR camera.

Production process slicing for a production effect can be modeled as a marked CEN/PAN/PDS sub-graph. For *static backward slicing*, CEN conditions annotate the *multi-aspect domain model*, e.g., material, energy, or information characteristics and location, like pre-/post-conditions of the *laser welding* process or between the *welding head* and *welding process*. For *conditioned slicing*, CEN conditions are combined with run-time data, e.g., the actual *welding temperature*. CEN conditions on PAN elements and artifacts are comparable to generalizing/applying assertions used on software code to multi-aspect model elements.

To evaluate MFCM meta-model application, the next section illustrates conducting the preliminary MFCM method (cf. Fig. 2) with practitioners.

6   Evaluation in a Feasibility Study

The proof of concept study [10] aimed to demonstrate the MFCM approach for meta-model design, focusing on the configuration and validation of multi-aspect risk knowledge in a MFCM model and its effectiveness to analyze a production effect with production process slicing. The study followed a preliminary MFCM method with three practitioners for the use case *welding of car body parts* [10]. Reflection with the practitioners evaluated their (i) traditional approach compared to MFCM, (ii) improved job performance using MFCM, and (iii) barriers to using MFCM, loosely applying the Technology Acceptance Model [8]. The practitioners provided the model content while a facilitator ensured adherence to MFCM, answered questions, and collected data on, e.g., model content and effort. The practitioners, a quality manager (lead quality investigator, FMEA and APIS tool expertise), a process expert (welding recipe and resource function tolerance expertise), and a production resource expert (camera vision and picture evaluation expertise), received initial training on the MFCM.

The domain experts conducted the preliminary MFCM method, supported by two researchers acting as MFCM facilitators and tool experts. They designed *MFCM models* for *welding of car body parts*, aiming at semi-finished car floor production (cf. Fig. 4), including the change of a CPPS resource, i.e., from an LCD camera to a LIDAR. MFCM steps were repeated to consider and validate new knowledge on target production effects and their causes.

Step 1. Specify I4.0 IS Scope. The lead expert specified stakeholder goals and questions in the production scope. The result was (i) a variability model for the production variants in the I4.0 IS family (cf. Fig. 1), (ii) stakeholder questions that the I4.0 IS shall answer using production knowledge (cf. Fig. 2), (iii) a PAN of a work line (cf. Fig. 2, blue elements), and (iv) a process description leading to the production effect, comparable to a cooking recipe (cf. Fig. 2, pink elements). The domain experts refined the stakeholder questions, e.g., *Why is the rework selection false positive rate high?*, to identify main causes of effects in a CEN (cf. Fig. 4, orange and violet elements). In total, the stakeholders formulated 5 questions with 10 conditions and 20 concepts in the CEN on a shared whiteboard and in an APIS FMEA failure net, which took the experts 46 person hours.

Step 2. Define FMEA Configuration with CEN Modules. The domain experts designed CEN modules that encapsulated slices of a stakeholder's effect and cause knowledge, and dependencies to neighboring stakeholders, backtracking from a production effect to main causes [6]. They linked effects and causes from several CEN modules into a system FMEA configuration (cf. Figs. 2 and 4, violet tags with matching IDs). The domain experts identified 7 CEN modules with 22 FMEA conditions, and 13 intra- and 12 inter-module CEN-to-CEN links. This took 26 person hours in three iterative rounds to address validation issues.

Step 3. Validate FMEA Concepts with Production Assets. The domain experts validated the concepts in the FMEA configuration linking them to the technical reality of PAN/PDS assets in three mapping and refinement iterations to address models with diminishing validation issues. They validated the

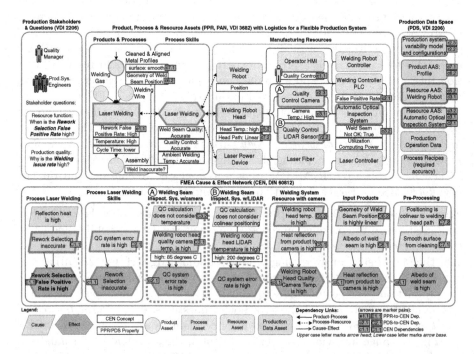

Fig. 4. MFCM PAN/PDS model with CEN modules for production effects *welding issues*: stakeholder concepts linked with FMEA conditions and data sources; model elements with bold frame, e.g., *Welding*, show a *production process slice*. (Color figure online)

FMEA's completeness regarding CEN paths from production effects to causes. They reported missing or wrong links between CEN and PAN/PDS and incomplete CEN paths to iteratively improve the linked models [6]. The result was (i) a validated FMEA configuration with CEN concepts (cf. Figs. 2 and 4, violet elements) linked to the PAN and to valid data sources in the PDS (cf. Fig. 4, violet and green/orange tags with matching IDs), in 72 links to PAN/PDS assets, and (ii) a list of model issues to resolve. This step took around 27 person hours.

MFCM Model, Highlighting a Production Process Slice. Figure 4 illustrates a production process slice for the effect *Rework Selection False Positive Rate is high* of the process *Laser Welding* (cf. MFCM elements with a bold frame). FMEA conditions in CEN modules describe cause-effect chains from an effect at the *Laser Welding* process and back to (1) input products, pre-processes and (2) resources, such as the *Welding Robot Head* and *Quality Control Camera*, similar to backward program slicing [12]. Therefore, CEN conditions refer to a slice's PAN assets and characteristics, which describe the impact of process and resource contributions to PAN characteristics, e.g., high *Welding Robot Head temperature* and the *Quality Control Camera*. The PDS contains the engineering artifacts and operation data sources for the slice. Compared to the hundreds of PPR assets in engineering a welding cell, the slice is, due to loose coupling, a small, well-focused graph to investigate likely causes for a production defect.

Change of FMEA Modules. To address quality control and analysis errors regarding the camera pictures due to high welding temperature, the domain experts proposed replacing the LCD camera with a LIDAR. This new CPPS configuration required updating the FMEA configuration from an LCD camera to a LIDAR FMEA module (cf. Fig. 4, CEN modules A & B, dashed contours). Therefore, the FMEA required adaptation to represent (i) the improvement regarding the quality control errors, and (ii) new dependencies that LIDAR introduced. The modular approach facilitated the efficient analysis and updating of FMEA and PAN dependencies. This step took around 5 person hours.

Industry 4.0 Information System Prototype. Based on stakeholder questions, the successfully validated FMEA configuration, and test data to evaluate the FMEA conditions, the IT expert and domain experts designed I4.0 IS user interface prototypes, access to required data, and queries to the CEN+PAN/PDS knowledge graph for an analysis of system effects and causes. The result was an I4.0 IS design and prototype of user interfaces, business logic, and data. To answer stakeholder questions, a researcher and an IT expert exported from APIS a *failure net* as a knowledge graph into a *Neo4J* graph database to configure queries and data access for a *Power BI* application.

Figure 5 shows the prototype of an I4.0 IS dashboard to illustrate the QM view based on multi-aspect production knowledge. The dashboard shows selected FMEA conditions with run-time data on CPPS parameters to evaluate the state of these conditions for production process slicing, similar to *conditioned program slicing* [12]. Parameters from these conditions can inform the detailed analysis of time series to indicate the change impact between variables, e.g., an increase of

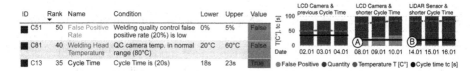

ID	Rank	Name	Condition	Lower	Upper	Value
■ C51	50	False Positive Rate	Welding quality control false positive rate (20%) is low	0%	5%	False
■ C81	40	Welding Head Temperature	QC camera temp. in normal range (80°C)	20°C	60°C	False
■ C13	35	Cycle Time	Cycle Time is (20s)	18s	23s	True

Fig. 5. I4.0 IS view on quality conditions with data from CPPS operation. (Color figure online)

temperature followed by an increase of the false positive rate for quality control (cf. Fig. 5, tags A and B), to identify likely causes for a process outcome.

MFCM Tool Support. FMEA tools, such as *APIS*,[4] facilitate eliciting FMEA configuration knowledge from domain experts, e.g., as a failure net. The PDS can be a cloud space, such as Google Drive, providing uniform data access. The CEN+PAN knowledge graph for FMEA configurations can be stored, managed, and queried in a graph database, such as *Neo4J/Cypher*.[5] An IS design tool, such as *MS Power BI*,[6] facilitates exploring I4.0 IS prototypes with advanced user interface and data analysis functions.

Comparison of MFCM to traditional best-practice FMEA regarding the requirements introduced in Sect. 3. The practitioners' approach involved in the feasibility study was *natural language FMEA without modules* (cf. Sect. 4).

The MFCM CEN and PAN models by design provided the capabilities to address *R1.i* by linking production contributions to production effect conditions; *R1.ii* by linking input products and processes in the PAN to cause conditions in the CEN; *R1.iii* by linking CPPS and human resource contributions in the PAN to FMEA conditions in the CEN; and *R1.iv* by providing a feature model in the production reconfiguration space. The MFCM CEN modules and method addressed *R2.i* by representing for a production effect the required dependencies and risk conditions coming from several stakeholders; *R2.ii* by representing the risk knowledge of stakeholders in a way that is easy to combine for CPPS variants; and *R2.iii* by validating FMEA conditions with PAN model elements and data sources in PDS artifacts. Further, MFCM resulted in actionable guidelines for evaluating FMEA conditions with data during CPPS engineering and run time by human and machine agents, similar to *conditioned program slicing* [12].

The traditional FMEA does not consider *R1* linking FMEA concepts to CPPS models and artifacts, making rigorous validation regarding completeness for a CPPS difficult and error-prone. Regarding *R2*, lacking traceability of FMEA conditions to stakeholder knowledge makes it easy to miss critical technical dependencies between production assets and processes. For example, stakeholders focusing on CPPS functions were not aware of production process dependencies, e.g., interaction of resources in different production steps. Therefore, it was hard to define and validate an FMEA configuration. CPPS configuration changes, e.g., a control camera change, can lead to inconsistencies in the traditional FMEA.

---

[4] APIS: https://apis.de/.

[5] Neo4J: https://neo4j.com/.

[6] MS Power BI: https://powerbi.microsoft.com/.

7 Discussion

This section discusses the results concerning the research question: *What is an effective meta-model to combine (1) the CPPS engineering and operation model with (2) the FMEA model required to analyze a production effect?* Therefore, we introduced the MFCM meta-model and reported on a proof of concept [10] for applying the MFCM in a feasibility study on *welding of car body parts.* MFCM represents multi-aspect risk knowledge by combining FMEA modules, encapsulating view-specific expert knowledge, into a system-level FMEA configuration that describes production effects and causes for a CPPS configuration. This system-level FMEA configuration can be effectively validated with CPPS engineering models and artifacts for completeness and semantic fit to data sources.

The MFCM study confirmed Razouk and Kern's findings [18] that FMEA conditions, formulated by expert teams, require validation to improve their usefulness. The study indicated that an FMEA validated with a domain model, typically a production process slice, can be a promising approach to provide high-quality input for efficiently analyzing conditions for a production effect. By providing integrated machine-readable FMEA and CPPS models, a MFCM knowledge representation clearly improves over a traditional quality board, where experts have implicit knowledge on partial domain models and work with knowledge elements scattered over heterogeneous, disconnected engineering documents. Introducing MFCM seems advisable to design I4.0 ISs in medium-to-large CPPS projects with good digitalization maturity, e.g., a PDS with digital twins for virtual commissioning of system components, where risk analysis based on modular FMEA configurations can be expected to be considerably faster and more effective than traditional FMEA without partitioning concepts for recombination.

Domain expert feedback regarding the perceived ease of use and usefulness [8] indicated that the MFCM model could improve job performance regarding efficiently evaluating causes of production effects with CPPS engineering and runtime data. The MFCM model, in particular, production process slicing, was found helpful to and answer stakeholder questions on (i) production conditions to prioritize data analysis, production, and maintenance tasks; and (ii) model issues that point to gaps required for data analysis. To this end, the modular MFCM model was found to outperform the traditional FMEA approach that required the interpretation of separate FMEA models by domain experts to inform the quality manager. Further, the quality manager pointed out (i) better insight on expert knowledge required to understand and address production risks; and (ii) good means to make production expert knowledge explicit in a group. Barriers to adopt and use the MFCM were (i) the extra effort for modeling and validation compared to the traditional FMEA; (ii) the extra training and guidance required from a MFCM facilitator; and (iii) working with complex, linked models that require tool support to hide complexity, such as the APIS failure network referring to PPR/PDS concepts. However, we argue that this issue could be overcome by tool support with a custom multi-aspect model editor.

This research builds on the dependency network design [6], on principles of software slicing [12], and concepts to combine FMEA and PAN models for CPPS engineering [6]. The results go beyond the state of the art in FMEA research in multi-aspect CPPS engineering [5,15,17,20] by (i) defining a meta-model for effective validation of modular FMEA configurations with the technical reality of CPPS engineering and operation, (ii) demonstrating an instance of the MFCM knowledge graph based on data from a digital CPPS engineering and operation environment, and (iii) considering the impact of structural change of a CPPS configuration, such as a component replacement, on the FMEA configuration.

Lessons Learned. The idea of validating FMEA concepts in modular FMEA configurations with engineering domain concepts in technical system configurations seems to be applicable to a wide range of problems, where experts coming from several disciplines cooperate based on mature domain-specific models of technical impact and dependencies that concern natural laws and engineering models or functions, e.g., general CPS engineering.

Production process slicing can decrease the complexity of debugging production processes, similar to software slicing. Combining engineering and run-time data support dynamic slicing to analyze defect conditions for a specific case. For example, production process slicing combined with FMEA conditions seems promising to determine the minimal required data for a production condition to model digital twins and for simulations and AI applications, e.g., for modeling and validating structured AI training data, in multi-aspect domains. Further applications concern the comprehension of multi-aspect production processes for a variety of technical domain architectures and facilitating the reuse of required contributions for a production effect across views on stakeholder artifacts, e.g., link to CAD assets related to a welding effect.

Limitations. The following limitations require further investigation. The feasibility study focused on a use case derived from projects at large CPPS engineering companies in the automotive industry. This may introduce bias due to the specific selection of requirements for production effects, FMEA concerns, and their validation, and of the alternative approaches considered, as well as the roles or individual preferences of the domain experts. To overcome these limitations, we plan empirical studies in a wider variety of application contexts.

The CPPS reconfiguration focused on the local change of a CPPS component and its impact on production, which is important but limited in scope. Hence, we plan to investigate the change impact of (i) larger CPPS resources and (ii) production process sequences and types. As CPPS engineering already manages working with heterogeneous, large artifacts and models in a collaboration of stakeholders focused by discipline, we expect production process slicing in an MFCM model to scale well and facilitate debugging multi-step production, even with large resources. In CPPS engineering, the automation hierarchy limits the length of dependency chains [7,14]: the number of relevant hierarchy levels is at most 10, while the number of possible dependencies on the same level is limited to 3, due to the sensor-controller-actor structure of control systems.

8   Conclusion and Future Work

This paper introduced the *MFCM* meta-model and preliminary method. They facilitate specifying and validating modular *FMEA* configurations to support the design of I4.0 ISs that inform domain experts. FMEA concept validation requires mapping production effect and cause conditions to CPPS engineering models and artifacts. The MFCM provides means to (i) structure FMEA configurations for validation and (ii) build on production process slicing, similar to program slicing [12], to effectively specify, collect, and validate the data required to evaluate the FMEA conditions during CPPS engineering, ramp-up, and operation [13].

In a real-world feasibility study, domain experts applied the MFCM meta-model in the context of *welding car body parts*. The results indicate that MFCM is effective for *production process slicing*, pointing out multi-aspect risk knowledge required to analyze conditions of a production effect. MFCM makes implicit production knowledge of senior domain experts explicit for interpretation by human and computer agents. This knowledge can be used to inform the data model for answering multi-aspect questions to design I4.0 ISs for validating system FMEAs with computer functions, e.g., empower AI-based CPPS engineering.

Future Work. We plan to investigate the efficient *reuse of FMEA configuration knowledge* in MFCM models for work lines that require similar capabilities, e.g., accurate welding. We plan case studies on the MFCM's applicability and scalability for a production family to reduce recurring risks. These studies shall clarify the adaptation effort of FMEA configurations for flexible CPPS and the effort required to adapt and validate the FMEA and associated I4.0 ISs.

We envision the MFCM's *application beyond the CPPS domain*. Therefore, we plan to investigate the concept in socio-technical systems with various stakeholder concerns, such as business process improvement or digital twins [6,13].

While MFCM focuses on unintentional causes of production effects, it provides a basis for analyzing information security, which deals with intentional wrongdoing. We aim to bridge security analyst concerns regarding relations of product quality to production resources for security monitoring.

Acknowledgment. The financial support by the Christian Doppler Research Association, the Austrian Federal Ministry for Digital and Economic Affairs and the National Foundation for Research, Technology and Development is gratefully acknowledged. This work has been partially supported and funded by the Austrian Research Promotion Agency (FFG) via the Austrian Competence Center for Digital Production (CDP) under contract number 881843.

References

1. VDI 3682: Formalised process descriptions. Beuth, 2015
2. IEC 60812: Failure Mode and Effects analysis (FMEA). IEC, 2018
3. VDI 2206: Development of mechatronic and cyber-physical systems. Beuth, 2021

4. Apel, S., Batory, D.S., Kästner, C., Saake, G.: Feature-Oriented Software Product Lines. Springer, Berlin, Heidelberg (2013). https://doi.org/10.1007/978-3-642-37521-7

5. Arévalo, F., MP, C.A., Ibrahim, M.T., Schwung, A.: Production assessment using a knowledge transfer framework and evidence theory. IEEE Access **10**, 89134–89152 (2022)

6. Biffl, S., Hoffmann, D., Kiesling, E., Meixner, K., Lüder, A., Winkler, D.: Validating production test scenarios with cyber-physical system design models. In: 2023 IEEE 25th Conference on Business Informatics (CBI). IEEE (2023)

7. Biffl, S., Lüder, A., Gerhard, D. (eds.): Multi-Disciplinary Engineering for Cyber-Physical Production Systems. Springer, Cham (2017). https://doi.org/10.1007/978-3-319-56345-9

8. Davis, F.D.: Perceived usefulness, perceived ease of use, and user acceptance of information technology. MIS Q. 319–340 (1989)

9. Dreyfus, S.E., Dreyfus, H.L.: A five-stage model of the mental activities involved in directed skill acquisition. Operations Research Center, University of California, Berkeley (1980)

10. Gregor, S., Hevner, A.R.: Positioning and presenting design science research for maximum impact. MIS Q. 337–355 (2013)

11. Grieves, M., Vickers, J.: Digital twin: mitigating unpredictable, undesirable emergent behavior in complex systems. Transdisciplinary perspectives on complex systems: new findings and approaches, pp. 85–113 (2017)

12. Harman, M., Hierons, R.: An overview of program slicing. Softw. Focus **2**(3), 85–92 (2001)

13. Liu, M., Fang, S., Dong, H., Cunzhi, X.: Review of digital twin about concepts, technologies, and industrial applications. J. Manuf. Syst. **58**, 346–361 (2021)

14. Lüder, A., Schmidt, N., Hell, K., Röpke, H., Zawisza, J.: Fundamentals of artifact reuse in CPPS. In: Biffl, S., Lüder, A., Gerhard, D. (eds.) Multi-Disciplinary Engineering for Cyber-Physical Production Systems, pp. 113–138. Springer, Cham (2017). https://doi.org/10.1007/978-3-319-56345-9_5

15. Meixner, K., Lüder, A., Herzog, J., Winkler, D., Biffl, S.: Patterns for reuse in production systems engineering. Int. J. Softw. Eng. Knowl. Eng. **31**(11n12), 1623–1659 (2021)

16. Monostori, L., et al.: Cyber-physical systems in manufacturing. CIRP Ann. **65**(2), 621–641 (2016)

17. Okazaki, S., Shirafuji, S., Yasui, T., Ota, J.: A framework to support failure cause identification in manufacturing systems. In: 2023 IEEE/ASME International Conference on Advanced Intelligent Mechatronics (AIM), pp. 858–865. IEEE (2023)

18. Razouk, H., Kern, R.: Improving the consistency of the failure mode effect analysis (FMEA) documents. Appl. Sci. **12**(4), 1840 (2022)

19. Rehman, Z., Kifor, C.V.: An ontology to support semantic management of FMEA knowledge. Int. J. Comput. Commun. Control **11**(4), 507–521 (2016)

20. Salah, B., Alnahhal, M., Ali, M.: Risk prioritization using a modified FMEA analysis in industry 4.0. J. Eng. Res. **11**(4), 460–468 (2023)

21. Sharma, K.D., Srivastava, S.: Failure mode and effect analysis (FMEA) implementation: a literature review. J. Adv. Res. Aeronaut Space Sci. **5**, 1–17 (2018)

22. Wu, Z., Liu, W., Nie, W.: Literature review and prospect of the development and application of FMEA in manufacturing industry. Int. J. Adv. Manuf. Technol. **112**(5), 1409–1436 (2021)

23. Xu, B., Qian, J., Zhang, X., Wu, Z., Chen, L.: A brief survey of program slicing. ACM SIGSOFT Softw. Eng. Notes **30**(2), 1–36 (2005)

Trusted Execution Environment for Decentralized Process Mining

Valerio Goretti[1] , Davide Basile[1(✉)] , Luca Barbaro[1] , and Claudio Di Ciccio[1,2]

[1] Sapienza University of Rome, Rome, Italy
{valerio.goretti,davide.basile,luca.barbaro,claudio.diciccio}@uniroma1.it
[2] Utrecht University, Utrecht, The Netherlands
c.diciccio@uu.nl

Abstract. Inter-organizational business processes involve multiple independent organizations collaborating to achieve mutual interests. Process mining techniques have the potential to allow these organizations to enhance operational efficiency, improve performance, and deepen the understanding of their business based on the recorded process event data. However, inter-organizational process mining faces substantial challenges, including topical secrecy concerns: The involved organizations may not be willing to expose their own data to run mining algorithms jointly with their counterparts or third parties. In this paper, we introduce CONFINE, a novel approach that unlocks process mining on multiple actors' process event data while safeguarding the secrecy and integrity of the original records in an inter-organizational business setting. To ensure that the phases of the presented interaction protocol are secure and that the processed information is hidden from involved and external actors alike, our approach resorts to a decentralized architecture comprised of trusted applications running in Trusted Execution Environments (TEEs). We show the feasibility of our solution by showcasing its application to a healthcare scenario and evaluating our implementation in terms of memory usage and scalability on real-world event logs.

Keywords: Collaborative information systems architectures ·
Inter-organizational process mining · TEE · Confidential computing

1 Introduction

In today's business landscape, organizations constantly seek ways to enhance operational efficiency, increase performance, and gain valuable insights to improve their processes. Process mining offers techniques to discover, monitor, and improve business processes by extracting knowledge from chronological records recorded by process-aware information systems, i.e., the *event logs* [13]. The vast majority of process mining contributions consider *intra-organizational* settings, in which processes are executed inside individual organizations. However, organizations increasingly recognize the value of collaboration and synergy in achieving operational excellence. *Inter-organizational* business processes

G. Guizzardi et al. (Eds.): CAiSE 2024, LNCS 14663, pp. 509–527, 2024.
https://doi.org/10.1007/978-3-031-61057-8_30

involve several independent organizations cooperating to achieve a shared objective. Process mining can bring the advantages of transparency, performance optimization, and benchmarking in this context [2]. Since different process data owners feed separate mining nodes, this setting characterizes what we call *decentralized process mining*.

Companies, though, are reluctant to share private information required to execute process mining algorithms with external parties [25], thus hindering its adoption. Letting sensitive operational data traverse organizational boundaries introduces concerns about data secrecy, security, and compliance with internal regulations [27]. To address this issue, the majority of research endeavors have focused thus far on the alteration of input data or of intermediate analysis by-products, with the aim to impede the counterparts from reconstructing the original information sources [15–18]. These preemptive solutions have the remarkable merit of neutralizing information leakage by malicious parties a priori. Nevertheless, they entail an ex-ante information loss, thus compromising downstream process mining capabilities [17,18], or require the execution of computationally heavy protocols undermining scalability [15,16].

To overcome these limitations, we propose CONFINE, a novel approach and tool aimed at enhancing collaborative information system architectures with secrecy-preserving process mining capabilities. To secure information secrecy during the exchange and elaboration of data, our solution resorts to *Trusted Execution Environments* (TEEs) [30], namely hardware-secured contexts that guarantee code integrity and data confidentiality before, during, and after their utilization. Owing to these characteristics, CONFINE lets information be securely transferred beyond the organizations' borders. Therefore, computing nodes other than the information provisioners can aggregate and elaborate the original, unaltered process data in a secure, externally inaccessible vault. Also, CONFINE is capable of providing these guarantees while demanding scalable computational overhead.

The decentralized architecture of CONFINE supports a four-staged protocol: *(i)* The initial exchange of preliminary metadata, *(ii)* the attestation of the mining entities, *(iii)* the secure transmission and secrecy-preserving merge of encrypted information segments amid multiple parties, *(iv)* the isolated and verifiable computation of process discovery algorithms on joined data. We evaluate our proof-of-concept implementation against synthetic and real-world data with a convergence test followed by experiments to assess the scalability of our approach. Since TEEs operate with dedicated memory pages shielded from access by external entities (operating system included), thus entailing a hardware constraint on computation space, we endow our experiments with an analysis of memory usage, too.

The remainder of this paper is as follows. Section 2 provides an overview of related work. In Sect. 3, we introduce a motivating use-case scenario in healthcare. We present the CONFINE approach in Sect. 4. We describe the implementation of our approach in Sect. 5. In Sect. 6, we report on the efficacy and efficiency tests for our solution. Finally, we conclude our work and outline future research directions in Sect. 7.

2   Related Work

The scientific literature already includes noticeable contributions to process mining in a decentralized setting with a focus on data secrecy, despite the relative recency of this research branch across process mining and collaborative information systems. The work of Müller et al. [28] revolves around data privacy and security within third-party systems that mine data generated from external providers on demand. To safeguard the integrity of data earmarked for mining purposes, their research introduces a conceptual architecture that entails the execution of process mining algorithms within a cloud service environment, fortified with Trusted Execution Environments. Drawing inspiration from this foundational contribution, our research work seeks to design a decentralized approach characterized by organizational autonomy in the execution of process mining algorithms, devoid of synchronization mechanisms taking place between the involved parties. A notable departure from the framework of Müller et al. lies in the fact that here each participating organization retains the discretion to choose when and how mining operations are conducted. Moreover, we bypass the idea of fixed roles, engineering a peer-to-peer scenario in which organizations can simultaneously be data provisioners or miners. Fahrenkrog-Petersen et al. [17,18] theorize the PRETSA algorithms family, namely a set of event log sanitization techniques that perform step-wise transformations of prefix-tree event log representation into a sanitized output ensuring *k-anonimization* and *t-closeness*. While these algorithms effectively minimize information loss, they introduce targeted approximations within the original event log, which may compromise the exactness of process mining results or inhibit mining tasks. In contrast, our research proposes an architecture wherein secure computational vaults collect event logs devoid of upstream alterations and protect them at runtime, thus generating results derived directly from the original information source. Elkoumy et al. [15,16] present Shareprom. Like our work, their solution offers a means for independent entities to execute process mining algorithms in inter-organizational settings while safeguarding the proprietary input data from exposure to external parties operating within the same context. Shareprom's functionality, though, is confined to the execution of operations involving event log abstractions [3] represented as directed acyclic graphs, which the parties employ as intermediate pre-elaboration to be fed into secure multiparty computation (SMPC) [12]. As the authors remark, relying on this specific graph representation imposes constraints that may turn out to be limiting in a number of process mining scenarios. In contrast, our approach allows for the secure, ciphered transmission of event logs (or segments thereof) to process mining nodes. Moreover, SMPC-based solutions require computationally intensive operations and synchronous cooperation among multiple parties, which make these protocols challenging to manage as the number of participants scales up [37]. In our research work, individual computing nodes run the calculations, thus not requiring synchronization with other machines once the input data is loaded.

We are confronted with the imperative task of integrating event logs originating from different data sources and reconstructing consistent traces that describe collaborative process executions. Consequently, we engage in an examination of

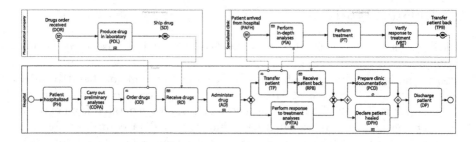

Fig. 1. A BPMN collaboration diagram of a simplified healthcare scenario (Color figure online)

Table 1. Events from cases 312 (Alice) and 711 (Bob) recorded by the hospital, the specialized clinic, and the pharmaceutical company

Hospital					
Case	Timestamp	Activity	Case	Timestamp	Activity
312	2022-07-14T10:36	PH	312	2022-07-15T22:06	TP
312	2022-07-14T16:36	COPA	711	2022-07-16T00:55	PRTA
711	2022-07-14T17:21	PH	711	2022-07-16T01:55	PCD
312	2022-07-14T17:36	OD	711	2022-07-16T02:55	DPH
711	2022-07-14T23:21	COPA	312	2022-07-16T04:55	DP
711	2022-07-15T00:21	OD	312	2022-07-16T07:06	RPB
711	2022-07-15T18:55	RD	312	2022-07-16T09:06	DPH
312	2022-07-15T19:06	RD	312	2022-07-16T10:06	PCD
711	2022-07-15T20:55	AD	312	2022-07-16T11:06	DP
312	2022-07-15T21:06	AD			

Pharmaceutical company		
Case	Timestamp	Activity
312	2022-07-15T09:06	DOR
711	2022-07-15T09:30	DOR
312	2022-07-15T11:06	PDL
711	2022-07-15T11:30	PDL
312	2022-07-15T13:06	SD
711	2022-07-15T13:30	SD

Specialized clinic		
Case	Timestamp	Activity
312	2022-07-16T00:06	PAFH
312	2022-07-16T01:06	PIA
312	2022-07-16T03:06	PT
312	2022-07-16T04:06	VRT
312	2022-07-16T05:06	TPB

$T_{312} = \langle$ PH, COPA, OD, DOR, PDL, SD, RD, AD, TP, PAFH, PIA, PT, VRT, TPB, RPB, DPH, PCD, DP $\rangle$

$T_{711} = \langle$ PH, COPA, OD, DOR, PDL, SD, RD, AD, PRTA, PCD, DPH, DP $\rangle$

methodologies delineated within the literature, each of which offers insights into the merging of event logs within inter-organizational settings. The work of Claes et al. [10] holds particular significance for our research efforts. Their seminal study introduces a two-step mechanism operating at the structured data level, contingent upon the configuration and subsequent application of merging rules. Each such rule indicates the relations between attributes of the traces and/or the activities that must hold across distinct traces to be combined. In accordance with their principles, our research incorporates a structured data-level merge based on case references and timestamps as merging attributes. The research by Hernandez et al. [20] posits a methodology functioning at the raw data level. Their approach represents traces and activities as *bag-of-words* vectors, subject to cosine similarity measurements to discern links and relationships between the traces earmarked for combination. An appealing aspect of this approach lies in its capacity to generalize the challenge of merging without necessitating a-priori knowledge of the underlying semantics inherent to the logs under consideration. However, it entails computational overhead in the treatment of data that can interfere with the overall effectiveness of our approach.

3   Motivating Scenario

To provide a running example and motivating scenario for our investigation, we focus on a simplified hospitalization process for the treatment of rare diseases.

The process model is depicted as a BPMN diagram in Fig. 1 and involves the cooperation of three parties: a hospital, a pharmaceutical company, and a specialized clinic. For the sake of simplicity, we describe the process through two cases, recorded by the information systems as in Table 1. Alice's journey (**case 312**) begins when she enters the hospital for the preliminary examinations (patient hospitalized, PH). The hospital then places an order for the drugs (OD) to the pharmaceutical company for treating Alice's specific condition. Afterwards, the pharmaceutical company acknowledges that the drugs order is received (DOR), proceeds to produce the drugs in the laboratory (PDL), and ships the drugs (SD) back to the hospital. Upon receiving the medications, the hospital administers the drug (AD), and conducts an assessment to determine if Alice can be treated internally. If specialized care is required, the hospital transfers the patient (TP) to the specialized clinic. When the patient arrives from the hospital (PAFH), the specialized clinic performs in-depth analyses (PIA) and proceeds with the treatment (PT). Once the specialized clinic had completed the evaluations and verified the response to the treatment (VRT), it transfers the patient back (TPB). The hospital receives the patient back (RPB) and prepares the clinical documentation (PCD). If Alice has successfully recovered, the hospital declares the patient as healed (DPH). When Alice's treatment is complete, the hospital discharges the patient (DP). Bob (**case 711**) enters the hospital a few hours later. His hospitalization process is similar to Alice's. However, he does not need specialized care, and his case is only treated by the hospital. Therefore, the hospital performs the response to treatment analyses (PRTA) instead of transferring him to the specialized clinic.

Both the National Institute of Statistics of the country in which the three organizations reside and the University that hosts the hospital wish to uncover information on this inter-organizational process for reporting and auditing purposes via process analytics [21]. The involved organizations share the urge for such an analysis and wish to be able to repeat the mining task also in-house. The hospital, the specialized clinic, and the pharmaceutical company have a partial view of the overall unfolding of the inter-organizational process as they record the events stemming from the parts of their pertinence. In Table 1, we show cases 312 and 711 and the corresponding traces recorded by the hospital (i.e., T_{312}^H and T_{711}^H), the specialized clinic (i.e., T_{312}^S and T_{711}^S), and the pharmaceutical company (i.e., T_{312}^C and T_{711}^C). Those traces are projections of the two combined ones for the whole inter-organizational process: $T_{312} = \langle$PH, COPA, OD, DOR, PDL, SD, RD, AD, TP, PAFH, PIA, PT, VRT, TPB, RPB, DPH, PCD, DP$\rangle$ and $T_{711} = \langle$PH, COPA, OD, DOR, PDL, SD, RD, AD, PRTA, PCD, DPH, DP$\rangle$. Results stemming from the analysis of the local cases would not provide a full picture. Data should be merged. However, to safeguard the confidentiality of the information, the involved parties cannot give other organizations open access to their traces. The diverging interests (being able to conduct process mining on data from multiple sources without giving away the local event logs in-clear) motivate our research.

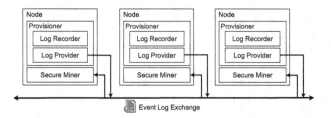

Fig. 2. The CONFINE high-level architecture

We remark that the problem we aim to solve spans across an array of domains beyond healthcare. It particularly applies to scenarios in which one or more parties are interested in process analytics outcomes based on data they bear but cannot be disclosed to the other process actors or to the miners. In the supply chain realm, e.g., the extraction of aggregate knowledge about trends and management guidelines is called for, but the acquisition of competitive advantage out of knowledge leakage must be prevented [33]. In personal informatics, company-wide work routine monitoring and analysis are desirable, though the details of individual participants should be sheltered from inquisitive inspections [31].

4   Design

Our goal is to enable the secure aggregation and elaboration of original, unaltered event logs from decentralized sources in dedicated environments that potentially lie beyond the individual organizations' information perimeter. With this objective in mind, we devise the `Secure Miner` component, which is capable of safeguarding data merge and processing by running certified code in an isolated execution vault. Thus, we decouple provisioning from treatment, and the two tasks can be carried out by distinct computing nodes. Here, we introduce CONFINE's key components, with a special focus on the `Secure Miner`.

The CONFINE Architecture at Large. Our architecture involves different information systems running on multiple machines. An organization can take at least one of the following roles: **provisioning** if it delivers local event logs to be collaboratively mined; **mining** if it applies process mining algorithms using event logs retrieved from provisioners. Figure 2 depicts the high-level schematization of the CONFINE framework. In our solution, each organization hosts one or more nodes encompassing diverse components (the names of which will henceforth be formatted with a `teletype` font). Depending on the played role, nodes come endowed with a `Provisioner` or a `Secure Miner`, or both. The `Provisioner` component, in turn, consists of the following two sub-components. The `Log Recorder` registers the events taking place in the organizations' systems. The `Log Provider` delivers on-demand data to miners. The hospital and all other parties in our example record Alice and Bob's cases using the `Log Recorder`. The `Log Recorder`, in turn, is queried by the `Log Provider` for event logs to be made available for mining. The latter controls access to local event logs by authenticating data requests by miners and rejecting those that come from unauthorized parties. In our motivating scenario, the specialized clinic, the pharmaceutical company, and the hospital leverage Log Providers to authenticate the miner before sending their logs. The Secure Miner component shelters external event logs inside a protected environment to preserve data confidentiality and integrity. Notice that Log Providers accept requests issued solely by Secure Miners. Next, we provide an in-depth focus on the latter.

The Secure Miner. The primary objective of the Secure Miner is to allow miners to securely execute process mining algorithms using event logs retrieved from provisioners (the specialized clinic, the pharmaceutical company, and the hospital in our example). Secure Miners are isolated components that guarantee data inalterability and confidentiality.

Figure 3 illustrates a schematization of the Secure Miner, which consists of four sub-components: *(i)* the Log Requester; *(ii)* the Log Receiver; *(iii)* the Log Manager; *(iv)* the Log Elaborator. The Log Requester and the Log Receiver are the sub-components that we employ during the event log retrieval. Log Requesters send authenticable data requests to the Log Providers. The Log Receiver collects event logs sent by Log Providers and entrusts them to the

Fig. 3. Sub-components of the Secure Miner

Log Manager, securing them from accesses that are external to the Secure Miner. Miners of our motivating scenario, such as the university and the national institute of statistics, employ these three components to retrieve and store Alice and Bob's data. The Log Manager merges the event data locked in the Secure Miner to have a global view of the inter-organizational process comprehensive of activities executed by each involved party. The Log Elaborator executes process mining algorithms in a protected environment, inaccessible from the outside computation environment. In our motivating scenario, the Log Manager combines the traces associated with the cases of Alice (i.e., T_{312}^{H}, T_{312}^{S}, and T_{312}^{C}) and Bob (i.e., T_{711}^{H}, T_{711}^{S}, and T_{711}^{C}), generates the chronologically sorted traces T_{312} and T_{711}, and feeds them into the Log Elaborator's mining algorithms (see the bottom-right quadrant of Table 1).

5   Realization

Thus far, we have outlined the main functionalities of each component at large. Here we discuss the technical aspects concerning the realization of our solution. We first present the technologies through which we enable the design principles in Sect. 4. Then, we discuss the CONFINE interaction protocol. Finally, we show the implementation details.

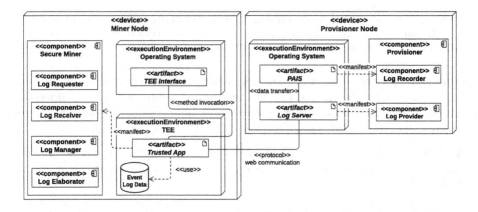

Fig. 4. UML deployment diagram of the CONFINE architecture

5.1 Deployment

Figure 4 depicts a UML deployment diagram [24] to illustrate the employed technologies and computation environments. We recall that the Miner and Provisioner nodes are drawn as separated, although organizations can host both. In our motivating scenario, e.g., the hospital can be equipped with machines aimed for both mining and provisioning.

Provisioner Nodes host the Provisioner's components, i.e., the Log Recorder and the Log Provider. The Process-Aware Information System (PAIS) manifests the Log Recorder [14]. The PAIS grants access to the Log Server, enabling it to retrieve event log data. The Log Server, on the other hand, embodies the functionalities of the Log Provider, implementing services that handle remote data requests and provide event log data to the miners. The Miner Node is characterized by two distinct *execution environments*: the Operating System (OS) and the Trusted Execution Environment (TEE) [30]. TEEs establish isolated contexts separate from the OS, safeguarding code and data through hardware-based encryption mechanisms. This technology relies on dedicated sections of a CPU that handle encrypted data within a reserved section of the main memory [11].

By enforcing memory access restrictions, TEEs aim to prevent one application from reading or altering the memory space of another, thus enhancing system security. These dedicated areas in memory are limited, though. Once the limits are exceeded, TEEs have to scout around in outer memory areas, thus conceding the opportunity to malicious readers to understand the saved data based on the reads and writes. To avoid this risk, TEE implementations often raise errors that halt the program execution when memory demand goes beyond the available space. Therefore, the design of secure systems that resort to TEEs must take into account that memory consumption must be kept under control.

We leverage the security guarantees provided by TEEs [22] to protect a Trusted App responsible for fulfilling the functions of the Secure Miner and its associated sub-components. Our TEE component ensures the integrity of the Trusted App code, protecting it against potential malicious manipulations and unauthorized access by programs running within the OS. Additionally, we utilize the isolated environment of the TEE to securely store event log data (e.g., Alice and Bob's cases). The TEE retains a private key in its inaccessible memory section, paired with a public key in a Rivest-Shamir-Adleman (RSA) [29] scheme for attestation (only the owner of the private key can sign messages in a way that is verifiable via the public key) and secure message encryption (only the owner of the private key can decode messages that are encrypted with the corresponding public key). In our solution, access to data located in the TEE is restricted to the sole Trusted App. Users interact with the Trusted App through the TEE Interface, which serves as the exclusive communication channel. The Trusted App offers secure methods, invoked by the Trusted App Interface, for safely receiving information from the OS and outsourcing the results of computations.

5.2   The CONFINE Protocol

We orchestrate the interaction of the components in CONFINE via a protocol, which consists of four subsequent stages: *(i) initialization, (ii) remote attestation, (iii) data transmission,* and *(iv) computation*. These stages are depicted in Figs. 5(a) to 5(c) and 6 respectively. They are mainly enacted by a Miner Node (multiple instances of which can be deployed in a decentralized fashion) and n Provisioner Nodes. We assume their communication channel is reliable [9] and secure [23]. In the following, we describe each of the above phases in detail.

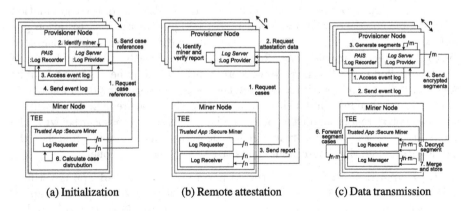

(a) Initialization   (b) Remote attestation   (c) Data transmission

Fig. 5. Unfolding example for the initialization, remote attestation and data transmission phases of the CONFINE protocol

Initialization. The objective of the initialization stage is to inform the miner about the distribution of cases related to a business process among the Provisioner Nodes. At the onset of this stage, the Log Requester within the

Trusted App issues n requests, one per Log Server component, to retrieve the list of case references they record (step 1 in Fig. 5(a)). Following sender authentication (2), each Log Server retrieves the local event log from the PAIS (3, 4) and subsequently responds to the Log Requester by providing a list of its associated case references (5). After collecting these n responses, the Log Requester delineates the distribution of cases. In the context of our motivating scenario, by the conclusion of the initialization, the miner gains knowledge that the case associated with Bob, synthesized in the traces T_{711}^H and T_{711}^C, is exclusively retained by the hospital and the specialized clinic. In contrast, the traces of Alice's case, denoted as T_{312}^H, T_{312}^C, and T_{312}^S, are scattered across all three organizations.

Remote Attestation. The remote attestation serves the purpose of establishing trust between miners and provisioners in the context of fulfilling data requests. This phase adheres to the overarching principles outlined in the RATS RFC standard [8] serving as the foundation for several TEE attestation schemes (e.g., Intel EPID[1] and AMD SEV-SNP[2]). Remote attestation has a dual objective: *(i)* to furnish provisioners with compelling evidence that the data request for an event log originates from a Trusted App running within a TEE; *(ii)* to confirm the specific nature of the Trusted App as an authentic Secure Miner software entity. This phase is triggered when the Log Requester sends a new case request to the Log Server, specifying: *(i)* the segment size (henceforth, *seg_size*), and *(ii)* the set of the requested case references. Both parameters will be used in the subsequent *data transmission* phase. Each of the n Log Servers commences the verification process by requesting the necessary information from the Log Receiver to conduct the attestation (2). Subsequently, the Log Receiver generates the attestation report containing the so-called *measurement* of the Trusted App, which is defined as the hash value of the combination of its source code and data. Once this report is signed using the attestation private key associated with the TEE's hardware of the Miner Node, it is transmitted by the Log Receiver to the Log Servers alongside the attestation public key of the Miner Node (3). The Log Servers authenticate the miner using the public key and decrypt the report (4). In this last step, the Log Servers undertake a comparison procedure in which they juxtapose the measurement found within the decrypted report against a predefined reference value associated with the source code of the Secure Miner. If the decrypted measurement matches the predefined value, the Miner Node gains trust from the provisioner.

Data Transmission. Once the trusted nature of the Trusted App is verified, the Log Servers proceed with the transmission of their cases. To accomplish this, each Log Server retrieves the event log from the PAIS (steps 1 and 2, in Fig. 5(c)), and filters it according to the case reference set specified by the miner. Given the constrained workload capacity of the TEE, Log Servers could

---

[1] http://sgx101.gitbook.io/sgx101/sgx-bootstrap/attestation. Accessed: May 22, 2024.

[2] amd.com/en/processors/amd-secure-encrypted-virtualization. Accessed: May 22, 2024.

be requested to partition the filtered event log into m distinct segments. Log segments contain a variable count of entire cases (3). The cumulative size of these segments is governed by the threshold parameter specified by the miner in the initial request (step 1 of the remote attestation phase, Fig. 5(b)). As an illustrative example from our motivating scenario, the Log Server of the hospital may structure the segmentation such that T_{312}^H and T_{711}^H are in the same segment, whereas the specialized clinic might have T_{312}^S and T_{711}^S in separate segments. Subsequently, the n Log Servers transmit their m encrypted segments to the Log Receiver of the Trusted App (4). The Log Receiver, in turn, collects the $n \times m$ responses in a queue, processing them one at a time. After decrypting a processed segment (5), the Log Receiver forwards the cases contained therein to the Log Manager (6). Data belonging to the same process instance are merged by the Log Manager to build a single trace (e.g., T_{312}) comprehensive of all the events in the partial traces (T_{312}^H, T_{312}^S and T_{312}^C). To do so, the Log Manager applies a specific *merging schema* (i.e., a rule specifying the attributes that identify a case) as stated in [10]. In our illustrative scenario, the merging schema to combine the cases of Alice is contingent upon the linkage established through their case identifier (312). We underline that our solution facilitates the incorporation of diverse merging schemas encompassing distinct trace attributes. The outcomes arising from merging the cases within the processed segments are securely stored by the Log Manager in the TEE.

Computation. The Trusted App requires all the provisioners to have delivered data referring to the same process instances. For example, when the hospital and the other organizations have all delivered their information concerning case 312 to the Trusted App, the process instance associated with Alice becomes eligible for the computation phase, illustrated in Fig. 6. The Log Manager forwards the cases earmarked for computation to the Log Elaborator (step 1). These cases may constitute either the entire merged event log or a subset thereof. The former setting entails a single computation routine, thus saving execution time but requiring a larger memory buffer

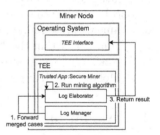

Fig. 6. Computation phase of the CONFINE protocol

in the TEE, whereas the latter necessitates multiple consecutive elaborations with a lower demand for space. Subsequently, the Log Elaborator proceeds to input the merged cases into the process mining algorithm (2). Notice that the above choice on the buffering of cases affects the selection of the mining algorithm to employ. If we elaborate subsequent batches, each containing a part of all merged cases, the mining algorithm must support incremental processing, enriching the output as new batches come along. An example of this class of algorithms is the HeuristicsMiner [36]. Otherwise, incrementality is not required. Ultimately, the outcome of the computation is relayed by the Log Elaborator from the TEE to the TEE Interface running atop the Operating System of the Miner Node (3). In our motivating scenario, the university and the national institute of statistics,

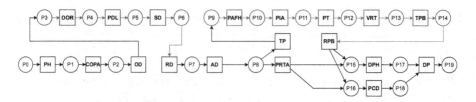

Fig. 7. HeuristicsMiner output with CONFINE (Color figure online)

serving as miners, disseminate the outcomes of computations, generating analyses that benefit the provisioners, although the original data are never revealed in clear. Furthermore, our protocol enables the potential for provisioners to have their own `Secure Miner`, allowing them autonomous control over the computed results. Notice that the CONFINE protocol does not impose restrictions on the post-computational handling of results.

5.3 Implementation

We implemented the `Secure Miner` component as an Intel SGX[3] trusted application, encoded in Go through the EGo framework.[4] We resort to a TLS communication channel [34] between miners and provisioners over the HTTP web protocol to secure the information exchange. To demonstrate the effectiveness of our framework, we re-implemented and integrated the HeuristicsMiner discovery algorithm [36] within the `Trusted Application`. Our implementation of CONFINE, including the HeuristicsMiner implementation in Go, is openly accessible at the following URL: github.com/Process-in-Chains/CONFINE/.

6   Evaluation

In this section, we evaluate our approach through our implementation. We begin with a convergence analysis to demonstrate the correctness of the data exchange process. As discussed in Sect. 5.1, the availability of space in the dedicated TEE areas is subject to hardware limitations. Therefore, we focus on memory consumption, as exceeding those limits could lower the level of security guaranteed by TEEs. Thus, we gauge the memory usage with synthetic and real-life event logs, to observe the trend during the enactment of our protocol and assess scalability. We discuss our experimental results in the following. All the testbeds and results are available in our public code repository (linked above).

Output Convergence. To experimentally validate the correctness of our approach in the transmission and computation phases (see Sect. 5), we run a *convergence* test. To this end, we created a synthetic event log consisting of 1000 cases of 14 events on average (see Table 2) by simulating the inter-organizational

---

[3] http://sgx101.gitbook.io/sgx101/. Accessed: May 22, 2024.
[4] http://docs.edgeless.systems/ego. Accessed: May 22, 2024.

Table 2. Event logs used for our experiments

Name	Type	Activities	Cases	Max events	Min events	Avg. events	Organization $\mapsto$ Activities
Motivating scenario	Synthetic	19	1000	18	9	14	$\mathcal{O}^P \mapsto 3,\ \mathcal{O}^C \mapsto 5,\ \mathcal{O}^H \mapsto 14$
Sepsis [26]	Real	16	1050	185	3	15	$\mathcal{O}^1 \mapsto 1,\ \mathcal{O}^2 \mapsto 1,\ \mathcal{O}^3 \mapsto 14$
BPIC 2013 [32]	Real	7	1487	123	1	9	$\mathcal{O}^1 \mapsto 6,\ \mathcal{O}^2 \mapsto 7,\ \mathcal{O}^3 \mapsto 6$

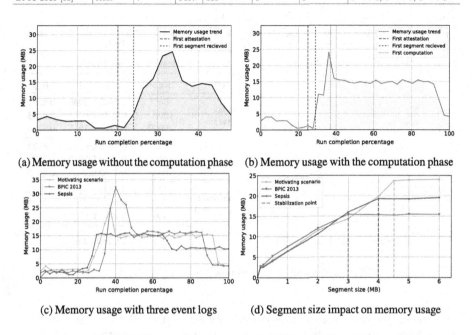

(a) Memory usage without the computation phase   (b) Memory usage with the computation phase

(c) Memory usage with three event logs   (d) Segment size impact on memory usage

Fig. 8. Memory usage test results (Color figure online)

process of our motivating scenario (see Fig. 1)[5] and we partitioned it in three sub-logs (one per involved organization), an excerpt of which is listed in Table 1. We run the stand-alone HeuristicsMiner on the whole log, and processed the sub-logs through our CONFINE toolchain. As expected, the results converge and are depicted in Fig. 7 in the form of a workflow net [1]. For clarity, we have colored activities recorded by the organizations following the scheme of Table 2 (black for the hospital, blue for the pharmaceutical company, and green for the specialized clinic).

Memory Usage. Figures 8(a) and 8(b) display plots corresponding to the runtime space utilization of CONFINE (in MegaBytes). Differently from Fig. 8(b), Fig. 8(a) excludes the computation stage by leaving the HeuristicsMiner inactive so as to isolate the execution from the mining-specific operations. The dashed

---

[5] We generated the event log through BIMP (https://bimp.cs.ut.ee/). We filtered the generated log by keeping the sole events that report on the completion of activities, and removing the start and end events of the pharmaceutical company and specialized clinic's sub-processes.

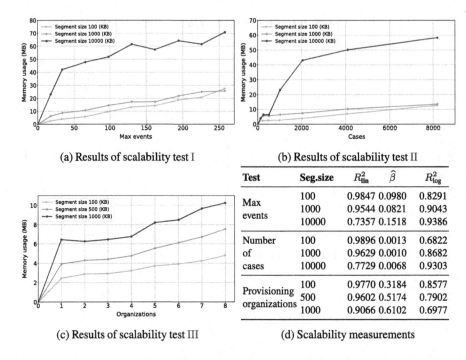

(a) Results of scalability test I

(b) Results of scalability test II

(c) Results of scalability test III

(d) Scalability measurements

Test	Seg.size	R^2_{lin}	$\hat{\beta}$	R^2_{log}
Max events	100	0.9847	0.0980	0.8291
	1000	0.9544	0.0821	0.9043
	10000	0.7357	0.1518	0.9386
Number of cases	100	0.9896	0.0013	0.6822
	1000	0.9629	0.0010	0.8682
	10000	0.7729	0.0068	0.9303
Provisioning organizations	100	0.9770	0.3184	0.8577
	500	0.9602	0.5174	0.7902
	1000	0.9066	0.6102	0.6977

Fig. 9. Scalability test results (Color figure online)

lines mark the starting points for the remote attestation, data transmission and computation stages. We held the segment size (*seg_size*) constant at 2 MB. We observe that the data transmission stage reaches the highest peak of memory utilization, which is then partially freed by the subsequent computation stage, steadily occupying memory space at a lower level. To verify whether this phenomenon is due to the synthetic nature of our simulation-based event log, we gauge the runtime memory usage of two public real-world event logs, too: Sepsis [26] and BPIC 2013 [32]. The characteristics of the event logs are summarized in Table 2. Since those are *intra-organizational* event logs, we split the contents to mimic an *inter-organizational* context. In particular, we separated the Sepsis log based on the distinction between normal-care and intensive-care paths, as if they were conducted by two distinct organizations. Similarly, we processed the BPIC 2013 log to sort it out into the three departments of the Volvo IT incident management system. Figure 8(c) depicts the results. We observe that the BPIC 2013 log demands the most memory during the initial stages, whereas the Sepsis log is associated with the least expensive run, but the polylines exhibit a matching shape with our synthetic dataset. To verify whether these trends are affected by the dimension of the exchanged data segments, we conducted an additional test to examine memory usage as the *seg_size* varies. Notably, the polylines displayed in Fig. 8(d) indicate a linear increment of memory occupation until a breakpoint is reached. After that, the memory in use is steady.

These points, marked by vertical dashed lines, indicate that the *seg_size* value that allows the providers to send their whole log partition in a single segment.

Scalability. To examine the scalability of the Secure Miner, we focus on its capacity to efficiently manage an increasing workload in the presence of limited memory resources (as it is the case with TEEs). We set three distinct test configurations by varying our motivating scenario log. In particular, we considered (I) the maximum number of events per case, (II) the number of cases $|\widehat{CID}|$, and (III) the number of provisioning organizations $|\widehat{\mathcal{O}}|$ as independent integer variables. To conduct the test on the maximum number of events, we added a loop back from the final to the initial activity of the process model, progressively increasing the number of iterations $2 \leqslant x_\circlearrowleft \leqslant 16$ at a step of 2, resulting in $18 + 16 \cdot (x_\circlearrowleft - 1)$ events. Concerning the test on the number of cases, we simulated additional process instances so that $|\widehat{CID}| = 2^{x_{cid}}$ having $x_{cid} \in \{7, 8, \ldots, 13\}$. Finally, for the assessment of the number of organizations, the test necessitated the distribution of the process model activities' into a variable number of pools, each representing a different organization ($|\widehat{\mathcal{O}}| \in \{1, 2, \ldots, 8\}$). We parameterized the above configurations with three segment sizes (in KiloBytes): *seg_size* $\in \{100, 1000, 10000\}$ for tests I and II, and *seg_size* $\in \{100, 500, 1000\}$ for test III (the range is reduced without loss of generality to compensate the partitioning of activities into multiple organizations). To facilitate a more rigorous interpretation of the output trends across varying *seg_sizes*, we employ two well-known statistical measures. As a primary measure of goodness-of-fit, we employ the coefficient of determination R^2 [5], which assesses the degree to which the observed data adheres to the linear (R^2_{lin}) and logarithmic (R^2_{log}) regressions derived from curve fitting approximations. To delve deeper into the analysis of trends exhibiting a high R^2_{lin}, we consider the slope $\widehat{\beta}$ of the approximated linear regression [4].

Figure 9(d) lists the obtained measurements, which we use to elucidate the observed patterns. Figure 9(a) depicts the results of test I, focusing on the increase of memory utilization when the number of events in the logs grows. We observe that the memory usage trends for *seg_size* set to 100 and 1000 (depicted by green and lilac lines, respectively) are almost superimposable, whereas the setting with *seg_size* = 10000 (blue line) exhibits significantly higher memory usage. With *seg_size* assigned with 100 and 1000, R^2_{lin} approaches 1, signifying an almost perfect approximation of the linear relation. With these settings, $\widehat{\beta}$ is very low yet higher than 0, thus indicating that memory usage is likely to continue increasing as the number of maximum events grows. The configuration with *seg_size* = 10000 yields a higher R^2_{log} value, thus suggesting a logarithmic trend, hence a greater likelihood of stabilizing memory usage growth rate as the number of maximum events increases. In Fig. 9(b), we present the results of test II, assessing the impact of the number of cases on memory consumption. As expected, the configurations with *seg_size* set to 100 and 1000 demand lower memory than settings with *seg_size* = 10000. The R^2_{lin} score when *seg_size* is assigned with 100 and 1000 indicate a strong linear relationship between the dependent and independent variables compared to the trend with $seg\_size = 10000$, which is better described by a logarithmic regression ($R^2_{\log} = 0.9303$). Differently from test I, the $\widehat{\beta}$ score associated with the linear approximations with seg_size set to 100 and 1000 approaches 0, indicating that the growth rate of memory usage as the number of cases increases is negligible. In Fig. 9(c), we present the results of test III, on the relation between the number of organizations and memory usage. The chart shows that memory usage trends increase as provisioning organizations increase for all three segment sizes. The R^2_{lin} values for the three seg_sizes are very high, indicating a strong positive linear correlation. The test with $seg\_size = 100$ exhibits the slowest growth rate, as corroborated by the lowest $\widehat{\beta}$ (0.3184). For the configuration with $seg\_size = 500$, the memory usage increases slightly faster ($\widehat{\beta} = 0.5174$). With $seg\_size = 1000$, the overall memory usage increases significantly faster than the previous configurations ($\widehat{\beta} = 0.6102$). We derive from these findings that the **Secure Miner** may encounter scalability issues when handling settings with a large number of provisioning organizations. Further investigation is warranted to determine the precise cause of this behavior and identify potential mitigation strategies.

In the next section, we discuss other future endeavors stemming from our work.

7 Conclusion and Future Work

In this paper, we described CONFINE, a decentralized approach to process mining. Based upon TEEs, it guarantees the secrecy and confidentiality of data transmitted to and elaborated by processing nodes outside the perimeter of the event log providers. Our research can spur a number of future investigations and improvements in the field. First, we aim to enhance our solution by readjusting it to the relaxation of underlying assumptions we made, including fair conduct by data provisioners, the absence of injected or maliciously manipulated event logs, the exchange of messages through reliable communication channels where no loss or bit corruption occurs, and the existence of a universal clock for timestamps. Also, we are extending our analysis with formal proofs of soundness and completeness of the protocol. Our future work encompasses the integration of usage control policies that specify rules on event logs' utilization, too. We plan to design enforcement and monitoring mechanisms to achieve this goal following the principles adopted in [6,7]. We remark that a possibly severe threat to data secrecy lies in the reconstruction of the original input information back from the mining output. Keeping this aspect in mind is crucial to determine the mining algorithm to be embedded in the **Secure Miner**. Studies in this regard have been conducted, among others, in [19,35]. Integrating the proposed recommendations with CONFINE paves the path for future investigations. Finally, we acknowledge that the focus of our implementation is on a specific process discovery task. Nevertheless, our approach has the potential to seamlessly cover a wider array of discovery techniques as well as other process mining functionalities like conformance checking and performance analysis. Showing their integrability with our approach, and drawing guidelines on the use of different algorithms, are research directions we plan to follow.

Acknowledgments. The authors thank Giuseppe Ateniese for the fruitful discussion and insights. This work was partly funded by MUR under PRIN grant B87G22000450001 (PINPOINT), the Latium Region under PO FSE+ grant B83C22004050009 (PPMPP), and Sapienza University of Rome under grant RG123188B3F7414A (ASGARD).

References

1. van der Aalst, W.M.P.: Verification of workflow nets. In: Azéma, P., Balbo, G. (eds.) ICATPN 1997. LNCS, vol. 1248, pp. 407–426. Springer, Heidelberg (1997)
2. van der Aalst, W.M.P.: Intra-and inter-organizational process mining: discovering processes within and between organizations. In: Johannesson, P., Krogstie, J., Opdahl, A.L. (eds.) PoEM 2011. LNBIP, vol. 92, pp. 1–11. Springer, Heidelberg (2011). https://doi.org/10.1007/978-3-642-24849-8_1
3. van der Aalst, W.M.P.: Federated process mining: exploiting event data across organizational boundaries. In: SMDS 2021, pp. 1–7 (2021)
4. Altman, N., Krzywinski, M.: Simple linear regression. Nat. Methods **12**(11), 999–1000 (2015)
5. Barrett, J.P.: The coefficient of determination-some limitations. Am. Stat. **28**(1), 19–20 (1974)
6. Basile, D., Di Ciccio, C., Goretti, V., Kirrane, S.: Blockchain based resource governance for decentralized web environments. Front. Blockchain **6**, 1141909 (2023)
7. Basile, D., Di Ciccio, C., Goretti, V., Kirrane, S.: A blockchain-driven architecture for usage control in solid. In: ICDCSW, pp. 19–24 (2023)
8. Birkholz, H., Thaler, D., Richardson, M., et al.: Remote ATtestation procedureS (RATS) Architecture (2023)
9. Cachin, C., Guerraoui, R., Rodrigues, L.E.T.: Introduction to Reliable and Secure Distributed Programming, 2nd edn. Springer, Heidelberg (2011). https://doi.org/10.1007/978-3-642-15260-3
10. Claes, J., Poels, G.: Merging event logs for process mining: a rule based merging method and rule suggestion algorithm. Expert Syst. Appl. **41**(16), 7291–7306 (2014)
11. Costan, V., Devadas, S.: Intel SGX explained. Cryptology ePrint Archive (2016)
12. Cramer, R., Damgård, I., Nielsen, J.B.: Secure Multiparty Computation and Secret Sharing. Cambridge University Press, Cambridge (2015)
13. De Weerdt, J., Wynn, M.T.: Foundations of process event data. In: van der Aalst, W.M.P., Carmona, J. (eds.) Process Mining Handbook. LNBIP, vol. 448, pp. 193–211. Springer, Cham (2022). https://doi.org/10.1007/978-3-031-08848-3_6
14. Dumas, M., La Rosa, M., Mendling, J., Reijers, H.A.: Fundamentals of Business Process Management, 2nd edn. Springer, Heidelberg (2018). https://doi.org/10.1007/978-3-662-56509-4
15. Elkoumy, G., Fahrenkrog-Petersen, S.A., Dumas, M., Laud, P., Pankova, A., Weidlich, M.: Secure multi-party computation for inter-organizational process mining. In: Nurcan, S., Reinhartz-Berger, I., Soffer, P., Zdravkovic, J. (eds.) BPMDS EMMSAD 2020. LNBIP, vol. 387, pp. 166–181. Springer, Cham (2020). https://doi.org/10.1007/978-3-030-49418-6_11

16. Elkoumy, G., Fahrenkrog-Petersen, S.A., et al.: Shareprom: a tool for privacy-preserving inter-organizational process mining. In: BPM (PhD/Demos), pp. 72–76 (2020)
17. Fahrenkrog-Petersen, S.A., van der Aa, H., Weidlich, M.: PRETSA: event log sanitization for privacy-aware process discovery. In: International Conference on Process Mining, ICPM 2019, Aachen, Germany, 24–26 June 2019, pp. 1–8 (2019)
18. Fahrenkrog-Petersen, S.A., van der Aa, H., Weidlich, M.: Optimal event log sanitization for privacy-preserving process mining. Data Knowl. Eng. **145**, 102175 (2023)
19. Fahrenkrog-Petersen, S.A., Kabierski, M., van der Aa, H., Weidlich, M.: Semantics-aware mechanisms for control-flow anonymization in process mining. Inf. Syst. **114**, 102169 (2023)
20. Hernandez-Resendiz, J.D., Tello-Leal, E., Marin-Castro, H.M., Ramirez-Alcocer, U.M., Mata-Torres, J.A.: Merging event logs for inter-organizational process mining. In: Zapata-Cortes, J.A., Alor-Hernández, G., Sánchez-Ramírez, C., García-Alcaraz, J.L. (eds.) New Perspectives on Enterprise Decision-Making Applying Artificial Intelligence Techniques. SCI, vol. 966, pp. 3–26. Springer, Cham (2021). https://doi.org/10.1007/978-3-030-71115-3_1
21. Jans, M., Hosseinpour, M.: How active learning and process mining can act as continuous auditing catalyst. Int. J. Account. Inf. Syst. **32**, 44–58 (2019)
22. Jauernig, P., Sadeghi, A.R., Stapf, E.: Trusted execution environments: properties, applications, and challenges. IEEE Secur. Priv. **18**(2), 56–60 (2020)
23. Kamil, A., Lowe, G.: Understanding abstractions of secure channels. In: Degano, P., Etalle, S., Guttman, J. (eds.) FAST 2010. LNCS, vol. 6561, pp. 50–64. Springer, Heidelberg (2010). https://doi.org/10.1007/978-3-642-19751-2_4
24. Koch, N., Kraus, A.: The expressive power of UML-based web engineering. In: IWWOST 2002, vol. 16, pp. 40–41 (2002)
25. Liu, C., Li, Q., Zhao, X.: Challenges and opportunities in collaborative business process management: overview of recent advances and introduction to the special issue. Inf. Syst. Front. **11**, 201–209 (2009)
26. Mannhardt, F.: Sepsis cases - event log (2016). https://doi.org/10.4121/UUID: 915D2BFB-7E84-49AD-A286-DC35F063A460
27. Müller, M., Ostern, N., Koljada, D., et al.: Trust mining: analyzing trust in collaborative business processes. IEEE Access **9**, 65044–65065 (2021)
28. Müller, M., Simonet-Boulogne, A., Sengupta, S., Beige, O.: Process mining in trusted execution environments: towards hardware guarantees for trust-aware inter-organizational process analysis. In: Munoz-Gama, J., Lu, X. (eds.) ICPM 2021. LNBIP, vol. 433, pp. 369–381. Springer, Cham (2021). https://doi.org/10.1007/978-3-030-98581-3_27
29. Rivest, R.L., Shamir, A., Adleman, L.M.: A method for obtaining digital signatures and public-key cryptosystems (reprint). Commun. ACM **26**(1), 96–99 (1983)
30. Sabt, M., Achemlal, M., Bouabdallah, A.: Trusted execution environment: what it is, and what it is not. In: 2015 IEEE TrustCom/BigDataSE/ISPA, pp. 57–64 (2015)
31. Sinik, T., Beerepoot, I., Reijers, H.A.: A peek into the working day: comparing techniques for recording employee behaviour. In: Nurcan, S., Opdahl, A.L., Mouratidis, H., Tsohou, A. (eds.) RCIS 2023. LNBIP, vol. 476, pp. 343–359. Springer, Cham (2023). https://doi.org/10.1007/978-3-031-33080-3_21
32. Steeman, W.: BPI challenge 2013, incidents (2013). https://doi.org/10.4121/UUID:500573E6-ACCC-4B0C-9576-AA5468B10CEE

33. Tan, K.H., Wong, W.P., Chung, L.: Information and knowledge leakage in supply chain. Inf. Syst. Front. **18**(3), 621–638 (2016)
34. Thomas, S.A.: SSL and TLS Essentials: Securing the Web. Wiley, Hoboken (2000)
35. von Voigt, S.N., et al.: Quantifying the re-identification risk of event logs for process mining - empiricial evaluation paper. In: Dustdar, S., Yu, E., Salinesi, C., Rieu, D., Pant, V. (eds.) CAiSE 2020. LNCS, vol. 12127, pp. 252–267. Springer, Cham (2020). https://doi.org/10.1007/978-3-030-49435-3_16
36. Weijters, A.J.M.M., van der Aalst, W.M.P., De Medeiros, A.K.A.: Process mining with the HeuristicsMiner algorithm (2006)
37. Zhao, C., Zhao, S., Zhao, M., et al.: Secure multi-party computation: theory, practice and applications. Inf. Sci. **476**, 357–372 (2019)

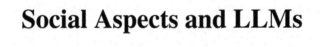

Social Aspects and LLMs

Identifying Citizen-Related Issues from Social Media Using LLM-Based Data Augmentation

Vitor Gaboardi dos Santos[(✉)][ID], Guto Leoni Santos[ID], Theo Lynn[ID],
and Boualem Benatallah[ID]

Dublin City University, Dublin, Ireland
{vitorgaboardidos.santos,guto.santos,theo.lynn,
boualem.benatallah}@dcu.ie

Abstract. Social media platforms, such as Twitter, offer an accessible way for people to share information and perspectives on a wide range of topics. Such citizen discourse can be a valuable source of information and offer policymakers and researchers insights into public sentiment, needs, and suggestions, guiding more informed and responsive planning and policy decisions. In this paper, we propose a novel approach using Large Language Models (LLMs) for data augmentation and multi-class classification to extract domain-specific data from tweets and identify issues raised by citizens thus providing policymakers and social science researchers with valuable data to formulate effective plans and policies for improving services. This approach involves initially collecting data from Twitter using specific keywords and manually labelling a subset of the acquired data. Then, we introduce a new data augmentation strategy employing a LLM that leverages the initial human-labelled data to enhance text diversity and address imbalances in the dataset. Finally, we use the manual-labelled and augmented data to fine-tune different LLMs to classify texts across multiple topics. We test our approach considering the identification of issues related to the cycling domain as case study, detecting tweets across eleven categories associated with infrastructure, safety, and accidents. Through fine-tuning BERT-based models and experimenting with zero- and few-shot prompts with GPT for tweet classification, we accomplished an accuracy of up to 90.9%.

Keywords: Tweet classification · BERT · GPT · LLM · Cycling

1 Introduction

Social media platforms, such as Twitter (currently known as X), provide a convenient and accessible way for citizens to express their opinions and engage in discussions about different topics [4]. They have been extensively used as a source of information, where users contribute with data that can be leveraged to

Supported by Dublin City University (DCU).

evaluate and monitor the quality of citizen services and infrastructure, including transport [24], traffic congestion [12], urban green spaces [23], and health [21]. The collection and analysis of citizen discourse can empower national and local governments, and others stakeholders to develop effective plans and policies for improving services. Nevertheless, obtaining data related to issues raised by citizens on social media presents significant challenges. Manual approaches are typically time-consuming and labor-intensive [24], emphasizing the need for automated solutions leveraging Natural Language Processing (NLP).

Traditional NLP solutions involve training or fine-tuning standard models for classifying public opinion presented in texts on different topics. In this case, it is necessary to collect and prepare a substantial amount of training and testing data, select a model architecture, train or fine-tune the model, evaluate its performance, and finally deploy it for usage after a satisfactory performance is achieved [20]. Moreover, the model performance relies heavily on the quality and quantity of training data samples, which can be expensive and challenging to obtain depending on the topic [1]. On the other hand, generative LLMs like GPT [2] have been recently employed for classification purposes using zero- and few-shot prompts without the need to collect extensive data [3,32]. In this approach, the developers leverage the model's conceptual understanding of language to write prompts detailing a specific behaviour that the LLM must follow to generate a desired output [28]. Although this strategy allows prototyping NLP applications without the need for extensive training data, it introduces challenges such as high dependence on prompt quality, high costs associated with commercial API inference, scalability issues in real-world scenarios due to slow processing time, and privacy concerns [28,30].

In this paper, we propose an innovative pipeline for identifying specific issues raised by citizens on Twitter using LLMs fine-tuned with training data obtained through a novel human- and GPT-based data augmentation approach. This approach explores the robust performance of traditional NLPs solutions while using the capabilities of generative LLMs to leverage the dataset for fine-tuning models. We initially identify domain-specific topics, gather tweets using related keywords, and manually label a subset of the gathered data. Then, we use GPT to create paraphrases and address the challenge of limited annotated data. This strategy focuses on increasing text diversity and balancing the class distribution, thereby improving generalisation when employing this training data for fine-tuning a multi-class classifier. Next, we combine the manually labelled and augmented data to fine-tune LLMs, specifically, BERT [6] and BERTweet [19], and test GPT [2] under zero- and few-shot prompts for classification.

We evaluate the effectiveness of our approach by considering the domain of cycling-related issues as a case study. Despite the benefits to individual health, economics, and the environment, urban cycling faces several obstacles, including lack of dedicated cycling infrastructure, secure parking and storage, safety concerns, and traffic problems [7,14,15]. Through the identification and monitoring of these challenges in tweets, authorities and other stakeholders may gain valuable insights, enabling them to formulate strategies for enhancing urban cycling policymaking. Furthermore, we assess the performance of the fine-tuned models by computing their accuracy on a test dataset that was manually curated by the authors. Results show that fine-tuning BERT achieved the highest performance with an accuracy of 90.9% in classifying among eleven cycling-related issues, highlighting that specialized models, fine-tuned on human-annotated and LLM-augmented data, generally outperform zero- or few-shot GPT classification.

In summary, we make the following contributions:

- Novel data augmentation pipeline using GPT-based prompts to address the challenge of limited annotated training data and leverage a balanced dataset to train or fine-tune domain-specific multi-class classifiers.
- Multi-class models to identify citizen-related issues by fine-tuning BERT and BERTweet using manual-labelled and augmented data, and prompting GPT under zero- and few-shot prompts employing only manual-labelled data.
- Collection of a dataset with cycling-related tweets labelled into multiple topics such as infrastructure, theft, parking, and accidents. The method to collect this dataset is applicable to other domains.
- Evaluation and comparison of the classifiers' performance considering both an augmented and manual-labelled data for BERT-based models, and different strategies for choosing samples in the GPT few-shot prompt.

2   Related Work

Text Classification: Several works have been developed on text classification using social media data. Plunz et al. [23] focused on tweets from New York City parks, employing a logistic regression classifier with embedding features to determine if tweets related to green urban areas expressed a positive sentiment. Park et al. [21] analysed Google Maps reviews of hub airports in the US to identify the public perception of COVID-19 policy using text clustering to identify four topics. Taleqani et al. [25] conducted sentiment analysis on tweets using naive Bayes, logistic regression, and support vector machine to evaluate public opinion on dockless bike-sharing systems. Das et al. [5] proposed a framework for understanding the emotions of cyclists towards cycling through content published in tweets. They employed standard NLP techniques, such as text mining and sentiment lexicon.

The adoption of LLMs in text classification has become increasingly popular given their remarkable performance [26]. BERT [6] is a pre-trained LLM that excels in comprehending the context of words within a sentence, leading to noteworthy language understanding [10]. BERT has been fine-tuned in many downstream applications using social media data, such as aiding public safety personnel during disasters [31], analysing political campaign messages [13], and detecting COVID-19-related fake news [22]. BERTweet [19] is another pre-trained LLM with the BERT architecture, but fine-tuned on a corpus of 850M English tweets using the RoBERTa [16] pre-training procedure. BERTweet has demonstrated effectiveness in hate, offensive and profane detection [11] and health misinformation detection [29]. Although these solutions demonstrate satisfactory performance, they require substantial training data, which may be difficult to acquire depending on data availability.

On the other hand, GPT is a generative LLM pre-trained on vast amounts of text data, enabling it to understand and generate human-like text with remarkable coherence [10]. GPT can be used as a classification tool through zero- or few-shot prompting without much training data, achieving noteworthy results in hate speech [3] and agriculture topic classification [32]. Nevertheless, employing GPT for classification under prompting has drawbacks, such as limited input token length, high cost of conducting online inference, and scalability issues [30].

Data Augmentation: GPT has also been employed as a data augmentation tool to increase training diversity without explicit data collection, and as a solution to improve model generalization and robustness for applications where collecting data is challenging [9]. Yoo et al. [30] proposed a method for synthesizing samples by including a specific number of real samples from each class in a GPT prompt and generating mixed sentences influenced by the included samples. Fang et al. [8] employed GPT-4 to augment student responses for automatic scoring using a prompt requesting for similar written-answers. They used the augmented samples and the original sentences to fine-tune a BERT variant model, leading to improved performance. Møller et al. [18] investigated the application of GPT-4 in generating synthetic data for low-resource domain applications in computational social science. Their findings highlight the benefits of data augmentation, particularly in improving performance on rare classes in multi-class tasks. Van Nooten et al. [27] leverage GPT 3.5 to create samples of anti-vaccination tweets in Dutch to augment a multi-label vaccine hesitancy dataset. They employed prompts that generate instances based on human-labelled data and assign labels to the augmented samples. They found that including the augmented data improves the overall classifier performance.

Our novel approach is designed to address applications with limited-available training data and unbalanced datasets by including a data augmentation pipeline that maximizes the use of input samples and enhances text diversity through paraphrase requests using GPT model. This allows leveraging data to fine-tune state of the art LLMs to identify citizen-related issues. Furthermore, we test our methodology in the case study of cycling-related topics, a domain with limited data availability [5]. We include detecting a broader range of topics than previous works [5, 25], such as infrastructure, theft, parking, accidents, and traffic.

3   Methodology

In this section, we present our approach for identifying citizen issues from social media using LLMs. As illustrated in Fig. 1, we use the Twitter API to collect tweets with topic-related keywords, and manually label a subset considering desired topics to monitor. Then, we employ GPT to augment the labelled tweets and use both human-annotated and augmented data to fine-tune BERT and BERTweet for multi-class classification, and employ some labelled data for zero- and few-shot classification using GPT. Finally, we evaluate all classifiers using a test dataset. We consider the case study of identifying cycling-related issues to evaluate our methodology.

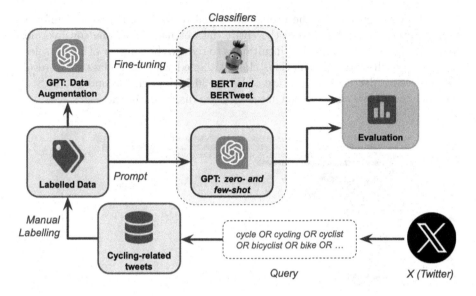

Fig. 1. Approach overview.

3.1   Data Collection and Human-Based Labelling

The Twitter data collected comprises 6,744,591 tweets posted between December 1st, 2022 and December 31st, 2022, acquired through the Twitter API. We collected tweets that mention one of the following terms: cycle, cycling, cyclist, bicyclist, bike, bicycle, cycle lane, cycle path, electric bike, city bike, ebike, e-bike.

Urban cycling faces many challenges, including inadequate infrastructure, insecure parking, safety concerns, poor way finding, and traffic issues [7,14,15]. In response to these issues, we selected the following categories for monitoring: *Accidents, Behaviour, Rental, Infrastructure, Journey statistics, Parking, Routes, Sales, Signage, Traffic, and Theft.* Moreover, we labelled tweets into these classes and "others", enclosing tweets unrelated to these topics.

We selected 1,650 tweets from the data collected and manually labelled them. However, we identified two issues after concluding this process. The first is the high number of False Positives (FP), accounting for 43.73% of the labelled data. This problem occurred due to the selection of keywords that occasionally identified tweets discussing other events related to "cycle", such as "cycle of life" or "cycle of abuse", instead of referring to the intended action of riding a bicycle. Moreover, there were FPs originating from product reviews, advertisements for bicycle accessories, and general tweets that did not align with any predefined categories. The second issue is the highly imbalanced dataset distribution.

To improve the dataset with high-quality samples, we manually labelled an additional 1,100 tweets. However, we employed a distinct approach when selecting the samples to label. We computed the most frequent sentence-level bigram

for each class considering the previously labelled data, and used this information to filter new samples from the entire dataset using only the top five most
frequent bigrams per class. The intuition is to reduce the number of FP by selecting tweets with word combinations closely aligned with each class. As a result,
we observed a decrease in the rate of FP to 36.53% in the second batch. Some
sentence-level bigrams and their frequency are displayed in the Fig. 2.

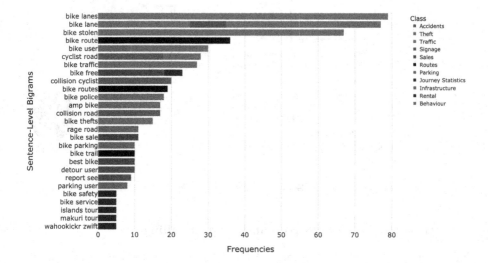

Fig. 2. Five most frequent sentence-level bigram per class.

Some sentence-level bigrams appear across multiple classes. For instance,
"bike" and "lane" are found in tweets belonging to the classes *Traffic*, *Signage*,
Infrastructure, and *Behaviour*. This happened because it is common for users to
refer to these topics using both words within the same sentence. This idea of
a sentence-level bigram belonging to multiple classes emphasizes how context-
dependent the classification of tweets in this application is, where pairing two
cycling-related words can lead to different classes.

Figure 3 displays the distribution of manually labelled samples across different classes. It is possible to observe that some classes still have a limited
number of tweets, notably *Rental* and *Signage*, each with less than 50 samples.
Finally, we pre-processed all tweets from this training dataset to remove URLs
and punctuation and replace username mentions with "@user".

3.2   Data Augmentation

The percentage of FP decreased after filtering the tweets to be manually labelled
based on sentence-level bigrams, which led to a higher number of samples for all
categories. However, the training dataset remains imbalanced and some classes
still have few samples. To address these challenges, we prompted GPT-3.5-turbo

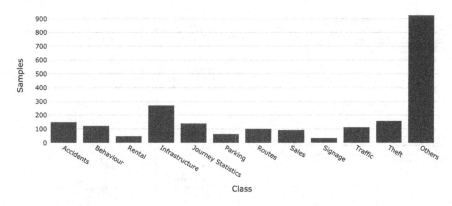

Fig. 3. Number of manually labelled samples per class.

model to perform data augmentation by creating paraphrases of tweets using the already labelled tweets as inputs.

The number of paraphrases requested for each tweet *(n)* varied based on the amount of labelled data available for a particular class. For instance, as shown in Fig. 3, the *Signage* class have few samples, so we requested more paraphrases for each tweet of this class when compared to the *Accidents* one, which had a larger sample pool. Our approach aimed to ensure that each class had a minimum of 400 tweets (number of desired samples per class). We chose this threshold because it demonstrated good performance when fine-tuning BERT for multi-class problems, as documented in Liu et al. [17]. Furthermore, we prompted GPT to create paraphrases considering all the samples from the labelled data, enabling a better text diversity when creating the new instances. We did this for every class except for *Infrastructure*, since it already contains many instances, allowing to accumulate 400 samples without using all labelled data.

An overview of our data augmentation process is shown in Fig. 4. We first extract all tweets of one particular class, and compute the number of paraphrases to be generated for every tweet within this class by considering the number of labelled data available and number of desired samples. Then, we iterate through each tweet within the selected class and request GPT to generate *n* paraphrases based on a specific prompt instruction, followed by few-shot examples specific to the class, and the tweet to be paraphrased. Next, we process the GPT's responses using the structure outlined in the prompt and integrate them into the dataset.

After testing multiple prompt instructions to generate diverse lexical and syntactical paraphrases, we used the following one: *You are an expert in paraphrases and creating tweets for cycling content. For each given tweet and subject, I want you to create other tweets that are lexically and syntactically different. You can change names, dates, and places, and you must make it as different as possible while maintaining the subject of the sentence.* This instruction was followed by a 3-shot prompt, including an example of a tweet and three

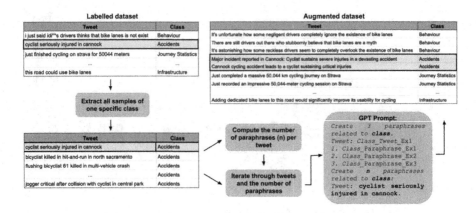

Fig. 4. Data augmentation process overview.

corresponding paraphrases. We manually crafted examples for each class with the goal of enhancing the model's contextual understanding.

Despite instructing GPT to generate diverse paraphrases with entity variations, the model often produced text using the same entities as the original tweet. Also, the writing style in these paraphrases tends to be more formal when compared to typical language used on Twitter. However, the content of the paraphrases remained accurate and effectively conveyed the intended meaning of the respective class in most instances. Finally, Fig. 5 displays the amount of training samples acquired by merging the manually labelled data and augmented datasets, resulting in a more balanced dataset and increased sample size. In total, the training dataset was composed of 5,599 tweets, of which 2,213 are human created and 3,386 are GPT created.

3.3   Test Dataset

To evaluate the classifiers' performance, we built a test dataset consisting of 220 unique tweets (20 per class) posted between September 5th, 2023, and September 7th, 2023. These tweets were manually gathered by the authors from the X website, using the name of each class as a keyword, along with the following terms: cycling, cyclist, bike, and bicycle. We selected tweets from a distinct timeframe than those in the training dataset to minimize potential biases of testing the models with similar content used during fine-tuning and better assess the robustness of the models.

3.4   Tweet Classification

To perform multi-text classification of cycling-related tweets, we will evaluate the performance of different LLMs and identify the most effective one. In particular, we employed GPT as classifier under zero- and few-shot prompt, and fine-tuned

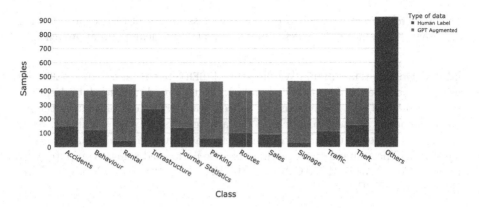

Fig. 5. Training data distribution.

BERT and BERTweet using the training dataset discussed in Sect. 3.2. Although tweets may cover multiple cycling-related topics, we treat the classes as mutually exclusive. Therefore, each tweet is assigned to a single class that best represents its content.

GPT-Based Classifier. While GPT is primarily known for its use in text generation, it can also be employed for classification tasks, despite its cost and resources [3,32]. In this configuration, we send GPT a prompt with instructions including all possible output classes, and request the model to classify a new input text into one of the mentioned classes. We assess GPT's performance as a classifier considering two configurations: zero-shot prompt, where only an instruction is provided to the model; and few-shot prompt, which include some few examples to enhance the model's contextual understanding of the task. In both cases, we used the following base prompt: *Classify the tweet related to cycling and delimited by triple backticks into one of the following 11 different categories: Accidents; Behaviour; Rental; Infrastructure; Journey Statistics; Parking; Routes; Sales; Signage; Traffic; Theft, and Others (if the tweet is not related to cycling). Return only the name of the class that represents the given tweet.*

We prompted `GPT-3.5-turbo` model for this task. Some parameters can be adjusted to improve GPT's performance as a classifier. The first parameter is the *"temperature"*, which controls the level of randomness in the model's output. Higher values result in a more random output, while lower values lead to a more deterministic outcome. We set the temperature value to 0 to ensure that the model consistently selects the class with the highest probability. Also, GPT can output any word from its extensive vocabulary, although our request is to generate only the class name. Consequently, there may be cases where the first token in the output does not correspond to any of the desired classes. To ensure that the output is consistent, we restricted the output tokens to be within a predefined set by increasing the *"logit bias"* of all tokens associated with the classes names and the *"end of text"* special token to 100. Lastly, it is better to request the model to output the class names instead of a numerical representation, since it provides a more semantically meaningful approach [2].

BERT-Based Classifier. We fine-tuned `BERT-base-cased` and `BERTweet` using the complete human-labelled and LLM-augmented training data described in Sects. 3.1 and 3.2. The fine-tuning process was performed considering the following hyperparameters: 5 epochs, 5^{-6} learning rate, AdamW optimizer, batch size of 8 samples, and early stopping if the accuracy does not improve after one epoch. The training and experiments were performed using a computer with Intel(R) Core(TM) i7-12700 CPU at 2.10GHz, 32 GB RAM, and Nvidia GeForce GTX 16660 SUPER.

4   Results

Table 1 summarizes the performance for each model. GPT zero-shot presents the worst results considering all metrics, including an accuracy of 77.27%. However, this outcome is particularly noteworthy as it was acquired without employing any training data for classification, and it serves as our accuracy baseline.

Table 1. Models comparison.

Model	Accuracy	Precision	Recall	F1-score
GPT zero-shot	0.7727	0.7710	0.7083	0.7074
GPT six-shot	0.8409	0.8062	0.7708	0.7755
BERTweet	0.8772	0.8156	0.8041	0.8062
BERT-base-cased	**0.9090**	**0.8418**	**0.8333**	**0.8345**

We provided six examples in the prompt to improve GPT's performance as a classifier, a configuration that we call GPT six-shot. The confusion matrix shown in Fig. 6(a) shows that GPT zero-shot had more misclassifications for two particular classes: 21 tweets were incorrectly categorized as *Infrastructure*, and 10 tweets were misclassified as *Routes*. This result indicates that GPT lacks context to differentiate both classes. To address this issue, we provided additional context by adding three samples for each of the *Infrastructure* and *Routes* classes in the prompt, which were randomly chosen from our manual-labelled training dataset. As shown in Table 1, the results with the six-shot examples improved the classification performance by approximately 7% in all metrics except precision.

Figure 6(b) shows the confusion matrix considering the GPT six-shot prompt. The number of correct classification for both *Routes* and *Infrastructure* classes decreased. However, the number of FP also decreased, leading to a better performance overall. We also tested other combinations of examples, such as including one tweet of all classes, but the results did not improve as much when compared to selecting samples from classes with the lowest performance.

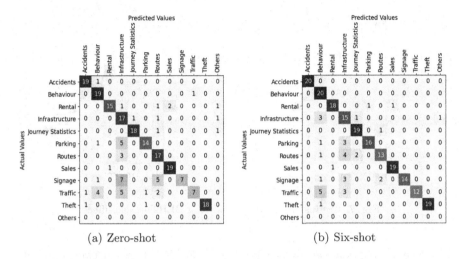

(a) Zero-shot (b) Six-shot

Fig. 6. Confusion matrix considering GPT as classifier.

We also considered fine-tuning BERT-based models. The BERTweet model outperformed both GPT prompts, obtaining more than 80% in all performance metrics. The vanilla BERT model obtained the best performance, being the only one that obtained an accuracy of over 90%. However, it is important to highlight that both BERT models were fine-tuned using the entire training dataset, while GPT used only a few samples.

Figure 7 displays the confusion matrix for BERT and BERTweet fine-tuned models. Both models demonstrated enhancements in the classification of *Infrastructure* class, where BERT exhibited no mistake of other classes with *Infrastructure*, while BERTweet had only one misclassification. For the *Routes* class, both BERT and BERTweet improved the true positive rates, although BERT and BERTweet confused *Signage* tweets with the *Routes* class on three and five occasions, respectively. Other notable results include BERT's confusion of *Infrastructure* with *Traffic* on three occasions, and BERTweet's misclassification of *Behaviour* with *Traffic* four times. Furthermore, the number of correct predictions (diagonals of the confusion matrices) also increased. For BERT, the class with the fewest accurate samples was *Infrastructure* (15 tweets), and for BERTweet, it was *Signage* (14 tweets).

Although this work involves tweet classification and BERTweet was fine-tuned considering English tweets, it had a lower performance when compared to the vanilla BERT. We suspect this occurred for two reasons. First, classifying tweets about cycling may not require specialized Twitter-related features that BERTweet is optimized for. BERT was pre-trained on a diverse corpus of text, including a wide range of topics and writing styles. This general pre-training

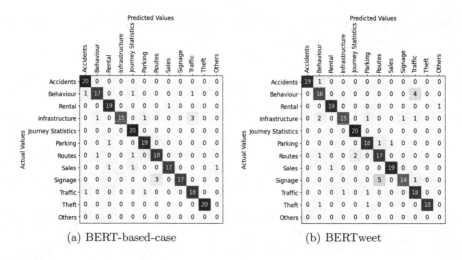

(a) BERT-based-case   (b) BERTweet

Fig. 7. Confusion matrix considering BERT as classifier.

can make it more adaptable to various text domains. Thus, our tweets probably have a writing style closer to standard written language, which would favour the BERT model. Second, when performing data augmentation, the writing style of the tweets were actually more formal than the usual Twitter language. Therefore, our training data may be more similar to the information trained on BERT.

Furthermore, it is important to note the challenge of classifying tweets considering the classes adopted in this paper, as some texts can be related to multiple classes. Table 2 illustrates some cycling-related tweets with the classification of each model considered in this paper.

The first tweet shown in Table 2 discuss mainly about the traffic consequences when introducing a new cycling lane. Therefore, we consider that this tweet belongs to the *Traffic* class, although it is understandable to be also assigned to *Infrastructure* since it discusses new cycle routes, as classified by the GPT six-shot. Similarly, we consider that the second tweet is related to *Infrastructure* class, as it discuss the need to construct cycling pavements for people safety. However, both BERT and BERTweet model classified it as *Behaviour*, which is also comprehensible given that the tweet also mentions the behaviour of drivers in the city of Harare. Finally, the third tweet showcases an example discussing about *Infrastructure*, where only the GPT six-shot model misclassified.

Therefore, despite our best model achieved an accuracy of 90.9%, we consider this performance outstanding given the complexity of classifying the specific classes. Furthermore, some errors are acceptable since certain tweets may carry multiple interpretations and can belong to two or more classes simultaneously.

Table 2. Classification results of some tweets.

Tweet	GPT 0-shot	GPT 6-shot	BERTweet	BERT
just where do you think Sheffield can handle new cycle routes? Taking away a lane of traffic purely for cyclists will make the already abysmal traffic problem worse and drive people away from the city altogether	Routes	Infra.	Traffic	Traffic
In the new Zimbabwe, we need to advocate for rights of runners in the road! City of Harare should plan & construct (cycling & running pavements) for safety of people who want to exercise! Running in the road is never safe! Harare drivers do not know how to drive	Others	Infra.	Behav.	Behav.
Kids in bike lanes are an indicator species for safe cycling infrastructure	Infra.	Behav.	Infra.	Infra.

5   Limitations and Future Work

A primary limitation in the data augmentation pipeline lies in using only OpenAI's `gpt-3.5-turbo` model. In future research, we plan to diversify our approach by integrating other generative LLMs like LLaMA and Falcon, aiming to reduce dependence on commercial models. Furthermore, a more comprehensive assessment of text diversity in the augmented dataset is necessary to ensure the creation of high-quality samples.

In the classification approach, we assumed that classes are mutually exclusive, indicating that tweets are labelled to a single class. However, some tweets may cover multiple topics simultaneously. For instance, in our cycling-related topics discussed in this paper, some tweets could be labelled as *Infrastructure* and *Behaviour*, or *Routes* and *Traffic*, among others. In future work, we plan to consider multi-label classification, assigning more than one class to a tweet.

Further research includes applying our method to other citizen-related issues, performing sentiment analysis to understand overall citizen opinion about each identified issue, considering other languages and input information such as video and images, and investigating alternative approaches involving multiple stages of manual labelling and fine-tuning to enhance the models' performance.

6   Conclusions

We proposed a novel technique for identifying citizen-related issues from social media using LLMs. Our approach involves gathering tweets of domain-specific topics raised by citizens, followed by manual annotation of a subset of the collected data. Then, an innovative GPT-based data augmentation pipeline creates more training samples from the annotated data. This strategy aims to balance the dataset while also introducing diverse paraphrases. Finally, we fine-tuned BERT and BERTweet using both manually annotated and augmented data, and tested zero- and few-shot GPT prompts for classifying tweets in distinct topics. We assessed this approach by identifying eleven different issues within the domain of cycling, a case study with limited data availability.

The data augmentation strategy worked satisfactorily, producing new text with similar meaning to the original tweets, despite resulting in a more formal tone and not altering entities when requested, resulting in a training dataset more balanced. The fine-tuned BERT model achieved the best accuracy of 90.9% among all tested classifiers. Furthermore, both fine-tuned models performance surpassed zero- or few-shot GPT prompt classification.

Acknowledgement. This work was supported by funding from the European Consortium of Innovative Universities Bicizen project. This work was also conducted with the financial support of the Science Foundation Ireland Centre for Research Training in Artificial Intelligence under Grant No. 18/CRT/6223.

References

1. Adadi, A.: A survey on data-efficient algorithms in big data era. J. Big Data **8**(1), 24 (2021)
2. Brown, T., et al.: Language models are few-shot learners. In: Advances in Neural Information Processing Systems, vol. 33, pp. 1877–1901 (2020)
3. Chiu, K.L., Collins, A., Alexander, R.: Detecting hate speech with GPT-3. arXiv preprint arXiv:2103.12407 (2021)
4. Daemi, A., Chugh, R., Kanagarajoo, M.V.: Social media in project management: a systematic narrative literature review. Int. J. Inf. Syst. Proj. Manag. **8**(4), 5–21 (2021)
5. Das, S., Dutta, A., Medina, G., Minjares-Kyle, L., Elgart, Z.: Extracting patterns from Twitter to promote biking. IATSS Res. **43**(1), 51–59 (2019)
6. Devlin, J., Chang, M.W., Lee, K., Toutanova, K.: BERT: pre-training of deep bidirectional transformers for language understanding. arXiv preprint arXiv:1810.04805 (2018)
7. Dill, J.: Bicycling for transportation and health: the role of infrastructure. J. Public Health Policy **30**, S95–S110 (2009)
8. Fang, L., Lee, G.G., Zhai, X.: Using GPT-4 to augment unbalanced data for automatic scoring. arXiv preprint arXiv:2310.18365 (2023)
9. Feng, S.Y., et al.: A survey of data augmentation approaches for NLP. arXiv preprint arXiv:2105.03075 (2021)
10. Ghojogh, B., Ghodsi, A.: Attention mechanism, transformers, BERT, and GPT: tutorial and survey (2020)

11. Glazkova, A., Kadantsev, M., Glazkov, M.: Fine-tuning of pre-trained transformers for hate, offensive, and profane content detection in English and Marathi. arXiv preprint arXiv:2110.12687 (2021)
12. Gu, Y., Qian, Z.S., Chen, F.: From twitter to detector: real-time traffic incident detection using social media data. Transp. Res. Part C Emerg. Technol. **67**, 321–342 (2016)
13. Gupta, S., Bolden, S., Kachhadia, J., Korsunska, A., Stromer-Galley, J.: PoliBERT: classifying political social media messages with BERT. In: Social, Cultural and Behavioral Modeling (SBP-BRIMS 2020) Conference, Washington, DC (2020)
14. Heinen, E., Maat, K., Van Wee, B.: The effect of work-related factors on the bicycle commute mode choice in The Netherlands. Transportation **40**, 23–43 (2013)
15. Iwińska, K., Blicharska, M., Pierotti, L., Tainio, M., de Nazelle, A.: Cycling in Warsaw, Poland-Perceived enablers and barriers according to cyclists and non-cyclists. Transp. Res. Part A Policy Pract. **113**, 291–301 (2018)
16. Liu, Y., et al.: RoBERTa: a robustly optimized BERT pretraining approach. arXiv preprint arXiv:1907.11692 (2019)
17. Liu, Y., Dmitriev, P., Huang, Y., Brooks, A., Dong, L.: An evaluation of transfer learning for classifying sales engagement emails at large scale. In: 2019 19th IEEE/ACM International Symposium on Cluster, Cloud and Grid Computing (CCGRID), pp. 542–548. IEEE (2019)
18. Møller, A.G., Dalsgaard, J.A., Pera, A., Aiello, L.M.: Is a prompt and a few samples all you need? Using GPT-4 for data augmentation in low-resource classification tasks. arXiv preprint arXiv:2304.13861 (2023)
19. Nguyen, D.Q., Vu, T., Nguyen, A.T.: BERTweet: a pre-trained language model for English Tweets. arXiv preprint arXiv:2005.10200 (2020)
20. Paleyes, A., Urma, R.G., Lawrence, N.D.: Challenges in deploying machine learning: a survey of case studies. ACM Comput. Surv. **55**(6), 1–29 (2022)
21. Park, J.Y., Mistur, E., Kim, D., Mo, Y., Hoefer, R.: Toward human-centric urban infrastructure: text mining for social media data to identify the public perception of COVID-19 policy in transportation hubs. Sustain. Urban Areas **76**, 103524 (2022)
22. Pavlov, T., Mirceva, G.: COVID-19 fake news detection by using BERT and RoBERTa models. In: 2022 45th Jubilee International Convention on Information, Communication and Electronic Technology (MIPRO), pp. 312–316. IEEE (2022)
23. Plunz, R.A., et al.: Twitter sentiment in New York City parks as measure of well-being. Landsc. Urban Plan. **189**, 235–246 (2019)
24. Qi, B., Costin, A., Jia, M.: A framework with efficient extraction and analysis of Twitter data for evaluating public opinions on transportation services. Travel behav. Soc. **21**, 10–23 (2020)
25. Rahim Taleqani, A., Hough, J., Nygard, K.E.: Public opinion on dockless bike sharing: a machine learning approach. Transp. Res. Rec. **2673**(4), 195–204 (2019)
26. Sun, X., et al.: Text classification via large language models. arXiv preprint arXiv:2305.08377 (2023)
27. Van Nooten, J., Daelemans, W.: Improving Dutch vaccine hesitancy monitoring via multi-label data augmentation with GPT-3.5. In: Proceedings of the 13th Workshop on Computational Approaches to Subjectivity, Sentiment, & Social Media Analysis, Toronto, Canada, July 2023, vol. 1, pp. 251–270 (2023)
28. Viswanathan, V., Zhao, C., Bertsch, A., Wu, T., Neubig, G.: Prompt2Model: generating deployable models from natural language instructions. arXiv preprint arXiv:2308.12261 (2023)

29. Wahle, J.P., Ashok, N., Ruas, T., Meuschke, N., Ghosal, T., Gipp, B.: Testing the generalization of neural language models for COVID-19 misinformation detection. In: Smits, M. (ed.) iConference 2022. LNCS, vol. 13192, pp. 381–392. Springer, Cham (2022). https://doi.org/10.1007/978-3-030-96957-8_33
30. Yoo, K.M., Park, D., Kang, J., Lee, S.W., Park, W.: GPT3Mix: leveraging large-scale language models for text augmentation. arXiv preprint arXiv:2104.08826 (2021)
31. Zahera, H.M., Elgendy, I.A., Jalota, R., Sherif, M.A., Voorhees, E.: Fine-tuned BERT model for multi-label tweets classification. In: TREC, pp. 1–7 (2019)
32. Zhao, B., Jin, W., Del Ser, J., Yang, G.: ChatAgri: exploring potentials of ChatGPT on cross-linguistic agricultural text classification. arXiv preprint arXiv:2305.15024 (2023)

Kicking Prejudice: Large Language Models for Racism Classification in Soccer Discourse on Social Media

Guto Leoni Santos[1]([✉]) [iD], Vitor Gaboardi dos Santos[1] [iD], Colm Kearns[1] [iD],
Gary Sinclair[1] [iD], Jack Black[2] [iD], Mark Doidge[3] [iD], Thomas Fletcher[4] [iD],
Dan Kilvington[4] [iD], Patricia Takako Endo[5] [iD], Katie Liston[6] [iD],
and Theo Lynn[1] [iD]

[1] Dublin City University, Dublin, Ireland
{guto.santos,vitorgaboardidos.santos,colm.g.kearns,gary.sinclair,
theo.lynn}@dcu.ie
[2] Sheffield Hallam University, Sheffield, UK
j.black@shu.ac.uk
[3] Loughborough University, Loughborough, UK
M.Doidge@lboro.ac.uk
[4] Leeds Beckett University, Leeds, UK
{T.E.Fletcher,D.J.Kilvington}@leedsbeckett.ac.uk
[5] Universidade de Pernambuco, Caruaru, Brazil
patricia.endo@upe.br
[6] Ulster University, Belfast, UK
k.liston@ulster.ac.uk

Abstract. In the dynamic space of Twitter, now called X, interpersonal racism surfaces when individuals from dominant racial groups engage in behaviours that diminish and harm individuals from other racial groups. It can be manifested in various forms, including pejorative name-calling, racial slurs, stereotyping, and microaggressions. The consequences of racist speech on social media are profound, perpetuating social division, reinforcing systemic inequalities, and undermining community cohesion. In the specific context of football discourse, instances of racism and hate crimes are well-documented. Regrettably, this issue has seamlessly migrated to the football discourse on social media platforms, especially Twitter. The debate on Internet freedom and social media moderation intensifies, balancing the right to freedom of expression against the imperative to protect individuals and groups from harm. In this paper, we address the challenge of detecting racism on Twitter in the context of football by using Large Language Models (LLMs). We fine-tuned different BERT-based model architectures to classify racist content in the Twitter discourse surrounding the UEFA European Football Championships. The study aims to contribute insights into the nuanced language of hate speech in soccer discussions on Twitter while underscoring the necessity for context-sensitive model training and evaluation. Additionally, Explainable Artificial Intelligence (XAI) techniques, specifically the Integrated Gradient method, are used to enhance transparency and interpretability in the decision-making processes of the LLMs, offering a comprehensive approach to mitigating racism and offensive language in online sports discourses.

Keywords: Tweet classification · Large Language Models · XAI · BERT · RoBERTa

1   Introduction

The United Nations International Convention on the Elimination of all Forms of Racial Discrimination (ICERD) defines racism as: "any distinction, exclusion, restriction or preference based on race, colour, descent, or national or ethnic origin which has the purpose or effect of nullifying or impairing the recognition, enjoyment or exercise, on an equal footing, of human rights and fundamental freedoms in the political, economic, social, cultural or any other field of public life" [50]. Interpersonal racism occurs when individuals from dominant racial groups, either socially or politically, behave in ways that diminish and harm people who belong to other racial groups [6]. It manifests in many different ways including pejorative name-calling including racial slurs, stereotyping racial or ethnic minorities as less intelligent or worthy, or enacting microaggressions, amongst others [45]. Racist speech and offensive language can perpetuate social division, reinforce systemic inequalities, and undermine community cohesion [18, 39, 46]. Furthermore, studies have consistently shown that being the target of interpersonal racism can affect mental and physical health [41, 54].

Online racism occurs on Internet-based social media or direct messaging platforms and includes disparaging remarks, symbols, images, or behaviours that inflict harm [16]. Like in the "real world", not only does being the target of racism on social media affect mental health [16], research suggests mere exposure to online racism may contribute to a variety of health issues [48].

Social media has become a ubiquitous platform for the global discourse on sports and has significantly impacted the delivery and consumption of sport [22]. It offers an unprecedented space for fans to engage with teams, players, and each other [21, 35]. Unfortunately, this virtual space has also witnessed a troubling surge in the propagation of hate speech and offensive language in sports discourses [20, 27]. The issue of racism and hate crime in soccer, the world's most popular sport, are well-documented [7, 26]. It is therefore unsurprising that this issue has also migrated to the soccer discourse on social media [15, 27, 36].

The debate on Internet freedom in the context of social media moderation centres on two primary and often conflicting values: the right to freedom of expression and the need to protect individuals and groups from harm [9, 28]. With the acquisition of Twitter by Elon Musk and changes in Twitter's moderation policies, now called X, the discussion on the role and responsibilities of social media platforms to moderate content on their platforms has once again come to the fore. Indeed, in January 2023, more than two dozen UN-appointed independent human rights experts called out for leaders of technology companies to "urgently address posts and activities that advocate hatred, and constitute incitement to discrimination, in line with international standards for freedom of expression" [19]. However, even where such platforms had the desire to moderate racist content and offensive language, such moderation is not without challenges not least due to the sheer volume of user-generated data, the nuances of language and context, and the global diversity of cultural norms, and indeed legal frameworks, regarding freedom of speech [23,43]. This is particularly the case in sporting contexts, and particularly soccer, where racist and offensive language are commonplace between fans offline and online.

In the last decade, transformer architectures such as Bidirectional Encoder Representations from Transformers (BERT) [17] and Robustly optimized BERT approach (RoBERTa) [33] have emerged that can be fine-tuned to classify text for specific domains or contexts including hate speech and offensive language [11,37,44,51]. It is well established that soccer should be treated as a unique context possessing its own linguistic idiosyncrasies [12,30]. It is characterised by domain-specific terminology with cultural and regional variations. Furthermore, soccer fans have idiosyncratic ways of interacting, including chants, slogans and specific metaphors and expressions [24,25,30,40]. Brown et al. [13] argue for the centrality of soccer supporters' identity to their lives: "being a supporter is a key part of their 'real' lives: a regular, structuring part of their existence that enables them to feel belonging in the relative disorder of contemporary social formations", attesting to the impact this identity has in shaping their linguistic idiosyncrasies. This is equally true in the context of hate speech and offensive language in online soccer discourse. The field of research into online hate speech and sport has grown significantly in recent years [27] and therefore should be treated as a distinct domain for training language models.

The aim of this paper is to evaluate different Large Language Models (LLMs) for classifying racist content in the Twitter discourse for the UEFA European Football Championships (the Euros). Using an approach similar to Nasir et al. [37], we first construct a dataset for training and testing LLMs performance and then fine-tune four LLMs - a basic version of BERT, a version of BERT pretrained for hate speech classification (BERT Hate Speech), a version of BERT pretrained for twitter classification (BERTweet), and a version of RoBERTa pretrained for offensive speech (RoBERTa Offensive Speech). To understand the relationship between the input data and output classification, we use an Explainable Artificial Intelligence (XAI) technique based on the Integrated Gradient method [47]. Our work contributes to in-domain and cross-domain classification of hate speech and establishes a need for fine-tuning LLMs for context-sensitive hate speech and offensive language detection in soccer discourses on Twitter. We demonstrate how XAI techniques can be used to fine-tune the models and make a labelled dataset for evaluation and benchmarking of LLMs available. Results showed that the RoBERTa Offensive speech achieved the best performance, outperforming other versions of BERT and RoBERTa.

The rest of this paper is organised as follows: Sect. 2 introduces LLM and XAI. Section 3 summarises related works on the detection of hate speech and offensive language on Twitter using machine learning models. Section 4 presents the data and the methodology used to evaluate the LLM models and how we use XAI to explain the models behaviour. The results for the evaluation of LLMs performance and the outcomes from the XAI analysis are presented in Sect. 5. Limitations and avenues for future research are presented in Sect. 6 and Sect. 7 concludes the paper.

2 Background

2.1 Large Language Models

Traditional language models, such as those based on Recurrent Neural Networks (RNNs), process text sequentially, which can limit their ability to effectively capture contextual nuances. In contrast, BERT marks a significant advancement in NLP [17]. Leveraging the power of the Transformer architecture [52], Transformers represent a paradigm shift in sequence modelling. They process input data in parallel using attention mechanisms, enabling efficient capture of long-range dependencies. BERT's utilisation of the Transformer architecture is particularly effective in tasks such as classifying racist content in different contexts on Twitter. Its bidirectional analysis comprehensively understands the context of tweets, considering both preceding and succeeding words simultaneously. BERT employs a two-step pre-training process: (i) masked language modelling (where a random subset of words in a sentence is masked, and the model predicts them), and (ii) next sentence prediction (where the model predicts if a sentence logically follows another). This pre-training equips BERT with a deep understanding of contextualised language representations. Having been pre-trained on large corpora, such as books or Wikipedia articles, BERT is fine-tuned for specific tasks like sentiment analysis, answering questions, or, in this case, classifying racist content on Twitter. Its ability to capture nuanced dependencies in language makes it adept at discerning sentiment and context, especially in dynamic domains like social media and discourses with linguistic idiosyncrasies, such as soccer discourses.

RoBERTa builds on BERT's by introducing several modifications to BERT's architecture and training methodology [33]. RoBERTa removes the Next Sentence Prediction task and trains the model on longer text sequences, thereby enhancing its contextual understanding. It also uses dynamic masking during pre-training, which helps in learning more generalizable representations.

2.2 Explainable Artificial Intelligence

XAI is crucial in understanding the decisions made by models like BERT and RoBERTa. XAI techniques improve user trust, aid in error correction, ensure compliance with regulations, and enhance collaboration between humans and artificial intelligence systems. They are particularly important in tasks like content moderation on social media, where transparency and accountability are essential. Integrated Gradients attribute model predictions to individual input features [47]. This is valuable in understanding which words or phrases are pivotal in a model's decision-making process, such as identifying racist content in discussions about the Euros on Twitter.

Integrated Gradients is a method designed to explain the predictions of machine learning models by attributing feature importance to input variables.

Considering the straight line path from the baseline x' to the input x, the gradients are computed at all points along this path. In particular, integrated gradients refer to the integral of gradients traced along a straight line path from the baseline x' to the input x. Mathematically, let $f(x)$ represent the prediction function of the model, and x denote the input vector. The attribution $IG_i(x)$ for the ith feature is computed as follows:

$$IG_i(x) = (x_i - x_i') \times \int_{\alpha=0}^{1} \frac{\partial f(x' + \alpha \times (x - x'))}{\partial x_i} d\alpha \tag{1}$$

where x' denotes the baseline input, x_i is the value of the ith feature in the input vector x, and x_i' is the corresponding value in the baseline. The integral term represents the accumulated gradients along the straight path from the baseline to the input x.

3   Related Works

Several research papers have been published on the use of machine learning and deep learning to detect hate speech on Twitter. Pitsilis et al. [42] applied multiple LSTM classifiers, combined with user characteristics, to classify hate speech on Twitter. Their approach combined outputs from various LSTM models using different ensemble strategies. The input considered was a combination of tweets and features related to the users' tendency towards hateful behavior, including racist, sexist, or neutral classes. Their results showed that different ensemble strategies yielded varying performance levels, with the highest F1-score for racism detection being 70.84%.

Benítez-Andrades et al. [11] compared five different deep learning models for detecting racist and xenophobic content in Spanish tweets. This included two BERT-based models - Multilingual BERT and BETO [14] - and three other deep learning techniques - Convolutional Neural Network (CNN), LSTM, and a model combining CNN and LSTM. The BETO model outperformed all models evaluated, achieving 84.28% precision, 87.30% recall, and an 85.76% F1-score.

Lee et al. [31] introduced a new architecture, GCR-NN, combining Gated recurrent units (GRU), CNN, and an RNN model to predict the sentiment of racist tweets. They annotated tweets with racist content using TextBlob based on polarity, and then classified them as positive, negative, or neutral. The GCR-NN architecture outperformed other models cited in the literature.

Wang and Islam [53] proposed a CNN model, TextCNN, to classify gender and racial discrimination on Twitter. Their analysis revealed that the most negatively connotated words were related to Muslim, Islam, religion, ISIS, Mohammed, Jew, and other sensitive racial and religious terms. The model achieved an accuracy of 96.9% for gender discrimination and 98.4% for racial discrimination, however the authors considered the sentiment analysis of the tweets in order to detect racism and sexism content.

Finally, Vanetik et al. [51] explored the performance of a variety of models for classifying racism in tweets in the French language. They developed a dataset using tweets collected with a vocabulary of racist speech keywords. The authors compared various models including BERT, Random Forest, Logistic Regression, and Extreme gradient boosting (XGBoost), using different text representation approaches like TF-IDF, N-grams, and BERT embeddings. They found that by combining BERT embeddings with logistic regression yielded the best for monolingual text representation and for cross-lingual and multilingual experiments.

Although all of these works make important contributions to the classification of racism on Twitter, none of them focus on the soccer context specifically. Furthermore, none of them presented XAI tools to help understand the behaviour of the models, i.e., the impact of input data on model prediction.

4   Data and Methods

Figure 1 presents the pipeline used to detect racism and identify impactful words in tweets featuring racist speech.

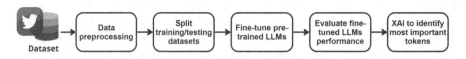

Fig. 1. Racism classification pipeline.

4.1   Dataset

For this study, we collected tweets associated with the Euros. Table 1 presents the hashtags used to define the dataset on Euro 2016 and Euro 2017. To define the tournament dataset for this study, we used hashtags and terms associated with each fixture (e.g., #ITAvIRL, #ITAIRL etc.) official championship hashtags (e.g., #euro2016 and 'euro 2016' etc.) and official Twitter accounts (e.g. @euro2016 etc.), and related variants. For each tournament, we collected tweets from one week before to one week after the tournament. In total, we generated datasets from eight tournaments, four women's tournaments and four men's tournaments from 2008 to 2022. We stored the tweets in a local database, allowing for advanced filtering through SQL queries.

To construct our datasets of hate speech samples, we first developed a dictionary of racist terms. The dictionary was initially populated with terms from the Hatebase project[1], a website created to assist organisations moderate online conversations and detect hate speech. We then expanded it with terms from extant literature on hate speech in soccer. Using this dictionary, we filtered potential racist tweets from our database with SQL queries. However, not all tweets selected necessarily contain racist content. Thus, a manual review by human coders was required. Ultimately, 1,048 racist tweets were identified.

---

[1] https://hatebase.org/.

Table 1. Example of hashtags and terms used to collect the tweets about the Euros 2016 and 2017.

Euro Year	Gender	Hashtags and Terms
2016	Men	#EURO2016 "Euro 2016" #euro16 #euros #euros2016 @euro2016 @uefa @fifa #FRAvROU #FRAROU #ALBvSUI #ALBSUI #WALvSVK #WALSK #ENGvRUS #ENGRUS #TURvCRO #TURCRO #POLvNIR #POLNIR #GERvUKR #GERUKR #ESPvCZE #ESPCZE #IRLvSWE #IRLSWE #BELvITA #BELITA #AUTvHUN #AUTHUN #PvISL #PISL #RUSvSVK #RUSSK #ROUvSUI #ROUSUI #FRAvALB #FRAALB #ENGvWAL #ENGWAL #UKRvNIR #UKRNIR #GERvPOL #GERPOL #ITAvSWE #ITASWE #CZEvCRO #CZECRO #ESPvTUR #ESPTUR #BELvIRL #BELIRL #ISLvHUN #ISLHUN #PvAUT #PAUT #SUIvFRA #SUIFRA #ROUvALB #ROUALB #SVKvENG #SKENG #RUSvWAL #RUSWAL #NIRvGER #NIRGER #UKRvPOL #UKRPOL #CROvESP #CROESP #CZEvTUR #CZETUR #HUNvP #HUNP #ISLvAUT #ISLAUT #ITAvIRL #ITAIRL #SWEvBEL #SWEBEL #SUIvPOL #SUIPOL
2017	Women	#WEURO2017 #euro17 #euros #euros2017 #weuros #WEUROS2017 #weuro @UEFAWomensEuro @uefa @fifa #NEDvN #NEDN #DENvBEL #DENBEL #GERvSWE #GERSWE #ITAvRUS #ITARUS #ESPvP #ESPP #ENGvSCO #ENGSCO #AUTvSUI #AUTSUI #FRAvISL #FRAISL #NvBEL #NBEL #NEDvDEN #NEDDEN #SWEvRUS #SWERUS #GERvITA #GERITA #SCOvP #SCOP #ENGvESP #ENGESP #SUIvFRA #SUIFRA #BELvNED #BELNED #NvDEN #NDEN #SWEvGER #SWEGER #RUSvITA #RUSITA #PvENG #PENG #SCOvESP #SCOESP #FRAvAUT #FRAAUT #ISLvSUI #ISLSUI #BELvN #BELN #NEDvDEN #NEDDEN #GERvDEN #GERDEN #SWEvNED #SWENED #ENGvFRA #ENGFRA #NEDvENG #NEDENG #DENvAUT #DENAUT #NEDvDEN #NEDDEN

In addition to racist tweets, we needed a sample of non-racist tweets to fine-tune our models to distinguish between racist and non-racist content. We selected these tweets using queries that excluded terms from our racism dictionary. Human coders also reviewed these tweets to ensure that they were not related to racism but rather to the soccer context. An equal number of racist and non-racist tweets were included to create a balanced dataset. Therefore, our final dataset is composed of 2,096 tweets (1,048 racist tweets and 1,048 non-racist tweets).

Some language models in our study can handle raw text, but we decided to apply text preprocessing techniques to increase text comprehension by removing useless parts of the text or noise [29]. Therefore, after data collection, we apply preprocessing which consists of converting the text to lowercase and removing stop words, user mentions, URLs, and emojis. The dataset was split into 80% for training and 20% for model evaluation.

4.2   Large Language Models

After preparing the training and testing datasets, we selected various pre-trained LLMs for fine-tuning, a process proven effective for achieving state-of-the-art performance in downstream tasks [32].

All LLMs we considered in this work are available on the hugging face platform[2]. The first model is the traditional BERT model [17]. We used the uncased

---

[2] https://huggingface.co/docs/hub/index.

version of this model[3], since we converted all text to lower case during the pre-processing phase.

Given our focus on racism, a type of hate speech, we also included BERT Hate Speech, a model fine-tuned on diverse hate speech categories using 16 datasets [3]. We selected the version trained in English language data. We also considered a widely-used variation of the RoBERTa model, BERTweet[4], optimized for the unique characteristics of tweets, including short length, informal grammar, and irregular vocabulary [38]. This model was trained on large datasets of English tweets, including a dataset related to COVID-19. Special tokens were used for user mentions and URLs. Finally, we used RoBERTa Offensive, an LLM trained for various text-related tasks including offensive and hate speech detection [10].

4.3   Explainable AI

Following the fine-tuning of LLMs, we applied XAI techniques, specifically Integrated Gradients, to elucidate the relationship between input data and output classification [47]. This method assigns a score to each word in the input text, indicating its impact on the model's classification. We applied Integrated Gradients to each tweet individually to understand the impact of each word on the model classification. Additionally, we used it to identify words more directly related to racism in a soccer context. By running the model on a dataset of tweets and calculating word scores, we identified and ranked words based on their frequency and impact on the model's classification.

It's important to note that due to BERT's wordpiece tokenization [55], some words are divided into sub-word units. Integrated Gradients assigns scores to each sub-word unit, so we averaged these scores to obtain a composite score for words split into multiple units.

5   Results

Table 2 presents benchmark results for the LLM models evaluated in this study. The BERT Hate Speech model showed the lowest performance, with all metrics falling below 90%. Its recall of 80.21% indicates a significant limitation in accurately identifying racist tweets. Consequently, its F1-score, at only 87.25% is also lower compared to other models.

The basic BERT model outperformed the model specifically trained to identify hate speech. This could be due to its training on diverse datasets and multilingual models, which may have exposed it to a broader range of hate speech vocabulary than that found in our specific soccer context. The basic BERT model achieved an accuracy of 94.75% and a recall of 92.19%, marking improvements of 7.27% and 14.92%, respectively, over the BERT Hate Speech model. The substantial improvement in recall directly contributed to a 7.91% increase in the F1-score.

---

[3] https://huggingface.co/bert-base-uncased.
[4] https://huggingface.co/vinai/bertweet-base.

Table 2. Comparison of Large Language Models.

Model	Accuracy	Precision	Recall	F1-score
BERT	94.75	96.20	92.19	94.15
BERT Hate Speech	89.26	95.65	80.21	87.25
BERTweet	95.47	96.76	93.23	94.96
RoBERTa Offensive Speech	**96.18**	**97.31**	**94.27**	**95.77**

The RoBERTa models surpassed both BERT models in our racism classification task. BERTweet demonstrated an accuracy of 95.47%, a precision of 96.76%, and a recall of 93.23%. Its relatively high and similar precision and recall led to a robust F1-score of 94.96%.

The RoBERTa Offensive Speech exhibited the highest performance among the evaluated models. It achieved an accuracy of 96.18%, which is 6.92% higher than that of the lowest-performing model (BERT Hate Speech). Its precision and recall were also superior, with the recall being 14.06% higher than the lowest observed. This resulted in the highest F1-score of 95.77%. The RoBERTa Offensive Speech model's training on a dataset of offensive tweets [56] likely contributed to its proficiency in recognising vocabulary relevant to soccer-related tweets.

Considering the tweets classified as racist by all models, most were indeed racist, as indicated by the high precision metrics. However, only the BERT, BERTweet, and RoBERTa Offensive Speech models were effective in correctly identifying racist content, as reflected in their high recall values. These results are echoed in the F1-score, which is the harmonic mean of precision and recall. Models with a high F1-score, such as the RoBERTa Offensive Speech (95.77%), can effectively minimise both false positives and false negatives in classifying racist content in tweets.

Figure 2 illustrates the embeddings for the last hidden layer considering the RoBERTa Offensive Speech before and after fine-tuning with the data presented in this paper, since it was the model the presented best results. Each point of the embedding is a vector with dimension 768, so we use the t-SNE technique to reduce the high dimensionality of the vectors to two dimensions [34]. The green dots are the racist tweets and the red crosses are the non-racist tweets. Figure 2a shows the embeddings before the fine-tuning, i.e., the embeddings with the knowledge of the RoBERTa model that was trained only to detect offensive speech. It is possible to note two different groups of tweets, since the model was trained to detect offensive speech and racist tweets tend to be offensive, showing that the model already has a good performance to represent racist and non-racist tweets. However, there is a large overlap between racist and non-racist tweets, meaning the model is not able to clearly differentiate between the two types of tweets, making classification difficult.

After fine-tuning (Fig. 2b), there is a clear difference between the two categories of tweets, showing that there are two groups of tweets. Although it is possible to see the difference between the racist and no-racist tweets, there are few racist tweets inside the non-racist tweet cluster, which compromised the performance of the model, resulting in the performance presented in Table 2.

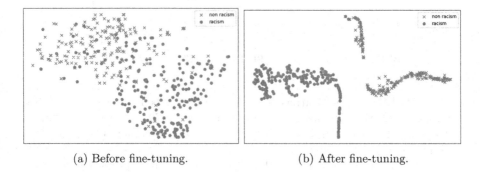

(a) Before fine-tuning.   (b) After fine-tuning.

Fig. 2. Embeddings calculated using the RoBERTa Offensive Speech. (Color figure online)

Figures 3 and 4 summarise Integrated Gradient results for racist and non-racist tweets, respectively. It is important to note that the words shown on the horizontal axis underwent preprocessing, explaining the absence of some original tweet words.

The non-racist tweet "*Im in tears right now, we are in the final #EURO2020 #ENGDEN #ENG*" highlights *final* and *#ENG* as impactful words, directly relating to the soccer context. Conversely, the word *tears* is the word that had a minor negative impact on the model's prediction. The racist tweet "*If it weren't for the "niggers" England wouldn't of got out of group stages. You lot are shite, be grateful #eng #Euro2020Final #euro2020*", shows *niggers* as having the most significant impact, a clear racist slur. Also, the word *shite* also positively influenced the prediction, likely due to the training of the RoBERTa Offensive Speech model on offensive language. Interestingly, the word "grateful" negatively affected racism prediction, as it's not typically linked to racist contexts.

Table 3 shows the more frequent words with a high impact on the model prediction of tweets that were classified as racist. Words that are usually used to discriminate black people appear as the most frequent words (e.g. *black, monkey, niggers*, and *negro*). Two terms related to England (*English* and *England*), and the justification is that England played the final of Euro 2020 and three black players missed the penalties, which resulted in the defeat of the English team, resulting in racist reactions against them on Twitter [8].

The term *French* is also notable, likely conflating the target of the racism and is potentially linked to racism against Kylian Mbappé after he missed a crucial penalty against Switzerland, leading to France's elimination in the round of 16. Similarly, *Muslims* is identified as a significant word in the context of racism, reflecting biases and discrimination in the dataset's specific context. Historically speaking, anti-Muslim speech is not a new phenomenon [2], and it is not surprising that words related to it in datasets about racism and hate speech.

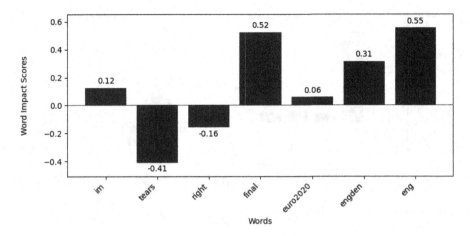

Fig. 3. Impact of words for the sentence: I'm in tears right now, we are in the final #EURO2020 #ENGDEN #ENG.

Table 3. Words that have high impact on the tweets that were classified as racist.

Word	Frequency
black	56
monkey	53
niggers	35
fucking	18
English	10
people	7
French	6
negro	6
England	6
Muslims	6

6 Limitations and Avenues for Future Research

In this study, we focused on four models based on BERT. Although these models have been applied successfully in different text classification tasks, including hate speech classification on Twitter, new LLMs have emerged in recent years. Meta's LLaMA, OpenAI's GPT LLMs, and PaLM 2, amongst others were proposed and are able to interpret natural language instructions and producing responses across a vast array of subjects. The last model released by OpenAI, GPT-4 [1], exhibits human-level performance on different benchmarks. Llama 2 [49] is a family of pretrained and fine-tuned open source LLMs proposed by Meta that outperformed others LLMs in the literature. PaLM 2 [5] is the model proposed by Google that was designed to deal with different languages and domains. LLMs

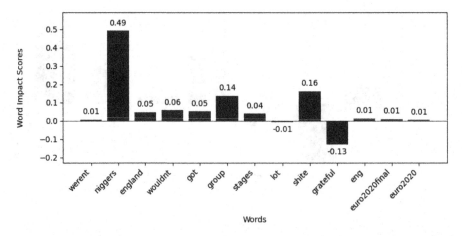

Fig. 4. Impact of words for the sentence: If it weren't for the "niggers" England wouldn't of got out of group stages. You lot are shite, be grateful #eng #Euro2020Final #euro2020.

are trained on a vast amount of public data, including tweets, which enables them to develop a deep understanding of the nuances of language, including those that may convey racist sentiments.

As well as evaluating other LLMs for racism detection, there is a significant opportunity for research on hybrid and ensemble models that combine various architectures like CNN, LSTM, BERT, and RoBERTa. These combined models may be more adept at capturing the subtle nuances of hate speech across different contexts and languages, thereby enhancing detection accuracy. The usage of these models can be also combined with different preprocessing techniques, from keep more information in the text (e.g. emojis) to try to change the text representation (e.g. stemming) [4]. This is critical given the negative consequences of labelling an individual incorrectly as a racist. Furthermore, it is vital to address potential biases in AI models and to uphold ethical standards in the detection and classification of hate speech. Future research must focus on developing fair and unbiased models that respect ethical guidelines and considerations.

We focus on one type of hate speech - racism. Future research should broaden its scope to encompass various forms of hate speech such as homophobic speech, ableist language, xenophobia, and religious-based hate speech, amongst others. Each of these areas presents unique linguistic characteristics and challenges, necessitating specialised attention in the development and training of models. Classifiers that distinguish between hate speech that meet the legal threshold for criminal or civil action as opposed to merely offensive language be of significant value for law enforcement, online platforms, and researchers. Furthermore, investigating both paradigmatic (stereotypical), non-paradigmatic (non-stereotypical), and appropriated slurs is another important research direction. Future studies should aim to classify these slurs effectively while also determining the targets and perpetrators of hate speech. This approach will provide a more detailed understanding of the dynamics and patterns of online hate speech and wider online abuse.

Given that our study was primarily focused on a dataset based on one international soccer championship limited to the European continent, it is crucial to recognise that these findings might have limited applicability in other different although related contexts, such as domestic league and cup competitions, championships on other continents e.g. AFCON and the World Cup, as well as different genders. Future studies should consider fine-tuning their models to these specific scenarios to ensure both relevance and accuracy. Moreover, our study was limited to the English language and one time period, extending research to include multi-lingual datasets is essential, considering that hate speech is a pervasive issue transcending language barriers. This expansion will allow for a more comprehensive and inclusive approach to understanding and combating hate speech globally. Longitudinal research across multiple tournaments may allow for new insights on the evolution of hate speech/offensive language in a soccer context and the effectiveness of platform moderation over time.

The creation of effective tools for monitoring social media and strategies for intervention is imperative. This includes developing systems capable of real-time detection and response to mitigate the proliferation of hate speech, especially during major sporting events, but also includes deriving insights on the evolution of hate speech, triggers, perpetrators, targets, and effective responses.

As social media's role in shaping global sports discourse continues to grow, addressing the rise in hate speech and offensive language becomes increasingly urgent. This study's insights emphasise the potential of LLMs in detecting and analysing such speech in the context of soccer. Moving forward, the challenge lies in expanding research to cover a wider array of hate speech types, employing more sophisticated AI models, and adapting these models to various contexts and languages. Through these endeavours, we can better understand and confront the escalating issue of hate speech in online sports conversations.

7   Conclusions

This study delved into the critical issue of hate speech and offensive language on social media, with a particular focus on the discourse surrounding soccer. By employing LLMs to detect instances of racism on Twitter, specifically related to discussions about the Euros, we were able to gain significant insights. Among the four pre-trained models that we evaluated, the RoBERTa model, which is tailored for detecting offensive speech, emerged as the most effective. Analysis using the Integrated Gradients algorithm highlighted that derogatory terms targeting black individuals and references to French and English nationalities had the most significant impact on the models' ability to identify racist tweets, reflecting the real-world incidents of racism that occurred during the Euro Cup 2020.

Acknowledgment. This work was supported by funding from the UK Arts and Humanities Research Council and the Irish Research Council (grant number AH/W001624/1), and the Federation Internationale de l'Automobile.

References

1. Achiam, J., et al.: GPT-4 technical report. arXiv preprint arXiv:2303.08774 (2023)
2. Acim, R.: Islamophobia, racism and the vilification of the Muslim Diaspora. Islamophobia Stud. J. **5**(1), 26–44 (2019)
3. Aluru, S.S., Mathew, B., Saha, P., Mukherjee, A.: Deep learning models for multilingual hate speech detection. arXiv preprint arXiv:2004.06465 (2020)
4. Anandarajan, M., Hill, C., Nolan, T.: Text preprocessing. In: Anandarajan, M., Hill, C., Nolan, T. (eds.) Practical Text Analytics: Maximizing the Value of Text Data. AADS, vol. 2, pp. 45–59. Springer, Cham (2019). https://doi.org/10.1007/978-3-319-95663-3_4
5. Anil, R., et al.: Palm 2 technical report. arXiv preprint arXiv:2305.10403 (2023)
6. American Psychological Association, et al.: APA resolution on harnessing psychology to combat racism: adopting a uniform definition and understanding (2021)
7. Back, L., Crabbe, T., Solomos, J.: The changing face of football: racism, identity and multiculture in the English game. Berg (2001)
8. Back, L., Mills, K.: 'when you score you're English, when you miss you're Black': Euro 2020 and the racial politics of a penalty shoot-out. Soundings **79**(79), 110–121 (2021)
9. Balkin, J.M.: Free speech is a triangle. Colum. L. Rev. **118**, 2011 (2018)
10. Barbieri, F., Camacho-Collados, J., Neves, L., Espinosa-Anke, L.T.: Unified benchmark and comparative evaluation for tweet classification. arXiv preprint arXiv:2020.12421 (2020)
11. Benítez-Andrades, J.A., González-Jiménez, Á., López-Brea, Á., Aveleira-Mata, J., Alija-Pérez, J.M., García-Ordás, M.T.: Detecting racism and xenophobia using deep learning models on twitter data: CNN, LSTM and BERT. PeerJ Comput. Sci. **8**, e906 (2022)
12. Billings, A.C.: Defining Sport Communication. Taylor & Francis (2016)
13. Brown, A., Crabbe, T., Mellor, G.: Introduction: football and community–practical and theoretical considerations. In: Football and Community in the Global Context, pp. 1–10. Routledge (2013)
14. Cañete, J., Chaperon, G., Fuentes, R., Ho, J.H., Kang, H., Pérez, J.: Spanish pre-trained BERT model and evaluation data. arXiv preprint arXiv:2308.02976 (2023)
15. Cullen, A., Williams, M.: Online hate speech targeting the England and Wales men's football teams during the 2022 FIFA World Cup (2023)
16. Del Toro, J., Wang, M.T.: Online racism and mental health among black American adolescents in 2020. J. Am. Acad. Child Adolesc. Psychiatry **62**(1), 25–36 (2023)
17. Devlin, J., Chang, M.W., Lee, K., Toutanova, K.: BERT: pre-training of deep bidirectional transformers for language understanding. arXiv preprint arXiv:1810.04805 (2018)
18. Dovidio, J.F., Gaertner, S.L.: On the nature of contemporary prejudice: the causes, consequences, and challenges of aversive racism (1998)
19. UN Experts: Freedom of speech is not freedom to spread racial hatred on social media. United Nations (2023)
20. Farrington, N., Hall, L., Kilvington, D., Price, J., Saeed, A.: Sport, Racism and Social Media. Routledge (2017)
21. Fenton, A., Keegan, B.J., Parry, K.D.: Understanding sporting social media brand communities, place and social capital: a netnography of football fans. Commun. Sport **11**(2), 313–333 (2023)

22. Filo, K., Lock, D., Karg, A.: Sport and social media research: a review. Sport Manag. Rev. **18**(2), 166–181 (2015)
23. Gillespie, T.: Custodians of the Internet: Platforms, Content Moderation, and the Hidden Decisions that Shape Social Media. Yale University Press (2018)
24. Glynn, E., Brown, D.H.: Discrimination on football Twitter: the role of humour in the Othering of minorities. Sport Soc. **26**(8), 1432–1454 (2023)
25. Hoffmann, T.: Cognitive sociolinguistic aspects of football chants: the role of social and physical context in usage-based construction grammar. Z. Angl. Am. **63**(3), 273–294 (2015)
26. Kassimeris, C., Lawrence, S., Pipini, M.: Racism in football. Soccer Soc. **23**(8), 824–833 (2022)
27. Kearns, C., et al.: A scoping review of research on online hate and sport. Commun. Sport **11**(2), 402–430 (2023)
28. Klonick, K.: The new governors: the people, rules, and processes governing online speech. Harv. L. Rev. **131**, 1598 (2017)
29. Kurniasih, A., Manik, L.P.: On the role of text preprocessing in BERT embedding-based DNNs for classifying informal texts. Neuron **1024**(512), 927–34 (2022)
30. Lavric, E., Pisek, G., Skinner, A., Stadler, W.: The Linguistics of Football, vol. 38. Narr Francke Attempto Verlag (2008)
31. Lee, E., Rustam, F., Washington, P.B., El Barakaz, F., Aljedaani, W., Ashraf, I.: Racism detection by analyzing differential opinions through sentiment analysis of tweets using stacked ensemble GCR-NN model. IEEE Access **10**, 9717–9728 (2022)
32. Lee, J.S., Hsiang, J.: Patent classification by fine-tuning BERT language model. World Patent Inf. **61**, 101965 (2020)
33. Liu, Y., et al.: RoBERTa: a robustly optimized BERT pretraining approach. arXiv preprint arXiv:1907.11692 (2019)
34. Van der Maaten, L., Hinton, G.: Visualizing data using t-SNE. J. Mach. Learn. Res. **9**(11), 2579–2605 (2008)
35. McDonald, H., Biscaia, R., Yoshida, M., Conduit, J., Doyle, J.P.: Customer engagement in sport: an updated review and research agenda. J. Sport Manag. **36**(3), 289–304 (2022)
36. Miranda, S., Gouveia, C., Di Fátima, B., Antunes, A.C.: Hate speech on social media: behaviour of Portuguese football fans on Facebook. Soccer Soc. **25**(1), 79–91 (2023)
37. Nasir, A., Sharma, A., Jaidka, K.: LLMs and finetuning: benchmarking cross-domain performance for hate speech detection. arXiv preprint arXiv:2310.18964 (2023)
38. Nguyen, D.Q., Vu, T., Nguyen, A.T.: BERTweet: a pre-trained language model for English tweets. arXiv preprint arXiv:2005.10200 (2020)
39. Pager, D., Shepherd, H.: The sociology of discrimination: racial discrimination in employment, housing, credit, and consumer markets. Annu. Rev. Sociol. **34**, 181–209 (2008)
40. Papadima, A., Photiadis, T.: Communication in social media: football clubs, language, and ideology. J. Mod. Greek Stud. **37**(1), 127–147 (2019)
41. Paradies, Y., et al.: Racism as a determinant of health: a systematic review and meta-analysis. PLoS ONE **10**(9), e0138511 (2015)
42. Pitsilis, G.K., Ramampiaro, H., Langseth, H.: Effective hate-speech detection in Twitter data using recurrent neural networks. Appl. Intell. **48**, 4730–4742 (2018)
43. Roberts, S.T.: Behind the Screen. Yale University Press (2019)
44. Sarkar, D., Zampieri, M., Ranasinghe, T., Ororbia, A.: fBERT: a neural transformer for identifying offensive content. arXiv preprint arXiv:2109.05074 (2021)

45. Staff, A.: Race and ethnicity guidelines in psychology: promoting responsiveness and equity12
46. Sue, D.W., et al.: Racial microaggressions in everyday life: implications for clinical practice. Am. Psychol. **62**(4), 271 (2007)
47. Sundararajan, M., Taly, A., Yan, Q.: Axiomatic attribution for deep networks. In: International Conference on Machine Learning, pp. 3319–3328. PMLR (2017)
48. Tao, X., Fisher, C.B.: Exposure to social media racial discrimination and mental health among adolescents of color. J. Youth Adolesc. **51**(1), 30–44 (2022)
49. Touvron, H., et al.: Llama 2: open foundation and fine-tuned chat models. arXiv preprint arXiv:2307.09288 (2023)
50. NATIONS UNIES: International convention on the elimination of all forms of racial discrimination. UN General Assembly (UNGA) (2006)
51. Vanetik, N., Mimoun, E.: Detection of racist language in French tweets. Information **13**(7), 318 (2022)
52. Vaswani, A., et al.: Attention is all you need. In: Advances in Neural Information Processing Systems, vol. 30 (2017)
53. Wang, L., Islam, T.: Automatic detection of cyberbullying: racism and sexism on Twitter. In: Jahankhani, H. (ed.) Cybersecurity in the Age of Smart Societies. ASTSA, pp. 105–122. Springer, Cham (2023). https://doi.org/10.1007/978-3-031-20160-8_7
54. Williams, D.R., Mohammed, S.A.: Discrimination and racial disparities in health: evidence and needed research. J. Behav. Med. **32**, 20–47 (2009)
55. Wu, Y., et al.: Google's neural machine translation system: bridging the gap between human and machine translation. arXiv preprint arXiv:1609.08144 (2016)
56. Zampieri, M., Malmasi, S., Nakov, P., Rosenthal, S., Farra, N., Kumar, R.: Predicting the type and target of offensive posts in social media. arXiv preprint arXiv:1902.09666 (2019)

Infonomics of Autonomous Digital Twins

Istvan David[1]($\boxtimes$) and Dominik Bork[2]

[1] McMaster University, Hamilton, Canada
istvan.david@mcmaster.ca
[2] TU Wien, Business Informatics Group, Vienna, Austria
dominik.bork@tuwien.ac.at

Abstract. High autonomy is challenging to achieve in digital twins. This is due to the lack of understanding of the socio-technical challenges and the information needs of digital twin autonomy. In this paper, we contextualize digital twin autonomy in terms of human and technical factors, identify novel socio-technical classes of digital twins with varying levels of autonomy, and define strategies that help improve autonomy across these classes. Our strategies are governed by information valuation models we developed specifically for digital twins. Our approach fosters a systematic top-down technique to improve the autonomy of digital twins.

Keywords: autonomy · digital transformation · information value

1 Introduction

Digital twins [20] are virtual representations of physical assets. By continuously collecting data from the physical asset, digital twins maintain a live model of the physical system, allowing for advanced computer-aided services, such as monitoring, predictive analytics, and automated decision-making [29]. Digital twins are also equipped with control capabilities over the physical system, further expanding the impact of having explicit, continuously maintained models of the system that allow for enhanced reasoning capabilities as to how to control the physical system for optimal behavior. Thanks to its beneficial properties that enable higher digital maturity, digital twinning is gaining popularity in an array of domains, especially in those where the system can be managed through closed-loop control. Pertinent examples include manufacturing systems [32], smart farming systems [19], and complex manufacturing processes, such as injection molding [4].

Autonomy is the ability to make a decision about the preferred course of action to control the underlying system in an optimal fashion [38]. Autonomy allows digital twins to respond to unexpected events, which is an important trait in controlling complex systems. Experience shows that achieving full autonomy of digital twins is often a challenging problem [18] and in some cases, it might not be feasible at all [12]. The lack of trust, understandability, and explainability can severely limit how much liberty organizations are willing to give to a digital twin [6]. In lower-digitalized sectors, autonomy is additionally influenced

G. Guizzardi et al. (Eds.): CAiSE 2024, LNCS 14663, pp. 563–578, 2024.
https://doi.org/10.1007/978-3-031-61057-8_33

by the sheer ability to deploy and maintain complex sensor networks, and manage voluminous data. Of course, full autonomy is not always desired. In many cases, human agency is required to become part of the system and the challenge is to understand how human factors align with autonomy ambitions [18]. Still, autonomy aspects should be planned early in the lifecycle of systems [6].

Providing systems with information of sufficient quality and volume is key in enabling autonomy [30]. Yet, it is currently not well-understood which classes of information contribute value to the autonomy of digital twins.

This work is the first to investigate digital twin autonomy from an information valuation perspective. We rely on *infonomics*, the discipline of asserting economic value to information [21]. Our contributions are as follows.

- We define a framework to classify levels of digital twin autonomy as the combination of the *ability* and the *liberty* to act. We identify two novel digital twin categories—*human-actuated* and *human-supervised digital twins*—to shed light on a more socio-technical view of digital twins. (Section 3)
- We define three information valuation models using well-established metrics to apply the principles of infonomics to digital twin autonomy. (Section 4)
- We define five digital twin autonomy strategies based on the information valuation models to guide organizations along their maturation journey and reach higher levels of digital twin autonomy. (Section 5)

Our work is motivated by the lessons learned from an industry project on digital twin engineering for cyber-biophysical systems [12]. We draw from this project and demonstrate the utility of our approach in Sect. 6.

The target audience of our work includes adopters, developers, and researchers of digital twins. Adopters can use the reference framework in Sect. 3 to position the status quo at their organization and subsequently, employ the strategies in Sect. 5. Developers can use the information valuation models in Sect. 4 to trace high-level autonomy ambitions to tangible concerns of data quality. Researchers can use this work to drive their research towards impactful directions.

2   Background

Digital twins are strongly coupled to their physical counterparts with the intent of controlling them for optimal behavior. For example, digital twins can be used for better control over sustainability goals [11], e.g., reduced energy consumption, reduced waste, and improved productivity. The digital twin's ability for real-time analysis, optimization, and control allows for deferring some design decisions to the operational phase and controlling the underlying asset based on data available only at operation. Most systems subject to digital twinning require real-time reasoning and control, which, in turn, necessitate elevated levels of autonomy. Rosen et al. [30] note that to achieve sufficient autonomy, digital twins require *"as much information as possible concerning the overall world state, the products to be manufactured, the geometry and affordances of the parts and tools to be used, as well as their own capabilities and configuration"*. Indeed, information is a key enabler of autonomy, yet, it is currently not well-understood which classes of information contribute value to the autonomy of digital twins. This paper aims to overcome this limitation of the state of the art.

ISO 23247 is a standard that provides general principles for developing digital twins in manufacturing.[1] Its second part, the ISO 23247-2:2021 defines a reference architecture with three functional and one extra-functional entity. Later in this work, specifically in Sect. 4, we relate digital twin information value models to the three functional entities. The *User Entity* provides user interfaces to interact with the digital twin. Here, the user may be a human or another application, e.g., simulators, analysis tools, or other digital twins. The *Core Entity* is comprised of sub-entities and functional entities that implement functionality for digitally representing and assessing components of the physical twin. Finally, the *Data Collection and Device Control Entity* contains functional entities for collecting data from the physical twin and for controlling and actuating it.

The reader is referred to Shao [32] for more details and use cases.

Infonomics is the discipline of asserting economic value to information, first defined by Laney [21]. Assessing the economic value of information helps organizations treat information as a financial asset. In our work, we rely on the **data quality metrics** of infonomics (see Table 1). Below, we give a brief excerpt of these metrics. The reader is referred to Laney [21, pp. 246–249] for details.

The first group of Laney's data quality metrics are *objective* metrics. *Validity* measures how well available data accurately represents reality. *Completeness* is the percentage of data recorded out of the total available data. *Integrity* measures the correctness of linkages between records. *Consistency* tells how much data formats vary. *Uniqueness* is the ratio of alternate forms of data that exist. *Precision* is the degree of exactitude of a value. (While a value may be completely accurate, its applicability may be suboptimal because of its lack of precision.) *Timeliness* is the likelihood that data is faithful to reality at any given time.

The second group defines *subjective* metrics. *Existence* measures if key ideas are represented in information assets. *Scarcity* is the likelihood that other organizations do not have the same data. *Relevance* is the number of business processes that could benefit from the data. *Usability* is the degree to which data is helpful in business functions. *Interpretability* is the degree to which data can be understood. *Believability* is the degree to which stakeholders trust data. *Objectivity* is the degree to which the data source is believed to be free of biases.

3 A Classification Framework of Digital Twin Autonomy

We now define a classification framework to relate different levels of digital twin autonomy. We argue that autonomy is not unidimensional, but rather, an artifact of orthogonal technical and human aspects. As shown in Fig. 1, in this frame of thinking, technical aspects determine the digital twin's *ability* to act. This includes, e.g., proper equipment, actuators, algorithms, and communication

---

[1] https://www.iso.org/standard/75066.html.

networks to be in place to control the physical twin. Human aspects determine the digital twin's *liberty* to act. This includes, e.g., the trust stakeholders have in the digital twin, which can be fostered, e.g., through explainability [9] and experimentability [5]. These dimensions give rise to classes of digital twins with different autonomy characteristics.

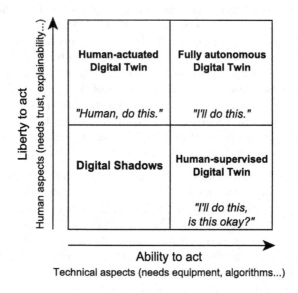

Fig. 1. Classification framework of digital twin autonomy.

3.1 Levels of Digital Twin Autonomy

Digital Shadow: No Ability and No Liberty. Digital shadows, as defined by Kritzinger et al. [20], are virtual replicas of physical systems that capture the prevalent state of the system but have no means to control the physical system. That is, a change in the state of the physical system will be reflected in the digital replica, but not the other way around. The limitation in control is clear in most works focusing on digital shadows, although the reasons are less obvious. In our classification framework, the reason for this limitation is twofold. First, digital shadows have no ability to act. That is, means of control, such as actuators and software might not be available. Second, digital shadows have no liberty to act either. This limitation might be by design when stakeholders do not require more elaborate functionality to support their goals. Often, digital shadows are seen as precursors of digital twins [3], with reduced functionality that is to be developed later as the system and the digital maturity of the organization evolves. Despite the limited autonomy, digital shadows are considered key enablers of important digitalization trends, such as Industry 4.0 [7].

Fully Autonomous Digital Twin: Ability and Liberty. At the other end of the autonomy spectrum, fully autonomous digital twins both possess the ability to control the twinned physical system (physical twin) and enjoy substantial liberty to do so. The ability to control the physical twin is due to the proper technical enablers in place both on the digital side (e.g., real-time simulators [14]) and on the physical side (e.g., actuation infrastructure for control). Fully autonomous digital twins had a transformational impact in many domains including production control [30], maintenance [10], and layout planning [34].

Human-Supervised Digital Twin: Ability but No Liberty. A distinct autonomy class of digital twins emerges when the technical underpinnings of the digital twins would enable it to act, however, the digital twin lacks the liberty to do so. This is one of the autonomy classes of digital twins exhibiting substantial interplay between human and machine, rendering it a true socio-technical system [15]. Removing the human from the loop to achieve full autonomy might not be possible for a number of human aspects. For example, an organization might decide, that human intelligence is vital in a given setting because business goals might be cumbersome to elicit and encode in the digital twin. Another example might be the lack of trust in the digital twin which is a typical scenario in lower-digitalized domains where stakeholders are less tech-savvy.

Levels of human supervision vary across domains, with reference frameworks being tied to specific sectors. In autonomous driving, for example, the SAE J3016 standard defines six levels of autonomy from no autonomy (Level 0)—e.g., providing warnings and momentary assistance, such as automatic emergency braking—to full autonomy (Level 5)—driving the vehicle without a driver [16]. Human supervision, oversight, or other forms of participation are particularly important when humans or societies are part of the twinned physical system. Caldarelli et al. [8] warn that digital twins designed or operated without proper explanation or human oversight might negatively affect citizenry, but designed human participation fosters adaptive and sustainable solutions.

Human-Actuated Digital Twin: Liberty but No Ability. Human-actuated digital twins emerge when stakeholders around the digital twin intend to allow high liberty however, the digital twin is not equipped with the ability to control the physical twin. In human-actuated digital twins, the digital twin makes decisions and the human staff executes them. Clearly, real-time actuation is not possible in these cases due to the delay and imprecision associated with this control mode. However, human-actuated digital twins can still be sufficient solutions. The first notion of human-actuated digital twins appears in previous work [12] in the context of smart agronomy, where the underlying system changes at a substantially slower rate than traditional engineered systems. Thus, slow actuation might be sufficient. Additionally, placing the human in the loop allows for recognizing potentially undesirable control decisions, often without the need to involve an expert. Another pertinent example is due to Wang et al. [36] who propose the notion of human digital twins. Human digital twins include *"physical representations and virtual models of humans to accurately track and reflect* *the human motion, perception, and manipulation activities and capabilities and to address the challenges in the human-centric manufacturing".*

3.2   What to Do with Levels of Autonomy?

The desired level of autonomy of a digital twin depends on the problem at hand and is heavily influenced by the digital maturity of the adopting organization.

Achieving full autonomy might not be the goal of every organization. Increasingly often, experts are calling for tighter integration of digital twins with human agencies, arguing that high levels of digital twin autonomy should be achieved without sacrificing human agency [18]. Indeed, digital twins are not meant to be solely technical implementations. In our work, we maintain the view that digital twins are typically socio-technical systems with the human in the loop.

In their interviews with experts, Muctadir et al. [25] encounter multiple opinions about humans playing an important role in a digital twin and therefore, they should be considered as components of digital twins. In this work, we maintain the view that there are classes of digital twins that should be viewed as socio-technical systems with substantial human effort in the loop and that autonomy and human involvement span a spectrum that organizations should consider when choosing their digital twinning journeys. Embracing the human in the loop aligns well with the core ideas of the new wave of industry practices, such as Industry 5.0[2], which attempt to bring the human back in the loop.

Independently from the targeted level, autonomy must be addressed in a systematic way. To this end, organizations need guidelines to improving the autonomy of their digital twins. To support such maturation journeys, Sect. 4 defines high-level information valuation models that improve digital twin autonomy while Sect. 5 defines five elementary digital twin autonomy strategies.

4   Information Valuation Models for Digital Twins

We now define three information valuation models for digital twins based on the data quality metrics of Laney [21] discussed in Sect. 2. We opt for defining new valuation models because the information valuation models of Laney's infonomics are either too general or too finance-focused to drive autonomy decisions about digital twins. However, as pointed out by Bendechache et al. [2] in their recent systematic survey of data valuation, Laney's metrics are still adequate and provide the most comprehensive, multi-dimensional view of data quality. Thus, we rely on published metrics, but use them in our new information valuation models. For completeness, we also consider the model quality metrics of Mohagheghi et al. [24], aligned with Laney's metrics. Our models are related to the three key entities outlined in the ISO 23247-2:2021 reference architecture and explained in Sect. 2: reasoning, control, and the user entity.

---

[2] https://research-and-innovation.ec.europa.eu/research-area/industrial-research-
   and-innovation/industry-50_en.

Table 1. Metrics of data and model quality, and their influence on the three information valuation metrics for digital twin autonomy.

	Data quality metrics (Laney [21])	Model quality metrics (Mohagheghi [24])	DT valuation model RVI	AVI	UVI
Objective	Validity		●		
	Completeness	C2-Completeness	●		
	Integrity	C3-Consistency	●		
	Consistency	C3-Consistency	●		
	Uniqueness		●		
	Precision			●	
	Timeliness			●	
Subjective	Existence	C1-Correctness			●
	Scarcity			●	
	Relevance				●
	Usability				●
	Interpretability	C4-Comprehensibility			●
	Believability				●
	Objectivity			●	
		C5-Confinement			●
		C6-Changeability	●		

A shortcoming of Laney's information models is that about half of them rely on subjective judgment and therefore, their actionability is questionable. This limitation renders them unsuitable for scalable, automated decision-making [2]. Therefore, we refrain from exactly defined formulas and instead, we define which metrics influence our models. This information is still sufficient to understanding how the improvement of metrics can drive digital twin autonomy.

For completeness, we also draw from the modeling domain and correlate the model quality metrics of Mohagheghi et al. [24] with Laney's metrics.

Table 1 shows the mapping of our three information valuation models onto the metrics of data quality [21] and model quality [24].

Reasoning Value of Information (RVI). RVI measures the value of the information at hand for automated reasoning, e.g., to analyze the physical twin and derive the appropriate control strategy. This class of information is crucial in developing complex reasoning that is primarily achieved through real-time analytics and simulation. Thus, the RVI is related to the *Core Entity* of ISO 23247, particularly to the *Digital Modeling, Simulation,* and *Analytic Service* Functional Entities (FEs). As shown in Table 1, RVI is primarily influenced by *objective* metrics, such as validity and consistency. This is intuitive, as the quality of the reasoning is contingent on the quality of the input data. Reasoning with invalid data leads to incorrect results, compromising automated decision-making.

This information model is best implemented by suppliers of digital twins who understand how much of the capabilities of reasoning-related FEs can a digital twin utilize under the prevalent RVI profile. To increase the RVI, suppliers can improve objective metrics, e.g., completeness, by increasing the ratio of recorded and total data; or integrity, by establishing links between data records.

Control Automation Value of Information (AVI). AVI measures how much value the information at hand provides for automating the control of the digital twin over the physical twin. This class of information is crucial in developing automated control capabilities that are typically achieved through precise actuation. Thus, the AVI is related to the Data Collection and Device Control Entity of ISO 23247, particularly to the Device Control Sub-Entity. As shown in Table 1, AVI is primarily influenced by two of Laney's *objective* metrics: precision and timeliness. Controlling a physical twin in an automated manner is only feasible if sensor data is available in adequate precision and timeliness as otherwise, the controlling actions steer the physical twin in inadequate or even misleading directions, potentially causing distortions like the bullwhip effect [22].

This information model is best implemented by experts with a proper understanding of the physical twin's actuation infrastructure, and preferably, with the ability to implement improvements in its instrumentation (data collection facilities and actuation). To increase the AVI, experts can improve the two influencing metrics—precision, e.g., by increasing the precision of sensor data; and timeliness, e.g., by automating data collection at every point of the system to shorten update periods of the digital twin.

User Value of Information (UVI). UVI measures how much value the information at hand provides for human users to comprehend the workings of the digital twin. This class of information fosters trust in the digital twin's working and allows the human to potentially become an active participant who works *with* the digital twin. Thus, the UVI is related to the User Entity of ISO 23247. As shown in Table 1, the UVI is primarily influenced by Laney's *subjective*—i.e., human-centered—metrics like usability, interpretability, and believability.

This information model is best implemented by working with the stakeholders of the digital twin—including expert users and decision-makers—to gauge their ability to comprehend the goals of the digital twin. Controlled experiments and focus groups are proper ways to measure the perceived value of the digital twin by the users. Improving the UVI might be achieved, e.g., through increasing interpretability by putting intuitive reporting interfaces in place; or through increasing believability by allowing experimentation with the digital twin.

5   Autonomy Strategies for Digital Twins

To highlight the utility of the information valuation models to drive the improvement of digital twin autonomy, we now define five digital twin autonomy strategies that leverage the information valuation metrics defined in Sect. 4 and span maturation trajectories towards more autonomous digital twins.

Table 2. Autonomy strategies for digital twins

Inf. value			Strategy	Improvement	
RVI	AVI	UVI		Inf. value	Dimension
Low		High	Externalize KPIs	RVI↑	Ability
High	Low	High	Improve actuation	AVI↑	Ability
High		Low	Improve explainability	UVI↑	Liberty
	High	Low	Enable experimentation	UVI↑	Liberty
High	High	High	Human-computer collaboration	* ↑	Ability&Liberty

The five strategies are summarized in Table 2. Different combinations of RVI, AVI, and UVI give rise to desirable strategies that improve the autonomy of a digital twin in one or both of the dimensions shown in Fig. 1. Strategies (1) and (2) focus on the technical aspect of improving the digital twin's *ability to act*. Strategies (3) and (4) focus on the human aspect of improving the digital twin's *liberty to act*. Finally, strategy (5) shows a combined strategy that acts in both dimensions of ability and liberty.

Externalize KPIs. Low RVI limits the ability of the digital twin to act. High UVI indicates that users still find the available information useful. Information with low RVI and high UVI indicates that users might have tacit knowledge that was not properly externalized. Externalizing tacit knowledge into explicit KPIs will drive the reasoning of the digital twin and increase its RVI.

Externalization of KPIs can be generally achieved by requirements elicitation, prototyping, and following the SECI knowledge creation model [27].

Improve Actuation. When RVI and UVI are high (e.g., followed by externalizing KPIs, as explained in the previous point), AVI can still be low. This means despite both the human and the digital twin find it useful, the information at hand is still insufficient to drive actuation at the right levels, limiting the digital twin's ability to act. Improving actuation capabilities increases the AVI of information and by that, fosters higher levels of autonomy.

Improving actuation might include instrumenting the physical twin with a better-performing actuator ensemble, relying on robotized means of actuation, and improving the precision and timeliness of actuation instructions.

Improve Explainability. When the UVI is low, the *liberty* of the digital twin to act is inevitably limited. A pertinent example of human factors that limit liberty is the lack of explainability of the digital twin's reasoning and actions. When the UVI is low but the RVI is otherwise high, i.e., the digital twin possesses the ability to reason at high levels, improving the explainability of reasoning is a beneficial strategy. By improving explainability, humans can gradually gain more trust in the reasoning capabilities and qualities of the digital twin.

Better explainability can be achieved, e.g., by visualizing the digital twin's reasoning, or by generating examples and counterexamples of simulation results.

Enable Experimentation. Low UVI can coincide with high AVI. This means the information at hand allows the digital twin to control the physical twin appropriately. However, low UVI indicates potential trust issues in the digital twin's capabilities. Enabling experimentation with the digital twin is a beneficial strategy in these cases. Through a series of experimentation scenarios, the human can gain trust in the digital twin's ability to control the physical asset properly.

The emerging field of experimentable digital twins [31] is focusing on enabler techniques in which humans can interactively simulate in the virtual space, or in the virtual-physical space [26].

Human-Computer Collaboration. There are cases when each of RVI, AVI, and UVI are high and the digital twin might have reached the Fully Autonomous level (Fig. 1). This fortunate situation allows for facilitating advanced mechanisms to further improve both the ability and liberty of digital twins. Human-computer collaboration is one of these mechanisms that requires strong foundations in each information valuation model.

Human-computer collaboration is considered the next generation of digital twin techniques as of today, including concepts such as human digital twins [36], human-centric digital twins [1], and citizen twins [28].

6   Illustrative Case

To illustrate the utility of our approach, we reconstruct the engineering process of one of our previous industry cases [12] and demonstrate how stakeholders can utilize the framework and autonomy strategies presented in this paper.

Setup. The case presents a smart farming company that operates production facilities (e.g., greenhouses). The company's goal is to automate decision-making in their production facilities. Decision-making includes controlling environmental conditions in the most efficient ways so that crop growth is appropriately stimulated. Their real-time decision-making and control capabilities position digital twins as the primary candidates to support the company's goals.

In lower-digitalized sectors, such as agriculture, employing digital solutions is substantially hindered by the lack of organizational capabilities and stakeholder trust. Therefore, change must happen in well-scoped incremental steps as the organization proceeds through its path of digital maturation.

The digital twinning journey in this case is sequenced into three phases: proof-of-concept (Sect. 6.1), prototype (Sect. 6.2), and deployment (Sect. 6.3).

6.1 Simulator Proof-of-Concept

Targeted Class of Autonomy. Digital shadow.

Aim. The company aims to kick off their digital twinning journey with a safe and cost-efficient prototype. There is no expectation in this phase to control the physical twin. Rather, the simulation facilities of the digital side must be developed and their capabilities must be demonstrated. The goal of the deliverable is to support the reasoning and decision-making of subject matter experts. In essence, the digital shadow is a simulator that takes real-time data and presents predictions to subject matter experts.

Goal. Improve RVI. This is a requirement for building faithful simulators.

Strategy. Externalize KPIs. This strategy (Table 2) improves the RVI. By that, it aids the development of more comprehensive and detailed simulation facilities. As a result, the ability of the digital twin will improve, but still not sufficiently to act autonomously or by the human in the loop.

Implementation. By Table 1, RVI is improved by eliciting domain knowledge from agronomists and engineers to increase (1) the completeness of externalized KPIs and (2) resolve any inconsistencies among them (e.g., by goal modeling [37]).

6.2 Prototype

Targeted Class of Autonomy. Digital shadow → human-supervised digital twin.

Aim. In this phase, the company aims to improve the digital shadow by developing mechanisms that would control the conditions in the production room.

Goal. Improve the AVI. Thanks to the previous stage, the RVI is sufficiently high, but the AVI is still low and needs to increase.

Strategy. Improve actuation. By that, the AVI will increase, allowing for finding partial autonomy scenarios in which the digital twin could make decisions. However, due to a lack of trust, the company decides for limited control by the digital twin. There is a human in charge who approves the decisions of the digital twin.

Implementation. Following Table 1, AVI is improved by (1) acquiring actuators that improve precision (e.g., irrigation equipment with refined positioning capabilities); (2) improving the timeliness of actuation (e.g., by tuning the temperature controllers to reach the desired room temperature faster).

6.3 Gradual Improvement and Deployment

Targeted Class. Human-supervised digital twin → human-actuated digital twin.

Aim. In the final phase, the company aims to remove the single decision-maker from the loop and push decision-making closer to staff members. Such a human-machine ensemble allows for complex control operations, e.g., manipulation of plants, without having to acquire precision robotics or hire specialized skills.

Goal. Improve liberty. The main challenge in this phase is that the stakeholders might not have enough trust in the digital twin to remove the subject matter expert from the decision-making process.

Strategy. Enable experimentation. By Table 2, liberty can be improved either by enabling experimentation or by improving explainability. In our case, the company opted for the former. Experimentation improves the UVI by allowing subject matter experts to gain an understanding of the digital and physical twin.

Implementation. Following Table 1, we improve UVI through increasing interpretability and believability. This is achieved by developing (1) interactive user interfaces that allow for advanced visualization, and (2) features for short-length what-if analysis that can be verified in the physical experimental setting.

6.4   Reflection

The above case demonstrated how our framework and autonomy strategies span a clear, systematic chain of arguments from high-level aims to specific implementation details. The framework was not available at the time of the project we draw from [12], but it would have aided our efforts greatly.

First, the framework helps identify quick wins. Scoping subsequent steps in a digital twin project is less complex and much safer if the current level of autonomy is well-understood and the required steps of evolution are tied to specific data quality metrics. These links foster better requirements that will deliver the desired evolutionary step. Second, the framework allows for articulating various kinds of high-level goals. In Sect. 6.1 and Sect. 6.2, the goals were related to specific information models. However, in Sect. 6.3, the goal was related to a dimension in the reference framework (Fig. 1). In each situation, the end-to-end correspondence to data quality metrics ensures sound technical outcomes. Third, although outside of the scope of this paper, the framework allows for composing and analyzing sequences of decisions. In Sect. 6.3, the *Enable experimentation* strategy was a viable option because, in previous phases, the RVI and AVI were sufficiently improved. Augmenting our framework with temporal semantics to allow for analyzing sequences of strategic decisions, potentially governed by digital twin evolution frameworks [13] are left for future work.

Threats to Validity. The main threat to the validity of our approach is that it has been validated only in one industry case. We attempted to mitigate this threat by sampling further digital twinning reports, but the scientific literature on the twinning itself does not offer sufficient details into the strategic decision-making of projects. Therefore, we resorted to validating our approach on a real, large-scale industry case in which we had access to every decision and were part of the strategic process. As a consequence of using one case, overfitting might occur. We attempted to mitigate this risk by maintaining a general discussion and drawing only conclusions that we felt confident to generalize.

7   Related Work

Tekinerdogan and Verdouw [33] define the digital autonomy architectural pattern for digital twins. Autonomy, in their terms, does not require manual human intervention as the digital twin reacts to changing conditions. They associate autonomy with the ability to learn from previously encountered situations and adapt control actions accordingly. Our framework focuses more on the human elements of digital twin autonomy. Hribernik et al. [18] focus on the *ability* dimension of autonomy and emphasize the crucial role of adaptation as autonomous systems must also act proactively with respect to their own purposes. Bradshaw et al. [6] discuss seven myths of autonomy. One of their key findings is that despite common belief, there is no such thing as a fully autonomous system. Humans usually cannot be fully removed from the system, nor is it always desirable to do so. Our work shares these views and exactly for these reasons, we advocate approaching digital twin autonomy from a socio-technical point of view and investigate the borders between digital twin and human autonomy, as recommended by Hribernik et al. [18]. Hexmoor et al. [17] define autonomy as an artifact of the human's individual trust in the system and the system's ability to execute its mission. In their framework, individual trust is further decomposed into factors such as benevolence and capability of subsystems, and investigate human-analogous traits of autonomous systems such as sociability, frustration, and disposition. These metrics might be useful in further refining and quantifying human-machine dynamics in our framework.

We based our work on the infonomics theory of Laney [21], but there are a number of other valuation models available. Lu and Zhu [23] propose evaluation methods for the Enterprise Value of Information (EVI), based on qualitative metrics (such as information authenticity and degree of coverage) and quantitative metrics (such as information flux and information cost). Viscusi and Batini [35] relate information value to metrics such as information quality, information structure, information infrastructure; and utility which is mostly determined by information diffusion. Neither of these information valuation models is specific to digital twins and seems to be focusing on qualitative metrics that, similarly to Laney's metrics, lack actionability. A comprehensive and recent review of data valuation models is due to Bendechache et al. [2].

8   Conclusion

In this paper, we have presented how different classes of information contribute to the autonomy of digital twins. We defined three novel information valuation models based on the established theory of infonomics [21] to understand the influence of information on autonomy. We have outlined five strategies to improve autonomy by increasing the value of information in the different valuation models. While likely not an exhaustive list of all possible digital twin information valuation models, the comprehensive nature of the ISO 23247 reference framework the models are linked to suggests an appropriate coverage of the main concepts and relationships among them. To situate digital twin autonomy efforts in a comprehensive framework, we proposed one in terms of two orthogonal dimensions: a more technology-focused dimension, *ability*; and a more human-focused dimension, *liberty*. We contextualized two traditional and identified two novel socio-technical classes of digital twins. Our information valuation models, digital twin autonomy strategies, and our framework foster a systematic top-down approach to improving the autonomy characteristics of digital twins.

In line with Bradshaw et al. [6], we argue that autonomy must be considered early in the engineering process of the digital twin. Our approach helps to reason about autonomy already at an early phase. At the same time, we emphasize that human agency should be considered as a first principle in digital twinning.

Future work will focus on augmenting our framework with temporal semantics to allow for reasoning about compositions of autonomy strategies, as well as applying the framework to more digital twin projects for validation purposes.

References

1. Asad, U., Khan, M., Khalid, A., Lughmani, W.A.: Human-centric digital twins in industry: a comprehensive review of enabling technologies and implementation strategies. Sensors **23**(8), (2023). https://doi.org/10.3390/s23083938. https://www.mdpi.com/1424-8220/23/8/3938
2. Bendechache, M., Attard, J., Ebiele, M., Brennan, R.: A systematic survey of data value: models, metrics, applications and research challenges. IEEE Access **11**, 104966–104983 (2023). https://doi.org/10.1109/ACCESS.2023.3315588
3. Bergs, T., Gierlings, S., Auerbach, T., Klink, A., Schraknepper, D., Augspurger, T.: The concept of digital twin and digital shadow in manufacturing. Procedia CIRP **101**, 81–84 (2021). https://doi.org/10.1016/j.procir.2021.02.010
4. Bibow, P., et al.: Model-driven development of a digital twin for injection molding. In: Dustdar, S., Yu, E., Salinesi, C., Rieu, D., Pant, V. (eds.) CAiSE 2020. LNCS, vol. 12127, pp. 85–100. Springer, Cham (2020). https://doi.org/10.1007/978-3-030-49435-3_6
5. Bonney, M.S., de Angelis, M., Dal Borgo, M., Wagg, D.J.: Contextualisation of information in digital twin processes. Mech. Syst. Signal Process. **184**, 109657 (2023). https://doi.org/10.1016/j.ymssp.2022.109657. ISSN 0888-3270
6. Bradshaw, J.M., Hoffman, R.R., Woods, D.D., Johnson, M.: The seven deadly myths of "autonomous systems". IEEE Intell. Syst. **28**(3), 54–61 (2013). https://doi.org/10.1109/MIS.2013.70
7. Braun, S., et al.: Engineering digital twins and digital shadows as key enablers for Industry 4.0. In: Vogel-Heuser, B., Wimmer, M. (eds.) Digital Transformation, pp. 3–31. Springer, Heidelberg (2023). https://doi.org/10.1007/978-3-662-65004-2_1
8. Caldarelli, G., et al.: The role of complexity for digital twins of cities. Nat. Comput. Sci. **3**(5), 374–381 (2023). https://doi.org/10.1038/s43588-023-00431-4
9. Chazette, L., Brunotte, W., Speith, T.: Exploring explainability: a definition, a model, and a knowledge catalogue. In: 2021 IEEE 29th International Requirements Engineering Conference (RE), Los Alamitos, CA, USA, pp. 197–208. IEEE (2021). https://doi.org/10.1109/RE51729.2021.00025
10. D'Addona, D.M., Ullah, A.M.M.S., Matarazzo, D.: Tool-wear prediction and pattern-recognition using artificial neural network and DNA-based computing. J. Intell. Manuf. **28**(6), 1285–1301 (2017). https://doi.org/10.1007/s10845-015-1155-0

11. Daoutidis, P., Zachar, M., Jogwar, S.S.: Sustainability and process control: a survey and perspective. J. Process Control **44**, 184–206 (2016). https://doi.org/10.1016/j.jprocont.2016.06.002

12. David, I., et al.: Digital twins for cyber-biophysical systems: challenges and lessons learned. In: 2023 ACM/IEEE 26th International Conference on Model Driven Engineering Languages and Systems (MODELS), pp. 1–12. IEEE (2023). https://doi.org/10.1109/MODELS58315.2023.00014

13. David, I., Bork, D.: Towards a taxonomy of digital twin evolution for technical sustainability. In: 2023 ACM/IEEE International Conference on Model Driven Engineering Languages and Systems Companion (MODELS-C), pp. 934–938. IEEE (2023). https://doi.org/10.1109/MODELS-C59198.2023.00147

14. David, I., Syriani, E.: Automated Inference of Simulators in Digital Twins. CRC Press, Boca Raton (2023). ISBN 9781032546070

15. Emery, F.E., Trist, E.L.: Socio-technical systems. Manag. Sci. Models Tech. **2**, 83–97 (1960)

16. Fard, N.E., Selmic, R.R., Khorasani, K.: Public policy challenges, regulations, oversight, technical, and ethical considerations for autonomous systems: a survey. IEEE Technol. Soc. Mag. **42**(1), 45–53 (2023). https://doi.org/10.1109/MTS.2023.3241315

17. Hexmoor, H., McLaughlan, B., Tuli, G.: Natural human role in supervising complex control systems. J. Exp. Theor. Artif. Intell. **21**(1), 59–77 (2009). https://doi.org/10.1080/09528130802386093

18. Hribernik, K., Cabri, G., Mandreoli, F., Mentzas, G.: Autonomous, context-aware, adaptive digital twins-state of the art and roadmap. Comput. Ind. **133**, 103508 (2021). https://doi.org/10.1016/j.compind.2021.103508

19. Koren, I., Braun, S., Van Dyck, M., Jarke, M.: Dynamic strategic modeling for alliance-driven data platforms: the case of smart farming. In: Nurcan, S., Korthaus, A. (eds.) CAiSE 2021. LNBIP, vol. 424, pp. 92–99. Springer, Cham (2021). https://doi.org/10.1007/978-3-030-79108-7_11

20. Kritzinger, W., Karner, M., Traar, G., Henjes, J., Sihn, W.: Digital twin in manufacturing: a categorical literature review and classification. IFAC-PapersOnLine **51**(11), 1016–1022 (2018). https://doi.org/10.1016/j.ifacol.2018.08.474

21. Laney, D.B.: Infonomics: How to Monetize, Manage, and Measure Information as an Asset for Competitive Advantage. Routledge, London (2017)

22. Lee, H.L., Padmanabhan, V., Whang, S.: Information distortion in a supply chain: the bullwhip effect. Manag. Sci. **43**(4), 546–558 (1997). https://doi.org/10.1287/mnsc.43.4.546

23. Lu, Y., Zhu, H.W.: An approach for quantifying enterprise value of information (EVI). In: 2009 International Conference on Management Science and Engineering, pp. 594–600 (2009). https://doi.org/10.1109/ICMSE.2009.5317369

24. Mohagheghi, P., Dehlen, V., Neple, T.: Definitions and approaches to model quality in model-based software development - a review of literature. Inf. Softw. Technol. **51**(12), 1646–1669 (2009). https://doi.org/10.1016/j.infsof.2009.04.004

25. Muctadir, H.M., Negrin, D.A.M., Gunasekaran, R., Cleophas, L., van den Brand, M., Haverkort, B.R.: Current trends in digital twin development, maintenance, and operation: an interview study (2023)

26. Niyonkuru, D., Wainer, G.: A DEVS-based engine for building digital quadruplets. Simulation **97**(7), 485–506 (2021). https://doi.org/10.1177/00375497211003130

27. Nonaka, I., Takeuchi, H.: The knowledge-creating company. Harv. Bus. Rev. **85**(7/8), 162 (2007)

28. Panetta, K.: Trends Appear on the Gartner Hype Cycle for Emerging Technologies. Gartner Inc., Stamford (2019)
29. Rasheed, A., San, O., Kvamsdal, T.: Digital twin: values, challenges and enablers from a modeling perspective. IEEE Access **8**, 21980–22012 (2020). https://doi.org/10.1109/ACCESS.2020.2970143
30. Rosen, R., von Wichert, G., Lo, G., Bettenhausen, K.D.: About the importance of autonomy and digital twins for the future of manufacturing. IFAC-PapersOnLine **48**(3), 567–572 (2015). https://doi.org/10.1016/j.ifacol.2015.06.141
31. Schluse, M., Priggemeyer, M., Atorf, L., Rossmann, J.: Experimentable digital twins - streamlining simulation-based systems engineering for industry 4.0. IEEE Trans. Ind. Inform. **14**(4), 1722–1731 (2018). https://doi.org/10.1109/TII.2018.2804917
32. Shao, G.: Use case scenarios for digital twin implementation based on ISO 23247. Technical report (2021). https://doi.org/10.6028/nist.ams.400-2
33. Tekinerdogan, B., Verdouw, C.: Systems architecture design pattern catalog for developing digital twins. Sensors **20**(18), (2020). https://doi.org/10.3390/s20185103
34. Uhlemann, T.H.J., Lehmann, C., Steinhilper, R.: The digital twin: realizing the cyber-physical production system for Industry 4.0. Procedia CIRP **61**, 335–340 (2017). https://doi.org/10.1016/j.procir.2016.11.152
35. Viscusi, G., Batini, C.: Digital information asset evaluation: characteristics and dimensions. In: Caporarello, L., Di Martino, B., Martinez, M. (eds.) Smart Organizations and Smart Artifacts. LNISO, vol. 7, pp. 77–86. Springer, Cham (2014). https://doi.org/10.1007/978-3-319-07040-7_9
36. Wang, B., Zhou, H., Yang, G., Li, X., Yang, H.: Human digital twin (HDT) driven human-cyber-physical systems: key technologies and applications. Chin. J. Mech. Eng. **35**(1), 11 (2022). https://doi.org/10.1186/s10033-022-00680-w
37. Yu, E.S.: Social modeling and *i**. In: Borgida, A.T., Chaudhri, V.K., Giorgini, P., Yu, E.S. (eds.) Conceptual Modeling: Foundations and Applications. LNCS, vol. 5600, pp. 99–121. Springer, Heidelberg (2009). https://doi.org/10.1007/978-3-642-02463-4_7
38. Zuehlke, D.: Smartfactory - from vision to reality in factory technologies. IFAC Proc. Vol. **41**(2), 14101–14108 (2008). https://doi.org/10.3182/20080706-5-KR-1001.02391

Model-Driven Engineering and Quantum Workflows

Comparing MDD and CcD in the Bug Localization Context: An Empirical Evaluation in Video Games

Isis Roca[1,2(✉)], África Domingo[1], Óscar Pastor[2], Carlos Cetina[1], and Lorena Arcega[1]

[1] SVIT Research Group, Universidad San Jorge, Zaragoza, Spain
{iroca,adomingo,ccetina,larcega}@usj.es
[2] PROS Research Center, Universitat Politècnica de València, Valencia, Spain
opastor@dsic.upv.es

Abstract. The development of video games usually involves two main methods: Code-centric Development (CcD) and Model-Driven Development (MDD). CcD uses code languages that provide more control but it requires more effort in order to deal with implementation details. MDD raises the abstraction level (avoiding implementation details) by means of software models that are transformed into code or interpreted at run-time. Raising the abstraction level favors the participation of non-technical roles such as level designers or artists that are essential for video game development. However, bug localization, which is crucial for identifying faults, is less explored in MDD despite its advantages. This work examines how MDD and CcD impact bug localization by using a commercial video game that has been released on PlayStation 4 and Steam. We compare bug localization in terms of performance, productivity, and user satisfaction. The results showed that bug localization in MDD led to higher satisfaction among subjects. However, the differences in performance or productivity depended on experience and favored CcD for professionals. Our findings suggest that bug localization practices performed suboptimally in models, indicating a knowledge gap in addressing bugs within MDD environments. With the rising popularity of MDD in video games, there is a need to explore alternative forms of bug localization for MDD.

Keywords: Experiment · Model-Driven Development · Code-centric Development · Bug Localization · Game Software Engineering

1 Introduction

The video game industry has evolved into a highly profitable segment[1]. The increasing popularity of video games has led to a rise in the complexity of creating

---

[1] T. B. R. Company, Gaming global market report 2023, https://www.thebusiness researchcompany.com/report/gaming-global-market-report.

Partially supported by MINECO under the Project VARIATIVA (PID2021-28695 OBI00) and by the Gobierno de Aragón (Spain) (Research Group S05_20D).

G. Guizzardi et al. (Eds.): CAiSE 2024, LNCS 14663, pp. 581–595, 2024.
https://doi.org/10.1007/978-3-031-61057-8_34

them. Video game development involves complex software that encompasses various aspects of gaming, such as game mechanics, graphics, and physics. As a result, a separate field of engineering, known as Game Software Engineering (GSE), emerged. Its focus lies in the creation and maintenance of software that is specifically tailored to meet the demands of video games [1].

Video games can be implemented using two primary methods: traditional Code-centric Development (CcD) or Model-Driven Development (MDD) [5]. In the case of CcD, game developers manually write and structure the code that is responsible for the game's behavior, mechanics, and graphics. This approach allows for fine-grained control and customization, but it can be complex and time-consuming. On the other hand, MDD involves creating high-level models that describe the game's structure, behavior, and components. These models are then transformed into executable code or interpreted at runtime.

Unfortunately, similar to traditional software, the increase in video game complexity is accompanied by an increase in the appearance of software bugs [2]. A good example of this is the blockbuster *Cyberpunk 2077*[2]. Hence, maintenance is becoming more and more important. Bug localization is one of the most important and common activities performed by developers during software maintenance and evolution. Bug localization aims to identify the location in the artifact that is pertinent to a software fault. When models are used for code generation, addressing bugs at the model level must not be neglected [3]. While MDD is acknowledged for its advantages in software development [16], particularly in terms of development effort and quality [12], the exploration of bug localization within the MDD context remains an underexplored area.

In this paper, we evaluate whether the development method (MDD or CcD) can have an impact on bug localization tasks by analyzing Kromaia, a commercial video game released on PlayStation 4 and Steam. We present an experiment in which we compare bug localization in MDD and in CcD, in terms of performance, productivity, and satisfaction. A total of 54 subjects (classified as students or professionals) performed the tasks of the experiment, locating bugs in two scenarios of Kromaia. The satisfaction of the subjects was greater when performing bug localization in MDD. However, the performance and productivity results of the students did not show significant differences, while the performance and productivity results of the professionals were better when performing bug localization in CcD.

Our results suggest that there exists a positive perception of MDD. However, the practices used for bug localization need to be evaluated in models due to their suboptimal results. This indicates a knowledge gap in addressing bug localization in models. Given the growing popularity of MDD in the video game domain (and its increasing use in industry-specific domains), there is a need to focus on how engineers perform bug localization in models.

The structure of this paper is as follows. Section 2 reviews the related works in the area. Section 3 presents the case study, Kromaia. Section 4 outlines the

---

[2] How buggy is Cyberpunk 2077, really? - https://www.pcgamer.com/how-buggy-is-cyberpunk-2077-really/.

experimental design. Section 5 presents the experiment results, followed by a discussion in Sect. 6. Section 7 summarizes the threats to the validity. Finally, Sect. 8 concludes the paper.

2   Related Work

Although there are no research efforts that empirically compare MDD and CcD from a bug location perspective, previous studies have emphasized the effectiveness of MDD in various domains, showcasing its benefits, especially in small-scale projects under favorable conditions [10,14]. Existing research has primarily compared MDD and CcD in software development scenarios [12].

Studies by Krogmann and Becker [12], Kapteijns et al. [10], and Mellegård and Staron [14] have provided insights into the efficiency and effectiveness of MDD in different contexts, shedding light on its potential advantages and the distribution of effort between models and other artifacts. Martínez et al. [13] explored the perceptions of undergraduate students regarding Model-Driven, Model-Based, and Code-centric methodologies, indicating that the Model-Driven approach was considered the most beneficial, although perceived as less aligned with developers' prior experiences. Pappoti et al. [18] further underscored the advantages of MDD, demonstrating shorter development times and fewer challenges when utilizing code generation.

Panach et al. [17] and Domingo et al. [8] delved into the contextual factors influencing the benefits of MDD. Panach et al. affirm its consistent delivery of higher-quality results. Chueca et al. [6] performed an empirical evaluation in the field of game development. They highlighted the enhanced correctness achieved through Software Product Lines (SPLs) based on MDD compared to other traditional methods.

The field of Game Software Engineering (GSE) is gradually becoming a focus, although studies in this specific area still need to be completed. Our work aims to extend the comparative analysis between MDD and CcD by focusing on bug localization in the context of a video game company.

3   Background

The case study that we used to assess this experiment focuses on the video game Kromaia[3]. It is a commercial video game that is accessible on both PC and PlayStation 4 platforms. It immerses players in a three-dimensional environment that combines elements of space exploration, action, and shooting genres.

The developers of Kromaia can follow the principles of MDD. They can employ a Domain-Specific Language (DSL) called Shooter Definition Modeling Language (SDML) to define the attributes and behaviors of the game's entities. The game's entities include bosses, environmental elements, weapons, defenses,

---

[3] For more information about Kromaia, you can view the official trailer released by Playstation: https://youtu.be/EhsejJBp8Go.

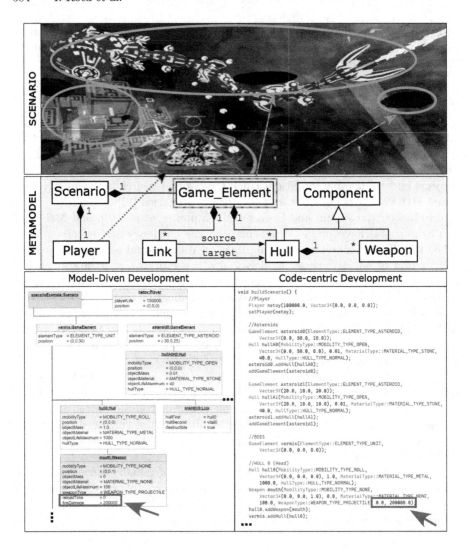

Fig. 1. Scenario Metamodel and Bug example in MDD and CcD.

and movement behaviors. SDML, which was initially designed for shooter-style video games, has proven to be adaptable for games with similar themes outside of this genre. A simplified subset of the SDML metamodel is shown in the central part of Fig. 1. The complete metamodel comprises more than 20 concepts, 20 relationships, and over 60 properties. SDML models are interpreted at runtime to generate the corresponding game's entities. In other words, software models created using SDML are translated into C++ objects at runtime using an inter-preter integrated into the game engine [5]. For more information on the SDML model shown in Fig. 1, a video presentation can be found here: https://youtu.be/Vp3Zt4qXkoY.

SDML allows the development of any game element, such as bosses, enemies, or environmental elements. An actual example of the scenario of a final boss of Kromaia is presented in the upper part of Fig. 1. The Serpent is the final boss that the player must defeat in order to complete Level 1. This boss is composed of one main hull (the head of the serpent) followed by eight hulls. The head has one weapon, and the tail (last hull) has three spike weapons.

In addition, Kromaia developers can also follow a CcD method. They can use the C++ programming language to create content for the game. Game elements created in C++ must have the same rules and structural patterns as those created with SDML in order to fit correctly with the rest of the game.

An actual example of a bug is illustrated in the bottom part of Fig. 1. The left part of the figure shows the bug in MDD, while the right part shows the same bug in CcD. In this particular case, a player reported: *"I am unable to fight the final boss of the first level, which is supposed to be the easiest. I die after being hit by a single shot, so I believe that something is wrong"*. A closer inspection reveals that the issue is attributed to an improper weapon configuration. On the one hand, the *fireDamage* attribute exceeds the player's life, resulting in the player's immediate death when attacked by the boss. On the other hand, the *reloadTime* attribute is set to zero, causing the boss to launch continuous attacks without pause. This bug significantly impacts the player experience.

4   Experiment Design

4.1   Objectives

According to Wohlin's guidelines [21] for reporting software engineering experiments, we have organized our research objectives using the Goal Question Metric template for goal definition [4]. Our goal is to **analyze** software development methods, MDD and CcD, **for the purpose of** comparison, **with respect to** performance, productivity, and user satisfaction, **from the point of view of** students and professionals developers, **in the context of** bug localization for a video game company.

4.2   Variables

In this study, the factor under investigation is the software development method (*Method*) in which the bug localization is performed. There are two alternatives: MDD or CcD, which are the methods used by the subjects to perform the bug localization tasks (BL tasks).

Since the goal of this experiment is to evaluate the effects of using different methods when performing bug localization in a scenario of a commercial video game, we selected *Performance* and *Productivity* as the objective dependent variables.

We evaluated *Performance* by calculating precision, recall, and F-measure based on the confusion matrix between subjects' solutions and the ground truth.

Precision reflects the accuracy of the identified bugs, recall captures how well all bugs were found, and F-measure balances these two aspects. To represent the *Performance* of the subjects in each BL task, we used the F-measure as the percentage of a BL task solved by a subject. We measured the time used by each subject to finish each task to calculate *Productivity* as the ratio of *Performance* to time spent (in minutes) to perform a BL task.

We also analyzed the methods with respect to *Satisfaction* using a 5-point Likert-scale questionnaire based on the Technology Acceptance Model (TAM) [15]. We use TAM adapted to bug location since it is the questionnaire previously used to measure variables related to satisfaction (comparing MDD and CcD) [9]. We decompose *Satisfaction* into three subjective dependent variables as follows: *Perceived Ease of Use* (PEOU), the degree to which a person believes that learning and using a particular method would require less effort. *Perceived Usefulness* (PU), the degree to which a person believes that using a particular method will increase performance, and *Intention to Use* (ITU), the degree to which a person intends to use a method when performing BL tasks. Each of these variables corresponds to specific items in the TAM questionnaire. We average the scores obtained for these items to obtain the value for each one of these variables.

4.3   Design

We chose a factorial crossover design with two periods using two different tasks, T1 and T2, one for each period. The subjects were randomly divided into two groups (G1 and G2). In the first period of the experiment, all of the subjects solved T1 with G1 using MDD and G2 using CcD. Afterwards, in the second period, all of the subjects solved T2 with G1 using the CcD and G2 using MDD.

This repeated measure design enhances the experiment's sensitivity, as noted by Vegas et al. [19]. By observing the same subject using both alternatives, between-subject differences are controlled, thus improving the experiment's robustness regarding variation among subjects. By using two different sequences (G1 used MDD first and CcD afterwards, and G2 used CcD first and MDD afterwards) and different tasks, the design counterbalances some of the effects caused by using the alternatives of the factor in a specific order (i.e., learning effect, fatigue). The effects of the factors period (Task), sequence (Group), and subject will be studied to guarantee the validity of this experiment.

To verify the experiment design, we conducted a pilot study with two subjects. The pilot study facilitated an estimate of the time required to complete the tasks and questionnaires, the identification of typographical and semantic errors, and the testing of the online environment used to create the experiment.

4.4   Research Questions and Hypotheses

The research questions and null hypotheses are formulated as follows:

RQ1 - Does the **Method** impact the *Performance* of the BL tasks? The corresponding null hypothesis is $H_{0,Per}$: The **Method** does not have an effect on the *Performance* of the BL tasks.

RQ2 - Does the **Method** impact the *Productivity* of the BL tasks? The corresponding null hypothesis is $H_{0,Pro}$: The **Method** does not have an effect on the *Productivity* of the BL tasks.

RQ3 - Does user satisfaction differ when developers use a different **Method** to solve BL tasks? To answer this question, we formulated three hypotheses based on the variables *Perceived Ease of Use*, *Perceived Usefulness*, and *Intention to Use*, with their corresponding null hypotheses. These are: $H_{0,PEOU}$, the **Method** does not have an effect on *Perceived Ease of Use*; $H_{0,PU}$, the **Method** does not have an effect on *Perceived Usefulness*; $H_{0,ITU}$, the **Method** does not have an effect on *Intention to Use*.

The hypotheses are formulated as two-tailed hypotheses since we have not found empirical studies that support a specific direction for the effect in the video game domain.

4.5 Participants

We selected the subjects using convenience sampling [21]. A total of 58 subjects with different knowledge about programming, modeling, and video game development performed the experiment, but only 54 decided to submit their answers and confirmed their agreement to be part of this study. In this study, the participants included 10 professionals working in video game development and 44 third-year undergraduate students who are taking a course in object-oriented programming from a technology program at Universidad San Jorge.

The experiment was conducted by two instructors. During the experiment, one of the instructors gave instructions and managed the focus groups. Both instructors clarified doubts and took notes during the experiment.

4.6 Experimental Objects

The tasks of our experiment were extracted from real-world software development, Kromaia [5]. The tasks consisted of localizing two bugs using textual descriptions of the bugs. Each bug was located in a scenario of Kromaia.

To solve the BL tasks using MDD, the subjects used UML diagrams of Kromaia scenarios and the metamodel. To solve the BL tasks using CcD, the subjects used C++ code of Kromaia scenarios and the files of the C++ classes.

A video game engineer who was involved in the development of Kromaia and a researcher designed the two tasks of similar difficulty and prepared the correction templates. In both CcD and MDD, the two tasks consisted of localizing the six error points of a bug given its description. The scenarios where the subjects had to localize the bug had a total of 223 possible error points in Task 1 and 200 in Task 2.

For data collection, we prepared two forms using Microsoft Forms (one for each experimental sequence) with the following sections:

I An informed consent form that the subjects must review and accept voluntarily. It clearly explains what the experiment consists of and that the personal data will not be collected.

II A demographic questionnaire was used to characterize the sample.

III A specific questionnaire for each sequence to collect the subjects' responses during the experiment (their solutions to the tasks, the start and end time of each task, and their answers to the satisfaction questionnaire).

The experimental objects used in this experiment (the training material, the tasks, the correction templates, and the forms used for the questionnaires), as well as the results and the statistical analysis, are available as a replication package at http://svit.usj.es/MDDvsCcD-BugLocalization.

4.7 Experimental Procedure

The experiment was conducted in two different sessions. The experiment was conducted face-to-face with a group of students in the first session. In the second session, the experiment was conducted online with professionals. During the online session, all of the participants joined the same video conference via Microsoft Teams, and the chat session was used to share information or clarify doubts. The experiment was scheduled to last for one hour and 45 min and was conducted following the experimental procedure described as follows:

1. An instructor explained the parts of the session and clarified that the experiment was not a test of the subjects' abilities. (5 min)

2. The subjects attended a video tutorial on the different methods used in Kromaia to develop the video game scenarios and the BL tasks in those scenarios. The information used in the experiment was available to the subjects. (10 min)

3. The subjects received clear instructions on where to find the links to access the forms for participating in the experiment. They were also told about the structure of these forms and where they could find information about the methods used in the experiment. The subjects were randomly divided into two groups (G1 and G2). (5 min)

4. The subjects accessed the online form, and they read and confirmed having read the information about the experiment, the data treatment of their personal information, and the voluntary nature of their participation before accessing the questionnaires and tasks of the experiment. (5 min)

5. The subjects completed a demographic questionnaire. (5 min)

6. The subjects performed the first task. The subjects from G1 had to use MDD to perform a BL task, and the subjects from G2 had to perform the same task but using CcD. After submitting their solution, the subjects completed a satisfaction questionnaire about the method used for bug localization. (maximum of 30 min)

7. The subjects performed the second task. The subjects from G1 used CcD, and the subjects from G2 used MDD. Then, the subjects completed the satisfaction questionnaire. (maximum of 30 min)

8. One instructor conducted a focus group interview about the tasks while the other instructor took notes. (10 to 15 min)
9. Finally, the tasks were corrected, and a researcher analyzed the results.

4.8   Analysis Procedure

We have chosen the Linear Mixed Model (LMM) [20] for the statistical data analysis. LMM handles correlated data resulting from repeated measurements, and it allows us to study the effects of factors that intervene in a crossover design (period, sequence, or subject) and the effects of other blocking variables (e.g., in our experiment, professional experience) [19]. In the hypothesis testing, we applied the Type III test of fixed effects with unstructured repeated covariance. This test enables LMM to produce the exact F-values and p-values for each dependent variable and each fixed factor.

In this study, **Method** was defined as a fixed-repeated factor to identify the differences between using MDD or CcD, and the subjects were defined as a random factor $(1|Subj)$ to reflect the repeated measures design. The dependent variables (DV) for this test were *Performance* and *Productivity*, and the three other variables correspond to *Satisfaction*: *Perceived Ease of Use* (PEOU), *Perceived Usefulness* (PU), and *Intention to Use* (ITU).

In order to take into account the potential effects of factors that intervene in a crossover design in determining the main effect of **Method**, we considered **Period** and **Sequence** to be fixed effects. In order to explore the potential effects of the subject's experience to determine the variability in the dependent variables in the statistical model, we also considered the fixed factors **Experience** and the combination of factors **Method** and **Experience**.

We tested different statistical models in order to find out which factors, in addition to **Method**, could best explain the changes in the dependent variables. Some of these statistical models are described mathematically in Formula 1. The starting statistical model (*Model* 0) reflects the main factor used in this experiment, **Method** and the random factor $(1|Subj)$. We also tested other statistical models (e.g., *Model* 1, *Model* 2, and *Model* 3) that included the fixed factors **Experience** (Exp.), **Period** (Per.) or **Sequence** (Seq.), which could have effects on the dependent variables.

$$
\begin{aligned}
&(Model\,0)\ DV \sim Method + (1|\,Subj.) \\
&(Model\,1)\ DV \sim Method + Exp. + Method*Exp. + (1|\,Subj.) \\
&(Model\,2)\ DV \sim Method + Seq. + Per. + (1|\,Subj.) \\
&(Model\,3)\ DV \sim Method + Exp + Method*Exp. + Seq. + Per. + (1|\,Subj.)
\end{aligned}
\tag{1}
$$

The statistical model fit of the tested models for each variable was evaluated based on goodness of fit measures such as Akaike's information criterion (AIC) and Schwarz's Bayesian Information Criterion (BIC). The model with the smallest AIC or BIC is considered to be the best fitting model [9,11].

The assumption for applying LMM is the normality of the residuals of the dependent variables. To verify this normality, we used Shapiro-Wilk tests as well as visual inspections of the histograms and normal Q-Q plots. To describe the changes in each dependent variable, we selected the statistical model that satisfied the normality of residuals and also obtained the smallest AIC or BIC value.

To quantify the differences in the dependent variables due to the factors considered, we calculated the Cohen d value [7], which is the standardized difference between the means of the dependent variables for each factor alternative. Values of Cohen d between 0.2 and 0.3 indicate a small effect, values around 0.5 indicate a medium effect and values greater than 0.8 indicate a large effect. We selected box plots to describe the results graphically.

5   Results

The **Method** factor produced changes in all of the dependent variables. However, its effect size was different between the objective and subjective dependent variables, and, for objective variables, it depended on experience. Table 1 shows the values for the mean and standard deviation of the dependent variables for each method and the corresponding Cohen d value measuring the effect size of **Method** for each variable. Positive values of Cohen d value indicate differences in favor of MDD, and negative values indicate differences in favor of CcD. Values indicating medium and high effects are shaded in light and dark gray, respectively.

Table 1. Values for the mean and standard deviation of the response variables and Cohen d values for the alternatives of Method (MDD and CcD)

		Performance	Productivity	Satisfaction $\mu \pm \sigma$		
		μ % $\pm\sigma$	μ %/min $\pm\sigma$	PEOU	PU	ITU
All Subjects	MDD	34.66 ± 27.17	1.88 ± 1.57	3.45 ± 0.93	3.39 ± 0.92	3.41 ± 1.17
	CcD	33.28 ± 26.15	1.72 ± 1.63	2.64 ± 0.89	2.57 ± 0.85	2.52 ± 1.11
	Cohen d	0.052	0.101	0.89	0.932	0.78
Students	MDD	37.64 ± 26.62	2.02 ± 1.55	3.53 ± 0.88	3.49 ± 0.89	3.57 ± 1.17
	CcD	31.94 ± 26.69	1.59 ± 1.53	2.72 ± 0.9	2.64 ± 0.86	2.63 ± 1.14
	Cohen d	0.214	0.282	0.908	0.971	0.818
Professionals	MDD	21.57 ± 27	1.24 ± 1.57	3.1 ± 1.09	2.99 ± 0.99	2.7 ± 0.92
	CcD	39.22 ± 23.99	2.27 ± 2.01	2.3 ± 0.76	2.28 ± 0.76	2.05 ± 0.86
	Cohen d	−0.691	−0.575	0.849	0.809	0.729

According to Cohen d values, we can state that when considering all of the subjects who participated in the experiment, the effect size of the **Method** factor in favor of MDD for *Performance* and *Productivity* was negligible, with Cohen d values of less than 0.2 in favor of MDD. When considering only the students, the Cohen d value of 0.21 indicates small effects in favor of MDD, whereas, for professionals, the negative Cohen d value smaller than −0.5 indicates medium effects in favor of CcD. On the other hand, when considering all of the subjects or distinguishing them by experience, the effect size of **Method** in favor of MDD was large, with Cohen d values around 0.8 for the variables related to satisfaction: *Perceived Ease of Use* (PEOU), *Perceived Usefulness* (PU), and *Intention to Use* (ITU). The box plots in Fig. 2 illustrate these results.

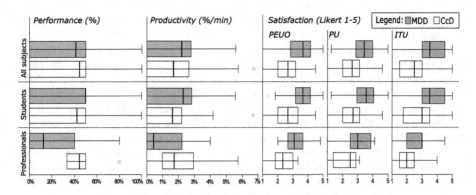

Fig. 2. Boxplots for dependent variables

All of the statistical models shown in Formula 1 verify the normality of the residuals. The statistical model that best explains the changes in the *Performance* and *Productivity* variables is *Model* 3 of Formula 1 since it is the one that obtained the lowest values for the AIC and BIC fit measures. *Model* 1 of Formula 1 is the one that best explains the changes for the variables related to satisfaction. Table 2 shows the results of the Type III fixed effects test for each of the dependent variables and for each fixed factor of the statistical model used in each case. Values indicating significant differences are shaded in grey.

Table 2. Results of Type III test of fixed effects for each variable and factor. NA = Not Applicable

	Method	Experience	Method * Exp.	Sequence	Period
Performance	F = .890; p = .350	F = .545; p = .464	F = 4.416; p = .041	F = 5.649; p = .021	F = 6.023; p = .018
Productivity	F = .821; p = .369	F = .044; p = .834	F = 5.357; p = .025	F = 7.103; p = .010	F = .666; p = .418
PEOU	F = 24.656; p < .001	F = 2.456; p = .123	F = .001; p = .974	NA	NA
PU	F = 22.731; p < .001	F = 2.760; p = .103	F = .172; p = .680	NA	NA
ITU	F = 7.620; p = .008	F = 7.620; p = .008	F = .258; p = .614	NA	NA

For *Performance* and *Productivity*, the factor **Method** obtained p-values that are greater than 0.05. Therefore, our first two null hypotheses are not rejected, at least when considering the aggregated data of students and professionals. The p-value of less than 0.05 for the combination of factors **Method * Experience** for *Performance* and *Productivity* indicates that, for both dependent variables, the effect of **Method** on students is significantly different from the effect of **Method** on professionals. By testing the results of the **Experience** separately, the **Method** factor obtained p-values of less than 0.05. However, for students, the differences due to the **Method** factor are significant only when using *Model* 0 of Formula 1. For students, the effects of **Sequence** or **Period** are larger than the effects of **Method**. Thus, a comprehensive answer to **RQ1** and to **RQ2** is that there are significant changes in *Performance* and *Productivity* due to the **Method** factor, although the direction and size of these changes vary depending on the subjects' experience, as shown by the descriptive statistics and Cohen d values.

On the other hand, the **Experience** factor obtained a p-value greater than 0.05 for *Performance* and *Productivity*, which indicates that there are no significant differences between the average results achieved by students and professionals on BL tasks. Nevertheless, as the **Method * Experience** factor indicates, these results are distributed in different ways between the different methods depending on experience. In addition, for *Performance*, the p-values of less than 0.05 obtained by the factors **Sequence** and **Period** indicate significant changes in this variable due to these two design factors. We obtained a Cohen d value of 0.474 between the two alternatives of **Sequence** (G1: MDD-CcD, G2: CcD-MDD), indicating medium differences in favor of G1. The subjects who began the experiment by locating bugs in MDD demonstrated better performance results than those who started with CcD. Similarly, the Cohen d value of 0.405 between the two alternatives of **Period** (Task 1, Task 2) indicates medium differences in favor of Task 1. The subjects performed better on the first task than on the second task. For *Productivity*, the p-values obtained by the factor **Sequence** are also lower than 0.5, indicating significant changes in the subjects' productivity depending on the method they use first during the experiment. The Cohen d value of 0.580 between the two alternatives of **Sequence** indicates medium differences in favor of G1. The subjects who started the experiment solving the BL task in MDD were more productive in both tasks than those who started the experiment solving the BL task in CcD. The differences that we observed in the subjects' performance between the first task and the second task were not reproduced in their productivity since the subjects spent more time on the first task than on the second.

For the variables related to satisfaction, *Perceived Ease of Use*, *Perceived Usefulness* and *Intention to Use*, the **Method** factor obtained p-values of less than 0.05. Therefore, our third null hypothesis is rejected, and the answer to **RQ3** is affirmative: The user satisfaction is significantly different when developers use a different **Method** to solve BL tasks. **Method** has significant large effects on *PEOU*, *PU*, and *ITU*, which confirms the statistical significance of the differences observed in the mean values of the variables related to satisfaction. In addition, the factor **Experience** obtained a p-value of less than 0.05 for *ITU*. The Cohen d value of 0.606 between students and professionals indicates a medium effect in favor of the students. The students gave higher scores than the professionals on *ITU* for both of the methods used in the experiment.

6   Discussion

Overall, both students and professionals reported greater satisfaction when using MDD for bug localization. However, the results of performance and productivity do not show significant differences when considering the group of students. In contrast, when considering the group of professionals, the results of performance and productivity show significant differences in favor of CcD. The results of satisfaction and the focus group comments suggest a positive perception of models in this context, although the results of performance and productivity are not aligned with the subjects' satisfaction.

This observation is consistent with the current state of the scientific literature in this field. Many research efforts make claims regarding the benefits of models, including bug reduction. Nevertheless, the effectiveness of bug localization in models has not been exhaustively evaluated, perhaps because of the assumption that it would be better to use models.

During the focus group, some subjects highlighted that having performed the location in the model before helped them to understand the C++ code. This led to improved performance and productivity in the bug localization tasks for those who had performed the MDD-CcD sequence. These outcomes are supported by the results and hypothesis tests. In addition, the students stated that they preferred to perform bug localization in the models. However, professionals who have a greater proficiency in software development prefer to perform bug localization in the C++ code.

It seems that in CcD, the subjects have a way of navigating (e.g., starting from a method relevant to the bug, they inspect the methods that call it or the methods it calls). However, in MDD, when a model element relevant to the bug is located, it is not clear to the subjects how to continue inspecting the model. One may think that graphically connected model elements (e.g. connected with relationships) are also relevant to the bug, but the bug may involve unconnected model elements. This suggests that it is not straightforward to transfer bug localization in CcD to bug localization in MDD.

Our findings suggest that there is a lack of knowledge on how to approach bug localization in models. This might mean that the established practices yield suboptimal results when they are applied to models. In fact, the students who are more unfamiliar with established practices in software development obtained better results when performing bug localization in models. In contrast to the professionals, the students used more intensively the metamodel to locate bugs, which can also explain why their results were better.

Considering the growing popularity of MDD in the video game domain and their increasing use in industry-specific domains, there is a critical need to focus on how engineers perform bug localization in models. It is important to move away from the current trend of assuming that models are inherently superior for bug localization, as empirical evaluations do not support this assumption.

7   Threats to Validity

To describe the threats to validity of our work, we use the classification of Wohlin et al. [21]. This section shows the threats that affected the experiment.

Conclusion Validity: The *low statistical power* was minimized because the confidence interval is 95%. To minimize the *fishing and the error rate* threat, the statistical analysis has been done by a researcher who did not participate in the task design or in the correction process. The *reliability of measures* threat was mitigated because the measurements were obtained from the data sheets that were automatically generated by the forms with the answers of the subjects when they performed the tasks. The *reliability of treatment implementation* threat was alleviated because the procedure was identical in the two sessions. Also, the tasks were designed with similar difficulty.

Internal Validity: To avoid the *instrumentation* threat, we conducted a pilot study to verify the design and the instrumentation. The *interactions with selection* threat affected the experiment because there were subjects who had different levels of experience, different levels of modeling or coding, and different levels of knowledge of the video game domain. To mitigate this threat, the treatment was applied randomly.

This threat also affected the experiment because of the voluntary nature of participation. We selected students from a course whose content was in line with the experiment activities to avoid student demotivation.

Construct Validity: To mitigate the *mono-method bias* threat, we mechanized the measurements as much as possible by means of correction templates. To weaken the *evaluation apprehension* threat, at the beginning of the experiment, the instructor explained to the subjects that the experiment was not a test of their abilities. The instructor also told the students that neither participation nor results would affect their grades in the course where the experiment took place. In order to mitigate the *author bias* threat, the tasks were extracted from a commercial video game and were designed by the same experts with similar difficulty for the two methods compared. The experiment was affected by the *mono-operation bias* threat since we worked with only two BL tasks from a specific video game.

External Validity: The *interaction of selection and treatment* threat affects the experiment because it involves a larger number of students than professionals, making students more represented in the overall results than professionals. The *domain* threat occurs because the experiment has been conducted in a specific domain (video game) and for a very specific type of task, i.e., to solve a BL task in a scenario of Kromaia video game. We think that other experiments in different games should be performed to validate our findings.

8 Conclusion

In this work, we present an experiment that compares MDD and CcD in terms of performance, productivity, and satisfaction. This work investigates the influence of MDD and CcD on bug localization, employing the video game Kromaia (a commercial video game) as a case study. Bug localization in MDD increased satisfaction, but professionals performed better in CcD. The subjects' techniques that were applied for bug localization showed suboptimal performance in models, highlighting a knowledge gap in MDD bug localization. With the growing popularity of MDD in video games, exploring effective bug localization methods specific to MDD is essential.

References

1. Ampatzoglou, A., Stamelos, I.: Software engineering research for computer games: a systematic review. Inf. Softw. Technol. **52**(9), 888–901 (2010)
2. Arcega, L., Font, J., Cetina, C.: Evolutionary algorithm for bug localization in the reconfigurations of models at runtime. In: Proceedings of the 21st ACM/IEEE International Conference on Model Driven Engineering Languages and Systems, MODELS 2018, New York, NY, USA, pp. 90–100. Association for Computing Machinery (2018). https://doi.org/10.1145/3239372.3239392
3. Arcega, L., Font, J., Haugen, Ø., Cetina, C.: An approach for bug localization in models using two levels: model and metamodel. Softw. Syst. Model. **18**(6), 3551–3576 (2019)
4. Basili, V.R., Dieter Rombach, H.: The TAME project: towards improvement-oriented software environments. IEEE Trans. Softw. Eng. **14**(6), 758–773 (1988)
5. Blasco, D., Font, J., Zamorano, M., Cetina, C.: An evolutionary approach for generating software models: the case of Kromaia in game software engineering. J. Syst. Softw. **171**, 110804 (2021)

6. Chueca, J., Trasobares, J.I., Domingo, Á., Arcega, L., Cetina, C., Font, J.: Comparing software product lines and clone and own for game software engineering under two paradigms: model-driven development and code-driven development. J. Syst. Softw. **205**, 111824 (2023)
7. Cohen, J.: Statistical Power for the Social Sciences. Laurence Erlbaum and Associates, Hillsdale (1988)
8. Domingo, Á., Echeverría, J., Pastor, Ó., Cetina, C.: Evaluating the benefits of model-driven development. In: Dustdar, S., Yu, E., Salinesi, C., Rieu, D., Pant, V. (eds.) CAiSE 2020. LNCS, vol. 12127, pp. 353–367. Springer, Cham (2020). https://doi.org/10.1007/978-3-030-49435-3_22
9. Domingo, Á., Echeverría, J., Pastor, Ó., Cetina, C.: Comparing UML-based and DSL-based modeling from subjective and objective perspectives. In: La Rosa, M., Sadiq, S., Teniente, E. (eds.) CAiSE 2021. LNCS, vol. 12751, pp. 483–498. Springer, Cham (2021). https://doi.org/10.1007/978-3-030-79382-1_29
10. Kapteijns, T., Jansen, S., Brinkkemper, S., Houet, H., Barendse, R.: A comparative case study of model driven development vs traditional development: the tortoise or the hare. From code centric to model centric software engineering Practices Implications and ROI (2009)
11. Karac, E.I., Turhan, B., Juristo, N.: A controlled experiment with novice developers on the impact of task description granularity on software quality in test-driven development. IEEE Trans. Softw. Eng. **47**(7), 1315–1330 (2019)
12. Krogmann, K., Becker, S.: A case study on model-driven and conventional software development: the Palladio editor. Softw. Eng. (2007)
13. Martínez, Y., Cachero, C., Meliá, S.: MDD vs. traditional software development: a practitioner's subjective perspective. Inf. Softw. Technol. **55**(2), 189–200 (2013)
14. Mellegård, N., Staron, M.: Distribution of effort among software development artefacts: an initial case study. In: Bider, I., et al. (eds.) BPMDS/EMMSAD -2010. LNBIP, vol. 50, pp. 234–246. Springer, Heidelberg (2010). https://doi.org/10.1007/978-3-642-13051-9_20
15. Moody, D.L.: The method evaluation model: a theoretical model for validating information systems design methods. In: ECIS 2003 Proceedings, p. 79 (2003)
16. Mussbacher, G., et al.: The relevance of model-driven engineering thirty years from now. In: Dingel, J., Schulte, W., Ramos, I., Abrahão, S., Insfran, E. (eds.) MODELS 2014. LNCS, vol. 8767, pp. 183–200. Springer, Cham (2014). https://doi.org/10.1007/978-3-319-11653-2_12
17. Panach, J.I., España, S., Dieste, Ó., Pastor, Ó., Juristo, N.: In search of evidence for model-driven development claims: an experiment on quality, effort, productivity and satisfaction. Inf. Softw. Technol. **62**, 164–186 (2015)
18. Papotti, P.E., do Prado, A.F., de Souza, W.L., Cirilo, C.E., Pires, L.F.: A quantitative analysis of model-driven code generation through software experimentation. In: Salinesi, C., Norrie, M.C., Pastor, Ó. (eds.) CAiSE 2013. LNCS, vol. 7908, pp. 321–337. Springer, Heidelberg (2013). https://doi.org/10.1007/978-3-642-38709-8_21
19. Vegas, S., Apa, C., Juristo, N.: Crossover designs in software engineering experiments: benefits and perils. IEEE Trans. Softw. Eng. **42**(2), 120–135 (2015)
20. West, B.T., Welch, K.B., Galecki, A.T.: Linear Mixed Models: A Practical Guide Using Statistical Software. Chapman and Hall/CRC, London (2014)
21. Wohlin, C., Runeson, P., Höst, M., Ohlsson, M.C., Regnell, B., Wesslén, A.: Experimentation in Software Engineering. Springer, Heidelberg (2012)

A Model-Driven Framework to Support Portfolio Management Under Uncertainties

Clara Le Duff[1,4]([✉]), Yohann Chasseray[1], Audrey Fertier[1], Raphaël Falco[2],
Anouck Adrot[3], Benoit Montreuil[4], and Frederick Benaben[1,4]

[1] Centre Génie Industriel, IMT Mines Albi, 81000 Albi, France
clara.le_duff@mines-albi.fr
[2] Lab R&D, Scalian, 31000 Toulouse, France
[3] Dauphine Recherches en Management (DRM), Université Paris Dauphine,
75016 Paris, France
[4] Physical Internet Center, Georgia Institute of Technology, Atlanta, USA

Abstract. Project Portfolio management has become a standard in the business world as a means of structuring and achieving corporate objectives. It enables the progress of a project portfolio to be monitored and evaluated using a wide range of techniques, in particular the risks management approach. However, due to the complexity and uniqueness of these portfolios, it's becoming increasingly difficult to predict the evolution of portfolios and assess the impact of every change on the performance regarding the predefined objectives. This leads to emerging uncertainties that portfolio managers must address at each stage of the portfolio management process. To address this problem, we focus on the execution phase of portfolio management process and present through the vision of uncertainty in a portfolio management context, a model-driven framework using the Physics of Decision paradigm to support the execution phase of a projects portfolio. This framework presents a new approach to monitor projects portfolios which add flexibility and information interpretation to the risk management principles and could serve as a basis for the development of future information systems.

Keywords: Project portfolio management · Uncertainty · Risk an Opportunity management · Information support system · Physics of decision

1 Introduction

Although projects have been a fundamental aspect of human civilization, and the need for collaboration has been recognized for centuries, the formalization of project management as a field emerged in 1950's [34]. This marked the beginning of the development of tools and methods for managing projects. Notable early figures in this development were Henri Ford and Henry Gantt who set up tools and framework for project management that are still widely used nowadays.

G. Guizzardi et al. (Eds.): CAiSE 2024, LNCS 14663, pp. 596–611, 2024.
https://doi.org/10.1007/978-3-031-61057-8_35

In increasingly volatile, uncertain, complex and ambiguous (VUCA) environment, companies from various sectors divided their activities into portfolios or programs, each containing multiple projects aimed at achieving strategic and financial objectives [1,7,19]. The Project Management Institute (PMI) has outlined four phases for Project Portfolio Management (PPM): *Initiation, Planning, Execution,* and *Optimization* [12]. Projects in the same portfolio are mainly interrelated, due to the sharing of the same resources and the dependencies between several tasks in different projects. The inherent complexity and dynamic nature of both the organization and its environment make these four phases complex to execute during portfolio management, these two factors create a climate conducive to uncertainty.

Uncertainty, defined by the Cambridge dictionary as "caused by the possibility of a sudden change in the current situation", plays an important role in this context. Portfolio management strategies need to be well-prepared to cope with and mitigate this uncertainty, in order to ensure the successful execution of projects and the achievement of the corresponding objectives. These challenges can be addressed through the implementation of information systems to enhance data collection, processing, storage, and information distribution in complex situations [8]. Moreover, several studies have highlighted the positive impact of computerized Information Systems in PPM for achieving successful performance [14], so it seems appropriate to use Portfolio Management Information Systems (PMIS) and to integrate uncertainty perception. The perception of uncertainty can be achieved through the creation of multiple scenarios by managers, enabling them to subsequently enhance their management practices. Despite the variety of frameworks and methods developed for PMIS, including those based on knowledge management, risk management, and optimization, organizations still struggle with the monitoring and control of their portfolios under uncertainties (induced by the increasing complexity and dynamics) [10,15,25]. **Is there a project management information system able to support managers in managing the risks and opportunities associated with the planning and execution phases of portfolio management, despite the uncertainties?** This question is addressed through a presentation of the related works regarding the monitoring of a portfolio and their limitations regarding uncertainties. Then, an approach inspired by the Physic of Decision (POD) paradigm will be detailed and adapted to the portfolio management context. Finally, the relevance of this approach will be demonstrate with an illustrative example.

2 Related Work

2.1 From Risk Management to Uncertainty Management

The traditional approach to risk management involves risk identification, assessment, mitigation and control. Methods developed in these fields have proved effective when fed by historical data, or with managers expertise. But in today's unique and complex portfolio, these traditional methods are no longer suited to their expectations [2]. With a weak background knowledge, it will be difficult, if not impossible, to manage risks, i.e. identify, assess, mitigate and control risks. In addition to a knowledge base, companies should include learning and flexibility to their risk management approach [20] and change their vision of risks [24]. The Standard for Portfolio Management [12] advises portfolio manager to "continually monitor changes in the broad environment". The study of uncertainty began in the early 20th century as a result of the unpredictable and dynamic turbulence with which managers and their companies were increasingly confronted. Uncertainty management is the future of portfolio and project management [2]: the ability to understand, assess, adapt and cope with the dynamic of unexpected changes [20]. Therefore, how to better understand and monitor portfolio evolution?

To answer this question, the subsections below present (i) existing methods for managing different sources of uncertainty and (ii) an existing approach for modeling and managing cascading effects, and risk management as well as opportunity management.

2.2 Sources of Uncertainties

Petit [24,25] identifies four sources of uncertainty in portfolio management due to: (i) changes at the level of a single project, (ii) changes at the level of the portfolio, (iii) the complexity of the organization, and (iv) the environment of the organization. To identify methods able to deal with these different type of uncertainty, we perform a literature review using the following query: (**TITLE("project*" OR "portfolio*") W/1 "management") AND TITLE (system* OR methodolog* OR framework*) AND TITLE-ABS-KEY (uncert*))**. The query was executed on SCOPUS, yielding 111 items. Subsequently, exclusion criteria were applied focusing on the studied phase of the portfolio management process (the execution phase was selected).

Change in a Single Project. Changes in a project includes the addition, modification, or deletion of a resource, a task, a planing or every component of the project. Simulations are widely used to assess and support the management of risks linked to a change within a single project. An ontology can be used to model a portfolio and its projects, then, based on expertise, inference rules can be defined to propagate the impacts of changes [9,16]. In more complex and unpredictable environment, a multi-agent model [3] or a system dynamic model [5] can be used to mathematically model the behaviour of a portfolio and its projects, including the impacts of changes. In addition, uncertainties in the inputs of simulation models lead to uncertainties in their outputs. As proposed by [23], fuzzy logic can be used to model these uncertainties.

Change in a Portfolio. Changes in a portfolio include the addition, modification, prioritization or deletion of a project [31]. Every portfolio's value is assessed by the manager and is subject to uncertainty. As with a change in a project, simulation and fuzzy logic can be used to support the management of risks at the portfolio level.

Organizational Complexity. Uncertainties are linked to the complexity of each project, its portfolio, the organization or its environment. These organizational complexities depend on the number, variety and interconnections of these components [13]. They can be structural, emergent and sociopolitical [18]. Simulation and fuzzy logic should also be used to support risk management despite the organizational complexity. This is illustrated in [16] and promoted by [17] who stresses the need for context-sensitive portfolio risk management.

External Environment. Changes in the environment of the organization include changes in its zone of influence, in its competitors' zones of influence, or in its global environment. [24,32] propose to include uncertainties in the management of risks linked to technical, market or costumer developments. It is evident that the sources of uncertainties are diverse, and their treatment varies across the literature. Is there a singular method to model these uncertainties and their impacts on heterogeneous and unique projects or portfolios?

2.3 Risk and Opportunity Management

Portfolio management information systems (PMIS) can support the management of risks during the *initiation* and *planning* phase of every project and portfolio, thanks to simulation and fuzzy logic approaches. They manage opportunities, as well as risks [33]. They could also support risks and opportunities management during their *execution* phase: the more uncertainties there are, the more important it is to monitor changes and their consequences during the execution of individual projects.

In the literature, the POD approach appears to be intriguing for addressing this question. In the POD approach, every evolution of a system is determined by the risks and opportunities it faces [4]. As illustrated in Fig. 1, the POD core ontology can model any cause and effect relationships with 3 concepts and 4 relationships. It can be supplemented by existing conceptualizations of uncertainty, such as those proposed by [27] (through complexity, equivocity, etc.). Therefore, can the POD approach be used to model and simulate the evolution of a portfolio, its organization, its environment, and the risks and opportunities associated with each, during both the project planning and execution phases?

3 Proposal

To provide some answers to this question, the research work presented in this paper proposes to combine:

- the Physics of Decision (POD) approach used by Le Duff [16] to model both the changes in a portfolio dynamically during the control process and propose a decision support system tool based on scenarios created by the portfolio managers. An ontology of this model is defined bellow;

– the domain ontology dedicated to Project Definition inspired by Stahl [29], the domain ontology dedicated to Project Monitoring of Dong [9] and the domain ontology dedicated to the portfolio of projects develop by Newton [22] in order to structure the data and the knowledge concerning portfolio project nature and context in order to identify the possible sources of uncertainties;
– the rule-based approach proposed by Tah [30] to model the behaviour of a portfolio project using the risks and opportunities that they faced. Notably, rules defined by [30] are revised and changed to include flexibility and dynamics;

Ontologies were developed following the four classical stages: Specification, Conceptualization, Formalization, and Implementation [26]. Leveraging the principle of utilizing POD (Principle of Ontology Dynamics), all dynamics must be articulated using the CORE ontology, positioned alongside the domain ontology. We translated the main paradigm of POD: "Every system evolution can be explained by risks and opportunities that the system faces, and these risks and opportunities can be expressed through characteristics of my system. Thus, we have the Core Ontology, and then we proceed to delineate, in the most general manner possible, the components and associations between these components.

3.1   The POD Framework

The Physics of Decision (POD) ontology [4], represented in Fig. 1, uses *Potentialities* to model the behaviour of any systems, from supply chains [6] to pandemics [21]. If the potentiality threatens to reduce the performance of a system, it is called a *Risk*, if it improves it, it is called an *Opportunity*. Usually, risks, i.e. Potentialities, are seen as a product of hazard, i.e. *Potential*, and exposure and vulnerability, i.e. *Susceptibility* [11]. A negative potential is a *Danger*, a positive potential is a *Favorability*. Three types of inference rules are define with conditions on characteristics. They are used to infer the creation of a potential, a potentiality, or the triggering of a potentiality. The *modifies* condition includes a condition and its implications for the characteristics of affected components.

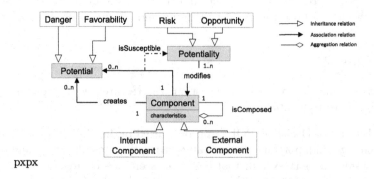

pxpx

Fig. 1. The ontology model of the POD paradigm.

3.2   The Domain Ontology Dedicated to Project Portfolios

To model the behaviour of project portfolios, we propose the domain ontology shown in Fig. 2. It is inspired from the Stahl model [29], who created a meta-model at the component level to enable the most comprehensive modeling of heterogeneous elements within a single formalism. Regarding Dong's model [9], we drew inspiration for the list of components and their associated association relationships within the portfolio of components. Regarding Newton's proposed ontology, it can be used to instantiate the model and determine the functionalities of a future Information System and whether they are compatible with the Core Ontology POD. A *Portfolio* is made up of *Projects*. A project is made up of *Tasks*. A task can group together other tasks, i.e. subtasks. Following SADT (Structured Analysis and Design Technique) notation principle [28], each task, project or portfolio, has *Inputs, Resources, Outputs* and *Objectives*. Portfolio, projects and tasks are *Portfolio components*. *Internal components* are internal to the project manager's organisation. Resources can be either human, financial, material or software resources. Then *Objective* concerns portfolio components. Two kind of *External Components* are considered: the *Contributing Components* and the *Contextual Components*. Contributing components are external resources that can be allocated to portfolio components. Contextual components cannot be controlled but can affect one or more project components. For example, weather conditions, seismic zones, networks (transport, energy, communication) and political contexts are considered as contextual components. The task concept is one of the lowest level concept of the ontology.

Association Relations Between Concepts. Inputs (such as a requirement or goods) *isNeeded* by a portfolio component, *uses* resources (human, material, money or a software for example) and *generates* outputs (goods, delivery, report). The A resource can *use* or be used by other resources (a machine *uses* one human resources) and external components *provides* internal components (external goods, external human, to help executing the portfolio component). Finally, a collaborator *provides* external resources. The availability of inputs and resources of a portfolio component conditions its ability to start. The completion a portfolio component generates outputs that can be reused as inputs for one or more portfolio components.

The novelty of this approach lies in the extension of a domain ontology by a Core ontology. The purpose of this Core ontology is to be able to serve as the extension for any domain ontology, this is what is reflected in Fig. 2. By creating rules that link instances related to our domain with the dynamics linked to the Core ontology, we are able to simulate any evolution of a system.

3.3   The Rule-Based Approach

Our framework includes how the POD model, extended to the portfolio project management domain, can be used to simulate the evolution of a portfolio given a chosen *timestep*. Following the research work of Tah [30] and [4] we propose to

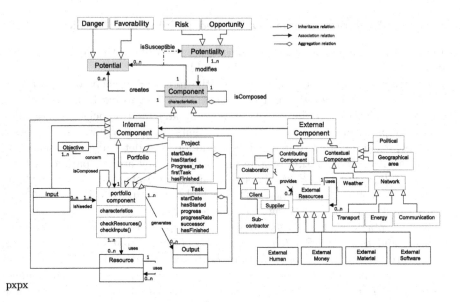

pxpx

Fig. 2. The POD ontology extended to the portfolio project management domain

model its dynamic using inference rules. These rules represent risks and opportunities: the *functional behaviour* (opportunities needed to simulate the execution of the portfolio of projects) and the *emerging behaviour* (emerging potentialities needed to simulate the execution of the portfolio subject to different sources of uncertainty).

Three rules are proposed to represent portfolios behaviours. To ensure genericity, these rules are first defined on the POD core ontology level: (**R1**) traduces the conditions for a Component to generate a Potential (Danger or Favorability); (**R2**) traduces the conditions for a Component to be susceptible to a Potential, thus generating a Potentiality (Risk or Opportunity); (**R3**) traduces the conditions for a Potentiality to be triggered and its consequences to be applied on components characteristics. These three upper rules are then specified according to the concepts of our domain ontology for each Potentiality. Each portfolio domain specification rule is presented below.

Modelling Functional Behaviours. We define functional behaviour (FB) as the behaviour that encompasses the classic (undisturbed) dynamic of a portfolio of projects (executing a planning and divide activities into tasks). We identified five functional behaviours proper to portfolio management that are described in Table 1. The mathematical description of the functional rules associated to these behaviours are described in Table 3). FB1 states that if a project is not started and can starts, it starts. FB2 states that if a project has started, its first task has not started yet but can start, then it starts. FB3 states that if a started task remains unfinished, and can continue, it goes on. FB4 states that if a task is finished, has a successive task which can start, then this task starts. Finally FB5

Table 1. Couple Favorability/Opportunity to model the functional behaviour of a portfolio.

generator type	Condition of generation (R1)	Fav	suceptible type	Condition of susceptibility (R2)	Opp	Condition of triggering (R3)
Project P_x	A project is not started	$F_1^{P_x}$	Project P_y	The project has inputs and available resources	$O_1^{F_1^{P_y},P_y}$	Project Manager trigger
Project P_x	Project started, first Task not started	$F_2^{P_x}$	Task T_y	The first task has inputs and available resources	$O_2^{F_2^{P_x},T_y}$	Project Manager trigger
Task T_x	Task has started and is not finished	$F_3^{T_x}$	Task T_y	The first task has inputs and available resources	$O_3^{F_3^{T_x},T_y}$	Project Manager trigger
Task T_x	Task is finished and has successor	$F_4^{T_x}$	Task T_y	The successor task has inputs and available resources	$O_4^{F_4^{T_x},T_y}$	Project Manager trigger
Task T_x	The last task is finished	$F_5^{T_x}$	Project P_y	The projects can generated outputs	$O_5^{F_5^{T_x},P_y}$	Project Manager trigger

states that if the last task of a project is finished, the project can be closed. The singularity of our approach is that each of these functional behaviours can be modeled through the execution of a set of rules specified from the generic rules defined in the previous section (R1 and R2, R3 being automatically triggered). The application of these rules is repeated as much as necessary at each timestep of portfolios life cycle automating the projects executions. The possibility to use these rules is ensured by the identification of functional behaviours components with Potential and Potentialities, as it is presented in Table 1. The following formalism is used to refer to the attribute of a concept: "*concept.attribute*".

The Emerging Behaviours. The emerging behaviours (the emerging risks and opportunities faced by the portfolio) depend on unexpected events (emerging risks or opportunities grouped under the Potentiality concept) as opposed to expected behaviour (functional behaviour, modeled by functional opportunities). Unlike functional behaviours, the number and variety of emerging behaviour make them more difficult to list and sometimes domain dependent. To do so, we propose the following method to implement these emerging behaviour through the same mechanism as before:

1. Identify a list of potentialities (risk or opportunity) that our portfolio can face using domain experts or literature.
2. Identify the components that generate each identified potential and define the generation condition using its characteristics.

Table 2. Example of couple Potential (P)/Potentiality(PO) to model the emerging behaviour of a portfolio.

generator	Condition of generation (**R1**)	P	susceptible	Condition of susceptibility (**R2**)	PO	Condition of triggering (**R3**)
Colab $Colab_x$	A new colaborator produces resources	$P_n^{Colab_x}$	Task T_y	The task uses this resources	$Po_n^{P_n^{Colab_x},T_y}$	To sign contract with
Task T_x	A task needed inputs	$P_m^{T_x}$	Project P_y	The project has no stock reserve	$Po_m^{P_m^{T_x},P_y}$	The number of input increase

3. Identify the components that are susceptible to these potentials and define the susceptibility conditions using characteristics.
4. Find the triggering conditions for the potentiality for each type of susceptible components, using characteristics of components of the portfolio.
5. Find the consequences of the potentiality as a change of characteristics, regarding all the characteristics of the portfolio.

To illustrate the proposed methodology, two examples of couple potential, potentiality are explain using language natural in Table 2 and the rules are written using first order logic in Table 3. The first example involves an opportunity through the association of a new collaborator to a given task. The collaborator is here a generator of a potential as he may produces some resources. The components identified as susceptible to this potential are all tasks that may need the produced resource. If one task actually needs the produced resource, then the potentiality linking them is created. The opportunity will be seize and will impact the task if the contract with this new collaborator is signed. The second example involves a risk under the change of an input on the task and so the project, and the portfolio. In this case, the fact that a task has started and has input created the potential danger of lacking a component. The susceptible component is identified as the project associated has no inventory buffer regarding this input. This will generates the potentiality (risk) of lacking resource. The risk is triggered if the change on this input has changed, and the consequences will be that the task can not continue. Table 2 and 3 is a sample of possible rules regarding the emerging behaviors of a portfolio; these rules can be created as long as the corresponding components and attributes exist in the model instance. Through a cascade effect, one can thus describe the behaviors and consequences of these uncertainties and changes at the portfolio scale (Fig. 3).

Table 3. Corresponding mathematical rules.

Corresponding mathematics rules

$\forall Project\ P_x,\ P_x.hasStarted() = No \wedge P_x.startDate <= now \rightarrow \exists F_1^{P_x},\ P_x\ generates\ F_1$ **(R1)**

et. $\forall F_1^{P_x}, \forall Project, P_y,\ P_y = P_x \wedge P_y.checkInputs() = 1 \wedge P_y.checkResources() = 1 \rightarrow \exists O_1^{F_1^{P_y},P_y}\ P_y\ susceptible\ to\ F_1^{P_x}$ **(R2)**

and $\forall O_1^{F_1^{P_y},P_y},\ ProjectManager.trigger() \rightarrow P_y.hasStarted() = Yes \wedge P_y.activeTasks = None$ **(R3)**

$\forall Project\ P_x,\ P_x.hasStarted() = Yes \wedge P_x.activeTasks = None \rightarrow \exists F_2^{P_x},\ P_x\ generates\ F_2$ **(R1)**

and $\forall F_2^{P_x}, \forall Task, T_y,\ P_x.firstTask = T_y \wedge T_y.checkInputs() = 1 \wedge T_y.checkResources() = 1 \rightarrow \exists O_2^{F_2^{P_x},T_y},\ T_y\ susceptible\ to\ F_2^{P_x}$ **(R2)**

and $\forall O_2^{F_2^{P_x},T_y},\ ProjectManager.trigger() \rightarrow T_y.hasStarted() = Yes \wedge P_x.activeTasks = T_y$ **(R3)**

$\forall Task\ T_x,\ T_x.hasStarted() = Yes \wedge P_x.progress \leq 1 \rightarrow \exists F_3^{T_x},\ T_x\ generates\ F_3$ **(R1)**

and $\forall F_3^{T_x}, \forall Task, T_y,\ T_y = T_x \wedge T_y.checkInputs() = 1 \wedge T_y.checkResources() = 1 \rightarrow \exists O_3^{F_3^{T_x},T_y},\ T_y\ susceptible\ to\ F_3^{T_x}$ **(R2)**

and $\forall O_3^{F_3^{T_x},T_y},\ ProjectManager.trigger() \rightarrow T_y.progress = T_y.progree + T_y.progressRate$ **(R3)**

$\forall Task\ T_x,\ T_x.hasStarted() = Yes \wedge P_x.progress \geq 1 \rightarrow \exists F_4^{T_x},\ T_x\ generates\ F_4$ **(R1)**

and $\forall F_4^{T_x}, \forall Task, T_y,\ T_x.successor = T_y \wedge T_y.checkInputs() = 1 \wedge T_y.checkResources() = 1 \rightarrow \exists O_4^{F_4^{T_x},T_y},\ T_y\ susceptible\ to\ F_4^{T_x}$ **(R2)**

and $\forall O_4^{F_4^{T_x},T_y},\ ProjectManager.trigger() \rightarrow T_y.hasStarted() = Yes \wedge T_x.hasFinished() = Yes$ **(R3)**

$\forall Task\ T_x,\ T_x.hasStarted() = Yes \wedge P_x.progress \geq 1 \wedge T_x.successor = end \rightarrow \exists F_5^{T_x},\ T_x\ generates\ F_5$ **(R1)**

and $\forall F_5^{T_x}, \forall Project, P_y,\ T_x.project = P_y \rightarrow \exists O_5^{F_5^{T_x},P_y},\ P_y\ susceptible\ to\ F_5^{T_x}$ **(R2)**

and $\forall, O_5^{F_5^{T_x},P_y},\ ProjectManager.trigger() \rightarrow P_y.hasFinished() = Yes \wedge T_x.hasFinished() = Yes$ **(R3)**

$\forall Collaborator, Collab_x, Collab_x.listproduct = Resource10 \rightarrow \exists P_n^{Collab_x}, Collab_x\ generates\ P_n$ **(R1)**

and $\forall P_n^{Collab_x}, \forall Task, T_y.usesResources = Resources10 \rightarrow \exists Po_n^{P_n^{Collab_x},T_y},\ T_y\ susceptible\ to\ P_n^{Collab_x}$ **(R2)**

and $\forall Po_n^{P_n^{Collab_x},T_y},\ ProjectManager.trigger() \rightarrow T_y.Collab = Collab_x$ **(R3)**

$\forall Task, T', Task.hasStarted() == Yes \wedge Task.hasInput() == yes \rightarrow \exists P_m^{T_x}, T_x\ generates\ P_m$ **(R1)**

and $\forall P_m^{T_x}, \forall Project, P_y, \forall Task, T_x,\ P_y.hasbuffer() == 0 \wedge T_x \in P_y.tasks \rightarrow \exists Po_m^{P_m^{T_x},P_y},\ P_y\ susceptible\ to\ P_m^{T_x}$ **(R2)**

and $\forall Po_m^{P_m^{T_x},P_y},\ T_x.inputs.hasChanged() == Yes \rightarrow O_3^{T_x,P_y} = False$ **(R3)**

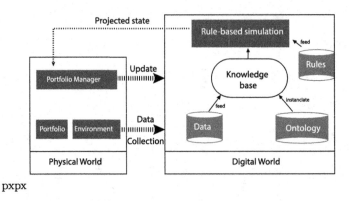

pxpx

Fig. 3. The rule-based simulation framework

3.4   Utilization Framework

Our framework combining the POD approach, our domain ontology and our rules, can be used at both design-time and at run-time. All the available data from environment and the portfolio itself (regarding projects and tasks) instantiate the digital model inside the information system. This digital model serves as a representation of the portfolio's actual state. The portfolio manager can use at least the opportunities define by the rules in Table 1 to model the dynamics of the portfolio and visualize the undisturbed execution of the portfolio. Then, for each known emerging behaviour and its associated potentiality (risk or opportunity), he can provide the information corresponding to the (**R1**), (**R2**), (**R3**) rules. Thank to our mechanism, their propagation and impact is automatically modeled. At run time, the framework can also be used to update the model. If the portfolio undergoes a change that has not been modeled by the potentialities, the portfolio manager can update the characteristics, or create new couple of Potential/Potentiality and this will be store and save on the rules set and will be taken into account during the subsequent execution of the rules. The portfolio's dynamics can therefore be simulated with its data and rules, and the portfolio manager can create simulations, with events or changes he wants to study, with the desired projection time. The aim is to: (i) add change due to risks and opportunities at any time during the portfolio's execution; (ii) be able to model the cascading effect, since a change in one characteristic can be the condition of existence of a potential, the condition to susceptibility of a component or to trigger a potentiality, generating this way a cascading effect; (iii) add flexibility to portfolio modeling, enabling us to cover a large number of scenarios for study through a generic and simple mechanism; (iv) decrease uncertainty due to the understanding and the formalization of the knowledge concerning the portfolio (risks and opportunities identification) execution.

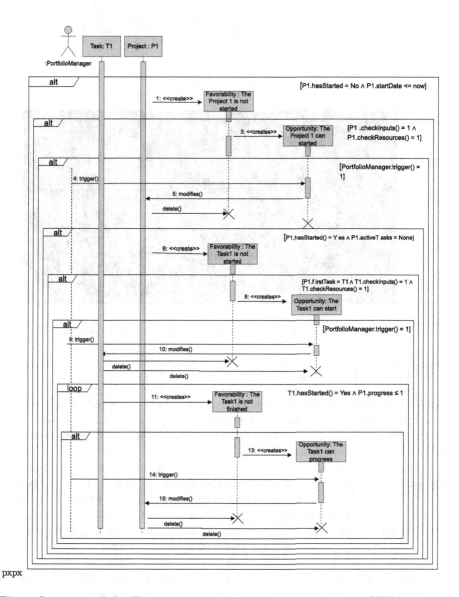

pxpx

Fig. 4. Beginning of the illustrative example of project progress using UML sequence diagram.

pxpx

Fig. 5. Interface of the risks and opportunities view of the prototype.

3.5   Application Example

We were able to simulate the evolution of a portfolio using only the five functional rules mentioned above. Subsequently, when modeling the evolution of the portfolio, we added the rules corresponding to emerging risks and opportunities to assess impacts and create response scenarios.

The example in Fig. 4 shows our framework applied to the simulation of a portfolio execution. It shows how certain concepts, such as favorability and opportunity, are created and how they contribute to the functional behaviour of the portfolio. It is modeled using a UML sequence diagram. Throughout the project's lifecycle, the favorability for project initiation ('The project can begin') is established if the project has not yet started. Upon meeting all necessary conditions, the opportunity to initiate the project emerges. Ultimately, the Portfolio Manager determines the activation of this opportunity, transitioning the project status to 'has started'. A similar mechanism applies to task initiation, followed by a loop that advances the task in accordance with associated favorabilities and opportunities. The scalability of this mechanism can simulate any portfolio, whatever their complexity, and whatever the emerging risks and opportunities. This approach facilitates a clear visualization of the cascading effects and their causes. A prototype has been developed incorporating these five rules and emerging potentialities rules to observe the evolution of a portfolio comprising two projects. When the rules are applied, the portfolio functions properly. Figure 5 is a screenshot depicting a moment during the execution of the portfolio in the prototype

4   Conclusion

We propose a new vision for integrating risk and opportunity management in portfolio execution. To do so, we adapted POD paradigm to our field as it allows to explain any change as a potentiality (risk or opportunity) that a portfolio may undergoes. This approach also assumes that the optimal functioning of a portfolio is in fact a sequence of opportunities that the manager has seized. With the current proposition, it is expected to model the evolution of a project portfolio using a single formalism. The ontology domain remains adaptable by the user; however, substantial work is still required on the model's dynamics. Since the dynamics are governed by rules, it is essential to ensure that the rules can be sequenced without causing infinite execution loops. This is why the paper suggests this simple formalism, which already allows for the consideration and customization of this proposition. As the proposed framework operates under the premise of known risks and opportunities, one of its limits resides in the needed domain specific description of emerging behaviour for a given portfolio. However, once these risks and opportunities have been listed, the automated dimension of our approach ensures the translation of their dynamic. These are the initial steps towards the generalization of models and the uniformity of portfolio management information systems. A first perspective is the transition towards a performance-based vision. This implies the definition of KPIs in order to better evaluate each potentiality or scenario. Through this performance-based approach supported by POD, a second perspective is the tracking of the real performance of a project portfolio, as multi-dimensional trajectories representing the difference between expectation and reality. A difference means that a potentiality has not been integrated yet. These two perspectives align with the long-term ambition of this work: a digital twin of a portfolio, allowing a manager to interact with the projects' execution, and foresee their evolution, despite their singularity, dynamics, complexity and uncertainty.

References

1. Arantes, A., Alhais, A.F., Ferreira, L.M.D.F.: Application of a purchasing portfolio model to define medicine purchasing strategies: an empirical study. Socioecon. Plann. Sci. **84**, 101318 (2022). https://doi.org/10.1016/j.seps.2022.101318
2. Aven, T.: Risk assessment and risk management: review of recent advances on their foundation. Eur. J. Oper. Res. **253**(1), 1–13 (2016). https://doi.org/10.1016/j.ejor.2015.12.023
3. Batkovskiy, A.M., Kurennykh, A.E., Semenova, E.G., Sudakov, V.A., Fomina, A.V., Balashov, V.M.: Sustainable project management for multi-agent development of enterprise information systems. Entrepreneurship Sustain. Issues **7**(1), 278–290 (2019). https://doi.org/10.9770/jesi.2019.7.1(21)
4. Benaben, F., et al.: Instability is the norm! A physics-based theory to navigate among risks and opportunities. Enterp. Inf. Syst. **16**(6), 1–28 (2021). https://doi.org/10.1080/17517575.2021.1878391

5. Calderon Tellez, J., Bell, G., Herrera, M.M., Sato, C.: Project management and system dynamics modelling: time to connect with innovation and sustainability. Syst. Res. Behav. Sci. (2023). https://doi.org/10.1002/sres.2926

6. Cerabona, T., et al.: The physics of decision approach: a physics-based vision to manage supply chain resilience. Int. J. Prod. Res. 1–20 (2023). https://doi.org/10.1080/00207543.2023.2201637

7. Cooper, R.G., Edgett, S.J., Kleinschmidt, E.J.: New product portfolio management: practices and performance. J. Prod. Innov. Manag. **16**(4), 333–351 (1999). https://doi.org/10.1016/S0737-6782(99)00005-3

8. DeLone, W.H., McLean, E.R.: Information systems success: the quest for the dependent variable. Inf. Syst. Res. **3**(1), 60–95 (1992). https://doi.org/10.1287/isre.3.1.60

9. Dong, H., Hussain, F., Chang, E.: ORPMS: an ontology-based real-time project monitoring system in the cloud. JUCS - J. Univ. Comput. Sci. **17**(8), 1161–1182 (2011). https://doi.org/10.3217/jucs-017-08-1161

10. Dvir, D., Lechler, T.: Plans are nothing, changing plans is everything: the impact of changes on project success. Res. Policy **33**(1), 1–15 (2004). https://doi.org/10.1016/j.respol.2003.04.001

11. Hochrainer-Stigler, S., et al.: Toward a framework for systemic multi-hazard and multi-risk assessment and management. iScience **26**(5), 106736 (2023). https://doi.org/10.1016/j.isci.2023.106736

12. Project Management Institute (ed.): The Standard for Portfolio Management. Advances in Business Strategy and Competitive Advantage (ABSCA), 4th edn. Project Management Institute, Newtown Square (2018)

13. Kaufmann, C., Kock, A.: Does project management matter? The relationship between project management effort, complexity, and profitability. Int. J. Proj. Manag. **40**(6), 624–633 (2022). https://doi.org/10.1016/j.ijproman.2022.05.007

14. Kock, A., Schulz, B., Kopmann, J., Gemünden, H.G.: Project portfolio management information systems' positive influence on performance - the importance of process maturity. Int. J. Proj. Manag. **38**(4), 229–241 (2020). https://doi.org/10.1016/j.ijproman.2020.05.001

15. Korhonen, T., Laine, T., Martinsuo, M.: Management control of project portfolio uncertainty: a managerial role perspective. Proj. Manag. J. **45**(1), 21–37 (2014). https://doi.org/10.1002/pmj.21390

16. Le Duff, C., Gitto, J.P., Jeany, J., Falco, R., Lauras, M., Benaben, F.: A physics-based approach to evaluate crisis impacts on project management, pp. 134–143 (2022)

17. Martinsuo, M., Korhonen, T., Laine, T.: Identifying, framing and managing uncertainties in project portfolios. Int. J. Proj. Manag. **32**(5), 732–746 (2014). https://doi.org/10.1016/j.ijproman.2014.01.014

18. Maylor, H.R., Turner, N.W., Murray-Webster, R.: How hard can it be?: Actively managing complexity in technology projects. Res. Technol. Manag. **56**(4), 45–51 (2013). https://doi.org/10.5437/08956308X5602125

19. Meskendahl, S.: The influence of business strategy on project portfolio management and its success - a conceptual framework. Int. J. Proj. Manag. **28**(8), 807–817 (2010). https://doi.org/10.1016/j.ijproman.2010.06.007

20. Meyer, A.D., Loch, C.H., Pich, M.T.: Managing project uncertainty: from variation to chaos. MIT Sloan Manag. Rev. **43**(2), 60 (2002)

21. Moradkhani, N., Benaben, F., Montreuil, B., Lauras, M., Jeany, J., Faugre, L.: Multi-criteria performance analysis based on physics of decision - application to COVID-19 and future pandemics. IEEE Trans. Serv. Comput. **16**(3), 1987–1998 (2023). https://doi.org/10.1109/TSC.2022.3187214

22. Newton, E., Girardi, R.: PROPOST: a knowledge-based tool for supporting project portfolio management. In: 2007 International Conference on Systems Engineering and Modeling, pp. 9–16 (2007). https://doi.org/10.1109/ICSEM.2007.373328

23. Oh, J., Yang, J., Lee, S.: Managing uncertainty to improve decision-making in NPD portfolio management with a fuzzy expert system. Expert Syst. Appl. **39**(10), 9868–9885 (2012). https://doi.org/10.1016/j.eswa.2012.02.164

24. Petit, Y.: Project portfolios in dynamic environments: organizing for uncertainty. Int. J. Proj. Manag. **30**(5), 539–553 (2012). https://doi.org/10.1016/j.ijproman.2011.11.007

25. Petit, Y., Hobbs, B.: Project portfolios in dynamic environments: sources of uncertainty and sensing mechanisms. Proj. Manag. J. **41**(4), 46–58 (2010). https://doi.org/10.1002/pmj.20201

26. Pinto, H.S., Martins, J.P.: Ontologies: how can they be built? Knowl. Inf. Syst. **6**(4), 441–464 (2004). https://doi.org/10.1007/s10115-003-0138-1

27. Ramasesh, R.V., Browning, T.R.: A conceptual framework for tackling knowable unknown unknowns in project management. J. Oper. Manag. **32**(4), 190–204 (2014). https://doi.org/10.1016/j.jom.2014.03.003

28. Ross, D., Schoman, K.: Structured analysis for requirements definition. IEEE Trans. Softw. Eng. **SE-3**(1), 6–15 (1977). https://doi.org/10.1109/TSE.1977.229899

29. Ståhl, D., Bosch, J.: Modeling continuous integration practice differences in industry software development. J. Syst. Softw. **87**, 48–59 (2014). https://doi.org/10.1016/j.jss.2013.08.032

30. Tah, J.H.M., Carr, V.: Knowledge-based approach to construction project risk management. J. Comput. Civ. Eng. **15**(3), 170–177 (2001). https://doi.org/10.1061/(ASCE)0887-3801(2001)15:3(170)

31. Teller, J., Kock, A., Gemünden, H.G.: Risk management in project portfolios is more than managing project risks: a contingency perspective on risk management. Proj. Manag. J. **45**(4), 67–80 (2014). https://doi.org/10.1002/pmj.21431

32. Voss, M., Kock, A.: Impact of relationship value on project portfolio success - investigating the moderating effects of portfolio characteristics and external turbulence. Int. J. Proj. Manag. **31**(6) (2013). https://doi.org/10.1016/j.ijproman.2012.11.005

33. Ward, S., Chapman, C.: Transforming project risk management into project uncertainty management. Int. J. Proj. Manag. **21**(2), 97–105 (2003)

34. Weaver, P.: The origins of modern project management. In: Fourth Annual PMI College of Scheduling Conference 15–18 April 2007 Marriott Pinnacle Downtown, Vancouver (2007)

Observability for Quantum Workflows in Heterogeneous Multi-cloud Environments

Martin Beisel$^{(\boxtimes)}$(iD), Johanna Barzen(iD), Frank Leymann(iD), Lavinia Stiliadou(iD), and Benjamin Weder(iD)

Institute of Architecture of Application Systems, University of Stuttgart, Universitätsstr. 38, 70569 Stuttgart, Germany
{beisel,barzen,leymann,stiliadou,weder}@iaas.uni-stuttgart.de

Abstract. Quantum workflows enable a robust, scalable, and reliable orchestration of hybrid applications comprising classical and quantum tasks. Varying availability and pricing of classical infrastructure and quantum devices promote adaptive deployments of required functionalities. While workflow engines enable to execute, monitor, and analyze quantum workflows, visualizing the information relevant to each specific user group is challenging, particularly within heterogeneous and adaptive multi-cloud environments. To overcome this issue, we present an approach enabling unified observability of quantum workflows, including details of the classical services and infrastructure, as well as the current characteristics of used quantum devices. To this end, we introduce different process views that facilitate workflow monitoring and analysis for quantum and deployment experts and discuss them for a typical use case from the quantum domain. Further, we provide a system architecture and a corresponding prototypical implementation supporting our approach.

Keywords: Observability · Quantum Computing · Quantum Workflows

1 Introduction

Quantum computing enables solving various complex problems, e.g., in chemistry and machine learning, more efficiently than their best-known classical counterpart [22]. Most quantum algorithms require classical pre- and post-processing, e.g., to prepare classical input data for the quantum device or to visualize the results, making them inherently hybrid [14]. Implementing the functionalities required for quantum algorithms following software engineering concepts, such as separation of concerns and modularization, commonly leads to services using different programming languages or data formats that must be orchestrated.

Workflows are an established technology for orchestrating the control and data flow of heterogeneous services [15]. Thus, they are a promising candidate for modeling quantum applications, as they provide many benefits, such as robustness, scalability, and transactional processing [36]. To execute a workflow, all

G. Guizzardi et al. (Eds.): CAiSE 2024, LNCS 14663, pp. 612–627, 2024.
https://doi.org/10.1007/978-3-031-61057-8_36

required services must be accessible by the workflow engine and are invoked when the corresponding task is executed [15]. However, especially in a rapidly evolving domain such as quantum computing, services are often custom-built. Thus, they are not always available via the cloud and must be deployed specifically for a workflow execution [35]. Thereby, the deployment targets of services depend on different factors, such as hardware availability, cost, or a company's privacy policies. As some factors, such as hardware prices and availability, frequently change, deploying services on-demand when they are required or adapting the execution environment based on these changes can be beneficial [31].

However, the high complexity of workflows containing various quantum and classical tasks, as well as today's heterogeneous multi-cloud deployments, complicate workflow monitoring and analysis. For example, data about the calibration of a quantum device, i.e., the metrics describing its behavior, e.g., error rates and decoherence times, are crucial for understanding the results of a quantum circuit execution [14,34]. However, quantum providers use different metrics to describe their devices, hindering users from accessing and analyzing the characteristics of the devices in a unified manner. Another example are heterogeneous multi-cloud environments, for which each cloud provider offers its own dashboard for observing the environment status [21]. Hence, for workflows that deploy services on-demand in various cloud environments, keeping track of where and when a service is deployed can become a challenge, as no unified access in the context of the workflow is available. To overcome these challenges and thus improve observability, all data about the workflow and its execution environment are stored by a *provenance system* [34]. To obtain insights from these large amounts of data, they need to be structured and comprehensively presented to the user. However, different user groups typically require different kinds of information and abstraction levels. For instance, a quantum expert is primarily interested in provenance data related to the results of quantum circuit executions, whereas a member of the operations team is mainly concerned with the status of the execution environment, i.e., the classical and quantum resources, used by the workflow.

In this paper, we present an end-to-end approach enabling observability in a unified manner when executing quantum workflows within an adaptive and heterogeneous multi-cloud environment. Thereby, our approach employs established concepts, such as on-demand deployment and provenance, and combines them with a new concept improving the monitoring and analysis of quantum workflows and their corresponding execution environments. To achieve this, we introduce custom abstractions for quantum workflows, so-called *process views* [3,26], that visualize relevant information in a comprehensive and role-based manner. The suitability of the process views is demonstrated by applying them to a use case orchestrating a typical quantum algorithm. To prove the practical feasibility of our approach, we provide a system architecture and a prototypical implementation.

The remainder of this paper is structured as follows: Sect. 2 discusses fundamentals and the problems tackled in this work. In Sect. 3, the approach for improving the observability of quantum workflows is presented. Section 4 introduces different process views for quantum workflows. Section 5 presents the system architecture and a prototypical implementation supporting our approach.

Section 6 discusses limitations and possible improvements for our approach. Finally, Sect. 7 presents related work, and Sect. 8 concludes the paper.

2 Fundamentals and Problem Statement

In this section, we present fundamentals about quantum computing, quantum workflows, service deployments, provenance, and process views. Furthermore, we discuss the problems tackled in this work and present our research questions.

2.1 Quantum Computing

Quantum computing enables computational advantages by leveraging quantum mechanical phenomena [22]. Algorithms for quantum devices are implemented in the form of quantum circuits [14]. However, the executability of these circuits is restricted by the limited number of qubits provided by current devices [22]. Moreover, today's devices are error-prone, leading to distorted results. Since the characteristics of quantum devices change regularly, e.g., due to device recalibrations and varying error rates, selecting a suitable quantum device based on the quantum circuit and current device data improves the quality of the result [25].

2.2 Workflows and QuantME

Workflows enable the modeling and execution of processes consisting of various tasks [15]. Thereby, workflow languages, such as BPMN and BPEL, can be used to model these tasks, as well as their partial order and the data flow between them. Utilizing workflows provides various benefits, such as advanced error handling, robustness, and transactional processing. Some workflow languages, e.g., BPMN, also provide a comprehensive graphical notation, facilitating the understandability of the workflow. Moreover, workflows can be executed automatically in a scalable and robust execution environment using *workflow engines.*

To ease modeling quantum-specific tasks in workflows, the *Quantum Modeling Extension (QuantME)* was introduced [1,33,36]. QuantME provides additional modeling constructs comprising task-specific properties that facilitate the modeling and configuration of commonly occurring quantum tasks. For example, the circuit execution task enables configuring the execution of a quantum circuit, e.g., by specifying the quantum device to use. To ensure portability, the approach includes a transformation step that transforms QuantME modeling constructs to native modeling constructs of the used workflow language via reusable workflow fragments stored in a repository [36]. Suitable fragments are selected by matching each QuantME task's configuration with a fragment's detector, which specifies the fragment's capabilities, e.g., circuit execution for IBM quantum devices.

2.3   Service Deployment

While some of the services required by a workflow are always-on and available, e.g., Google Maps and PayPal, application-specific services are typically self-hosted [31]. However, deploying self-hosted services manually is a complex, time-consuming, and error-prone task requiring deep technical expertise [11]. Therefore, various technologies for automating the deployment of services and applications have emerged, e.g., Kubernetes and OpenTOSCA [2]. These deployment automation technologies use reusable *deployment models*, which are executed to set up and configure the services and their execution environment. To reduce costs and unnecessary consumption of infrastructure resources, self-hosted services that are used irregularly should be deployed *on-demand* once they are required by a task of the workflow [31]. Selecting deployment targets on-demand provides various benefits, such as the opportunity to deploy services on cheap spot instances [16] that are available only at specific times or the possibility to determine a deployment target based on non-functional requirements or runtime data [31].

2.4   Provenance and Process Views

Provenance refers to the collection of all data associated with an object and can be used to gain insights into quantum workflows and their executions [10]. For example, keeping track of changing quantum device error rates and intermediate results of quantum workflows is crucial [34]. The collected provenance data can then be used to review and understand results, improve reproducibility, or detect patterns. Provenance data is typically stored in *provenance graphs* which store data objects as nodes and define their relations using typed edges. An established concept for comprehensively visualizing provenance data of a workflow are process views [3,26]. They reduce the complexity of the workflow by generating additional abstraction layers that, e.g., hide all unnecessary details, filter data, or aggregate information depending on the user-specific requirements. Provenance data can be used to improve an application's observability, i.e., the capability to understand the state of an application by utilizing its outputs [20].

2.5   Problem Statement

The selection of suitable deployment targets for quantum and classical services at design time is often not possible for today's adaptive multi-cloud environments, as infrastructure availability and pricing change. Further, the heterogeneous data, e.g., different data formats and metrics, provided by various cloud offerings complicate monitoring and analysis. This leads us to our first research question:

> *RQ 1:* *"How to enable flexible deployments of quantum workflows with their required quantum and classical services in adaptive multi-cloud environments, and how can they be observed in a unified manner?"*

As stated above, process views are used to visualize workflows at different levels of granularity. In the quantum domain, different abstraction levels are especially important as it is an interdisciplinary area involving experts with different backgrounds. However, there is a lack of process views cooping with the specialties of quantum workflows, e.g., QuantME modeling constructs or heterogeneous classical and quantum hardware. Thus, our second research question is as follows:

> **RQ 2:** *"Which information should be abstracted, aggregated, and enriched in process views to ease the understanding of quantum workflows?"*

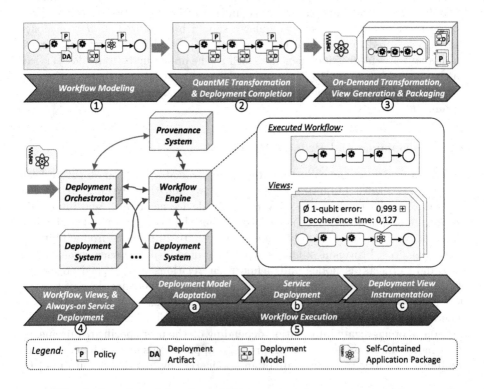

Fig. 1. Overview of the observability approach for quantum workflows

3   Observability for Quantum Workflows

To address RQ 1, we present our approach for enabling unified observability when executing quantum workflows within adaptive multi-cloud environments. Figure 1 showcases the different steps of our approach. To discuss these steps, we utilize the widely known concepts and graphical notation of BPMN.

3.1   Workflow Modeling

First, the quantum workflow is manually modeled using QuantME modeling constructs and native modeling constructs. During workflow modeling, service implementations can be attached to service tasks [35]. Thereby, they can either be provided as *deployment models*, defining where and how the included implementation shall be deployed, or as *deployment artifacts* that solely contain the implementation, e.g., as a ZIP file comprising a Python service. To configure the deployment, *policies* can be specified and assigned to a task. For example, a policy can define that a service should be deployed on-demand, is stateful, and hence must not be undeployed once it is deployed, or imposes privacy constraints. By assigning a policy to a QuantME modeling construct, it is applied to the whole workflow fragment that is used for its replacement (see Sect. 2.2).

3.2   QuantME Transformation and Deployment Completion

In the second step, it is ensured that all deployment artifacts and models are ready for deployment. Initially, all QuantME modeling constructs must be transformed into native modeling constructs [36]. Afterward, also deployment artifacts and models contained in their replacements can be processed. As deployment artifacts only contain service implementations and information about their dependencies, a suitable deployment model enabling automatic deployment must be generated for each of them. This deployment model has to define a suitable infrastructure and install the dependencies of the service. To enable the flexible deployment of services, e.g., based on changing infrastructure availability and pricing, as well as varying policies, incomplete deployment models can be specified, missing concrete definitions about the infrastructure. Thus, incomplete deployment models are completed based on current provenance data and given policies [11].

3.3   On-Demand Transformation, View Generation and Packaging

For each service task whose corresponding service shall be deployed on-demand, a transformation step generating a new sub-process is required. The generated sub-process comprises tasks managing the on-demand deployment and the original task calling the service. Additionally, different process views are generated to abstract the workflow visualization for different user groups. The process views introduced as part of this work are discussed in detail in Sect. 4. Finally, the workflow, the generated views, as well as all contained deployment models and policies are bundled in a self-contained application package.

3.4   Workflow, Views, and Always-On Service Deployment

To set up the execution environment of the workflow, the self-contained application package is utilized: First, the *deployment orchestrator* utilizes *deployment systems*, such as Kubernetes or the OpenTOSCA Container [2], to deploy all self-hosted services, which shall be always available during the workflow runtime. Subsequently, it binds their endpoints to the corresponding tasks in the workflow. Afterward, the updated workflow is uploaded to the *workflow engine*. Finally, the different views of the workflow are connected to the executable workflow, enabling live monitoring and analysis of the workflow using these views.

3.5   Workflow Execution

In the last step of our approach, the deployed workflow is instantiated by passing the required input data, e.g., the problem instance to solve and tokens for accessing quantum devices. During the entire workflow execution, the *provenance system* tracks all available data about the workflow and its execution environment.

For each task requiring on-demand service deployment, the corresponding deployment model is sent to the deployment orchestrator, which adapts the model if the hardware is no longer available, policies are no longer fulfilled, or current provenance data leads to a more suitable deployment target (see a). Additionally, the deployment orchestrator checks if instances of the resulting deployment model are already running and accessible, which can then be reused to execute the task. If none are available, the adapted deployment model is sent to a deployment system, which instantiates the service (see b). To enable service monitoring, live data, e.g., about the deployment status and hardware utilization, is continuously retrieved and utilized to dynamically update and instrument views, e.g., the *deployment view*, which provides details about the status of all deployments (see c). Once the service is successfully deployed and the views have been instrumented, the task is executed. In addition to the on-demand deployed services, the data collection and view instrumentation are also done for services deployed in the fourth step of our approach, enabling unified observability for all services. The collected provenance data is analyzed by the provenance system to improve the efficiency of service deployments, e.g., deploy services with long idle times on-demand instead of prior to the workflow execution or vice versa.

4   Process Views for Quantum Workflows

To address RQ 2, we first identify which information should be abstracted, aggregated, and enriched to improve the understandability of quantum workflows for different user groups. Thereby, we established a baseline of relevant information by analyzing the literature, which we then discussed in semi-structured interviews with five partners from academia and industry, respectively. The partners have backgrounds in software engineering, workflow technologies, and quantum computing. Their insights could be transferred into four novel process views: The (i) *quantum view* supports quantum experts in observing quantum-related tasks and the used quantum devices. The (ii) *deployment view* facilitates the monitoring of self-hosted services utilized by a workflow in a unified manner. The (iii) *pattern view* shows which patterns, e.g., the cloud computing patterns [9] and quantum computing patterns [13], are realized within a workflow. Thereby, mnemonic icons and the comprehensive description of the patterns can be leveraged to ease the understanding of the concepts implemented by the tasks. The (iv) *provenance graph view* enables users to observe the incremental expansion of the provenance graph corresponding to the workflow during execution [10].

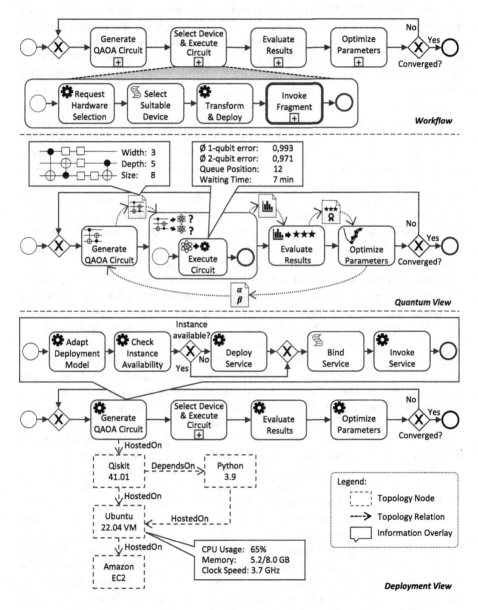

Fig. 2. Overview of a workflow and its generated quantum and deployment views

In the following, we will discuss the quantum and deployment views in detail, as they were assessed as the most important by our partners. To demonstrate the practical feasibility of these views, we present them for a typical use case from the quantum domain, solving the *Maximum Cut (MaxCut)* problem with the *Quantum Approximate Optimization Algorithm (QAOA)* [8]. As shown at the top of Fig. 2, the first step of the quantum algorithm is the generation of a quantum circuit. QAOA utilizes parameterized circuits, whose parameters are iteratively improved to find the solution. Once generated, the quantum circuit is executed on a suitable device. Afterward, the quality of the execution results is evaluated, such that the circuit parameters can be optimized. These tasks are repeated until no improved parameters can be found and the optimization converges.

The workflow contains the sub-processes managing the on-demand deployment and service invocation, as well as the sub-process handling the quantum hardware selection and circuit execution. The sub-process used for on-demand deployment is discussed in detail in the paragraph discussing the deployment view. The quantum hardware selection does not require a deployment step, as the *NISQ Analyzer* [25], which is used for retrieving a list of suitable devices for the circuit that shall be executed, is available as a part of the system architecture (see Sect. 5). After requesting a list of suitable devices, a script task is used to select one of them, e.g., by prioritizing short queue times. Subsequently, QuantME tasks contained in the hardware selection sub-process are transformed based on the selected quantum device [33]. The resulting transformed workflow is deployed independently and is then invoked by the final BPMN call activity.

The *quantum view* abstracts from the executable workflow by visualizing the QuantME modeling constructs that were originally used to model the workflow. Thereby, complex multi-step tasks are shown in a comprehensive manner, e.g., the selection of a suitable quantum device is visualized by a single *quantum hardware selection sub-process*. Furthermore, QuantME task types and data objects are enriched with additional information facilitating the understanding and monitoring of these tasks. For example, the *quantum circuit execution task* provides live data about device error rates enabling quantum experts to gain insights about the faultiness of execution results. Moreover, analyzing the structure of the circuit shown in the *quantum circuit object* or the visualization of the probability distribution contained in a *result object* allows quantum experts to already draw conclusions during the execution of an algorithm, enabling them to adapt to unexpected situations on the fly, e.g., by modifying parameters.

The workflow resulting from transforming all QuantME modeling constructs is shown in the *deployment view*. The quantum hardware selection sub-process is replaced by a sub-process, whereas all other QuantME tasks are implemented by service tasks whose implementations shall be deployed on demand. However, to enable the on-demand deployment of these service tasks, the workflow must be transformed again, introducing sub-processes for each of them. Each generated sub-process first adapts the deployment model based on current provenance data and then checks if a suitable instance is already running. If no instance is

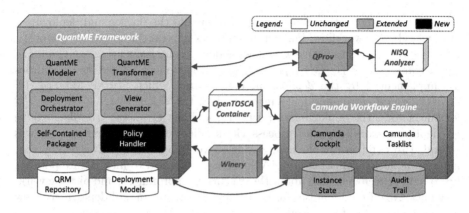

Fig. 3. System architecture for the observability approach for quantum workflows

found, the adapted deployment model is used to provision the service. Next, the endpoint of either the existing or the new service instance is bound to the service task before invoking it as the final step of the sub-process. To facilitate the monitoring of deployed resources, information about the deployment process of a service task and the topology of deployed services is shown in the deployment view. Moreover, live data, as well as the properties of topology nodes, can be observed. For example, the service for generating the QAOA circuit is hosted on an Amazon EC2 instance, which runs an Ubuntu VM that first installs Python and then Qiskit.

The quantum and deployment views are based on the structure of the workflow prior to the respective transformations. To visualize the views, supplementary workflows, e.g., realized as distinct BPMN diagrams, that include the pre-transformation states are uploaded to the workflow engine in addition to the executable workflow. The overlays within the views are generated based on the respective task's properties, e.g., its type. The synchronization of the executed workflow and the views is achieved by matching the identifiers of the corresponding modeling constructs. Additional details about all introduced views, as well as a list of corresponding visualized information can be found at GitHub [29].

5   Architecture and Prototype

In this section, we introduce a system architecture supporting the presented approach and discuss the details of our corresponding prototypical implementation.

An overview of the system architecture realizing our approach is depicted in Fig. 3. Unchanged components are colored in white, expanded components are depicted in gray, and newly added components are highlighted in black. On the left, the *QuantME framework* is shown, enabling modeling and transforming quantum workflows. The contained *QuantME modeler* is a graphical BPMN-based workflow modeler, which was extended to support the attachment of policies and deployment artifacts. The *QuantME transformer* was extended with additional transformation functionalities to enable the on-demand deployment of services by the workflow. Further, it supports the transformation of QuantME modeling constructs to native workflow modeling constructs using the *QuantME Replacement Model (QRM) repository* [36]. Deployment-related functionalities are implemented by the *deployment orchestrator*, which utilizes *Winery* [12] for storing and retrieving deployment models, the *OpenTOSCA Container* [2] for automating the deployment of services, and the *Camunda workflow engine* for deploying workflows and process views. The deployment orchestrator was extended to complete deployment models leveraging Winery. The deployment model completion functionality of Winery was extended to incorporate policies, up-to-date provenance data about the execution environment, and historic workflow data. New functionalities for generating the quantum and deployment view during the workflow transformations were added to the *view generator*. The *self-contained packager* was extended to support the packaging of policies in quantum applications. Thereby, we utilize the packaging mechanisms of TOSCA for all attached deployment models and bundle them with the executable workflow, the policies, and the supplementary workflows employed for visualizing the views. Finally, the newly added *policy handler* maps the policies attached to the tasks to the requirements of the incomplete deployment model.

The provenance system *QProv* [34] collects and stores data in a provenance database during the entire modeling and execution process and was extended to incorporate deployment data. To execute quantum workflows, the state-of-the-art Camunda workflow engine is used. It comprises the *Camunda cockpit*, which provides insights into running and completed workflows, e.g., current variable values, and was extended to visualize the newly added views. Thereby, it instruments the views with current provenance data about quantum devices and service deployments provided by *QProv* and instance data stored in the *instance state* database during runtime or *audit trail* after termination, respectively. The *Camunda tasklist* provides a graphical user interface that allows users to manage and work on human tasks within a business process and remains unchanged. The *NISQ Analyzer* [25] is used to select suitable quantum devices during runtime.

All components of our system architecture are prototypically implemented and publicly available as open-source projects on GitHub [30]. The QuantME framework is a web-based BPMN workflow modeling tool that extends bpmn-js. Its plugin system enables adding custom modeling constructs or transformation algorithms, e.g., to support on-demand service deployment. To enable unified observability during workflow execution, the Camunda workflow engine was extended to support custom views. These views are serialized using the BPMN XML syntax. A detailed description of our prototype as well as a comprehensive step-by-step guide on setting up and executing the use case introduced in Sect. 4 are available on GitHub [30]. Furthermore, a demonstration video showcasing our prototype for the presented use case is available on YouTube [28].

6   Disucussion and Limitations

In this section, we analyze and discuss the limitations of our approach concerning (i) the selection of suitable hardware for the quantum and classical services invoked by the workflow, (ii) the maintenance of process views when adapting the workflow after view generation, and (iii) the aggregation of provenance data visualized within process views to gain insights about the overall process. Furthermore, we present possible extensions for addressing these limitations.

Using incomplete deployment models enables an automated selection of suitable quantum and classical infrastructure during runtime. However, to perform this selection, mechanisms for choosing a suitable option based on the given requirements as well as current data about available hardware are required. In our approach, we employ three steps for selecting suitable cloud offerings: (i) available cloud offerings are filtered based on credentials provided by the user, (ii) mandatory policies are enforced, e.g., that a private cloud must be used, (iii) a suitable option is chosen based on current data, e.g., the pricing, retrieved from the cloud provider APIs by the provenance system. Thereby, information about the hardware requirements of the corresponding service is taken into account when historic performance data for the corresponding service is available in the provenance system or manually provided by the user. Additionally, automatic scaling policies are provided by many cloud providers to optimize resource usage.

Since workflows are no static artifacts and are commonly adapted after the initial modeling, e.g., to incorporate additional process steps or modify existing ones, an approach for maintaining associated process views is required. In our approach, the process view generation and maintenance is complicated by the automated transformation procedures modifying the workflow irreversibly. As editing a transformed workflow is complex and error-prone, we differentiate between the working copy of the workflow and the transformed workflow. Once transformed, the workflow must no longer be edited, and further changes must be made in the working copy, which can then be transformed again. To generate the views, the connection between modeling constructs across different views and the executed workflow is established by preserving the task identifiers during workflow transformation and view generation. However, our current approach does not enable a modification of the views after their generation. To overcome this limitation, all modifications in the workflow can be tracked utilizing a provenance system. The collected data can then be used to inject, modify, or delete the corresponding modeling constructs in the supplementary workflows used for the process views.

The views introduced in this work improve the understandability of the process for different user groups by abstracting, aggregating, and enriching data for specific tasks. However, they do not provide a simplified view of the entire workflow that enables users to get an overview of the workflow without investigating it manually. For example, the provenance data collected for the service deployments can be aggregated to give the user an overview of the total costs or the infrastructure utilization currently incurred by the process execution.

7   Related Work

Various approaches and dedicated scientific workflow management systems were presented to enable dynamic service deployments. Vukojevic-Haupt et al. [31] introduce an approach for context-aware service selection and provisioning of on-demand services in scientific workflows using an enterprise service bus. However, their approach neither enables the adaptation of deployment models based on current provenance data and policies nor supports the unified observability of deployed services. Dörnemann et al. [7] propose an approach to dynamically schedule service calls based on the load of the execution environment and deploy additionally required instances on demand. *Kepler* [17] enables the on-demand deployment of services using EC2 resources. However, the entire deployment process, including the setup of virtual machines or installation of required programs, must be manually modeled within the workflow, leading to a cluttered workflow model. Moreover, the approach is limited to EC2 resources, restricting users from utilizing other cloud offerings. *Pegasus* [6] enables selecting resources, e.g., virtual machines, which are used to deploy services on demand. However, their approach is limited to existing resources and can not deploy new instances.

Views are utilized in different works to support the monitoring and analysis of workflow executions. Biton et al. [3] introduce an approach to generate user-specific process views based on their requirements automatically. Furthermore, Schumm et al. [26] introduce various process viewing patterns which describe different techniques for composing views. These techniques comprise structural changes to the workflow as well as adaptations in its presentation. Similarly, the *Proviado* monitoring framework [23] uses process views to ensure the compliance of process visualizations with the access rights of specific user groups. Cohen-Boulakia et al. [5] ease the analysis of collected provenance data by abstracting unnecessary data or aggregating it to improve understandability. Sonntag et al. [27] introduce a collection of views easing the understanding of different aspects of scientific workflows, e.g., the data flow or infrastructure information. In contrast to their infrastructure view, our deployment view also incorporates arbitrary deployment models and the service deployment process.

Approaches for dynamically adapting workflow models have been presented by Bucchiarone et al. [4], who annotate tasks with goals, preconditions, and effects, and Mundbrod et al. [18], who enable a context-aware selection of suitable workflow fragments, e.g., based on current loads of available components. Moreover, adaptive workflow engines, such as *AristaFlow* [24] and *AgentWork* [19], have been presented. For example, they enable an automated migration of workflow instances to new versions of the corresponding workflow model or dynamic exception-handling mechanisms, which can add and remove activities on the fly.

In previous work [32], we introduced a concept to rewrite quantum workflows for so-called hybrid runtimes, improving their efficiency. However, by automatically adapting the workflow, the understandability for the user decreases. To circumvent this issue, process views were used to visualize the original workflow, including the intermediate results received from the hybrid runtime. Building upon this concept, we added additional overlays in the quantum view to emphasize important information, e.g., calibration data of the used quantum device, and added three new views, namely the deployment, pattern, and provenance graph views.

8 Conclusion and Outlook

Quantum workflows enable robust, scalable, and reliable orchestration of hybrid quantum applications. Due to the varying availability and pricing of classical and quantum resources provided via the cloud, as well as the changing characteristics of quantum devices, hybrid quantum applications benefit from multi-cloud deployments. While workflow engines support the execution of quantum workflows using adaptive execution environments, monitoring and analyzing them becomes increasingly challenging. All information relevant to a specific user must be visualized comprehensively without decreasing the understandability by showing unnecessary details. To overcome this issue, we presented an approach enabling the unified observability of quantum workflows with their execution environments, including details of the classical services and infrastructure, as well as the used quantum devices. For this, different process views were identified, and their suitability was demonstrated for a typical use case. Finally, we presented a system architecture and a prototypical implementation supporting our approach.

In future work, we plan to evaluate our approach and the introduced views in a broader user study, enabling us to improve their usability and granularity of the visualized information. Further, we plan to collect provenance data from quantum workflow executions over a large timeframe. This enables us to gain valuable insights into interrelationships and correlations of data in quantum workflows, which can be utilized to improve the presentation of the shown process views.

Acknowledgments. This work was partially funded by the BMWK projects *EniQmA* (01MQ22007B) and *SeQuenC* (01MQ22009B).

References

1. Beisel, M., Barzen, J., Bechtold, M., Leymann, F., Truger, F., Weder, B.: QuantME4VQA: modeling and executing variational quantum algorithms using workflows. In: Proceedings of the 13th International Conference on Cloud Computing and Services Science (CLOSER), pp. 306–315. SciTePress (2023)
2. Binz, T., et al.: OpenTOSCA - a runtime for TOSCA-based cloud applications. In: Basu, S., Pautasso, C., Zhang, L., Fu, X. (eds.) ICSOC 2013. LNCS, vol. 8274, pp. 692–695. Springer, Heidelberg (2013). https://doi.org/10.1007/978-3-642-45005-1_62
3. Biton, O., Davidson, S.B., Khanna, S., Roy, S.: Optimizing user views for workflows. In: Proceedings of the 12th International Conference on Database Theory (ICDT), pp. 310–323. ACM (2009)

4. Bucchiarone, A., Marconi, A., Pistore, M., Raik, H.: Dynamic adaptation of fragment-based and context-aware business processes. In: Proceedings of the 19th International Conference on Web Services (ICWS), pp. 33–41. IEEE (2012)

5. Cohen-Boulakia, S., Biton, O., Cohen, S., Davidson, S.: Addressing the provenance challenge using ZOOM. Concurr. Comput. Pract. Exp. **20**(5), 497–506 (2008)

6. Deelman, E., Vahi, K., Juve, G., Rynge, M., Callaghan, S., Maechling, P.J., et al.: Pegasus, a workflow management system for science automation. Future Gener. Comput. Syst. **46**, 17–35 (2015)

7. Dörnemann, T., Juhnke, E., Freisleben, B.: On-demand resource provisioning for BPEL workflows using Amazon's elastic compute cloud. In: Proceedings of the 9th IEEE/ACM International Symposium on Cluster Computing and the Grid (CCGRID), pp. 140–147. IEEE (2009)

8. Farhi, E., Goldstone, J., Gutmann, S.: A quantum approximate optimization algorithm. arXiv:1411.4028 (2014)

9. Fehling, C., et al.: Cloud Computing Patterns: Fundamentals to Design, Build, and Manage Cloud Applications. Springer, Vienna (2014). https://doi.org/10.1007/978-3-7091-1568-8

10. Herschel, M., Diestelkämper, R., Ben Lahmar, H.: A survey on provenance: What for? What form? What from? VLDB J. **26**, 881–906 (2017)

11. Hirmer, P., Breitenbücher, U., Binz, T., Leymann, F.: Automatic topology completion of TOSCA-based cloud applications. In: Proceedings des CloudCycle14 Workshops auf der 44. Jahrestagung der Gesellschaft für Informatik e.V. (GI). LNI, vol. 232, pp. 247–258. Gesellschaft für Informatik e.V. (GI) (2014)

12. Kopp, O., Binz, T., Breitenbücher, U., Leymann, F.: Winery – a modeling tool for TOSCA-based cloud applications. In: Basu, S., Pautasso, C., Zhang, L., Fu, X. (eds.) ICSOC 2013. LNCS, vol. 8274, pp. 700–704. Springer, Heidelberg (2013). https://doi.org/10.1007/978-3-642-45005-1_64

13. Leymann, F.: Towards a pattern language for quantum algorithms. In: Feld, S., Linnhoff-Popien, C. (eds.) QTOP 2019. LNCS, vol. 11413, pp. 218–230. Springer, Cham (2019). https://doi.org/10.1007/978-3-030-14082-3_19

14. Leymann, F., Barzen, J.: The bitter truth about gate-based quantum algorithms in the NISQ era. Quantum Sci. Technol. **5**(4), 1–28 (2020)

15. Leymann, F., Roller, D.: Production Workflow: Concepts and Techniques. Prentice Hall PTR (2000)

16. Lin, L., Pan, L., Liu, S.: Methods for improving the availability of spot instances: a survey. Comput. Ind. **141**, 103718 (2022)

17. Ludäscher, B., Altintas, I., Berkley, C., Higgins, D., Jaeger, E., Jones, M., et al.: Scientific workflow management and the Kepler system. Concurr. Comput. Pract. Exp. **18**(10), 1039–1065 (2006)

18. Mundbrod, N., Grambow, G., Kolb, J., Reichert, M.: Context-aware process injection: enhancing process flexibility by late extension of process instances. In: Debruyne, C., et al. (eds.) OTM 2015. LNCS, vol. 9415, pp. 127–145. Springer, Cham (2015). https://doi.org/10.1007/978-3-319-26148-5_8

19. Müller, R., Greiner, U., Rahm, E.: AgentWork: a workflow system supporting rule-based workflow adaptation. Data Knowl. Eng. **51**(2), 223–256 (2004)

20. Niedermaier, S., Koetter, F., Freymann, A., Wagner, S.: On observability and monitoring of distributed systems - an industry interview study. In: Yangui, S., Bouassida Rodriguez, I., Drira, K., Tari, Z. (eds.) ICSOC 2019. LNCS, vol. 11895, pp. 36–52. Springer, Cham (2019). https://doi.org/10.1007/978-3-030-33702-5_3

21. Noor, A., et al.: A framework for monitoring microservice-oriented cloud applications in heterogeneous virtualization environments. In: Proceedings of the 12th International Conference on Cloud Computing (CLOUD), pp. 156–163 (2019)

22. Preskill, J.: Quantum computing in the NISQ era and beyond. Quantum **2**, 79 (2018)

23. Reichert, M., Bassil, S., Bobrik, R., Bauer, T.: The Proviado access control model for business process monitoring components. Enterp. Model. Inf. Syst. Archit. (EMISAJ) **5**(3), 64–88 (2010)

24. Rinderle-Ma, S., Reichert, M.: Advanced migration strategies for adaptive process management systems. In: Proceedings of the 12th IEEE Conference on Commerce and Enterprise Computing (CEC), pp. 56–63. IEEE (2010)

25. Salm, M., Barzen, J., Breitenbücher, U., Leymann, F., Weder, B., Wild, K.: The NISQ analyzer: automating the selection of quantum computers for quantum algorithms. In: Dustdar, S. (ed.) SummerSOC 2020. CCIS, vol. 1310, pp. 66–85. Springer, Cham (2020). https://doi.org/10.1007/978-3-030-64846-6_5

26. Schumm, D., Leymann, F., Streule, A.: Process viewing patterns. In: Proceedings of the 14th International Conference on Enterprise Distributed Object Computing (EDOC), pp. 89–98. IEEE (2010)

27. Sonntag, M., Görlach, K., Karastoyanova, D., Leymann, F., Malets, P., Schumm, D.: Views on scientific workflows. In: Grabis, J., Kirikova, M. (eds.) BIR 2011. LNBIP, vol. 90, pp. 321–335. Springer, Heidelberg (2011). https://doi.org/10.1007/978-3-642-24511-4_25

28. University of Stuttgart: Demonstration Video: Observability for Quantum Workflows (2024). https://www.youtube.com/watch?v=XpChXXgAr_0

29. University of Stuttgart: Detailed View Description (2024). https://github.com/PlanQK/workflow-modeler/tree/master/doc/views

30. University of Stuttgart: Quantum Workflows, MODULO, and QuantME Use Cases (2024). https://github.com/UST-QuAntiL/QuantME-UseCases

31. Vukojevic-Haupt, K., Haupt, F., Karastoyanova, D., Leymann, F.: Service selection for on-demand provisioned services. In: Proceedings of the 18th International Conference on Enterprise Distributed Object Computing (EDOC), pp. 120–127. IEEE (2014)

32. Weder, B., Barzen, J., Beisel, M., Leymann, F.: Provenance-preserving analysis and rewrite of quantum workflows for hybrid quantum algorithms. SN Comput. Sci. **4**(233), 1–19 (2023)

33. Weder, B., Barzen, J., Leymann, F., Salm, M.: Automated quantum hardware selection for quantum workflows. Electronics **10**(8), 984 (2021)

34. Weder, B., Barzen, J., Leymann, F., Salm, M., Wild, K.: QProv: a provenance system for quantum computing. IET Quantum Commun. **2**(4), 171–181 (2021)

35. Weder, B., Breitenbücher, U., Képes, K., Leymann, F., Zimmermann, M.: Deployable self-contained workflow models. In: Brogi, A., Zimmermann, W., Kritikos, K. (eds.) ESOCC 2020. LNCS, vol. 12054, pp. 85–96. Springer, Cham (2020). https://doi.org/10.1007/978-3-030-44769-4_7

36. Weder, B., Breitenbücher, U., Leymann, F., Wild, K.: Integrating quantum computing into workflow modeling and execution. In: Proceedings of the 13th IEEE/ACM International Conference on Utility and Cloud Computing (UCC), pp. 279–291. IEEE (2020)

Tutorials

Data-Driven Business Process Simulation: From Event Logs to Tools and Techniques

Orlenys López-Pintado[✉] and David Chapela-Campa

University of Tartu, Tartu, Estonia
{orlenys.lopez.pintado,david.chapela}@ut.ee

Abstract. Business Process Simulation (BPS) is a common approach to, among other goals, estimate the impact of changes to a business process on its performance. The potential of BPS goes from predictive applications – e.g., assessing the impact on the cycle time if the number of new cases per day doubles – to process optimization – e.g., finding the resource configuration that optimizes a certain KPI. This tutorial navigates through BPS core principles, simulation types, practical uses, and benefits, deepening into discrete-event simulation and data-driven techniques to automatically discover and model different aspects of the process, such as resource allocation. In addition, the tutorial incorporates an interactive component, demonstrating the use of tools for automated BPS model discovery and simulation.

Keywords: Process simulation · process mining · resource scheduling

Business Process Management (BPM) is a widespread discipline offering a set of techniques to optimize the performance of processes. One relevant task within BPM is predicting the process performance, either under the current configuration (as-is model) or a hypothetical configuration after applying some changes (to-be model). As part of BPM, Business Process Simulation (BPS) is a common approach to, among other goals, estimate how changes to a business process impact certain performance measures. For example, enabling analysts to answer "what-if" questions such as "What would be the cycle time of a process if the number of daily new cases increases by 20%?" or "What would be the impact of switching some resources from full-time to part-time on the process?".

The starting point of BPS is a process model enhanced with simulation parameters (a BPS model), e.g., capturing the resource availability, activity processing times, arrival rate of new cases, and branching probabilities at decision points in the process. Indeed, the usefulness of BPS hinges on the quality of the BPS model used as input. Traditionally, BPS models are manually created by modeling experts. However, this task is time-consuming and error-prone [6]. To tackle this shortcoming, several studies have advocated using process mining techniques to automatically discover BPS models from event logs recorded by (process-aware) information systems [1, 7]. These data-driven approaches automatically discover and calibrate simulation models from execution data to ensure the model is better aligned with the observed reality [2].

G. Guizzardi et al. (Eds.): CAiSE 2024, LNCS 14663, pp. 631–632, 2024.
https://doi.org/10.1007/978-3-031-61057-8

Simultaneously, the configuration described in the BPS model needs to be interpreted by a system, a simulation engine, that simulates the execution of the system, enabling its performance analysis [5]. Different simulation techniques have focused on modeling more realistic and complex behaviors. Regarding resource availability and performance, traditional approaches propose to treat resources as undifferentiated entities [1], e.g., pools of resources where each resource in a pool shares the same performance and availability. Conversely, more recent approaches model resources as individuals by independently assigning a performance and availability calendar to each one of them [4, 5]. Regarding the specific schedule of each resource, traditional research – e.g., the BPSim standard [8] – adopt a binary view of resource availability, i.e., at a specific time instant, resources are either available or not to perform process activities. More recently, some studies proposed to model the availability of resources in a probabilistic manner, i.e., defining the likelihood of a resource being available at any time with a probability function, instead of a boolean value [3].

This tutorial focuses on the theory behind traditional and modern techniques for (data-driven) BPS, emphasizing the motivation and benefits of novel proposals. The explanations are supported by the use of tools for the automated discovery of BPS models from event logs, their modification, their simulation, and the analysis of the results. The tutorial concludes by reflecting on the advantages, disadvantages, and open challenges in the field of BPS.

References

1. Camargo, M., Dumas, M., González, O.: Automated discovery of business process simulation models from event logs. Decis. Support Syst. **134**, 113284 (2020)
2. Chapela-Campa, D., Benchekroun, I., Baron, O., Dumas, M., Krass, D., Senderovich, A.: Can I trust my simulation model? Measuring the quality of business process simulation models. In: Di Francescomarino, C., Burattin, A., Janiesch, C., Sadiq, S. (eds.) BPM 2023. LNCS, vol. 14159, pp. 20–37. Springer, Cham (2023). https://doi.org/10.1007/978-3-031-41620-0_2
3. López-Pintado, O., Dumas, M.: Discovery and simulation of business processes with probabilistic resource availability calendars. In: ICPM 2023, pp. 1–8. IEEE (2023)
4. López-Pintado, O., Dumas, M., Berx, J.: Discovery, simulation, and optimization of business processes with differentiated resources. Inf. Syst. **120**, 102289 (2024)
5. López-Pintado, O., Halenok, I., Dumas, M.: Prosimos: discovering and simulating business processes with differentiated resources. In: Sales, T.P., Proper, H.A., Guizzardi, G., Montali, M., Maggi, F.M., Fonseca, C.M. (eds.) EDOC 2022. LNBIP, vol. 466, pp. 346–352. Springer, Cham (2022). https://doi.org/10.1007/978-3-031-26886-1_23
6. Maruster, L., van Beest, N.R.T.P.: Redesigning business processes: a methodology based on simulation and process mining techniques. Knowl. Inf. Syst. **21**(3), 267–297 (2009)
7. Rozinat, A., Mans, R.S., Song, M., van der Aalst, W.M.P.: Discovering simulation models. Inf. Syst. **34**(3), 305–327 (2009)
8. Workflow Management Coalition. BPSim: business process simulation specification. Document number WFMC-BPSWG-2016-1 (2016). https://www.bpsim.org/specifications/2.0/WFMC-BPSWG-2016-01.pdf

Designing Virtual Knowledge Graphs

Diego Calvanese[1,2] and Davide Lanti[1(✉)]

[1] Free University of Bozen-Bolzano, Bolzano, Italy
{diego.calvanese,davide.lanti}@unibz.it
[2] Umeå University, Umeå, Sweden

1 Goal

Complex data processing tasks, including data analytics and machine/deep learning pipelines, in order to be effective, require to access large datasets in a coherent way. Knowledge graphs (KGs) provide a uniform data format that guarantees the required flexibility in processing and moreover is able to take into account domain knowledge. However, actual data is often available only in legacy data sources, and one needs to overcome their inherent heterogeneity. The recently proposed Virtual Knowledge Graph (VKG) approach is well suited for this purpose: the KG is kept virtual, and the relevant content of data sources is exposed by declaratively mapping it to classes and properties of a domain ontology, which users in turn can query. In this talk we introduce the VKG paradigm for data access, present the challenges encountered when designing complex VKG scenarios, and discuss possible solutions, in particular to deal with the complexity of the mapping layer and its relationship to domain ontologies.

2 Scope

Intended Audience: This tutorial is meant for students interested in Knowledge Graphs for data-intensive applications, with particular focus on the *virtual* scenario, that is, on the scenario for which data is kept in the sources and access is provided through query-rewriting techniques proper of the literature from Ontology-based Data Access.

Level: Basic

Prerequisites: Basics about relational databases, first-order logic, and data modeling, as typically taught in BSc-level Computer Science courses. A background in logics for knowledge representation, description logics, and complexity theory might be useful to establish cross-connections, but is not required to follow the course.

3 Structure of Contents

1. Motivation
   We motivate the need for a principled approach to data management in complex scenarios, where multiple, typically heterogeneous, data sources needs to be accessed in a uniform and integrated way.

G. Guizzardi et al. (Eds.): CAiSE 2024, LNCS 14663, pp. 633–634, 2024.
https://doi.org/10.1007/978-3-031-61057-8

2. VKGs for Data Access

2.1 VKG Framework

We present the key components of VKGs, namely a domain ontology, (possibly wrapped) data sources, and the mapping layer between the two, justifying the usefulness of each component and of virtualization in the context of data access; we further provide the formalization of VKGs in terms of logic and their grounding in the Semantic Web W3C standards.

2.2 VKG Systems and Usecases

We present various systems implementing the VKG paradigm, and discuss industrial use-cases where VKGs have been successfully deployed.

2.3 Query Answering over VKGs

We present the key ideas behind the query answering approach in VKGs, which is based on query rewriting and mapping unfolding.

3. Designing VKGs

3.1 Query Optimization in VKGs

We present the most important query optimization techniques in VKGs, showing that their application requires the VKG system to be well-designed.

3.2 Mapping Patterns

Mappings constitute the most specific component of a VKG system, and they are also the most critical one, affecting performance of query evaluation. We present a set of mapping patterns that have a direct correspondence with traditional principled ways of designing the data layer in information systems.

3.3 Guidelines for VKG Design

By relying on the identified mapping patterns, we present a series of guidelines that ensure that a VKG system is well-designed and does not incur in unnecessary loss of performance when processing queries.

4. Conclusions

How to Conduct Valid Information Systems Engineering Research?

Jan Mendling[1,2,3] ⓘ, Henrik Leopold[4](✉) ⓘ, Henning Meyerhenke[1] ⓘ,
and Benoit Depaire[5] ⓘ

[1] Department of Computer Science,Humboldt-Università zu Berlin,Berlin, Germany
[2] Department of Information Systems and Operations Management,
Vienna University of Economics and Business,Wien, Austria
[3] Weizenbaum Institute, Berlin, Germany
[4] Kühne Logistics University,Hamburg, Germany
henrik.leopold@klu.org
[5] Hasselt University,Hasselt, Belgium

Abstract. Algorithms play an important role for information systems engineering research as they are the foundational building block of many techniques. At the same time, specific methodological guidance on how to design, evaluate, and present algorithm-based research is scarce. This tutorial addresses the needs of doctoral students and early career researchers to understand how they can establish a solid research contribution based on established methodological guidelines. No specific background knowledge is required. The content of the tutorial focuses on general challenges of information systems engineering research. The objective of this tutorial is to provide early career researchers with a profound understanding of basic concepts from the philosophy of science and specific strategies how algorithms can be scientifically investigated and presented in a systematic manner.

Keywords: Algorithm engineering · Evaluation of algorithms · Design and Analysis of Algorithms

Algorithms play an important role for information systems engineering. In 2023, over 90% of the accepted papers at CAiSE dealt with algorithms in one or another way. Algorithms are the foundational building blocks of many techniques that address task requirements of certain types of users in a specific application domain [2].

In our research, we have observed that doctoral students of computer science find it less challenging *to conduct* research on algorithms, but the more difficult *to express what they actually achieve* with their work. On the one hand, this difficulty stems from a gap of methodological education in computer science

The research of the author was supported by the Einstein Foundation Berlin under grant EPP-2019-524, by the German Federal Ministry of Education and Research under grant 16DII133, and by Deutsche Forschungsgemeinschaft under grant ME 3711/2-1.

curricula. On the other hand, computer science overall has made little effort in framing its work in the philosophy of science. One of the rare examples is [3] who establishes his concepts on ideas of Popper. These concepts are considered in [1] for the development of a methodological framework for algorithm engineering.

In our tutorial, we build on this recent framework for researching algorithms [1] with a specific focus on information systems engineering. In turn, we discuss its foundations in ontology, epistemology, and methodology. Each of these different types of contributions faces validity concerns. We highlight specific validity concerns of research on different types of algorithms and corresponding strategies to address them. By clarifying the ideas of this framework based on examples from information systems engineering research, we help early career researchers to express what their research provides, which in turn helps them to structure their research and the presentation of their papers.

This tutorial addresses the needs of *doctoral students and early career researchers* to understand how they can establish a solid research contribution based on established methodological guidelines. *No specific background knowledge* is required. The content of the tutorial focuses on *general* challenges of information systems engineering research. The objective of this tutorial is to provide early career researchers with a profound understanding of basic concepts from the philosophy of science and specific strategies how algorithms can be scientifically investigated in a systematic manner. The tutorial will be structured along the perspectives of our framework. The framework integrates an ontological, an epistemological, and a methodological perspective, and identifies corresponding validity concerns. We will make use of several research articles from different areas of computer science to illustrate the framework.

References

1. Mendling, J., Leopold, H., Meyerhenke, H., Depaire, B.: Methodology of algorithm engineering. arXiv preprint arXiv:2310.18979 (2023)
2. Munzner, T.: A nested model for visualization design and validation. IEEE Trans. Vis. Comput. Graph. **15**(6), 921–928 (2009)
3. Staples, M.: Critical rationalism and engineering: ontology. Synthese **191**(10), 2255–2279 (2014)

FAIR Data Train: A FAIR-Compliant Distributed Data and Services Platform

Luiz Olavo Bonino da Silva Santos[1,2](✉)

[1] Semantics, Cybersecurity and Services group, University of Twente,
Enschede, The Netherlands
l.o.boninodasilvasantos@utwente.nl
[2] Biosemantics group, Leiden University Medical Center, Leiden, The Netherlands

The Findable, Accessible, Interoperable, and Reusable (FAIR) principles have become essential in modern data management practices. However, achieving FAIRness in data management remains a challenge, particularly in distributed environments where data and services are scattered across various platforms and organizations. Traditional data analysis approaches require data to be copied and moved to a central location where it would eventually be combined with data from other sources. From technical and economic perspectives, it is increasingly unlikely that a single organisation or individual is allowed or can afford to collect and store all the needed data and maintain their required infrastructure. Another argument against data centralisation comes from a social perspective related to the ethical and legal restrictions to the sharing of privacy-sensitive data. Regulations such as the European General Data Protection Rules (GDPR) define rules to protect the access of personal data and have an impact on the way data can be stored and processed. Therefore, to comply with these regulations and, at the same time, harness the potential of the massive amount of data available, a distributed and privacy-preserving data analysis approach is necessary.

Distributed learning offers a flexible approach to analyzing data from various sources without the need to move them in a central location [2]. In the healthcare domain, the concept of the Personal Health Train (PHT) [3] has gained momentum in recent years. Originating in 2016 from discussions among life sciences researchers in the Netherlands, the PHT initiative envisioned a decentralized, privacy-preserving infrastructure for data and services, aligning with the FAIR principles [4] to ensure the findability, accessibility, interoperability, and reusability of not only the data but all relevant infrastructure components.

Central to the PHT approach is the notion that algorithms travel to the data rather than vice versa. Drawing on the analogy of a train system, where trains represent analysis algorithms and stations where data can be processed, this approach enables analysis to be conducted on distributed data sets, including sensitive ones, without breaching organizational boundaries. Thus, data privacy, control, and adherence to ethical and legal standards are upheld [1]. The PHT vision foresees data stations of different sizes and capabilities. For instance, large hospitals would have large stations containing data from a significant number of patients, while small medical practices would have a station containing only the data of their patients.

G. Guizzardi et al. (Eds.): CAiSE 2024, LNCS 14663, pp. 637–638, 2024.
https://doi.org/10.1007/978-3-031-61057-8

Through early discussions and implementations of the PHT, its potential applicability in diverse domains such as agriculture, finance, legal affairs, and security has become evident. While these domains differ in data types and applicable regulations from personal health data, the platform's design remains agnostic, accommodating various data types, access conditions, and policies. Hence, we introduce the FAIR Data Train, a term that shifts focus from healthcare to emphasize the platform's commitment to facilitating FAIR data practices across different sectors. For detailed specifications, visit https://specs.fairdatatrain.org.

This tutorial introduces the FAIR Data Train, a distributed data and services platform designed to promote FAIR data practices in distributed environments. The goal of this tutorial is to provide participants with comprehensive insights into the FAIR Data Train, its architecture, functionality, and implementation, as well as strategies for leveraging the platform to enhance data integration, collaboration, and knowledge discovery in distributed environments. The tutorial is targeted at researchers, data scientists, data managers, system architects, policymakers, and industry practitioners interested in FAIR data and services management, distributed data integration, and system interoperability.

References

1. Beyan, O., et al.: Distributed analytics on sensitive medical data: the personal health train. Data Intell. **2**(1-2), 96–107 (2020)
2. Rieke, N., et al.: The future of digital health with federated learning. NPJ Digit. Med. **3**(1) (2020). https://doi.org/10.1038/s41746-020-00323-1
3. Bonino da Silva Santos, L.O., Ferreira Pires, L., Graciano Martinez, V., Rebelo Moreira, J.L., Silva Souza Guizzardi, R.: Personal health train architecture with dynamic cloud staging. SN Comput. Sci. **4**(1), 14 (2022). https://doi.org/10.1007/s42979-022-01422-4
4. Wilkinson, M.D., et al.: The fair guiding principles for scientific data management and stewardship. Sci. Data **3**(1), 160018 (2016)

Engineering Information Systems with LLMs and AI-Based Techniques

Massimo Mecella$^{(\boxtimes)}$ (ID)

Sapienza Universitá di Roma,Rome, Italy
mecella@diag.uniroma1.it

Abstract. The current evolution of AI, and of Generative AI in particular, namely Large Language Models (LLMs), makes it possible to adopt them as supporting tools for the engineering of information systems, in particular for their design, development and dimensioning. The goal of this tutorial is to instruct the attendees about AI and Generative AI and LLMs, with an IS engineering attitude, and then to focus on recent approaches and applications for their usage during the design of ISs and the development of ISs.

Keywords: Large Language Models · Information Systems Engineering · Artificial Intelligence · Software Architectures

The tutorial will be given by Massimo, with the support of his research group and postdocs/PhD students who are providing specific techniques and practical cases; in particular, the tutorial is partly presented by Francesca de Luzi, Flavia Monti, Jerin Mathew, Mattia Macrì, Marco Calamo, Jacopo Rossi, Matteo Marinacci, Filippo Bianchini, and Giovanni Della Pelle.

The outline of the tutorial is as it follows:

– **An introduction to Gen AI**, consisting of the following parts:

- AI, from the winters to the summers;
- A quick&dirty introduction to Deep Learning, GenAI, LLMs and chatbots;
- What about prompt engineering, RAG and fine tuning?

– **A survey of GenAI for Information systems**, which includes:

- LLMs for extracting information from documents;
- Merging LLMs with knowledge graphs, how symbolic and subsymbolic work together;
- LLMs for conceptual modeling of applications;
- LLMs for extracting business process specifications;
- LLMs for evaluating the dimension of applications;
- LLMs for drafting the software architecture of applications;
- LLMs for generating software code;

G. Guizzardi et al. (Eds.): CAiSE 2024, LNCS 14663, pp. 639–640, 2024.
https://doi.org/10.1007/978-3-031-61057-8

- LLMs for dynamically executing pipelines composing different run-time tools.

All the above points will be presented by surveying existing work and comparing them according to different dimensions, including repeatability, quality of the outcomes, etc.

- **Real experiences and tools.** On the basis of current research activities we are conducting, we will present some case studies and proof-of-concepts (PoCs) that we are experimenting with. They include also published work and others under submission.

- **Challenges and concluding remarks**, in which future work and interesting research challenges to be addressed in the future will be outlined.

References

1. De Giacomo, G., Favorito, M., Leotta, F., Mecella, M., Silo, L.: Digital twin composition in smart manufacturing via Markov decision processes. Comput. Ind. **149**, 103916 (2023)
2. Calamo, M., De Luzi, F., Macrí, M., Mencattini, T., Mecella, M.: CICERO: A GPT2-Based Writing Assistant to Investigate the Effectiveness of Specialized LLMs' Applications in e-Justice. ECAI, pp. 3196-3203 (2023)
3. Bianchini, F., Calamo, M., De Luzi, F., Macrì, M., Mecella, M.: Enhancing complex linguistic tasks resolution through fine-tuning LLMs, RAG and knowledge graphs. In: CAiSE 2024 2nd Workshop on Knowledge Graphs for Semantics-driven Systems Engineering
4. Liu, J., Xia, C.S., Wang, Y., Zhang, L.: Is your code generated by ChatGPT really correct? Rigorous evaluation of large language models for code generation. In: NeurIPS (2023)
5. Chang, Y., et al: A survey on evaluation of large language models. ACM Trans. Intell. Syst. Technol. (2023.) https://doi.org/10.1145/3641289
6. Liang, J.T., Yang, C., Myers, B.A.: A large-scale survey on the usability of AI programming assistants: successes and challenges. In: ICSE (2024). https://doi.org/10.48550/arXiv.2303.17125

Author Index

A

Adrot, Anouck 596
Agostinelli, Simone 248
Ali, Syed Juned 107
Alkhammash, Hanan 87
Alman, Anti 178
Amiri Elyasi, Keyvan 124
Andersson, Kent 336
Andolina, Salvatore 284
Arcega, Lorena 581

B

Bakhtina, Mariia 475
Barba, Irene 456
Barbaro, Luca 509
Barberio, Anna 284
Barzen, Johanna 612
Basile, Davide 509
Beerepoot, Iris 371
Beisel, Martin 612
Benaben, Frederick 596
Benatallah, Boualem 531
Benvenuti, Dario 248
Biffl, Stefan 492
Black, Jack 547
Bork, Dominik 107, 563
Brockhoff, Tobias 20

C

Cai, Rujian 55
Cappiello, Cinzia 284
Casciani, Angelo 248
Ceravolo, Paolo 71
Cetina, Carlos 352, 581
Chapela-Campa, David 631
Chasseray, Yohann 596
Chen, Dan 319
Christfort, Axel Kjeld Fjelrad 440
Corea, Carl 161
Cosma, Vlad Paul 440

D

da Silva Santos, Luiz Olavo Bonino 637
David, Istvan 563
De Luzi, Francesca 248
Del Valle, Carmelo 456
Depaire, Benoit 635
Di Ciccio, Claudio 509
Di Francescomarino, Chiara 423
Doidge, Mark 547
Domingo, África 581
Donadello, Ivan 423
dos Santos, Vitor Gaboardi 531, 547

E

Endo, Patricia Takako 547

F

Fahland, Dirk 141
Falco, Raphaël 596
Falconi, Matteo 300
Felli, Paolo 161
Fertier, Audrey 596
Fletcher, Thomas 547

G

Ghidini, Chiara 423
Gianola, Alessandro 3
Giebler, Corinna 267
Goretti, Valerio 509
Gröger, Christoph 267

H

Haarmann, Stephan 195
Hildebrandt, Thomas T. 440
Hoffmann, David 492
Hoos, Eva 267
Huang, Shuwei 319

G. Guizzardi et al. (Eds.): CAiSE 2024, LNCS 14663, pp. 641–643, 2024.
https://doi.org/10.1007/978-3-031-61057-8

J
Jiménez-Ramírez, Andrés   456
Junior, Sylvio Barbon   71

K
Kearns, Colm   547
Kilvington, Dan   547
Klijn, Eva L.   141
Kropatschek, Sebastian   492
Kvapil, Jan   475

L
Lama, Manuel   215
Lanti, Davide   633
Lapeña, Raúl   352
Le Duff, Clara   596
Leemans, Sander J. J.   36
Leopold, Henrik   371, 635
Leymann, Frank   612
Li, Bing   55
Li, Duantengchuan   55
Li, Tian   36
Liston, Katie   547
Liu, Lin   319
Lombardo, Giacomo   300
López-Pintado, Orlenys   631
Lu, Xixi   231, 440
Lüder, Arndt   492
Lundberg, Jan   336
Lynn, Theo   531, 547

M
Maggi, Fabrizio Maria   178, 423
Mannhardt, Felix   141
Marinacci, Matteo   248
Marrella, Andrea   248
Matera, Maristella   284
Matulevičius, Raimundas   475
Mecella, Massimo   639
Meixner, Kristof   492
Mendling, Jan   387, 635
Meyerhenke, Henning   635
Mitschang, Bernhard   267
Moffat, Alistair   87
Montali, Marco   3, 36, 161
Montreuil, Benoit   596

O
Oyamada, Rafael Seidi   71

P
Pastor, Óscar   352, 581
Patrizi, Fabio   161, 215
Pérez, Francisca   352
Plebani, Pierluigi   300
Polyvyanyy, Artem   36, 87
Pucci, Emanuele   284

R
Rama-Maneiro, Efrén   215
Reichert, Manfred   456
Reijers, Hajo A.   231, 371, 440
Rinderle-Ma, Stefanie   178, 403
Rivkin, Andrey   178
Rizzi, Williams   423
Roca, Isis   581
Rossi, Jacopo   248
Rubensson, Christoffer   387

S
Sancricca, Camilla   284
Santos, Guto Leoni   531, 547
Schwarz, Holger   267
Seidel, Anjo   195
Sinclair, Gary   547
Slaats, Tijs   440
Smit, Tim K.   231
Stein Dani, Vinicius   371
Stiliadou, Lavinia   612
Stirna, Janis   336
Stuckenschmidt, Heiner   124
Švenda, Petr   475

T
Tavares, Gabriel Marques   71
Tessaris, Sergio   423

U
Uysal, Merih Seran   20

V
van der Aa, Han   124
van der Aalst, Wil M. P.   20
van der Werf, Jan Martijn E. M.   371

Verón, Javier   352
Vidal, Juan   215

W
Wais, Beate   403
Wang, Chong   55
Wang, Jian   55
Weber, Barbara   456
Weder, Benjamin   612
Weidlich, Matthias   387

Werner, Sebastian   300
Weske, Mathias   195
Winkler, Sarah   3
Winter, Karolin   178

Y
Yang, Jingwei   319

Z
Zheng, Chao   55

Printed in the United States
by Baker & Taylor Publisher Services

Printed in the United States
by Baker & Taylor Publisher Services